Economics
PRINCIPLES IN ACTION

3392

Economics

PRINCIPLES IN ACTION

FOURTH EDITION

Philip C. Starr

Chaffey College

Wadsworth Publishing Company
Belmont, California
A Division of Wadsworth, Inc.

(415) 595-2350

Economics Editor: Stephanie Surfus
Production: Del Mar Associates
Designer: Louis Neiheisel
Copy Editor: Lillian Rodberg
Cartoons: Paul Slick and Janet Colby
Technical Illustrators: Steve Harrison and
Pam Posey
Photographer: Bill Call

Printed in the United States of America

1 2 3 4 5 6 7 8 9 10—88 87 86 85 84

ISBN 0-534-03189-7

Library of Congress Cataloging in Publication
Data

Starr, Philip C.
    Economics, principles in action.

    Includes bibliographical references and
index.
    1. Economics. 2. Economics—Examina-
tions, questions, etc.   I. Title.
HB171.5.S78   1984   330   83–14829
ISBN 0-534-03189–7

For Wendy, An, and Hugh

Introduction for Instructors

First, a word for instructors unfamiliar with this text: *Economics: Principles in Action* grew out of a one-term course we created at Chaffey (community) College called Economics 110: An Introduction to Economics. The course has become so popular that enrollment in it accounts for more than one-third of total enrollment in all economics courses.

Special Features of the Book

THE BOOK IS NONTECHNICAL. Students taking economics courses for the first time sometimes have a built-in fear that economics will be largely made up of charts, graphs, equations, and statistics. In this text, I have used as nontechnical an approach as possible. There are no algebraic symbols, few abbreviations, and scant use of formulas. The charts and graphs have been kept as simple as possible (for instance, there are no references to x and y axes—only "horizontal" and "vertical"). A short chapter (Chapter 4) is designed to help those students who are "turned off" by graphs.

THE BOOK IS EASY AND ENTERTAINING TO READ. I have tried to make the text pertinent, newsworthy, and simple to read. I used many examples from daily newspapers and weekly news magazines such as stories on energy problems and air pollution. One of the greatest compliments students have paid me after reading earlier editions of this text was that "all that stuff in the newspaper is beginning to make sense."

A CAST OF CHARACTERS KEEPS THE BOOK LIVELY AND HUMAN. Concepts such as demand and supply, profit maximizing behavior, progressive and regressive taxes, and prisoners' dilemma are explained via anecdote and imaginary people. In addition, there are biographies of Adam Smith, Karl Marx, and John Maynard Keynes.

THE BOOK EXPOSES STUDENTS TO AN ABUNDANCE OF ISSUES. Rent control laws, minimum wage laws, the behavior of cartels, unions, the Monetary Control Act, the underground economy, the Laffer Curve, supply-siding, rational expectations, the "Reagan Experience," as well as the trade offs between clean air and unemployment, between equality and efficiency, and between unemployment and inflation are included. Students learn of the great debates within the economics profession: about the economic role of government, about monetary versus fiscal policy, and about the cures for "stagflation."

ECONOMIC TERMS, CONCEPTS, AND THE "THREAD OF THE ARGUMENT" ARE CONTINUALLY REINFORCED. If there is one thing I learned from the education courses I once took, it is that we constantly need to explain *why* we're doing what we're doing. Chapter 1 begins the approach toward this objective with a discussion of why one should study economics, what employment opportunities there are in the profession, and how economists think about many important problems of general interest to citizens (not just to professional economists).

This effort continues through the book. Each of the six parts opens with a description of what is to come. Each chapter opens with a list of "key words" that signal the principal concepts readers will encounter in the chapter. (These words appear in boldface in the text.) Immediately following the list of key words is a paragraph or two giving an overview of the chapter that explains why the chapter is located where it is, why it is important, and how it is organized. Each chapter is followed by a summary and discussion questions.

Presenting the Material: Possible Sequences

The book is divided into six parts (instead of five as in the third edition) for maximum flexibility. Instructors who wish to emphasize macro could assign Chapters 1 through 3 in Part 1, Chapter 4 in Part 2, and then jump to Chapter 12, which opens Part 4. Instructors wishing to emphasize micro could assign Parts 1 through 3 (micro) and then a stripped-down version of macro by assigning Chapters 12, 16, 17, and 18 (omitting the appendices to Chapters 16 and 18). The appendices—16A, 18A, and 20A—also permit greater flexibility than the third edition by permitting instructors to include or exclude a few relatively esoteric topics such as the Keynesian Cross (16A), the Keynesians vs. the Monetarists (18A), and exchange rates (20A).

Changes in the Fourth Edition

In the introduction to the third edition, I said, "It cannot be stressed enough that this edition is a major overhaul. Almost every page and certainly every topic has been revised in some way to clarify meanings, to look at ideas from a fresh angle, or drop unnecessary material, as well as to include new and pertinent material." At the time of *that* rewriting, I remember having an ill-conceived fantasy that, at last, I had arrived on a plateau where future editions could be handled with minimal adjustments. Nothing could have been further from the truth. This edition has been through a far more rigorous process of review and revision than the third edition, testimony without doubt to the fact that economics is an exciting and ever-changing field of study. The goals of the book and its basic structure are the same as ever, but many internal changes have been made. Some examples:

■ Chapter 1 now includes a new cost-benefit section to show more clearly how economists think.

■ To make students aware earlier in the book that our particular brand of market-price system is but one of many systems, Chapter 2 now includes a new historical section, and Chapter 3 (formerly Chapter 19) is an updated description of the economies of the Soviet Union and the People's Republic of China. (The latter description involves considerable change from the Maoist influence of the third edition.)

■ The appendix about understanding graphs was poorly placed in the third edition. In the fourth edition, this material has been fleshed out into a more complete and concise chapter (Chapter 4). The chapter now precedes the first discussion of graphs (demand-supply) in Chapter 5.

■ The introductory exposition of demand and supply has been improved, using multiple suppliers. Applications of demand-supply theory in the "real world" have been expanded.

■ To improve continuity, several box essays have been incorporated into the text. In fact, I have deliberately tried to avoid box essays under the theory that they interrupt the flow of material and tend to disorient students. One example: the minimum-wage discussion, a box essay in the third edition, is now part of the text in Chapter 7. Its placement there, in connection with elasticity, is new, and the discussion more realistic than before.

■ Discussions with reviewers revealed that labor markets, income distribution, and discrimination in labor markets needed more intensive treatment than that given in past editions. Accordingly, two almost entirely new chapters have been written: Chapter 10 on labor markets and Chapter 11 on income distribution and discrimination. These two chapters do not add to the length of the book because obsolete material has been replaced and existing material reorganized.

■ The order of the first three chapters in the macro section has been changed to a more logical sequence, namely, (1) the link between micro and macro, (2) how the performance of the economy is measured, (3) the historical record of that performance, and (4) the economic role of government (budgets and taxes).

- The macro section has a much improved organization because the material about inflation and unemployment, previously scattered among three chapters, has been gathered in one place: Chapter 13.
- The treatment of macro theory and practice is improved and updated, both made necessary by the current battles between the Keynesians, monetarists, supply-siders, and rational expectationists. All of these schools of thought appear longer on the stage in this edition than in previous ones.
- Following the discussion questions at the end of each chapter there is a new feature, the question "Did you ever wonder why . . . ?" This question is designed to uncover paradoxes, expose myths, and introduce ways of applying economic concepts that are relevant to students' interests. *This question is answered in the study guide* to help students see how economists handle such questions. Similar questions appear in the instructor's manual with suggested answers.

The back matter of the text contains a glossary of all key words with a short definition of each and the chapter and page numbers in the text where the term is explained. We have tried to make the index more extensive and helpful than in previous editions; it also includes the key words in boldface type.

The Study Guide and Instructor's Manual

The study guide and instructor's manual that accompany the text have also, like the text, been through a major overhaul. We believe now that they will be far more useful than ever before.

The study guide is written by Dale Sievert and David Martin of Milwaukee Area Technical College. It is a complete rewrite of the previous guide. Each of the 28 self-instructional units consists of eight parts:

- a statement of the unit's behavioral objectives, titled "At the very least . . ."
- a summary of the objectives of each unit called "In a nutshell"
- a series of exercises aimed at the objectives
- <u>answers to the exercises</u>
- a related newspaper or magazine headline with two or three questions designed to connect the headline to the unit
- a posttest
- <u>answers to the posttest</u>
- a suggested answer to the "Did you ever wonder why . . . ?" questions from the text.

Martin and Sievert have also provided a much more extensive instructor's manual. The material in the manual associated with each chapter in the text is divided into six parts:

- an outline of the text chapter
- a paragraph summarizing the purpose of the chapter
- teaching tips that highlight areas in the chapter that have proven difficult for students in the past
- a cross-reference guide that couples the study guide unit number(s) with each chapter
- <u>50 objective questions consisting of 35 multiple-choice and 15 true-false items</u>
- additional "Did you ever wonder why . . . ?" questions with answers.

Enlarged copies of conceptually important technical art are located at the back of the instructor's manual. These pages are suitable for reproduction or conversion to transparencies.

Acknowledgments

My indebtedness is multiple and heavy, especially to Dale Sievert, Milwaukee Area Technical College. I am grateful for his many intensive, detailed reviews of the manuscripts, the "Did you ever wonder why . . . ?" questions, the first version of Chapter 10 about unions, as well as his work on a much improved study guide and instructor's manual. In all of these matters, he has generously given excessive amounts of his time and energy.

I am also indebted to colleagues S. Craig Justice for his help with Chapter 18 (Monetary Policy), and to colleague Charles S. Miller for photographic research.

As already indicated, the manuscript for the fourth edition went through a very rigorous review and revision process. For their helpful and often multiple reviews, I want to thank: Kristi Weir, Bellevue Community College; James Dietz and John Lafky, California State University at Fullerton; Robert Payne, Portland Community College; Michael Johnson, California State University at San Luis Obispo; Ralph Worthington, St. Petersburg Community College; Donald Schaeffer, Washington State University; Leonard Peterson, Lansing Community College; George Uhimchuk, Clemson University; Eugene Phillips, Moorhead State University; and Robert Strain, California State University at Long Beach.

Lillian Rodberg, manuscript editor, was also a powerful force in the revision process. She scrutinized every word with great care and made many valuable corrections, additions, and suggestions for research and rethinking. I owe her much.

Ann McCleary once again expertly typed the manuscript many times. Bonny McLaughlin has again provided a fine index, much more extensive this time, as well as the list of key words with definitions. Judy Cooke assisted Bonny with the typing of these two difficult but important chores.

I am also grateful to the staff of Wadsworth, especially Bill Oliver and Stephanie Surfus, economics editors, and Jerry Holloway, production services coordinator. I thank them for their encouragement and support.

When the manuscript was ready for production, it passed into the hands of an unusually gifted team of people called Del Mar Associates. My view of their work is one of gratitude and admiration. They are Nancy Sjoberg and Frankie Wright, production managers; Louie Neiheisel, designer (cover and text); Paul Slick, illustrator; Pam Posey and Steve Harrison, technical illustrators; and Bill Call, photographer.

I also want to thank the library staff at Chaffey College, who, now for the fourth round, have saved many hours of hunting.

And again, I want to thank my long-suffering wife, Emily, who has contributed many hours of her own professional expertise to this project.

Contents

PART **IV**

THE MACRO VIEW AND THE ROLE OF GOVERNMENT/233

12 The National Economy: Measuring Its Performance 234

13 Changes in GNP, Employment, and Prices: Problems in the Macroeconomy 249

14 The Economic Role of Government: Its Size and Impact 268

The purpose of Part I of this book is to explain the meaning of economics, to describe how economists think, and to help you think about our world in terms of a patchwork of different economic systems. This part consists of three chapters. Chapter 1 describes typical problems economists try to analyze, what economics means, and how the word

INTRODUCTION: WHAT ECONOMICS IS ABOUT

"economics" is defined. Chapter 2 outlines how different types of economic systems try to overcome scarcity, with emphasis on the origins and major characteristics of the system now operating in the United States. Chapter 3 describes other economic systems with emphasis on the Soviet Union and the People's Republic of China.

1
What Is Economics?
Trying to Improve Our
Material Welfare

KEY WORDS
Inflation
Rule of 72
Scarcity
Cost
Free good
"Real" terms
Opportunity cost
Trade-off
Secondary job market
Primary job market
Foregone income
Cost-benefit analysis
Economics
Microeconomics
Macroeconomics
International economics

L ook at the front page of any large-city newspaper. Usually it will present you with a bewildering variety of economic issues as well as the conflicts they give rise to: <u>battles between environmentalists and industrialists</u>, be-<u>tween unions and management;</u> arguments among politicians over taxes, welfare, inflation, energy conservation, land use, or unemployment; and on and on.

Behind the scenes you will usually find economists helping to advise or to influence one side or the other. A famous English economist, John Maynard Keynes, once said that we are, without realizing it, "usually the slaves of some <u>defunct</u> economist." Without realizing it, we also are often the slaves of living economists who occupy positions of great influence in universities, large corporations, and government. <u>The main purpose of this book is to help you think about personal, business, and public issues as economists do.</u> The main purpose of this first chapter is <u>to explain what economics is.</u>

Most people have heard the word "economics" often enough—and certainly we are often told to "economize." Consequently, most of us have an intuitive grasp of one of the central meanings of economics: to be careful about spending. We are admonished to be careful about spending because by doing so we will (we hope) become better off. And this *is* what economics means. Economics is a social science that studies ways to improve human welfare in material terms, by which we mean the goods and services we buy (or produce ourselves) to satisfy our wants. Nonmaterial aspects of human welfare like personal and social adjustment to one's own values or aspirations, to members of the opposite sex, or to one's contemporaries are left to other branches of the social sciences like anthropology, sociology, and psychology. However, it has been shown that, at least in the United States, income levels and degrees of happiness tend to rise or fall together.[1] It's easier to be happier with more material things than with less.* Therefore, although economics is not directly connected with curing unhappiness, the chances are that economists can help make us happy if they can find ways to improve our material welfare.

This chapter is divided into two main parts—(1) why we study economics and (2) what economics is all about—and a concluding note on how this book is organized.

WHY STUDY ECONOMICS?

There are at least two ways of thinking about why we should study economics: (1) from our point of view as citizens, where we look at economics as a tool to improve local, national, or international welfare; and (2) from our point of view as private individuals who ask, "How does this affect *me*?" Let's consider these two points of view.

What Is My Interest as a Citizen?

Here are two important economic problems that affect us as citizens: a local problem and a national/international problem.

---

* This statement has to be qualified. Among people living at the same time in the same economic system, those who "have" will usually be happier than those who "have not." But comparing one generation with those in another in terms of happiness is much more difficult. Who is to say that we are happier than our grandparents were, even though we use Cuisinarts, drive Corvettes, and play PacMan, while they pushed carpet sweepers, cranked Model T's, and played Monopoly.

A Local Economic Problem: Rental Housing

One of our severest problems is urban housing. For example, in the Bronx area of New York City there are acres of burned-out and vandalized housing. Poor people still live there despite continual muggings and burglaries because they can't afford to pay more than the low rents imposed by rent control. Yet rent controls discourage investors from building new housing units. Who wants to invest in a new building if the rental income from the building yields no profit after expenses?

Moreover, as property values in the area decline, a city's revenues from property taxes decline—revenues that are used to support local schools, police forces, and fire departments. As these services decline, people have an incentive to leave the area, further increasing the number of abandoned buildings, and so it goes.

This problem is by no means unique to New York City. Recently, it was reported that there were 4,000 unoccupied housing units in South-Central Los Angeles.[2] The explanation: absentee owners—speculators who bought and sold low-rent units for quick profits and were uninterested in maintaining the units in livable condition. Discouraged tenants either vacated voluntarily or were forced out by city authorities when the housing units failed to meet health standards.

Note that in New York, the source of the problem was at least partly the result of government-regulated rent ceilings, whereas in Los Angeles the problem apparently resulted from nonenforcement of government regulations concerning maintenance of the buildings. Thus, two cases in which the obvious problem—abandoned buildings—was the same, fueled arguments for opposing factions: those economists who want to reduce government involvement and those who want to increase it. We'll discuss examples of this debate throughout this book.

Many other economic problems face local governments, such as how to provide public education, police and fire protection, street maintenance, trash collection, flood control, zoning for land use, public health and welfare—issues we cannot discuss in detail here. Let's turn now to a major national and international problem of concern to all citizens.

A National/International Problem: Inflation

Simply defined, **inflation** means a rise in the general price level. (We discuss inflation in greater detail in Chapters 13 and 19.) Inflation is extremely important to understand because, within the United States, the presence of inflation means that a redistribution of income is taking place. When you have to pay a higher price for an item, the store where you buy it takes in more income. Of course, the store's costs may be higher because suppliers or employees are receiving more money. The trick, when studying inflation, is to discover who wins and who loses.

Internationally, inflation is important because rising prices in the United States mean that foreigners will be reluctant to buy our products. In 1982, we exported about $350 billion worth of goods and services to other countries. If foreigners take a dislike to our prices, approximately five million workers in export-related industries may lose their jobs.

Moreover, if foreigners take a dislike to our prices, their demand for our dollars with which to buy U.S. products will fall. (A full explanation of the

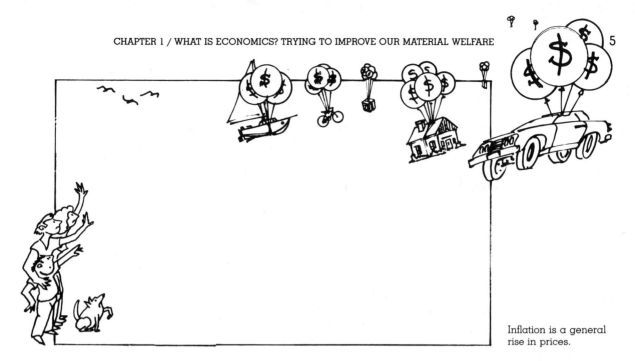

Inflation is a general rise in prices.

financing of foreign trade and the exchange-rate mechanism is in Chapter 20.) When that happens, the dollar will exchange for fewer Japanese yen, German marks, and so on, and products from these foreign countries or travel in them for U.S. citizens becomes more expensive. Finally, if it becomes more expensive to buy, say, a Datsun or Arabian oil, U.S. prices will tend to rise because U.S. auto producers don't have to compete as hard with the Japanese car manufacturers and because increases in the cost of oil tends to raise the price of almost everything.

Inflation usually hurts the people the most who can afford it least: retired people living on savings or on fixed incomes and young people in nonunion jobs whose wages do not keep up with price increases. These groups of people find that increases in price usually exceed increases (if any) in their wages. Consequently, as the years go by, each paycheck buys fewer and fewer groceries, rents less and less attractive apartments, affords less and less entertainment, and so forth. As a result, the standard of living of these groups falls; they are forced to live on less.

What's In It for Me?

We'll turn now from our involvement in economics as citizens to our private concerns and ask, "What is studying economics going to do for me?" It can do two main things: (1) It can help you think more intelligently about personal economic decisions, such as buying, selling, saving, or investing. (2) It can help you function more successfully as an employee of a business firm. Chapter 10 deals with the problems of employees as union members. Chapter 9 discusses economic decision making by the managers of business firms.

You may also want to consider seeking a job as an economist. Over 120,000 persons worked as economists in 1982; about three out of every four of these were employed in private industry or research organizations. Of the remainder, about half were teachers and half worked for government agencies.

Business firms offer a wide range of activities for economists: planning the location of gas stations, supermarkets, telephone exchanges, or banks; helping banks to invest depositors' money wisely; helping corporations plan long-term growth or helping them with price and output decisions to obtain desired profit; helping union executives bargain more effectively with management; helping stockbrokers advise their customers.*

In the preceding section we have reviewed some of the issues of interest to economists (and to our public and private selves). In the next section, we will examine one of the central questions that help define economics as a field of study.

WHAT ECONOMICS IS ALL ABOUT

Economics exists because of the multitude of serious problems that affect our material welfare, such as unemployment, inflation, pollution, energy shortages, starvation in poor countries, and so on. A crucial question arises: Are these problems short-term accidents, or are they symptomatic of long-term problems facing future generations? A number of circumstances occurring in the 1960s and 1970s made us realize that many of our most serious problems are of the long-term variety. Two of them are: (1) the post-World War II demand for natural resources, and (2) the growing needs of the poor countries.

The Post–World War II Demand for Natural Resources

By the mid-1960s, the industrial countries that had been involved in World War II demonstrated full recovery from the damage they had suffered, and in the early 1970s most of these countries enjoyed a business boom. This post-war recovery led to enormous increases in demand for resources (like oil) that often were not available in sufficient quantities. In addition, widespread drought and two oil crises (1973 and 1979) helped to aggravate shortages and to accelerate price increases.

Total world production of all goods and services exploded between World War II and the early 1980s—from $1 trillion worth to about $10 trillion in 1982. By the late 1960s, signs of stress appeared: pollution became a front-page concern, and food-production capacity was strained as demand for food grew by 30 million tons per year.

In the fall of 1973, most nations suddenly became aware that there might not be enough oil to sustain current needs. Arab nations placed an oil embargo on the countries that had been trading with Israel. In the United States there were long lines of cars at gas stations waiting to fill up. The people living in the northeastern United States had a cold winter as stocks of heating oil were exhausted. Many families used their fireplaces for warmth and for cooking.

We began to realize that our planet might not be capable of giving us the essentials of life. Why? Mainly because the demands of an increasing population have begun to outrun the resources needed for production.

The Growing Needs of the Poor Countries

Estimates are that by the year 2020, the earth's population will jump to 8 billion.** To appreciate this astounding increase, consider that it took *4 million*

---

* For descriptions of several private-sector jobs for economists, see *Business Economics Careers*, National Association of Business Economists, 28349 Chagrin Boulevard, Cleveland, OH 44122. Single copies of this twenty-one-page pamphlet are free. Additional copies are 30 cents each, as of this writing.

** According to the World Bank, world population will be 6.3 billion by the end of the century, 8 billion by 2020, and will peak and stabilize around 11 billion by 2050.

BOX ESSAY
The Handy "Rule of 72"

Today we are in a period of rapid, geometric population increase, and within the next 36 years or so—within your lifetime—the population of the world is expected to double. During the 1960s and early 1970s, the world's population increased at the rate of 2 percent a year, reaching nearly 4.7 billion people in 1982. At this rate, it will double in 36 years, according to the "Rule of 72."*

The **Rule of 72** is a convenient method of roughly determining how fast your money, or any number, will double at any rate of increase or any interest rate compounded annually.

The rule is as follows:
Divide any annual interest rate into 72; the answer gives you the number of years required to double the number.

Thus, if the world's population increases at a rate of 2 percent annually, the world's population will double in $72 \div 2 = 36$ years. If the interest rate is 3 percent, the principal (money) will double in 24 years ($72 \div 3$). If your money is in a savings and loan account paying 8 percent compounded annually, it will double in 9 years. The same formula can be used in studying inflation. If the rate of inflation is, say, 6 percent, in 12 years prices will double and the dollar will have lost half of its purchasing power. We used the Rule of 72 below: an average rate of population increase of 2.3 percent means that population will double in about 31 years ($72 \div 2.3 = 31.1$).

---

*A note for instructors and math-minded students who might wonder why the Rule of 72 works. What is so magic about the number 72? Thanks to statistician Richard Penfield Ament, we have an answer: "The number 72 is an approximation (for convenient figuring) of a number that ranges from 69.3 to 74.3 for interest or growth rates ranging from near-zero to 15 percent, compounded *annually*. If interest is compounded daily or continuously, the number is exactly (to the nearest tenth) 69.3 for any rate of interest. This number is the natural logarithm of 2 multiplied by 100." Clear?

---

years to reach today's population, but it will take only *36 years* to double that!

Tragically, the growth rate is higher among the 93 poorest countries of the world, which contain about 75 percent of the globe's population. During the 1970s the population increase in these countries was 2.3 percent per year, while the increase in developed countries like the United States was only 0.8 percent. The higher rate for the poorer countries means their population will double in about 31 years, whereas in the United States doubling will take 90 years (see Box Essay).

The problem is that the high rates of population increase in poor countries cut into any gains they make in food or industrial production. In one sense, aid from foreign countries (such as technical assistance or medical experts) makes the situation worse. Such aid helps to assure that more people will live to reproductive age, meaning that unless population is controlled, there are more mouths to feed. Even with foreign aid, there is widespread starvation; population experts estimate that as many as 20 million people in the poorer countries starved in 1982. The problems of the poor countries are discussed in some detail in Chapter 21.

There is nothing new about the problems of the poor countries. High rates of population increase, poor life expectancy, illiteracy, poverty, and starvation have been around a long time. What makes the present situation different is the growing awareness among these poor people that they are on the bottom rung of the world's income ladder. The people in the poor countries are now engaged in what is called a "revolution of rising expectations." Socialist and

Marxist governments have helped them achieve political independence, and thus they are challenged to solve their own problems. The richer countries will have to help, but filling the needs of the poor countries will put still greater pressure on the world's scarce resources.

The Costs of Economic Decision Making

The worldwide food and energy shortages that made headlines in the early 1970s help to illustrate what economics is all about. Economics exists as a field of study because the supplies of many things do not keep up with human wants. If, for example, the supply of oil is limited, economists ask, "Shall we use what oil there is for heating or for power, for plastics or for asphalt?" Because there is not enough oil to satisfy all these wants at once, the supply is called scarce. **Scarcity** exists whenever human wants exceed available supplies.* Scarcity forces us to choose among alternatives. Economists try to estimate the effects (**costs**) such choices (decisions) will have on the material aspects of human welfare.

Does every decision necessarily involve a cost? Yes, almost every decision does involve a cost. The term "cost" means that time and effort must be expended to obtain the good or service desired. One way to appreciate this fact of life is to consider what economists mean by a **free good**. A free good (or service) is one that exists in such abundance that people can take or use as much of it as they please without any effort or cost, and there will still be enough left to satisfy the wants of everyone else.

We used to call air and water free goods, but most of us who live in or near cities realize that *clean* air and water do not exist in unlimited quantities; there is usually a cost connected with obtaining sterilized, piped, purified, or bottled water and a cost connected with filtering air in our homes or, optionally, hiking to the nearest mountain peak. And so, sad but true, everything is to some extent *scarce*. When something is scarce, someone has to be paid to provide it; the price covers the costs borne by the supplier for supplying the scarce good or service, and the price also helps to determine which buyers will be able to obtain it.

When goods and services are scarce, there is also a cost involved in choosing which ones we want to use. A cost of using more of our scarce oil supplies for home heating is that car drivers won't have as much gasoline or diesel fuel, or that there won't be as much fuel for power stations and industry. The cost of the decision to refine more oil for heating is measured by the effects that less gasoline, diesel fuel, and so forth, will have on individuals and on the economy.

No matter how many goods we have—cars, stereos, whatever—there is always something else we want. Because our incomes are limited, when we buy one item we give up the chance to buy anything else we could have bought with the same amount of money. So the *cost* of that item is measured by the sacrifice we made in giving up the satisfaction we might have gotten from the goods or services given up. In short, any purchasing decision has a cost in

---

* There is need for a caution here. Scarcity doesn't exist uniformly or at the same time across the world. Our tastes change at different times and in different places, as does our ability to satisfy them. And certainly there are vast discrepancies in supply. For example, in July 1882 a newspaper reported a glut in canned Alaskan salmon while noting in another article that people in the African country of Chad were starving.

"real" terms. The word "real" in this sense means that the cost is measured not by money, but by the actual goods or services sacrificed.

We can also measure the cost of intangibles such as time. Because your time is limited, you cannot do all the things you would like to do. When you decide to spend your time doing one thing, you give up the opportunity to do all other things you could have done in that time.

Opportunity cost is the value of what we give up for something we want.

Measuring the Costs of Our Decisions

How should we measure the cost of anything—of a new motorcycle, a new freeway, or a rapid-transit system? Economists use a concept called **opportunity cost**.

To determine opportunity cost, we measure the value of the *next most* desirable opportunity we must sacrifice in order to take the course of action we have selected. When you go to class or decide to study in the library, you give up the opportunity to watch television at home. The opportunity cost of attending class or studying in the library is the value you place on the television program you miss.

What is the cost of the $1,000 motorcycle you want? It is not the price. The opportunity cost to you if you buy it is not $1,000 but the next most desirable product or service you might have bought with that $1,000. Notice that the money (price) is *not* the cost itself. The cost is your evaluation of the "real" things sacrificed.

So, money is a *means* of getting the things we want, price is a *measure* of how much money is required, and cost is the value of what we *forego*. The question economists ask is how much in actual products and services must be sacrificed to build whatever is being considered—a dam, hospital, school, rocket, weather satellite, and so on.

We can look at the opportunity costs of any decision, but one of the most frequently underestimated costs is the cost of war. The obvious costs are lost lives, destroyed property, and interrupted careers, as well as wasted resources in the form of helicopters, guns, bullets, uniforms, trucks, and all the rest of the military paraphernalia. Less obvious costs are the slum clearance, antipollution, public health, and welfare projects that might otherwise have been undertaken. Consider also the costs in hospitals, doctors, medicine, and equipment devoted to veterans' care long after the war is over, as well as the costs of the benefits paid to dependents. For instance, in 1967 more than 1,300 dependents of veterans of the American Civil War—a war that ended 102 years before—received *annual* benefits totaling more than $1 million. Veterans' benefits for the Spanish-American War amounted to $5.3 billion, or twelve times the original cost of that war.*

Economists use one other term to refer to opportunity cost: **trade-off**. What do we trade off—or lose—if we decide to do this or that? In a later chapter we will consider one of the most famous trade-offs, inflation versus unemployment. Some economists believe that in order to get prices to fall—to reduce inflation—the government must slow down the economy to such an extent that unemployment may increase.

Every personal decision involves many calculations, but you should consider, at least briefly, the idea of opportunity costs when you make a decision. These are your personal trade-offs. Since you are a student, the opportunity cost of doing your homework may be the sacrifice of a tennis game, drinking beer with your friends, or just goofing off, while the opportunity cost of marriage, children, or social activities may be poor grades.

Costs of Work, Study, or Play

The opportunity costs of choosing a job are especially important to college students. There is a kind of triangular relationship between (1) part-time work or work in a **secondary job market**, (2) work in a **primary job market**, and (3) a college education.

Secondary-market jobs are those with low pay, high turnover, little required skill, and little training by employers, such as waiting on tables, pumping gas, or clerking in stores. Primary-market jobs are those involving skill, investment by employers in training, higher pay, avenues for promotion, career possibilities for employees, and low turnover.

Frequently, college students take jobs in secondary markets because primary market jobs require more time than commitment to a college education will permit. One college student (we'll call him Kirk) took a night job as a security guard in a manufacturing plant so that he could spend some of the time studying. The job required little skill or training. The company's executives knew Kirk, realized that he was management material, and were ready to promote him to a "primary" job. Kirk preferred to stay where he was in order to finish college.

The opportunity cost of Kirk's going to college can therefore be estimated as the sum of his college expenses plus the extra income he lost by staying in his security-guard job (rather than taking a better-paying job) plus the chances of

---

* World War I benefits did not begin to decrease until 1966. World War II benefits are not expected to decline until the year 2000. Benefits to dependents of Vietnam veterans are expected to continue beyond 2100. See James L. Clayton, "Vietnam: The 200-Year Mortgage," *The Nation*, 26 May 1969, p. 661.

promotion he may also have lost. Economists have estimated that half of the cost of going to college is in the form of lost earnings (often called **foregone income**). Or, to put it another way, the true cost of going to college is double the money costs to students, parents, or taxpayers. Most economists believe that the college degree *is* worth it, and that investing in one's education has a higher return than that earned by savings accounts or by financial investments like stocks and bonds.

Social Costs of Individual Decisions

A personal decision may impose costs, not just on oneself, but also on others. Consequently, the total cost to society (social cost) is measured by the opportunity costs borne by individuals for their own decisions *plus* additional costs that may be borne by others. Examples are the purchase of a car that pollutes the atmosphere, a powerful stereo that keeps the neighbors awake, the noise and smoke trails from jet planes, disease-producing wastes from industrial production. Economists try to uncover these additional costs that may not be part of a buyer-seller transaction in order to estimate the total social cost of decisions to produce, buy, sell, use, or discard products or services.

Cost-Benefit Analysis

The preceding section has emphasized the costs of every decision. This view of economics is, as you might guess, only one side of the coin. Usually, there are both gains and losses (costs) in most decisions. (Possible exceptions are wars and suicide pacts.) Consequently, economists are faced with the job of measuring the benefits to society as well as the costs of business and government decisions.

A simple example may help. You are trying to decide about spending an evening with an attractive member of the opposite sex. There are, inevitably, both actual (monetary) and opportunity costs involved. On the other hand, the evening promises benefits in the form of an improved relationship. So, as a budding economist, you compare the expected costs with the expected benefits of the decision to go out with Mr. or Ms. Z. This comparison of costs and benefits is called **cost-benefit analysis**. It is an extremely important approach to problems in economics.

But, just as it is hard to analyze the costs and benefits of, say, the Concorde jet plane, it is hard to identify *all* the costs and benefits of most decisions. Often, as we analyze economic problems, we reach a point where we want to say, "Ah, now I understand. This is the answer." The feeling is like that of finding the secret room of an Egyptian pyramid where the treasure is hidden. But, inevitably in economics and, we suspect, in any course of study, the more we look at the secret room the more we find (in the dim light of our ignorance) that the treasure isn't really there after all; that the secret room really has many doors leading to many other rooms that might hold the treasure.

Let's go back now and look once more at our two problems—rental housing and inflation—to appreciate this problem.

ECONOMIC ANALYSIS IS LIKE A NEVER-ENDING TREASURE HUNT

Let's assume that the "treasure" in the case of rental housing is a solution that provides plentiful, clean, healthy, beautiful, low-cost housing to low income groups at a low cost to society. Or, in the case of inflation, we'll assume that the treasure is a cure for inflation that manages to bring prices down without hurting anyone's welfare. The difficulty in both cases is that there are many "rooms," detours, or hurdles on the way to either treasure. It's very hard to find solutions to either problem that lead to improved welfare for everyone. Very often in economics, we find that a solution that helps one group hurts another.

For example, in the case of housing, rent control laws are designed to keep rents low so that low-income people can afford inexpensive apartments. A praiseworthy idea. But rent control laws—designed to help poor people—will certainly hurt landlords. And the landlords may defend themselves against loss by refusing to maintain their apartment buildings (or by refusing to build new ones). Ultimately, the poor may become worse off—as in New York City—by having no choice but to live in substandard housing.

If we recommend the other extreme, no rent control, the landlords will certainly be satisfied. But the poor may fare even worse under this policy than under rent-control laws. Witness the slum conditions in our large cities that evolved when there were no rent control laws, and laws guaranteeing healthy places to live were not enforced. We will discuss this difficult problem again in Chapter 6.

In no case is the difficulty of the "treasure hunt" better illustrated than in the search for ways to control inflation. During 1981–1982, the government tried to correct the inflationary problems described in Chapters 13 and 19. The method adopted for the attack on inflation is called "tight money." (We'll explain the theory and practice of this idea in more detail in Chapter 18.)

The purpose of the tight money policy (engineered by the Board of Governors of the Federal Reserve System) was to give the banks less money to lend. The idea was that if the banks had less money to lend, everyone would be less able to borrow and would, therefore, spend less. And if there were less borrowing and spending, business firms would find selling their goods and services more and more difficult. Increasingly, the business firms would have to run clearance sales or offer discounts and rebates. Prices would have to come down.

By this measure, the policy was a huge success. Prices still went up, but the year-to-year increase in prices fell from 13.3 percent in 1979 to 4 percent in 1982. Inflation seemed to be licked. The "treasure" was found. But was it?

As it turned out, there were probably only a few groups of people who were happy: U.S. travelers to foreign countries and people with large savings accounts. Just about everyone else was, to put it mildly, very unhappy.

Business firms were unhappy with falling sales and profits. The number of business failures doubled from 11,742 in 1980 to over 22,000 in 1982.[3] Workers were very unhappy as the number of unemployed workers increased from 7.6 million in 1980 to nearly 12 million in 1982, an increase of 58 percent! The banks were unhappy because they made fewer loans (even though interest rates were high), and because they had to pay higher interest rates to savers to attract their money. Typically, the higher rates went to savers with large amounts of money who could afford to leave their funds in savings accounts six months or longer. Consequently, this group of people was made happy by the tight-money decision.

And U.S. travelers to foreign countries were delighted to find that their U.S. dollars could, on the average, buy 25 percent more in most other countries.

This happened because the high interest rates in the United States enticed foreign savers to put their money in U.S. banks rather than in banks in their own countries. And whenever they did, the U.S. dollar grew in value relative to their own currencies. Thus, more English pounds, French francs, or German marks had to be offered for each dollar foreign savers wished to put in an American bank account. (This mechanism will be explained in some detail in Chapter 19.)

As foreign currencies flowed into U.S. banks, international exchange rates changed. To give you one example, at the beginning of 1980, an American traveler could exchange one dollar for 4.16 French francs. In 1982, an American traveler could exchange one dollar for 6.9 French francs, an increase of 65 percent.* (*Vive la France!*)

And so we found lots of happy overseas American travelers heading for Europe in 1982. What about the people of other countries?

Some will be happy; some won't. All the people who cater to Americans, like hotel and restaurant people, will be happy. Foreign business firms that sell products to the United States *may* become happier because Americans will find that their dollars buy more French champagne, French perfume, or whatever. We have emphasized "may" because lower incomes in the United States will tend to reduce our purchases from other countries.

Many other foreign business firms will certainly be unhappy. Why? Because, first of all, they will find it hard to borrow money at their own banks because of the flight of savings to U.S. banks. And second, they will find their own banks charging higher and higher interest rates in an effort to compete with U.S. banks; in short, to keep the money at home.

And foreign business firms that buy American products will find American prices are too high because they have to pay more of their currencies for each American dollar. (And thus, American business firms that sell to firms in other countries will also be unhappy.)

Figure 1-1 sketches the effects of a tight-money policy on the welfare of many groups of people. Imagine that each group is a room in that pyramid we mentioned earlier. When examined closely, each reveals doors to rooms involving other groups of people. Without question, the sketch is incomplete. Perhaps you can think of still more groups of people who will be affected. To uncover the whole array of the effects of any decision is the challenge facing economists. Then, when economists have displayed all the evidence of costs and benefits, the people (the government in this example) must decide what to do.

This discussion of cost-benefit analysis is an example of what economics is all about.

Putting It All Together

So far in this chapter we have shown that: (1) The industrial countries and the poor countries both want a great deal more of everything than they are getting. (2) And because we all want more than is available at some-times or places, such things are scarce. (3) And when things are scarce, we have to make choices. (4) But those choices involve opportunity costs. (5) And those oppor-

---

* Unfortunately, we can't assume the American traveler can actually *buy* 65 percent more in France without taking into account the inflation rate in France. Still, the American travelers were *much* better off in 1982 than they were in 1980.

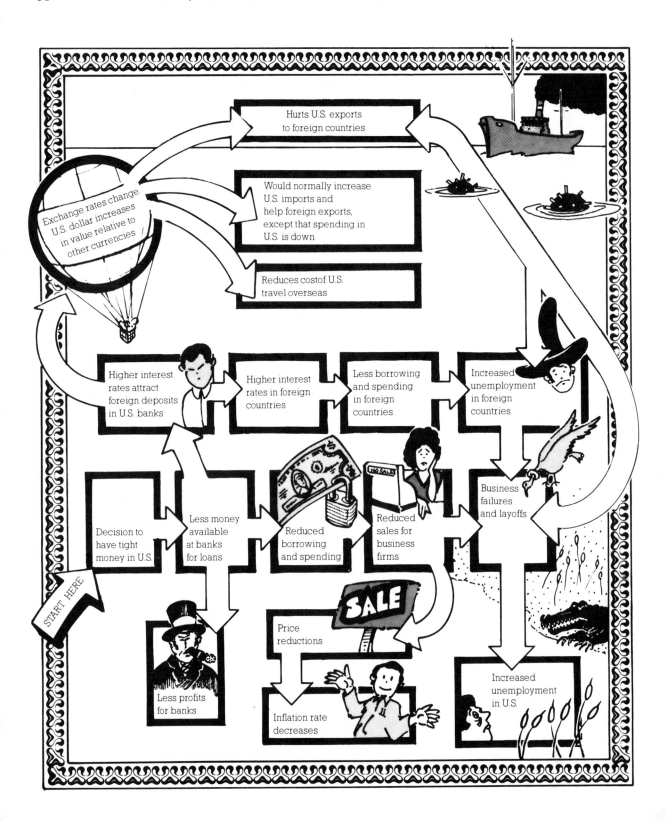

tunity costs are not shared equally; after choices are made, we usually find that some people win and are happy and some people disproportionately bear the cost of the decision and are unhappy. (6) Thus, economics is finally a study of the costs and benefits of decision making to individuals and to society.

Now we are ready for a definition of economics.

A Definition of Economics

First, a reminder: We can never judge the costs or benefits of any decision with certainty because the consequences of our decisions lie in the future. Economists like to say, "We live in a world of risk and uncertainty." Consequently, economic studies lead to estimates about *expected* future costs or benefits.

Economics can therefore be defined as a social science that analyzes the expected effects of private and public decisions on human material welfare. Economists measure the effects of these decisions by comparing social benefits with social costs.

Once that comparison is made, any individual, state, or nation will profit by pursuing a course of action wherein expected benefits exceed expected costs. This common-sense principle is the golden rule (sometimes called the "decision rule") of economics. But common-sense rules like this one are often easier stated than followed. This one has two grave difficulties:

1. The dollar cost of building a freeway may be known, but we usually cannot measure all of the opportunity costs of the project, such as the intangible effects on a community's morale when it is divided by a highway, or the costs borne by those who live near the new highway and have to suffer from increased air pollution and noise. And the benefits of the freeway will be hard to measure. How can we measure the benefit to a community of reduced driving time? (Economists have tried to make such measurements, but the results are subject to considerable error.)

2. Estimates of costs and benefits are difficult because of time span problems. Should we include costs and benefits for the next generation, or the generation after that? How can we know what the future will bring? New methods of transportation might be developed that would make freeways obsolete.

HOW THIS BOOK IS ORGANIZED

This text is organized into three major areas: microeconomics, macroeconomics, and international economics.

Microeconomics (discussed in Parts II and III) refers to a microscopic view of the economy—to bits and pieces rather than to the economy as a whole. Microeconomic theory is concerned with how prices of individual products and services are determined. Prices in turn determine what is produced and who is able to buy.

Macroeconomics (the subject of Parts IV and V) is concerned with the functioning of the whole economy—particularly the federal government's efforts to manipulate the economy to provide jobs and stable prices.

International economics (Part VI) is concerned with the problems of international trade and the unequal distribution of income around the world.

At the back of the book is a list of all the important abbreviations used throughout the text and an alphabetical list of key words with definitions. The

Figure 1-1.
(*Opposite*) Some cost-benefit effects of tight money.

list of key words is taken from those appearing at the beginning of each chapter. With each key word you will see numbers to show the chapter and page on which the term first appears. For example, **demand 0; 00** means that *demand* is discussed in Chapter 0, page 00.

After the list of key words you will find an index; those items that also appear in the list of key words are in boldface.

SUMMARY

Economics is a discipline concerned with improving human material welfare. The world is currently faced with many attacks on welfare: inflation, unemployment, oil and food shortages, pollution, and urban flight are only a few. This book is written to help you understand these challenges.

Economics exists as a field of study because growing numbers of people want more and more of what is available. And when human wants exceed what is available, scarcity exists. When products are scarce, we have to decide how best to use them. And the decisions we make always have a cost, called opportunity cost.

Opportunity cost consists of whatever could have been done if a particular course of action had not been chosen. In every decision, we should consider the opportunity cost involved. These costs occur because of scarcity: we do not have unlimited time, goods, or services available to us.

Economics is an exciting and necessary field of study that seeks to improve human welfare by helping us make wiser decisions. The economist helps people to decide what to do by analyzing the expected costs and benefits of their decisions.

Discussion Questions

1. Is there a danger that the Western countries might some day suffer from an inadequate food supply? Give your reasons why or why not.

2. What are the costs and benefits involved in buying a motorcycle? making or accepting a date? going to college? getting a job instead of going to college? working and going to college? living at home or in an apartment? Consider the costs and benefits to others as well as to yourself.

3. What are the costs and benefits of a welfare program? of not having a welfare program? of building highways? of fighting a war? of having a democratic system of government?

4. Try a "treasure hunt" yourself. Identify all the consequences of a decision to increase parking fees at your college.

DID YOU EVER WONDER WHY . . .

. . . the expression "Anything worth doing is worth doing well" isn't always true?

References

1. Norman M. Bradburn, *The Structure of Psychological Well Being* (Chicago: Aldine, 1969).

2. Henry Weinstein, "707 W. 82nd—Portrait of an L.A. Slum," *Los Angeles Times*, 3 August 1978.

3. Lawrence R. Klein, "Recession Exacts Too High a Toll," *Los Angeles Times*, 6 July 1982, Part IV, p. 3.

2

How Different Economic Systems Deal with Scarcity

KEY WORDS

Economic system
Traditional systems
Command/planning systems
Market-price systems
Market
Adam Smith
Usury
Schoolmen
Canon Law
Just price
Just wage
Factors of production
Enclosure movement
Capital
Entrepreneur
Social goods

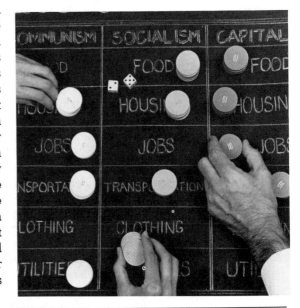

The message of Chapter 1 was that scarcity forces us to measure the inevitable costs and hoped-for benefits of every decision. This chapter describes the different routes societies take in making those decisions. After some preliminaries, most of the chapter is devoted to describing our kind of economic system, its history, and some of its successes and failures. The chapter is divided into four sections: (1) the three questions every economic system must answer, (2) three different ways of answering those questions, (3) a brief history of our market-price system, and (4) an evaluation of our market-price system.

THE THREE QUESTIONS EVERY ECONOMIC SYSTEM MUST ANSWER

First, what do we mean by **economic system**? An economic system is the particular body of laws, habits, ethics, and customs (religious or otherwise) that a group of people observe to satisfy their material wants.

All systems, from primitive to advanced, face three fundamental questions: (1) What goods and services should be produced (and in what quantities)? (2) How should they be produced? (3) For whom should they be produced? Let's now examine each of these questions.

What Goods and Services Should Be Produced?

Every economic system must decide, consciously or not, what goods (TV sets or stereos or bicycles) and services (medical care or legal advice or plumbing) are to be produced and in what quantities. These decisions require, of course, an evaluation of opportunity cost. If we decide to devote more of our resources to making cars, we will have fewer resources for building rapid transit systems. The opportunity cost of each new car is measured by the amount of rapid transit we could have provided but did not.

This observation must be qualified. For example, if people are unemployed, we might be able to use some of them to build cars without having to divert people already employed in rapid transit. Also, if new technology (new machines, tools, or production methods) makes it easier to produce cars, that will release some people from automobile production to work on rapid transit. A surplus of workers and/or new technology enables us to have more of both products.

How Should the Goods and Services Be Produced?

Every society must decide not only what products and services it wants (and in what quantities) but also *how* it should produce them. The question of how involves choosing some combination of machines and people. For example, should we use large numbers of people working with garden tools to cultivate potatoes or a much smaller number of people working with tractors?

Either way, we have to consider the opportunity costs of employing the machines and people in growing potatoes. We have to measure this cost in terms of the lost production of something else.

But the problem is more complex than that. Let's take a very simple example. A potato farmer is understandably tired of cultivating his fields by hand. He wants to purchase a "machine"—in his case, a horse and plow. To buy the horse and plow, he will have to sell some of his potatoes. Consequently, the opportunity cost of the horse and plow is measured by the sacrifice the farmer and his family have to make in not consuming some of their potatoes. In some cases, this opportunity cost may be severe—the family may not get enough to eat. Of course, the decision to buy the horse and plow is made with the expectation that future benefits will make up for these present costs.

In poor countries, this kind of trade-off is an excruciating problem. If the government in one of these countries decides to build a hydroelectric dam, many hundreds of people may have to be taken away from food-producing activities. The opportunity cost of the dam may be further starvation of the people. Thus, the question of *how* may involve some very difficult decisions.

For Whom Should the Goods and Services Be Produced?

Every society must decide who receives the products and services produced, which is another way of saying that a society must decide how income will be distributed among its people. Needless to say, whether by design or circumstance, the world's production and income are very unequally distributed. About 60 percent of the world's population receives only about 10 percent of total income, whereas 10 percent of the people receive about 50 percent of total world income.

In the United States, the lowest 20 percent of families receive only 5 percent of total income, while the highest 20 percent of families receive over 40 percent of the total. And, roughly 25 million people in the U.S. are classified as poverty-stricken. More on the distribution of income in Chapter 11.

Part of the "for whom?" question involves deciding which generation, present or future, should receive the goods and services produced. Decisions to use resources for long-term projects like the Tennessee Valley Authority or cancer research often mean a sacrifice for today's generation in favor of some expected benefit for tomorrow's. Most of the working population pays Social Security taxes for the benefit of older people. Research expenditures on power from hydrogen fusion are expected to be $1 billion per year for twenty years; commercial use of hydrogen fusion is not expected until the year 2015. Again, we must measure opportunity cost.

THREE WAYS TO ANSWER THE THREE QUESTIONS

Economic systems through history fall into three broad categories depending on the method they employ to answer the three questions about goods and services: what? how? for whom? The three categories are traditional, command/planning, and market-price system.

In the real world, economic systems are rarely 100-percent examples of any one category. The United States economy is best described as a market-price system, but it contains many command elements like regulatory agencies and executive orders issued by governors or presidents. And many traditional elements are present also, as in the way many young people choose their parents' occupations. Consequently, most systems are *mixed* systems, but most systems also are identifiable as being predominantly of one type or another.

Traditional Systems

Societies with **traditional systems** find the answers to the three questions by copying the decisions made by previous generations. The best examples of traditional systems are seen in primitive tribes. The decisions about what crops will be produced (or what game will be hunted) and how this food will be

The traditional behavior of tribal societies—copying what has has always been done—exists even in modern societies.

produced and distributed are made by copying what the tribe has always done. Change is slow. Everyone's role in the tribe is understood. Tasks are assigned to members of the tribe in the same way those tasks were assigned in previous generations.

Although primitive tribes provide the best examples of traditional behavior, we often find such behavior in modern societies—particularly in the way we copy one another's dress and, despite having our consciousness raised by the Women's Movement, continue to train and hire female rather than male secretaries or male rather than female airline pilots.

Command/Planning Systems

Command/planning systems are systems where the three questions are answered by the central government. The purest form of command/planning systems are dictatorships or those nations governed by an elite group. Examples are the People's Republic of China, the Soviet Union and, in varying degrees, its satellites, plus Albania and Cuba. These countries are so-called "communist" countries operating, in theory, according to the ideas of Karl Marx. Other *1867* examples of command/planning are military dictatorships like Argentina and some of its neighbors. In both types of command/planning systems the three questions are answered by those in command.

But national economic planning also appears in some of the Western democracies like France. In France, business executives, government officials, and labor union leaders meet annually to discuss economic goals for industry for the next five-year period. Compliance is voluntary. For that reason, French planning is sometimes called "indicative planning" to convey the idea that goals are "indicated," not necessarily required. Consequently, there is great diversity among countries in the amount of planning they do, as well as in the amount of "commanding" done by their central governments.

Market-Price Systems

Economic systems based on prices and the bargaining that occurs between buyers and sellers are **market-price systems**. When a price is agreed upon and a sale is made, the three questions are answered. The buyer's agreement to pay determines what is produced, how it is produced, and, of course, for whom it is produced. Each buyer and seller represents an economic unit (individual, family, business firm, government agency, or country) that is motivated by self-interest to make the best deal (or profit) it can for itself.

When buyers and sellers come together to agree on a purchase or sale, the transaction takes place in what economists call a **market**. The term "market" describes any method by which, or place at which, buyers can communicate with sellers. A good or service is purchased or sold for a price, and the price helps to determine what kinds of economic activity will take place in a market-price system.

The decisions made by buyers and sellers help to determine prices. And prices in turn signal the ways our society decides what to produce, how to produce, and for whom to produce. The quantity and quality of lettuce on hand in Los Angeles, for instance, is determined by hundreds of freely made producing and buying decisions. Each one of these decisions involves someone's conscious or unconscious assessment of opportunity cost. The farmer may wonder whether to grow lettuce or beets; the buyer may wonder whether to buy lettuce or spinach.

The Market-Price System Is Really an Auction

Many observers liken market-price systems to an *auction*, because somewhere behind the scenes, buyers bid among themselves for the goods and services sellers want to sell. When you go to the supermarket, no bidding is apparent. The prices of all the products are shown. You decide to buy or not to buy, or how much to buy, depending partly on price.

Where, then, is the auction? Your buying decisions cause changes in the store's inventory. When the inventory drops below desired levels, those who buy for the store must then *bid* (against other stores) for supplies offered by farmers (or brokers).

The Markets for Resources

Your buying decisions will also influence farmers in their decisions about what crops to grow and how much land to devote to each crop, leading to decisions about what fertilizers, insecticides, delivery systems, and machinery they will need. These decisions will in turn influence the production decisions of firms that supply farmers.

The farmer's decisions about the amounts and types of land, fertilizers, and other necessities of production are decisions that answer the "how" question. These decisions are made in many so-called "resource" markets. These markets do not deal in the product or service finally sold to the consumer; rather, they deal in all of the things (like the land, the workers, the tools and machines) that producers require for production.

In short, in pure market-price systems, *everything* is for sale—products, services, and resources. The haggling that leads to a purchase or sale answers the three questions.

Self-Interest—The Driving Force

More than two hundred years ago, a famous economist named **Adam Smith***
wrote (1776) that "it is not from the benevolence of the butcher, the brewer, or the baker, that we expect our dinner, but from their regard to their own inter-

---

* Adam Smith is introduced more formally on page 31.

est. We address ourselves, not to their humanity but to their self-love. . . . Nobody but a beggar chooses to depend chiefly upon the benevolence of his fellow citizens."[1]

Smith was identifying what he felt was the fuel that drove our market-price system—the force of self-interest. We work, according to Smith, primarily to satisfy our own wants, not out of "benevolence" for someone else. This self-interest makes the market-price system work. Self-interest forces producers to produce at a profit and the people, generally, to buy those things and work at those trades that give them the greatest satisfaction.

One wonders if we operate this way out of a natural human instinct, perhaps like fear of falling. If so, we can expect our market-price system to continue through the ages, perhaps with a few adjustments but with the same basic engine, driven by the same fuel. If not, on the other hand, we should view our system as merely one stopping place on a path leading to something else, to another system, fueled perhaps by an urge to protect long-term survival of the human race—rather than by more immediate self-interest.

In support of this second view, there is evidence to show that self-interest and the widespread use of markets are new phenomena. As one writer puts it, "The notion of making the motive of gain universal never entered the heads of our ancestors. At no time prior to the second quarter of the nineteenth century were markets more than a subordinate feature in society."[2] But, around 1825, there was a startlingly "abrupt change." Suddenly, land, labor, and capital became available in markets. Also, the widespread use of money replaced the barter system that had been in operation throughout Europe.

Consequently, our present market-price system can be viewed as simply one rung on a ladder leading to something else. We don't know yet what the next rung looks like, or where the ladder leads. But we do know what the last rung was like. The next section is devoted to a description of this immediately preceding "rung." The purpose of the section is to provide you with a basis for thinking critically and constructively about our present way of answering the three questions.

A BRIEF HISTORY OF OUR MARKET-PRICE SYSTEM

Market-price systems as we know them today did not make their appearance in Europe until well after the end of the Middle Ages, or roughly 1750. Prior to that time, many things were not for sale; there were no prices established for many products; money was much less important than it is today. The absence of prices is particularly noticeable in the absence of markets for land and for labor: land was acquired by conquest or inheritance, and laborers did not change jobs.

The Status of Land from the Middle Ages to 1750

Visualize a Europe dotted with small towns and villages, often clustered around a nobleman's house or castle. The scene is primarily rural and agricultural.

Farming is done on small strips that fan out like spokes of a wheel from the nobleman's house. On each of the strips, a serf and his family live and work the soil.

A portion of the crops is delivered to the nobleman as rent for the use of his land; the serf and his family can keep and consume the remainder. The relationship of the serf to his noble is mutually helpful in that the noble provides military defense for the serf in exchange for the serf's food production and military service in time of war.

The land is not for sale. The crops are generally not for sale either—except that, as larger, nonself-supporting towns grow, a portion of the crops will leave the noble's domain* and appear in small cash markets in the towns. (This exception is one of the forces that signalled the end of the Middle Ages.)

The land did not change ownership unless the change was made by conquest (the principal means of expanding land and wealth). And usually the serfs stayed right where they were, under the new "owner."

When the nobleman died, his land was not sold but was given to his eldest son under the laws of primogeniture (resulting in many intrigues and murders by those left out—to say nothing of providing the plots for many old movies).

The Status of Labor in the Middle Ages

The people and their descendants stayed in the same occupation for many generations. A serf remained on his land for life. His children were expected to do the same.

The attitude of the serf and his family were traditional. They did not aspire to anything better for themselves or for their children.

The status of workers in the towns was comparable. Young workers were generally apprenticed to work for a guild**—to engage in, say, the making of cloth. The apprentice lived in the house of the guild "master." The apprentice's wages were his room and board.

Like the serf, the apprentice was expected to stay put. In fact, the rigid Apprenticeship Laws prevented the apprentice from leaving the guild where he was employed.

Even after promotion to journeyman, the worker was bound by tradition to stay with the same trade. Moreover, tradition required the workers' sons to learn that trade, so that families would frequently be involved with the same occupation for many generations.

One sees here a society where explicit rules and implicit tradition prevent anyone from "getting ahead," from trying to improve his station in life. This idea so interested Irish historian John Bagnell Bury that he wrote a book called *The Idea of Progress* (1920) to show that man's desire to improve his material welfare is recent; that throughout the Middle Ages, man's search for happiness, if any, was concerned with success after death rather than before it.

This point indicates the power of the Roman Catholic Church. The people were generally more interested in getting to heaven with the aid of the Church than in amassing wealth while alive. The teachings of the Church served to strengthen this attitude, as the next section will indicate.

The Attitude of the Roman Catholic Church during the Middle Ages

The attitudes of the people who dominated religious thought during the Middle Ages were greatly influenced by the Greek philosopher Aristotle (384–322

---

* The noble's enclave is called a "manor." We are describing the manorial system here.

** The medieval guilds were forerunners of the modern factory. They were large houses where thirty to fifty boys and men worked. The guilds specialized in particular tasks; that is, one guild would make cloth, another jewelry, and so forth. Usually, the output of the guilds was not intended for sale in markets but was produced at the request of some wealthy personage in the area.

B.C.). In particular, Aristotle had condemned people for wanting to amass large sums of money and for lending money to earn interest. In his time and during the Middle Ages, the practice of lending money to earn interest was called **usury**. (Nowadays, the term "usury" applies only to rates of interest considered excessive.)

Aristotle's feelings about money came from his belief that, by itself, money was useless. (After all, what can one do with money in a desert wilderness?) Consequently, it was ethically correct to use money where goods and services were available in exchange. But it was not correct to let money by itself earn additional money. Aristotle wrote that "the most hated sort [of transaction between people], and with the greatest reason, is usury, which makes a gain out of money itself, and not from the natural use [exchange for purchases] of it."[3]

In the Middle Ages the Church revived and supported Aristotle's view, because it helped the Church focus its followers' attention on spiritual matters rather than on the evil business of getting rich. Church doctrine was formulated by an elite group of priests called the **Schoolmen** (or, often, the Scholastics). The Schoolmen* did not address congregations of people in the churches, as did the regular priests. The Schoolmen were aloof and apart. Their job was to interpret previous, written doctrine and distribute to the ministering priests what was considered "the last word" on all matters of ethical behavior. Their writings formed what is called **Canon Law**. And, although the origin was the Church, this body of rules was enforced by the nobles, just as if the rules had been passed by a civil authority like a parliament.

The provisions of Canon Law that interest us here are the just price, the just wage, and the doctrine of usury. All three served to delay the appearance of a true market-price system.

The Just Price

The Schoolmen wanted to be sure that every exchange involved a trading of equivalent value; in particular, that a buyer was never cheated into paying more than something was worth. But how did the Schoolmen determine "what something was worth"? That question stirred much thought and discussion. Finally, they decided that the **just price** was whatever the community thought a product was worth (the "common estimate"). The Schoolmen wanted to be sure that sellers never made undue profit through fraud, monopoly advantage, or the buyer's ignorance.

One can see here the Church's disapproval of financial success. Moreover, we can see the Church's endorsement of the general rule that no one should get ahead too fast.

The Just Wage

Much more than the just price, the **just wage** served to keep everyone in his place. Whereas the just price applied primarily to the sellers, the just wage applied both to seller and *buyer*. From the point of view of the buyer (the employer) the wage could not be more than that necessary to maintain the worker's *present station* in life (or that of his parents). From the worker's point of view, he should not ask for more than this amount.

If you were a lord, it was perfectly correct for you to expect to maintain a

---

* Thomas Aquinas (1225–1274) is the best known.

The elite Schoolmen ordained that God allowed no upward mobility from the ordered ranks.

lord's way of life. Thus, the Schoolmen believed men were placed by God in ordered ranks, each permitted to maintain a given lifestyle. There was no upward mobility. Anyone aspiring to move up in the ranks was guilty of *avarice*—one of the Seven Deadly Sins.

The Usury Doctrine

The usury doctrine prohibiting the charging of interest on loans differed from the just-price and just-wage doctrines. The latter were attempts to insure a fair price. The usury doctrine prohibited all interest, with some carefully noted exceptions.

The Schoolmen's argument originated with Aristotle. It was based on the notion that there are two kinds of products: "fungibles" (durable goods like land or farm implements) and "consumptibles" (perishable goods like food).

The usury doctrine permitted rent payments for the use of fungibles, because the Schoolmen argued that, in this case, the object itself and the use of it were separate and distinct. One could verify this distinction between use and ownership by observing that after a fungible like land was used by someone else, the land itself would revert to the original owner. But, the Schoolmen went on to argue, it was impossible to lend the use of a consumptible—say, an apple—to someone else, because the lender could not expect the return of the *same* article.

The Schoolmen called money a consumptible, because the lender of one coin could not expect the same coin back. Interest charged for such a good was immoral.

EFFECTS OF THE USURY DOCTRINE. The usury doctrine was important because it kept money from being available for borrowing. This slowed the industrial development of Europe and the resulting emergence of a full-fledged market-price system. More than anything else, the doctrine reduced the supply of funds that could have been used to finance expanding enterprises and the commercial development of new ideas.

Because the supply of money available for loans was sparse, the interest rates that were allowed were high.* People needing money couldn't afford the high interest rates, even though the Church was sympathetic to their needs.

Nevertheless, as the Middle Ages wore on, the doctrines of the just price, just wage, and usury weakened and were compromised increasingly. By A.D. 1700, the doctrines were in shambles and could no longer halt the emergence of market-price systems. The compromises affecting the usury doctrine help to illustrate what happened.

THE WEAKENING OF THE USURY DOCTRINE. In the later stages of the Middle Ages, commerce among various parts of Europe increased. There were famous town fairs where food and many kinds of goods were sold. Ships had found their way to the Americas and to the Orient. Spanish ships brought gold and silver to increase the amounts of cash available. All of these gradual changes put pressure on the doctrine of usury. The doctrine was weakened in three ways:

1. The Schoolmen began to allow interest to be charged to compensate the lender for the risk of nonrepayment or the risk of delay in repayment. What especially hurt the prohibition against interest was that the Schoolmen eventually allowed the lender and borrower to agree on a "conventional penalty" to cover the risks of such delays. The conventional penalty could be written into the loan contract. Thus, in effect, interest was permitted.

2. Matters were made even more complicated by the emergence of silent partnerships, where silent partner A provided funds to finance a venture carried on by B and C. Somehow, A had to be rewarded without calling the reward interest. At first, the Church approved the arrangement by calling A's share profit. But this view broke down with the development of a three-way contract between A, B, and C, in which A was promised a minimum amount for his risk taking *and*, in addition, a share of the profits. The Church had to give way here, because if one amount reserved for A was profit, the other had to be interest.

3. The Church became a lender itself when it set up charitable loans in Northern Italy. The Church discovered (perhaps to its embarrassment) that, like other lenders, it had to charge something extra to cover the risk of nonrepayment plus the administrative costs of investigating the borrower's credit.

The weakening of the usury doctrine paved the way for rapid industrial development and the appearance of a market-price system. When the prohibitions against usury were dropped, money became available at much lower rates of interest for the financing of new ventures and for the expansion of existing ones. As markets grew in size, larger and larger amounts of money were needed to finance ever larger enterprises.

---

* This point is confusing. The usury doctrine prohibited all charging of interest, yet interest rates were high. The explanation for this apparent contradiction is that there were some illegal loans—a black market for borrowing money. And, the Schoolmen did permit interest in exceptional cases, as the section on "weakening" indicates.

And as money became increasingly available, the calculations of business progress in money terms became the rule. The lock-step constraints of the just wage and the just price gradually disappeared as business owners juggled their costs and prices to expand their profits. Thus the freer use of money helped the economic activity of the times to escape the strictures of Canon Law.

This section has helped to explain how increased use of money enabled Europe to move from a system of tradition mixed with command toward a market-price system. In the next section, we will consider how land, labor and capital became members of the newer system.

The Factors of Production Join the Market-Price System

Nowadays, it is commonplace for us to speak of renting or buying land, renting or buying buildings, or hiring or firing laborers. These resources were generally not available for sale in the Middle Ages, but now they are. And in economics we call them the **factors of production**.

Many writers believe that the availability for sale of the *factors* in markets signals the real beginning of our present market-price system, because cash markets for *goods* and *services* are almost as old as the human race. But the widespread availability of the factors in markets is new, beginning only about 200 years ago. The development of these factor markets are described briefly.

Land

During the Middle Ages, as we have noted, land was divided up into large estates. The ownership of these estates did not change unless the existing owners were thrown off the land by a victorious army. No member of the owning family would dream of selling even a parcel to someone outside the family. The land was definitely not part of the market scheme.

But eventually something happened that forced many landowners to sell their ancestral homes and estates. What happened was the arrival in Europe of large quantities of gold and silver from the Americas. For example, during the years 1501 to 1660, roughly 17 billion grams of silver and 181 million grams of gold arrived in Europe,[4] with a combined value of $14 billion (valued at today's prices). The impact of this relatively gigantic amount of cash on an essentially barter economy enabled many of the newly rich to bid up prices for goods and services they wanted to buy. And, during the period, average prices rose, by one estimate,[5] 4.3 times.*

What does this rise in prices have to do with the land ownership? Typically, the landowner-serf relationship was one of a creditor to a debtor. During a period of rising prices, a debtor wins; the creditor loses. If the debtor owes the creditor periodic payments, fixed in amount, each payment has less and less purchasing power as the months go by. To whatever extent the serf had rent payments to make that were in money** terms (instead of in bushels of grain), the landlord found that with each payment he could not buy as much as with the previous one. By 1650, the lord who received money payments from his serfs found that those payments could buy only one-fourth as much as they had for his ancestors in 1500.

---

* Clough calls it the "European Price Revolution of 1450–1659"; see notes 4 and 5 under references.

** A change that had taken place gradually.

The landlords were "land poor," living in fancy houses with rich furnishings but short of cash to buy the necessities of day-to-day living. And so, many landlords went bankrupt and had to sell out to those who held the cash—typically the merchants—who soon became known as the "merchant-princes." Land became available in the marketplace as a factor of production that could be bought and sold.

Labor

It is true that, during the Middle Ages, workers were paid a wage, but usually the wage was in "kind." Apprentices in the guilds received their room and board, although the skilled journeymen received money wages. The serfs working in the fields earned their livelihoods by being able to keep a portion of their crops.

But nowhere in that setting do we find a pool of labor one could hire. As a new business owner, you could not hire people away from other enterprises. The Apprenticeship Laws made it illegal. And the serfs were bound to keep working for the lord who protected them.

Nevertheless, this unavailability of unattached labor began to change. Beginning in about 1500, large landowners, particularly in England, became aware of increases in the demand for wool and the opportunities for large profits in sheep-raising. Accordingly, they changed the character of their estates.

Up to this time, large landed estates existed primarily for self-support for the lord's family, his staff, and his serfs. The serfs worked the strip farms and watched over a few farm animals allowed to graze on communal fields owned by the lord. These activities produced very little cash income for the lord.

With the possibility of large profits from the sale of wool, many large landowners fenced ("enclosed") their estates, brought in thousands of sheep, and forced many of the serfs to leave the land. This action by the landowners is called the **enclosure movement**. The movement continued at an irregular pace for 350 years until about 1850.

No precise figures are available as to the number of people forced to leave the land. But we can guess that the number was in the many thousands because, by 1850, half of the arable land in England was enclosed.

The people forced off the land gradually moved to the cities. Called the "wandering poor," they became the members of a pool of very cheap unemployed laborers looking for work. Their presence helped the formation of early mass-production factories like textile mills. The factories, in turn, gradually replaced the guilds where the emphasis had been on highly skilled hand work—on quality, not quantity.

Significant in this tale is the role of profit. The spirit of Canon Law was that no one should profit unfairly at the expense of another. In contrast, the enclosure movement was motivated by self-interest, a symbol of a new era when the search for profit became more important than spiritual sanctity.

The creation of a pool of unattached, readily available labor by the enclosure movement was given added momentum by increases in population, beginning about 1800, and by increased use of machinery, improved seeds, fertilizers, and water systems on farms. The large estates, now devoted to sheep grazing, couldn't absorb more people. Improvements in farming methods led to a dramatic decrease in the number of workers needed on farms. In the Middle Ages each serf and the working members of his family supported perhaps two or

To gain profits from wool sales, landowners enclosed their estates, brought in thousands of sheep, and forced the serfs to leave.

three other people. In modern times, one farmworker in the United States can support fifty other people. The increase in population and improvements in farming guaranteed the availability of a surplus of labor for sale.

Capital

The remaining factor of production that is needed to produce anything, besides land and labor, is a building containing manufactured tools and equipment. For example, to make a tapestry one needs a building containing one or more looms. Economists call the buildings, machines, trucks, filing cabinets, and other equipment used in production **capital**.

Nowadays, when we want to start a business, these forms of capital are available in markets. We can buy them. But during the Middle Ages, as we have seen, the land and the buildings on the land didn't change hands until landowners were forced by rising prices to leave. The traditional rule was that families did not sell their land or their buildings.

Consequently, the buildings on such land didn't change ownership. Moreover, it was virtually impossible to build a new building or buy one in the towns because the existing guilds had monopoly rights to produce everything that was produced.

And so a number of forces combined to make capital available to markets:

1. The enclosure movement provided the labor force needed to staff mass-production factories. The factories competed with the guilds and eventually broke the guilds' power to regulate production. As the guilds died, the barriers preventing new enterprises from creating—and/or obtaining—capital crumbled.

2. The influx of gold and silver created a *new* class of rich merchant-princes who could offer irresistible amounts of cash for the capital they needed.

3. And the cash needed to finance new enterprises (or expand old ones) became available with the death of the doctrine of usury.

And so all the elements (the factors) needed for production became available in markets. But this availability isn't quite enough. Someone is needed who has the gumption to purchase the factors and start an enterprise. This person (or group of people) is called an entrepreneur.

Entrepreneurship

The **entrepreneur** is the person with the gleam in his or her eye who risks everything to start a new enterprise. The Middle Ages would have discouraged that person's appearance. It was wrong to try anything new. (For example, for decades the tapestry-making guilds followed rules declaring there had to be just so many threads per inch in the cloth.) What was important in the Middle Ages was the blessing of the Church, not the amassing of wealth. But as we have seen, the decline of Canon Law and the availability of land, labor, and capital made the new risk-taking, profit-seeking adventurer possible. And so the entrepreneur arrived.

In the modern world, identifying the entrepreneur is sometimes difficult. In a family-owned hardware store, the husband and wife are the owners and risk-takers and are, therefore, the entrepreneurs. But because they work in the store and pay themselves wages, they are also laborers.

The distinction becomes more difficult when we think of a large corporation. Who is the entrepreneur? Technically, the stockholders are, because they bear the risk of loss, hoping for profit. Their money started the business; it purchased the necessary factors of production. Like the hardware store owners, the corporation president may be both a labor factor of production (earning a wage to manage the corporation) and an entrepreneur (a stockholder). Regardless of who, or what group, the entrepreneur is, the entrepreneurial spirit of risk-taking, driven by the search for profit, is the force that fuels the operation of the true market-price system.

As the Middle Ages drew to a close, a champion of the new era of free-wheeling markets appeared. We think of him now as the originator of modern economic theory.

Adam Smith

Eighteenth-century economist Adam Smith (see Box Essay on page 31) believed that the market-price system would provide the most efficient possible allocation of resources and that all forms of land, labor, capital, and entrepreneurship would be employed to maximum advantage under such a system. He believed that the price system and the movement of resources to the most profitable use would lead to the highest possible total production and standard of living. If one occupation or product became more profitable than another, he stated, resources would begin to flow toward it, bringing the price down and the quantity up so that consumers would always benefit and no entrepreneur could earn any unusual profit for long. These ideas were expressed in Smith's 1776 book, *An Inquiry into the Nature and Causes of the Wealth of*

BOX ESSAY

Adam Smith, 1723–1790:
The Man with the "Invisible Hand"

The year 1776 marked the birth of a political revolution in America, and its birth certificate was the Declaration of Independence. In England the year marked an intellectual revolution. Modern economic theory was born, and its birth certificate was Adam Smith's *The Wealth of Nations.*

Smith's beliefs are subject to controversy. Some people claimed he was a truly religious man. Others called him a cynical realist. Some said his sympathies lay with the laboring class. Others believed his way of life precluded any action that would harm the elite.

The son of a customs official who died before he was born, Smith was kidnapped by gypsies at the age of four and abandoned by the side of the road. He recovered, and by age fourteen enrolled at Glasgow College. Three years later, he received a scholarship to Oxford, where he stayed for six years, even though he was miserable

much of the time.

(The university was at that time operating under a "do your own thing" system, with students literally teaching themselves whatever they wanted to know, a custom Smith thought was an exercise in futility.)

After Oxford he spent two years searching for a job and finally, in 1748, he was appointed to a lectureship in English literature at the University of Edinburgh. He did so well that three years later, at the age of 28, he received the professorship of logic at Glasgow College and the next year ascended to the professorship of moral philosophy.

After thirteen years in Glasgow, Smith became a traveling private tutor to the Duke of Buccleuch, ward of Charles Townshend, the Chancellor of the Exchequer (and the man who was to help precipitate the American revolution). This position provided generous remuneration, as well as many side

benefits in places visited and people met, and during this time Smith began writing *The Wealth of Nations.* Unfortunately, the job unexpectedly terminated after two-and-a-half years, and he returned to Scotland.

In Scotland he became Commissioner of Customs and settled down purposefully for the next ten years to writing his book. He also, unpurposefully, began perpetuating his reputation for absentmindedness. One morning, for instance, while strolling in his dressing gown in his garden, he became so engrossed in his thoughts that he walked fifteen miles from home before he became aware of his surroundings.

Adam Smith is especially noted for his theory of the "invisible hand" and his advocacy of free trade even though, in his position as Commissioner of Customs in Scotland, he dealt with import taxes.

Nations, considered the beginning of modern economic theory. In one famous passage, he concluded that the market-price system would take care of itself if left alone. If each participant pursued his own self-interest, the system as a whole would produce the maximum quantity of goods, just as if an "invisible hand" were leading society to the best of all worlds. Smith's statement formed the basis for the laissez-faire* political philosophy—noninterference by government in the workings of the economic system.

Here are his words:

As every individual, therefore, endeavors as much as he can both to employ his capital in the support of domestic industry, and so to direct

---

* The French term "laissez-faire" means "let the people do as they please." In Smith's day, the laissez-faire idea was a plea of the Physiocrats, a group of economic thinkers in France who wanted to free French business firms from a tangle of government regulations and tariff barriers. Since those days, the phrase is used commonly to indicate minimal government interference with a market-price system.

that industry that its produce may be of the greatest value; every individual necessarily labors to render the annual revenue of the society as great as he can. He generally, indeed, neither intends to promote the public interest, nor knows how much he is promoting it. By preferring the support of domestic to that of foreign industry, he intends only his own security; and by directing that industry in such a manner as its produce may be of the greatest value, he intends only his own gain, and he is in this, as in many other cases, *an invisible hand* to promote an end which was no part of his intention. Nor is it always the worse for the society that it was no part of it. By pursuing his own interest he frequently promotes that of the society more effectually than when he really intends to promote it.[6]

Smith's statement that a laissez-faire market-price system promotes the interest of society was based on his belief that, in such a system, entrepreneurs would battle (compete) intensely with one another for the consumer's money. In a society where entrepreneurs and workers are free, he stated, competition among them will force them to produce the goods and services that consumers want most. Only in a free, competitive society where entrepreneurs and workers are free to pursue their special talents, and where consumers are free to choose products from a number of competitive firms, will the consumer know whether or not he or she is getting the best deal. If, as in a planned economy, you can buy only one type of coat, you have no way of comparing the coat offered (and its price) with another.

Free choice and competition not only give each consumer the best deal, they ensure the most efficient and most profitable use of each resource. Furthermore, the fluctuation of prices (and profits) ensures the production and distribution of the quantities consumers will buy in each geographical location. Thus, says Smith, freedom of choice, spurred on by self-interest, an absence of government interference, and competition, will provide the greatest benefits for consumers and society.

AN EVALUATION OF OUR MARKET-PRICE SYSTEM

The great advantage of the market-price system is that no planning mechanism is necessary in Washington, D.C., to produce the goods and services people want, in the right quantities, in the right times and places, and at the right prices. And, entrepreneurs will want to use the factors of production as efficiently as possible in order to maximize their profits. Inefficient entrepreneurs will be weeded out by competitors and forced into bankruptcy. More important than anything else for those who live in it, a market-price system is compatible with democracy and political freedom. The system organizes production in a way that enables its people to be free to pursue their own self-interest—to "pursue" their own version of "happiness."

For 144 years this view of the benefits of a market-price system prevailed, despite opposition from critics like Karl Marx (1818–1883). It was not until after the Great Depression of the 1930s that the theory of a free, unregulated market-price system came under serious attack. Since then, the system has been criticized for failing in five areas: (1) preserving competition, (2) preventing "boom-and-bust" cycles, (3) distributing income evenly, (4) producing social goods, and (5) preventing pollution.

Decline of Competition

The motivation of self-interest causes a competitive economic system to become increasingly less competitive. No entrepreneur wants to be subjected to ruinous competition from a competitor. Instead, entrepreneurs want to insulate themselves from competition by becoming bigger (meaning that new firms will need to invest more if they are to compete), by participating in combinations, by advertising, by engaging in franchise agreements, by promoting licensing laws, by obtaining patent rights, and by otherwise erecting barriers to entry that prevent other firms from competing. Smith recognized these monopolistic tendencies and condemned them.

As competition lessens, the existing firms no longer need to worry so much about producing as efficiently, or producing as good a product, or charging the lowest possible price. There is evidence that competition is lessening in the United States. More on this in Chapter 8.

Boom and Bust

The very fact that a market-price system is operated by self-interested groups of entrepreneurs and workers in conflict with one another produces unstable levels of employment and prices. History has shown that the market-price system does not guarantee full employment. In 1933, when government participation in the private economy was negligible, the unemployment rate reached 24.9 percent. It was never below 14 percent in the years 1931 to 1940.

During the 1970s most segments of the economy suffered from losses in real income caused by inflation that continued into the 1980s. There is also evidence that inflation may result in unemployment because some people may buy less when prices go up (with any given income), and less buying means fewer jobs. Supporters of the Adam Smith view argue that inflation is caused by government interference with free prices (price controls) and excessive government spending. Some of the critics, however, insist that inflation and unemployment are the inevitable consequences of conflict fueled by self-interest.

Income Distribution

The market-price system guarantees no particular level of income distribution. As we pointed out, 20 percent of the people in the United States receive only about 5 percent of the total income. The market-price system is really an *auction* on the buyer's side. Suppose there are thirty students on an island and one six-pack of beer. Who gets it? In a primitive society, custom would decide. In a planned society, the planners would decide. In a market-price system, the beer would go to the people able and willing to pay the highest price. The market-price system is simply another way to ration scarce goods and services.

This point deserves greater emphasis. We know that in any system there are not enough goods and services to satisfy everyone's wants. So how do we decide who gets what? In our market-price system, the people with larger incomes will be more apt to be able to buy what they want. People with lower incomes will be more apt to be *unable* to buy some of the things they want. As economists put it, some of the low-income people will be "excluded" from the market.

Any price excludes some people from buying. Either (1) these people are unable to buy because they can't afford the price, or, (2) their desire to buy, given their particular incomes, isn't intense enough to outweigh the cost. Consequently, a market-price system is simply a way of rationing the things produced among people who want them and can afford them.

And so in market-price systems there will tend to be differences in satisfaction resulting from differences in the ability to buy. But, these differences in satisfaction will occur for another, less evident, reason. When we look at the array of goods and services produced by a market-price system, we may find that the array is biased against the wants of the poorest people. If you are an entrepreneur, will you be interested in producing goods or services for people who have little money to buy them? Probably not. So, market-price systems may exclude poorer people from buying while the goods and services produced may be designed to serve the wants of people with more money.

Social Goods

Because the market-price system produces only what people are willing to pay for, it may not provide goods and services when profit is absent or is not apparent to potential entrepreneurs. Goods and services in this category are national defense, police forces, fire departments, roads, public schools, hospitals for poor people. These goods and services are often called **social goods** or public goods.

Pollution

Closely associated with a market-price system's failure to provide social goods is the problem of pollution. Entrepreneurs are often uninterested in protecting the environment, because efforts to do so usually increase the costs of production and reduce profits. It's much cheaper for entrepreneurs to dump waste into local streams or lakes or to allow toxic fumes to escape up their chimneys than to install costly devices to prevent these attacks on the environment.

Pollution is discussed again in Chapter 6. The problem is an example of what economists call "market failure." Another instance of market failure involves conservation of scarce resources, because entrepreneurs may, in some cases, be more interested in short-term profit today than in conserving to provide benefits tomorrow for a future generation. When market failure does occur, some nonmarket action is often taken to solve the problem. By nonmarket action we mean the enactment of environmental protection legislation like the Clean Air Act or the establishment by the federal government of storage reservoirs for oil to provide us with oil in the event of future interruptions in the flow of imported oil.

We have highlighted the major problems faced by market-price systems. The most important point to remember, however, is that every problem has a cost, and the solution to every problem has a cost. Unemployment has a cost in human suffering. Reducing unemployment may involve the cost of additional taxes to finance programs for the unemployed. The job of the economist is to estimate the costs of problems, the costs of the solutions to those problems, and the chances of success of any proposed solution.

SUMMARY

Every society must make three decisions: what goods and services to provide in what quantities, how they are to be produced, and for whom. The manner in which societies answer the what, how, and for whom questions determines the character of their economic systems; that is, whether the system is traditional, planned, or market-price.

The distinguishing characteristic of market-price systems is that not only are goods and services for sale but so also are the factors of production—land, labor, and capital. The appearance of full-fledged market-price systems is recent, beginning around 1750.

This appearance followed a long period during the Middle Ages when economic affairs were conducted by tradition or command. Church doctrine called Canon Law, controlled prices, and wages; charging interest, with a few exceptions, was prohibited.

Toward the end of the Middle Ages, Canon Law was weakened by the enclosure movement, the arrival of cash from the Americas, and inflation which forced many landowners to sell their land. These changes made way for the arrival of the market-price system.

Adam Smith, a Scottish philosopher, endorsed the idea of a market-price system in his book, *The Wealth of Nations.*

Although Adam Smith believed that the market-price system would operate as if "by an invisible hand" to give an ideal solution to the questions of what, how, and for whom, in actuality the system allows many problems to exist, such as unemployment, poverty, pollution, and inflation.

Discussion Questions

1. Are you a factor of production? If you are, what is the opportunity cost of doing what you are doing? Does the benefit gained from what you are doing more than offset the loss of all the other opportunities you have given up?

2. If you were the dictator of a small country, how would you decide how to use each parcel of land? What job should each of your citizens be ordered to perform? How much effort should be put into capital formation at the expense of current consumption? (Assume your country is at peace, with no foreseeable threat of war.)

3. Does the "invisible hand" work? Why or why not?

4. What decisions is the market-price system good at making? What decisions does it fail to make or make poorly?

DID YOU EVER WONDER WHY . . .

. . . it isn't wasteful for restaurants to use disposable plastic "silverware"?

References

1. Adam Smith, *An Inquiry into the Nature and Causes of the Wealth of Nations* (Chicago: Encyclopaedia Britannica, 1952), p. 7.

2. *Primitive, Archaic, and Modern Economics Essays of Karl Polanyi,* George Dalton, ed. (Boston: Beacon Press, 1968), p. 67.

3. From "On the State, Property, and Money," *Politics,* in Philip C. Newman, Arthur D. Gayer,

Milton H. Spencer (eds.), *Source Readings in Economic Thought* (New York: Norton, 1954), p. 11.

4. Shepard B. Clough, *European Economic History,* 2nd ed. (New York: McGraw-Hill, 1968), p. 150.

5. *Ibid.,* p. 151.

6. Adam Smith, p. 194.

3

Socialism, the U.S.S.R., and the People's Republic of China

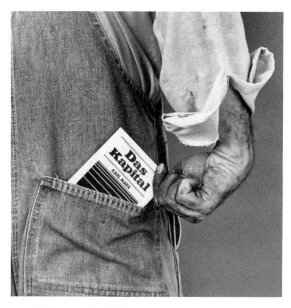

KEY WORDS
Capitalism
Socialism
Communism
Karl Marx
Proletariat
The Communist Manifesto
Alienation
Gosplan
Turnover tax
Nomenklatura
Mao Tse-tung
Commune
Brigade
Team

Most of Chapter 2 was about the ancestry of the market-price system. The United States and many of its major trading partners are predominantly* market-price systems, but many dozens of other nations are not.

This chapter is about those systems where the three questions are answered by other than market forces. Most of these other systems operate under what is called socialism. We need, very much, to understand socialist systems, because many of them were formed out of dislike for the way market-price systems operate. We should study these other systems to help us better understand our own and to improve it.

There are other good reasons for studying socialism. In the United States, socialism is often a bad word. In some circles, to be called a socialist is *almost* equivalent to being called a traitor. Various administrations are accused of leading the country down a disastrous road toward socialism because of such public works as the Tennessee Valley Authority or welfare-oriented legislation like Medicare. Socialism is depicted as a fate worse than death. Yet to many of the world's people, socialism means something good and positive. Primarily it means that their country is trying a system that is intended to correct faults sometimes associated with the market-price system. Over fifty countries with more than 40 percent of the world's population are governed by socialism.

Our discussion of socialism is divided into four sections: the first defines terms, the second talks about Karl Marx, the ''Father of Socialism,'' and the last two describe socialism in practice in the Union of Soviet Socialist Republics (the U.S.S.R.) and the People's Republic of China (the P.R.C.).

DEFINITIONS OF TERMS

In Chapter 2, we discussed three terms commonly used to describe economic systems: traditional, command/planning, and market-price. These terms are timeless in the sense that they are applicable to both ancient and modern societies. Within the last 200 years, three other terms, also designed to label types of societies, have become part of our vocabularies: capitalism, socialism, and fascism. All six terms describe different ways of answering the three basic questions (what? how? and for whom?). But the last three terms are more complex in that they imply types of governments and particular sets of goals.

Capitalism

Capitalism has four aspects, as follows:

1. Private ownership is a generally accepted institution. Factories, land, goods, and services are privately owned by individuals or by groups of individuals like stockholders.

2. Most people are free to pursue their own economic self-interest; that is, to work for personal gain. For this reason, capitalism is often called the *free enterprise system*; most people are free to choose their own occupations.

3. Because people are motivated by self-interest, they will compete with one another to get ahead, to make a better product, to dominate markets in order to obtain a bigger profit. The struggle for bigger profits leads (usually but by no means always) to a high degree of competition between business firms.

---

*We use the word ''predominantly'' to indicate that all systems involve a mixture of ingredients, of capitalism and socialism, or of free markets and command. ''Predominantly'' means that in the United States the three questions are, more often than not, answered by free markets.

4. The three questions are answered by the freely made decisions of buyers and sellers.

The description we have just given is of "pure" capitalism—capitalism without the command elements of tax laws, licenses to buy, and vast numbers of government regulations. But that is clearly not the capitalism that exists in twentieth-century America. Economists frequently call our system *mixed capitalism*. That means our system is a mixture of free, privately owned enterprise on the one hand and government participation on the other.

Socialism

A good way to start an argument is to try to define socialism. Every socialist country has its own version, and there are many socialistic elements in systems we think of as market-price systems. Rome University historian Rosario Romeo once said, "Everyone imagines socialism in his own way." [1] Nevertheless, we will hazard a definition: **Socialism** is a system in which the means of production are owned by the people *as a group*, usually through their government, rather than by individuals. Thus, we distinguish between capitalism and socialism mainly by identifying whether the productive enterprises of a country are privately or publicly owned.

In the countries that have adopted socialism, its supporters hope to overcome what they consider to be capitalism's two major problems: (1) the unequal distribution of wealth, and (2) the uneven course of economic growth with periods of "boom or bust."

For both purposes, socialist countries tend to have a high (relative to capitalist countries) degree of economic planning and government regulation of the economy.

Socialist countries belong to three general categories, depending on their origins and intentions:

1. So-called "communist" countries like the People's Republic of China or the Soviet Union (U.S.S.R.) and its satellites. These countries claim to have abolished private property. They have nationalized the means of production—in most cases by revolutionary means, and their governments often urge others to do the same. However, as we shall see, elements of the market-price system are surviving and in some cases growing even in these countries.

2. So called "market-socialist" countries like West Germany, Great Britain, most countries of Western Europe, and Japan. Note that socialism does not necessarily imply authoritarian government. The market-socialist countries have democratic governments.

3. So called "third-world" countries like Algeria, Libya, Syria, Iraq, Tanzania, and Guyana. Despite their great differences, these countries have two attributes in common: (1) They are all former colonies and are anxious to rid themselves of the colonial practices that exploited them, and (2) they are pursuing policies aimed at reducing the importance of private property.

Fascism

During World War II, the terms "fascism" and "Nazism" were used to describe capitalistic systems under the control of dictators like Hitler and Mussolini.

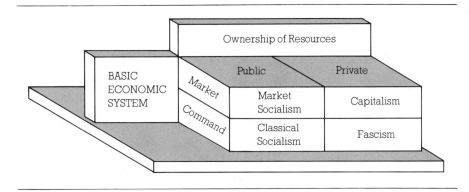

Figure 3-1.
A classification of economic systems.

Curiously, Hitler's drive to power in the 1930s was based on an appeal to the workers and promises to improve their welfare. (In German, the word *Nazi* is an abbreviation for *Nazionalsoziolist*, or "national socialist.") But when Hitler gained power he switched his allegiance to the large corporations that had financed him. Ownership of property stayed in private hands, although many controls were imposed.

Figure 3-1 classifies economic systems according to both their ownership of resources and the political aspects of the system. Thus market-socialist economies combine some kind of market-price system with public ownership. Marxist socialist systems are command systems. Fascism, which combines so-called private ownership with a high degree of government control, is a command system.

The Presence of Markets in All Systems

These terms can be confusing. Should we label a country a market-price system, or call its system capitalism, or what? Just remember that the label "market-price system" describes one of the three methods nations use to answer the three questions, and that capitalism* and socialism are classifications in terms of who owns the means of production. Consequently, market-price systems can exist in either capitalistic or socialistic countries.

Although the United States is more nearly a market-price system than anything else, it is a mixture of systems just as it is a blend of capitalism and socialism. Many choices are not made through markets but are dictated by tradition, like having turkey for Thanksgiving or requiring male workers in department stores to wear coats and ties. And command elements are present in the government's enforcement of safety and environmental standards as well as its regulation of many agricultural prices (the prices of dairy products, for example). And finally, elements of socialism are present in publicly (government) owned enterprises like municipally owned airports and utilities.

And while a market-price system is inevitably found in capitalistic countries, it is found also in traditional and in socialistic countries. Tribal cultures have marketplaces where exchange often takes the form of barter. And socialist countries, as already mentioned, have some forms of private enterprise like small shops or private plots on farms.

---

*Fascism is not mentioned separately here because we think of fascism as a variant of capitalism.

Marx believed that entrepreneurial self-interest leads to the exploitation of labor.

Socialist countries all have one trait in common. Even though they are pursuing their goals in a wide variety of revolutionary or peaceful ways, they adopted their present systems because of the ideas of **Karl Marx.**

KARL MARX, THE FATHER OF SOCIALISM

We usually think of Marx as the father of communism, not of socialism. But as you will see, Marx thought of socialism as a transition stage in society's path toward his true ideal—a communist world. To a Marxist, communism represents the purest form of socialism. For this reason, many of the world's socialist countries like to believe they are following the Marxian path to communism. (You will find a short biography of Karl Marx in the box on page 41.)

Communism and Socialism Compared

The ideal of **communism**, like that of socialism, is that the means of production are owned and operated by "the workers." But communist theory goes considerably further than socialist theory in emphasizing ownership and control by "labor."

Communists believe the institution of private property is the cause of what they consider the most important defect of capitalism: unequal distribution of income. As long as entrepreneurs own the means of production and hire others to work for them, the communists say, there will be separate classes of people, and entrepreneurs and landowners will exploit the industrial workers and agricultural laborers. Because the entrepreneurs own the land and capital, according to communist theory, they can keep the workers trapped in a condition of slavery, for the workers cannot earn a living without using factories or land owned by the entrepreneurs.

Socialists generally believe that people should be paid in proportion to their contribution to production: "From each according to his ability, to each according to his *work.*" Communists view socialism as a transitional phase, during which the state will have to set up planning agencies to answer the three

BOX ESSAY

Karl Heinrich Marx, 1818–1883: The Father of Communism

Karl Marx's father was born Hirschel Levi and was the descendant of a long line of rabbis. However, because of anti-Semitism in the German town of Trier, where he lived, he changed his name to Heinrich Marx and joined the Christian church. His wife, who was also of rabbinical lineage, remained faithful to her religion until 1825 when, after seeing all of her seven children baptized into the Lutheran church, she decided to follow suit. Perhaps because he witnessed the religious dissension between his father and mother, Karl Marx became an enemy of all religious dogma.

Gifted from early childhood, young Karl turned for friendship and intellectual stimulation to his father, who was a successful lawyer and philosopher, and to a family friend, Ludwig von Westphalen, the Royal Prussian Privy Councillor. Although von Westphalen was far removed from the Marx family socially, he was much impressed by the young Karl Marx, and so was his daughter, Jenny. Eventually, Marx's father worried that Karl and Jenny's infatuation with each other might cause friction with the von Westphalens, so he was happy when his son went away to the University of Bonn in the fall of 1835.

On his own, and away from home, Marx immediately began sowing wild oats, running up debts, and neglecting his studies. He was also arrested for noisiness

and drunkenness. His involvement in a duel led to a state investigation, and as a result Marx left Bonn and returned home. He and Jenny von Westphalen became engaged, which may have been a deciding factor in his later life, for he went to Berlin for another try at university work and eventually earned a doctorate in philosophy.

The death of his father in 1838 left Marx with no close family ties because his mother refused to support him, and he had never liked his other relatives. To earn a livelihood, in 1842 he became associated with the *Rhine Gazette*, a left-wing newspaper, and became its editor. Never noted for his tact, Marx soon alienated German government officials with his editorials, and in 1843 the *Gazette* was officially suppressed, leaving Marx a self-styled martyr with an interest in socialism. He was forced to leave Germany for Paris. Against his mother's wishes, he married Jenny von Westphalen and embarked upon a life of poverty.

The year 1844 was a turning point in Marx's life, for it was then he met Friedrich Engels, son of a German cotton manufacturer, who was working in one of his father's factories in England. Engels had had the opportunity (as Marx had not) of observing firsthand the plight of industrial workers in England—the fifteen-hour days, starvation wages, and unsafe working conditions.

In 1845, Marx and his family moved to Belgium, where he founded the first Communist Party organization with no membership formalities, no political program, and no members of the proletariat. Still, it was a move from theoretical to active socialism. In the following years, Marx was occupied with constant writing and political struggle, culminating in *The Communist Manifesto*, which he and Engels drafted in 1848.

Failing to get communism established on the Continent, Marx moved to London in 1849. In 1852 he became a political correspondent in England for the *New York Tribune*. He earned very little and was almost completely dependent upon Engels for support during the last thirty-four years of his life. Even with Engels' help he remained so poor that several of his children died. Despite these difficulties, the first volume of *Capital*, his most famous work, was published in 1867.

Marx continued to work on additional volumes of *Capital* but was unable to complete them. When his wife died in 1881, he said, "The Moor [as his children called him] is dead, too." He died fifteen months later. Engels edited the rest of the material of *Capital* and brought out the second and third volumes after Marx's death.

questions of what, how, and for whom to produce. After its planning is done, the theory goes, the state and its supervisory agencies will "wither away," leaving a classless society of workers and peasants all equal with one another and all owning the means of production. When this true communism has arrived, workers will live by a new philosophy: "From each according to his ability, to each according to his *need*." Thus, in communist/Marxist theory, the workers gradually abandon a what's-good-for-me attitude (Adam Smithian self-interest) and learn to work for the general good of society.

Because today, of course, true communism has not yet arrived, a communist is a socialist who is, at least in theory, working toward a stateless, classless society. Thus, the two most famous examples of communism—the Soviet Union and the People's Republic of China—are actually socialist countries.

To understand how communism came to be opposed to capitalism, we need to understand how communism originated.

Marx's Attack on Capitalism

Karl Marx believed that labor's contribution to production was the source of all value, but that the wages received by laborers were purposely kept far below the value of the products they labored to make. The reason for this disparity, he thought, was that capitalists "expropriated" this "surplus value"* in the form of profit.

Moreover, according to Marx, the capitalists' desire for more and more profits caused them to pay lower and lower wages so they could extract the maximum possible surplus value from the working people. And the capitalists' desire to grow richer, as well as their egotistical desire for a display of wealth, motivated them to invest their profits, wrung from labor in the form of surplus value, in bigger factories and more machinery.

As production continually increased and wages were constantly depressed, Marx thought, sooner or later people would be too poor to buy the flood of goods produced. As demands for goods slackened, the working people making them would be laid off, so that there would be even fewer people earning wages to buy goods. This would cause a depression (like the Great Depression in the 1930s in the United States). Depression would follow depression, each worse than the previous one because of the continually lessening demand for the increasing supply of products coming from bigger and bigger factories.

With each depression, Marx predicted, the plight of the working class—which he called the **proletariat**—would become worse, because of lower wages and higher unemployment, until finally it would become so bad that the working people would overthrow the capitalists and establish a socialist state. Thus, ***The Communist Manifesto,*** which Marx wrote with his friend Friedrich Engels, ends with these ringing exhortations:

> They [the communists] openly declare that their ends can be attained by the forcible overthrow of all existing social conditions. Let the ruling

---

*According to Marx, all value is created by labor. The land is worthless until labor is applied. Capital (machines and factories) represents "embodied labor" because people create it. Therefore, the laborer is entitled to the whole product of his labor. But the greedy capitalist pays him only a portion of the value he creates—just enough for his subsistence. The remainder—in the form of profits, interest, or rent—goes to the capitalist. It is that remainder that Marx called "surplus value." As you can see, Marxist theory does not consider entrepreneurial talent or risk-taking to be a factor of production.

classes tremble at a communist revolution. The proletarians have nothing to lose but their chains. They have the world to win. Working men of all countries, unite!

Marx's attack on capitalism was particularly directed at the concentration of the ownership of private property in one class, that of the capitalists. It was strongly influenced by Engels' observations of the early stages of the factory system, when child labor, in particular, was often abused. He believed the capitalists would accumulate capital (the "means of production") at the expense of a growing number of propertyless proletarians. He also believed that the one way such laboring men could improve their status was to seize the capitalists' wealth and property and control the means of production themselves.

This violent solution is not inevitable, however. History has proved Marx wrong by showing that overt force is not necessary to redivide income and wealth. Through a combination of labor unions and social and economic legislation, the lot of many working people has improved over the years in the United States. In the years between 1939 and 1982, real spendable weekly earnings (earnings adjusted for inflation and after taxes) doubled.*

Still, though Marx might concede that the worker's lot might improve a bit under capitalism, he would insist that capitalism involves a fundamental conflict between the owners (capitalists) and nonowners (proletariat) of the means of production. This conflict, he would say, inevitably produces economic instability in capitalistic countries, as indicated by their periodic recessions. Workers would continue to be paid less than the value of their work and to be deprived of power to make production decisions. These ideas are the essence of Marx's most famous work, *Capital* (*Das Kapital*).

Marx might also correctly point out that, while average real per-capita income has grown, income and wealth are still not distributed equally. Moreover, to any assertion that the working person's lot has improved, Marx might reply, "Why? Because of the market-price system? Or because of labor unions and social-welfare legislation?"

Marx was particularly interested in the way industrial capitalism tended to separate workers from the products they created. Today, workers in large factories find themselves on an assembly line working on only a small part of the whole—say the door assembly of the automobile they produce. No one worker or group of workers is in a position to enjoy the act of creating a whole automobile. Individual workers lose their pride in creativity, the kind of pride skilled artisans like painters, plumbers, or farmers have when they can see their productive efforts "come to life." Industrial workers, Marx pointed out, begin to feel that their jobs and their own existence are meaningless—and this feeling of meaninglessness is worsened by the fact that a capitalist, not the worker, owns and controls the means of production.

Psychologists now call this sense of meaninglessness and powerlessness **alienation**, and Marx is to be given much credit for identifying the problem. However, alienation is not just a capitalist problem. The same sense of power-

---

*But we have to admit that this statement is misleading. All of the improvement in real spendable earnings occurred between 1939 and 1960. Since 1960, real spendable weekly earnings have fluctuated up and down with no long-term improvement.

lessness is found in socialist countries among industrial workers under the control of a central authority.

Marx has left a valuable legacy for social scientists by pointing out that (1) the exploitation of any class is dangerous; (2) capitalism may have a tendency to breed periods of unemployment and human suffering; and (3) a system based on entrepreneurial self-interest sometimes produces ever larger enterprises that may stifle competition and concentrate economic power in the hands of relatively few people. Marx reminds us also that violent revolution is always possible if a large class of people begins to believe it is powerless to achieve the same standard of living enjoyed by many others.

Two Marxist societies born in revolution are the Soviet Union and the People's Republic of China. Let's look at both to see how communist theory has worked in practice.

THE UNION OF SOVIET SOCIALIST REPUBLICS

The Soviet Union grew out of a revolution in 1917 against the almost feudal conditions under the tsars of Russia, where the majority of the people were exploited laborers or peasants working on land that did not belong to them. Since the revolution, the U.S.S.R. has been gradually transformed into an economic system in which more than 95 percent of all enterprises are owned by the state, the rest being only a few shops and markets selling produce from private agricultural plots. (However, the socialist planners have repeatedly found that Adam Smithian self-interest keeps produce on the table in Moscow: Food production from private plots is an important part of the Soviet lifestyle.)

Like many socialist states, the Soviet Union operates under a central economic plan. Production goals are given in a series of five-year plans (produced by a bureaucracy called the **Gosplan**), which are broken down into hundreds of targets or quotas each industry must meet. Three to four million people are involved in the Gosplan planning mechanism, using elaborate inventories to measure the quantities of goods produced and sold and complicated computer operations to decide how to obtain and use resources.

Wages vary from occupation to occupation, although not as much as they do in the United States. Socialist theory espouses equal distribution of income, but reality in the Soviet Union is very much otherwise. (Indeed, high progressive income taxes in market-socialist democracies probably produce a more even distribution than prevails in the Soviet Union.) Basic wages are low by U.S. standards, but bonuses may quadruple a worker's income, and they are widely used to push production beyond specified quotas. Piece-rate systems are also used to push workers harder, and a variety of extra privileges are used as incentives, such as better housing and access to products in short supply.[2]

An overriding goal in the Soviet Union has been the creation of heavy machinery and factories to provide the equipment necessary for industrial growth. The Soviet government is also committed to a program of military spending. To achieve these goals, the government has had to direct resources away from consumer products; that is, it has demonstrated that the opportunity cost of capital formation is sacrificed consumption. For a long time, Soviet women could not buy lipstick, and there are frequent shortages of fresh meat, chicken, and fresh vegetables. When products people want suddenly appear—shoes, for example—there are long lines of people waiting to buy. Some statistics may give you an idea of the burden on the Soviet consumer. In the period 1975-79,

The Soviet government's commitment to military spending led to shortages of consumer products.

the United States spent about 5.3 percent of its gross national product (GNP) for military purposes; the U.S.S.R. spend 14.3 percent.* More significant than the percentages are the absolute sums. In 1979 the U.S.S.R. spent $167 billion out of a GNP of $1,260 billion; the United States spent $122 billion ($45 billion less) out of nearly double the GNP, or $2,374 billion.

How do the Russians take resources away from producing the consumer products people want? A heavy sales tax called a **turnover tax** is put on consumer goods, usually at the wholesale level. Sometimes this tax amounts to as much as 44 percent of the retail price of a product. By varying the amount of the tax, Soviet planners can raise or lower the retail price of consumer goods and encourage or discourage their purchase. Discouraging the consumption of, say, automobiles releases resources for building trucks. In other words, price is still used as a mechanism for rationing, but the high price is less a function of actual scarcity than of masked command decisions.

The turnover tax illustrates a fundamental economic principle: In any society, more capital goods must be produced if the economy is to grow. But, the production of more capital goods requires resources—people, land, steel, and so on—that might have been, at the moment, producing consumer goods. Thus, one of the opportunity costs of producing more capital goods is sacrificed consumption. (In a free-market economy, money for capital goods comes from the reinvested profits of entrepreneurs and the savings—in bank accounts, stock funds, and so on, of many individuals. This is voluntarily forgone consumption.)

Soviet industrial statistics are difficult to evaluate, since they come from government sources alone, and the U.S.S.R. practices strict censorship of its own news media as well as news dispatched by foreign media. There is also evidence of a huge "underground economy" in the U.S.S.R. Economists generally agree that the Soviet rate of economic growth has equaled or exceeded that of the United States, particularly during the 1930s, and that Soviet living standards have risen in recent years. Nevertheless, because the U.S. economy produces almost twice as much as the Soviet economy, any given U.S. growth rate would still provide vastly more goods per year than an equal Soviet rate. (A 5 percent growth rate on $1 is only a nickel, whereas a 5 percent growth on $5 is a quarter.)

*Statistics given are from various tables in the *Statistical Abstract of the United States*, 1982–1983.

The gains of socialist planning have had their costs. Citizens under a socialist-planning system have little or no political and economic freedom—to choose an occupation, start a business, or vote for opposition candidates. Also, socialist planning may build in mistakes on a large scale. A Czechoslovakian economist once told us that he was working with a computer operation that attempted to keep track of 1.5 million items! Imagine trying to estimate the quantities, sizes, colors, and so on of just the items people wear and eat! Mistakes in planning will produce shortages of desired goods and surpluses of things no one wants. The desire to fill quotas may cause factory managers to produce items that cannot be sold. If you are running a nail factory and your quota is expressed in weight, you will probably produce only the heaviest nails. You will pay little attention to producing a variety of shapes and sizes.

An engineer who emigrated from the U.S.S.R. in the late 1970s tells of a factory manager who developed some procedures that greatly reduced the number of defective metal fittings his assembly line produced. Eventually, workers were assigned to destroy perfectly good parts in order to meet the factory's scrap metal quota. During the Soviet prohibition on lipstick manufacture, some employees falsified their plant's inventories and sent materials to an illegal factory where lipstick could be secretly produced at night. (The "lipstick entrepreneurs" were eventually caught and jailed.)

The foregoing stories illustrate a basic difficulty facing control planners: No matter how carefully a plan is drawn, some of the citizens involved will find ways to circumvent or change the plan if the plan does not coincide with their own self-interest. Another basic difficulty is that although central planners can specify goals, the methods they specify for producing those goals may not work. Central plans lack the flexibility to adapt to changing circumstances. The following section helps to explain this point.

COMMAND/PLANNING AND MARKET-PRICE SYSTEMS COMPARED: A LOOK AT FOOD PRODUCTION

The Soviet Union is constantly in need of more food to feed its people. On the other hand, in the United States, we produce more food than we need, and food has become one of our most important exports. A look at how food-production decisions are made in the two countries will help you to visualize some important differences between command/planning and market-price systems.*

During much of the nineteenth century under the tsars, Russia produced most of the food it needed with some left over for export. Indeed, the Ukraine, now part of the U.S.S.R, was called the "breadbasket of Europe." Until 1970, the Soviet Union *exported* grain. Now (in 1983) the Soviet Union will *import* 46 million tons of grain, one-quarter of its grain supplies for both people and livestock. The Soviets especially need grain to feed animals, because shortages of dairy products and meat are particularly visible to the average Soviet consumer.

Recent food shortages in the Soviet Union can no longer be blamed on "bad" years, because the Soviets are now importing grain *every* year, and the

---

*This section depends heavily on Lester R. Brown, "The Food Connection: Transforming the U.S.-Soviet Relationship," *The Futurist*, December 1982. Mr. Brown is president of World Watch Institute, a privately endowed "think tank." *The Futurist* article is an 8-page summary of a 48-page article which can be obtained by writing for Paper 51, "U.S. and Soviet Agriculture," October 1982, World Watch Institute, 1776 Massachusetts Avenue, N.W., Washington, D.C. 20036. The price as of December 1982 was $2.00.

grain imports have not been planned. In 1982, the *planned* amount of grain production was 238 million tons; *actual* production was 170 million tons, a 68-million ton gap.

When we compare grain production in the U.S.S.R with the United States, significant differences become apparent. To rule out differences in climate and differences in the amount of land under cultivation, let's look only at the output per hectare* under cultivation in the two countries in 1950 and again in 1982. In 1950, the Soviets produced 0.8 metric tons of grain per hectare. By 1982, they had increased that figure to 1.4 metric tons, a hefty gain of 75 percent. During the same period, grain production in the United States increased from 1.6 metric tons per hectare to 4.2 metric tons, a gain of 263 percent!

How can there be such differences—given the same amount of land under cultivation? Let's examine just one aspect of farming—fertilization of the soil. In the Soviet Union, farmers are told how much fertilizer they are going to use—say, phosphate—because the production of phosphate is spelled out in a five-year plan. In the United States, a farmer will first test the soil in each of his fields and then decide on a variety of fertilizers and methods and times of applying the fertilizer depending on the particular crop, the soils, and the climate. If the growing season is unusually cold or wet, the farmer may reduce the amount of phosphorus used on vegetable crops, or the farmer might increase the amount of nitrogen used in corn-growing regions to help his corn withstand the late-summer effects of drought.

This kind of flexibility and individual tailoring of fertilizer use is one reason why, in 1981, the Soviets used 26 million tons of fertilizer to harvest 170 millions of grain, while Americans used 21 million tons (19 percent less) to harvest 315 million tons (185 percent more).

There are signs that authorities in command/planning systems are beginning to recognize that top-down decision making lacks the ingenuity and adaptability that individual decision making has, especially when the individual gets to keep some of the profits.

WILL SOVIET SOCIALISM CHANGE DIRECTION?

Well, yes and no. It seems clear now that the Soviets (and also the Chinese) recognize some of the possible weaknesses of central planning. To cure these ills, Soviet planners (and the Chinese) are permitting many enterprises, particularly farms, to operate in private markets. Given carefully described limits, farmers can grow what they want to grow and decide how they want to do it. The restrictions placed on them are (1) a limit on the amount of land that can be used for private purposes, and (2) a formula specifying that some fraction of the amount produced be given to the State. In both countries, the increases in production as a result of such changes have been phenomenal. Do these changes mean that these socialist countries are becoming more like market-price systems? We doubt it, because central authorities retain control and can change or revoke these new freedoms at any time.

Will the Soviets move along the socialist path toward communism? At present, this seems unlikely. They have apparently adopted a system of wage payments and awards of privileges that has created different classes of people with different standards of living—somewhat like what happens in a capitalist coun-

---

*A hectare is a metric measure of land area. One hectare equals roughly 2.5 acres.

try, except for differences in who gets what. Furthermore, Soviet-style planning requires totalitarian government. The people who have such powers will not want to give them up—especially since officials and bureaucrats are at the top of what Hedrick Smith, former *New York Times* correspondent in Moscow, describes as a pyramid-shaped Soviet society with a small elite class at the top.[3] A secret roster of this elite is called the ***nomenklatura*** (nomenclature). These people enjoy all the privileges once reserved for the tsar and his nobles. The *nomenklatura* is found on all levels and at all places, from villages to the Kremlin. According to Smith, it "operates like a self-perpetuating, self-selecting fraternity, a closed corporation."[4] Those who run the show reserve for themselves the privileges of chauffeur-driven cars, villas, and deluxe apartments, which are not available to others at any price.

THE PEOPLE'S REPUBLIC OF CHINA

On October 1, 1949, **Mao Tse-tung*** (1884–1976) announced to the Chinese people that Chiang Kai-shek's armies were defeated. The Chinese people call this day a day of liberation, and today when they talk of history they speak of "before liberation" and "after liberation." They have good reason.

Before and After Liberation

Before liberation, people died in the streets on cold nights. An American newspaper in Shanghai ran an article in early 1949 stating that eighty corpses had been found in the morning after a cold wind the night before. Young girls were forced to become prostitutes. Drug addiction from opium was widespread. Rich peasants charged 100 percent interest every six months on loans to tenant farmers. Taxes were repeatedly collected by warlords until the people were paying taxes a year in advance. Large cities like Canton, Nanking, Peking, and Shanghai were divided up into walled "concessions" owned by foreign companies or governments. In one such concession in Shanghai there was a park with a sign that read NO CHINESE OR DOGS ALLOWED.

People were often treated like beasts of burden, forced to work in the factories and fields from the age of seven. Work was long, averaging twelve hours a day, and wages were barely sufficient to maintain life. Workers and peasants were so poor they could not maintain their families and often sold their babies into slavery for a few pennies. No wonder the Chinese were ready to overthrow their economic system.[5]

Today, the Chinese economy is growing rapidly. Despite the fact that there are tremendous masses of people—more than four times the number in the United States in a country only 2.5 percent larger geographically—all receive, at minimum, a subsistence diet; all have a place to live, adequate clothing, medical care, and free education. Illiteracy, starvation, prostitution, sexually transmitted disease, and drug addiction have, with some exceptions, been reduced or eliminated. Cities are clean. Flies, mosquitoes, and other common pests have almost disappeared. A near-miracle seems to have occurred.[6] How has this come about?

---

*The spelling of Mao Tse-tung is from the Wade-Giles system. At the start of 1979, the Chinese officially adopted a new system called the "Pinyin" (phonetic) system which more closely approximates Chinese pronunciation. Under the Pinyin system, Mao Tse-tung becomes Mao Zedong; Peking becomes Beijing; Teng Hsaio-ping becomes Deng Xiaoping, and so forth. We'll stick with the older, Wade-Giles system on the theory that it is still more familiar to most readers.

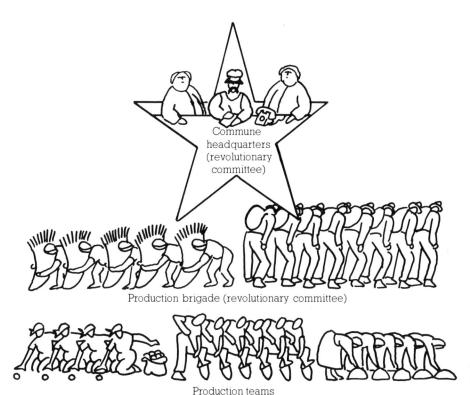

Commune
headquarters
(revolutionary
committee)

Production brigade (revolutionary committee)

Production teams

Figure 3-2.
How an agricultural
commune is
organized.

The Communes

Mao fought for control of China for roughly twenty-two years, from 1927 to 1949. Conversion of the countryside to socialism took about ten years after liberation, and most agricultural land is now organized into **communes** (Figure 3-2). One example is Ping Chow commune near Canton. It is situated on 50,000 acres of land, of which 12,000 acres are under cultivation, and has 69,000 people living in 16,000 households.

The commune is divided into 20 production **brigades**, each consisting of 14 teams with about 200 members each. The **team** is the basic accounting unit for measuring production and determining how food, shelter, and pay will be divided among the people. Communes, brigades, and teams are headed by revolutionary committees elected by the people. The election is not by ballot but by a process of discussion that continues until consensus is reached.

Mao constantly called for self-reliance, and the communes reflect this principle. Most of them have their own schools, hospitals, power sources, machine shops, and metalworks. Except for production of sophisticated machinery, a commune is almost self-sufficient.

The Ping Chow commune's crops are rice, vegetables, fruit, peanuts, and sugar beets. Farm animals are pigs, water buffalo (seen everywhere as draft animals), dairy cows, and poultry. The commune has a printing plant, a peanut oil refinery, and factories where food is processed and lime, cement, textiles, and rattan baskets are produced.

The commune system allows large areas to be organized and this permits much specialization and pooling of equipment.

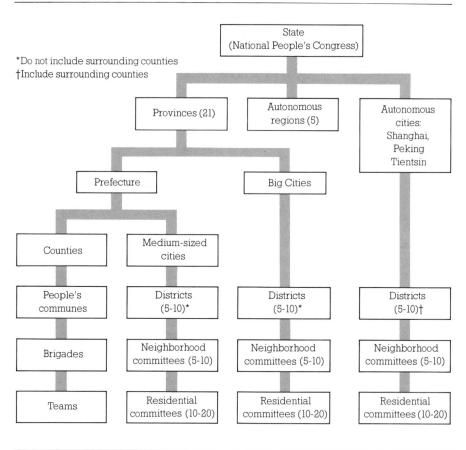

Figure 3.3
Political organization
of the People's
Republic of China.

The Cities

The cities in China are organized much like communes with their brigades and teams. They are divided into districts, neighborhood committees, and finally residential committees (Figure 3-3). Like the team, the residential committee is responsible for about 200 people.

The state owns all enterprises, although the workers are encouraged to feel pride in their commune or factory. Answers to the three basic questions (what? how? for whom?) are determined by an exchange of information between enterprises and ministries located in cities, counties, provinces (states), and the national government in Peking. Enterprises seem to have much more say in what and how to produce in China than in the Soviet Union. There is also less pressure to fulfill production targets; consequently, there is less cheating.

Because the entire society is organized into these small groups of 200, people can share their feelings about the national tasks that confront them and can have a small-town sense of community despite the enormous population. The small-town type of grouping also helps the authorities maintain discipline, for everyone knows what everyone else is doing and people who get out of line are soon discovered. Mistakes, crimes, marital or other interpersonal problems, and "capitalist-roader" thinking are dealt with by the revolutionary committees responsible for each team or residential area. Crime is rare and, despite power struggles in Peking, the people appear to be remarkably united.

Whether they are happy is a different question. A recent article by an American who had lived and worked in a Chinese city (Zhengzhou) for a year suggests they are not happy. This man spoke the language fluently and came to know the people. His conclusion was that their living surroundings were drab; that they were constantly beseiged by political indoctrinators; that the diet was unvaried and entertainment nil; that when traveling, the people were packed like animals in trains; and on and on in considerable detail.[7]

Income and Saving

Although wages are very low, the Chinese people have enough because expenses are minimal. In a family of four with both husband and wife working, combined income is about $50 per month. Each month they pay about $8 for food, $3 for rent, $2 for heat, $1 for electricity, and 10 cents for water. Medical care runs a few dollars a year. Once or twice a year they spend about $10 for clothing (everyone's outer garments are almost alike). Thus, as much as a quarter of family income can be put in a bank and saved for highly prized items—bicycles or sewing machines for example. Unlike the basic necessities, for which the government sets low prices, such luxuries are expensive. A bicycle or sewing machine at $70 represents more than 10 percent of a family's yearly income.

Mao's Great Contribution

Mao's great contribution to China was in giving the peasants a feeling that their status was just as important as a technician's or a scientist's. Mao's philosophy was like that of a coach who belives that it's more important for everyone on the team to play—and to have the right spirit—than to let only the best players play. "Indeed," writes Professor John Gurley, "Maoists believe that rapid economic development is not likely to occur *unless* everyone rises together."[8]

This point is considerably more profound than those few quoted words indicate. At the core of Maoism we find a rejection of Adam Smithian individual self-interest, the incentive that drives market-price systems to produce ever more and more. Market-price systems are based on the idea that economic growth will occur through the efforts of individuals competing with one another in the marketplace. Maoism is based on the categorically different thesis that groups (or nations) will succeed in overcoming scarcity to whatever extent they help all members of the group. (Chinese culture has always placed great emphasis on this kind of mutual help within families. One might say that Mao's doctrines presented the nation or the Chinese society as a whole as a kind of extended family.) A beautiful idea: that we will improve our own material welfare *best* by making sure our friends share *equally* with us in any improvements in material welfare that may occur. Yet, the beautiful idea did not last long.

After Mao

After Mao's death in September 1976, this point of view was drastically revised by Teng Hsaio-ping, Vice Chairman of the Communist Party and Army Chief of Staff.

Teng initiated a new program calling for "Four Modernizations"—of China's agriculture, industry, science and technology, and defense. To accomplish his goals, Teng abandoned Mao's egalitarianism with its let-everyone-play-on-the-team philosophy. Teng decided that winning the game with the *best* players was what counted.

Some examples will help to dramatize the change. Prior to Mao's death, the universities were open to any "worker-peasant-soldier" recommended by his or her team or neighborhood committee. Examinations had been eliminated and students were chosen for ideological (Maoist) purity in an attempt to destroy the elitism that had characterized Chinese higher education, when only the elite could afford preparatory schooling. Teng reinstituted a strict examination policy. The universities became reserved for China's most able.

Teng also revised Mao's doctrine of keeping China's economy self-reliant. During 1978, 530,000 tourists visited China, including thousands of business executives looking for new markets. Coca-Cola was granted exclusive rights to sell in the People's Republic. And what would have been considered the height of "capitalist-roading" during Mao's regime is now being built near Peking—a golf course!

China has entered into a $20 billion trade agreement (oil for steel) with Japan, a $13.5 billion agreement with France (which includes the construction of two nuclear power plants), and other smaller trade agreements with Denmark, Sweden, and Great Britain. The United States is involved in several agreements including building a chain of hotels and establishing landing rights at various airports for Pan Am.

Teng—or his heirs—has a long way to go. In 1978, there were 630,000 students enrolled in China's universities (versus 10 million in the United States). Teng's program for agriculture requires the purchase or building of nearly 5 million pieces of farm machinery; for industry, the replacement of machines often twenty years old; for defense, the modernization of an air force whose most recent bomber was made in 1954.

The Long March

Table 3-1 shows that by most measures of a modern society China is still far from catching up with the Soviet Union and the United States. The section about agriculture reveals the gravity of China's problem. Chinese production of grain is not much more than that in the United States, but China has more than four times as many people (an estimated 1.2 billion in 1982). And most of China's people (85 percent) are needed to work in agriculture because there are very few tractors. Somehow food production will have to be increased and mechanized to release people for work in other activities. Achieving a food *surplus* is the first, necessary step toward economic growth.

Change in the Communes

Prior to 1979, the provincial or regional governments of China gave the communes quotas for each of the crops they produced. The quotas were based on output for previous years and were generally not difficult to meet.* Production under the quota was sold to the government at one price. Production over the

---

*This section draws from Martin and Kathleen Feldstein, "China Gambles on Incentives," *Los Angeles Times*, 20 July 1982, Part IV, p. 3, and Stephen E. Cohen, "Lenin Economics in China, Red Faces in the Kremlin," *Los Angeles Times*, 29 May 1983, Part IV, p. 5.

Table 3-1. A Long March

	U.S.	U.S.S.R.	China
Area	3.6 million square miles	8.6 million square miles	3.7 million square miles
Population	220 million	262 million	1 billion*
GNP	$2.1 trillion	$1.2 trillion*	$444 billion*
Industry			
Steel production	135 million tons	166 million tons	34 million tons
Oil production	474 million tons	629 million tons	110 million tons
Coal production	654 million tons	796 million tons	651 million tons
Auto production	9.2 million	1.3 million	15,000*
Computers in use	340,000	30,000*	2,000*
Agriculture			
Percentage of work force engaged in agriculture	3.3	25	85*
Grain production	294 million tons	259 million tons	325 million tons
Tractors	4.4 million	2.5 million	225,000*
Communications			
Telephones	155 million	22 million	5 million*
Television sets	133 million	60 million	700,000
Paved roads	3.1 million miles	200,000 miles	161,000 miles
Air-passenger miles	193 billion	84 billion	1 billion
Social indicators			
Average yearly industrial wage	$13,400	$3,000	$360*
Average life expectancy	73 years	69 years	65 years
Residential living space per capita	450 square feet*	133 square feet	30 square feet*
Day's earnings to buy bicycle	1¼	7	67
Percentage of population under 20	35	37	40-45*

*Estimates

Source: Adapted from *Newsweek,* 5 February 1979, p. 43. With permission from Fenga & Freyer, Inc.

quota was sold to the government at a higher price. It was the commune's responsibility to divide whatever revenues came in.

In 1979, the central government in Peking decided that the system was not solving persistent food shortages. A new system was adopted called the production responsibility system. Under this system, the communes were given moderate quotas, as before, but once the quota was met, the land was turned over to teams, or, in some cases, to individual families to grow whatever they pleased. This production, in excess of the quotas, could be sold at the family's discretion, either to the government or to private, cash markets. Apparently the Chinese felt that Adam Smithian self-interest and the individual rewards of the market-price system would increase food production. Reportedly, the new incentives have indeed produced substantial increases in agricultural output. Annual growth of agricultural output has tripled and peasant income has doubled since the new system was introduced.

The Chinese concede that the production responsibility system has at least three defects: (1) It stresses production now at the expense of long-term, community-wide projects like irrigation; (2) the emphasis on production in the present neglects the long-term problem of soil depletion; (3) the new system is rapidly leading to considerable differences in income.

In fact, two brothers near Canton were jailed for making $10,000 per year on a truck farm. Later they were released by a high official who commented, "What is wrong with peasants relying on their own effort. . . . We must not get scared and jealous as soon as we see others getting high incomes."[9] That story illuminates the conflict taking place in China between believers in centralized planning (who jailed the brothers) and believers in decentralized, individual incentives (who released them). This conflict between Maoism and capitalism will continue, and the outcome will be crucial to China's future economic and political development.

A TENTATIVE CONCLUSION

Let's sum up our impressions of the Soviet Union and China. We cannot make positive measurements about the success of Soviet versus Chinese planning. In both cases the planning mechanism attempts to coordinate production of all major products—grain, oil, steel, electrical power, and so forth. Observers have commented, however, that lines of people trying to buy scarce items are common in the Soviet Union but are not seen in China. Somehow the Chinese have adjusted incomes and prices so that the quantities demanded do not exceed quantities supplied.

Of course, the pushing and shoving for scarce goods one sees in the Soviet Union is a measure of the people's ability to buy, whereas the absence of lines in China *may* be an indication of the people's inability to buy. But, although the Chinese are terribly poor by American standards, what there is is divided among the people so that everyone is surviving.

Which state is closer to the communist ideal? There is no doubt that China was, prior to Mao's death, working for a classless society far more diligently than the Soviets. Now, the Chinese are dabbling with many market-price "capitalist-roader" experiments. And apparently the central planners in Peking are more willing than their counterparts in Moscow to give up some of their authority. A possible explanation: The communist revolution in China is relatively recent (1949), compared with that of the Soviet Union (1917). Being newer, the Chinese bureaucracy is less set in its ways and is readier to try new ideas. But both countries seem more interested in the near-term goal of economic growth than in the communist ideal of a classless society.

SUMMARY

Socialism is an economic system in which the public, through its government, owns the major enterprises in a state, allocates resources through central planning, and attempts an equitable distribution of wealth and income. Socialist countries in the West are examples of mixed systems—mixtures of capitalism and socialism.

In other socialist countries the term "communism" is used to indicate that the country is following the principles and writings of Karl Marx, one of the earliest leaders of the Communist Party (1847).

Communist theory states that socialism is an interim stage leading eventually to a classless society in which the state has withered away.

Socialism exists in many forms among over fifty nations, involving more than 40 percent of the world's population. Most socialist countries try to equalize incomes; those countries considered communist also try to do away with private property so that all industry and agriculture are collectively owned by the people.

The Soviet Union and the People's Republic of China are both examples of socialism. In both cases almost all property is owned by the state. The Chinese economy, and its whole social fabric, are undergoing a period of fundamental change from egalitarianism under Mao to emphasis on growth.

Discussion Questions

1. Why did Karl Marx believe capitalism would destroy itself?

2. What are the distinctions between socialism and communism?

3. How does the People's Republic of China differ from the Soviet Union?

4. In what respects is the Soviet Union "capitalistic"? China?

5. How are the people motivated to believe in equality in China?

6. What has happened to the goal of equality since Mao's death?

7. What conclusion might you draw about the effects of central planning on productivity?

References

1. "Socialism: Trials and Errors," *Time*, 13 March 1978, p. 24.

2. For many examples, see Hedrick Smith, *The Russians* (New York: Quadrangle/New York Times Book Co., 1976).

3. Smith, *The Russians.*

4. Ibid., p. 29.

5. See Edgar Snow, "Why China Went Red," *The Other Side of the River* (New York: Random House, 1962).

6. The author was able to observe many of these developments during a visit to China for twenty-two days in April and May of 1976, on a trip arranged by the United States–China Peoples Friendship Association. The trip involved visits to agricultural communes, schools, hospitals, factories, stores, and a bank. Of course, twenty-two days do not an expert make. There are many descriptions of the Chinese economy but little official information. See James Tobin, "The Economy of China: A Tourist's View," *Challenge*, March/April 1973; J. K. Galbraith, *A China Passage* (Boston: Houghton Mifflin Co., 1973); Joseph Kraft,

The Chinese Difference (New York: Saturday Review Press, 1972); Joan Robinson, *Economic Management in China* (London: Anglo-Chinese Educational Institute, 1973); Thomas G. Rawski, "Chinese Industrial Production 1952 to 1971," *The Review of Economics and Statistics*, May 1973; John W. Gurley, "The New Man in the New China," *The Center Magazine*, May 1970; K. P. Wang, *The People's Republic of China—A New Industrial Power with a Strong Mineral Base* (Washington, D.C.: U.S. Bureau of Mines, 1975); Christopher Howe, *China's Economy* (New York: Basic Books, 1978); Frederic M. Kaplan, Julian M. Sobin, and Stephen Anders, *Encyclopedia of China Today* (New York: Harper & Row, 1979).

7. James Kenneson, "China Stinks," *Harper's*, April 1982.

8. Professor John Gurley (Stanford University) quoted in "Capitalist and Maoist Development," in *America's Asia*, Edward Friedman and Mark Seldon, eds. (New York: Random House, 1971).

9. Michael Parks, "Dissent Grows Over China's Farm Reforms," *Los Angeles Times*, 19 July 1982, Part I, p. 1.

I n this part we begin our discussion of the market-price system that we see in operation in the United States. The chapters in this part describe the basics of microeconomics (often called price theory). Microeconomics is concerned with economic decision making by consumers, business enterprises, and local agencies, as opposed to economic decisions made by national governments. And because the price of everything is so important to these decisions, microeconomics asks how prices are determined and

PART II

PRICES AND HOW THEY WORK

how prices answer the three questions—what? how? and for whom?—in a market-price system.

"Prices and How They Work" contains four chapters. The first (Chapter 4) is designed to help you understand graphs. The second (Chapter 5) shows how prices are determined. Chapter 6 discusses how prices change in response to changes in markets. Finally, Chapter 7 describes what happens when buyers react strongly to price changes or, conversely, when price changes have little effect on buying decisions.

4

The Economist's Tool Kit: How to Use Models and Graphs

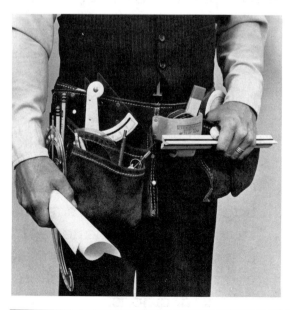

This chapter will help you understand all the chapters that follow. It describes two basic tools economists (and other social scientists) use to explain their ideas. These tools are models and graphs. Some students are immediately turned off by graphs, but, like pictures, graphs are often worth a thousand words. In any case, they are not difficult; and the real purpose of this chapter is to explain graphs at the level they are used in this book.

First, however, we must take up a touchy question: Is economics a science?

IS ECONOMICS REALLY A SCIENCE?

The discussion in Chapters 2 and 3 about different economic systems and the pros and cons of our own system tempts us to take sides—to say one is better than the other. However, we should be sensitive to the idea that economics is valuable to whatever extent it is a science.

A scientist must draw conclusions from observed data: Two apples and two apples make four apples; people buy less at higher prices than at lower prices. These are examples of **positive reasoning**; they are conclusions drawn from observations. There is no attempt to say that the conclusions are good or bad—just that they *are*.

Conclusions drawn from positive reasoning contribute to our understanding because they can be tested. If the same data produce the same conclusions over and over again, we can conclude that those conclusions are true. Then we can use this information to predict future events or to cause future changes to occur.

If, on the other hand, we ask, "Do we *want* those future changes to occur?" then we are engaging in **normative reasoning**; that is, deciding whether or not we believe something is desirable. If you believe the government deprives you of freedom, then you may tend to believe that the causes of our economic woes are not faults of a market-price system but rather the result of undesirable government interference with the system. The problem is that we cannot test these judgments because they are based on personal values, which are difficult if not impossible to measure.

Normative judgments often creep into a discussion. If one says: "Prices are too high," the statement is normative, because the statement implies that there is some lower level of prices that is desirable. "Taxes hurt me worse than you," or "Taxes hurt the poor more than the rich," or "People aren't free in a socialist country" are normative statements. Not only do they imply that we can measure people's feelings, but the word "hurt" implies injury—something bad.

If, on the other hand, we say, "A $1,000 tax is a larger percentage of a $10,000 income than of a $20,000 income," or "In China, professors make about what laborers do," we have made a positive statement, one that can be tested, and one that does not suggest good or bad. However, we all find it impossible to engage in "pure" positive reasoning. Normative judgments usually creep in.

To whatever extent we can keep economics "positive," economics is a science. Economists try to analyze the world in as "positive" a way as possible. Their job is to describe, predict, and offer alternatives. And this brings us to our discussion of models and graphs, for economists and other social scientists engage in model building in order to avoid normative judgments as much as possible.

WHAT MODELS ARE

A **model** is a simplified version of the world requiring a set of assumptions. Consider a recipe:

> Take 2¾ cups whole-wheat flour. Add 1½ cakes yeast dissolved in 3 tablespoons lukewarm water. Add 1 cup lukewarm water, 2 tablespoons brown sugar, 1½ teaspoons salt, 3 tablespoons melted shortening. Shape into a ball. Bake 45 minutes at 375°F. You'll have a 5″ × 10″ loaf of whole-wheat bread.

This is a model because it has ignored many details present in the real world. The thermostat on the oven could be faulty. The oven could have an air leak. Some person could come along and peek in and change the cooking time. The yeast could have lost its oomph. The water used could be full of chlorine and might change the taste. And so on.

Thus, the recipe is a model in that it is a simplified version of the real world, and—without saying so—the recipe or model assumes that none of these dangers exist. If we assume they do not exist, we can say as a matter of positive reasoning that the recipe will produce bread.

This is what economists try to do. By building models they try to arrive at a conclusion. The danger, of course, is that the model will involve so many assumptions that it no longer represents the real world. Consequently, a model is a theory that the creator hopes involves only positive reasoning. The usefulness of the model depends on how well it explains or predicts outcomes in the real world. Research economists spend much of their time developing models to reduce unemployment and inflation, for example, and then testing them, using current and past data to see if they work.

Sometimes, social scientists use the Latin phrase ***ceteris paribus***—"all other things remain the same"—to remind readers that a model is being used. In our example, *ceteris paribus* would mean that everything that goes into the oven is exactly what the recipe calls for; that nothing else changes in the real world (in the oven or outside the oven) to disturb the model.

WORKING WITH GRAPHS

Economists often use graphs to illustrate their models. There are many different types of graphs. We will use two of the most common types in this book: functional graphs and time series graphs. Functional graphs show the effect of one variable on another. Sometimes they show opportunity cost; that is, how the decision to buy more of one thing means the loss of something else. Sometimes they show how changes in income or prices cause changes in spending. The term "functional" is taken from the vocabulary of mathematics to convey the idea that changes in one variable are "functions of" (caused by) changes in the other.

A **functional graph** is a picture of the relationship between two variables. A **variable** is simply a quantity whose numerical value is allowed to change. One variable is shown on the horizontal axis, and the other is shown on the vertical axis (Figure 4-1).

To take a simple example, suppose you have $10 in your pocket. With it you can buy five $2 movie tickets or ten $1 six-packs of a soft drink. If you buy five movie tickets, you can buy zero six-packs. If you buy four movie tickets ($8),

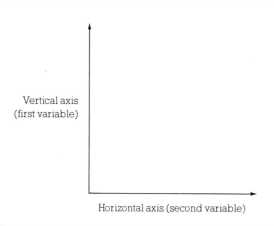

Figure 4-1.
How economists use graphs to picture relationships between two variables.

Table 4-1. Movie Tickets or Six-Packs?

No. of $2 movie tickets	No. of $1 six-packs	Total $ spent
5	0	$10
4	2	10
3	4	10
2	6	10
1	8	10
0	10	10

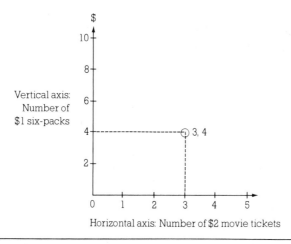

Figure 4-2.
How to locate a point on a graph.

you will have $2 left and can buy two $1 six-packs. We can represent this relationship by a table (Table 4-1).

Let us graph the relationship by putting the number of movie tickets on the horizontal axis and the number of six-packs on the vertical axis (Figure 4-2). Note that in each case we start with 0 at the intersection of the horizontal and

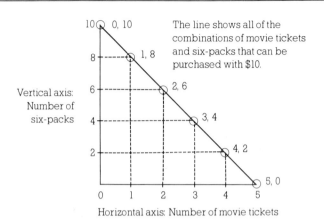

The line shows all of the combinations of movie tickets and six-packs that can be purchased with $10.

Vertical axis: Number of six-packs

Horizontal axis: Number of movie tickets

Figure 4-3.
Example of an inverse relationship.

vertical axes (called the **origin**) and increase the numbers at equal intervals, moving right on the horizontal axis and up on the vertical axis.

Suppose we want to represent the option 3 movie tickets and 4 six-packs. We read up from the horizontal axis at 3 to a point opposite 4 on the vertical axis, and we find a point that represents the combination of 4 six-packs and 3 movie tickets on the graph. If we find all of the points in the table and connect them by a line, we have a graph that slopes downward from the left to the right, as shown in Figure 4-3. This is called an **inverse relationship**, because the more movie tickets we buy the fewer six-packs and vice versa. As one variable increases, the other decreases. (This example also illustrates opportunity cost: Each additional movie ticket costs two six-packs; each additional six-pack costs one-half of a movie ticket.)

Figure 4-3 shows the combination of six-packs and movie tickets that can be purchased with a fixed amount of money ($10). In this type of graph, the quantities of each item that can be purchased are determined by something that the graph does not show; that is, by a third variable. In this case, that third variable is the amount of money we have to spend. If the amount changes to more or less than $10, the line will shift to the right or left. Consequently, the line as presently shown depends on the *ceteris paribus* assumption: that nothing outside the graph (like the amount of money we have to spend) changes.

To make this point clear, let's show what happens if the amount we can spend increases from $10 to $20. Figure 4-4 illustrates this increase. (The line shifts to the right. Visualize the line shifting to the left if the amount we can spend becomes less than $10.)

Now let us illustrate a **direct relationship**, one in which, as one variable increases, so does the other. In this example, the two variables are spending and income. The graph is a functional one because it shows the degree to which spending is a "function" of changes in income; that is, that changes in income cause changes in spending. Suppose you are taking home $200 a week of your earnings. You spend $180 and save $20. Now suppose you get a series of $5 raises—to $205, $210, $215, and so forth. With each $5 raise, you increase your spending $4—to $184, $188, $192 . . . This time we will cut out the part of the graph from 0 to $200 on the horizontal axis and from 0 to $180 on the

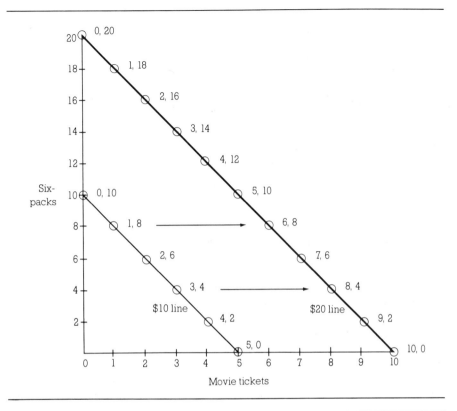

Figure 4-4.
The combinations of six-packs that can be purchased at $10 and at $20.

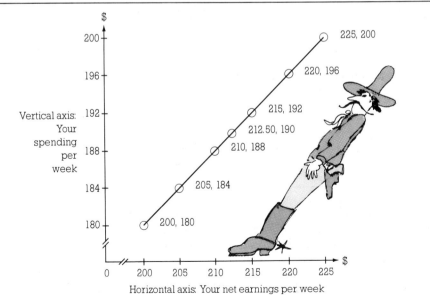

Figure 4-5.
Example of a direct relationship.

vertical axis to save space; the broken lines illustrate this omission. As Figure 4-5 shows, the line connecting the points now slopes upward from left to right

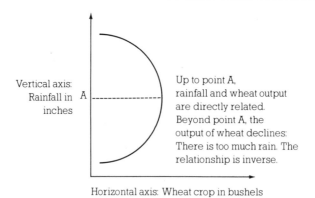

Figure 4-6.
A changing
relationship between
two variables.

Vertical axis:
Rainfall in A
inches

Up to point A,
rainfall and wheat output
are directly related.
Beyond point A, the
output of wheat declines:
There is too much rain. The
relationship is inverse.

Horizontal axis: Wheat crop in bushels

and represents a direct relationship. Graphs are handy to use because with a single line we can represent many points—$200,$180; $205,$184; and so on—and even points in between, $212.50,$190.

Even when we don't know the exact numbers, a graph is a picture showing us instantly what the relationship is between two variables. What if the graph looked as shown in Figure 4-6?

Functional graphs can also tell us whether one variable has a large or small effect on the other. Let's consider the response of buyers to price changes for boxes of toothpicks:

Price per box	Quantities an average family will buy every six months
10¢	2
15¢	2

The graph would look like Figure 4-7.

Suppose, however, we change the quantities as follows:

Price per box	Quantities purchased
10¢	5
15¢	2

The graph would then look like Figure 4-8. In other words, as the line becomes more horizontal, changes in the vertical-axis variable cause larger changes in the horizontal-axis variable. The slope of the line tells us as much as the direction of the line.

TIME-SERIES GRAPHS

Time-series graphs are also two-variable graphs, but one variable is always some measure of time: weeks, months, or years. These graphs are very useful in displaying historical data to show what our performance has been in the past, to enable us to guess about the future. There are a variety of ways to show time-series information. To illustrate, we'll pretend that we want to plot the tempera-

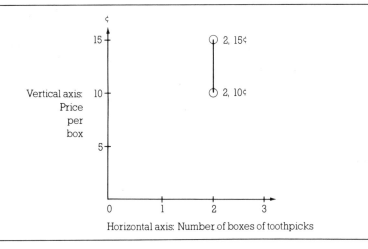

Figure 4-7.
When the line is straight up and down, changes in the vertical-axis variable have no effect on the horizontal-axis variable.

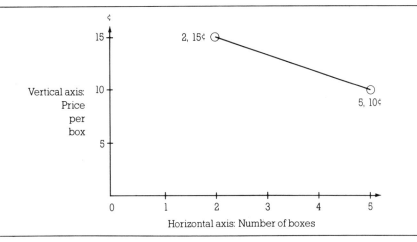

Figure 4-8.
A small change on the vertical axis produces a large change of the horizontal axis.

tures in a desert community called Palsied Palms in California. (We're thinking of building a desert hideaway there.)

We find that in year X, the temperatures during the months from February through June are 105°F in February, 95°F in March, 102°F in April, 98°F in May, and 110°F in June. One way of displaying this information is shown in Table 4-2. This same information can also be displayed in a graph as shown in Figure 4-9 on the next page.

As you can see, this figure takes up a great deal of unnecessary space because there are no readings below 95°F. The customary way to get rid of the unneeded space is shown in Figure 4-10.

Figure 4-10 presents the same information that Table 4-2 and Figure 4-9 do but in much less space. A broken line on the vertical axis solves the problem, as it does in Figure 4-5. But, a caution is worthwhile. The broken-line trick no longer shows the relationship of the temperatures to zero. If you need to show how high all of the numbers are (how hot it really is!), avoid the broken line and take all the space you need.

Now suppose that the long-run average for each of these months is 100°F and that we want to show variations from this norm. As you can guess, we're

Table 4-2. Temperatures during the Months February to June, Year X, in Palsied Palms, California Daytime Averages*

Months	Temperatures (in degrees Fahrenheit)
February	105
March	95
April	102
May	98
June	110

*Note that in this table and the graphs that follow, we're trying hard to be precise in stating what is being measured.

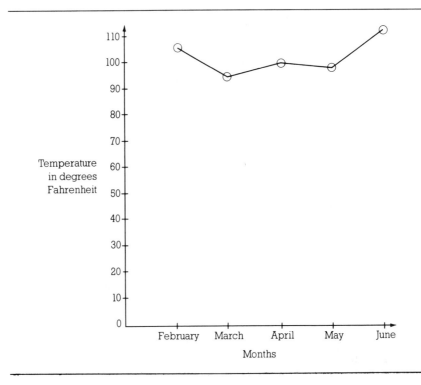

Figure 4-9. Temperatures during the months February to June, year X, in Palsied Palms, California; daytime averages (data based on Table 4-2).

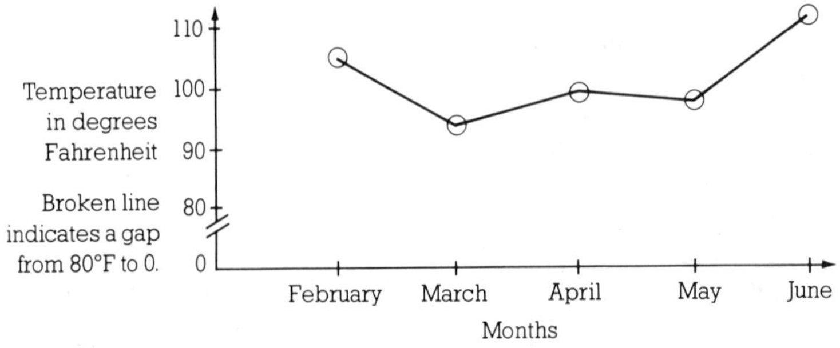

Figure 4-10. Temperatures during the months February to June, year X, in Palsied Palms, California; daytime averages (data based on Table 4-2).

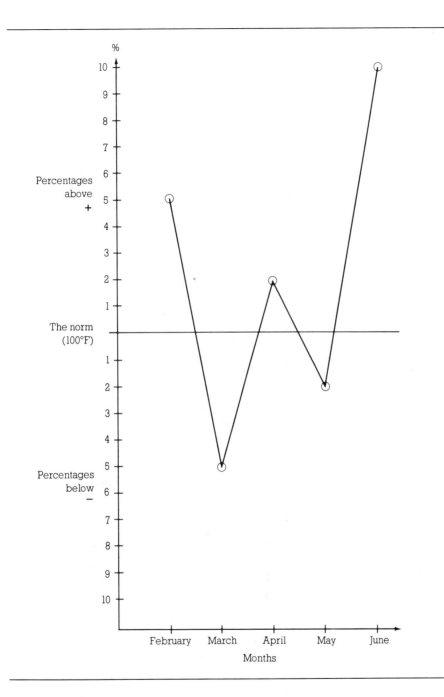

Figure 4-11.
Temperatures during the months February to June, year X, in Palsied Palms, California; months percentage variations from the norm (average) in year X (data based on Table 4-2).

using the number 100 to make it easy to show percentage variations. February is 5 percent above the average (norm); March is 5 percent below; April is 2 percent above; May is 2 percent below; and June is 10 percent above. We can easily show these variations as in Figure 4-11.

Finally, we can show the percentage increase or decrease of the temperature

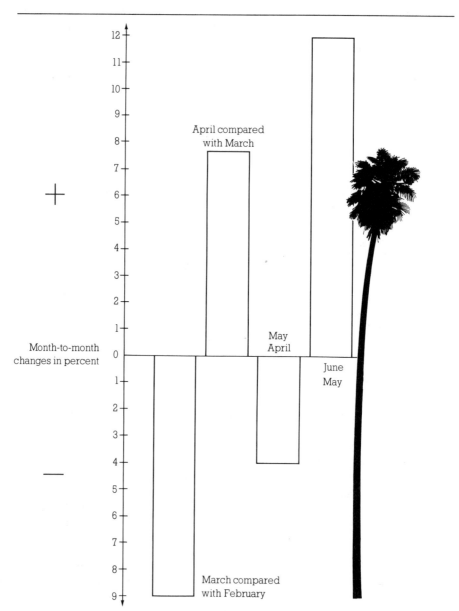

Figure 4-12.
Month-to-month
percentage changes
in temperature,
February to June,
year X, Palsied
Palms, California
(data based on Table
4-2).

in each month relative to that of the previous month. (We can't do February because we don't have January figures.)

Thus, March is 9.5 percent below February (the 10-degree drop divided by the February temperature of 105 = 10 ÷ 105 = 9.5 percent). The April temperature is 7/95 or 7.4 percent above March. The May temperature is 4/102 or 3.9 percent below April. Lastly, the June temperature is 12/98 or 12.2 percent above May. Figure 4-12 illustrates these changes.

Figure 4-12 is a bar chart, a very common type of graph. Typically, cost-of-living changes are shown in bar charts if the purpose is to show how fast prices are rising. Sometimes, also, the same method is used to show year-to-year percentage changes in a nation's total output.

We hope this brief explanation has made you feel more comfortable with graphs. Remember that they are just pictures designed to show the effect of one variable on another—like the effect of caloric intake on weight, or, as in the next chapter, the effect of prices on the quantities of things people will buy or sell. You will be looking at many more graphs throughout this book. We hope you will find them understandable, interesting, and useful.

SUMMARY

Economists try hard to be scientists by using positive (from observation) rather than normative (judgmental) reasoning. By using positive reasoning they can reach conclusions that can be tested.

Economists use simplifications of the real world called models to reach their conclusions. Models involve many assumptions, the most important being *ceteris paribus*, which means that variables outside the model don't change. Graphs are often used to explain models.

Graphs are pictures that show how variables change with respect to one another. The graphs in this book are limited to those involving two variables, which are measured on the two axes of the graph, the vertical axis and the horizontal axis.

The graphs in this book are of two types, functional graphs and time-series graphs. Functional graphs show how changes in one variable are associated with changes in the other. Time-series graphs show changes of one variable plotted against time changes.

Discussion Questions

1. Why is it difficult to avoid normative judgments?

2. Invent a model involving bike riding. What assumptions do you have to make before you can draw conclusions?

3. Suppose you are the owner of a factory making barrels of Kickapoo Joy Juice. You record how the output of the factory varies with the number of workers. Your record shows:

Number of workers	Output of barrels per week
5	20
10	50
15	75
20	90

You draw this information on a graph.
  a. What kind of graph is it?
  b. Is the line straight?
  c. If not, how can you account for its shape?

DID YOU EVER WONDER WHY . . .

. . . you should not advise a friend to see a certain movie?

5

Demand and Supply: The Contest Between Buyers and Sellers

KEY WORDS

Barriers to entry
Exclusion principle
Demand
Demand schedule
Law of demand
Income effect
Substitute effect
Demand curve
Substitute goods
Complementary goods
Inflation psychology
Self-fulfilling prophecy
Supply
Capital formation
Investment
Supply schedule

Supply curve
Shortage
Surplus
Equilibrium price
Market power

This chapter continues our discussion of the market-price system. In it we will assume that prices are being determined in an Adam Smithian market-price system; that is, with a high degree of competition among self-interested buyers and sellers and a minimum of government regulation. Later on, in Part III, we will drop this assumption.

This chapter first discusses the three functions of prices, then demand, supply, and how prices are determined.

THREE FUNCTIONS OF PRICES

Prices have three main functions in a market-price system: (1) directing the use of resources, (2) rationing goods and services and resources, and (3) establishing the relative values of all resources and goods and services. We will consider each of these.

Directing the Use of Resources

By "directing the use of resources," we mean that prices determine the method of production; that is, the selection of the resources to be used and the quantities of each resource to be used. The example that follows shows how prices determine what mixtures of labor and capital will be used in production.

How Prices Determine Production Methods
Suppose an entrepreneur can buy a wallet-making machine for $10,000 and that the life of the machine is one year. The machine has to be operated by one worker who makes $40 per day. This employee works, on the average, 220 days per year and therefore earns $8,800. Excluding other costs of raw material, electricity, fuel, maintenance, and so on, the total cost of the worker and the machine per year is $18,800 ($10,000 + $8,800). Together, the worker and the machine produce 10,000 wallets per year at a cost of $18,800, or $1.88 per wallet.

Let's suppose that the entrepreneur has the alternative of hiring 9 workers at $10 per day to do the same job without the machine. Excluding the cost of hand tools, total costs are, we will assume, $10 × 9 workers × 220 days = $19,800. Assume that the 9 workers can make 12,000 wallets per year. By using workers instead of a machine, the cost per wallet can be cut to $1.65 ($19,800 ÷ 12,000).

What will the entrepreneur do? He will hire the workers. The point is that the price system has determined how the wallets will be made, who receives the income for the job, and who can afford to buy them. The price system has determined which resources will be used and in what quantities.

Is everyone happy? No. The manufacturer of the machine did not sell it and may have to lay off employees. The skilled operator of the machine did not get the job.

This anecdote illustrates a fact of life. The price system provides the measuring stick that enables the entrepreneur to make choices. These choices may make some people happy, others unhappy. However, if the system works perfectly—with no barriers to entry—it may make consumers happier by providing wallets at lower cost. And lower costs to consumers mean (1) that resources have been used efficiently in satisfying consumers' wants, and (2) that consumers can have a higher standard of living with the same income.

A **barrier to entry** is anything that prevents the free movement of a resource as, for example, people into a chosen occupation. Typical examples are academic hurdles (teaching credentials, bar exams, medical exams), occupational licenses (barbers, food vendors), franchise agreements, discriminatory hiring policies, patent rights, and capital requirements (necessary to start a factory). In New York and many other major cities, anyone who wants to own a taxicab must purchase a "medallion," or license. The number of these licenses is limited and the medallions cost many thousands of dollars—a formidable barrier to entry for many minority groups who might otherwise become small entrepreneurs in this way.

For a moment, let's consider a price system in which there *are* barriers to entry and which therefore does not work perfectly. Suppose that the 9 workers make only 10,000 wallets instead of 12,000. The cost per wallet is then $1.98 ($19,800 ÷ 10,000) instead of $1.65. Suppose now that the workers are all related to the entrepreneur. To keep peace in the family, the entrepreneur hires the workers anyhow. Now, barriers to entry block the purchase of the machine and the hiring of the skilled operator. Consumers will probably have to pay a higher price for wallets.

Rationing Goods and Services and Resources

Suppose that the price of top-quality sirloin steak is about $5 per pound. Who gets the steak? Only those who want it and can afford it at that price. Is everyone happy? Of course not. At that price many of us are excluded from the market for steak and are obliged to buy hamburger. The higher the price, the more people are excluded. This idea is called the **exclusion principle**. The price system determines who can buy goods and services and who cannot. In this way, the price system again performs the "for whom" function by rationing goods and services.

Establishing Values of Resources and Goods and Services

Prices establish a relationship between all resources and all goods and services. If a sweater sells for $20 and a pair of socks for $2, our society values ten pairs of socks as the equivalent of one sweater. In this way, prices measure the relative values of everything in our society. The price measure helps us consciously or unconsciously to figure the opportunity cost of the next purchase we make.

We have noticed that the system does not necessarily make everyone happy. It is simply one way—an amoral, sometimes cold-blooded way—of making choices. Would you rather have the choices made by some planner? Or by voting? Because we live in a mixed system, our choices are made in many ways, but it is important to recognize the problems (or costs) of choosing one system over another.

DEMAND:
HOW MUCH CONSUMERS BUY
DETERMINES PRICES

Prices are determined by the forces of demand and supply. Let us first consider a model of demand. **Demand** is defined as the number of units of a product you (or a group of people) will buy at various prices during some period of time.

Table 5-1. Fred's Demand Schedule

Number of beers	Price Fred is willing and able to pay for each additional beer
1	$30
2	25
3	18
4	10
5	2
6	1

The Demand Schedule

Once upon a time, a man we will call Fred wandered alone in the Sahara Desert. He had been abandoned by his faithless wife and his best friend, who had departed with the only means of transportation, their one and only camel, and with all the food and water. The temperature rose to 130°F. Fred was on the verge of collapse from thirst when suddenly a truck appeared. As it approached, Fred began to make out lettering on the side of the truck. Could it be? Was it a mirage? The lettering spelled out: COLD BEER.

In a haze of semiconsciousness, Fred heard the driver ask, "Would you like an ice-cold beer?" Fred could hardly believe his ears. He answered, "Please, please, I'll give you *anything* for a beer."

The driver, Sinbad, replied, "Well, would you pay $100?"

Fred considered this. He had only $86 in his wallet, which certainly was not doing him any good in the desert. But he was reluctant to give up the whole $86 at once. He answered, "Thirty dollars."

Sinbad said, "Okay, have one."

Fred clutched the beer can with shaking hands. It was cold—perfect. He opened it clumsily and gulped it down, spilling precious ounces on his sand-caked face and hair.

There was a pause. Sinbad said, "Perhaps you'd like another?" Fred gasped, "My God, would I!" Sinbad, stone-faced, inscrutable, answered, "It all depends. The price is $30."

Fred considered. He was less thirsty now. He finally answered, "I'll pay $25."

Sinbad handed over the second beer, which Fred immediately drained, spilling less with steadier hands.

Let us now assume that Fred consumes six beers, but as his thirst and cash diminish he persuades Sinbad to accept a lower price for each successive can. We can show this on a table (Table 5-1). This table is called a **demand schedule**. It tells us how many units of a product a buyer (Fred) will be willing and able to buy during some period of time at various prices.

You might think that the price of two beers should be shown as $30 + $25 ÷ 2, or $27.50 each, but the table represents the price Fred is willing to pay for each beer if he can purchase them one at a time.

The Law of Demand

Notice that, in the *demand schedule*, as price falls, the quantity bought increases. This is called the **law of demand**. Price and quantity are inversely

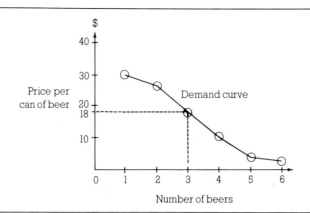

Figure 5-1.
Fred's demand curve.

related. Economists speak of *three reasons for the law of demand*—that is, why the quantity purchased increases as the price falls.

First, as the price falls, we can afford to buy larger quantities out of any given income. This is called the **income effect**. Pretend for a moment that you spend your entire income on tennis balls and that you make $100 per week. If the price of a can of three tennis balls is $2.50, you can afford to buy 40 cans per week. If the price should fall to $2, you can afford to buy 50 cans per week (and/or more of other things too).

Second, as the quantity purchased increases, we are not willing to pay as much for each additional unit. Why not? Because the satisfaction we receive from each additional unit is less than the satisfaction given by the one before. As our thirst is gradually quenched, each additional beer becomes less important—we will not offer as much for it.

Table 5-1 explains this point. How much is Fred willing to pay for three beers? Seventy-three dollars. This is a good measure of total satisfaction—to Fred. But we ask, "What is the third beer worth to Fred?" the answer is, of course, $18. This is a measure of the satifaction provided by the third beer only.

Third, as the price of a product falls, we will use it for other purposes. This point is not evident in our beer example, but let's suppose we are talking about paint thinner or diamonds. If the price of paint thinner fell far enough, some people would use it for weed killer. If the price of diamonds were $1 per cubic yard, we would substitute diamonds for gravel in making concrete. This is called the **substitution effect**. As the price falls, we increase our purchases because we find more and more uses for a product and substitute it for others.

These reasons for the law of demand should not be considered as if they were independent of one another. They all operate together in varying degrees of importance in each situation. If the price of phonograph records should fall, we will (1) buy more out of any given income, (2) tend to substitute them for cassette tapes, and (3) find that our satisfaction declines with each additional record, so that still lower prices are needed to motivate us to buy.

The Demand Curve

Fred's schedule (Table 5-1) can also be presented in the form of a graph (Figure 5-1). The price that Fred is willing and able to pay during some period of time is shown on the vertical axis. The number of beers (quantity) he is willing

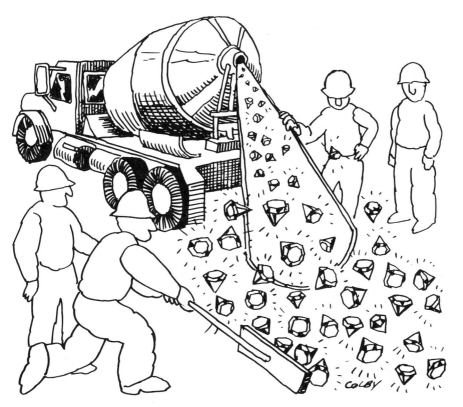

If the price of diamonds fell far enough, they could be used to make concrete.

to purchase at each price is shown on the horizontal axis. The line sloping down from left to right is called a **demand curve**. The dotted line at $18 shows that at that price he will buy 3 cans of beer.

Demand with Multiple Buyers

Fred and Sinbad were two individuals haggling. But the forces of demand (and supply) often represent the buying (or selling) decisions of many buyers and sellers. The example that follows helps to explain how a demand curve can be drawn to represent the buying decisions of several people.

Suppose that a student in your economics class appears one day with a coffee mug in her hand and announces the mug is for sale. She has crafted it beautifully and decorated it with the college emblem, a stalking black panther. The student—we'll call her Amelia—explains that she made it in her ceramics class and would like to sell it.

Your economics instructor is naturally delighted to be able to show off the workings of the market-price system, and an auction is organized. (To make this illustration as simple as possible, we'll pretend that there are just seven students in the class; we'll call them A, B, C, D, E, F, and G.) The instructor decides to encourage everyone to bid something by conducting the auction by secret ballot. Students write their names and what they *would pay* for the mug on slips of paper. We emphasize "would pay" because the concept of demand means not merely that we *want* something but that we are *ready, willing, and able* to pay for it. The slips are given to Amelia, who finds that the bids are as shown in Table 5-2.

Table 5-2. The Bids for Amelia's Coffee Mug

Student	Bid
A	$ .40
B	2.40
C	0
D	4.00
E	.80
F	0
G	3.20

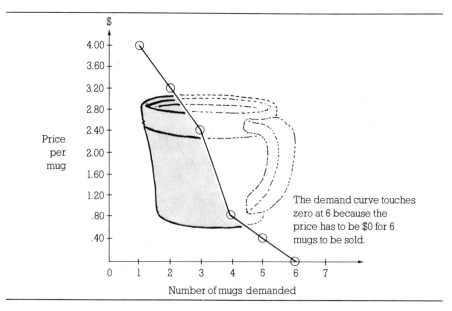

Figure 5-2.
Demand curve for
coffee mugs at
different prices.

The demand curve touches
zero at 6 because the
price has to be $0 for 6
mugs to be sold.

Table 5-3. Demand Schedule for Coffee Mugs at Different Prices

If the price were . . .	Number of students who would buy	Student(s) who would buy at each price
$4.00	1	D
3.20	2	D and G
2.40	3	D, G, and B
.80	4	D, G, B, and E
.40	5	D, G, B, E, and A
0	7	Everyone

Believe it or not, we can construct a demand *schedule* with this information. First we will arrange the bids in order, highest to lowest. Then we'll ask, "How many mugs could have been sold at each price?" Table 5-3 illustrates.

The demand curve would look like Figure 5-2. Note that, like any demand curve, the curve shows the number of coffee mugs that *could have been sold* at various prices to a specific group of people, during a specific period of time (a particular time on a particular day, for example), at a particular place. Change the people, the time, or the place and the schedule in Table 5-3 may change. After we discuss Figure 5-2, we'll go on to discuss the major causes for these changes in demand schedules. (Amelia will, of course, sell the coffee mug to the highest bidder, student D.)

Notice that the demand curve for Amelia's coffee mugs is shaped very much like Fred's demand curve for beer in Figure 5-1. The line slopes down from left to right because of the law of demand explained on pages 73 and 74.

Another way of describing the line is to say that it has a negative slope; it runs downhill. And still another way is to say that the line shows an *inverse* relationship between price and quantity. As the price falls, the quantity demanded increases and vice versa.

Table 5-4. A Change in Demand

Student	Old bid	New bid
A	$ .40	$ .80
B	2.40	3.20
C	0	.40
D	4.00	4.80
E	.80	2.40
F	0	1.20
G	3.20	4.00

Table 5-5. Old and New Demand Schedules for Coffee Mugs

If the price were . . .	Old number of students who would buy	New number of students who would buy
$4.80	0	1
4.00	1	2
3.20	2	3
2.40	3	4
1.20	3*	5
.80	4	6
.40	5	7
0	7	7**

*The number of students who will buy doesn't increase from 3 to 4 until the price drops to $.80; consequently, the number of students who will buy stays at 3 whether the price is $2.40 or $1.20.
**The number of students who will buy stays at 7 because there are only 7 students.

Changes in Demand

Assume that by some miracle everyone in the economics class gets some extra money to spend—say $50. Everyone can now bid more for the coffee mug. The old bids from Table 5-2 and the new ones are shown in Table 5-4.

With this information we can revise Table 5-3 to make Table 5-5.

Figure 5-3 shows in graph form how the new schedule compares with the old one.

The new demand curve in Figure 5-3 indicates that for every quantity the students are willing to pay a higher price; and, at every price they are willing to buy a larger quantity. In this situation the demand curve shifts to the *right*, indicated by the three arrows. If, on the other hand, the students had less money to spend, they would probably bid less than the prices given in the old schedule. In that event, the demand curve would shift to the *left*.

In other words, the demand curve shifts to the right because of an *increase* in demand. The curve shifts left because of a *decrease* in demand.

Shifts in Demand versus Movements Along a Demand Curve

Now we must explain a fine point that has bothered and confused economics students for decades. If we look at Table 5-3 we see that as the price falls from $4.00 to $3.20 to $2.40 and so on, the quantity (number) of mugs the class is

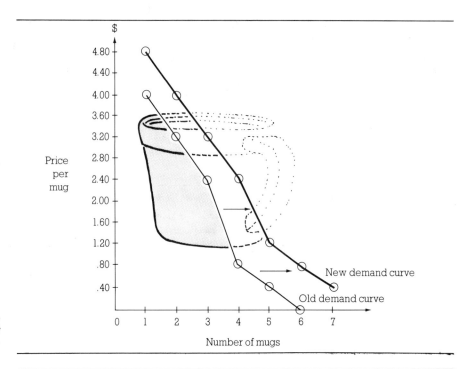

Figure 5-3.
Example of a change
in demand.

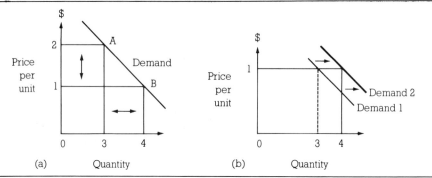

Figure 5-4.
(a) Change in the
quantity demanded
(movement along a
given demand curve,
from A to B). (b)
Change in demand
(movement or shift of
the demand curve
itself).

willing to buy increases. This increase is a movement *along and down* the demand curve. The increase is caused by a drop in the price, *not by a change in everyone's income.* Consequently, the increase in the number of mugs the class is willing to buy does not result in a shift in the curve.

Moving along a given curve is called a *change in the quantity demanded;* it is *not* called a change in demand. Economists speak of a change in demand only when the line shifts to the left or right—that is, when the buyer will buy larger or smaller quantities at each and every price. The distinction between a "change in the quantity demanded" and a "change in demand" is further explained in Figure 5-4.

The difference between a movement along the line (change in the quantity demanded) and a shift in the line (change in demand) may seem like much ado about nothing. But the difference is important. Changes in the quantity demanded occur because of changes in price—shown in Figure 5-4(**a**). But in (**b**), people will buy more without any drop in the price. They will buy more at every price (and pay a higher price for every quantity). What causes people to buy more (or less) even when the price does not change? To put it another way, what causes the demand curve to shift (to the right or left)? There are at least five possible reasons for shifts in demand. They may occur all together or in any combination: (1) Changes in present or expected income, (2) changes in tastes, (3) changes in the prices of substitute or complementary goods, (4) changes in buyers' expectations, and (5) changes in the number of buyers. Let us examine each reason.

Changes in Present or Expected Incomes

If the money you have to spend increases, your demand curve will shift to the right. You can afford to buy larger quantities at every price. Conversely, if you have less money—or expect to have less—your demand curve will shift to the left.

Changes in Tastes

Buyers' tastes change constantly as fads and styles come and go. If a fad makes a product more popular, the demand curve for it will shift to the right. When something goes out of style, the demand curve will shift to the left.

Changes in the Prices of Substitute or Complementary Goods

Our demand for anything will change when prices of other products change. These products may be either substitute goods or complementary goods.

Substitute goods are goods that compete with one another—for example, two brands of essentially the same product, such as two brands of similar coffee. Suppose each brand sells 10 pounds per week in Pop's Grocery Store. Also suppose both sell at $4.00 per pound, as in Figure 5-5. Now suppose that Brand 2 lowers its price to $3.75, as in Figure 5-6. The demand curve for Brand 2 indicates that the quantity demanded increases from 10 pounds to 13. Where will this extra business come from? On the assumption that Brand 1 does not lower its price, Brand 2's gain will come from Brand 1's loss of business. This result is shown in Figure 5-7. If Brand 1 does not lower its price, demand for it will *decrease*. People will reduce their purchases of it from 10 to 7 pounds as they increase their purchases of Brand 2 from 10 to 13 pounds.

To summarize: A drop in the price of one substitute good, with no change in the price of the other, leads to a decrease in demand for the second product.

Complementary goods are goods that go together, like cars and tires. Consider the demand per month for cars and tires. A drop in the price of automobiles will *increase* (shift to the right) the demand for tires. Figure 5-8 illustrates the point. The two diagrams show that if the price of automobiles drops, people will demand more of them. (Has there been a change in demand? No, there has only been a change in the *quantity* demanded—the demand has not shifted.) But now consider the tires. With more cars on the road, people will demand more tires *at every price*. With the price of tires unchanged at $60, people will increase their purchase of tires from 400 to 480 per month.

Substitute and complementary relationships may also work together. For instance, in August 1976 it was reported that gasoline had become so scarce in

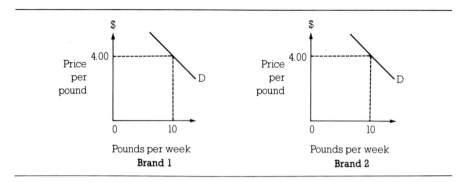

Figure 5-5.
Competing substitute
goods.

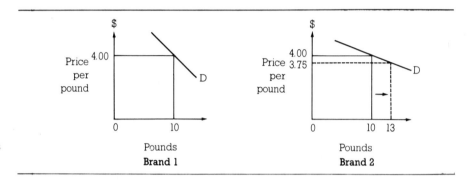

Figure 5-6.
Brand 2 lowers its
price.

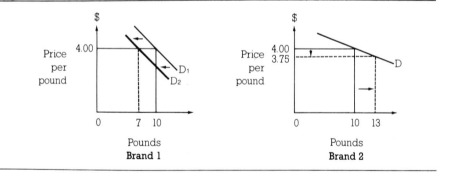

Figure 5-7.
Demand falls for
Brand 1.

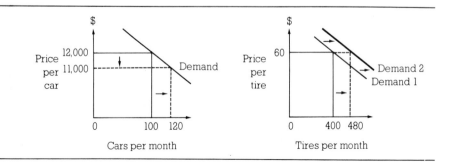

Figure 5-8.
Effect of a price
change of one
complementary good
on demand for
another.

Saigon, Vietnam, that the price per gallon had risen to $12! Can you guess what happened? Gasoline and motorcycles are complementary goods. Motorcycles and bicycles are substitute goods. Thus, when the price of gasoline went up, the *quantity demanded* for gasoline decreased. And the decrease in the *quantity demanded* for gasoline caused a *decrease in demand* for any vehicle using gasoline, such as motorcycles and automobiles. On the other hand, the demand for people-powered bicycles skyrocketed. In fact, it was reported, the price of bicycles went to *$600* apiece, whereas motorcycles, once in great demand, were selling for about a third of that.

Changes in Buyers' Expectations

Buyers also increase or decrease their demand with changes in expectations. If we expect prices to be lower next week, our demand will shift to the left this week; we will prefer to wait. If we worry about being laid off next week, our demand will also shift to the left; we will try to save to prepare for a period of unemployment. Conversely, if we expect to become more secure or prosperous in the future, we will "live it up"; our demand will increase this week.

These movements of demand with changes in expectations illustrate another fact of life. If we believe the future will be rosy, we will increase our purchases. Entrepreneurs will become more prosperous and hire more people. The belief will become reality. Unfortunately, there is a connection here with what economists call **inflation psychology**. If people believe prices are rising, they will increase current purchases—demand will shift to the right. This will cause prices to rise even more as people try to buy before another round of price increases occurs. This price increase will again increase demand, and so on, resulting in an upward spiral of prices.

If we believe the future will be bleak, on the other hand, the spiral effect may plunge us downhill into depression or at least recession. (We use *recession* to mean a mild depression—see the Glossary at the end of the book for a more exact definition.) When buyers wait to buy at lower prices, entrepreneurs have to lay off employees. As people become unemployed, they and those still employed worry about the future and try to increase their savings (which may be difficult at lower incomes), further causing demand curves to shift to the left, which causes more people to be laid off. Social scientists call this tendency for a popular belief to become true a **self-fulfilling prophecy**.

Changes in Number of Buyers

Demand curves may change if the number of buyers changes. If a new factory is built and draws an influx of factory workers into a town, the increased number of people (buyers) will tend to cause prices to rise in the town because larger quantities of foodstuffs, housing, and so on, may be demanded. This result is true of the world in general. As the population of the world increases, our demands increase and prices tend to rise.

A Quick Review

Let us not forget the idea of a model and the *ceteris paribus* assumption. The law of demand states: "As the price falls, the quantity demanded increases (or vice versa)." We should add "*ceteris paribus*" to that statement. What we mean is that the quantity demanded will increase as the price falls *provided nothing else changes*—like incomes, tastes, prices of other products, expectations, or

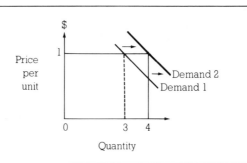

Figure 5-9.
An increase in
quantity at every
price.

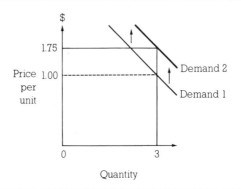

Figure 5-10.
An increase in
demand with no
change in quantity.

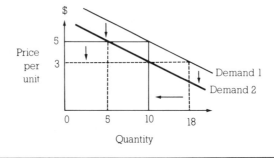

Figure 5-11.
A decrease in
demand.

the number of other buyers. If any or all of these five variables changes, we could have either an increase or a decrease in the quantity demanded *without* a change in price.

We can interpret an increase in demand in two ways: (1) It can be thought of as an increase in *quantity* at every price (Figure 5-9). The specific numbers have been chosen arbitrarily, but the illustration shows that, at a price of $1, people will increase their purchases from 3 to 4 units. (2) An increase in demand can be thought of as the buyer's willingness to pay a higher *price* for every quantity (Figure 5-10). Here the buyer is willing to pay $1.75 instead of $1 per unit when he or she buys 3 units.

We can interpret a decrease in demand the same way: (1) The decrease can be thought of as a reduction in the quantities demanded, with no change in price. Thus, Figure 5-11 shows that if the price stays at $5, the quantity demand-

Because consumer attitudes, products, and prices change, entrepreneurs can never be sure of the elusive demand curve.

ed will drop from 10 units (Demand 1) to 5 units (Demand 2). (2) The decrease in demand can be thought of as a drop in the price necessary to cause the buyer to demand the same quantity. Thus, when the price is $5, Demand 1 shows the quantity demanded to be 10 units. After the decrease in demand (Demand 2), the price will have to fall to 3 to persuade the buyer to buy the same 10 units.

Is There Really a Demand Curve?

In the real world, the demand curve is as elusive as that famous pot of gold at the end of a rainbow. Entrepreneurs can never be sure what the demand curve for their products looks like or whether or not it is shifting. People's attitudes, other products, and other prices are changing constantly. But even if a demand curve for any particular product is hard to chart, it does exist. Knowing what controls the demand curve will help intelligent entrepreneurs study their markets—the attitudes of people who buy their products—so that after experimentation and experience they can begin to forecast what will happen when prices are changed or when important buying habits of their customers change. Many entrepreneurs who may never have studied economics probably have an intuitive "feel" for their buyers' demand.

SUPPLY:
HOW MUCH SUPPLIERS OFFER AT VARIOUS PRICES

The other important force that determines price is supply. A supplier is anyone who produces or sells a good or service. **Supply** is defined as the maximum number of units suppliers of a product will offer for sale at various prices during some period of time.

Let's return to Amelia and her coffee mug. Amelia is, of course, the supplier. When she finds that her coffee mug is worth $4 to someone (student D—see Table 5-3 on page 76), she considers making mugs in quantity to earn some extra money. But, what should she charge? She can think of four costs of production: (1) the ceramics course fee to cover materials and use of the kiln, (2) the opportunity costs of making each mug in terms of lost study time and lost leisure time, (3) the added costs of making molds (which she needs for mass production), and (4) a reasonable profit to cover her entrepreneurial risk-taking.*

As she jots down estimates of these costs, Amelia realizes she can forget about (1), the course fee. It would be a mistake to count something she is doing anyhow, for fun, as a cost of production. Moreover, the opportunity cost of producing *some* of the mugs would be zero, because she could make them in regular class time. She would only have to count the opportunity cost of the extra time she put into mug-making when she went into mass production.

From what she learned in economics class, she realizes that the molds she would make herself are *capital*, just like any a tool or machine she would create to increase production and profit. In making them she is engaging in **capital formation**, or what economists call **investment**. (For those who might not know, a ceramic mold receives liquid clay, called "slip." Molds permit mass production of many shapes.)

On the other hand, the mold-making would have its own opportunity cost: loss of income from the mugs she might have made by hand and sold in the time it took to make the molds.

Even assuming the extra clay and glazes, and the plaster for the molds, do not cost Amelia an additional fee, she finds that her estimated opportunity costs are quite high. Finally, though, she decides that she can afford to make 10 coffee mugs a week, using molds, provided she receives at least $2 per mug.

The college bookstore agrees to sell them at a small profit. A new enterprise is born!

Success is almost immediate. The mugs, with their menacing black panther emblem, are an instant hit. After 3 days, the first 10 mugs are gone.

Then, two significant events occur:

First, Amelia is pleased and proud of her success but realizes she can afford to make more coffee mugs per week only if the price rises. Each additional hour spent at mug-making means one less hour of leisure. Moreover, the opportunity cost of lost leisure increases, because each lost hour of leisure becomes more important to Amelia. Of course, this situation doesn't apply just to Amelia. Usually, when we work at some task, the task eventually becomes costlier to us in terms of fatigue, and, correspondingly, each additional hour of leisure time sacrificed is more valuable.** Amelia decides to produce mugs, but only if the price rises. She explains this problem to the store manager and agrees to the production schedule shown in Table 5-6.

We have labeled Table 5-6 Amelia's **supply schedule**, because that's what it is: It is a schedule showing the quantities per week she will produce (supply) at various prices. Notice that although the price rises are in even increments of fifty cents, the number of additional mugs she will make is less each time. When the price rises from $2.00 to $2.50, she will make 5 additional mugs. But

---

*The costs of production are covered in more detail in Chapter 9.

**This fact of life helps explain why employers would probably have to pay hourly-paid employees time-and-a-half for overtime even if it were not the law. (Salaried employees are usually expected "to give their all" without overtime pay in return for such actual or presumed incentives as managerial status, "career potential," a bigger stake in the company's future, and so on.)

Table 5-6. Amelia's Supply Schedule (Quantities per Week)

If the price is	Amelia will make this many mugs
$1.50	0 (At $1.50 Amelia won't make any)
2.00	10
2.50	15
3.00	19
3.50	22
4.00	24
4.50	25
5.00	25

Table 5-7. Greg's, Nick's, and Sue's Supply Schedules

Price	Quantities supplied		
	Greg	Nick	Sue
$1.50	6	0	2
2.00	14	0	6
2.50	21	6	10
3.00	27	10	14
3.50	32	13	17
4.00	36	15	19
4.50	39	16	20
5.00	40	17	21

when the price rises from $4.50 to $5.00, she will still make only 25. The opportunity cost of lost leisure has risen to the point where she refuses to make more mugs.

The second significant event is that other members of Amelia's ceramics class watch Amelia's success with great interest. Three of them—Greg, Nick, and Sue—decide to compete. Each one has a meeting with the store manager and agrees to the supply schedules in Table 5-7.

Now let's add Amelia's quantities to the quantities of the others and add up the totals available at each price (Table 5-8).

Figure 5-12 is a graph of the total quantities supplied at each price. The result is called a **supply curve**.

Compare the supply curve in Figure 5-12 with the demand curves in Figures 5-1, 5-2, and 5-3. Notice that the supply curve rises from left to right (a direct relationship), indicating that as the price rises the quantity supplied increases. The demand curve, on the other hand, falls from left to right. Price and quantity are inversely related on anyone's demand curve (or schedule).

The rising supply curve in Figure 5-12 has a message that may not be obvious: The quantities offered for sale will increase—but only when the price increases. Why is that? For some reason, coffee mugs must get more expensive to make as the quantity increases. In other words, a rising supply curve shows

Table 5-8. Total Supplies of Coffee Mugs per Week

Price per mug	Amelia	Greg	Nick	Sue	=	Total quantities supplied
$1.50	0	9	0	6		15
2.00	10	16	4	7		35
2.50	15	22	7	11		55
3.00	19	27	10	14		70
3.50	22	32	13	17		84
4.00	24	36	15	19		94
4.50	25	39	16	20		100
5.00	25	40	17	21		103

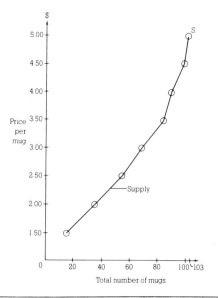

Figure 5-12.
Total production per week of coffee mugs at College X at various prices.

that the *cost of production is increasing.** What cost is that? We already know. It is the rising opportunity cost of lost leisure.

Moreover, look at the line from the price of $3.50 to $5.00. The line becomes steeper; the last segment is almost vertical. In this part of the curve, opportunity cost rises rapidly as the quantities increase by smaller and smaller amounts. Finally, in contrast to the demand curve with its negative slope indicating an inverse relationship, the supply curve is *positively* sloped to show a direct relationship between price and quantity.

Changes in Supply

Just as demand does not change as we move along the demand curve, supply does not change as we move along the supply curve. As the price rises, the

---

*Supply curves do not *always* rise. In some situations they may be flat if costs remain constant, or they may even fall if costs fall. These cases usually occur in mass production situations. However, costs will eventually rise as output approaches the capacity of a plant.

Table 5-9. Old and New Quantities Offered for Sale after an Increase in the Cost of Production

Price per mug	Old quantities supplied	New quantities supplied
$1.50	8	0
2.00	35	20
2.50	55	35
3.00	70	55
3.50	84	65
4.00	94	75
4.50	100	85
5.00	103	90

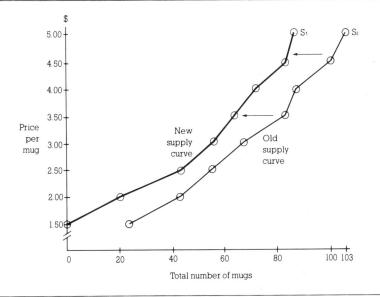

Figure 5-13. Old and new supply curves after an increase in the cost of production.

students are willing to produce more coffee mugs, but there has been no change in supply. The supply curve—the number of coffee mugs produced at each price—changes only when those quantities produced change, with no change in price. If *that* happens, there has been a change in supply—there will be a whole new supply curve.

Why might the supply curve shift? Let's suggest one possibility. Suppose that the authorities at Amelia's college, as well as the ceramics instructors, get fed up with the stream of students in and out of the ceramics lab and, particularly, with the unbudgeted amounts of clay being used. To slow the clay-drain down, a new fee is instituted: $1 per pound of clay. Our student-entrepreneurs are faced with a new ballgame—just as if in the real world they had suddenly been hit with a new tax or higher prices for clay. After the students adjust to this rise in costs, the supply schedule changes as shown in Table 5-9.

Figure 5-13 shows the old and new supply curves. Note that the increase in

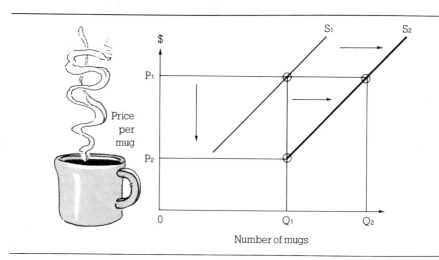

Figure 5-14.
An increase in supply.

the cost of clay causes the curve to shift to the left. When the curve shifts to the left the quantity is less at every price. Moreover, see that on the new curve, the price has to be $3.00 before the students will produce 55 mugs. The old curve shows they will produce that many when the price is $2.50, not $3.00. There-fore, the shift also means that, for *every* quantity, there is a higher price.

Just to complete the story, pretend for a moment that the students find a cheaper or faster way to make their molds. Now they will be willing to offer larger quantities with no change in price. They might even be willing to pro-duce the same quantities of mugs at lower prices. These changes are shown by a shift in the supply curve to the *right*. Figure 5-14 shows this change.

In Figure 5-14 we have adopted some shortcuts. The two supply curves are labeled S_1 and S_2. When the curve shifts to the right, the quantity produced at P_1 is Q_1. But after the change in supply, the quantity produced at price P_1 is Q_2, a larger quantity. Also, the diagram shows that the students will be willing to produce quantity Q_1, at the lower price of P_2.

Why would these changes occur? There are three reasons for changes in supply, which may occur singly or in combination: (1) Changes in production costs, (2) change in number of suppliers, and (3) changes in suppliers' expec-tations.

Changes in Production Costs

If production costs rise (owing to a tax increase, say, or a new union contract), the supply will generally shift to the left. Economists usually refer to this shift as a decrease or reduction in supply because less will be offered at each price. If costs fall because of a technological improvement or because of lower prices for resources or materials, the supply curve will shift to the right.

The shift to the right might also occur because a government subsidy offsets some of an entrepreneur's costs. That entrepreneur will be willing to increase the quantities offered at each price because the cost of production is lower.

Production-cost changes would also include any change in the entrepre-neur's evaluation of the opportunity cost of sacrificed leisure—or a shift in preference from money to leisure (or vice versa).

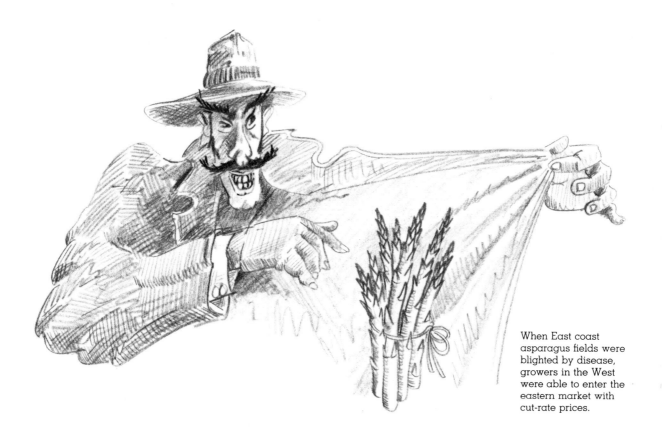

When East coast asparagus fields were blighted by disease, growers in the West were able to enter the eastern market with cut-rate prices.

Change in Number of Suppliers

Generally, an increase in the number of suppliers (more competition) will cause the supply curve to shift to the right, driving the price down for any given quantity, because some of the new competitors will offer to sell at lower prices. A shift to the left will occur if there are fewer suppliers—less competition— enabling the remaining suppliers to raise prices for any given quantity. For example, when a disease wiped out most of the asparagus fields in New Jersey, growers from the West were able to enter the East Coast market at premium prices.

Change in Suppliers' Expectations

Any change in entrepreneurs' expectations about the future will shift the supply curve. If they expect future misfortune (bankruptcy) they may be willing to work harder now to salt away some money, and the supply curve will shift to the right. Entrepreneurs who expect future sales to drop may reduce output. If the future looks bright and secure, entrepreneurs might say, ''Great, we'll take it a little easier,'' and their supply curve will shift to the left.

As a beginning economics student, you may find it helpful to think of demand and supply as separate forces, representing the desires of consumers on

Table 5-8. (repeated)

Price per mug	Total quantities supplied
$1.50	15
2.00	35
2.50	55
3.00	70
3.50	84
4.00	94
4.50	100
5.00	103

the one hand and producers on the other. The capability of a producer to supply is often independent of what consumers may wish to purchase. In the real world, however, particularly in a relatively free society like our own, demand and supply are usually interdependent. Supply may shift because suppliers expect future changes in demand, and demand may shift because buyers expect future changes in supply.

HOW PRICES ARE DETERMINED

We have come to the point of this chapter. In market-price systems, prices *usually* answer the questions of what will be produced, how those products and services will be produced, and for whom. We have to say "usually," because often the three questions are answered in accordance with tradition or in response to command (laws and government regulations). Prices, too, are "usually" determined by the forces of demand and supply operating in free markets. Again we have to say "usually," because prices are often determined by forces other than demand and supply; for example, by government agencies, monopolies, or groups of companies who cooperate with one another to fix prices.

In the example that follows of how prices are determined we will assume that the forces of demand and supply do operate, free of these hindrances.

Let's begin with the supply schedule that shows how many coffee mugs will be available at the college bookstore before the supply decreases because of the extra fee for clay. We're thinking of the totals supplied at each price in Table 5-8. (See top of this page.).

This supply schedule doesn't tell us, by itself, what the price will be. We will also need a demand schedule that shows how many coffee mugs will be demanded at each price. Table 5-10 is an assumed demand schedule; it has nothing to do with the auction among the seven students in the classroom.

Shortages and Surpluses

We are almost there—at the climax when the price will be revealed. But, we have to make a crucial assumption: We have to assume that the bookstore manager will change the price frequently, responding to observations of demand and supply. In other words, we have to assume that the bookstore manager prices the mugs so that all the mugs are sold each week at the highest possible price. To be very explicit, we will assume that if the quantities de-

Table 5-10. An Assumed Demand Schedule for Coffee Mugs at College X (Figures Are in Quantities Demanded per Week)

Price per mug	Quantities demanded
$1.50	130
2.00	120
2.50	110
3.00	100
3.50	90
4.00	80
4.50	70
5.00	60

Table 5-11. The Supply and Demand Schedules Compared (Data Taken from Tables 5-8 and 5-10)

Price per mug (1)	Quantities demanded (2)	Quantities supplied (3)	Shortages (−) and surpluses (+) (4)
$1.50	130	15	− 115
2.00	120	35	− 85
2.50	110	55	− 55
3.00	100	70	− 30
3.50 } 3.65*	90 } 88*	84 } 88*	− 6 } 0*
4.00	80	94	+ 14
4.50	70	100	+ 30
5.00	60	103	+ 43

*At some price between $3.50 and $4.00, the quantities demanded and supplied will be exactly equal. See further explanation in the text.

manded exceed the quantities supplied (called a **shortage**), the manager will raise the price. If the quantity supplied exceeds the quantity demanded (called a **surplus**), the manager will lower the price.

This assumption is another one of those economic facts of life. It doesn't make people any happier, but it's logical. If there is a shortage of parking spaces at your college, the quantity demanded must exceed the quantity supplied. The present fee must be too low. What to do? Raise the fee. The shortage will disappear.

If, on the other hand, your local department store has a surplus of sheepskin coats in June, what to do? Hold a "sale"; that is, lower the price. (An alternative might be to pay the costs of storing them until next winter.)

Table 5-11 combines the demand and supply schedules for coffee mugs and shows the shortages and surpluses at each price.

What price will the bookstore manager choose? Remember that he or she must find the highest price at which all of the mugs will be sold each week.

The fourth column of Table 5-11 helps to show how the store manager will find the right price. That column shows the shortages (−) and the surpluses

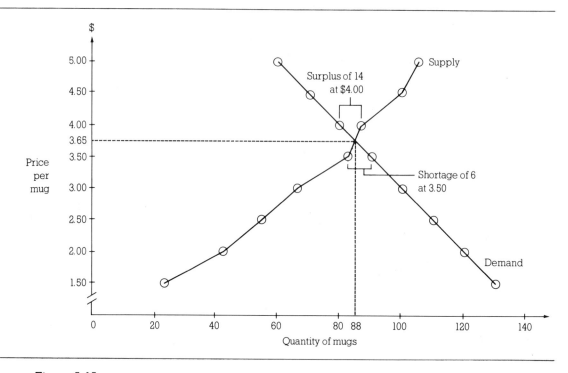

Figure 5-15.
Quantities of coffee mugs demanded and supplied at College X per week.

(+) at each price. The store manager will want to find the highest price at which there is no shortage or surplus—a price where the difference between the quantity demanded and quantity supplied is zero. The fourth column shows how the shortage gets less and less as the price rises above $1.50, and how the surplus disappears as the price falls from $5.00.

The fourth column indicates clearly that the store manager will have to choose some price between $3.50 and $4.00. The store manager will have no way of knowing for sure what the exact price will be, because demand and supply schedules do not necessarily change in any uniform way. But we'll assume that, through trial and error, the store manager discovers that at $3.65, the same number of mugs is supplied and sold (demanded). That magic quantity is, we'll assume, 88 mugs per week. Figure 5-15 illustrates this conclusion.

The Equilibrium Price

Figure 5-15 is a diagram famous in economics. Back around 1900, an English economist, Alfred Marshall (1842–1924) said the demand and supply curves are like two blades of a pair of scissors. Neither "blade" can determine the price; both are necessary.

Let's review and elaborate on what Figure 5-15 means. At the intersection of the two curves the quantities demanded and supplied are equal. At any price above $3.65, there will be a surplus. At $4.00, for example, 94 coffee mugs will be supplied, but only 80 will be demanded—a surplus of 14 mugs. At $3.50, just below the intersection of the two curves, 90 coffee mugs are demanded, while only 84 are supplied—a shortage of 6 mugs. Somewhere between $4.00 and $3.50 the quantities demanded and supplied will be equal.

The climax of our story is that the store manager will eventually arrive at a price close to $3.65 for the mugs. That price is the **equilibrium price**. At that price, as shown by the dotted line drawn to the horizontal axis, the students will want to make 88 mugs, and all the mugs will be sold each week. Thus, finally, we have seen how prices are determined in free markets and how prices answer the three questions.

Equilibrium: The Automatic Mechanism

The idea of an equilibrium price is like that of water seeking its own level. If the price gets away from equilibrium, there will be an automatic tendency to return to the equilibrium price and quantity.

At any price *above* the $3.65 equilibrium, the quantity supplied exceeds the quantity demanded. In that situation, the price will fall, probably for two reasons: (1) The store manager will drop the price to get rid of any surplus, and/or (2) some of the students making the mugs, in their eagerness to increase sales, may offer their mugs to the store at lower prices. In this event *competition among sellers* helps the price to fall.

At any price *below* equilibrium, the quantities demanded exceed those supplied. At these low prices, the students have little incentive to make the mugs even though more mugs could be sold. The store manager will have to raise the price, and then the students will produce more mugs than can be sold.

The store manager may also notice one other phenomenon. As long as the price remains below equilibrium, some of the students who wish to buy mugs, but who can't because there are not enough available, will offer to pay more than the going price. Remember, that even at the equilibrium price of $3.65, there are some people willing to pay prices as high as $5.00. Thus, the price will tend to rise if it is below equilibrium for two reasons: (1) The store manager will want to encourage more production to reduce the shortage, and/or (2) buyers with more money will offer more than the going price. In such a case, *competition among buyers* helps the price to rise.

Economists use the word *equilibrium* to mean that automatic forces in the market will cause the price to move toward the price at which the quantity supplied will equal the quantity demanded. The equilibrium price sets the *value* of a product in our society. With our mug example, it determines the quantities of resources (land, labor, capital, and entrepreneurship) necessary to produce 88 mugs and the sacrifices consumers are prepared to make to buy those mugs.

Because at the equilibrium price the quantity demanded equals the quantity supplied, with no shortage or surplus, economists speak of the equilibrium price as the price that "clears the market" of any surplus. All goods produced are sold. The arrows in Figure 5-16 indicate the automatic movements of price and quantity if the price is temporarily above or below the equilibrium price.

It is well to stress that surpluses and shortages are unlikely as long as the price is *free* to change; that is, there is always some price where the quantity demanded and the quantity supplied are equal. If, at a given price, the quantity supplied exceeds the quantity demanded, the price will fall. If, at a given price, the quantity demanded exceeds the quantity supplied, the price will rise. If these adjustments are not prevented (by price controls, for example), the price will reach a point where the quantity demanded equals the quantity supplied.

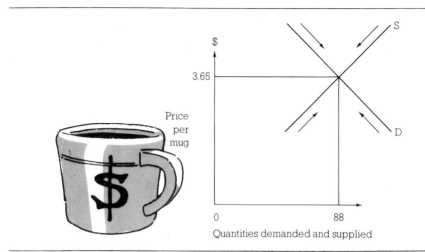

Figure 5-16.
The equilibrium price
mechanism.

The Exclusion Principle (Again)

Notice again that at prices below $3.65 many more mugs might be sold—many who were unwilling to pay $3.65 or who could not afford to pay $3.65 would be ready to buy. When the price is $3.65, however, these people are excluded from the market. Remember the exclusion principle: Any price excludes some people, because the market-price system is a rationing device. The higher the price, the more people are excluded.

At any price higher than $3.65, the students would have been eager to produce more mugs—perhaps even by hiring some helpers. But if they try collectively to sell more than 88 mugs at any price higher than $3.65, they will not succeed; buyers will not go along. Any students who cannot, or will not, make mugs for $3.65 or less will be excluded from the market. Once again we note that a market-price system efficiently rations scarce goods and resources, but that does not mean everyone is happy.

The Importance of Competition

Throughout this discussion we've omitted saying anything about *how fast* a market for any good or service will adjust to the equilibrium price.

Suppose for a moment that the price is below equilibrium and that there is only *one* buyer—you, for example. At the below-equilibrium price, suppliers aren't willing to supply the quantity you want to buy. From your point of view, there is a shortage at that price. If there were other buyers in the market, some of them might offer a higher price, and you would be forced to compete with them exactly as if you were participating in an auction. The price would surely rise. But if no other buyers are present, you can say to the supplier, "Either sell your products to me at the price I'm offering, or you won't sell any." The supplier can, of course, reply, "You're not going to get the quantities you want at this low price. My production costs won't permit it."

So, a period of haggling will ensue. The speed—and magnitude—of the price movement upward will depend on the power each one can exert on the other. The extent of this power—often called **market power**—will depend on whether or not you, the buyer, can find a reasonably close substitute at a price you are willing to pay and on whether or not the seller can locate any other, more willing buyers.

By the same token, if the price is above equilibrium, a supplier who is the *only* supplier might not worry about the resulting surplus. Such a supplier can say, "I'll wait and see if I can't force more buyers to meet my price." But if there are lots of suppliers and there is a general surplus in the market, then competition surely will force the price down. The magnitude of the price decrease will depend on the number of suppliers and how intensely they compete.

Consequently, we can see that price movements in the market are the result of competition among buyers and sellers. The speed and magnitude of price adjustments will depend on the intensity of this competition.

Competition in markets has a particularly important bearing on movements of the supply curve. Suppose that the students find a cheaper or faster way to make their molds, as illustrated in Figure 5-14. Will the students *necessarily* be willing to make more mugs at every price? Will they necessarily be willing to make the same quantities of mugs at *lower* prices? Why not keep the price and quantities the same as they were on the old supply curve? Then they would make *more* money in *less* time.

The answer is that the students will have no reason to make more mugs or drop the price, *unless* one or more of them makes such an offer to the store manager. If *that* happens, competition among them will force the price down. On the other hand, they might all sign a pact (in blood) not to drop the price. If they hang together, *the supply curve will not shift*.

Suppose that in the "real world" an oil company, steel company, automobile manufacturer, or any enterprise that is likely to have considerable market power finds a way to produce more of its product at no increase in (or perhaps even lower) cost. Will that firm shift its supply curve to the right and lower its prices? Why not simply use the opportunity to increase profits and keep prices where they were? Or even raise them? Answer again: No reason unless the firm has competitors who are offering the same, or almost the same, goods or services at lower prices.

This question of competition is particularly acute in the oil business. Why should an oil company increase its production (even if prices are higher) if it is not forced to do so by competitive oil companies? We mention this point because the oil companies have been accused of cooperating with one another in determining price and output policies. More on this in Chapter 6.

Price competition may therefore force firms to move their supply curves to the right. Lack of price competition tends to keep supply curves where they are or even to cause them to shift to the left (for example, a decision by OPEC, the Organization of Petroleum Exporting Countries, to reduce oil production so oil prices can be further increased).

SUMMARY

Prices serve three purposes in the market-price system: (1) They direct the use of resources; (2) they ration goods and services; and (3) they establish the relative values of everything in a society.

Prices are determined by demand and supply. Economists define demand as the number of units of a product a buyer will be willing and able to buy during some period of time at various prices. The law of demand holds that, as the price falls, the quantity demanded increases. This occurs because (1) a consumer can afford to buy more if the price is lower (income effect); (2) the satisfaction a consumer derives from each additional unit decreases with each additional unit he or she purchases; and (3) as the price of a product decreases, a consumer will buy it instead of other products he or she might have bought (substitution effect).

On a graph, economists usually represent demand by a line sloping down from left to right, with prices on the vertical axis and quantity on the horizontal. When demand increases—when buyers will pay more for every quantity—the line shifts to the right. When demand decreases, the line shifts to the left. Demand changes when (1) buyers' income increases or decreases; (2) buyers' tastes change; (3) the prices of other products change; (4) buyers' expectations about the future change; or (5) the total number of buyers changes.

There is an important distinction between movement along a demand or supply curve and a change in the curve. Changes in demand and supply occur only when the curve changes. The significance of this idea is that when the curve changes, more or less will be demanded or supplied without changes in price.

Supply is defined as the number of units a producer or seller of a product will offer for sale at various prices during some period of time. Economists represent supply graphically by a line sloping up from left to right. This direction of slope indicates that, as higher prices are paid for a product, more will be supplied.

A change in supply is represented by a shift in the supply curve. When the line shifts to the left, supply decreases because a smaller quantity will be offered at each price and a higher price is necessary for any given quantity. When the line shifts to the right, supply increases because a larger quantity will be offered at each price and because the same quantities will be offered at lower prices.

The two forces, supply and demand, operate together to determine all prices and quantities of everything bought and sold, thereby determining how much value our society attaches to any good, service, or resource. When shortages occur at a given price, the price tends to increase, causing the quantity supplied to increase until an equilibrium price is reached. When the equilibrium price is reached, the quantity demanded equals the quantity supplied—there is no shortage or surplus, and the market is "cleared." Similarly, when a surplus occurs at a given price, the price tends to decrease, causing the quantity demanded to increase until an equilibrium is reached.

The degree of competition in a market will determine how fast price adjustments occur.

Discussion Questions

1. What is your demand curve for something you buy regularly (perhaps phonograph records or tapes)? Is it a straight line? Is the slope of the line steeper at lower prices than it is at higher prices? Why might this be? Jot down some prices and quantities of what you would buy over some period of time and try plotting a demand curve on some graph paper.

2. If the price of coffee rises from $4 to $4.50 per pound, will a change in demand occur? Why or why not?

3. If your employer offers you a raise and you decide to increase your working hours from 30 hours to 40 hours per week, what happens to your personal supply curve? What happens to your employer's demand for your services? See if you can diagram what happens and explain.

4. Why is competition important in analyzing shifts in supply?

5. Assume that the table at right provides weekly demand and supply data for gasoline at your local gasoline station:

Quantities demanded (thousands of gallons)	Price per gallon	Quantities supplied (thousands of gallons)
40	$1.10	5
30	1.30	15
20	1.50	25
10	1.80	30
5	1.90	40

a. First graph the data on graph paper.

b. What will the equilibrium price be? Why? (Note that you won't find the exact price in the table, but you should be able to find the two prices between which equilibrium is located.)

c. At what prices will there be lines of waiting cars with angry drivers? Why?

d. What would you do to get rid of the lines? Would everyone be happy?

DID YOU EVER WONDER WHY . . .

. . . the law of demand doesn't work with designer clothes and diamond rings?

6

Prices in Action: Shortages, Surpluses, Oil Crises, and Pollution

KEY WORDS
Price floor
Price ceiling
Nonrenewable resource
Private (internal) costs
External effects
External costs (or benefits)
Social costs
Effluent charges
Allocative efficiency

The previous chapter showed you how the forces of demand and supply, if allowed to operate freely in competitive markets, determine equilibrium prices. In this chapter, we will discuss why equilibrium prices change, what happens when they are prevented from changing, and how they can be used to solve a problem like pollution. Before we begin, we should take note of some fundamental issues.

Prices change for three reasons: (1) Because of shifts in demand and supply; (2) because of government regulations forcing them to be above or below some limit; (3) or, at times, because powerful business firms can set prices independently of supply-demand forces. Here we will discuss reasons (1) and (2); the third issue is discussed in Chapters 8 and 9.

Remember what you learned in Chapter 5 about supply and demand curves, and you will understand an important priniciple that underlies this discussion: Changes in price do not cause changes in demand and supply; rather, *it is changes in demand and supply that cause changes in price*.

Recall the three causes of shifts in supply: (1) Changes in production costs, (2) changes in number of suppliers, (3) changes in *suppliers'* expectations (pp. 86–90). Now recall the five causes of shifts in demand: (1) Changes in current or expected spendable funds, (2) changes in taste, (3) changes in prices of *other* products, (4) changes in buyers' expectations, (5) changes in number of buyers (pp. 77–81). In none of these cases are shifts in demand or supply *caused* by changes in the price of the product under consideration. Clearly, the reverse is true.

Bear this in mind as you read the three sections of this chapter: (1) How price changes are caused by shifts in demand and supply, (2) the effects of government price fixing, and (3) an example of economic theory in action— pollution control.

PRICE CHANGES CAUSED BY SHIFTS IN SUPPLY AND DEMAND

We'll discuss shifts in supply first and then shifts in demand.

Price Changes Caused by Shifts in Supply

Back on page 78, you saw Figure 5-4. The left-hand sketch in that figure looks like Figure 6-1. The sketch describes movements up or down a demand curve. A drop in the price would result in an increase in quantity; a price rise would result in a decrease in quantity. These changes were called changes in the "quantity demanded," *not* changes in demand.

What is missing from that sketch is an explanation of *why* the price changes. Why *do* we move along the demand curve from Point A to Point B? The missing explanation is that movements from Point A to Point B on any demand curve have to be caused by shifts in supply. Figure 6-2 provides the missing link.

Figure 6-2 shows how an increase (shift to the right) in supply causes the movement from Point A to Point B along the demand curve. (In this case, the figure shows an increase in supply causing a drop in the price and an increase in the quantity demanded.)

In Figure 6-2, we're following a common practice: P_1 and P_2 mean first and second prices. Q_1, Q_2, and Q_3 mean first, second, and third quantities. S_1 and S_2 mean first and second supply curves. If there had been more than one demand curve, we would have labeled them D_1, D_2, and so forth.

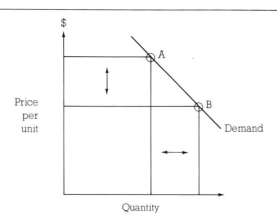

Figure 6-1.
Part (a) of Figure 5-4.

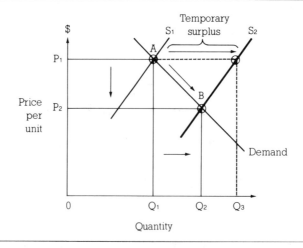

Figure 6-2.
Changes (shifts) in
supply cause
movements along a
demand curve.

Does Figure 6-2 make sense? Imagine there is an unusually large crop of cantaloupes (as there is when this is being written). The increase in supply, given any demand curve, will cause the price of cantaloupes to fall, in this case from P_1 to P_2.

We have added some additional lines to the figure to explain further why the price falls. Suppose, for a moment, the price remains at P_1. At P_1, the quantity demanded is Q_1, but after the increase in supply the quantity supplied is Q_3. Thus, if the price stayed at P_1, there would be surplus of unsold cantaloupes indicated by the distance from Q_1 to Q_3. The price has to fall for suppliers to get rid of the surplus. They find that at P_2 the surplus disappears. The quantities demanded and supplied are again equal.

In this example, the increase in supply (about which some suppliers may be unhappy) came from (we'll assume) an unusually healthy combination of perfect weather and an absence of pests. We mention this as a reminder that the increase in supply means an increase in the quantity offered for sale at *every* price. Consequently, we have what might seem a paradoxical situation: Suppliers offer more goods as the price falls, because (1) cantaloupes can't be stored

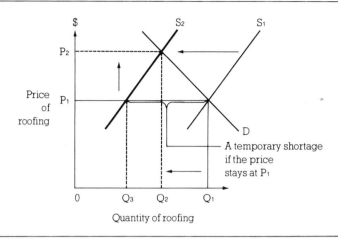

Figure 6-3.
A decrease in supply.

(withheld from the market), and (2) each cantaloupe grower is forced by other, competitive growers to drop his or her price. (We'll come back to this vulnerability of farmers in the next chapter.)

To summarize, this section has shown how increases in supply—given no change in demand—cause prices to fall. Conversely, we can visualize prices rising if supply decreases.

Suppose roofing contractors face higher costs because of the higher prices they must pay for tar (a petroleum product). As Figure 6-3 shows, the supply curve shifts to the left because of increases in the cost of production. The equilibrium price of roofing rises from P_1 to P_2, assuming no change in demand, and the quantity demanded falls.

Once again, why does the price change? If the price doesn't change, but remains at P_1, Q_1 will be demanded but only Q_3 will be supplied. Thus at P_1, there is a *shortage*. Suppliers will find they can charge more; some demanders will bid the price up. This combination of forces will surely cause the price to rise.

If roofing contractors find it cheaper to install new roofs because oil and tar have become cheaper, visualize the supply curve shifting to the right, causing a drop in the price and an increase in the quantity demanded.

Price Changes Caused by Shifts in Demand

This time let's begin with a supply curve. In Figure 6-4, we see there is a movement along a supply curve from Point A to Point B, owing to an increase in price and, also, an increase in the "quantity supplied." *Supply does not change*.

Again the question is: What causes the movement from Point A to Point B? Answer: an increase in demand. Figure 6-5 illustrates.

Now we'll try a real-world example of the situation described in Figure 6-5. Pretend we're thinking about the demand for, and supply of, gasoline at your local gas station. The current demand and supply schedules are shown in Table 6-1. Equilibrium price and quantity are clearly at $1.60 per gallon. At that price, the quantities demanded and supplied are equal.

Now let's assume a reason for an increase in demand. The increase is caused

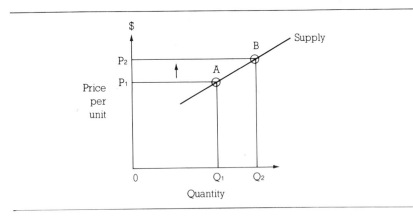

Figure 6-4.
An increase in the
quantity supplied.

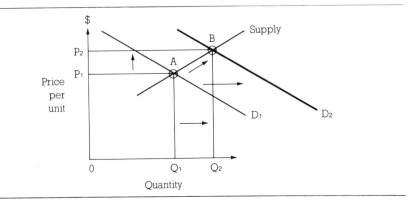

Figure 6-5.
An increase (shift to
the right) of the
demand curve cause
a movement up the
supply curve.

Table 6-1. Demand and Supply of Argonaut Gasoline at Your Local Station (per Week)

Price per gallon	Gallons supplied	Gallons demanded	
$1.20	4,000	8,000	
1.40	5,000	7,000	
1.60	6,000	6,000	Equilibrium
1.80	7,000	5,000	
2.00	8,000	4,000	
2.20	9,000	3,000	

by fears in the United States of a war in the Middle East that may involve our major supplier, Saudi Arabia. Such thoughts would cause drivers to fill up with gasoline in expectation of future shortages. Thus, an increase in demand occurs because buyers expect a future shift (to the left) in supply. The increase in demand means that drivers will try to buy more gasoline—*at every price.* Supply need not change at all. The increase in demand occurs because drivers are afraid supply *might* change.

Table 6-2 shows what happens. The new equilibrium price is now $1.80, where the quantities supplied and demanded (Column 4) are equal at 7,000 gallons per week.

Table 6-2. Demand and Supply of Argonaut Gasoline at Your Local Station (per Week)

(1) Price per gallon	(2) Gallons supplied	(3) Old gallons demanded	(4) New gallons demanded	
$1.20	4,000	8,000	10,000	
1.40	5,000	7,000	9,000	
1.60	6,000	6,000	8,000	
1.80	7,000	5,000	7,000	New equilibrium
2.00	8,000	4,000	6,000	
2.20	9,000	3,000	5,000	

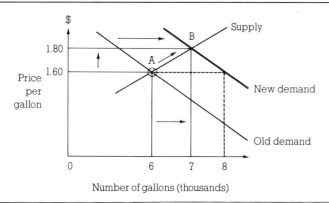

Figure 6-6.
Effect of an increase in demand on prices and sales of Argonaut gasoline (per week). Note that if the price stays at $1.60, there will be a shortage: 8,000 gallons will be demanded only only 6,000 supplied. Only if the price rises to $1.80 can there be a new equilibrium.

Figure 6-6 shows the increase in demand graphically. Remember that there is no change in supply, because the supply curve has not shifted; there is only a *change in the quantity supplied.*

What conclusions can we draw from this model of a gasoline market? When an increase in demand (shown by the horizontal arrows) occurs with no change in supply, there will be—*ceteris paribus*—an increase in the equilibrium price (shown by the vertical arrow) and an increase in the quantity bought and sold.

Now let's think about blue jeans. What would happen if dermatologists announced that wearing blue jeans causes skin cancer? Assuming no change in supply, a decrease in demand will occur; the equilibrium price will fall, and the quantities demanded and supplied will also fall. Figure 6-7 illustrates this effect. The arrows help to show the changes in demand, price, and quantity.

Shifts in Both Supply and Demand

If both supply and demand change, the result is difficult to forecast. It all depends on the direction of the shifts and whether or not supply shifts *more* or *less* than demand. (In the following figures, the two equilibriums are circled.) Let's assume that supply shifts more than demand and that both increase (Figure 6-8). The price falls as the quantity rises.

What happens if supply and demand both increase, as in Figure 6-8, but demand rises more than supply, as in Figure 6-9? This time the increase in demand offsets the increase in supply, and the price rises. In both cases, quantity rises.

Figure 6-7.
Effect of a decrease in
demand: Price and
quantity decrease. In
this case, if the price
stays at P₁, the
quantity demanded
will be Q₃ and the
quantity supplied, Q₁.
This surplus will
cause suppliers to
drop the price and
decrease the
quantities they
produce.

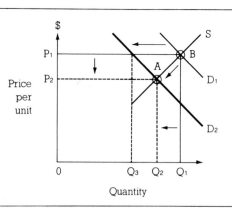

Figure 6-8.
Supply increases
more than demand.

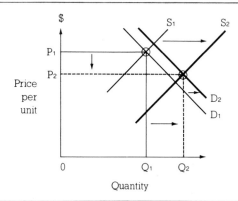

Figure 6-9.
Demand increases
more than supply.

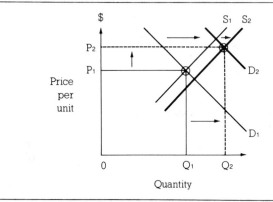

Saigon Again

The situation in Saigon in August 1976 (see page 81 in Chapter 5) is a good way
to recap this section on changes in demand and supply. Remember that the
price of gasoline had gone to $12 a gallon, leading to a drop in the demand for
motorcycles and an increase in the demand for bicycles. We can diagram these
changes as follows:

First, the supply of gasoline decreased tremendously when the American

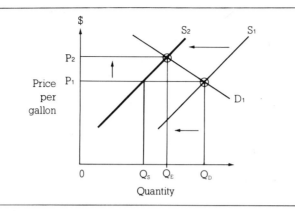

Figure 6-10.
The supply of gasoline decreases in Saigon when the Americans leave.

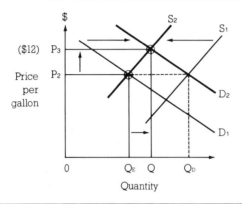

Figure 6-11.
The demand for gasoline increases after the supply decreases.

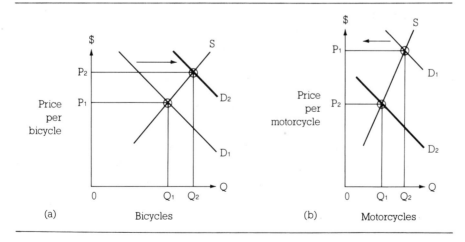

Figure 6-12.
The demand for bicycles increases; the demand for motorcycles decreases.

forces left, and when refineries, pipelines, and so on were destroyed. The reduction in supply led to an increase in demand from those who wanted to hoard gasoline in expectation of still greater shortages. Figures 6-10 through 6-12 show step by step what happened.

When the supply of gasoline decreases, a shortage develops at price P_1, because at that price, the quantity demanded, Q_D, exceeds the quantity supplied, Q_S. But, as long as the price is free to change, the shortage will cause a price rise to P_2 and a new equilibrium quantity at Q_E. (The shortage will encourage profiteering sellers to charge more and wealthy gasoline users to pay more.)

But, as this change takes place, gasoline users fear future shortages and decide to hoard gasoline. The demand for gasoline increases as Figure 6-11 shows.

In Figure 6-11 we can see that if the price stays at P_2, there will again be a shortage. Q_D, the new quantity demanded, exceeds the quantity supplied at Q_E. This shortage leads to a still higher price at P_3 (which we know is $12) and a new equilibrium quantity at Q.

Finally, the exorbitant price of gasoline leads to increase in demand for bicycles and a decrease in demand for motorcycles—shown in Figure 6-12.

Figure 6-12 shows no changes in supply (although there could very well be some) but only changes in demand leading to changes in the *quantities supplied*. All of these changes took place because gasoline and motorcycles are complementary goods. Gasoline and bicycles, and bicycles and motorcycles, are substitute goods.

The Efficiency of Market-Price Systems

The Saigon story demonstrates the efficiency of market-price systems in solving (in this case) shortages. When the supply of petroleum products decreased, the demand for petroleum-using vehicles eventually fell, as shown by Figure 6-12**b**. And as people substituted bicycles for motorcycles, suppliers of bicycles were given an incentive to increase production—the quantities of bicycles increased along with price increases. When all these forces had worked themselves out, new equilibrium prices were reached where the quantities of bicycles supplied and demanded were equal and where the quantities of motorcycles supplied and demanded were also equal. Free markets had efficiently—without bureaucratic control—solved the difficult problem of a severe oil shortage.

Of course, not everyone was happy. In particular, those without bicycles who could not afford the $600 price were excluded from the market. As always, the market-price system favors people with more money to spend.

Soon after the events discussed here, the market-price system in Vietnam was, to a great extent, replaced by a system of prices set by the government. The next section discusses the effects of government-set prices in the United States.

EFFECTS OF GOVERNMENT PRICE FIXING

From time to time, if the lobbies in Washington push hard enough, Congress may be persuaded that the equilibrium price is too low to give suppliers a satisfactory income. Congress (or a state legislature) obliges by passing a law that establishes a minimum price, below which prices are not allowed to fall. The object is, of course, to ensure continued political support from the affected suppliers.

Congress may also, on occasion, take the view that the equilibrium price is inflationary or that it excludes too many poor people. In that event, Congress will pass a law that sets a maximum price, above which prices cannot rise. Let's examine, first, government-set minimum prices and, second, government-set maximum prices.

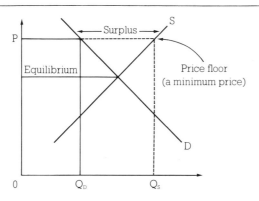

Figure 6-13.
Picture of a surplus
cause by a price floor.

Government-Set Minimum Prices:
Price Floors and Surpluses

When the government legislates a minimum price, that price is called the
price floor. The price is not permitted to fall below that minimum.

The price floor the government sets is independent of the forces of demand
and supply. In fact, the price floor might be above, below, or equal to the
equilibrium price that prevails at any particular time. However, the government
officials' usual reason for setting a minimum price is that they believe the
equilibrium price is too low. If, then, the price floor is set at some level above
the equilibrium price, the quantity supplied will exceed the quantity demanded, and a *surplus* will result.

The government may then take the surplus (typically farm surpluses) off the
market, probably by buying it at the price floor. The public as taxpayers are
faced with the cost of buying, storing, and disposing of the surplus, and the
public as consumers must pay higher prices for the smaller quantities farmers
will sell to them.

Figure 6-13 is a picture of a surplus. P stands for the price floor per unit sold.
Q_D represents the quantity demanded. Q_S is the quantity supplied. The difference between Q_D and Q_S is the surplus in number of units.

There may be political reasons behind the government's decision to assume
the headaches of a surplus: Members of a powerful interest group like farmers
may demand protection from an equilibrium price that they consider too low.
Lobbies and political pressure may lead to the passage of a price-floor law.

"Buttering Up the Farmers"[1]

The price floors for dairy products are among the best known examples of
government interference with market prices in the United States. Ever since
1949, Congress has set price floors for dairy products to help dairy farmers
through "dry" winters when their cows don't give as much milk as in other
seasons. The price floors have been generous.

In 1981, the price floor for butter was 50 cents per pound above the world
price; the price floor for milk powder was 70 cents per pound higher than the
world price. Milk and butter producers were given every incentive to overpro-
duce, because of these high prices.

And this the dairy producers did. "Aided by ultra-modern farming techniques, today [cows] have become milk-making marvels . . .,"[2] some of whom produce four times as much milk as they did in 1955.* The result, in 1980 alone, was a surplus of about 8.2 *billion* pounds of milk that was purchased by the government at taxpayers' expense.

If you were a dairy farmer, what would you do? Produce as much as you can. Whatever you can't sell to consumers at the price-floor price, the government is obligated to buy. This example of dairy industry price floors illustrates four economic facts of life:

1. Any economic decision is apt to benefit some people and hurt others, as we saw in Chapter 1. The dairy-price program undoubtedly helped dairy farmers but hurt consumers. The fact that the government-guaranteed prices produced surpluses is sufficient proof that dairy prices were above equilibrium. Consumers paid higher prices than they would have without the price floors. Taxpayers were hurt because they bore the burden of the cost of buying and storing the surpluses.

2. In any program like the dairy price-support programs, the benefits are not equally shared. In 1977[3] (the latest available figure at this writing), there were about 1,500 producers of fluid milk.** The largest *50* of them sold *60* percent of all the fluid milk produced in that year. These are the companies who received the lion's share of the extra dollars the government paid out.

3. The pursuit of self-interest provides countless examples of human ingenuity. (Perhaps the first example that comes to mind is the billions of dollars Americans spend to avoid income taxes.) In the context of this chapter, however, we're thinking of the incredible efforts made by dairy farmers to increase production, given the incentive of high, guaranteed prices. A market-price system provides the incentive, as no other system does, to motivate people to produce and to find new solutions to economic problems. The larger and more conspicuous the potential profits, the more they will spur production. And the freer producers are to innovate and improvise as they please, the more they will produce. This fact of life is surfacing in many socialist countries (as we saw in the case of China), where central governments are using free market incentives like private garden plots to encourage the people to produce more.

4. The milk story also reminds us that economic decisions are never made in a vacuum. They are often made because of political forces; once made, they are shaped by political action. Politics and the economics of milk production are certainly intertwined. The dairy industry lobby in Washington is one of the most powerful forces affecting Congressional decision making. A few examples of that power: After the dairy industry pledged $2 million to President Nixon's reelection campaign in 1971, the President reversed the decision of his own Secretary of Agriculture[4] and raised the price floor for milk. President Carter raised it again after a $126,000 contribution from the dairy industry to his election campaign. During the Reagan administration

---

*In 1979, there were about half as many milk cows as there were in 1960, but they produced just as much milk. *Statistical Abstract of the United States, 1980,* p. 727.

**In many cases, dairy farmers belong to cooperatives, each of which counts as one producer. That is the reason for the apparently low figure of 1,500.

Congressmen received more than $1 million before the milk price floor vote.

(1981), 110 members of the House voted to raise the floor again. The organization Common Cause discovered that 243 congressmen had altogether received more than $1 million, an average of $4,000 each, from the three largest dairy cooperatives immediately prior to the vote. (The measure lost, but the price floor was still at 1980 levels as of 1983.)

Disposing of the Surplus

You must be wondering what any government does with the surpluses created by price floors. By 1982, the warehouses holding dairy products were overflowing with butter, cheese, and nonfat dry milk, all of which were threatening to spoil. In a series of moves, the Reagan administration did its best to reduce the hoard.

About 100 million pounds of cheese were given to poor people, and later butter was also given away. You may recall TV news films showing lines of elderly and poor people waiting to receive these products. In a much less well publicized incident, the Administration sold 200 million pounds of butter to New Zealand for about half what dairy farmers were originally paid for it (butter that likely was sent on to the Soviet Union in some form). The Department of Agriculture was routinely selling up to 10 percent of its total stock of nonfat dry milk back to farmers for use as animal feed "where it is often given to dairy cows to produce more milk."[5] Despite these efforts, the surpluses will continue to accumulate as long as the price floor is above the equilibrium price—and retail prices of milk, butter, cottage cheese, and yogurt will stay high.

Government-Set Maximum Prices: Price Ceilings and Shortages

When the government legislates a *maximum* price, the maximum legal price is called a **price ceiling**.

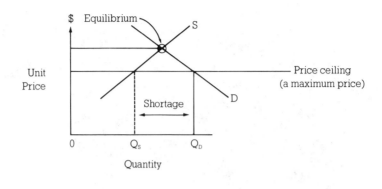

Figure 6-14.
Picture of a shortage
cause by a price
ceiling.

Keep in mind that the price ceiling may be above, below, or equal to the equilibrium price. Usually, however, the government believes the equilibrium price will reach a point that is too high.

Economic reasons (the need to control inflation, for example) may cause the government to set a price ceiling by freezing prices if it believes the equilibrium price is too high for people with low incomes. Or the government may want to discourage the production of some item by reducing or eliminating profits for the producer (for example, cars and gasoline for consumer use in wartime).

Even if the government has benevolent reasons for setting price floors or price ceilings, it faces enormous consequences when it interferes with equilibrium prices.

Assuming the government's maximum price, the price ceiling, is *below* the market-determined equilibrium, the quantity demanded will exceed the quantity supplied. A *shortage* will result.

Figure 6-14 is a picture of a *shortage* caused by a price ceiling. This time, P stands for price ceiling per unit sold, and the quantity demanded (Q_D) exceeds the quantity supplied (Q_S). The difference is the shortage in number of units.

The Case of Rent Controls

Rent controls are an example of price ceilings. Tenants often begin to call for rent controls when landlords have been raising rents to catch up with rising maintenance costs and taxes and to maximize their profits. In a number of major cities, rent control laws have stopped landlords from raising rents or placed many legal barriers in their way.

What happens? Figure 6-14 tells the story. Any price below equilibrium, like a ceiling on the maximum rents a landlord can charge, creates a shortage (or perhaps worsens an already existing one). When landlords find they can't increase rents, they may simply abandon older buildings, or they may convert their apartment buildings to cooperatives or condominiums.* The National As-

---

*Buyers of a "cooperative" buy shares in a corporation that owns the building and land; the individual buyer does not actually own the apartment and consequently cannot mortgage it. A condominium buyer owns the individual apartment outright and owns the land around the building jointly with other owners. "Condo" buyers can mortgage their property.

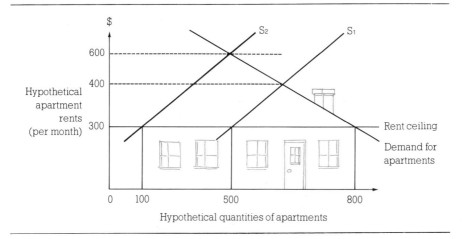

Figure 6-15.
Rent controls with a decrease in supply of apartments.

sociation of Home Builders estimates that the number of rental units in the United States is declining at the rate of 1.5 percent—or 420,000 apartments—a year.[6]

During the years 1970–1978, for example, the supply of rental units in Washington, D.C., dropped from 199,100 to 175,900; in New York City, landlords abandoned 30,000 units annually because they couldn't afford the upkeep. Only about 2,000 new units a year were built.[7]

Some of these reductions were undoubtedly decreases in the quantities supplied; that is, movements down a given supply curve as a result of the lower prices forced by price ceilings. But when existing apartment units are taken off the market, fewer units are available at *any* price. When that happens, supply decreases. Figure 6-15 shows the effects of a decrease in supply coupled with a price ceiling.

We can modify Figure 6-14 with Figure 6-15 to show not only the rent ceiling but also the decrease in supply.*

S_1 represents the supply of apartments before landlords convert them to cooperatives or condominiums. The rent ceiling is set at $300 per month. The equilibrium rent is at $400. In that situation the (hypothetical) shortage is 300 apartments, because at the rent ceiling of $300, demand will call for 800 units but only 500 will be supplied.

S_2 shows what happens when landlords, frustrated by rent control laws, abandon their buildings or convert them to cooperatives or condominiums. The decrease in supply of rental units now means that at the ceiling price of $300, only 100 units will be supplied, but 800 units are still demanded. The shortage is now (800−100) 700 units instead of 300.

Oil Prices

The gyrations of oil prices over the last decade have provided us with another example of demand and supply movements coupled with price ceilings. During the 1970s, three factors combined to create severe shortages and periodic

---

*Some economists argue that the rent ceiling causes a movement down a supply curve, a change in the quantity supplied, rather than a shift in the supply curve. We take the view here that a shift occurs because fewer apartments are available at *every* price.

lines of angry motorists at gas stations: (1) two interruptions in the flow of Middle Eastern oil to the United States, (2) a very complicated set of price ceilings, and (3) increases in the American demand for oil accompanying a decrease in the production of oil in the United States. Here is a very brief review of these three factors.

In November 1973, during negotiations to halt the Arab-Israeli war, the Arabs announced an embargo on oil shipments to countries friendly to Israel. Because the United States had been supplying arms and dollars in support of Israel, it was the main target of the embargo. Suddenly the United States did not have enough oil to satisfy the demand for heating, transportation, and myriad industrial uses.

The Arab action forced Americans to respond to an energy shortage that had been developing over decades. As early as 1952, the Paley Commission appointed by President Eisenhower had forecast the energy crisis by projecting increased energy use and diminishing supplies. In the mid-sixties, blackouts and brownouts occurred in the northeastern states. Thus, the Arab announcement merely precipitated a crisis that would probably have occurred at some time during the 1970s in any event.

Another oil crisis made the world shiver during the winter of 1978–1979. The revolution in Iran suddenly deprived oil-consuming nations of about 6 million barrels per day, about 10 percent of total world consumption of 64 million barrels per day. For the United States the crisis meant a loss of 900,000 barrels per day, nearly 5 percent of our daily consumption of 19 million barrels.

Both crises caused shock waves of considerable magnitude. Because both occurred in winter, homes in New England ran short of heating oil. Blackouts and brownouts occurred when power companies couldn't get enough diesel fuel. Despite measures like 55-mph speed limits and alternate days for gasoline purchasing (depending on the last number of one's license plate), there were long lines of car drivers waiting for gasoline at those stations that had it. Many didn't.

OIL CEILING PRICES. Let's remember at this point that when market prices are free to change, shortages and surpluses will disappear. But in this case, the shortages and the lines of frustrated car drivers did not easily disappear, because gasoline prices were held down by a set of complicated price ceilings.

The arithmetic of oil pricing has been, and is, confusing. Just prior to the Arab oil embargo, the federal government regulated oil prices under the Emergency Petroleum Act of 1973. Since the embargo of 1973–1974, the regulations covering oil prices have become enormously complicated. Table 6-3 summarizes the rules covering old and new oil in 1979. As you can see, there were price ceilings that regulate "old oil" and "new oil," "new new oil," and "stripper oil." OPEC* prices are also shown.

Table 6-3 shows that when the world price of oil was about $20 per barrel, price ceilings in the United States were far below that figure. In most European countries and in Japan, where there were no price ceilings, the price of gaso-

---

*OPEC, the Organization of Petroleum Exporting Countries, has thirteen members: Saudi Arabia, Iran, Iraq, Venezuela, Kuwait, United Arab Emirates, Qatar, Libya, Algeria, Ecuador, Nigeria, Gabon, and Indonesia. See *U.S. News & World Report*, 12 March 1979, for a summary of the oil production for each OPEC country.

Table 6-3. A Paradise for Lawyers and Accountants (Ceiling Prices for 42-gallon Barrels of Oil as of April 1979)

Type of oil	Ceiling price
1. "Old oil" (from wells drilled before May 1973)	$ 5.75
2. "New oil" (from wells drilled after May 1973)	12.66
3. "New, new oil" drilled after January 1979, 2.5 miles away from, or 1,000 feet deeper than, an existing well	14.00
4. "Stripper oil" from wells producing less than 10 barrels per day	14.55
OPEC World Price	about 20.00

Source: Time, 16 April 1979, p. 67.

line at the pump was two and three times the U.S. price. In those countries, there were no lines at the gasoline stations (equilibrium prices were $2 to $3 per gallon).[8] In the United States, where the price was $1 per gallon or less, car drivers in long lines swore at the oil companies, the government, and one another.

We have titled Table 6-3 a "paradise" for lawyers and accountants because the price ceilings provided the incentive for much legal and accounting interpretation. You can see why from the table. The price ceilings gave the oil companies enormous rewards if they could make their oil fit into higher-priced categories. Thus, they spent millions to prove that "old" oil was really "new" oil, that new oil was really "new-new" oil, and/or that their oil was really stripper oil. The government's efforts to prove otherwise were often fruitless. Old oil, new oil, or new-new oil could all come out of the same well. Old oil, new oil, new-new oil, and stripper oil were sometimes produced by different wells in the same field. It was a mess. And the mess caused resources to be wasted in trying to prove the oil companies' (or the government's) interpretation of the regulations.

INCREASES IN DEMAND FOR OIL BUT A DECREASE IN THE PRODUCTION OF OIL IN THE UNITED STATES. The effects of the price ceilings were predictable: Increases in the quantities demanded were encouraged; increases in the quantities supplied were discouraged. During the period from 1960 to 1978, the number of 42-gallon barrels of oil consumed in the United States almost doubled. Yet during that same period of time the population of the United States increased only 21 percent. Each of us used more oil directly for driving as well as indirectly for fueling our factories and our power stations for the running of our gadgets (our hair dryers).

Many of our friendliest trading partners—Japan and the democracies in Western Europe—were unhappy about our low oil prices and excessive use of energy. They saw the United States as contributing to high gasoline prices because of our demand for OPEC oil.

And they were right. During the 1970 through 1979 decade our own production of oil declined 10 percent while our oil imports grew by 500 percent. Table 6-4 shows how our dependence on foreign oil increased from 1970 to 1979, and then declined again by 1981—as our total dependence on oil declined—in response to higher prices and their effects on oil use.

Table 6-4. Trends in U.S. Oil Use and Prices

	1970	1979	1981
Percentage of total energy from oil	44%	50%	43%
Percentage of oil imported	15%	50%	34%
Price per 42-gallon barrel	$2	$15-$40	$32
Total cost of imported oil per year	$1 billion (483 million barrels)	$50 billion (2.4 billion barrels)	$62 billion (1.6 billion barrels)

Source: U.S. Departments of Energy and Commerce

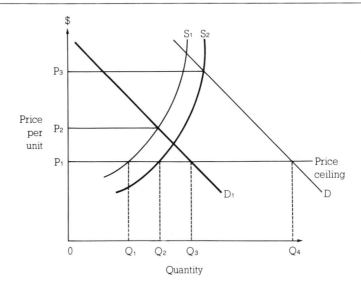

Figure 6-16.
A small increase in supply, a large increase in demand, with a price ceiling.

PUTTING IT ALL TOGETHER. When small increases in supply,* occasionally interrupted by external shocks, are coupled with large increases in demand *and* price ceilings, the reasons for shortages become very visible. Figure 6-16 shows a modest increase in supply from S_1 to S_2, but a large increase in demand from D_1 to D_2.

The two equilibrium prices necessary to remove the shortages are shown at P_2 and P_3. P_1 represents a price ceiling imposed by the government. Before the increase in demand and supply, the shortage is the distance between Q_1 and Q_2. But after the changes in demand and supply, the shortage, caused by the ceiling, is much greater—the distance between Q_3 and Q_4.

THE END OF THE OIL CRISES—OR IS IT? By mid-1982, the oil shortages had disappeared. Oil companies actually had an oversupply; their storage tanks were full. Two events helped: (1) In 1980, President Carter signed into law a measure

_____

*We are assuming small increases in supply here under the theory that more oil has gradually become available in this country and from other countries. Our purpose is to show how shortages can occur even when supply does increase, but precise data were not available at this writing.

(the Crude Oil Windfall Profit Tax Act of 1980) to eliminate all price ceilings on oil (whereupon gasoline prices at the pump increased rapidly from about $1 to $1.50 per gallon); and (2) a worldwide recession during the 1980–1982 years reduced world demand for oil, and prices settled down to a new equilibrium of around $1.15 per gallon. Nevertheless, the oil crises of the 1970s served to remind us of what happens when controls are placed on free markets.

The oil crises of the seventies also serve to emphasize the difference between renewable and **nonrenewable resources**. A nonrenewable resource is one that exists in limited, finite quantities. Once that quantity is used up, the resource is gone forever. Oil and coal are nonrenewable resources. Both commodities were formed millions of years ago. When we find all there is to find, there will be no more. On the other hand, the sun, the wind, the tides, or plants and trees that we can grow, all provide us with sources of energy we can renew indefinitely. For example, we are becoming aware of the difference between cotton clothing (renewable) and polyester clothing that is nonrenewable because the polyester is made from oil. The 1980s will be a period of great development of renewable resources.

Solving Shortages

When there is a shortage, some form of rationing becomes necessary. One way to eliminate the shortage is by allowing the price to rise. If there is a shortage of parking spaces at your college, for instance, the administration may decide to raise student and faculty parking fees. We talked about this in Chapter 5. Some people will be unhappy about the solution, of course, but the higher fees will force more car-pooling and bike-riding and the shortage will disappear.

Another way to overcome shortages is simply to overlook the problem and allow people to stand in long lines (as at gas stations) waiting to buy. This kind of rationing system (called queueing) excludes those at the end of the line when supplies run out.

The government may also devise an elaborate distribution system. It may issue food or gasoline ration cards; it may ask buyers to fill out forms in quintuplicate; and it may set criteria for buying. During World War II, one had to establish proof of need to obtain a new car or a telephone.

One way an individual may overcome shortages caused by rent controls is to follow a practice common in New York City: Pay the landlord a "key charge"— a "bonus" for handing you the key. A similar, well-recognized way to get the bank to give you a Federal Housing Administration (FHA) mortgage that often carries a below-equilibrium rate of interest is to pay the bank "points"—each point being 1 percent of the mortgage. This kind of add-on charge excludes those without the financial means to engage in these activities, thus defeating the original purpose.

The eventual result of rationing may be that some suppliers will engage in illegal "black-market" activities (selling at prices above those legally set by the government), which in turn entail costs to taxpayers in the form of policing, trying criminals, and so forth. During World War II, a time of extensive price ceilings and widespread shortages, black markets in nylon stockings, gasoline, tires, and new or used cars were commonplace.

Some Implications of Price Ceilings and Price Floors

Before leaving the topic of government interferences with free-market prices, we should think about the costs or benefits of such interferences to a nation that permits them. The costs and benefits of price ceilings are particularly apparent in command-planning countries like the Soviet Union and its satellites. In these countries the State dictates most prices including food prices. To make sure that the people stay alive and that they continue to accept their government, the planning authorities will usually impose price ceilings (low prices) on necessary foods like milk, cereals, bread, margarine, potatoes, some form of meat (usually canned or smoked) and certain vegetables. But as we know from our own experience with oil prices, ceiling prices discourage production and encourage consumption. The inevitable result is that the people will complain about food shortages. And as we have seen in Chapter 3, food shortages are chronic in the Soviet Union. And, very often the shortage works itself out—to some extent—through unofficial private production and private markets. Often these private sources are part of a large underground economy. (More on this subject in Chapter 12.)

But, as the dictator of such a country, what do you do? You want the people, especially low-income people, to have essential foods at low prices, but *enforced* low prices will guarantee that there won't be enough.

One solution is clearly to go the U.S. route: Use *price floors* to encourage production (and allow the farmers to keep the profits). Here too there are costs, but these costs are not as visible as hunger.

One cost is that taxpayers have to provide funds for the price floor. Another cost is that the people will have to pay a higher price for what they get. And another cost is the cost to taxpayers of storing and/or distributing surpluses. But, least visible of all, is the cost to the people of allowing resources to flow to a tax-supported industry in amounts that exceed the quantities a free market would provide.

Nevertheless, as a dictator, you might be tempted to use price floors, because these costs are less visible. But . . . but . . . but . . . will you be able to rest easy? Probably not. The price floors will create a class of wealthy, powerful farmers who will gain increasing political clout and who may want to replace you with someone else. And low-income people will become increasingly unhappy with high food prices. One solution for them is food stamps. In justification for such a policy you mention the combination of price floors and food stamps in the United States. (You do this privately with your advisors, because officially you hate the United States). But . . . but . . . this policy will have its problems because taxpayers will dislike having to pay for the policy two ways: (1) They will have to pay the cost of the price supports and the surpluses, and (2) they will have to pay the cost of the food stamps.

What, finally, do you do? About all you can do is to admit to yourself that any economic decision has both costs and benefits, and that your job is to find a policy that will keep you in your job.

This chapter ends with one more example of price theory. It is a somewhat different kind of example in that it involves a free-market solution to a problem that exists because free markets have failed to deal with it. The problem is pollution.

ECONOMIC THEORY IN ACTION: POLLUTION CONTROL

In an Adam Smithian, self-interested world, entrepreneurs are expected to enlarge their profits as much as possible. The natural way to do this is to produce

The bedrock of 19th century industry.

at the lowest possible cost. But at whose cost? It is obviously cheaper for entrepreneurs to dump waste into the nearest stream or into the atmosphere than to truck waste to some waste-disposal facility or to filter it coming out of their chimneys. Therefore, what may be sensible for entrepreneurs may not be desirable for the community.

And our views of what is desirable for the community change over time and as we acquire new knowledge (for example, understanding the relationship of pollution to various diseases). Back in the 1890s, when heavy industry was becoming dominant in the United States, lawsuits were brought against polluters on the grounds that they were violating the rights of property-owners downstream from them. Some lower courts agreed, but eventually the Supreme Court rejected this argument on the grounds that industrialization was a "public good" that superseded the rights of those whose water was being polluted. Now that we have the industrialization and its advantages, the courts can, apparently, afford to address the disadvantages—although the tactic being used is regulatory law.

Here is a classic trade-off: We can force entrepreneurs "to clean up their acts," but when we do, entrepreneurs have to adopt more expensive means of production or waste disposal. Inevitably they will charge higher prices, and, given no change in demand, the quantity demanded will drop and workers will be laid off. The trade-off is therefore cleaner air and water *or* more unemployment. Here is how economists think about this problem.

Private Costs + External Costs = Social Costs

The costs associated with the manufacturer's production or buyer's use of any product are called **private (internal) costs**. They are borne by the seller and the buyer and are included in the market price or in the costs of using the product after purchase.

Normally, transactions involve only a buyer and a seller. When a seller sells a pad of paper to a buyer, only two people are apparently involved in the transaction. But if the factory that makes the paper contributes to air or water pollution, economists say that people *outside the transaction* are affected or that the transaction has **external effects**. Because paper production in this instance is harmful to people unconnected with the production or purchases of paper, **external costs** are involved.

The term **social costs** refers to the total impact on society of the production, distribution, and use of whatever is produced. Thus, social costs are private or internal costs plus external costs.

External effects may involve benefits as well as costs. Two examples of external benefits: (1) the education of a biochemist helps to prevent disease in thousands of children; such education has a private benefit for the biochemist but also great benefit for others external to that transaction. (2) Person A receives a vaccination for some contagious disease. The vaccination gives A a private benefit but also an external benefit (protection) to others with whom A has contact.

The problem is that prices in a market-price system usually reflect only private (internal) costs and benefits. If buyers and sellers don't have to consider environmental regulations, the equilibrium price will be below that necessary to cover external costs. The true costs to society are left out of price determination.

The Reserve Mining Company Case

A famous and long-drawn-out case that demonstrates the issue of private versus social costs came to public attention during the late 1960s and dragged out through most of the 1970s. It involved the Reserve Mining Company, located in the small town of Silver Bay, Minnesota.

The company mines a type of iron ore, called taconite, near Babbitt, Minnesota, and then ships it 50 miles to Silver Bay, on the shores of Lake Superior. There the iron content of the taconite is extracted, and, until the late 1970s, the wastes, or "tailings," were dumped into the water at the rate of 67,000 tons per day. Any time that Reserve Mining was attacked for polluting the lake—and the attacks were continual from 1967 to 1978—the company replied that it might have to close the plant if ordered to stop polluting. That would have caused economic havoc, because the company employed 3,200 workers in the area—at least 90 percent of the local work force. But in February 1972, the U.S. Justice Department decided to sue for a cleanup anyway. The trial began in the summer of 1976.

Public health became the key issue. Asbestos fibers were discovered in the drinking water that five communities (including Duluth, 60 miles down the shoreline) drew from Lake Superior. Federal scientists pinpointed Reserve's taconite tailings as the source of the asbestos. If ingested or inhaled—and particles were detected in the air over Reserve's Silver Bay plant—asbestos fibers can cause cancer.

The end of the story was finally written. Following many court battles in 1977 and 1978, the Reserve Mining Company agreed on July 7, 1978, to build a $370 million facility to process taconite waste on land and to cease dumping wastes into Lake Superior by a federal court deadline of April 15, 1980.

The Costs of Pollution Control

Reserve Mining's acceptance of the court order made lots of people happy. Company employees in Silver Bay kept their jobs. People living on or near Lake

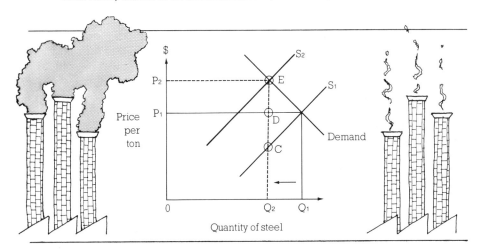

Figure 6-17.
Example of demand and supply when antipollution equipment is installed in a steel mill.

Superior breathed easier with less fear of cancer caused by ingestion of asbestos fibers. But, obviously, Reserve will try to shift the $370 million cost of the waste treatment facility to someone else.

Economic theory has a way of looking at this problem. If, say, a steel mill is forced to put in antipollution equipment, the company's product costs will rise. Its supply curve will shift to the left because a higher market price is necessary now to induce the mill to produce any given quantity. Assuming no change in demand, the shift in supply will cause the product price to rise and the quantity demanded to fall. Figure 6-17 shows what happens:

Higher production costs are shown by the shift of the supply curve from S_1 to S_2. The price rises from P_1 to P_2, causing the quantity demanded to decrease from Q_1 to Q_2. As the quantity demanded falls, the steel mill will buy fewer resources, among them labor. Employees will be laid off. Note also that the higher price that buyers must pay may or may not be socially desirable, depending on how different income groups are affected.

Ideally, the vertical distance between the two supply curves (the distance CE in Figure 6-17) reflects the external cost of producing the steel. We have to say "ideally" because of external costs may be extremely difficult to measure. (We can never be sure, for example, if the lung cancer of people in the community hospital has been caused by emissions from the steel mill's stacks or by excessive smoking.)

Nevertheless, we shall assume that an estimate of external costs can be made and that we can force the steel company to absorb all external costs by installing, say, a filtration system for its chimneys at an average cost of CE per system. The diagram now tells how this cost will be split between the mill and the buyer. At the new quantity, Q_2, the vertical distance between the supply curves, the additional cost of producing each unit at Q_2 is distance CE. We notice that the price rises from P_1 to P_2, the same as from point D to point E, or only about half the full distance CE. It is apparent, therefore, that the additional costs of production are *shared* by the buyer (who absorbs part of the cost in the form of higher prices) and by the steel mill (that is, by its stockholders).

The analysis of pollution highlights a typical economic problem. Measures to correct pollution will raise the prices of those products whose production, use, or disposal pollutes the environment. The increased prices of these products will cause a decrease in the quantity demanded (assuming no change in demand), a move upward along the demand curve. At higher prices, more people will be excluded from buying, and less of the product will be sold. The drop in sales will cause an increase in unemployment in that industry.

We can hope that eventually all prices will reflect the total social cost of production, distribution, use, and disposal of all goods and services and that therefore consumer choice will be based on prices that include all of these costs. Eventually, too, but after difficult periods of adjustment, the unemployment effects of pollution control will diminish as those who become unemployed as a result of the controls find jobs in nonpolluting industries or perhaps with business firms that manufacture pollution-control devices.

Methods of Pollution Control

The Reserve Mining Company story ended with the company's agreement to stop dumping taconite waste into Lake Superior and to build a new waste treatment facility. The Company was forced to accept a solution imposed by others.

Most economists prefer another approach to pollution control. They reason that no one understands better how to control pollution than the polluting business firm itself. Given the right incentives, the polluting firm is in the best position to determine the cheapest way of solving the problem.

For example, many economists prefer to charge polluting firms so much a pound for the waste they spew into the air or water. Such charges are called **effluent charges**. They are based on the legal idea that the firms are trespassing on property rights all of us share—the rights to clean air and water—and should pay for doing so. The economist's preference for the effluent charge is that business firms are thereby given the freedom to find their own best solution to the problem—or pay the charge.

A second approach is called the *bubble plan.*[9] A local environmental quality agency ("EQA") pretends there is a glass bubble, or lid, covering or surrounding all the chimneys and sewage outlets of a factory. The waste materials coming out of the factory are weighed annually. If the factory succeeds in reducing this quantity, it is given a "credit," stated in number of tons of waste, equal to a certain percentage (say, 70 percent) of the reduction the factory achieved during the year. This credit is put into a "bank account" kept with the EQA.

The only way a factory can expand and increase the waste it produces is to withdraw its own credits from its bank account. Or, it may buy credits from another firm. In this way, the EQA prevents total emissions in the area from exceeding the starting figure. Even new firms, when they come to the area, have to obtain credits from existing firms. Over the long term, total emissions in the area will decrease because the credits are some fraction (like 70 percent) of actual waste reductions. The plan has a provision to satisfy those worried about lack of growth in industrial output, employment opportunities, payrolls, and tax receipts. If not used within, say, eight years, all credits have to be sold to other firms to permit *them* to expand. The eight-year limit prevents participating firms from "banking" the credits for indefinite periods. The credits must either be used to make additional expansion possible or sold to enhance the firm's profits.

The possible uses of the credits are what put the bubble plan into the framework of a market-price system. However the firm uses the credits, it has a strong incentive to earn lots of them in order to increase the number of options available in the future. The more the firm reduces pollution, the more credits it receives.

The effluent-charge and bubble plans are efforts to reduce pollution with market-price methods. Whereas free markets, operating within the limits set by laws and court decisions, once permitted uncontrolled pollution, now market tactics are proposed for reducing it. The success or failure of the two plans is still in doubt. Many business firms resent the limits placed on their own growth, and many communities worry about unemployment.

The difficulty is that it's easy to place a value on private goods. Our willingness to pay the price of a television set measures the set's private benefit. It's much harder to measure the private benefit of a good held in common like air, or water in the local river or lake, or to *agree* along with other members of our community how much it's worth to keep the air and water clean.

What Is Our Goal?

To restate the question, what do we really want a price system to do? The pollution example highlights the importance of the question. If entrepreneurs can forget about pollution, their costs of production will be lower, their selling prices will be lower, they will sell more of their products, and as a result they will produce more, hire more people, and use more resources. Consequently, firms that pollute are a heavier drain on resources than if they were prevented from polluting. Society would be better off if some of these resources were used in industries where production is cleaner. Society might also be better off if more resources went to some industries that are producing products having widespread social benefit. Either way, free-market prices may not bring about an allocation of resources that best serves society. Economists will generally agree that resources are allocated to their best uses when the prices charged cause all industries to buy and use resources up to the point where the social benefit conferred by the last unit produced is equal to or exceeds the social cost of producing it. Such an allocation of resources is what economists mean by **allocative efficiency**. Effluent charges and bubble plans may be one step toward that goal.

SUMMARY

Equilibrium prices change because of shifts in demand and supply. Movements up and down a given demand curve are caused by shifts in supply. If the supply increases, the price will fall and vice versa. Movements up and down a given supply curve are caused by shifts in demand. If demand increases, the price will rise and vice versa.

If both curves increase, the *quantities* demanded and supplied will certainly increase, but the final *price* change depends on whether the shift in demand is greater or less than the shift in supply. If the former, the price will increase; if the latter, the price will fall. If both curves decrease, the *quantity* will certainly decrease, but again the final *price* change depends on whether the decrease in demand is greater or less than the decrease in supply. If the former, the price will fall; if the latter, the price will rise.

There may also be situations where one curve increases and the other decreases. In these cases, price movements are predictable, but quantity changes are not. If supply decreases and demand increases, the price will rise. If supply increases and demand decreases, the price will fall. Changes in quantity in both cases depend on whether the demand change is greater or less than the price change.

If the government legislates a minimum price, the price is called a price floor, and the result is usually a surplus. The most familiar examples of price floors are those for agricultural products. If the government legislates a maximum price, the price is called a price ceiling, and the result is usually a shortage. The most familiar examples of price ceilings are rent controls and gasoline-price controls during the 1970s.

Supply and demand analysis can be used to help solve or clarify many contemporary problems. In the case of pollution, the market-price system has not resulted in an efficient use of resources because the external costs of transactions—the pollution of air, oceans, or streams, or the disposal of used items by consumers—are not included in the price of products or services. If polluters are required to stop polluting, the opportunity cost of cleaner air may be increased unemployment in such polluting industries. If polluters had to pay effluent charges for the use of the air, water, or land they despoil, then the products they sell or use would include the cost of removing pollution, and more efficient, less polluting methods of production or distribution would probably be developed. Bubble plans have been started in some cities to reduce pollution. Effluent charges and bubble plans may help us to achieve allocative efficiency, where the social cost of using all resources in particular ways is matched by the social benefit of each use.

Discussion Questions

1. If you owned a restaurant, would you charge the same price for a top-sirloin steak dinner every night of the week? Why or why not? Illustrate your answer with a diagram.

2. If more electric power is used in the summer than in the winter because of air conditioning, what would you suggest that the power companies do?

3. What will be the effects of requiring automobiles to be pollution free? (What will happen to supply curves?)

4. If we wanted to help the poor by putting a price ceiling of 20 cents on a loaf of bread, what would happen?

5. Are there transactions with no external effects? What about the purchase of toothpaste or deodorant?

6. What are the external effects of education?

7. What is your definition of an efficient allocation of resources? How do you want everything divided among everyone? (Don't neglect external effects, which may involve either social costs or benefits.)

8. If we raised the minimum wage to $5 to help unskilled worders stay off welfare, what might happen? Illustrate your answer with a diagram. Would you call such a minimum wage a price floor or a price ceiling?

9. If there were an interest ceiling of 4 percent to help the poor obtain low-cost loans, how would the banks react? Who would get the money? What might the government have to do?

DID YOU EVER WONDER WHY ...

... once the price of something has risen, consumers cannot force the price down by buying less of it?

References

1. *Time*, 6 July 1981, p. 53.

2. "Price Supports—Milk: U.S. Drinks Less, Pays More," *Los Angeles Times*, 23 March 1981.

3. *Statistical Abstract of the United States, 1981*, p. 794, Table 1427. In 1963, the combined market share of the 50 largest companies was 48 percent, as of 1977, that share had been steadily increasing.

4. *Consumer Reports*, June 1982, p. 293.

5. Ellen Haas, "The Great Cheese Giveaway: Poor Are Last in Line Again," *Los Angeles Times*, 2 April 1982.

6. "Apartments Wanted," *Newsweek*, 4 June 1979, p. 79.

7. *Ibid.*

8. "Gasoline Abroad Plentiful but Costly, Survey Shows," *Los Angeles Times*, 22 May 1979, Part IV, p. 1.

9. The bubble plans are described in *Fortune*, 12 February and 4 May 1981.

7

Price Elasticity: How Price Changes Affect Our Buying Decisions

KEY WORDS
Price-elastic
Price-inelastic
Total revenue
Absolute change
Relative change
Coefficient of elasticity
Perfect inelasticity
Perfect elasticity

In the last chapter we saw that price changes will occur with changes in demand and supply. In this chapter we will look at the effects that increases or decrease in price have on buyers. The responsiveness of buyers to price changes is called "price elasticity."

Few topics in economics have so many, and such important, applications in decision making. One example: Suppose we want Americans to reduce their consumption of gasoline (or of anything) by 25 percent. How much will the price have to rise, in percentage terms, for this to happen?

Our discussion of elasticity is divided into three major parts: (1) price elasticity defined, (2) the price elasticity of demand: how it works, and (3) applications in the real world.

PRICE ELASTICITY DEFINED

Suppose a large department store drops the price of nylon jackets from $12 to $10. Sales thereupon increase from 100 jackets per month to 150. Revenue from sales increases from $1,200 ($12 × 100) to $1,500 ($10 × 150). Provided additional production costs or additional advertising and other selling expenses do not wipe out this gain, the sale is a success.

In such a case, the demand for the product is thus described as being **price-elastic**. If the demand for something is price-elastic, entrepreneurs will take in more money if they lower the price, because the increased volume of purchases will more than make up for the lower price received per unit. "Price-elastic" means that the *percentage change in the quantity purchased* is large relative to the *percentage change in price;* that the price change motivates consumers to increase their purchases by more than enough to offset price decreases.

Demand is also shown to be price-elastic when entrepreneurs raise the price and sales revenues fall. Suppose, for instance, the department store raises its price on nylon jackets from $10 to $12. Consumers respond by reducing purchases from 150 per month to 100, and sales revenue falls from $1,500 to $1,200. That sequence demonstrates that demand is price-elastic. Again, consumer response is large relative to the price change.

If, however, the store lowers its price from $12 to $10 and sales increase only from 100 jackets per month to 110, demand is **price-inelastic**. The sale has laid an egg. **Total revenue**—which is defined as price times quantity—has dropped from $1,200 ($12 × 100) to $1,100 ($10 × 110). The drop in price was not offset by a sufficient increase in the quantity demanded. Consumers were relatively indifferent to the price change.

Revenues versus Profits

A caution is necessary at this point. In the examples above we're thinking only about entrepreneur's *income* from sales—the money that goes into the cash register—not about the entrepreneur's *profit*. The price-elasticity of demand refers to the responsiveness of buyers (changes in the *quantity* demanded) to price changes. The concept says nothing about production costs. Of course, a change in the number of units sold will change the cost of production. If increased sales cause production costs to rise, and if the increase in cost is greater than the increase in revenue, profits will fall. Similarly, a reduction in sales volume could also be accompanied by lower production costs, and profits could rise. Thus, we must take *both* costs and revenues into account when we decide whether the price change was a good idea.

You will often hear economists referring to the "demand side" or the "supply side." These terms help distinguish discussions of responsiveness of buyers or from those about changes in production costs. Both "sides" have to be looked at to determine profit, but right now we are talking only about total revenue.

Percentage Changes in Quantity and Price

It is time now to define price elasticity more precisely. (In the discussion that follows, we will often drop the word "price" and simply use "elasticity." Just remember we are talking about responses to *price changes*.)

Elasticity refers to the interplay between *percentage* changes in quantity and *percentage* changes in price. We must use percentages because we need to show the *relative* importance of price and quantity changes. A 10-cent price change is small if the price is $10 (only 1 percent). But if the price is 20 cents, a 10-cent price change is 50 percent. The price change measured in money terms (10 cents) is called an **absolute change**. The price change measured in percentage terms in relation to some starting point ($10 or 20 cents) is called a **relative change**.

Changes in the *quantity* bought or sold are measured in percentage rather than absolute terms for the same reason. If the percentage change in quantity exceeds the percentage change in price, demand or supply is price-elastic. If the percentage change in quantity is less than the percentage change in price, then demand or supply is price-inelastic.

THE PRICE ELASTICITY OF DEMAND: HOW IT WORKS

Now, let us see how the price elasticity of demand works in practice. There are four possibilities, which we'll call Situations I, II, III, and IV.

Situation I: Increase in Quantity Exceeds Decrease in Price

Suppose you own the Dazzle Toothpaste Company, and you decide to sell more toothpaste by lowering your price. You have been selling 100 tubes of toothpaste per week to retail stores at a price of $1 each. You try reducing the price 10 percent, to 90 cents. Thereafter, sales increase 20 percent to 120 tubes per week. Demand is *elastic*; that is, the percentage increase in quantity exceeded the percentage decrease in price; buyers (the stores) are relatively responsive to your price change.

Notice an important point. You are taking in more money than before. Before the price change, you were taking in $100 per week (100 tubes at $1 each). After the price decrease, you are taking in $108 (120 tubes at 90 cents)—$8 more than before. The price drop has been more than offset by an increase in sales.

Situation II: Decrease in Quantity Exceeds Increase in Price

We can also tell the story in reverse. Suppose you have been selling 120 tubes per week at a price of 90 cents each. You try increasing the price to $1. What happens? Sales drop from 120 to 100 tubes per week, and you take in less money. Demand is *elastic*.

Table 7-1. Elasticity of Demand: Four Situations

Situation	Price per tube	Quantity (sales in tubes per week)	Total revenue	Elasticity of demand
I	$1.00	100	$100.00	
	.90	120	108.00	Elastic
II	$ .90	120	$108.00	
	1.00	100	100.00	Elastic
III	$1.00	100	$100.00	
	.90	105	94.50	Inelastic
IV	$1.00	100	$100.00	
	1.10	95	104.50	Inelastic

Situation III:
Increase in Quantity Is Less Than the Decrease in Price

Consider another possibility. You are selling 100 tubes per week at $1 each, and you decide to lower the price to 90 cents. This time sales increase, but only to 105 tubes per week. Total revenue falls from $100 per week to $94.50. In this case, the price was dropped 10 percent, but quantity increased only 5 percent. Demand is now *inelastic*; consumers were relatively indifferent to the price decrease. They did not jump to buy.

Situation IV:
Decrease in Quantity Is Less Than the Increase in Price

There is one more possibility. Suppose you increase the price from $1 to $1.10. Sales drop—the law of demand is alive and well. Now you are selling 95 tubes a week, a 5 percent drop. Your total revenue is now $104.50 (95 tubes at $1.10). That is, even though you sold fewer tubes, your total revenue went up. Why? Because this time, while price went up 10 percent, the number of units purchased went down only 5 percent. The price increase more than offset the drop in sales. Consumers were relatively indifferent to the price increase—they wanted the toothpaste badly enough to go on buying almost the same quantity. Demand was inelastic.

Table 7-1 summarizes the four situations showing elasticity of demand.

What Conclusions Can We Draw?

Our first conclusion is: When demand is elastic, the entrepreneur takes in more revenue from sales when the price is lowered and less revenue when the price is raised. (Again, keep in mind that we are thinking *only* about change in revenue, not about profit.)

Our second conclusion is: When demand is *inelastic*, the entrepreneur takes in less revenue when the price is lowered and more revenue when the price is raised.

A third conclusion: If you are a good entrepreneur, you should lie awake nights asking yourself whether the demand for your product is elastic or inelastic and what price changes will cause your total revenue to increase or decrease. But before you come to a decision, you must consider changes in costs, and therefore profits, that occur with changes in sales volume.

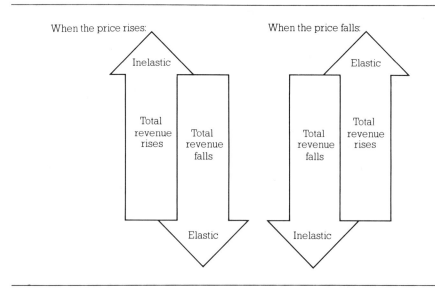

Figure 7-1.
Total revenue
movements compared
to price movements.

Table 7-2. Demand Schedule and Total Revenue for Dazzle Toothpaste

Price per tube	Quantity demanded per week	Total revenue per week (price times quantity)
$2.00	20	$ 40
1.80	40	72
1.60	60	96
1.40	80	112
1.20	100	120
1.00	120	120
.80	140	112
.60	160	96

Figure 7-1 provides a reminder of how total revenue changes when the price changes and when demand is elastic or inelastic. Note that when demand is elastic, total revenue goes in an opposite direction to price changes, but when demand is inelastic, total revenue and price change in the same direction.

Changing Elasticities along a Demand Curve

Let us now imagine that the demand schedule for Dazzle toothpaste looks like Table 7-2. Notice that as the price falls, quantity constantly rises (the law of demand), but total revenue first rises and then falls. Why? At first, the percentage change in price is small compared with quantity changes. The price drop from $2 to $1.80 is 10 percent (the 20-cent change relative to $2) yet the quantity doubles from 20 to 40—an increase of 100 percent.* Because the

---

*The base quantity is 20, and the difference between the old quantity and the new (40 − 20) is 20. Thus 20 ÷ 20 = 1 or 100 percent.

percentage increase in quantity is larger than the percentage decrease in price, consumer demand is responsive to the price change—demand is elastic. Further, as the price falls, total revenue rises because the quantity increase *more than makes up for* the price decrease.

At the bottom of the table, as the price falls from 80 cents to 60 cents, a drop of 25 percent (the 20-cent change relative to 80 cents), the increase in the quantity is about 14.3 percent (the 20-tube sales increase relative to 140 tubes).

If you examine Table 7-2 carefully, you'll see an odd and perhaps confusing situation. If we were to *graph* this demand schedule, our line would be straight, because the relationship between the two variables, price and the quantity demanded, is constant. Every time the price changes by 20 cents, the quantity changes by 20 units. Yet the *elasticity* along the straight line is *constantly changing.* Why? Relative (percentage) change may be different even though the absolute number remains the same.

A quick example will help. While the absolute difference between 10 and 9 is 1, the relative percentage difference is 10 percent. What is the absolute difference between 1 and 2? Answer: again 1—but this time the relative percentage difference is 100 percent. Again we are reminded of the difference between relative and absolute changes.

The Coefficient of Elasticity

Economists have developed a formula to determine whether demand is elastic or inelastic, and consequently whether total revenue will rise or fall in response to changes in price. The formula compares the percentage change in the quantity demanded with the percentage change in price. The number produced by the formula is called the **coefficient of elasticity**, usually abbreviated as E_D.

The formula* is:

$$E_D = \frac{\text{Percentage change in the quantity demanded}}{\text{Percentage change in price}}$$

Thus if the quantity demanded increases by 25 percent when the percentage price decrease is 10 percent, we have:

$$E_D = \frac{+25}{-10} = -2.5$$

---

* The percentage changes in the formula are computed by dividing the quantity change by the average quantity and dividing the price change by the average price. In each case the average is obtained by adding the two quantities or prices together and dividing by two. The whole formula for the coefficient is:

$$E_D = \frac{Q_1 - Q_2}{(Q_1 + Q_2)/2} \div \frac{P_1 - P_2}{(P_1 + P_2)/2}$$

For example, using the first two quantities and prices in Table 7-2, the calculation is:

$$E_D = \frac{20 - 40}{(20 + 40)/2} \div \frac{\$2.00 - \$1.80}{(\$2.00 + \$1.80)/2} = \frac{-20}{30} \div \frac{\$.20}{\$1.90} = \frac{-20}{30} \times \frac{\$1.90}{.20} = \frac{-19}{3} = -6.33$$

Using the last two quantities and prices, the calculation is:

$$E_D = \frac{140 - 160}{(140 + 160)/2} \div \frac{\$.80 - \$.60}{(\$.80 + \$.60)/2} = \frac{-20}{150} \div \frac{\$.20}{\$.70} = \frac{-20}{150} \times \frac{\$.70}{\$.20} = \frac{-70}{150} = -.47$$

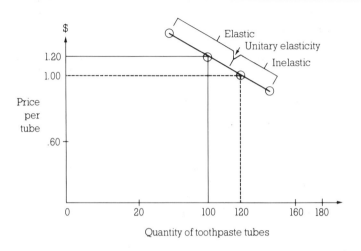

Figure 7-2.
Changing elasticities
along a demand
curve.

Note that the 2.5 figure is negative. This must be so because prices and quantities along a demand curve move in opposite directions. In this case, a price decrease (−) has caused a quantity increase (+), and any time minuses and pluses are multiplied or divided, the answer must be minus. *Having noted that, we will ignore the minus sign from now on.*

What does the 2.5 coefficient mean? It tells us that demand is *price-elastic;* that total revenue will rise as the price falls, or that total revenue will fall as the price rises. The number 2.5 means literally that, if the price rises 1 percent, quantity (sales) will fall 2.5 percent. The number also means that, if the price falls 1 percent, sales will increase 2.5 percent. The percentage change in quantity is two and a half times the percentage change in price. Remember that price and quantity move in opposite directions because the demand curve slopes down from left to right and price and quantity are inversely related.

On the other hand, a 0.5 coefficient would tell us that demand is *price-inelastic* (because the coefficient is less than 1), and that total revenue will fall as the price falls and rise as the price rises. Can you translate the 0.5 coefficient? It tells us that the percentage quantity change will be only half of the percentage price change (see Table 7-3, p. 133).

Finally, notice in Table 7-2 that as the price falls from $1.20 to $1, the quantity increases from 100 to 120, and total revenue does not change. The 20 percent increase in the quantity demanded exactly offsets the 20 percent decrease in the price. At that point in the table the elasticity is *unitary*, and the coefficient is one.

One more observation. Remember that the coefficient changes all along a given demand schedule or curve, as Table 7-2 indicates. We cannot call any given demand curve all elastic or all inelastic. The general pattern is shown in Figure 7-2. Because the coefficients of elasticity vary all along the line, coefficients will be greater than one in the elastic portion, less than one in the inelastic portion, and equal to one in the unitary portion.

The entrepreneur will of course be thinking not in terms of changing price as large ,as, say, $2 to 60 cents. Changes are usually made in small amounts, perhaps from $1.20 to $1.30. The point is, then, that a specific coefficient is relevant only to small changes in price and quantity at a particular time.

Four Tests of Price Elasticity

No one can accurately forecast why people want what they want, or why they want something badly enough to be unaffected by price increases (inelasticity) or strongly motivated to buy more because of price decreases (elasticity). Nevertheless, economists are generally agreed that there are four important tests of the price elasticity of demand. Every good entrepreneur should consider these tests and try to relate them to his or her product. As we proceed through the tests, think about Dazzle toothpaste. Is it elastic or inelastic with respect to each test? What do the results of all four tests reveal?

Test 1: Does the Product Have Many Substitutes?

The availability of close substitutes is by far the most important test of elasticity. If many substitutes are available, people will switch from Dazzle to Dentobrite or Glisten if Dazzle raises its price (assuming *ceteris paribus*, nothing else changes). In such a case, the percentage drop in Dazzle's quantity demanded would exceed the percentage increase in Dazzle's price; Dazzle's total revenue would fall. The more close substitutes there are, the greater the elasticity.

Remember also that if Dazzle lowered its price relative to the prices of competing brands, sales might increase more than enough to offset the price decrease. Why? Because people would stop buying Dentobrite, Glisten, and the like, and buy Dazzle.

On the other hand, if there are no close substitutes, consumers will buy about the same quantity regardless of price changes. Demand is inelastic.

Test 2: How Expensive Is the Product Relative to the Buyer's Income?

What percentage of the buyer's annual income does the price of the product represent? If the product is very *in*expensive, if the price represents a small portion of the buyer's income, the chances are that the demand will be price-*in*elastic.

An example: A highly advertised brand of cupcakes is sold two to a package. A few years ago, a pair sold for 10 cents. In one jump, the price was raised to 13 cents—a 30 percent increase in price. Did anyone complain? Probably not. The point is that we tend to be indifferent to price changes of inexpensive items—paper clips, matches, bobby pins, and the like.

If, on the other hand, we are considering buying a car on a salary of $20,000 per year, a $12,000 car represents over seven months' work. A 10 percent change in the price of the car, $1,200, represents more than three weeks' pay. The price change may affect us strongly. If the increase is $1,200, we may decide not to buy. Or, a $1,200 decrease may cause us to buy. We are strongly influenced by the price change either way.

Test 3: Is the Product a Luxury or a Necessity?

If the product is a necessity, demand will tend to be price-inelastic. Buyers will be relatively indifferent to price changes. Where habits are so strong that products *become* necessities (like heroin!), demand may be extremely price-inelastic. To a lesser extent, the same argument applies to people who insist on a certain brand of cigarettes, soap, deodorant, or toothpaste.

The demand for luxury goods will tend to be price-elastic—the more luxurious, the more elastic. Since we can take a luxury or leave it, we will be strongly influenced by price changes.

Test 4: How Much Time Does the Buyer Have to Compare Prices?

The longer the time period, the more elastic demand will become. As time passes, price differences may cause a habit to weaken, and demand to become more price-elastic. For instance, a smoker who is used to a particular brand of cigarettes pay 5 cents more per pack for a while, but eventually the smoker may start wondering whether the brand is worth the extra cost. The smoker may then drop the favorite brand and adopt a cheaper one. What about our Dazzle toothpaste? If Dazzle is more expensive than other brands, we can expect some loyal Dazzle users gradually to switch to other brands. In the short term, though, many products like cars, houses, gasoline, natural gas, and electricity tend to be demand-*ine*lastic, because people need plenty of time to find substitutes.

Now, what about Dazzle toothpaste? What does each test tell us about it?

- *Test 1: Are there substitutes?* Yes, many. Vote: elastic.
- *Test 2: Percent of buyer's income?* The toothpaste price is a negligible percentage of income. Vote: inelastic.
- *Test 3: Luxury or necessity?* To people who customarily brush their teeth, toothpaste is probably a necessity. But is any one brand like Dazzle a necessity? Probably not. Vote: elastic.
- *Test 4: Time?* Probably relevant. Unless the price change is large, toothpaste users probably stick to a brand they are used to, for a while. Demand is inelastic. But as time passes, if the price of Dazzle is above that of other brands, many people will switch. Demand becomes elastic.

What is the overall result? We have two votes for elastic and two votes for inelastic (provided we stick to a short time period). Are the elastic votes more important than the inelastic? Touchy question. If Dazzle toothpaste, a relatively inexpensive item, is well established, with a fair number of customers habituated to using it, a price change of perhaps 1 percent one way or the other probably will not affect sales much over a short period of time.

Then, what should you, the entrepreneur, do? You might experiment with slightly higher prices. Chances are that sales will not drop by as large a percentage as your percentage increase in price. With increased prices, your total revenue should rise.

Table 7-3 presents some short-run coefficients of the elasticity of demand. These coefficients are certainly not engraved in stone. They are estimates of what was going on during the period of each study. Whether they are still valid as you read this is another question.

Let's speculate briefly about the meaning of some of the coefficients. Remember, we're discussing the short run. Toilet articles are inelastic because we're in the habit of using a variety of cosmetic products like toothpaste, deodorants, eye shadow, lipstick, hair spray, and so forth. We're so much in the habit of using these products, and of using particular brands, we will tolerate *some* increases in price. If you're a smoker, the same principle applies. But

Table 7-3. Selected Coefficients of Demand Elasticity (Short-run)

Toilet articles	0.2
Tobacco products	0.5
Marijuana	1.5
Cabbage	0.4
Fresh tomatoes	4.6
Canned tomatoes	2.5
Natural gas	0.1
Medical care	0.3

Sources: D. Milton Shuffet, "The Demand and Price Structure for Selected Vegetables," Technical Bulletin No. 1105, U.S. Department of Agriculture, 1954. H. S. Houthaker and L. D. Taylor, *Consumer Demand in the United States* (Cambridge: Harvard University Press, 1970). T. C. Misket and F. Vakil, "Some Estimates of Price and Expenditure Elasticities among UCLA Students," *Review of Economics and Statistics*, November 1972.

apparently not so with marijuana. There are readily available substitutes for marijuana like tobacco cigarettes and/or alcoholic beverages.

Utilities are certainly a necessity for us, as is medical care. Inelasticity is logical. As for the tomatoes, both the fresh and the canned variety are elastic, indicating that there are substitutes. Apparently, though, we find canned tomatoes somewhat more necessary than fresh tomatoes. (We can guess it's because canned tomatoes are used in preparation of many dishes like casseroles, and, in summer, people can grow their own fresh tomatoes.)

We have completed our discussion of the price elasticity of demand. The four main points to remember are:

1. If demand is price-elastic, total revenue will rise if the price falls, and fall if the price rises.
2. If demand is price-inelastic, total revenue will rise if the price rises, and fall if the price falls.
3. Elasticity should only be associated with small changes in price and quantity, since there will usually be different elasticities along any given demand curve or schedule.
4. If the coefficient is greater than one, demand is price-elastic; exactly one, elasticity is unitary; less than one, demand is price-inelastic.

SOME GRAPHING SECRETS

In the balance of this chapter, there are several demand-supply drawings to illustrate the effect of different elasticities. An introduction to these graphs may be helpful.

In general, an elastic demand curve is shown with a relatively horizontal line, as in Figure 7-3.

The elasticity of the demand curve is apparent because when the price falls from P_1 ($25) to P_2 ($20), there is a relatively large increase in the quantity demanded. As we move from point A to B, there is a large change from Q_1 (100 units) to Q_2 (200 units).

The price drop also leads to an increase in total revenue. Total revenue is indicated by the area of the rectangles formed by the two axes and the price

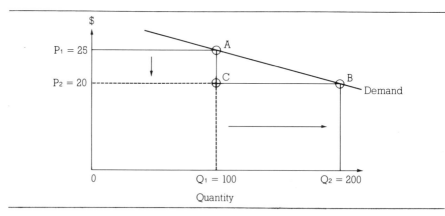

Figure 7-3.
An elastic demand
curve (imaginary
prices and quantities).

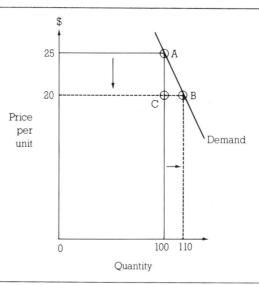

Figure 7-4.
An inelastic demand
curve.

and quantity lines. In Figure 7-3, total revenue is first shown by the rectangle $25 \times 100 = \$2,500$. When the price falls, total revenue has increased ($20 \times 200 = \$4,000$) with the price decrease, a clear indication of an *e*lastic demand curve.

Conversely, inelastic demand curves are usually shown with relatively vertical lines, as in Figure 7-4.

This time the decrease in price results in a very small increase in the quantity demanded. Total revenue actually falls from $2,500 to $2,200 ($20 \times 110$). The drop in total revenue, resulting from the price drop, confirms the inelasticity of demand, as well as the relative unresponsiveness of buyers to the price change.

But, the point of this story is that graphs can fool you. We started by saying that relatively horizontal demand curves indicate *e*lasticity; vertical curves indicate *ine*lasticity. Unfortunately, graphs are not that easy to interpret. We have to look carefully at how the two axes are scaled. Look for a moment at Figures 7-5(a) and (b).

Both figures say the same thing: As the price changes from P_1 ($3) to P_2 ($2)

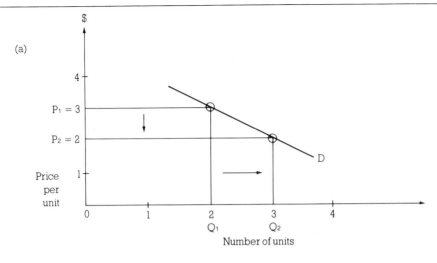

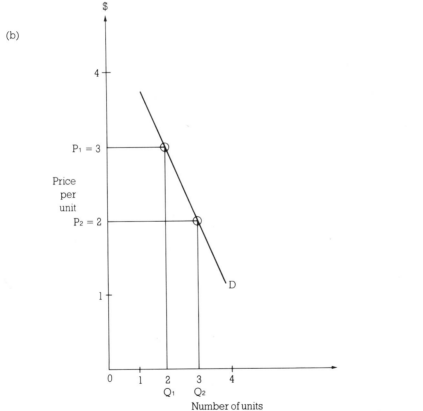

Figure 7-5.
Graphs can fool you.

per unit, the quantity demanded changes from Q_1 (2 units) to Q_2 (3 units). The coefficient in both cases is unitary because total revenue doesn't change; total revenue is $6.

The two graphs illustrate unitary elasticity, because they tell us that at some

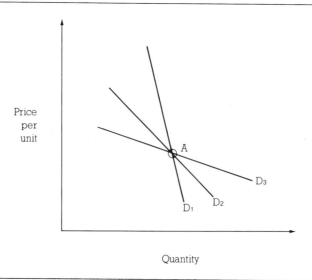

Figure 7-6.
Flatter demand
curves are more
elastic than vertical
demand curves.

point in the $2 to $3 price range the percentage change in the quantity demanded is the same as the percentage change in the price.* Yet in Figure
7-5(**a**), the demand curve is fairly horizontal; in Figure 7-5(**b**), the curve is
fairly vertical. So we have to be careful not to draw impulsive conclusions from
the slope of the line. Elasticity depends on the changes in price and quantity,
relative to one another, in a small portion of the line, not over the whole length
of the line.

To make you more comfortable, there is an easy rule to follow: If two or
more demand curves are drawn through the same point, the flatter ones will
indeed be more elastic than the more vertical curves. Figure 7-6 illustrates.

And so, with the caution presented in Figures 7-5 (**a**) and (**b**) firmly in
mind, we will assume from now on that flatter curves mean *more* elasticity;
steeper curves mean *less* elasticity.

Two special cases need to be mentioned because they reappear in Chapters
8 and 9. Demand curves may be either completely vertical like the one on the
left or completely horizontal like the one on the right:

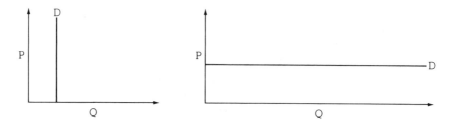

* If we use the method explained in the footnote on page 129, we can verify the fact that elasticity is
unitary, and that the coefficient is, therefore, 1:

$$E_D = \frac{2-3}{(2+3)/2} \div \frac{\$3 - \$2}{(\$3 + \$2)/2} = \frac{-1}{2.5} \div \frac{\$1}{\$2.5} = \frac{-2.5}{2.5} = -1$$

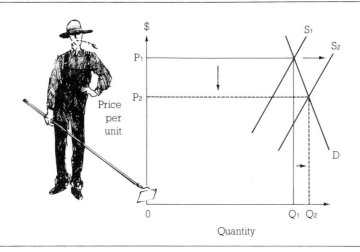

Figure 7-7.
Inelastic demand with increases in supply.

The left diagram indicates that a particular quantity will be demanded, *regardless* of the price. When the price doesn't affect the quantities demanded, the demand curve is called **perfectly inelastic**. A diabetic's demand for insulin is extremely inelastic when the next injection is required.

The right diagram indicates that buyers will buy as much as is available at price, P. The right diagram represents what is called **perfect elasticity**. A perfectly elastic demand curve exists when even the tiniest increase in price causes buyers to quit buying. The reason is, of course, that the greater the elasticity, the greater the availability of good substitutes. The best example of perfect elasticity is the demand for a small farmer's wheat. Every other farmer's wheat in the area is a perfect substitute. Any price increase by any *one* of the farmers will immediately cause buyers to buy their wheat from someone else.

APPLICATIONS IN THE REAL WORLD
Let us now take a look at a few common situations in which elasticity affects the welfare of buyers and sellers.

Elasticity and Agriculture
In the United States the demand for agricultural products is inelastic. We buy about the same amount of food regardless of change in food prices or our own incomes. The price elasticity of U.S. demand for all food is estimated to be only 0.25. That is, a 1 percent drop in food prices would increase food sales by only one quarter of 1 percent. To put it another way, food prices would have to drop 40 percent to increase food sales 10 percent.

What does all this mean for the farmer? When demand is inelastic, the farmer is subject to wide swings in price and income. If supply increases (because good weather, say, or a new fertilizer has resulted in the production of a bumper crop), prices fall sharply and the increase in quantity purchased is small, owing to the inelasticity of demand. Total revenue, or income for the farmer, drops with the fall in price. Figure 7-7 illustrates the farmer's problem.

Increases in supply have been typical in agriculture mainly because of technological breakthroughs. In the 1929–1983 period, farm production per farmworker person-hour increased more than five times.

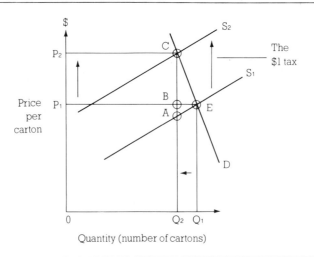

Figure 7-8.
A $1 tax on cartons of
cigarettes.

Constant downward pressure on farm prices and incomes because of over-production has led to increasing difficulties for small, less efficient farmers and to consolidation of small farms into large units often owned by major corporations. It has also led to considerable price and income support from government, as in the case of price floors for the dairy industry outlined in Chapter 6.

Elasticity and Taxes

Branches of government will find it easier to raise money by taxing a product having an inelastic demand than one with an elastic demand. When a product is taxed (as in the case of a sales tax), the price the consumer must pay rises, but if demand is inelastic consumers will continue to buy almost the same quantities as before the tax. Consequently, the government is relatively successful in collecting tax revenues from the sales of such products.

Kings in medieval times taxed salt because people and animals must have salt to live, and also because of its value as a preservative. The demand for salt today (all brands combined) is still very inelastic. Other favorites today for heavy taxes are gasoline, cigarettes, and alcoholic beverages. In some states, state and federal taxes account for half of the price of cigarettes and alcoholic beverages. Many of us are so habituated to cigarettes and alcohol that when the price rises we continue to buy almost the same quantities.

To illustrate, let's assume that the government needs additional revenue and decides to tax cigarettes $1 per carton. In demand-supply diagrams, a "lump-sum" tax like this is shown by a shift of the supply curve to the left. The vertical distance between the two supply curves is the amount of tax—in this case, $1. Figure 7-8 illustrates.

Figure 7-8 tells us that the tax causes the price to rise from P_1 to P_2. Suppliers require a higher price for *every* quantity they produce because they have to give $1 per carton to the government. Second, the figure tells us that the demand curve is quite steep, to represent our assumption that the demand for cigarettes (all brands together) is inelastic. Third, given this inelasticity, consumers buy fewer cartons (and presumably smoke less), as shown by the de-

If the government raises the minimum wage above equilibrium, the result may be higher teenage unemployment.

crease in the quantity demanded from Q_1 to Q_2. Fourth, because the decrease in sales is quite small, the government is happy because the tax raises a great deal of money. Fifth, producers are happy because most of the cost of the tax has been shifted to consumers. This last point requires some explaining.

At the new quantity demanded, Q_2, the tax is shown by the vertical distance between the two supply curves; that is, by the distance AC. We can also see that the price increases by almost that much—by the distance P_1–P_2, which is the same as distance BC. Consequently, the higher price to consumers absorbs almost the whole tax (AC). Producers are left with a relatively small amount to absorb: distance AB. The general rule is that, given any supply curve, the more *ine*lastic the demand curve, the more buyers will pay the cost of the tax in higher prices.

There is still a sixth point to be made about Figure 7-8. Can you see what it is? Yes, people are smoking less, *but* they are spending more of their budgets on cigarettes than before. Before the tax, the public's total expenditures are (the same as total revenue) shown by the rectangle, OP_1EQ_1. Now, the public spends OP_2CQ_2 for cigarettes. We know this second rectangle is larger, because demand is inelastic, and when the price rises, total revenue (expenditures) rises.

ELASTICITY AND PRICE FLOORS: THE MINIMUM WAGE
In this section we want to bring in one of the principles learned in Chapter 6 and show how elasticity applies. Price floors, like those in the dairy industry, usually produce surpluses. The same conclusion can be drawn from an analysis of minimum wages.

Under the Fair Labor Standards Act, the government can set minimum hourly wages for all workers employed in interstate industries. The minimum wage is a price floor, because it is apparently above the equilibrium hourly wage for at least one age group—those between 16 and 19.

At the end of 1981, when the federal minimum hourly wage was $3.35, about 9 million people were unemployed, and the unemployment rate for all workers

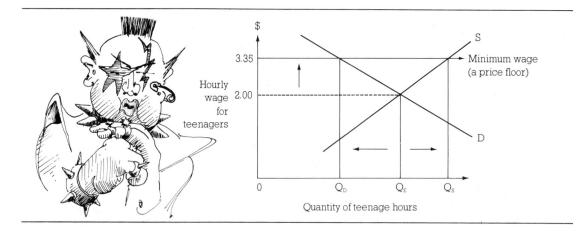

Figure 7-9.
Picture of a minimum
wage law.

was about 9 percent. In that year, the unemployment rate among those between 16 and 19 years of age was about 22 percent—about 2.4 times the national average.

The benevolent intention behind minimum wage laws is to help poorer workers by guaranteeing higher wages. But what if the minimum wage is higher than equilibrium? The result may be unemployment.

Figure 7-9 illustrates the problem. S represents the supply of teenagers who will work at various hourly wages. D represents the demand for teenage labor. Q_D stands for the person-hours of teenage labor demanded and Q_S for the number available. At the minimum wage of $3.35, the number of teenage hours offered for hire (Q_S) is clearly larger than the number demanded (Q_D). One can see that the quantity demanded declines from Q_E to Q_D as employers decide to substitute capital (like automatic dishwashers in fast-food restaurants) for labor (human dishwashers) when the wage-rate rises. On the other hand, as the wage-rate rises, teenagers decide to substitute work for leisure, and the quantity supplied increases from Q_E to Q_S. The result is a surplus, in this case a surplus of labor. The size of the surplus represents the number of teenagers who will be unemployed at the minimum wage.

For Q_D workers—those hired—everything may be fine; the minimum wage may have raised their income. But the minimum wage, the price floor, has produced a surplus of unemployed labor. Economic theory tells us we could have less unemployment and more employment if the wage fell. How far must the wage fall? There is no exact way of knowing (see the question mark at equilibrium).

Suppose the equilibrium wage is $2. At $2 there would be no teenage unemployment, a reminder that there is always an equilibrium price where the quantity demanded is equal to the quantity supplied. Would you favor that? The answer probably depends on whether or not you are unemployed. In any case, the cost of more unemployment may be increased welfare payments. This combination of rising unemployment and increased resort to welfare usually affects those people who are unskilled. The irony is that these are the people the minimum wage law is supposed to protect.

The government can, however, take various measures to deal with the labor surplus created by the minimum wage. Just as it can clear the market by buying

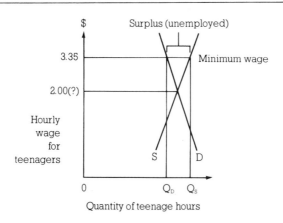

Figure 7-10.
Figure 7-9 redrawn with inelastic demand and supply curves.

surplus milk and giving it away, it can eliminate the newly created unemployment by hiring some of the unemployed to work on government projects. This shifts the excess cost of employing them from individual firms to taxpayers in general. The government can also lessen the economic loss to those put out of work by providing unemployment insurance, or it can increase the skills of those laid off by offering training programs. Or it can do nothing and allow the newly unemployed to fend for themselves. Recent amendments to the Fair Labor Standards Act have softened the unemployment effect for some groups of workers, by setting lower minimum wages for students and young people under 18 than for adult full-time workers. This change has led to accusations by some that "cheap" labor below age 18 is being substituted for more expensive adult labor, an effect that may be the cost of this particular decision.

Minimum Wage and Inelasticity

Figure 7-9 is drawn to show a substantial surplus at the minimum wage. But the size of the surplus (the number unemployed) depends on elasticity. If the demand for of teenage labor is *in*elastic, the surplus will be quite small (Figure 7-10).

Here we can see that the amount of unemployment is much less than in Figure 7-9, and indeed, some experts do believe that the minimum wage has little effect on teenage unemployment; that a 10 percent increase in the minimum wage probably causes an increase in teenage unemployment of *less* than 1 percent.[1] The authors of one study (see references) believe factors other than the minimum wage (like high turnover in low wage industries) may explain the high unemployment rates among teenagers.

And, if the demand for teenage labor *is* *in*elastic, most teenagers will be happy with the minimum wage. If we attach some numbers to Figure 7-10, you'll see why (Figure 7-11).

To show why teenagers might be happy with the minimum wage, we'll assume that $2 an hour is the equilibrium wage. At $2, we assume 4.1 million* teenagers will want to work and they all have jobs. Their total earnings per hour

*The figures on the horizontal axis approximate the real world as of December 1981.

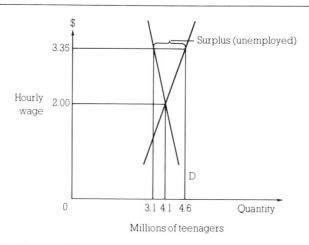

Figure 7-11.
Figure 7-10 with
numbers.

are $2 × 4.1 million = $8.2 million. After the passage of the minimum wage law, only 3.6 million are hired; that is, 0.5 million (500,000) lose their jobs. And at $3.35, another 0.5 million want to work; that is, another 500,000 join the labor force, so that the surplus is now 1.0 million teenagers who want to work but can't.

But, happiness is for those who keep their jobs. Total earnings per hour are now $3.35 × 3.6 million = $12.06 million, roughly $4 million more than before the minimum wage. This increase more than makes up for the loss (at least in dollars) suffered by those who lost their jobs: 0.5 million teenagers × $2 an hour = $1 million. The welfare of teenagers as a group increased by $3 million ($4 million − $1 million). In fact, with increased incomes, teenagers might spend more money. GNP (gross national product) might increase, and the demand for teenage labor might increase by enough to wipe out the surplus of unemployed teenage labor. This scenario depends on the *in*elasticity of demand for teenager labor. If demand is *e*lastic, teenagers as a group would lose.

Before we leave this topic, picture the idea that elasticity will also have an effect on the size of shortages caused by price ceilings. If demand is *in*elastic, the shortages will be less than if it is *e*lastic.

SUMMARY

When relatively small changes in the price of a product result in relatively large changes in the quantity demanded, demand is said to be price-elastic. When, on the other hand, relatively large changes in the price of a product have little effect on the quantity purchased, demand is said to be price-inelastic. An entrepreneur who manufactures a product for which the demand is price-elastic will take in more money by lowering its price, because the increase in volume of sales will more than make up for the loss in revenue for each item sold. On the other hand, if the demand for the product is price-inelastic, the entrepreneur will take in more money by increasing the price, because the additional revenue from each item sold will make up for the decrease in the number of items purchased at the new price.

Price elasticity can be expressed by the coefficient of elasticity—the relative change in quantity divided by the relative change in price. If the coefficient is greater than 1, relative changes in quantity are larger than relative changes in price, and demand is price-elastic. If the coefficient is less than 1, relative changes in quantity are smaller than relative changes in price, and demand is price-inelastic.

The demand for a product tends to be price-elastic if (1) substitutes for the product are available; (2) its price represents a large percentage of the buyer's income; (3) it is a luxury product; (4) buyers have plenty of time to compare prices.

The concept of elasticity helps to explain why farmers often experience large changes in income and why governments prefer to tax products for which the demand is price-inelastic.

The concept of elasticity also helps us to forecast the size of surpluses or shortages caused by price floors and price ceilings, as well as to analyze changes in demand caused by changes in income or changes in the prices of other products.

Discussion Questions

1. What is the price elasticity of demand for Crest toothpaste as compared with the elasticity for all toothpaste?

2. What is the price elasticity of demand for BMW motorcycles, Sony tape recorders, Zenith TVs? Explain, using the four tests.

3. If you are operating a hot-dog stand and you figure that the coefficient of elasticity of demand is greater than 1 for your hot dogs, should you experiment with higher or lower prices? Explain.

4. Explain the connection between changes in total revenue and elasticity. If you, a manufacturer of Kickapoo Joy Juice, believe the demand for your product is elastic, should you consider raising or lowering your price? Explain.

5. Assume that the coefficient of elasticity of demand for your Kickapoo Joy Juice is 1.2. Fill in the following blanks: For every _____ percent change in price, there will be a _____ percent change in the quantity demanded.

6. Assume that the coefficient of elasticity of demand for gasoline is 0.2. How much will the price have to rise to cause us to reduce our purchases of gasoline by 10 percent? (This question is essentially the same as the one posed on the first page of the chapter. Answer it by using the formula on page 125.)

DID YOU EVER WONDER WHY . . .

. . . poor growing weather makes farmers richer?

References

1. Charles Brown, Curtis Gilroy, and Andrew Kohen, "The Effect of the Minimum Wage on Employment and Unemployment," *Journal of Economic Literature*, June 1982.

Part III contains four chapters designed to explain real-world problems. The first chapter (8) describes the struggle by business firms to achieve market power. The chapter goes on to explain how this struggle for power is shaping our market-price system; it attempts to answer the question "Where are we headed?" Chapter 9 explores

PART III

MICRO-ECONOMICS IN THE REAL WORLD

strategies business firms can use to increase their profits when they can exercise market power. Chapter 10 continues the theme of market power from the point of view of workers. What can workers do

to gain power over their employers to raise wages and improve working conditions? The last microeconomics chapter (11) shows how our market-price system distributes income in the United States.

8

Doing Business in the Real World: The Struggle for Market Power in Product Markets

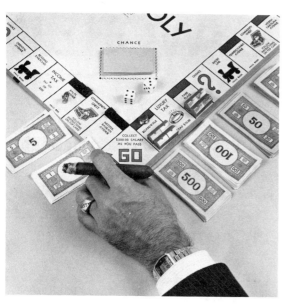

KEY WORDS

Market power
Price taker
Explicit costs
Implicit costs:
    wages, interest, rent,
    and normal profit
Economic profit
Perfect competition
Information costs
Monopolistic competition
Nonprice competition
Law of Diminishing Returns
Marginal product
Economies of scale
Diseconomies of scale

Oligopoly
Concentration ratio
Monopoly
Natural monopoly
Cartel

Back in Chapter 2 we mentioned that there are two major classes of markets, one for products or services and the other for resources (the factors of production). In the first market, consumers buy goods and services for final use. In the second market, business firms buy or rent land or capital and capital goods, and they hire workers to produce the things consumers want.

This chapter is about the behavior of business firms in product markets. As sellers, business firms try to strengthen their own position and to weaken that of competing sellers so that they, the winners, can charge higher prices and reap bigger profits. Their intention is to give buyers as few options as possible by reducing the number of suppliers. To whatever extent a buyer's options are reduced, a seller can control the market price. The seller's power to influence the price is called **market power**.

The chapter is divided into three sections: (1) What do economists mean by profit? (2) four kinds of markets, and (3) where are we headed?

WHAT DO ECONOMISTS MEAN BY PROFIT?

When we say that most firms seek to enlarge their profits, a first question is naturally: "What do we mean by profit?" The answer is not as simple as it might seem because accountants and economists have somewhat different views of profit. This section describes the economist's view.

To explain, let's assume a chicken farm owned by Jane Pennyworth. She has 8,000 hens that faithfully lay 4,900 eggs each day (or nearly 150,000 dozen per year). We will assume that Jane's share of the total egg market in the nearby large city is so small that she has no control over the market price. She has to accept the price offered her each day in the wholesale market where millions of eggs are bought and sold. Jane is what economists call a **price taker**.

During the time of our story, we'll assume that the wholesale price is 60 cents per dozen. Given this price, over which she has no control, the question for Jane is: How much profit must there be in the 60-cent price for her to be willing to buy and operate the factors of production (land, labor, and capital) and provide her entrepreneurship? Figure 8-1 illustrates Jane's situation. The demand curve is horizontal* at 60 cents, meaning that regardless of the amounts Jane supplies, the price remains at 60 cents.

Figure 8-1 tells us that Jane's total revenue will be 60 cents × 150,000 dozen eggs per year, or $90,000. Now let's assume that all Jane's money costs (every cost that requires paying someone some money), all expenses, even including taxes, are $70,000. These money costs are called **explicit costs**.

Apparently, Jane has made $20,000 ($90,000 − $70,000) as profit. The $20,000 is called *accounting profit*, not economic profit.

To determine Jane's economic profit, economists first ask, "What would Jane have made if she had done something else with her resources—her labor, land, and capital?" The foregone income from employing resources in some other way is called the **implicit cost** of doing business. Implicit costs are the opportunity costs of using an entrepreneur's resources (capital, land, time) in a particular way. They represent what *could* have been earned some other way.

---

*The demand curve pictured here is for *one* egg ranch. The demand curve for all eggs from *many* egg ranches will be downward sloping. See page 170 in Chapter 9 for clarification.

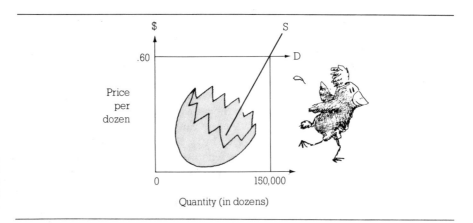

Figure 8-1.
Jane's supply curve:
The dozens of eggs
she will want to sell at
each price.

The Implicit Costs of Doing Business

First, what could Jane have earned in wages and fringe benefits if she had gone to work for someone else? The answer involves some thought and a good deal of guesswork. Assume she could have made $12,000 a year in a nice, safe, 40-hour-a-week job. This is what she gave up to produce eggs, and egg raising involves perhaps far more of her time, nervous tension, and energy than that kind of job. But perhaps Jane places a high value on independence. She might adjust the $12,000 figure downward to reflect the fact that the job she has foregone is not really that great a sacrifice after all. In any case, economists call the wages she could have earned in another employment **implicit wages**.

If the egg business includes a building or land Jane owns, she must also calculate the rental income she might have received if she had rented the land or building or both. Let us assume that she estimates the rental income she has sacrificed in this manner at $5,000 per year. As you might guess, this is called **implicit rent**.

Now assume that Jane has $30,000 tied up in her egg business in the form of buildings and equipment. Clearly Jane has lost the income her $30,000 might have earned.

Jane's purchase of $30,000 worth of capital for her egg business has two opportunity costs. One opportunity cost results from the interest she could have earned by putting her money in a savings account. The other opportunity cost results from the profit she could have earned by buying all or part of *another* business.

These two opportunity costs sound like the same thing, but there are important differences between them: (1) Money put in a bank earns interest because the bank must pay Jane for her sacrifice in foregoing the use of it. (2) When we become entrepreneurs like Jane, money used to purchase a business is expected to earn a "return" (profit) sufficient to reward us for the possibility of losing the money if the business fails. Thus interest is a *return* for foregoing consumption; profit is a *reward* for assuming the risk of loss.

Imagine that Jane's $30,000, now tied up in the egg business, had been split into two parts, and that one part, $10,000, had been put in a savings account earning 8 percent per year, or $800. This sacrificed income is called **implicit interest**. And further imagine that the remaining $20,000 of Janes's $30,000 had been "invested" in *another* business, and that this investment could have earned a profit of, say, $1,800 per year.* This opportunity cost of $1,800 is called **normal profit**, and it is also an implicit cost because, like implicit wages, implicit rent, and implicit interest, it does not entail any actual payment of money.

If we add up all of these implicit costs of using Jane's resources in the production of eggs, we have the following:

Implicit wages	$12,000
Implicit rent	5,000
Implicit interest	800
Normal profit	1,800
Total implicit costs	$19,600

The sum of the implicit costs—the $19,600—is viewed as a *cost of production*, not as profit of any kind, because Jane's egg business must earn at least $19,600 to offset the opportunity cost (implicit cost) of using the resources she owns. If the egg business doesn't earn at least $19,600 after taxes, then Jane might be better off doing something else with her time and capital.

Now where do we stand?

Income from sales	$ 90,000
Explicit (money) costs	−70,000
Accounting profit	$ 20,000
Implicit costs	−19,600
Remainder (economic profit)	$ 400

The remainder—$400—is called **economic profit**. It is also called pure profit. It means that the enterprise is earning more than enough to offset the opportunity costs of using the entrepreneur's resources in a particular way.

What Economic Profit Meant in Adam Smith's World

The existence of *economic* profit suggests that the resources employed in producing eggs are earning a surplus over and above what they could have earned if used some other way. This surplus (economic profit) suggests that some entrepreneurs not presently in the egg business will make the same calculations and conclude that the egg business will make money for them. As new entrepreneurs enter, the supply curve will shift to the right, driving the price down (assuming no change in demand). As the price falls, the economic profits will be squeezed out.

How far will the price fall? As it falls, some less efficient firms will find that their accounting profit does not cover the implicit costs. These firms will leave the egg industry. The firms that decide to remain will earn just enough to cover implicit costs and no more. All economic profit will be squeezed out because, as long as it exists, new entrepreneurs will continue to enter the industry and compete, forcing the price down to one that just covers the explicit plus implicit costs.

This Adam Smithian view of a market-price system is beautiful from the

---

*The $1,800 dollar return is 9 percent of $20,000, one percent higher than Jane can earn in a savings account. Therefore, why not put *all* the $30,000 into another business? Good question. Answer: Jane may not want to put all of her money into another business because the risk of loss is higher than when the money is in a bank.

point of view of consumers. They will always win by being able to buy goods and services at bargain prices. But what a bleak, cold world for entrepreneurs! Consequently, the first item of business on any intelligent entrepreneur's agenda is to discover how to prevent competing entrepreneurs from driving prices down.

THE FOUR MARKETS

In order to analyze these movements away from intense competition, economists use four terms to describe the level or degree of competition among sellers: *perfect competition, monopolistic competition, oligopoly,* and *monopoly.* The latter three represent movement to avoid competition. These terms do not describe separate categories but rather four areas on a spectrum, from lots of competition to none.

Perfect Competition

In the language of economics, there are four quite specific characteristics of a **perfect competition** in an industry.

Many Small Firms That Cannot Affect Price

In a perfectly competitive industry, there are thousands of small firms, but each is so small that it has no influence over the market price. Regardless of how much or how little the firm supplies, it cannot, alone, change the market price. Examples of such firms are small farmers, like Jane, who must accept the market price for their produce on any given day.

Firms That All Make the Same Product

All of the perfectly competitive firms in the industry make exactly the same product, so the only reason consumers have for choosing one firm's product over another is the product's price, not its packaging, advertising, smell, or anything else.

Mobile Resources

In the perfectly competitive world it is assumed that resources are instantly mobile. Thus, if profit suddenly appears in an industry, entrepreneurs will instantly rush into that industry. It is also assumed that there are no barriers to entry. As new entrepreneurs move in, supply shifts to the right. Given no change in demand, the price will fall.

At this point there may be some confusion. Whereas no *one* entrepreneur can influence the price, if substantial numbers of firms move into or out of an industry, the market price will fall or rise with changes in the total supply provided by all firms. The market price might also change because of a change in consumer demand.

Knowledge of Other Profitable Opportunities

The last requirement in the definition of perfect competition is that knowledge of more profitable opportunities for any of the resources is immediately and freely available. For example, suppose that you earn $10 an hour working in a television-manufacturing plant in Boston. The rate for the same job in Miami suddenly hits $20 an hour because of an increase in demand for TV sets there and a local shortage of workers with your particular skill. In the world of perfect competition, you would know of this opportunity immediately.

Resources would be perfectly mobile, so you could move to Miami with perfect ease and get the job with no difficulty (you would, for example, have no trouble joining a local union). As you and others move to Miami, the labor shortage will ease. Wages may very well come down as the supply of labor shifts to the right. As labor costs fall, TV entrepreneurs may be willing to sell more TV sets at lower prices. The end result is that, again, the change in consumer demand has been answered by a satisfying and immediate response in the form of an increase in production made possible by an increase in the supply of labor.

Note the emphasis on the information being freely available. Suppose you have to fly to Miami on a "scouting trip" to find out about the job. Even making phone calls to Miami to inquire about the job constitutes some kind of barrier to entry. Economists are becoming more and more interested in such **information costs** as computer data banks become more prevalent. Indeed, computer "matching services" are being used by both private industry and government to match everything from jobs and applicants to prospective dates.

Information costs can be found in almost every transaction. For example, when you shop for a car, comparing the deals and dealers, driving around or phoning involves both actual costs (gas and phone tolls) and opportunity costs (time).* When information costs are high, business firms can charge more than they could in markets where information costs are low. (Whenever you can easily compare prices, no one entrepreneur can "get away" with a price that is too far out of line.)

How Efficient Is Perfect Competition?

Economists not only criticize the market-price system's failure to provide full employment, stable prices, social goods, an equal distribution of income, and so forth (see end of Chapter 2), but they also stress the failure of perfect competition to improve the quality of products or to produce goods and services as efficiently as possible. (Of course, absolutely "perfect" competition has never existed, and very little "real-world" competition is based only on prices. Even with basic commodities, factors such as service, location, and even the order clerk's manner enter in.)

If there are no barriers to entry, if resources are instantly mobile, if information is immediate and free, and economic profits are continuously wiped out, entrepreneurs will be unable to put resources aside for research and development to improve the quality of their products or their methods of production. Large firms often use this argument against perfect competition to justify their size. In fact, however, many important inventions— air conditioning, automatic transmissions, power steering, the gyrocompass, the helicopter, the jet engine—have come from individuals or small companies rather than large corporations. One reason for this is that large firms often seem to choke on red tape and errors of judgment that are perpetuated by many people with vested interests. The research and development departments of large firms are often better at improving existing products than making new ones, and advances are almost always introduced by "hungry" newcomers. For example, the electric typewrit-

---

*These costs are not included in the car prices you consider and should be taken into account before you buy the car (or anything else). If you are planning to buy something inexpensive and the cost of information about the quality (or the prices of other brands) is high, you might want to save yourself the cost of obtaining all the information and buy the first version of the product or service you see.

er was developed by "upstart" IBM. When IBM grew up, it ignored the "micro-computer revolution" that a younger generation of upstarts began. Moreover, many new inventions are "happy accidents" that don't seem to happen in large corporate R&D departments.

Another argument against perfect competition is that low entry barriers can make it so easy for new entrepreneurs to compete that many of them will not be qualified to manage a business. Miscalculations of this sort mean wasted resources—empty stores, vacant offices, and factory buildings standing idle for months until other entrepreneurs find a way to make them pay. Finally, because the barriers to entry are low enough to let in unsophisticated or inexperienced entrepreneurs, the production methods used by many of them may not be very efficient. Because of this, a perfectly competitive price may be *higher* than it would be if less competition were present.

Why Economists Usually Prefer Competitive Markets

The difficulty is that one can never be sure whether a price is "high" or "low" unless competitive substitutes are available to buyers. The noncompetitive markets in utilities (gas, electric power, telephone) are good examples of common situations in which buyers have no choice. In such situations, we often have no reliable way to compare price and service, as we could if there were other, competing companies. Consider also the marketplace of ideas. If there is only one newspaper to read or only one or two (government-controlled) television stations to watch (or only one economics instructor to listen to), how can we compare information and arguments to arrive at the truth? We can't. The availability of alternative services or viewpoints for comparison is extremely important. For these reasons, most economists favor more competition rather than less.

Monopolistic Competition

The world of perfect competition is a cold, hard world for entrepreneurs. They are faced with a continuous life-or-death struggle for survival. If they succeed in making an economic profit, this brief moment of comfort evaporates as competing entrepreneurs force the market price down. Against all these forces, they are powerless because they are too small to influence the price. They have no market power.

What do normal entrepreneurs do? As long as they remain entrepreneurs—as opposed to giving up and working for someone else—they must find a way to remove themselves from this daily struggle. A good way to do this is to convince consumers that their products are in some way different from, and superior to, all others in the industry. If they can sell the idea of this difference, they may be able to charge higher prices than those given to them by the impersonal forces of the market.

In the real world, most firms escape from perfect competition just this way. Competing firms do not make identical products; differentiation via brand names is common. In some cases—grain markets are one example—there are no brand names. Such markets are often dominated by major producers who have great influence over the market price. (For instance, Far-Mar-Co, based in Kansas City, represents 250,000 wheat farmers and controls 15 percent of the wheat output of the United States.)

In the real world, then, virtually all markets are to some extent imperfect because: (1) Most firms are, to some extent, *price-makers* rather than price-

Entrepreneurs are faced with struggles for survival in a world of perfect competition.

takers; they determine (within a wide range of market power) the prices they will charge; (2) resources are not instantly mobile; (3) there are always some barriers to entry; (4) some information costs are always present. Thus, any market not carefully defined as perfectly competitive is called an "imperfect market."

The first of the imperfectly competitive markets is called **monopolistic competition**. Monopolistic competition is defined as a market in which there are many sellers—typically small stores, small service enterprises, small manufacturing firms—and the product of each seller is slightly different. This is the market we see every day in the older shopping areas of cities. Competition among large numbers of small clothing stores, drug stores, hardware stores, barber shops, grocery stores, dry cleaning establishments, and restaurants is often fierce. Each firm tries to persuade its prospective customers that it has something special to offer—perhaps easy credit, better service, or free delivery—that its competitors do not have.

The term *monopolistic competition*, therefore, describes a world where many entrepreneurs operate and barriers to entry are still low. But the products produced by different firms in a particular industry are no longer exactly alike: *Brand names* are attached to them.

As a toothpaste entrepreneur in a world of monopolistic competition, you might first give your product a snappy brand name like Dazzle and then launch a sales campaign to convince buyers that Dazzle really is special and worth its higher-than-market price. Your sales campaign might begin with an eye-catching label and local newspaper advertising extolling the qualities of Dazzle. The sales campaign would tout Dazzle's "special ingredients" that whiten and brighten teeth, making the user irresistible to the opposite sex. With the help of an advertising agency, you might develop a sales slogan: *Dazzle Does It!*

Think of all the ways sellers differentiate their products. Brands of gasoline advertise special ingredients or features, as do nationally advertised soaps, detergents, shaving creams, razor blades, cigarette filters, and so on. The object, of course, is to lift oneself above the jungle of price competition. Competition among competing brands, not in terms of price but in terms of special ingredients or services (such as free delivery), is called **nonprice competition**.

The world of monopolistic competition has plenty of price competition because entry barriers, such as capital requirements and franchises to buy, remain low. If economic profit appears, other firms can enter and compete without too much difficulty. We are still not far away from Adam Smith's world of perfect competition; entrepreneurs have little market power.

The Reasons for Large Size

In a few pages, we will leap from the world of small shops to that of giant corporations. In the real world, the leap isn't really there. The real world is a spectrum of every size of firm from the neighborhood lemonade stand to General Motors (once described as having a total output exceeding that of all but nine foreign nations). The four markets mentioned on page 150 are merely convenient stopping places on our guided tour of the real-world spectrum.

Business firms can become large in two main ways:

1. If they manage to keep competitors out by creating barriers to entry in the form of patents, franchises, licensing agreements, or perhaps control of key resource supplies.

2. If they can adopt mass-production methods that reduce the unit (average) variable costs of production, particularly the per-unit costs of labor and energy. We want to explain this second reason for large size in more detail.

The Law of Diminishing Returns

Most of us are familiar with the famous **Law of Diminishing Returns**. We speak of reaching the point of diminishing returns as we fall asleep over a textbook. The law applies just as well to business firms. At some point in production, business firms bump into a kind of sound barrier. Increases in output become more difficult and more expensive to achieve. Given one crucial assumption, *every* business firm will sooner or later bump into that barrier.

Let's now define the law and you'll see the assumption: If increasing amounts of one resource are added to other resources, with one or more of the latter *held constant in both quantity and quality*, a point will be reached where successive increases in output will become more difficult to achieve.

The crucial assumption is in italics. A familiar example of the law is that of a farmer adding fertilizer to an acre of ground. The acre of land is the resource held constant in quantity and quality. As additional pounds of fertilizer are added to the fixed amount of land, the land may at first become more and more productive, in terms of, say, bushels of wheat. But as we continue to add fertilizer, the increases in output will begin to slow down. Table 8-1 illustrates.

The column labeled **marginal product** (column 3) shows the extra production each pound of fertilizer contributes. The greatest increase in production occurs when the third pound of fertilizer is added to the land. After that, the increases slow down.* Ultimately, with the seventh pound of fertilizer, the marginal product becomes negative as the fertilizer begins to burn the soil.

---

*The Law of Diminishing Returns is often called the Law of Diminishing *Marginal* Returns to indicate that the law describes the behavior of marginal returns, not total returns.

Table 8-1. The Law of Diminishing Returns (Fertilizer Costs $3 per Pound)

Pounds of fertilizer (1)	Total bushels of wheat (2)	Marginal product (3)	Fertilizer cost per bushel (4)*
1	2		$1.50
		4	
2	6		1.00
		5	
3	11		0.82
		2	
4	13		0.92
		1	
5	14		1.07
		0	
6	14		1.29
		−1	
7	13		1.62

*Column 4 = Column 1 × $3 ÷ Column 2

The point of diminishing returns occurs at the third pound of fertilizer. Notice also that between the second and third pounds of fertilizer, returns *increase*. Up to the point of diminishing returns, increases in output become easier (and therefore cheaper) to achieve. After the point of diminishing returns, increases in output become more difficult and more expensive to achieve.

The changes in costs are shown in column 4. Assuming the cost of fertilizer is $3 per pound, we can find the average fertilizer cost per bushel of wheat by multiplying the number of pounds of fertilizer (column 1) by $3 and dividing the result by the number of bushels (column 2).

Notice that the fertilizer cost per bushel first goes down, and then at the third pound, the fertilizer cost per bushel increases. Consequently, the Law of Diminishing Returns is also called the *Law of Increasing Cost* because the cost per bushel turns up at the point of diminishing returns.

The point of diminishing returns arrives in *any* operation as long as one of the resources (one of the factors of production) is fixed in quantity and quality. The fixed factor in this case is the acre of land. To take another example, assume that a factory with a number of machines is the fixed factor (capital) and that we add workers (the variable factor). As we add workers, output may actually increase for a while at an increasing rate. But then the point of diminishing returns is reached, and the increases in output slow down.

The Reason for the Law

The *reason for the law* is that each successive unit of the variable factor has less of the fixed factor to work with. Translation: As we add workers to the factory, each worker has less of the factory to work with. (Not everyone can be at a machine.) As we add workers, at some point they will become increasingly less productive. The last workers hired will have to be assigned menial tasks like sweeping the floor.

The fertilizer/wheat example illustrates the same point as the workers/factory example. In the latter case, each additional worker has less of the fixed factor (the factory) to work with. In the fertilizer/wheat example, each additional pound of fertilizer has less unfertilized land (the fixed factor) to work with. Sooner or later, each additional pound of fertilizer becomes less productive.

Note that this phenomenon *has to take place* at some point in production as long as we hold the size of the factory and the number of machines in it (or the size of the farm) constant.

Economies of Scale and the Size of Business Firms

The Law of Diminishing Returns is like a sound barrier that tends to keep business firms small. In a small operation like Jane Pennyworth's, Jane's horizons are limited by the size of her acreage and the size of her hen house. Any attempt to increase the size of her flock within those constraints risks increases in mortality among her chickens and higher costs of production.

On page 154, we mentioned that business firms can become large if they find ways to reduce the costs of production. One example of how this is done is given at the end of this chapter. The simple invention of a cage for egg-laying hens has enabled egg ranchers to house and care for 1 *million* hens with a small number of workers tending automatic equipment.

The result of such technological changes pushes the point of diminishing returns to much larger outputs. But, of course, any long-run change for the better would do it—newer buildings, more land, more skillful workers, better feed, better vaccines, and so forth.

When the breakthrough (like the cage for egg-laying hens) occurs, the first firm to make the change can quickly grab larger and larger shares of the market. With lower costs it can undersell its smaller competitors, who may be forced to leave the industry.

Frequently, the breakthrough firms enjoy **internal** and **external economies of scale**. An internal economy of scale occurs when an X percent increase in all inputs results in an increase of more than X percent in output. If output increases by 11 percent after inputs are increased by 10 percent, the firm making such a change enjoys an economy of scale.

An economy of scale usually exists when one company can produce the output previously produced by two or more companies at lower unit costs. The classic example of an economy of scale is an automobile assembly line. If an automobile is assembled by an individual or even by a small company, much time is lost while workers pick up one tool and put down another. By contrast, if the entire assembly is done on a long, *moving* assembly line with many separate operations, each worker can be assigned one small task. No time is lost switching (or looking for) tools. Each worker becomes very adept at some specialty. The overall assembly of the car is far less expensive than if performed without the assembly line. But using an assembly line is feasible only for very large firms that can afford the initial investment of a billion or more dollars.

Computerized scanners at supermarket cash registers are another example of an economy of scale at work. The scanners not only give the customers a printout of their purchases but keep a continuous and automatic record of inventory changes. Such use of computers gives large business firms tighter control of their inventories and of their money. The ability to buy just the right item at the right time and in the right quantities may save millions in purchasing and labor costs, and in the explicit and implicit interest costs of money tied up in inventory.

External economies of scale are often enjoyed by large firms. These economies may be provided by local government in the form of better streets, harbors, and often schools for training employees. For example, a local community

college may put in a curriculum for training students in computer operation and repair. Many local firms benefit from such almost-on-the-job training courses while the cost is shared by other taxpayers. External economies of scale can also occur when the location of large firms motivates suppliers to move closer, thus reducing shipping costs.

All of these economies—both internal and external—help firms to become larger. And, as their production costs drop, the resulting increases in profit can be used to finance research into new breakthroughs that will provide additional economies of scale, and on and on.

Do Business Firms Then Become Ever Bigger?

At this point one would think that growth of large firms continues unabated, self-fueled by large profits generated by economies of scale. Not so. At some point the large firm may become too big for its location in terms of traffic snarls, noise, and pollution. Local governments may become disenchanted and impose costly regulations. The firm may lose some of its better employees who find jobs elsewhere with more attractive surroundings. And top management may become less efficient. As the firm grows, more managers are needed. Eventually the chief executive finds that too many people are reporting to him/her and hires another level of managers to manage the managers. Areas of responsibility gradually become less clear-cut, communication worsens, and the firm begins making poor decisions. These difficulties are called **diseconomies of scale**. Diseconomies of scale can limit the growth of large business firms.

The foregoing section has analyzed the cost advantages of large size. Unfortunately, there is no guarantee that those cost advantages will be passed on to consumers in the form of lower prices. Lower prices usully occur because competitors force business firms to lower prices. But in the last two markets we now examine, there is not apt to be much price competition. The first of these markets is called oligopoly.

Oligopoly

Oligopoly means that just a few producers or sellers supply a major portion of an industry's output. (The prefix *mono-* means one, and the prefix *oligo-* means few.) An oligopolistic industry is one in which there are three or four large firms, each one of which is large enough and has sufficient market power to influence the market price and total industry output.

Table 8-2. Percentage of U.S. Output Produced in the United States by the Four Largest Manufacturing Firms in Selected Industries

Industry	Percent of output
Lead	93%
Flat glass	92
Cereal breakfast foods	90
Chewing gum	87
Cigarettes	84
Gypsum products	80
Aluminum	70
Copper	72
Aircraft	66
Metal cans	66
Soap	62

Source: Bureau of the Census, 1972.

The best-known oligopolies in the United States are shown in Table 8-2, which uses a measure familiar to economists called the concentration ratio. The **concentration ratio** shows the share of U.S. output produced by the four largest firms in each industry. The concentration ratios in the table do, however, somewhat *over*state the degree of concentration, because the share of U.S. markets produced by foreign firms is not included.

Within the industries listed in the table, each firm must be extremely wary of the price and output decisions of the others. A price cut by one may cause the others to lower prices, resulting in lower revenues for all. If one firm raises its price and the others do not go along, it may lose customers to the firms with lower prices. However, some evidence, particularly in the automobile industry, indicates that when one firm raises its price, the others also raise theirs. When they act in concert, each of the firms maintains its share of the market.

Although deliberate collusion is illegal, economic theory suggests that oligopolistic firms cooperate by tacit agreement, so that each firm's sales and profits remain relatively stable. Lack of cooperation by any one firm involves too many risks for all. For example, on September 21, 1976, General Motors announced a 4.9 percent increase in the average base price of its new big-model cars for 1977. (GM earlier had announced an average 5.9 percent price boost for all its 1977 models.) One week later, Ford raised its average prices 5.6 percent. Chrysler then followed with a 5.9 percent increase and American Motors with a 4.8 percent increase.[1] Again, in 1979, the four firms went through four rounds of increases that raised prices an average of 8.5 percent over 1978. More recently, the auto-makers have copycatted one another's rebate and low-interest promotions.

Brand Acceptance Is Another Barrier to Entry

Just as competitors struggle to free themselves from the bleak prospects of perfect competition, so do competitors try to circumvent the discipline of monopolistic competition. If you, the Dazzle toothpaste entrepreneur, convince the public that your product is superior, you may be able to use the economic profit you earn thereby to remove yourself even further from competition. You will be able to afford large advertising campaigns. You will have money to purchase the capital goods you need to produce your product more efficiently. The more successful you become, the more difficult it is for other firms to compete. Think of how tough it would be to compete with a nationally advertised soft drink, cereal, or cigarette.

Among oligopolists the battle to get one's product before the public's eye is often intense. This battle takes place in the media and in retail stores. Some of its consequences are described in the next section.

The Battle for Shelf Space

To capture the public's attention, Campbell Soup now makes three lines of soup with 80 varieties. The last time we looked, old reliable chicken noodle and chicken with rice were almost crowded out by chicken gumbo, chicken noodle O's, curly noodle with chicken, cream of chicken, creamy chicken mushroom, chicken vegetable, chicken alphabet, chicken and stars, chicken 'n' dumplings, and chicken broth.

Why? To hog shelf space and prevent competitors from reaching the public.

Coca Cola's foods division recently added two new lines of drip coffee, two new varieties of fruit juice, and two new lines of powdered drink mixes. The drink mixes come in nine flavors and two sizes. The company has also added a tenth and eleventh flavor (punch and tangerine) to its existing Hi-C line of canned drinks.

Not to battle risks disaster. The Liggett & Myers Tobacco Company held 20 percent of the market thirty years ago. Now its market share has dropped to 3 percent. The company failed to match its rivals in introducing new brands of cigarettes to the public.

Before 1950, most smokers smoked Camels, Luckies, Old Gold, or Chesterfields, all uniformly 2 3/4 inches long. Now retailers must stock 58 varieties taking up 33 feet of shelf space. They also would have to provide 176 feet of shelf for candy and chewing gum, 1,983 feet for soft drinks, 210 feet for dog and cat foods (up 80 percent in 7 years), 229 feet for refrigerated foods, and 290 feet for frozen foods in order to accommodate all brands of these items.

Some experts believe that consumers sometimes become so confused by the variety of "choices" that they leave the store without buying or buy less than they had planned. But the chances are that no one firm can trust its rivals to give up the battle, and advertising agencies, whose total revenue was $55 billion in 1980, are unlikely to discourage their customers from continuing to add brand names to their offerings.[2]

The Power of Oligopolies

Almost twenty years ago, the well-known economist John Kenneth Galbraith stated that oligopolies are the "characteristic market of the industrial system."[3] There is no doubt that he is right.

The share of total manufacturing assets held by the 100 or the 200 largest firms is called the *aggregate* concentration ratio. The crucial question is: Have the shares been rising? Table 8-3 shows a steady increase in the shares held by both groups from 1950 to 1970, a slight dip in 1975, and a slight increase in 1980. We have to conclude that the trend since 1970 is not clear. The main point to notice, however, is that, regardless of any trend, the size and power of

Table 8-3. Largest Manufacturing Corporations: Percent of Assets Held, 1950 to 1981

Corporation rank group	1950	1955	1960	1965	1970	1975	1980	1981
100 largest	39.7	44.3	46.4	46.5	48.5	45.0	46.7	46.8
200 largest	47.7	53.1	56.3	56.7	60.4	57.5	59.7	60.9

Source: *Statistical Abstract of the United States, 1982–1983.*

large corporations is awesome. In 1981, there were roughly 200 thousand corporations in manufacturing. One hundred of them—one twentieth of one percent—owned almost half of all the assets of the group.

Monopoly

The last type of market is **monopoly**.

The term means that there is only one seller of a product or service in the market and that no good substitutes for its products or services are available. The firm need not be large. It might be the only drugstore in a town so small and geographically isolated that consumers cannot afford to drive to a competing drugstore in another town. Or the monopoly may be a giant. Until World War II, the Aluminum Company of America (Alcoa) was the only producer of aluminum in the United States.

When an industry has a monopoly and there is no competition, its power may be great. ("May be" because being a monopoly does not guarantee success—it could be the only supplier of something no one wants.)

With some monopolies, other products may provide a form of competition. For example, with aluminum there is competition from other metals, plastics, and fiberglass.

Utilities are probably the purest form of monopoly because available substitutes for electricity, natural gas, piped water, and telephone service are not very satisfactory. There are two main reasons why we are not permitted to buy utility service from more than one firm: (1) It would be clearly inconvenient to have the streets in continuous disrepair from constant tearing up by competing water companies, gas companies, power and telephone companies. (2) Utilities are usually **natural monopolies** because the conditions that justify their existence seem natural or attributable to nature.

A firm is a natural monopoly when it can produce the entire needs of a market at lower average cost than the combined average cost of two or more smaller firms. A natural monopoly achieves this advantage via the economies of large-scale production.

In the case of electrical power companies, for example, once the main (high tension) lines are built, the extra cost of adding additional customers decreases over a wide range of output. In such a case, we want to let the power company be a monopoly but to pass on its cost savings to customers in the form of lower prices. To make sure the natural monopolist acts accordingly, the firm is supervised by a "PUC" (a public utilities commission). The monopolist/utility can raise prices only with the permission of the PUC.

One so-called natural monopoly seems to have escaped government regulation: the U.S. Postal Service. The Postal Service has an absolute monopoly in the delivery of first-class mail under the theory that the more mail the Postal

Service handles, the cheaper the mail handling becomes. The argument is the familiar decreasing cost/economy of scale argument. But many economists are skeptical. Eighty-five percent of the costs of handling first-class mail are labor costs. As long as that is true, economies of scale are doubtful. We might be just as well off to have many competing postal-delivery services.

Is Bigness Badness?

Despite the urgency of brevity, we need to say something about society's responses to bigness. In general, we are suspicious of oligopoly and monopoly for at least four reasons:

1. Unless business firms truly compete on price, there is no guarantee that oligopolistic and monopolistic prices will not be above those available in competitive markets. In oligopolistic industries, the firms may cooperate with one another to keep the price up. Nor is there any guarantee that the profits generated by high prices will be used to finance new ideas.

2. In the absence of competition, there is no guarantee that the product or service will be of sufficiently high quality. (Already noted on page 152.)

3. Monopolists and oligopolists are price makers. When prices are set high, the public will not be able to buy as much. Thus, to some extent, output is lower in less-than-perfectly competitive markets than in perfectly competitive markets. Most economists believe that oligopolists and monopolists restrict output to keep prices up.

4. Large firms are often politically powerful. Frequently, our representatives in Washington are pressured to help them. Public welfare may suffer. The last section of this chapter discusses this point.

Laws have been passed to soothe these public concerns. Three famous laws deserve mention: the Sherman Anti-Trust Act of 1890, which made it illegal for firms to conspire to combine "in restraint of trade"; the Clayton Act of 1914, which tried to plug loopholes in the Sherman Act "where the effect would

Table 8-4. Summing Up the Four Markets

Market characteristics	Perfect competition	Monopolistic competition	Oligopoly	Monopoly
Product differentiation (brand names)	No	Yes	Yes, but less so if the oligopoly supplies a raw material like copper	Yes
Price competition	Intense: must meet prices of other firms	Intense	Occasional, but coopera-tive behavior often present	Occasional, with producers of substitute goods and services. Prices of natu-ral monopolies subject to regulation
Advertising (nonprice competition)	None	Intense	Intense	Often, to pro-mote public good will
Barriers to entry	None	Low	High	High
Information costs	None	Low	High	High
Opportunities to earn and keep economic profits	None	Few	Many	Many, though often regulated

substantially lessen competition"; and the Celler-Kefauver Anti-Merger Act of 1950, which tried to block the acquisition of one company by another—again where the effect would lessen competition.

There is much debate about how successful these laws have been. The courts have had great difficulty in defining such phrases as "substantially lessen competition." Nevertheless, economists generally believe that the laws—like a traffic cop—prevent the more flagrant attempts by firms to monopolize markets. But such a conclusion depends on the political climate of the moment.

We have completed the discussion of the four markets. Table 8-4 reviews the major characteristics of each.

WHERE ARE WE HEADED?

We have seen that entrepreneurs have very good reasons to graduate from high-ly competitive markets to those where they can earn and keep economic profits over a long span of time. Now the question is, "Where is our market-price system headed?"

One expert believes that a major change has occurred in the relationship between large business firms and government agencies. In 1900, "the line of demarcation" between public and private ownership could be "confidently distinguished" but now there is a "blending" of the two sectors: "The dividing line between public and private enterprise, never too distinct, has all but van-ished. The two sectors, to put it baldly, are becoming increasingly amalga-mated."[4]

The Blending of Public and Private Enterprise

"Blending" does not necessarily come from outright government ownership. Only about 2 percent of total output is generated by publicly owned enterprises such as the Tennessee Valley Authority.

Much of the blending occurs in joint ventures by government and private industry. In many cases, federal installations such as the atomic energy plants are contracted out to private concerns like General Electric, Westinghouse, and the Union Carbide Corporation. In the Communications Satellite Corporation (COMSAT), the federal government shares ownership and control with American Telephone and Telegraph (AT&T) and International Telephone and Telegraph (ITT).

Another type of blending occurs when the government is the major customer of many large corporations and countless small ones, as in the field of defense. Defense Department purchases usually account for more than 75 percent of the sales of seven major aircraft manufacturers. Many observers believe that aircraft and missile firms are so closely connected to the Defense Department that they have roughly the same status as the Postal Service.

The dependence of these firms on military contracts gave rise to the famous caution in President Eisenhower's farewell address shortly before he left office in 1961:

> This conjunction of an immense military establishment and a large arms industry is new in the American experience. . . . In the councils of government we must guard against the acquisition of unwarranted influence, whether sought or unsought, by the *military-industrial complex*. [Author's emphasis]

The federal government also supplies about 60 percent of the funds for all research and development (R&D) by industry, universities, and hospitals. Increasing reliance on these funds has fostered the ardent pursuit of key government officials by business and institutional suitors.

Not only have corporations become increasingly dependent on the federal government as purchaser of their goods and services and supplier of R&D funds. On several occasions, corporations have asked federal agencies for financial assistance. Examples are Chrysler's U.S. government loan guarantee of $1.5 billion in 1980, a smaller but similar guarantee for Lockheed in 1970, loans to Franklin National (the nation's 20th largest bank) in 1974, and a $4 billion subsidy to savings and loan banks in 1980. In 1979, after the Wheeling-Pittsburgh Steel Corporation requested a $105 million loan guarantee, one observant reporter commented:

> The drift is unmistakable. The government—through its loan-guarantee program—is acquiring an increasingly large steel investment that it will need to protect. Industry and labor are eager for the protection, and urge it through a variety of administrative and technical proposals. We will continue to have the mantle of free enterprise and the reality of government control.[5]

The blending of government and business in the United States is a fact of life. What is less clear is how it happened. The following story about the egg industry will help to show what pressures sometimes induce business firms to seek government assistance.

A Case of Eggs: Whatever Happened to Adam Smith?*

On a typical American family farm of the 1930s the husband worked in the fields and his wife tended a hen house and raised chickens. Perhaps a few dozen eggs a day were sold to neighbors, passersby, and perhaps to some small grocer. The "egg money" was traditionally the wife's source of a few luxuries.

This was a world of perfect competition. The farmers were selling an undifferentiated product. Everybody's eggs were like everyone else's. There were virtually no barriers to entry, and capital investment was small; the purchase price of a laying hen very small. Egg raising was a real business on a few farms of the period. Such a farm might have a flock of 2,000 hens laying approximately 100 dozen eggs per day. On the whole, however, each egg producer provided a tiny portion of the total supply and thus had no control over the market price.

Beginning in the early 1940s, this almost perfectly competitive industry went through a period of extremely rapid change. Today, the egg business has become an industry of mammoth farms each owning more than a million laying hens—often as many as 5 or 6 million. The birds are kept in completely automated climate-controlled hen houses where machines feed them, clean their cages, and collect, sort, grade, and package their eggs. Two men, whose main job is to keep the machinery running, can now take care of 200,000 hens. These gigantic firms are oligopolies, in many cases regulated and protected by government agencies.

How did these changes come about? Our story starts in 1940 in Southern California, where grocery stores began growing into chains of supermarkets. The big stores were not interested in dealing directly with any ranchers who delivered less than 500 cases** of eggs a week (180,000 eggs). In those days, the largest ranch could supply only 50 cases, and 500 cases of eggs constituted the entire weekly production of 32 egg ranches. To deal with the supermarket chains, local associations of egg ranchers joined together and formed the Council of Poultry Cooperatives, which functioned successfully for several years.

With the formation of the council, the perfectly competitive scene began to disappear, and the large egg ranches began to dominate the business. Southern California, with its temperate climate, was a perfect place for poultry. The high profits and high rates of return attracted entrepreneurs and also encouraged technological change. The key innovation—a cage—sounds terribly simple, but up to that time, chickens had typically been kept in a house with a floor. They were fed and watered by hand, eggs were gathered by hand, and the floor and roosts were cleaned by hand. The cage, where four hens were crammed into a space 12 inches by 18 inches, permitted the beginning of automated feeding, cleaning, and egg gathering. The cage also made it much easier to check each hen's production and health. The cage led to many economies of scale.

---

*The author is extremely grateful to two Southern California egg ranchers, Ronald S. Rossitter and Walter Zentler, for the details of this story. The author is, of course, fully responsible for any errors.

**One case of eggs contains 30 dozen eggs: $30 \times 12 = 360$ eggs.

At first, profits increased as the egg ranches adopted the cage and increased output. But soon the increases in supply caught up with them. Prices began to fall, and, as they fell, each producer had to produce more to maintain any level of income.* As the increases in supply accelerated, prices fell faster and faster.

At the same time, producers found that the demand for eggs, as for many other agricultural products, was extremely inelastic. As egg prices fell because of shifts in supply, consumers did not proportionately increase their purchases. If demand is inelastic and the price falls, what happens to total revenue? It falls.

It took about five years for the egg surplus in California to become a real problem, because the ranchers were able to export the surplus to eastern markets. Soon, however, the technology of producing eggs spread eastward. Climate-controlled hen houses made it just as easy to produce eggs in the Midwest and East as in Southern California.

The Egg Cartel

In 1965, to meet the challenge of falling prices and the surplus of eggs, the Southern California ranchers formed a new voluntary association, the Southwest Egg Producers (SWEP).

Each member of SWEP was given an equitable production base—a kind of weekly quota expressed in numbers of cases. SWEP agreed to buy this quota at prices it fixed and then sell the eggs to retail grocery stores. Prices on quota quantities were called "Pool 1" prices. If the market became glutted—say, oversupplied by 20 percent—Pool 1 prices then applied only to 80 percent of each rancher's base. The other 20 percent was sold at substantially lower prices—called "Pool 2" prices—with the understanding that Pool 2 eggs would not appear in California grocery stores.

The ranchers called this process a *surplus disposal* program. The objective, of course, was to limit the supply of eggs sold in California and thereby keep prices at profitable levels.

For a while the SWEP plan worked. Retail prices climbed to a high of $1 per dozen in some stores in late 1969. But then rising profits and improved technology caused the supply to continue its rapid increase. Even at SWEP's zenith, its members controlled only 70 percent of all the eggs produced in Southern California, and the surplus eggs produced by nonmembers could often be sold at prices higher than Pool 2 prices. Dissension grew in SWEP ranks. The largest and most influential producers who had grown the fastest resented the quota system. After trying a variety of plans, SWEP finally dissolved because the ranchers were unable to agree to limit production and to stick together.

Like the OPEC countries, SWEP was a **cartel**: an association of companies formed to prevent competition among its members and to control the overall quantity supplied and therefore the market price. In the United States, most cartels are illegal, but many agricultural products are exempted from antitrust laws, and agricultural cartels are often legal.

---

*These statements clearly contradict the idea that supply curves are always upward-sloping from left to right. In this situation, the supply curve slopes downward from left to right because the quantity supplied increases as the price falls. Sounds strange, but it does happen, particularly when crops (like eggs) are perishable. If the crop isn't perishable, the farmer may elect to store his crop until the price rises. But of course that decision depends on how badly the farmer needs income from sales to pay his bills. Sooner or later he will have to sell, whether the price rises or falls. In the long run, if prices continue to fall, the farmer will have to declare bankruptcy, join a cartel, or seek government assistance as the following discussion will indicate.

Being in a cartel requires discipline. Members must agree not to undersell one another no matter how tempting price cutting may be. The temptation is enormous because one member can steal large amounts of business from other members by offering to sell at a lower price—let's say, to a large supermarket chain. Because each rancher's eggs are excellent substitutes for every other rancher's eggs, the demand for any one rancher's eggs becomes extremely elastic if he or she cuts the agreed-upon price. "Cheating" becomes irresistible.

Price-cutting and lack of cooperation caused the break-up of SWEP. The individual ranchers went back to an "every-man-for-himself" philosophy. As a result, the oversupply grew, and prices went down and down.

Egg Producers and Government Assistance

By 1971–1972 the oversupply was so huge and egg prices were so low (they fell to Depression levels) that farmers, instead of earning $3 or $4 per year per hen, lost money. Many ranchers went bankrupt, and low prices forced others to merge into all kinds of associations and combinations in desperate attempts to control the market. But the ranchers could still not get together on price, and the surplus of eggs kept growing.

California ranchers solved their problem by invoking a 1937 state law permitting producers of many agricultural products to band together and vote to subject themselves to state control in the form of marketing boards. The egg ranchers voted in June 1972 to give control over egg production and pricing to a state marketing board, which in turn issued a "marketing order" aimed at removing nearly 10 percent of California eggs from the market. The order permitted each producer to sell 200 cases per week at any price he or she pleased. Any production over 200 cases had to be reduced by 10 percent or the surplus had to be turned over to the marketing board at a low price. The board then could dump it or sell it for animal feed. The immediate effect of the program was to increase egg prices by 3 to 4 cents a dozen[6] and to yield the typical egg rancher additional revenue of $600,000 per year. Thus, in accepting compulsory regulation, the California egg ranchers found a way to control prices.

Who is on the marketing boards? Egg ranchers. (Who else understands the business?) The result is, of course, controlled supply and higher prices. Free enterprise died in the California egg industry.

Conclusion

The egg case helps to show why entrepreneurs move along the spectrum of markets from perfect competition to oligopoly. Part of the urge comes from a natural desire to escape the zero-economic-profit world of perfect competition. Part of the movement comes from the success of a technological breakthrough like the cage for egg-laying hens.

But the bigger the firms become, the more they find reason to cooperate, perhaps to form cartels. If these attempts fail, then large firms often seek the protection of a government agency. Indeed, without government to "make them stick," cartel agreements generally do fail in the long run. Ironically, as economist Robert Heilbroner observes, though both socialistic and capitalistic views of society assumed that economic systems control their politics, now capitalism is "continuously subject to political direction."[7] In fact, many economists believe that our study of economics should now be called "political economics."

SUMMARY

Until 1930, the prevailing economic opinion of free enterprise was Adam Smith's: That of all economic systems, perfect competition provided the best allocation of resources, the most efficient production, and the largest possible output of goods and services at the lowest prices. Perfect competition exists only when (1) there are enough entrepreneurs in an industry so that no single firm can influence the price of the product; (2) products sold by all firms are exactly the same; (3) resources needed in production are instantly mobile; and (4) knowledge of more profitable opportunities for any of the resources is instantly available. No entrepreneur would receive economic profit above and beyond her or his implicit costs because, whenever a person developed a profitable business, others would rush into the business until it became no more profitable than any other business.

Despite the appeal of perfect competition, economists sometimes argue that, if no one receives economic profit, there will be no money to put aside for research or expansion. Also, perfect competition may be an inefficient system for allocating resources if many unqualified people enter into business (in the absence of entry barriers) and then fail.

Because of the lack of market power they have in competitive industries, entrepreneurs try to escape into other market situations that economists classify as monopolistic competition, oligopoly, and monopoly. Under monopolistic competition, each firm attempts to differentiate its product from other similar products by labeling it and advertising it. Because few barriers to entry exist, however, there is still a high degree of competition and little market power. An oligopoly is said to exist where a few companies become so big and powerful that they control most of the market, where any one of the companies can influence the market price, and where outside firms have difficulty entering the industry because of barriers, such as the large amount of capital required. In the least competitive system of all, monopoly, there is only one seller. Utilities are called natural monopolies because they are decreasing-cost industries—each additional unit costs less than the previous one to produce—and because the inconvenience and inefficiency of allowing competing firms to supply services to a given area seems too great to permit.

The tendency has been for government to become more and more involved in business, through outright ownership, joint public and private operation, attempts to influence government decision making, or government regulation.

The egg industry provides a case study of what has been happening (though not necessarily what *had* to happen) in many sectors of the economy for the last 100 years. Adam Smith's world no longer exists (if it ever did). Today, giant companies, initimately related to government, control large sectors of the economy.

Discussion Questions

1. Would a perfectly competitive system be ideal? Why or why not?

2. Under what circumstances would a perfectly competitive industry exist for a long time (say, 100 years)?

3. Would the products produced under this system be as high quality and/or as low-priced as those produced under conditions of oligopoly? That is, would consumers be better or worse off?

4. Suppose you buy a home worth $100,000. The remaining balance of your mortgage is $60,000. Other than taxes, insurance, and maintenance, what are the implicit costs of living in your home?

5. Estimate the implicit costs of owning a business in which you have invested $50,000. Assume you work in the business full time.

6. If you had been an egg rancher in "Case of Eggs," what would you have done?

7. Name as many entry barriers as you can. Are they all bad? To what extent is sheer size a barrier?

DID YOU EVER WONDER WHY...

... there were thousands of garages and breweries in the 1920s, while today there are still thousands of garages but only a handful of breweries?

References

1. *Facts on File*, 1976.

2. See A. Kent MacDougall, "Market-Shelf Proliferation—Public Pays," *Los Angeles Times*, 27 May 1979, Pt. I, p. 1, and "Madison Avenue Takes on Washington," *U.S. News & World Report*, 18 June 1979.

3. John Kenneth Galbraith, *The New Industrial State* (Boston: Houghton Mifflin, 1967), pp. 179–180.

4. Morton S. Baratz, *The American Business System in Transition* (New York: Thomas Y. Crowell, 1970), p. 5.

5. Robert J. Samuelson, "Steel: A Free Enterprise That Really Isn't," *Los Angeles Times*, 5 April 1979, Pt. II, p. 7. Reprinted with permission from *National Journal.*

6. Robert Fairbanks, "New Program May Boost Egg Prices 3–4 Cents a Dozen," *Los Angeles Times*, 1 September 1972.

7. Robert L. Heilbroner, "The Future of Capitalism," *World*, 12 September 1972.

Business Strategies to Increase Profits

KEY WORDS
Fixed costs
Variable costs
Market period
Short run
Long run
Shut-down point
Marginal revenue (MR)
Marginal cost (MC)
Variable pricing
Variable supply
Fixed supply
Price discrimination
Consumer surplus
Monopsony
Private labeling
Clayton Act of 1914
Robinson-Patman Act of 1936

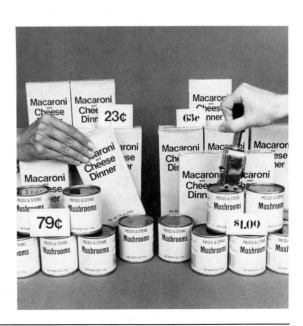

The previous chapter described how business firms try to escape the bleak world of perfect competition. Our emphasis was on why business firms tend to become large and monopolistic. This chapter analyzes the way economists think about operating a business: When should the business fold up and quit? When should the business expand? What can the business do to make more money? Of all the chapters in this book, this one is probably the most valuable for those of you who are already in business, or who are planning to start a business, or are planning to join a business firm with an eye toward participating in management.

The chapter is divided into three sections: (1) the economic theory of business profits, (2) why charging different prices for the same product or service is a good rationing device, and (3) why business firms charge different prices for the same good or service to increase their profits.

THE ECONOMIC THEORY OF BUSINESS PROFIT

Although economic theory has very little to say about how we as individuals should try to get rich, it has a good deal to say about how business firms should try to increase their profits. The economic theory of business operation is often called "profit-maximizing" theory. Profit-maximizing theory can be applied to many different kinds of firms.

In this section, we will discuss profit-maximizing theory in terms of Jane Pennyworth's egg farm, the example used at the beginning of the previous chapter. Recall that Jane had a relatively small egg farm. She was selling eggs at a wholesale price of 60 cents a dozen, and her share of the market in her city was so small that she had no control over the market price.

Under these conditions the demand curve for her eggs was horizontal—she could sell all the eggs she could produce at the market price of 60 cents. When the demand curve is horizontal, the curve is perfectly elastic at the market price, because her share of the market is too small to affect the price and because all of the other egg ranches supply perfect substitutes for Jane's eggs.

Figure 9-1 shows the demand curve for Jane's eggs compared with the total demand and total supply curves for all eggs in a large market like Chicago's or New York City's.

The equilibrium market price is 60 cents. No matter whether Jane supplies Q_1, Q_2, or Q_3, her selling price will always be 60 cents. She has no reason to sell for less, because she can sell all she has at 60 cents. If she tried to sell at a higher price, say, 61 cents, she wouldn't sell *any*. Why not? Because there are large numbers of small firms whose selling price is 60 cents. People will prefer buying from these other firms at 60 cents to buying from Jane at 61 cents. If demand or supply changes for the egg industry as a whole, the equilibrium price will change, and Jane's demand curve will rise or fall along with the demand curves of all the other small firms. Jane is a *price taker;* her only chance to control her profits or losses comes from her supply decisions.

Jane's Supply Decisions

Jane's supply decisions—that is, what quantities she will sell at each market price—are based (like those of any supplier) on the costs of production, exactly like the supply decisions of the students making coffee mugs back in Chapter 5. This section explains why some production costs are more important than others in making supply decisions.

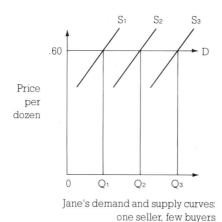

Jane's demand and supply curves:
one seller, few buyers

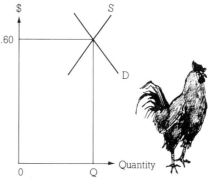

Total industry demand and supply:
thousands of sellers and buyers

Figure 9-1.
Jane's demand and
supply curves
compared with those
for the egg industry
as a whole.

Costs are divided into fixed costs and variable costs. **Fixed costs** are those costs that do not vary with changes in output (the number of eggs Jane decides to produce). **Variable costs** are those costs that change with output—with each additional egg she decides to produce.

A particular item like chicken feed may be a fixed or a variable cost, depending on whether or not Jane has made a *legal commitment* to pay the cost. If she has a contract with a feed company to buy so many pounds a week, then the feed is a fixed cost because it doesn't matter whether she produces one egg or 100,000; she still has to pay the bill.

Therefore, it is more accurate to say that fixed costs are those involving a past commitment; variable costs are those about which entrepreneurs can change their minds. Because past or future decisions are involved, economists like to divide time into three periods: the market period, the short run, and the long run.

In the **market period** all costs are in the past; the eggs have been put in cartons, trucked to the market, and displayed for sale. Because all costs have been incurred in the past, all costs are fixed. At this point, Jane has no more decisions to make; she takes what she can get.

For example, it doesn't matter whether Jane's production costs were $100 or $10,000; once she arrives at the market (and assuming she can't store the eggs) she will have to accept any price in order to unload her eggs. If demand is strong (no other egg producers come to market that day), she will get a good price. If there are more egg sellers than usual or fewer buyers, she will receive a low price. The important point is that her costs no longer influence her decision to sell once she is at the market.

The **short run** is defined as a period that includes both fixed and variable costs. We usually assume here that Jane's buildings and equipment (capital) have fixed costs (taxes, insurance, mortgage payments), but she can vary other costs like the amount of feed she decides to buy and the number of workers she decides to hire.

In the **long run,** Jane can vary *any* of the factors of production, including capital. She can sell her business, reduce its size, or add to it. She can make any decision she wishes to about any of her costs. Thus *in the long run all costs are variable*.

To simplify this discussion, let's consider only the profit-making decisions Jane should make in the *short run*.

The Operating Rule: To Operate or Not to Operate

First, Jane has to decide whether she should produce any eggs at all at the market price of, we'll assume, 60 cents per dozen. Now we're going to play a game involving a model. Assume that Jane is operating in the short run. That is, she is faced with both fixed and variable costs, and she can make only two decisions: to produce no eggs at all or to produce 100 dozen per day.

Now suppose she realizes one morning that whereas her selling price is 60 cents per dozen, her total production cost is 70 cents per dozen. Remember that Jane is making decisions in the short run. What should she do?

Her total revenue is 100 dozen × 60 cents per day = $60. Her total cost is 100 dozen × 70 cents = $70, a loss of $10 per day.

Jane reaches for her handy hand calculator and determines that her variable costs (feed, workers, electricity) are $50 per day and that her fixed costs (taxes, insurance, mortgage payments) average $20 per day. Should Jane produce zero eggs or continue producing the 100 dozen per day?

Notice that while she produces, her loss is $10 per day, but that if she stops, her fixed costs of $20 per day will continue—in the short run. Thus, she is clearly better off continuing to produce the 100 dozen eggs—as long as we assume the *short* run.

(Obviously she can't go on losing $10 per day forever, but a decision to sell out is a long-run decision and our game is limited to the short run.)

Here is another example. Assume that Jane's total costs are $120 per day. Her variable costs are still $50 per day, but her fixed costs are now $70 a day. What should she do?

If she doesn't operate at all, she will lose the $70 per day in fixed costs. If she does operate, her total revenue will still be $60. Her loss will be $60 − $120 = −$60. She will lose $60 if she operates and $70 if she does not. She is $10 better off operating than not operating.

Notice that in the first example Jane's fixed costs were $20. In the second example her fixed costs were $70. Yet in both instances her *operating loss* (the loss incurred if she produced and sold the 100 dozen eggs) was the same, −$10.

Where does the $10 come from? The total revenue of $60 is, in both cases, $10 more than the variable costs. Thus Jane's revenue from sales more than covers the variable costs of producing the eggs. Jane can use the extra $10 to help pay her fixed costs.

Figures 9-2 and 9-3 may help you to visualize why Jane is $10 better off operating than not operating in the short run. Figure 9-2 illustrates the situation discussed first.

Figure 9-2 shows that Jane's decision to operate brings in enough total revenue to pay all variable costs plus half (see the shaded area) the fixed costs. She's definitely better off to operate in the short run.

The second situation with fixed costs at $70 is shown in Figure 9-3. Here we can see again that Jane is $10 better off to operate. Total revenue exceeds the variable costs by $10 (see the shaded area) and reduces the fixed costs by that

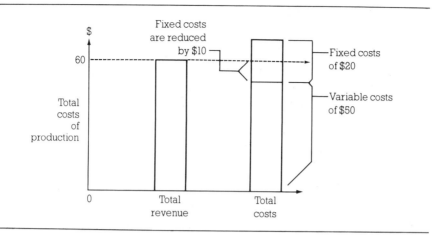

Figure 9-2.
Jane's total revenue is $60; fixed costs are $20; variable costs are $50.

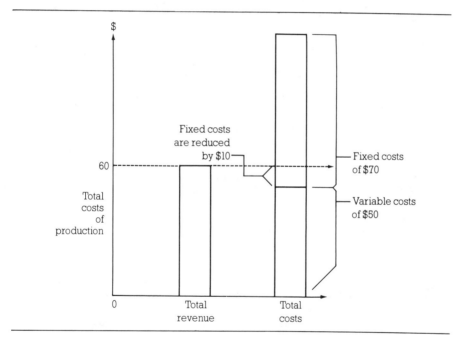

Figure 9-3.
Total revenue is $60; fixed costs are $70; variable costs are $50.

amount. Clearly, the key question in the short run is whether or not total revenue is sufficient to cover variable costs. Fixed costs are less important.

This discussion brings us to the rule for operating or not operating *in the short run.*

When total revenue is greater than variable costs in the short run, a business firm should continue to operate, even it it is losing money. If total revenue is less than the variable costs in the short run, the firm should not operate. The point at which total revenue is just equal to variable costs is called the **shut-down point**.

The discussion here is limited to the short run. If, in the long run, total revenue doesn't cover both variable *and* fixed costs, then the entrepreneur ought to sell out.

But the problem faced by many entrepreneurs with losing businesses is that they can't sell out as fast as they would like.* Then the question arises: Should they try to keep going even if the business is losing money? The operating rule says *yes* as long as the total revenue each day covers the variable costs of staying open. If total revenue doesn't cover variable costs, then board up the place and sell out as fast as possible.

This analysis leads us to the next rule. It explains how many units of a product a firm should produce in the short run in order to maximize profit or minimize loss. (We can drop the assumption that Jane must either produce zero or 100 dozen eggs.)

The Supply Decision Rule

Let's assume that the operating rule is satisfied and that Jane considers expanding production from 100 dozen per day to 120 dozen per day. Remember that Jane is too small to influence the market price, so the price, remains at 60 cents per dozen. The additional revenue she will get is 60 cents × the extra 20 dozen = $12. The extra revenue from the sale of each of these 20 dozen is called **marginal revenue** (MR). Marginal revenue is defined as the change in revenue when *one* more unit (of anything) is sold. In Jane's case, marginal revenue is 60 cents because total revenue increases by that much every time Jane sells one more dozen.

But what about Jane's costs of production? Fixed costs will remain the same, but variable costs (perhaps more chickens, feed, electricity, and labor) will change. The change in variable costs when *one* more dozen is produced is called **marginal cost** (MC).

Suppose marginal cost for the extra 20 dozen is 50 cents per dozen. The decision to produce 20 extra dozen will increase variable costs by 20 × 50 cents = $10, $2 less than the $12 of extra revenue Jane will receive when the 20 dozen are sold. Jane will be $2 better off to expand production by 20 dozen eggs.

> The supply decision rule is probably pretty obvious by now: Expand production as long as the extra revenue from increased sales exceeds the extra cost of production. More formally, economists say, *"Expand production in the short run as long as marginal revenue (MR) exceeds marginal cost (MC)."*

Applying the Supply Decision Rule

Once upon a time, Continental Airlines asked itself whether it should continue flying from city X to city Y even though it was losing money. To answer the question, it first determined what costs were marginal—extra costs solely connected with flying from city X to city Y. Then it determined the fixed costs associated with airport expenses, salaries, insurance, and depreciation—costs that would be incurred whether the flight went or not.

---

*We have in mind here a shopping area where many of the stores are going broke. Many are already boarded up with "For Sale" signs. Should the remaining entrepreneurs do the same, or continue to operate?

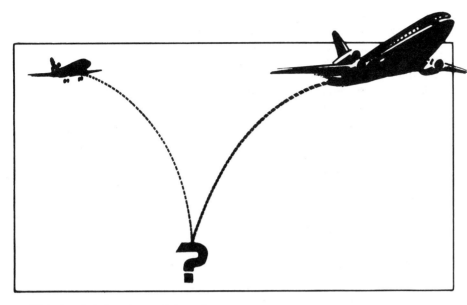

Continental Airlines had to analyze marginal and fixed costs for one of its flight routes.

This is what Continental found:

Total cost of one flight, city X to city Y	$4,500
Marginal costs only	2,000
Marginal revenue from the flight	3,100

Decision: Go—continue flying the route. Although the flight would lose $1,400 ($4,500 − $3,100), Continental would lose $2,500 if the flight *did not* go. Why? If total costs were $4,500 and marginal costs were $2,000, fixed cost that would be incurred, go or no-go, would be the difference—$2,500. By continuing the flight, Continental would earn $3,100—an excess of $1,100 over the marginal costs of $2,000. This extra $1,100 could be used to reduce the loss from $2,500 to $1,400.

So far, we have described a golden rule that all entrepreneurs should follow, whether they are in highly competitive markets or markets having some degree of monopoly. But the golden rule works just as well in everyday life. All it says is, "If the extra benefit of doing something is greater than the extra cost, then do it."

Suppose you are driving east from Los Angeles to Flagstaff, Arizona. Your eventual destination lies beyond: the Grand Canyon, Bryce Canyon, and Zion National Park. Should you take a twenty-mile detour north of Flagstaff to see the Sunset Crater National Monument? In deciding, should you consider the costs of getting to Flagstaff? No. These are fixed costs that will not change whether you visit the Sunset craters or not. They have already been incurred. You should consider only the extra or marginal cost of the detour (gas and oil plus opportunity cost of time spent) and compare that extra cost with the extra satisfaction of seeing the craters.

What's your vote? *You* decide. This question brings up a problem we mentioned before. We often have difficulty measuring the extra costs and benefits because they're unknown. Entrepreneurs are in the same boat. They have to estimate as best they can.

The Importance of "Thinking Marginal"

The idea of "marginality"—of looking at the costs and benefits of any decision to do something extra or additional—is one of the most important ideas in economics, right up there with demand, supply, and elasticity. "Marginal" refers to the last or extra unit of something. We look at this extra unit and try to decide whether the increase in satisfaction it provides will exceed the increase in the cost of obtaining it.

When economists analyze a public issue like an energy crisis or pollution, the bottom-line question is, "Will the additional (marginal) social benefit that results from XYZ policy justify the additional (marginal) cost of doing it?"

Economists also refer to "marginal" people. For example, if your college decides to raise parking fees (or any fee), there will be some students for whom that last expense is the "last straw" that causes them to change their behavior in some important way—perhaps even to drop out. Another usage: If gas prices go up and rapid transit becomes more available, some people "at the margin" will switch from cars to rapid transit. Economists will try to estimate how many people there are at the margin in determining whether or not taxpayers should subsidize rapid transit and if so, how large the subsidy should be.

We have seen the two golden rules of profit-maximizing theory: (1) Operate only if total revenue exceeds total variable costs; and (2) expand production as long as marginal revenue exceeds marginal cost. In the next two sections we want to explain the benefits to society and often to business firms of charging different prices (often called "variable prices") for the same product or service.

In the first of these two sections we'll show how variable prices can ration scarce goods and services when many different demand curves exist for the same good or service. In the second section we'll show how business firms can take advantage of variable pricing to increase their profits.

WHY VARIABLE PRICING
IS A USEFUL RATIONING DEVICE

All but one of the supply curves so far involve the assumption that the quantity supplied increases as the price increases; the supply curves rise from left to right. (An exception occurs in the "Case of Eggs" discussion on page 165.) What does this mean? It means that entrepreneurs (1) are able and (2) have the time to increase production when the price rises. The rising supply curve also indicates that higher and higher prices are necessary to persuade the entrepreneur to increase production. Consequently, the rising supply curve usually means that the per-unit costs of production are increasing. (Can you visualize a supply curve that slopes *down* from left to right? What would that suggest about production costs? Costs per unit must be decreasing, perhaps because of automation—more efficient production at larger outputs.)

When entrepreneurs can change the quantities they supply in response to changes in demand, we say that supply is **variable**. However, there are many examples in the real world of **fixed** supply—situations where the quantity supplied cannot change, particularly in a short period of time.

Examples of fixed supply are the number of parking spaces at your college or in your town, the number of hospital beds, theater seats, miles of roads or freeways, airport runways, TV repairmen, power lines, doctors, miles of sewer pipe, and so on. On any given day, the quantity of these things or people is

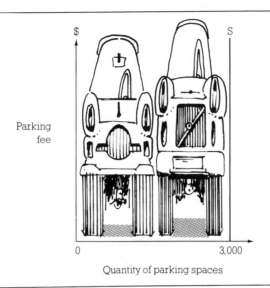

Figure 9-4.
Fixed supply at 3,000
parking spaces.

fixed regardless of the price people are willing to pay for them. Another good example of fixed supply is a work of art or a famous landmark. There is only one original Mona Lisa or Leaning Tower of Pisa. Finally, fixed supply frequently involves land. In your community there is a fixed amount of land available, whether it is used for industrial expansion, home building, or golf courses. Still another example of fixed supply occurred in Chapter 5. When Amelia brought her first coffee mug to her economics class, supply was fixed. There was only one coffee mug.

When supply is fixed, what does the supply curve look like? Answer—it's straight up and down, given one important assumption: We have to assume we're dealing with an instant in time. For that instant, the number of plumbers, gardeners, doctors, theater seats, and parking spaces in your community is fixed—regardless of the market price. Here is a picture of a supply curve showing that at an instant in time (say, today at 9 A.M.) there are 3,000 parking spaces at your college. Supply is fixed at that quantity (Figure 9-4).

It doesn't matter what the parking fee is; for a moment in time there will be only 3,000 spaces. On another day, the number could be different, if the college has sufficient time to develop more parking spaces.

Variable Prices and Parking Spaces

Now suppose that the parking fee is $15 per semester. At peak hours, 5,000 students want to park. Figure 9-5 illustrates the problem: At $15 there is a shortage of 2,000 parking spaces. E stands for the equilibrium price (parking fee). What can we do to eliminate the shortage? One solution is to raise the parking fee. There is some fee—at equilibrium—that will eliminate the shortage. Here again the exclusion principle plays a role. Poorer students ("at the margin") will be forced into car-pooling or other means of transportation. This is a short-run solution. The college may eventually have to build more parking lots or garages (shifting supply to the right).

This kind of problem can often become more complicated. Suppose you live in a town with 3,000 parking spaces. The parking meters charge 10 cents per

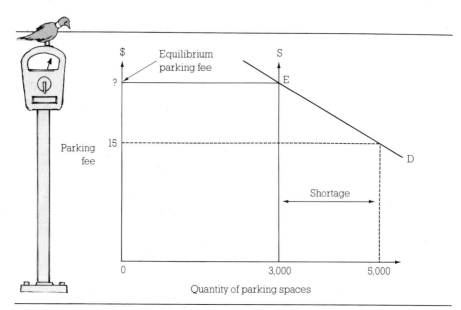

Figure 9-5.
Fixed supply and
equilibrium price for
parking spaces.

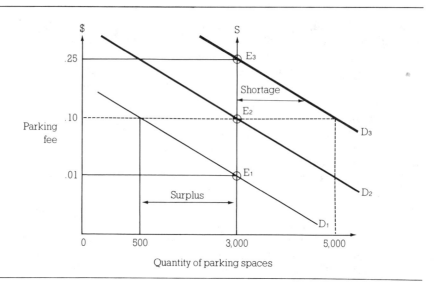

Figure 9-6.
Fixed supply and
changing demand.

hour. Between the hours of 9 P.M. and 9 A.M., 500 people want to park. Between 9 A.M. and 4 P.M., 5,000 people want to park. And between 4 P.M. and 9 P.M., 3,000 people want to park. Figure 9-6 illustrates the situation. D_1 represents the 9 P.M. to 9 A.M. demand, D_2 the 4 P.M. to 9 P.M. demand, and D_3 the 9 A.M. to 4 P.M. demand. E_1 represents the equilibrium price for D_1, E_2 the equilibrium price of D_2, and E_3 the equilibrium price of D_3.

At 10 cents per hour, D_1 shows us there will be a surplus of 2,500 parking spaces (the difference between the 500 demanded and the 3,000 available). During those hours, the parking fee could be lowered to 1 cent per hour without causing a shortage of space. The 10-cent charge is just right for D_2, but for D_3 there will be a shortage of 2,000 spaces at 10 cents. Raising the fee to perhaps 25 cents during the most popular shopping hours might solve the

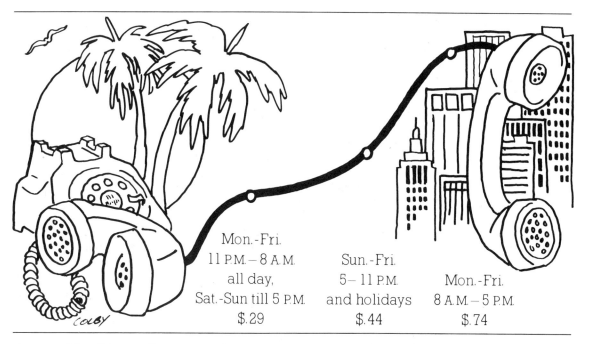

Mon.-Fri.
11 P.M. – 8 A.M.
all day,
Sat.-Sun till 5 P.M.
$.29

Sun.-Fri.
5– 11 P.M.
and holidays
$.44

Mon.-Fri.
8 A.M. – 5 P.M.
$.74

Figure 9-7.
Long distance
telephone rates for
direct-dial calls from
Los Angeles to New
York (first minute only
as of August 1982).

shortage. The diagram illustrates an important principle: Variable prices will solve shortages and surpluses at different times or places. What the town needs is a parking meter designed to show "violation" unless money is inserted in an amount appropriate for the time of day.

Telephone Charges

A familiar real-world example of the use of variable prices (where the supply is fixed) is the long distance telephone rate schedule. Supply is fixed because at any moment in time there are only so many telephone circuits between two points. Figure 9-7 shows how the telephone company uses variable prices.

As in the parking-space example, variable prices can help ration a scarce resource regardless of different demand curves (and, undoubtedly, different elasticities) at different times of the day or night. Lower charges reward telephone-users for phoning during off-peak hours.

Two more examples: We could get rid of freeway traffic jams by charging people variable prices for using the freeway—higher prices during peak hours; lower prices or no prices for driving during off-peak hours. Suppose each car had a small transmitter sending signals to networks of computers indicating time and distance traveled. At the end of each month, the driver would get a bill based on miles of freeway driving with variable charges based on time of day. The British use such a system for keeping track of railway cars—and recently a similar system began a "trial run" on a toll highway in Hong Kong. Similarly, traffic jams on toll bridges could be eliminated by charging high prices at peak hours; low prices otherwise.

The Economic Theory of Variable Pricing

Let's return to Figure 9-6 and look at D₂, the demand for parking spaces during the 4 P.M. to 9 P.M. evening hours. During that time period, 10 cents is the equilibrium parking fee. If we turn the clock back to, say, 10 A.M., we find that the number of potential buyers (demanders) of parking spaces has increased tremendously. At 10 A.M., the demand for parking spaces has increased, and a new equilibrium price is necessary to equalize the quantities demanded and supplied.

And so our first, and probably obvious, economic concept is that variable prices are needed to ration scarce resources where there are differences in demand. The differences in demand occur because of differences in time (telephones and parking spaces), differences in location (parking lots close to football games), differences in activity (hot dogs at baseball games, popcorn at movies), and so forth. At the right time and place or during the right activities, resource-owners (entrepreneurs) can charge lots more than usual for their scarce commodities.

Perhaps less obvious is the fact that each demand curve is the summation of individual demand curves having different elasticities. Figure 7-2 on page 130 is a reminder that at higher prices, any given demand curve is more elastic than at lower prices. Consequently, as the price goes up (to squeeze more money out of those who can pay), elasticity increases. The increase in elasticity is simply another way of saying that higher prices result in greater variations in the quantities demanded.

The reason for greater elasticity at higher prices is that one of the important measures of elasticity is the price as a percentage of the buyer's income. The greater this percentage, the greater the elasticity, and the greater the buyer's reaction to price changes. Moreover, the *lower* one's income, the greater the price will be as a percentage of income. *To recap:* The higher the price and the lower the income, the greater the elasticity of demand.

Now we can make the point: The higher the price, the lower the income, the more lower-income people will respond to higher prices by excluding themselves from the market, the more elastic their demand curves will be, and the more apt they will be to refuse to pay a higher price. Consequently, variable prices will have greater effect on people with higher elasticities of demand, the cause of which is lower income.

Nonetheless, variable prices are an efficient and often socially desirable means of rationing scarce resources. Variable phone rates mean less inconvenience to phone users from busy circuits, and the telephone company doesn't have to build as many new phone lines that, moreover, would stand idle during times of low demand. Variable tolls for toll bridges mean fewer traffic jams and less need for new bridges. But remember that there is always a cost for any economic decision. Variable prices will mean that some people "at the margin" will be forced to change their behavior in some, for them, unwanted way.

WHY BUSINESS FIRMS ENGAGE IN VARIABLE PRICING TO INCREASE THEIR PROFITS

The previous section has illustrated how variable prices can be used to ration a scarce resource. The probable motive of the resource-owner was as much to conserve a scarce resource as to delight stockholders with bigger profits. In this section, we want to show how variable prices can increase profits.

The practice by which entrepreneurs charge different prices for the same product is often called **price discrimination**. The entrepreneur is discriminating *against* the buyer who had to pay the high price and *in favor* of the buyer who is charged the low price.

Our discussion of price discrimination is divided into six parts: (1) The definition of price discrimination, (2) why entrepreneurs discriminate, (3) a case study of the Velvetex Paint Company, (4) marginal-cost pricing, (5) private labeling, and (6) the question of legality.

Price Discrimination: What It Is

Price discrimination is the sale of essentially the same product or service to different buyers, or even the same buyer, *by the same seller* at different prices. Typically, price discrimination occurs when a manufacturer sells a given product (say, a brand of lipstick) to different stores at different prices. A common form of price discrimination is the quantity discount. For example, a store may charge the same buyers less per can for, say, Coca-Cola, when it is bought in a six-pack than when a can is bought singly—and still less per can in case lots. Cartons of cigarettes cost less per pack than single packs. The price per ounce of *anything* is usually less, the larger the container. And if you find that a size 8 dress sells for the same price as a size 18, the cost per yard of material is much less in the larger-size dress.

Other examples of price discrimination are lower prices for movie and theater matinees than for evening performances. The theory here is that the demand for theater seats is not as high in the daytime as at night. Differences in demand may also account for differences in movie ticket prices for adults and children.

We need to be careful about one point. If *different stores* sell a given brand of, say, frozen orange juice at different prices, no price discrimination is involved because there are many sellers. The stores are simply competing with one another. But if the *manufacturer* of a given brand sells at different prices to different stores, then the manufacturer is practicing price discrimination in favor of some buyers and against others.

In the strictest economic sense, price discrimination is defined as charging different prices for exactly the same good or service. We will expand this definition to include the sale of *essentially similar* products that may vary somewhat in costs of production, delivery, or sales.

For example, consider a two-door, six-cylinder, stick-shift, 100-horsepower, compact car with radio and heater that sells for $11,000. This is the economy version. Now assume the manufacturer adds some chrome, racing stripes, and more expensive seat covers. These added features cost the manufacturer perhaps $350, but this deluxe version sells for $12,000. The two cars are *almost the same*, but they are styled and priced to appeal to two different kinds of buyers.

This form of price discrimination is used widely on deluxe and economy versions of appliances of all types. It is also used in marketing many household products.

We define price discrimination, therefore, as the sale of the same, or almost the same, products or services by the same seller at different prices, where the price differences cannot be accounted for by cost differences.

Why Does the Entrepreneur Discriminate?

What would you say if you paid $1 for toothpaste and then learned from a friend

Table 9-1. Prices Six Students Would Pay for a Stereo Set

If the price were . . .	Number of students who would pay this price or a higher price
$650	0*
600	1
500	2
450	3
400	4
300	5
150	6

* At $650, no students want to buy.

that, on the same day, from the same store, he had bought the same toothpaste for 60 cents? You might be angry enough to complain to the store owner. If a similar incident involved a large amount of money, you might take the store owner to court and sue him for unfair treatment. Yet entrepreneurs engage in such practices all the time. The reason is simple: By doing so they will make more money.

To help you understand where the extra money comes from, imagine six college students, each wanting very badly to buy the same brand-new stereo set. Without knowing the price at the local stereo store, each student says to him or herself, "I would be willing to pay . . . for the stereo." The maximum amounts each student would pay are shown in Table 9-1.

Table 9-1 is a demand schedule, because it shows the number of stereo sets that would be purchased at each price. If we were to graph this schedule, the demand curve would slope downward from left to right. More stereos can be sold at lower prices. A sloping demand curve* means that the market is "imperfect" and that entrepreneurs have sufficient market power to select their own price (a necessary condition for price discrimination).

Let's look at Table 9-1. If the stereo store has announced a price of $400, only four of the six students will buy the stereo set; two students will be excluded. The store's total revenue will be 4 × $400 = $1,600. *But,* why shouldn't the store consider what its total revenue could be if it sold the stereos *one at a time?* To put it another way, what if the entrepreneur could extract from each purchaser a price that matched the amount each purchaser was willing to pay? If the entrepreneur could find variable prices that would accomplish this noble objective, he would take in the amounts shown in Table 9-2.

Suppose the stereo store could extract all the money over $400 that each student was willing to pay. The store's total revenue would rise from $1,600 (400 × 4) to $1,950 ($600 + $500 + $450 + $400). The latter route, **variable pricing,** is obviously the only way to fly if consumers can be approached one at a time. Figure 9-8 illustrates this situation.

The demand curve starts at $650 to show that at $650 no stereo sets could be sold to the six students. The demand curve continues past the store's price of

---

*When the demand curve for a firm's product is perfectly flat, as it was in Figure 9-1 on page 171, the firm has no control over the price; the firm is a price *taker.* When the demand curve has a slope, the firm can decide (be a "price maker") whether to sell more units at lower prices or fewer at higher prices.

Table 9-2. Variable Prices for Stereo Sets

	Price	Number of students who would pay each price in excess of $400
	$600	1
	500	1
	450	1
	400	1
Totals	$1,950	4

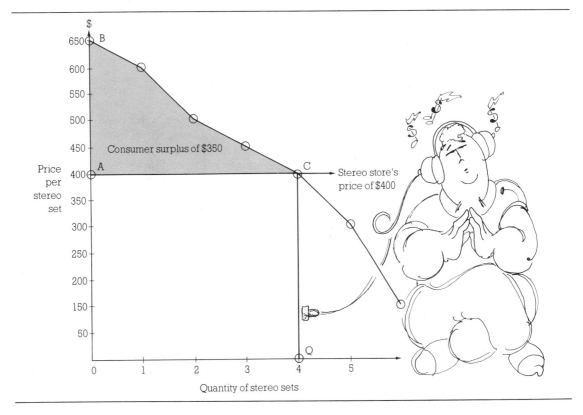

$400 to show the lower amounts two of the students would pay. At $400, these two students are excluded.

With uniform pricing at $400, the store's total revenue will be $1,600, as indicated by the rectangle, 0ACQ. But if the store can engage in variable pricing, its total revenue will rise to $1,950, as shown in Table 9-2. This extra $350 is shown by the irregular, shaded triangle ABC in Figure 9-8. The shaded triangle is called the **consumer surplus.** The consumers who would have been willing to pay a higher price than $400 receive a *surplus* of satisfaction over and above the cost of the set.

Clearly, all good entrepreneurs should spend a good deal of time planning how they can pocket the consumer surplus.

To be successful, price-discriminating firms must satisfy two prerequisites:

Figure 9-8.
Total revenue with uniform pricing versus total revenue with variable pricing.

1. They must have the market power to set prices. Price discrimination isn't possible in highly competitive markets; buyers would be stupid to pay high prices when many firms are offering the same product at lower prices.

2. Somehow, price-discriminating firms must be careful not to let those paying the high price become aware of the existence of the low price. One firm in our experience learned this principle the hard way, as the following story indicates.

The Perils of Price Discrimination: The Case of Velvetex Paint

Once upon a time (in the 1940s) there was a paint manufacturing company called Velvetex.* The Velvetex Company was one of the early discoverers of water-base paint—no fuss, no muss, the paint dries in thirty minutes, etc., etc. The company introduced its line of water-base paint with extensive advertising. The label on the paint can was colorful and expensive.

At first, competition was minimal, and the name and the paint soon caught on. Three hundred paint stores in the Los Angeles area bought the line. But soon other companies began to compete, because water-base paint is easy to make (the entry barriers are low). Dozens of competitors entered the fray. The supply curve shifted to the right, driving the price down. Gradually, Velvetex began to lose sales because it no longer had something special to offer.

At about this time, Velvetex paint was retailing at $6.95 per gallon. Paint stores purchased the paint from the factory for $4.50 a gallon. In order to increase sales, Velvetex decided to price-discriminate—to sell some of the paint in plain cans at lower prices as a new line for paint contractors. The "new" line of paint was called Commercial Formula. The black-and-white label was austere, businesslike. The paint received almost no advertising and was attractively priced for volume sales; paint stores bought Commercial Formula for $3.50 and sold it to painting contractors for $4.95.

Can you guess what happened? Probably. Since the same stores were buying Velvetex and Commercial Formula, they eventually realized that the two lines of paint were the same. (Information costs were not high enough.) They stopped buying Velvetex, bought only Commercial Formula, and sold it to retail customers for $5.95 while continuing to price it at $4.95 for contractors.

Velvetex's paint-store clients gradually substituted Commercial Formula for Velvetex, and the company found that it was selling no more paint than before and was making less money doing it. Furthermore, the paint stores became steadily angrier as more and more reports circulated that Velvetex could be purchased at retail at a variety of prices below $6.95. Velvetex's formerly loyal customers began to drop the line and pick up others with more uniform sales policies.

What was the colossal mistake? It was that Velvetex did not sell at different prices in *different markets*. The same paint stores bought both lines and merely substituted the cheaper line for the more expensive one.

Sales of both lines began to plunge, and so Velvetex made one last attempt at price discrimination. This time Velvetex decided to sell some of the paint to Premier Paint Stores, a large chain of discount paint dealers, at a much lower

---

*The company and brand names are fictitious; the story is sad but true.

Premier painted Velvetex out of its marketing picture by producing its own line of vinyl finish paint.

price. The agreement was that Premier would bring truckloads of its own cans with its own "Vinyl Finish" label to the Velvetex factory. Velvetex would fill the cans at a price of $1.50 per gallon. Premier would retail the paint through its chain of stores for $2.95, with an excellent profit margin of 49 percent of the retail price (excluding the cost of the can, transportation, and handling).

One would think that Velvetex's regular customers would hear of this and threaten to discontinue the line. Curiously, that did not happen. Velvetex had found a separate market. (Information costs about Premier's operations were high.) Few complaints were heard at the factory. The business with Premier almost doubled Velvetex's sales, reaching 40,000 gallons of paint per month to Premier alone.

But after six months, a Premier executive phoned Velvetex and said, "Awfully sorry, we've decided to make our own line of Vinyl Finish. It's been nice doing business with you." One year later, after continuing loss of sales, Velvetex gave up and went out of business.

The Supply Decision Rule Again

Was the Premier agreement a good idea? From the standpoint of price discrimination, it was. Judging from the very few complaints received, the Premier stores constituted a separate market. Sales to Premier, while they lasted, were *extra* sales; they did not subtract from regular sales.

But how profitable was the arrangement? Counting everything, executive salaries, taxes, insurance, and other expenses, it cost Velvetex about $2.50 to manufacture a gallon of paint. Why would Velvetex want to sell it for $1.50?

It happened that the *extra* (marginal) variable costs of producing the paint—mainly materials—were $1.40 per gallon. (The additional paint could be produced with the same number of workers.) When Premier agreed to pay

$1.50 per gallon, marginal costs of $1.40 were exceeded by 10 cents. By selling 40,000 gallons of paint per month to Premier, Velvetex made an extra $4,000 (40,000 × 10 cents) that could be used to pay some of its fixed costs. Even though the transaction was a losing proposition, Velvetex's loss was $4,000 less than it would have been if it had not sold to Premier. Of course, Velvetex could not continue this practice indefinitely (beyond the short run), because it was losing money. But for a while, it makes sense to heed the idea that one should expand output up to the point where the extra (marginal) revenue exceeds or is equal to marginal cost (see page 174 for a refresher). Velvetex's decision making was just as valid as Continental's when it decided to fly between Cities X and Y.

Premier's Power over Velvetex

One other point needs to be made. Velvetex allowed itself to become heavily involved with one buyer, Premier, which bought half of its output.

This was a risky arrangement. At any time, Premier could have asked for extras like special packaging or free delivery and Velvetex would have been stuck with higher costs. Velvetex depended too strongly on Premier and unwisely neglected to develop other markets.

When buyers of a product are powerful enough to exercise control over a seller, economists say there is an element of **monopsony** present. Whereas monopoly means one seller, monopsony means one buyer. Monopsony also exists in labor markets if employers (buyers of labor) are large enough to influence the wage rate. Velvetex should have been wary of the monopsonistic relationship with Premier.

Another Kind of Price Discrimination: Private Labeling

The Velvetex story, however disastrous, provides an example of another business practice, one that is extremely common. When the Premier Paint Store chain sold Velvetex under its own "Vinyl Finish" label, it was engaging in **private labeling**. There are probably very few large manufacturers who do not engage in a private labeling arrangement with firms that can provide large retail sales.

When a store puts its name on a package rather than the manufacturer's brand name (that is, when it is engaging in private labeling), there is no way of telling who made the product. At another store or even in the same store (as in the Velvetex case) the identical product may be on display under a different label.

The most visible examples of private labeling occur at large chain supermarkets and drugstores. Why do manufacturers choose large chain stores for private-label arrangements? If manufacturers must furnish privately labeled products for too many small accounts, their production lines are constantly interrupted to permit label switching. A manufacturer needs long production runs with a few large accounts to make private labeling pay.

Unfortunately, there is no way of determining that the private-label item is exactly the same as the national brand. Even when appearance, listed ingredients, and many other visible clues suggest that the two versions of the product are identical, one never knows for sure. Information costs are present. With this caution in mind, Table 9-3 shows some examples of national brand and private label prices at the local supermarket (August 1982).

Table 9-3. National Brand Prices vs. Private Label Prices

Item	Size	National brand price	Store label price	"Econo-buy" label*
White bread	1 lb.	$ .83	$ .59	
Monterey Jack cheese	1 lb.	2.83	2.59	
Low fat cottage cheese	1 pint	1.09	.88	
Butter	1 lb.	2.29	1.99	
Sandwich bags	150	1.03	.82	
Paper towels	120 sheets	.89	.71	
Pineapple juice	46 oz.	1.09	.99	
Sweet peas	17 oz. can	.53	.49	
Tea bags	100	2.19	1.94	$1.61
Facial tissue	200	.89	.65	.59
Diet drink	14 oz. can	.30	.24	
Frozen orange juice	16 oz.	1.75	1.29	

*The "Econo-buy" label did not even have the store's name on the container.

It is precisely because there will be some doubt in buyers' minds about the possible differences between national brands and their private-label counterparts that manufacturers can often successfully sell the same product under different labels at different prices. Some buyers will be motivated more by the advertising that pushes the national brand than they will be by the lower price on the private label. They will be willing to pay a higher price for the security they feel in buying a brand name. Other buyers will be willing to take a chance on the lower-priced, private-label brand. The two kinds of buyers support the "separateness" of the two markets—even in the same store.

Any manufacturer who engages in extensive private labeling must be aware of the possibility that consumers will stop buying the more expensive, nationally advertised version and buy only the cheaper, private-label version. On a national scale, manufacturers can undoubtedly get away with this practice because they sell to thousands of small accounts that carry only the national-brand version. Only a few very large accounts will be given the opportunity to buy at lower prices for private labeling purposes. In this way, the separateness of the low-priced and high-priced markets is preserved.

Private labeling may seem vaguely dishonest to you; but remember, if entrepreneurs can price their products so as to cover the marginal costs of the extra production involved in private-label sales, there is sound economic reason for engaging in this extra business.

The Question of Legality

Ever since John D. Rockefeller, Sr., founded Standard Oil, price discrimination has been, for many, a sinful term. In 1867, Rockefeller had gained control of a large oil refinery in Cleveland and was using railroads as his main method of transporting refined oil to other states. To lower the freight costs, he went to certain railroad companies and proposed to each one that he would ship all of his company's oil on that railroad in return for a special discount on freight rates. Since there were several competing rail lines anxious for his business, Rockefeller got his way and soon was receiving a rebate of 15 cents a barrel on the oil that he shipped. (In fact, he even received a similar rebate for every barrel his competitors shipped!)

Having thus persuaded certain railroads to price-discriminate in his favor, Rockefeller then went to competing oil refineries and offered to get the same shipping rebates for them in return for being allowed to buy controlling interest in their refineries (usually at a very low price). If they refused to sell, he told them that he would make sure that the railroads continued to charge them higher freight rates. Because freight charges were such a large portion of oil refining costs, one refinery after another gave in and sold control to Rockefeller. By 1904, Rockefeller's Standard Oil Company was refining more than 84 percent of the crude oil in the United States.[1]

The Clayton Act of 1914

Published exposés of Rockefeller's practices and similar tactics ultimately led to passage of the **Clayton Act of 1914,** briefly mentioned in the previous chapter. The Clayton Act made several business practices illegal, such as price discrimination, rebates, exclusive sales contracts, and interlocking directorates. The difficulty was that Congress qualified their illegality by adding a "weasel" phrase: The acts were illegal only "where the effect will be substantially to lessen competition or tend to create a monopoly." Because the courts have had an impossible job in trying to decide what "lessen competition" really means, the Clayton Act has been largely ineffective. Nevertheless, the Clayton Act created a powerful weapon: the Federal Trade Commission. Today the Federal Trade Commission (FTC) is responsible for prosecuting violators of the Clayton Act as well as violators of many other federal laws. Among other things, the FTC tries to make sure that advertising is truthful.

The Robinson-Patman Act of 1936

In 1936, Congress again attempted to curb price discrimination by passing the **Robinson-Patman Act.*** The Clayton Act was supposed to eliminate the practice whereby producers charged different prices to different buyers in order to put competing producers out of business. Called the "chain store law," the Robinson-Patman Act tried to prevent wholesalers from giving extra discounts to chain stores, a practice contributing to the failure of small retailers.

If anything, the Act further muddied the waters,** because the Act helped to spell out situations where price discrimination was possible. The Act provided three legal loopholes for price discrimination:

1. The Robinson-Patman Act retained the Clayton Act's weasel phrase about "substantially lessening competition."
2. The Act excuses price discrimination where the seller can show differences in the cost of sales.
3. The Act excuses price discrimination where the seller can show that the lower price is necessary to meet the equally low prices of competitors.

---

*The Robinson-Patman Act was an amendment to Section 2 of the Clayton Act.

**Several books have been written about the Robinson-Patman Act and the case law stemming from it. A short but over-condensed (for nonexperts) source is: Cyrus Austin, *Price Discrimination and Related Problems Under the Robinson-Patman Act* (Philadelphia: American Law Institute, 2nd rev. ed., 1959). In a preface, Mr. Austin calls the Robinson-Patman Act "an ineptly drawn statute, containing many ambiguities and inconsistencies."

SUMMARY

If entrepreneurs can learn to identify fixed costs, average costs, marginal costs, and marginal revenue, they can cut their losses or increase their profits. Two rules should be observed: (1) enterprises should shut down if total revenue is less than total variable cost, and (2) output should be increased as long as marginal cost is less than marginal revenue.

Variable prices can be used by companies or government agencies to ration scarce resources like parking lots, toll bridges, or, possibly, freeways. Companies like the telephone company can use variable prices to persuade people to make more calls in off-peak hours.

If an entrepreneur's market is sufficiently imperfect, the practice of price discrimination can further be used to increase profits or to cut losses. Price discrimination is defined as the sale of the same, or almost the same, products or services by the same seller at different prices, where the price differences cannot be accounted for by cost differences.

Enterprises use price discrimination to increase total revenue. If enterprises can find some buyers for their product at higher prices and other buyers at lower prices, they stand to take in more money than if they charge the same price to all customers.

Price discrimination may be accomplished in several ways—by charging different amounts for the same product at different times, in different places, for different quantities, or for different groups of customers or by selling deluxe and standard versions of essentially the same item. When different groups are charged different rates, the producer needs to keep these groups separate so that those who pay the higher rate do not become hostile or start buying at the lower rate. Information costs must be high. Many producers keep their buyers separate by selling their product under different brand names or labels—selling the product with a well-advertised brand name at a higher price than a similar item that is distributed by a chain store under the chain store's label. When a chain store or other distributor puts its own label on a product, the practice is called private labeling.

A producer may be willing to sell a product at less than its full cost so long as the price is above the marginal cost of production. The producer has to pay fixed costs anyway, and sales at prices above the marginal cost reduce fixed costs by the amount the price exceeds marginal costs. A marginal-cost pricing policy can lead to price discrimination if a manufacturer sells the bulk of his production at a high price, covering his total costs, and an additional portion at a lower price that still exceeds his marginal costs.

Laws like the Clayton Act have been passed to limit price discrimination, but they have not been very effective. The Robinson-Patman Act permits price discrimination in some situations.

Discussion Questions

1. Assume that you operate a business; that total revenue per week is $10,000, total fixed costs per week are $8,000, and total variable costs per week are $9,000. Should you continue to operate in the short run or not? How much do you lose if you do operate? Or if you don't operate? Be able to explain your answers.

2. What conditions are necessary for price discrimination to be successful? Why did Velvetex fail?

3. Are there types of price discrimination that may help the poor? Suppose your doctor charges the rich more than the poor. Ask him if he does and why.

4. If you were a small manufacturer producing Immortality, a skin cream for women over forty, would you engage in price discrimination? Why or why not? How would you go about it? Assume your production is 100 three-ounce jars per hour.

5. Again, as the manufacturer of Immortality, what should you think about if a chain of local health food stores asks you to sell the product to them under a private label?

6. Do you think it is fair for manufacturers to sell their products to big stores at lower prices than they charge small stores? Explain.

DID YOU EVER WONDER WHY . . .

. . . theaters have lower ticket prices for children and the aged?

References

1. Arthur S. Link, *American Epoch,* 3rd ed., Vol. 1 (New York: Alfred A. Knopf, 1963), p. 6.

2. Cyrus Austin, *Price Discrimination and Related Problems Under the Robinson-Patman Act,* 2nd rev. ed. (Philadelphia: The Joint Committee on Continuing Legal Education of the American Law Institute and the American Bar Association, 1959), p. 6.

CHAPTER

10

Power to the Worker:
A Study of Labor Markets

KEY WORDS
Derived demand
Labor productivity
Labor union
Open shop
Wagner Act (1935)
Closed shop
Taft-Hartley Act (1947)
Union shop
Landrum-Griffin Act (1958)
Quality circle
Theory Z

In the last two chapters we focused on the efforts of business firms to achieve market power and to use that power to increase their profits. Now we will shift our attention to problems faced by workers. Like the business firms that hire them, workers also want to escape the conditions imposed on them by the impersonal forces of competitive markets. Exactly as in the "case of eggs," workers try to increase their market power over employers by banding together ("SWEP" was, in effect a producers' "union") and by pressuring legislators to enact legislation that will improve their bargaining power, their wages, and their working conditions.

In all previous chapters our emphasis has been on the markets for products, on the attitudes of buyers (demanders) and sellers (suppliers) of those products. The goal has always been to see how the forces of demand and supply determine the price of the product, and how the price, in turn, determines how many units will be bought and sold. This chapter continues that same line of inquiry but with one major difference: We are no longer dealing with product prices but with the price of a factor of production—in this case, labor. And when we analyze labor markets, we find that the business firm is no longer the seller but is now the buyer, the demander of labor. And workers are now the sellers, the suppliers of their services.

In order to show how workers obtain market power and what they do with it when they get it, we have divided the chapter into four sections: (1) How wages are determined when workers have no market power, (2) how wages can be increased above free-market levels, (3) the labor union movement, and (4) recent changes in labor markets.

WAGE DETERMINATION WHEN WORKERS HAVE NO MARKET POWER

In this section we will pretend that the labor market is perfectly competitive, that no labor unions exist. By a perfectly competitive labor market, we mean one in which (1) the market price (the wage) is free to change without interference by any government agency, trade association of employers, or group of workers (like a union); (2) no one employer or worker has any power to change the prevailing wage of those in a given occupation—say, babysitters; (3) no forces prevent employers from wanting to buy (hire workers) or prevent workers from offering their services. By this last condition we mean that employers are ready to hire any worker regardless of skin color, age, or race, and that workers do not face any barriers to entry into an occupation, like occupational licenses to buy, tests to pass, or unions to join.

Under these circumstances, the wage is determined entirely by the forces of demand and supply. Suppose we are thinking of the wage for babysitters. Like any price, this wage will be determined at that point where the number of babysitters demanded by parents exactly equals the number of babysitters who wish to work (supply their services) at that wage. The analysis of how the wage is determined is exactly like the analysis an equilibrium price back in Chapter 5.

Assume Figure 10-1 represents the demand for and the supply of babysitting labor (a perfectly competitive market) in some city on a Saturday night.

As the figure indicates, the wage for babysitters will tend toward an equilibrium level of $1.50. Above that wage, the number of babysitters who want to work exceeds the number demanded; the unemployed babysitters will offer to

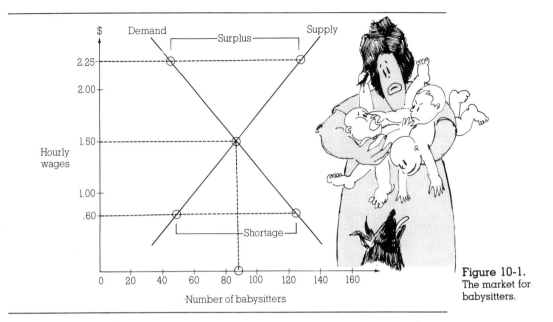

Figure 10-1.
The market for babysitters.

work for less as long as the wage is above $1.50. Below the wage of $1.50, the number of babysitters demanded exceeds the number supplied. The parents who fail to find babysitters at wages below $1.50 will bid the wage up. Ultimately, this market for babysitters will reach an equilibrium wage of $1.50 where 90 babysitters want to work and where that many are demanded.

In highly competitive labor markets, equilibrium wages are determined in this way. The *actual* wage may be higher or lower, depending upon other noncompetitive conditions we will discuss later. However, the level of this competitive wage and the number of jobs depends upon the relationships of labor demand and labor supply. Graphically, the wage level depends upon the location of the demand and supply curves.

The Demand for Labor

To understand the demand for labor, remember Chapter 5: think again about your demand for some major purchase—one that takes a lot of thought. For example, consider buying an expensive guitar, one costing over $1,000. (A conversation about such a purchase took place recently between a student and the author.) What *are* the major factors in making such a purchase? We settled on three factors:

   1. The price of the guitar.
   2. The opportunity cost of the guitar. (What is the value of all the things sacrificed when the guitar is purchased?)
   3. The student's *present and expected* levels of income and wealth.

If we assume that all these factors are favorable and that our student buys the guitar, we know that one point on the student's individual demand curve has been located. When the same factors are considered by everyone in the market

for such guitars, a market demand curve for many such guitars can be visual-
ized. Our point is that the three factors that dictate *anyone's* demand for *anything* determine the initial location of the demand curve.

A very similar set of three factors determines any employer's demand for
labor:

1. The price of labor; that is, the wage the employer will have to pay.
2. The opportunity cost of using labor, as compared with producing the
employer's product or service some other way; for example, with less labor
and more land or capital (machines).
3. The employer's *present and expected* level of profit from the use of
labor.

These three factors will determine the location of the employer's demand
curve for labor, precisely as they did the student's for the guitar. But notice an
important difference between the demand for the guitar and the demand for
labor. The third factor, the employer's present and expected level of profit,
indicates that an employer's demand for labor *depends* on the profitability of
the product or service that the employer product or service that the employer
produces. If demand for the product or service is high, the chances are that
profits will increase and that the employer will demand more labor (and more
of other resources). And vice versa. Because the demand for labor depends so
much on the demand for the product or service being produced, we call the
demand for labor (and the demand for any resource) a **derived demand**.

And now a definition of the demand for labor: *The demand for labor is a
schedule that shows us the number of workers that will be hired at all possible
wages during some period of time.*

Now we need to explain (1) why the demand for labor (like any demand
curve) slopes downward from left to right, and (2) what causes shifts in the
demand for labor.

Why the Demand Curve
Slopes Downward from Left to Right

The demand curve for labor acts exactly like the demand curve for Fred's beer
back in Chapter 5. The demand for labor is simply another example of the
general law of demand. The law states that more will be demanded at low
prices (wages) than at high prices. As in the case of Fred's beer, there are three
reasons for the law of demand as it applies to labor: (1) The income effect, (2)
the law of diminishing returns, and (3) the substitution effect. These three
reasons explain why the demand curve for labor slopes downward from left to
right.

The income effect says that demanders (employers of labor) will hire more
people as the wage falls, because out of any given revenue from sales (income), employers can afford to hire more people at lower wages. The law of
diminishing returns says that if *capital* (for example, a factory) is held constant
in quality and quantity, a point will be reached (the point of diminishing returns) where each additional worker will be less productive than the preceding
one. Consequently, under such circumstances, employers will *not* hire these
less productive workers unless the wage falls. Finally, the substitution effect
says that as the price (wage) rises, sensible employers will try to substitute

Rising wages may mean some workers will be replaced by computers or robots.

machines for labor and hire fewer workers; that if the wage falls in relation to the cost of purchasing and operating machines, sensible employers will try to use more workers and fewer machines.

One can see the substitution effect at work in offices today. Rising wages for bookkeepers and accountants may mean that some of them will be replaced by computers. Manufacturers may replace workers with robots or computer-operated machines. The substitution effect is also at work when American firms manufacture some or all of their products overseas. Less-costly foreign labor is substituted for more-costly American labor. In making any kind of resource substitution, firms are merely trying to make scarce resources stretch as far as possible—a logical objective.

Shifts in the Demand for Labor

The demand for labor changes (shifts) whenever the present or expected profitability of using labor changes. Changes in the profitability of using labor (see the third determinant of the demand for labor) will change (1) if the price of the product changes or (2) whenever the productivity of labor changes. An explanatory word on each:

Changes in the Price of the Product

As we already know from Chapter 6, the price of the product the workers are making will change whenever the demand for or the supply of the product changes. Suppose the product price increases. Employers will want to increase production in search of greater profits. Their demand for all of the factors of production—including labor—will probably shift to the right. And vice versa if the product price falls.

An example involving ballpoint pens will help to explain the relationship of wages to product prices. Suppose that the production costs for pens is 30 cents but that the pens can only be sold for a nickel. Clearly, no firm would hire

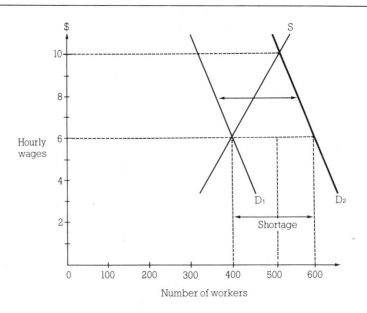

Figure 10-2.
An increase in the
demand for labor.

anyone, no matter what the wage. If, however, the pens sold for $4, firms would
search the ends of the earth for workers—even at sky-high wages. Thus, the
price of the product influences the location of the labor demand curve. A large
demand for pens, for example, makes possible a high enough price for firms to
find it profitable to hire workers.

What happens if product prices rise? Labor demand then rises. This result is
shown in Figure 10-2. Suppose that the pens originally sold for 20 cents, and
consequently firms wanted to hire 400 workers at $6 per hour. This quantity
demanded represents represents one point on D_1. This same point also represents the quantity of labor supplied at $6 per hour, the 400 people who want
jobs. Equilibrium exists. But what if the pen price rises to 40 cents? Then
demand for labor increases, represented by the higher demand of D_2. Firms
now want to hire 600 workers at $6 per hour, but at $6 per hour, only 400
people want jobs, resulting in a labor shortage. Consequently, wages will rise
to some new equilibrium like $10 per hour. At this higher wage an increased
number of workers—say, 120 more workers—will want to make pens, and at
the new equilibrium wage of $10 per hour, employers will demand 520 work-
ers, not the 600 they were willing to hire if the wage had stayed at $6 per hour.

Alternatively, if the price of ballpoint pens dropped from 20 to 15 cents, the
demand for labor would fall as shown in Figure 10-3. Here, the demand for
labor shifts leftward from D_1 to D_2. Wages fall from the original equilibrium at
$6 per hour to $4, and employers demand fewer workers so that even at the
lower wage, the number hired falls from 400 workers to 300.

Changes in the Productivity of Labor
The demand for labor will also change if **labor productivity** changes. The
productivity of labor is a measure of output per worker per hour. Increases in
the productivity of labor will influence the employer to demand more labor

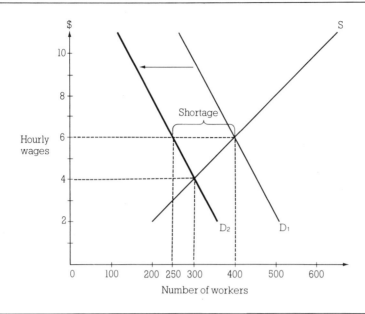

Figure 10-3.
A decrease in the demand for labor.

because expected profits will increase (and vice versa). Figure 10-2 shows how higher productivity shifts demand from D_1 to D_2, leading to both higher wages and more employment.

A good example of such a shift occurred in 1913 when Henry Ford introduced the moving assembly line in the production of Model T's. Assembly time for the chassis shrank from twelve and one-half hours to one hour and thirty-three minutes. The dramatic improvement in productivity led Ford to hire *more* workers—not fewer—despite the mechanization. This increase in employment was partially because Ford's demand for labor rose sharply as productivity rose. But additionally, falling Model T prices vastly increased car sales—which boosted the need for workers. Henry Ford also raised wages to $5 per day—more than double the normal factory rate at the time.

Figure 10-3 shows the opposite. Falling productivity indicates that expected profits will fall. Both labor demand and wages will fall. One example: the declining performance (productivity) of an aging baseball player results in lower demand for his services and a lower salary.

There are many factors determining labor productivity. Some of the main ones are:

1. *Education and training*—a higher quantity and quality of education and training tend to increase productivity.

2. *Worker attitudes*—one may have skills, but to what extent will they be used? This depends upon how the worker feels about the job, about work in general, and about life as a whole. Workers' poor attitudes may lead to decreased productivity.

3. *Working conditions*—many studies show that output increases with well-lit factories, carpeted offices, and safer working conditions.

4. *Capital per worker*—this refers to the tools and machines at the dispos-

al of workers. Workers today are more productive than their parents were, and their wages are higher, primarily because today's workers have more capital to work with.

The Supply of Labor

Why would anyone want to work? In general, for the same reason a rational person does anything—more can be gained than must be given up. That is, the benefits exceed the opportunity costs. To simplify matters we will assume initially that the benefits of work are solely related to money. The benefit of working is therefore the satisfaction from the goods and services bought with one's wages.

And the opportunity cost? Is it playing tennis? Visiting friends? Traveling? The cost varies with the person and the alternatives to work that are available.

Suppose a student is offered a dishwashing job at $4 per hour. He thinks: "With the job I can buy a car and enjoy the benefits of more dates with more different girls. But—what do I have to give up? Probably good grades. I'd better say no. I'd lose more than I'd gain." But what if the offer is $8? Or $12? Sooner or later our student will sacrifice grades. Eventually, the higher wage that permits the purchase of a car provides benefits that exceed the opportunity costs of having the car.

One can visualize the law of supply in operation here. The supply curve says that as the wage rises, laborers are willing to offer more work.* In Chapter 5, we saw that firms offer more output as the price rises because increasingly costly production becomes profitable. Here, too, the student eventually finds it "profitable" to work.

Two of the most important influences on the supply of labor are (1) the degree of skill needed, and (2) the nonmonetary aspects of the work.

Let's look at a hypothetical market for library aides in Connecticut as shown in Figure 10-4.

Assume a high level of reading and spelling is required and that only 20 percent of the work force qualify. Of that group, only 400 want the job at $6 per hour. That is the same number of aides libraries want. We are at equilibrium, shown by the intersection of S_1 and D. But suppose the libraries buy electronic readers, spelling-error correctors, and other machines that *reduce* the skills needed. Now let's assume that 30 percent of the work force qualifies, and that from this extra 10 percent there are 200 more people who want to work at $6 per hour. There is now a new labor supply curve at S_2. But there is now a labor surplus at $6 with 600 people trying to fill 400 job openings. Competition will force the wage to a lower equilibrium position—$4 per and 520 jobs. Why 520? First, the quantity demanded by libraries will increase as the wage falls. Second, some of the 600 people, in fact 80 of them, will feel that the $4 wage for a library aide is too low and will no longer offer their services.

Generally, an occupation requiring a few skills has a larger supply, as shown by S_2. We say "larger" because the positions of supply curves of different occupations are all relative to one another. A large supply simply means that, com-

---

* Remember that there are exceptions to the law of supply. We saw in Chapter 8 that egg ranchers might try to increase the quantities they supply when the price *falls*. Similarly, in labor markets, when wages rise, at some point, high-wage earners may decide to work *less*, by taking time off during the week or by retiring early.

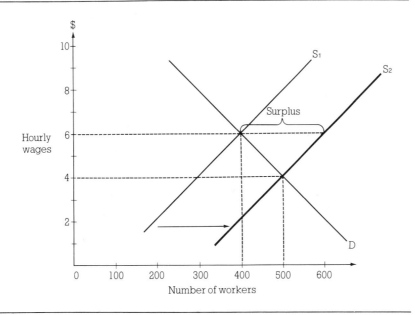

Figure 10-4.
An increase in the
supply of labor.

pared with most other occupations, a larger number of people can and will work at each wage. In turn, a large supply *tends* to result in lower wages, but one can never predict what an occupational wage will be merely by looking at the supply of labor available. The demand for labor in any occupation is equally important in determining what the wage will be. Nevertheless, we can safely predict that wages will be low when workers do not need sophisticated skills to hold the job in question. On the other hand, wages will be high in highly skilled jobs because fewer people qualify.

The second determinant of supply concerns the *nonmonetary aspects* of an occupation. Nonmonetary aspects that are favorable include such factors as the challenge presented, good working conditions, job interest, prestige, convenient working hours, long vacations, travel opportunities, pleasant fellow workers, good job location, and intellectual stimulation. Often such benefits are called *psychic income*—income of the mind rather than the pocketbook.

Favorable job aspects lead to an increase in the number of people wanting such positions at each wage. Figure 10-4 shows the results. The larger supply leads to a lower wage. In fact, some occupations pay so little that we say they are a "labor of love." For example, nursery-school teachers and nurses' aides are "paid" very well—in love, but not money. Some less extreme examples are national forest and park workers, photographers, artists, horticulturists, and public-school teachers.

All occupations also have some *unfavorable aspects.* They include boredom, stress, danger, close supervision, bad job locations, poor hours, low prestige, or little challenge. These negative aspects lead to a decrease in the number of people wanting such positions at each wage: The lower supply leads to a higher wage. Examples include: night-shift workers, skyscraper builders, foundry workers, coal miners, and central-city workers. Such jobs are not always *high* paying—but they are *higher*-paying because of such aspects.

This concludes the discussion of the *competitive* labor market. In it, wages always moved to equilibrium levels under the forces of labor surpluses or shortages. We assumed that laborers were mobile and informed about alternatives and that market adjustments were rapid. In reality, however, some labor shortages exist for years (teachers in the sixties, nurses in the seventies); so do labor surpluses (teachers and autoworkers today). Also, the law of demand can work slowly. Rising wages, rather than leading to immediate layoffs, can lead to fewer workers through *attrition* (not replacing those who quit or who retire). Thus, labor market adjustments in the real world can take months or years.

HOW WAGES CAN BE
INCREASED ABOVE FREE-MARKET LEVELS

Nonunion workers like babysitters and library aides may come to realize that they are in a tough spot; that they, as individuals, have little control over their wages. They may see that their situation parallels that of business firms trying to escape from the hard, cruel world of perfect competition, where, in the long run, economic profits are *zero*. Like business firms, workers over the years have tried to gain sufficient market power to improve their incomes; the equilibrium wage during most of the 1880s was barely enough for workers to live on. The workers' avenue to market power was by way of labor unions.

A **labor union** is an association of workers who join together to negotiate a labor-management contract with an employer. Individual workers can easily be fired over, say, a wage demand, but when the workers form a group, they become more difficult to fire. The group has the power to interrupt the employer's business through a strike if the group's demands are not met or at least negotiated.

When workers gain market power by joining unions, they can raise wages above the levels that would otherwise exist in competitive markets; that is, above the levels that would exist in labor markets where the wage is determined entirely by the impersonal forces of demand and supply. Three basic methods are used: (1) Increasing the demand for labor, (2) decreasing the supply of labor, and/or (3) simply forcing employers to pay a higher-than-equilibrium wage by exercising market power or using political power to make the government enact laws favorable to the unions.

Increasing the Demand for Labor

We can use Figure 10-2 again to show how wages can be raised by increasing the demand for labor. D_1 is the original demand for labor. D_2 represents the increase in demand after (1) the exercise of power by a union or (2) the enactment by the government of legislation favorable to unions. As Figure 10-2 indicates, the increase in demand for labor makes it necessary for firms to hire 600 workers instead of the 400 seeking work at $6 per hour. The resulting labor shortage at the $6 wage will drive the wage up to a new equilibrium at $10 per hour. Jobs will be more plentiful and up to 520 workers will be hired. Such an increase in the demand for *union* labor can be accomplished by:

■ Establishing *work rules,* by which unions force business firms to hire more workers than are generally required. For example, some musicians' unions require musicians to be hired even if only recorded music is to be played. This method is commonly called *featherbedding.*

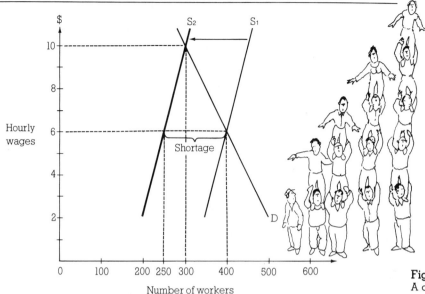

Figure 10-5.
A decrease in the
supply of labor.

- Claiming *jurisdiction*—an exclusive right to do certain types of work. For example, members of the Teamsters Union may be the only laborers allowed to move materials in a factory.
- Advertising. For example, a plumbers' union might try to convince the public that even minor plumbing problems should be solved by expert plumbers (who are union members).
- Persuading Congress to enact favorable legislation like the Davis-Bacon Act (1931), which essentially requires that workers on federally funded projects be paid union wages, thus eliminating the cost advantage of nonunion construction firms.

Restricting (or Decreasing) the Supply of Labor

Wages can also be raised by *de*creasing the supply of labor. Here, the union's intent is to restrict the number of people who are willing and qualified to work as compared with the number available in free, competitive conditions. Figure 10-5 shows the result. S_1 represents a free, competitive supply; S_2 is a restricted supply. The wage with restriction is $10, higher than in competitive conditions. However, fewer people are hired—300 rather than 400.

Restricting the supply of labor increases the cost of labor just as restricting the supply of eggs (discussed in Chapter 8) increased the cost of eggs. Supply is restricted in labor markets by (1) creating barriers to entry and (2) discriminating against certain groups of workers.

Many barriers to job entry exist, like credentials (degrees, licenses) that can be required of workers before they enter the market. In many states, barbers and chemical applicators (those applying herbicides and insecticides) must be licensed. Age and physical requirements are commonly imposed on workers such as airline pilots and police officers. Examinations are required for entering some occupations—nursing, certified public accounting, and legal practice. Long apprenticeships or training programs at low pay are commonly required in the skilled trades like carpentry.

The supply of workers in an occupation can also be restricted by requiring the payment of large fees or limiting the availability of training facilities. Unions sometimes require members to pay very high initiation fees, thereby discouraging joining. The American Medical Association, an organization of physicians, strongly influences whether new medical training facilities are built, the curriculum that is offered, and the length of the training. These restrictions are designed to maintain physician competency, but they also restrict the number of physicians that are trained, thus restricting supply and raising incomes. In 1981, the average physician earned $86,210.[1]

Discrimination* is still another way of restricting the supply of labor. Suppose that in a labor market for bricklayers, 300 people are willing and qualified to work at $7 per hour. Assume that 40 are black, 30 Chicano, 30 Oriental, and 200 white. Also, suppose that firms want to hire 300 workers at $7 per hour. The supply and demand for bricklayers should be at equilibrium.

But suppose that to work as a bricklayer, a worker has to be a union member and that nonwhites are not allowed to join. Then the quantity supplied at $7 per hour is only 200, not 300. There is a labor shortage. Wages will rise to a higher equilibrium. Nonwhites will enter other labor markets where they *are* allowed, and the supply of labor in those markets will be abnormally large. Consequently, wages there will be lower. Although discrimination is illegal now, complete enforcement of antidiscrimination laws is virtually impossible.

Methods of Forcing Employers to Pay a Higher-Than-Equilibrium Wage

A third way to raise wages is to make employers pay wages that are *above* equilibrium levels, regardless of the forces of demand and supply. Such wage increases can be obtained in two ways: (1) By enacting minimum wage legislation (or securing increases in current minimum wages), or (2) by using collective bargaining to force wages up.

Because the effects of minimum wage legislation were discussed in Chapter 7, we will not spend time on that topic here. Suffice it to say that minimum wage laws *do* force all wages, both union and nonunion, to increase. Once the minimum (which affects unskilled workers) has been raised, workers with some skills can justifiably demand more than that minimum.

Labor-management contracts, the end result of collective bargaining, prohibit individual workers from bargaining with the employer over wage rates. When bargaining collectively, workers bargain as a unit, acting much as a monopoly supplier does in product markets. The employer, by law, must deal with a union once it has been certified by the National Labor Relations Board to represent a majority of the workers. If denied its wishes, the union can pressure the employer by calling a strike—by asking its members to refuse to work until a settlement is reached. The employer, unable to produce goods or make a profit without workers, often agrees to pay the higher wage.

The results of collective bargaining are shown in Figure 10-6. Initially, before unionization, the wage paid was the equilibrium wage, $6 per hour. At that wage, there was no surplus or shortage of workers.

---

* This topic is discussed in more detail in Chapter 11.

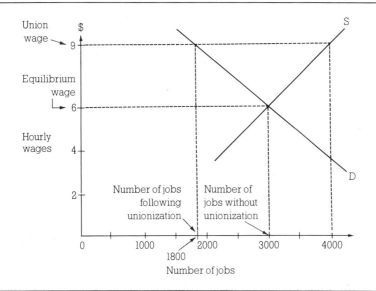

Figure 10-6.
The effects of
collective bargaining
by unions.

If the union succeeds in getting a wage of $9 per hour, the number of jobs falls from 3,000 to 1,800. The laid-off workers may be replaced by other resources such as capital (more mechanization), or possibly by foreign workers.* As more workers now want the job at the higher wage, there is a labor surplus of 2,200 workers. But the labor-management contract** prevents the wage from falling, just as do minimum wage laws.

This concludes the discussion of wage determination. Figure 10-7 summarizes in a flow chart all the factors discussed above. The chart shows the wage of an occupation to be partially the result of the interaction of the demand for and the supply of labor. The supply and demand, in turn, are influenced by competitive conditions (in single-outlined boxes) and by noncompetitive conditions (in shaded boxes). The wage is also partially the result of the noncompetitive conditions (double-ruled box, far right), like those arising from minimum wage legislation and from collective bargaining.

THE LABOR UNION MOVEMENT

During most of the 1800s, workers were often forced to accept wages that were barely sufficient to sustain their combined existence. Examples abound, particularly in England, of children working 16-hour days before the age of 10. Children were often forcibly loaded into wagons and taken to farms where they were "rented" to farmers for long days of drudgery. Men and women worked 14-hour days in coal mines and in the textile mills.†

---

* Meaning that the American factory may have some of its manufacturing done in other countries.

** Collective bargaining by unions is not unlike the actions of a cartel such as OPEC. Just as union members agree not to accept employment at less than a certain wage, the members of OPEC try to avoid selling below a given price.

† The current U.S. example of such conditions is the "sweatshop," often in the textile industry, where the workers are illegal immigrants working for wages that are below the legal minimum. In this instance, the workers may be content with their wage because it exceeds the wage they would receive in their home countries.

As time went by, and as the discontent of the working class increased, labor unions gradually came into being. The new labor unions of the late 1800s were quite different from their earlier counterparts, the guilds of the Middle Ages, mentioned in Chapter 2. The guilds had been associations of workers, dominated by a guild master. They existed primarily to preserve the production standards of the past. The tapestry-making guilds, for example, maintained rules concerning the number of threads per inch and the precise making of dyes. In contrast, the new labor unions were understandably, and primarily, interested in improving their wages and their working conditions.

In the early 1900s, union negotiations leading to a labor-management contract emphasized pay and hours of work. Bargaining still covers these issues, but as unions have gained power, they have become concerned with fringe benefits involving medical, dental, and optical care; pension funds (in addition to Social Security); and many job-related issues such as *job descriptions,* which rigidly prescribe exactly who does what and with what tools; *seniority rules,* which state who is laid off or promoted first; and the *check-off,* the company's agreement to deduct union dues from the workers' paychecks and to turn the money over to the union.

All of these areas for negotiation were usually interpreted by employers as interferences with management, and until 1935, employers did everything they could to prevent the formation of unions. During the 1920s, employers banded together in associations under what they called the *American Plan* to try to crush the unions by getting their employer-members to support the **open shop**—that is, a workplace where an employer could assert the right to hire anyone, whether union member or not. Because none of the employers wanted a union, "open shop" really meant no union. In addition to the open shop, employers often asked newly hired workers to sign contracts whereby the workers agreed not to join a union or engage in union activities. Workers who signed these contracts were called "yellow dogs" by union supporters; thus the contracts came to be known as yellow-dog contracts.

During the 1920s, both sides fought—literally. There was much violence and people were killed. In the West Virginia coal mines, for instance, miners formed an army of 4,000 men, which was crushed by another army of federal troops. In Illinois, two miners were killed during a battle between striking mine workers and strikebreakers brought in by the Southern Illinois Coal Company, and miners retaliated by killing nineteen of the strikebreakers. Violence also occurred in many other industries.

The Legal Status of Unions

Finally, in 1935, Congress passed the National Labor Relations Act (**Wagner Act**), which gave workers the legal right to form unions and to bargain collectively if they voted to do so. Voting was supervised by the National Labor Relations Board, which is still in operation today.

The Wagner Act gave unions tremendous power by permitting the **closed shop**. A closed-shop agreement requires the employer to hire only those who are already members of the union. The act also spelled out many restrictions on what were called *unfair labor practices.* Employers who pressured employees in any way to stay away from unions were found guilty of "unfair labor practices."

Although the Wagner Act imposed all kinds of restrictions on employers, it

Figure 10-7.
(Opposite page) Major factors in wage determination for an occupation.

imposed virtually none on labor. In 1947, the passage of the Labor-Management Relations Act of 1947 (**Taft-Hartley Act**) signaled a shift in public sentiment away from labor by outlawing the closed shop. The Taft-Hartley Act did, however, permit **union shop** agreements, under which newly hired workers did not have to be union members *before* employment but had to join the union some specified time *after* employment (usually thirty days). The Taft-Hartley Act also gave individual states the right to pass so-called *right-to-work laws* that prohibited union shops, and about half the states have passed such laws. Although the phrase "right to work" was intended to signify that workers should have the right to work whether they joined a union or not, the effect was to seriously damage union power.

The act also included a no-strike clause for certain industries (such as aircraft and others connected with national defense) deemed by the President of the United States to be involved with the national "safety and well-being." This clause provides an 80-day cooling-off period, during which a union cannot strike even after a contract with its employer has expired. (The best-known instance of the cooling-off provision occurred in 1959 when President Eisenhower initiated steps to halt a steel strike that had been in progress for 116 days. After the President's order, the workers went back to work. The conflict was then settled, in favor of the union, in slightly under two months.)

In 1958, Congress took another "swipe" at unions with the enactment of the **Landrum-Griffin Act** (officially, the Labor-Management Reporting and Disclosure Act). With this Act, Congress tried to prevent union bosses from assuming dictatorial control of their unions and from misappropriating union funds. The Act limited borrowing from union funds by union officials to $2,000, made embezzlement a federal offense, and provided several regulations related to voting and the use of the secret ballot to protect the rights of rank-and-file members. The Act helped Attorney General Robert F. Kennedy to convict Teamster boss Jimmy Hoffa in 1964 of misuse of union funds, among other crimes.

Membership in Unions

By far the largest organization of unions is the AFL-CIO. Until the 1930s, the A.F. of L. (American Federation of Labor) consisted of craft unions of workers such as carpenters, electricians, plumbers, and others involved with specific trades. Workers in a given factory often were fragmented into many of these craft unions, and there were times when they could not agree with one another during negotiations with the employer. For instance, in 1919 the unions tried to coordinate a steel strike with a committee representing more than twenty crafts. Even today the carpenters and machinists are still unable to settle some of the differences that resulted from this experience.

To overcome this splitting of union power, in 1935 John L. Lewis of the United Mine Workers and Sidney Hillman of the Amalgamated Clothing Workers formed the Congress of Industrial Organizations (CIO). The CIO aimed at unionizing entire factories with one union and became so successful that the A.F. of L. felt obliged to copy it with some industrial organizations of its own.

After considerable fighting among themselves involving *jurisdictional strikes*—strikes to force workers to join one union or another—the two giant organizations merged into one federation in 1955. In 1978, 17 million workers belonged to the AFL-CIO, out of a total of 20.3 million Americans in all unions.

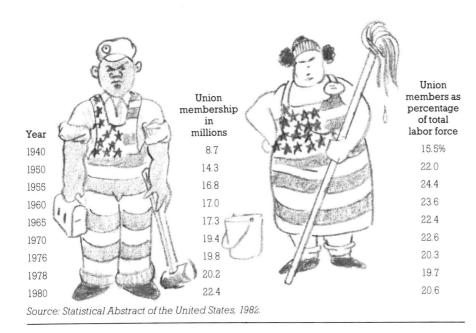

Year	Union membership in millions	Union members as percentage of total labor force
1940	8.7	15.5%
1950	14.3	22.0
1955	16.8	24.4
1960	17.0	23.6
1965	17.3	22.4
1970	19.4	22.6
1976	19.8	20.3
1978	20.2	19.7
1980	22.4	20.6

Source: Statistical Abstract of the United States, 1982.

Figure 10-8.
U. S. membership in national and international unions, 1940–1980.

There are still two large unions that do not belong to the federation, however—the Teamsters Union (1.9 million members) and the United Automobile Workers (1.4 million).

The AFL-CIO, with its offices in Washington, D.C., exists mainly to exert political influence on the President and the Congress. However, the real power of the federation lies in the locals, organizations of workers in specific towns and factories. The locals belong to national organizations and sometimes international ones (Canadian locals belong, too), both of which belong to the AFL-CIO.

Since 1968, union membership in the United States (excluding union members in Canada) has been growing slowly in numbers but, with exception of 1980 data, declining slowly as a percentage of the total labor force. The numbers are shown in Figure 10-8.

New Directions for Unions

The Wagner and Taft-Hartley acts did not include agricultural workers. Farm workers, particularly the migrant workers who move from crop to crop, have suffered from low wages, substandard housing, and lack of medical care. One dramatic example of an effort to bring these workers into the mainstream of American labor began in 1962 with the work of Cesar Chavez and the United Farm Workers of America (UFWA). In 1975, after much pressure from Chavez and the UFWA, California passed the first collective bargaining law for agricultural workers.

The growth of unions in agriculture is only one example of a new trend toward unionization of low-income workers in areas not previously unionized or where the unions lacked market power. Other examples are the Laborers and Service Employees, Retail Clerks, and the National Union of Hospital and Health Care Workers. The International Ladies' Garment Workers' Union has started working among illegal aliens on the West Coast. White collar workers have also organized in recent years. Government employees now have the American Federation of State, County, and Municipal Employees (AFSCME). Teachers' unions—the American Federation of Teachers (AFT) and the National Education Association (NEA)—are growing* and are insisting that the states pass collective bargaining laws for teachers.

RECENT EVENTS AND ISSUES—AND THE FUTURE

Like anything else, the labor market changes constantly, and not always in the interest of laborers, as some of the following topics indicate. Nevertheless, these issues will likely remain with us throughout the 1980s.

"Givebacks" and Concessions

Decades of increases in wages and in fringe benefits led many union members to believe that such increases might continue indefinitely. But the sharp economic slowdown of the late 1970s and early 1980s, the significant decline in the inflation rate, and the increasing competition of foreign manufacturers changed matters. These circumstances forced many unions to give up some of their market power.

In the early 1980s, one heard increasingly of *"givebacks"*—meaning that labor unions had to agree to *concessions;* that is, to reductions in wages, vacations, and fringe benefits. In March 1983 the United Steel Workers agreed to an immediate cut of $1.25 per hour with partially offsetting gains.[2] The steel firms are faced by severe competition. During 1982, imports reached 22 percent of U.S. sales of steel.[3] One reason U.S. firms find it hard to compete is the high cost of labor, about $26 per hour when all costs like fringe benefits are included.

In 1980, in order to save Chrysler Corporation from bankruptcy, 50 percent of its employees agreed to accept total concessions of $622 million dollars in the form of delayed pay increases, delayed COLAs (cost-of-living adjustments), and other benefits.[4] Many other smaller firms obtained similar concessions.

The reasons that labor unions were in trouble in 1981–1983 are many and complicated—a good deal more complicated than the fact of high wages. American steel manufacturers had become less competitive because they did not adopt new production methods.[5] Although economic theory tells us that high labor costs will motivate business firms to substitute capital for labor, substitution isn't that easy in firms requiring very expensive machines. Resource substitution doesn't take place smoothly because resources, like large machines, are often "lumpy," as economists like to say. The decision to substitute a new blast furnace or rolling mill for a few hundred workers may require millions of dollars. In addition, high interest rates during the 1981–1983 period made of borrowing for such improvements extremely expensive. The substitution of labor with capital is sometimes postponed for good reason. And finally, the worldwide recession reduced the demand for steel. All these factors, along with the high cost of labor, contributed to the softening of union demands.

---

*AFT membership rose from 165,000 in 1968 to 551,000 in 1980, and AFSCME from 364,000 to 1.1 million during the same period (*Statistical Abstract of the United States, 1982–1983*). These are both gigantic increases compared with other unions.

Through job enrichment programs, many companies try to improve employees' feelings about their jobs.

Similar factors also influenced the behavior of unions in the automobile industry.

For whatever reason, as the unions came under increasing pressure to soften or withdraw some of their demands, other forces were at work to reduce workers' feelings of conflict with their employers. Many versions of these new directions exist. For the sake of brevity we mention only three of them: job enrichment, new labor-management concepts borrowed from the Japanese, and so-called Theory Z management.

New Directions in Labor-Management Relations

Job Enrichment Programs

Many employers are now striving to improve workers' feelings about their work through what is sometimes called job enrichment; to enhance some of the favorable job aspects referred to on page 199—or at least to reduce the unfavorable ones. The film *9 to 5,* dealing with poor worker morale in a large office, showed how labor productivity can be increased by work sharing, by encouraging suggestions, by rotating jobs, and by involving workers in pay-increase decisions. Much of what is called job enrichment seeks to eliminate the boredom that results from a too highly refined division of labor. Other more sophisticated efforts try to improve the employee's identification with the firm's goals by increasing the motivation to work and by increasing the employee's self-esteem.[6]

The Quality-Circle Approach

Another approach is to introduce Japanese concepts of labor management in the United States. One such approach is the **quality circle**, a small group of workers who meet regularly to identify and solve worksite problems. Use of quality circles has been common in Japan since the 1960s and was first introduced to the United States by Lockheed Corporation's Sunnyvale plant in the mid-1970s. The circles are typically introduced by a management steering committee that enlists a coordinator to establish the circles and train the leaders. The seven or eight members of each circle are randomly selected from the workers who express an interest in participating. The regular on-the-job supervisor serves as the group leader. Groups typically meet for an hour a week during regular working hours, and members receive their regular pay for participating. Groups may discuss ways to increase worker morale such as starting baseball leagues, repainting the lunchroom, or putting in vending machines, or they may discuss ways to improve product quality or reduce inefficiency. After groups have met for a period of time, they report to management. The groups thus help develop worker leadership, encourage worker involvement, and improve manager-worker relations. They can also suggest money-saving improvements. For example, a quality circle at the Northrup Corporation saved the company $28,000 a year by recommending a new drill bit to reduce breakage, and a quality circle at Hughes Aircraft saved the company $45,000 a year by designing new procedures for cleaning parts.[7]

The Theory-Z Approach

A third approach is called **Theory Z**. The designation "Z" is used because more traditional management approaches had been designated previously as "X" and "Y." Theory Z has five key principles: (1) Workers need to have goals. (2) Workers need to be motivated. (3) Managers need to correct errors promptly. (4) Business firms need well-understood personnel policies to be successful. (5) Employee goals need to be revised regularly.

Theory Z management is an American version of a Japanese form of organization. Workers have long-term employment; they are given individual responsibility, but decisions are reached collectively; evaluation is informal and promotion infrequent; and the people in the organization develop a broad interest in and knowledge of each other as "whole" persons both on and off the job. A comparison of two electronics companies, one having a typical American work organization and one having a Type Z organization, revealed that the typical American executives were most concerned about profit margins and with the latest scientific developments in their respective professional fields, whereas the Type Z executives were more concerned with the loyalty, honesty, ability, and morale of their employees and expressed more attachment to their companies than to their own individual performance. The Theory Z approach is designed to achieve increased productivity by improving workers' emotional well-being.[8]

A Tentative Last Word

The past has been characterized by conflict between labor and management in which each side regarded the other as an adversary.

Increasing competition among nations and among individual business firms for world markets may force reappraisals of the need for such adversary relationships—as quality circles and Theory Z management approaches are demonstrating.

In addition to quality circles and Theory Z management systems, one can see in some countries evidence of a marriage of worker-management objectives. These marriages occur because union pension funds are heavily invested in corporate stocks and bonds to the point where the corporation's success is of great interest to the union. (The workers are coming to own the means or production in ways that Marx never anticipated.) And some corporations have found that productivity improves when workers participate in management decisions by being represented on boards of directors or management committees. This latter practice is sometimes called *industrial democracy*. The practice is growing in the United States and is prevalent in West Germany and the Scandinavian countries. These aspects of labor-management relations also represent a movement away from the "us versus them" attitude that has long characterized labor-management relations.

SUMMARY

In a market-price system, the level of resource prices helps a firm to select efficient production techniques. This chapter examined how markets determine the price of one resource, wages for labor, as well as the level of employment in a labor market.

Wages are determined by competitive and noncompetitive forces. In a freely competitive market, the supply of and the demand for labor determine the competitive equilibrium wage. The demand is influenced by the price of the item made as well as the productivity of labor, or output per man-hour. Productivity, in turn, is determined by worker skills and attitudes, working conditions, and the amount of capital invested per worker. Because the demand for labor partly depends on the demand for the goods or services produced by labor, we say that labor demand is a derived demand. Labor supply is determined by the skills needed as well as by the job's nonmonetary aspects. Other things being equal, an occupation will tend to have a high wage if its product price is high, if its workers are highly productive and highly skilled, or if it has some unfavorable aspects. Opposite conditions will lead to lower wages.

Workers and occasionally governments try to raise wages above competitive levels (1) by increasing the demand for labor (by advertising or by establishing work rules), (2) by decreasing the supply of labor (by raising skill requirements, restricting union membership, toughening worker training, or by discrimination), or (3) by establishing a wage floor or minimum that is placed above the equilibrium wage. Governments do this directly with minimum wage laws and indirectly by granting labor unions the right to bargain collectively.

Although workers began to organize in the 1800s, labor unions did not become powerful until after the Wagner Act of 1935. Unions lost some strength with the Taft-Hartley Act of 1947. Since the 1950s membership has grown slowly.

Unions have several goals, but foremost are increases in wages, improvements in fringe benefits, and improvements in working conditions. Labor unions obtain these objectives by threatening strikes, although labor-management contracts are usually signed without strikes through negotiations or intervention by third parties.

Labor markets are changing rapidly. Some unions are making concessions owing to foreign competition and a sluggish economy. Finally, new techniques are being introduced to improve the treatment, well-being, and the productivity of workers.

Discussion Questions

1. Does a job requiring a high degree of skills always pay well? Under what circumstances would it not?

2. What are some ways a laborer can influence his own wage by influencing the demand for his labor?

3. Can you give some past or present examples of labor surpluses or shortages? Why did they or do they not disappear?

4. How does the Taft-Hartley Act differ from the Wagner Act?

5. How do union policies affect the level of employment?

6. What are some occupations of today that are likely to be greatly diminished by the year 2000?

DID YOU EVER WONDER WHY . . .

. . . artists, authors, and forest rangers earn low incomes relative to their skills?

References

1. *Information Please Almanac,* 1982.

2. *Newsweek,* 14 March 1983.

3. "Selected Steel Industry Data," leaflet obtained from American Iron and Steel Institute, Washington, D.C., 7 January 1983.

4. *Wall Street Journal,* 21 January 1981.

5. Larry Green, "Rust Bowl: Steel Mills Waste Away," *Los Angeles Times,* 25 April 1983.

6. Richard E. Walton, "Work Innovation in the United States," *Harvard Business Review,* July–August 1979.

7. Kenneth A. Muir, "The Appropriateness of Quality Circle Financial Rewards," unpublished master's thesis, Claremont Graduate School, Claremont, California, 1982, pp. 15, 18, 20–23.

8. William G. Ouchi and Jerry B. Johnson, "Types of Organizational Control and Their Relationship to Emotional Well Being," *Administrative Science Quarterly,* 23, 1978, pp. 293–317; see also Jeremiah J. Sullivan, "A Critique of Theory Z," *The Academy of Management Review,* January 1983, pp. 132–142.

11

For Whom?
The Distribution of Income

Wealth versus income
Poverty
Exploitation
Discrimination
Marginal tax on work
Negative income tax

This chapter is the last of the *micro*economic chapters; after this we will be talking about "macro" and international problems. The topic of this chapter, the distribution of income, could belong to either micro- or macroeconomics. If, for example, we consider the influence of a particular labor union, say, the steelworkers, on wages in the steel industry, we are dealing with a microeconomic topic—a topic that is confined to a particular "piece" of the pie. If, on the other hand, we discuss the distribution of income among the entire population, or if we discuss what to do about poverty, we are then viewing a topic from a national, macroeconomic perspective.

This chapter has some of both viewpoints. It is an extremely important one because it explains how well—or poorly—we in the United States answer one of the three fundamental questions facing every society. The questions (discussed first in Chapter 2) are:

1. What goods and services (and what quantities) should we produce?

2. Having answered question 1, how shall we produce those goods and services? (What combinations of the factors of production shall we use?)

3. For whom should we produce? (How should we divide up everything that is produced?)

This chapter is about that last question. The chapter is divided into five sections: (1) ground rules, (2) inequality in the United States, (3) why people are poor, (4) the economic theory of discrimination, and (5) government efforts to soften the blow.

GROUND RULES

We need this section to clear up a few preliminaries. Here are the ground rules:

1. Our market-price system does not deliberately set out to answer the "for whom" question. There is no national plan for income distribution. Even when new economic measures are before Congress, and everyone knows that some people will benefit and some will be hurt, there is no consensus about how the present distribution of income should be changed.[1] Consequently, this chapter reviews what is happening to the distribution of income and will indicate only briefly what can be done.

2. Although the distribution of *wealth* is important, this chapter will focus on the distribution of income. **Wealth** consists of assets we own, like real estate, stocks, bonds, bank accounts, equities in life insurance policies, and personal property like jewelry. (In 1972, the top 1 percent of those who owned such assets owned 24.1 percent of the total.) Interesting as such information may be, we will limit our examination in this chapter to the distribution of income. By **income**, we mean the *flow* of dollars that comes to us, most often in the form of paychecks for work. And when we speak of inequality, we mean the unequal distribution of income in the United States.

INEQUALITY IN THE UNITED STATES

In this section we want to touch four bases: To present data showing the distribution of income, to review the arguments in favor of and against efforts to

Table 11-1. Money Income of Families: Percentage of Total Income Received by Each Fifth

	1950	1981
Lowest fifth	4.5	5.0
Second fifth	12.0	11.3
Middle fifth	17.4	17.4
Fourth fifth	23.4	24.4
Highest fifth	42.7	41.9
	100.0	100.0

Source: Statistical Abstract of the United States, 1982–1983.

equalize incomes, to define poverty (as well as we can), and to think about whether or not the number of people defined as poverty stricken is increasing or decreasing.

Income Distribution Data

One standard way to measure the distribution of income is to divide the 60 million or so families in the United States into 5 equal groups, rank them in terms of income from the lowest income group to the highest; and then show the percent of total income received by each group. Table 11-1 shows this information and compares 1950 with 1981 so that you can see whether or not the distribution of income is changing.

Let's see what these figures mean. The 4.5 figure under 1950 means that in 1950 the lowest fifth (20 percent of families—about 12 million) received only 4.5 percent of total income. Did their situation improve by 1981? Yes, but only a little. The highest fifth received more than 40 percent of total income in both years.

Although Table 11-1 presents as accurate a picture as is obtainable these days, economists are not happy with it. The problem is that the table *does* include the effects of *cash* subsidies to poor people (like welfare, Social Security, and unemployment compensation), but it does *not* include subsidies "in kind" like food stamps, school lunches, low-cost public housing, and Medicare and Medicaid. These subsidies (both cash and in-kind) have grown rapidly since the late 1960s and would probably increase the share of income going to the lowest fifth if they were included in the income figures.

Measuring in-kind subsidies is extremely difficult, but omitting them seriously distorts any comparisons we make. In January 1983, a financial magazine stated that "non-cash subsidies now go to one U.S. household in six, and they account for two of every three federal dollars spent to aid the poor. Any measure that ignores them fails to reflect the real world."[2] We do know that noncash subsidies are very unevenly distributed. In 1982, 29 percent of the poor received none; 22 percent received at least three kinds. By 1985, the Census Bureau hopes to have a formula for measuring income from in-kind subsidies. More on this point in the next section.

Arguments in Favor of and
Against Making Incomes More Equal

Now that you have seen the income-distribution picture, the question naturally arises: What should we do about it, if anything? As you will become increasingly aware in the "macro" section, economists are an argumentative lot, and they are not in agreement about how to answer this question (and many others).

Some economists will cite one main argument in favor of equalizing incomes. Others will cite three arguments against making any such effort.

The argument in favor of equalizing incomes is based on one of the three reasons given for the slope of the demand curve downward from left to right. (See page 74 in Chapter 5.) The idea is that when we buy increasing quantities of something—water, beer, ice cream sundaes, or whatever—each additional unit consumed is less and less satisfying. The connection between this idea and the demand curve is this: Because additional items that we buy are increasingly less important to us, the price must fall before we will buy them. Therefore, the demand curve must slope downward from left to right.

Consequently, the demand curve can be viewed, as always, as a schedule of the quantities we will buy at various prices during some period of time. But the demand curve can also be viewed as a schedule that shows the declining importance (or satisfaction obtained from) additional purchases of some good or service.

The connection between this idea and the distribution of income is that the more income we acquire, the less important additions to that income become. An increase in income of $10 means much less to a millionaire than a $10 increase in income does to a poor person. In the millionaire's case, the $10 might represent the purchase of a Beethoven symphony on a cassette tape; in the poor person's case the $10 might represent food for two or three days or a pair of blue jeans at a thrift shop.

Given this line of reasoning, the millionaire can give $10 to the poor person and *there will be a net increase in welfare for the two of them*. The reason is simply that the millionaire gives away much less satisfaction than the poor person receives. This example, therefore, provides a basis for arguing that transfers of income from higher-income people to lower-income people will increase the nation's welfare (the total satisfaction of its people). Here we have the basis for engaging in programs that do equalize incomes like unemployment compensation, general welfare, Social Security, and food stamps, as well as progressive income taxes. But despite this theoretical basis for income redistribution, there are three strong objections:

1. The assumption that $10 is less important to the rich person than to the poor person might be quite wrong. There is no way we can accurately measure satisfaction. The rich person's desire for the Beethoven symphony might be just as powerful as the poor person's desire for blue jeans. We simply cannot weigh these emotions. People *are* different, with different tastes and values. We cannot say for sure *which* way the nation's total satisfaction changes when income is transferred. Such judgments are normative (see Chapter 4) and are outside the realm of economics.

2. Any plan to redistribute incomes invites the creation of bureaucratic empires—empires of officials to decide who shall get the money taken from the better off, and in what form—dollars and/or food stamps, public housing, medical care. Consequently, some of the transferred income does not find its way to the poor. Well-known economist Arthur Okun once used the analogy of a "leaky bucket" to describe the inevitable failure of any plan to carry 100 percent of the redistributed income from one group to another.

3. To some extent, any redistributional plan may reduce the nation's ability to produce goods and services. The taxes necessary to transfer incomes may cause some highly taxed people to work less (or to engage in less entrepreneurial activity).* The payments the poor receive may cause them to shirk productive labor.

This third argument illustrates a possible trade-off between equality and efficiency. Those who support this view will argue that efforts to increase equality will reduce economic efficiency by reducing the incentive to work. And if total national output is reduced, the poor will suffer because there will be less to share; it's easier to share a larger pie than a smaller one. But, as always in economics, it isn't that simple. Some of the Scandinavian countries have larger public assistance programs than we do, and these countries also produce more on a per person basis than we do. And so, this third argument has not been settled.

Summing it up: What conclusion can we draw from this discussion? The main conclusion is that efforts to help the poor, if any, must come as the result of political, not economic, decision making. Voters have to determine what distribution of income they consider desirable.

A special case within this topic is the question of poverty, because, in some situations, people classified as poverty stricken are not just more unequal than others; they may not have the necessities of life. This is the problem to which we now turn.

Poverty

The term *poverty* is, to say the least, a most inexact term. The dictionary defines poverty as the condition of "being poor" or "in need." But poverty is a relative term in the sense that some people will always be poorer or needier than others. And poverty or "need" in the United States certainly has a different meaning than it has for starving millions of Africans near the Sahara Desert. In the United States, a poverty-stricken person may have a furnished house or apartment with indoor plumbing, appliances, a television set, and a car. And so any definition of poverty is necessarily arbitrary, and the definition depends on the standards of living of the country in which the poverty-stricken person resides. Nevertheless, the definition is extremely important in the United States, because it often determines whether or not a person or a family is eligible for welfare assistance.

In the United States the definition of **poverty** is based on the cost of a nutritionally balanced diet as determined by the Department of Agriculture. This cost is then multiplied by three to arrive at a figure that includes not only food but housing and related expenses plus the costs of clothing, necessary transportation, and medical care. Since 1969, this poverty-line figure has been adjusted upward each year to reflect increases in the cost of living. In 1982, the poverty-line figure for a nonfarm family of four was $9,287.

The number of people defined as below the poverty line is apparently going down, both in absolute numbers and as a percentage of total population. Table 11-2 compares poverty figures for 1959 with 1981.

---

* There is much argument in the economics profession about the effects of taxes on richer people. High taxes may actually invite them to work harder and to be more venturesome (because of tax write-offs).

Table 11-2. Persons* below Poverty Level, 1959 and 1981

Year	Poverty line	Number (millions)	Percentage of total population
1959	$2,973	39.5	22.4
1982	$9,287	38.8	14.0*

* Estimates for nonfarm family of four.

Source: Statistical Abstract of the United States, 1982–1983.

Although Table 11-2 presents a hopeful sign that poverty is diminishing, the numbers are the subject of much argument. There are two major problems: (1) Many poor people aren't counted, and (2) the poverty-line figures don't include subsidies in kind. A word on each.

Inaccuracies in Data
Government figures tend to overlook a large number of undocumented workers, many of whom are from Latin America or the Caribbean. Those who work usually do so on farms or in light industries, but many are unemployed. Most of those who work receive substantially less than American workers. Estimates of their number vary from 6 to 12 million. These numbers are missing from the poverty estimates. The undocumented workers are members of the "underclass."[3] Most of them are male.

Omission of In-Kind Subsidies
Once again we bump into the argument that the poverty-line income figure includes cash subsidies but not subsidies in kind. Consequently, three possible measures of the poverty line exist: (1) Earned income alone without cash subsidies or subsidies in kind, (2) earned income plus cash subsidies but not including in-kind subsidies (this is the present official measure), and (3) earned income plus cash subsidies *and* subsidies in kind.

In early 1982, the Census Bureau, at the request of Congress, attempted to compare the number of people officially designated as poverty stricken with what the number would have been if in-kind subsidies had been included. The Census Bureau found was that the number of people officially defined as poverty stricken would be cut approximately in half if in-kind subsidies were included.

Such a conclusion is appealing to those who want to reduce the government's aid to poor people. Others argue that the inclusion of in-kind subsidies may cause analysts to reach a conclusion exactly the opposite of the truth. Said one spokesman: "It's a lousy idea. How do you put a value on health assistance? Using that theory, an elderly woman who required $20,000 in Medicaid benefits would be considered wealthy. The sicker you are, the richer you aren't."[4]

Has Any Progress Been Made?
The question of progress in the war on poverty is a tricky one. Individuals move into and out of poverty, but if the *first* measure of poverty is used—earned income only without subsidies of any kind—the percentage of the population below the poverty line has not improved since 1965. In 1965, that percentage was 21.3 percent; in 1980 it was 21.9 percent, a slightly higher figure. The only

real progress in the poverty war has been the result of cash subsidies and in-kind subsidies. The *cash* subsidies are largely responsible for the drop in the percentages in Table 11-2 from 22.4 percent to 14 percent.

Moreover, the facts tend to confirm the unlikelihood that the problem will somehow go away. At least 70 percent of today's poor, according to economics professor Timothy Smeeding, are aged, disabled, or in households headed by a lone female parent with at least one child under school age. "These people can't be expected to work much," Smeeding commented.[5] We are left with the uncomfortable conclusion that there will always be people who need *some* form of outside assistance.

WHY ARE PEOPLE POOR?

You already have a good idea *who* the poor people are—women, minorities, old people, undocumented workers. This section takes up the causes of inequality with emphasis on one particular cause—discrimination.

People are poor for at least five reasons:

- They were born with the wrong genes. They lacked the basic equipment, the muscular coordination and brains to be successful in the occupations open to them.
- After birth, they lacked either the opportunity or the motivation to obtain education and training. Differences in the income, wealth, and motivation of their parents played a major role.
- Or, once on the job, they lacked the motivation, the "drive," to work hard and succeed.
- They were unlucky. They bought the wrong stocks, the wrong real estate, the wrong bright idea. They missed having the "right connections" with people who could give them a hand.
- Or, when the time came for obtaining a job, they could have been the wrong age, sex, religion, race, or color. It is this last cause of inequality we wish to emphasize in this section, primarily in connection with the economic status of women and minorities.

The Economic Status of Women and Minorities

When we say that some employers may "prefer" white adult males over other groups of workers, we mean that some employers "exploit" their workers or "discriminate" against some workers in favor of others.

Exploitation exists when workers are paid less than they would have been paid in perfectly competitive labor markets. A competitive market exists (1) when many employers are present to compete for every worker's services, and (2) where every worker has perfect knowledge of job opportunities, and (3) where no barriers prevent workers from seeking the job they want.

Thus, exploitation in labor markets can exist when (1) employees don't have sufficient information about what other employers might offer them; (2) employees may be prevented from considering employment elsewhere because of barriers to entry like the cost of moving, licenses to buy, or unions to join (high initiation fees); or (3) other employers fail to compete or have agreed not to compete for an employee's services. (Professional team owners used to agree among themselves not to compete for star players.) When these elements exist in labor markets, employees may be trapped, knowingly or unknowingly, in exploitative jobs.

Discrimination exists when workers with the same skills are treated differently by employers. Employers may discriminate against workers in hiring or promotion on the basis of sex, race, or age (*job discrimination*) or by paying workers differently for doing the same job (*wage discrimination*).

Discrimination can be enormously difficult to identify or prove. The employer can always argue, "I'm not turning Mary down because she's a female and Bob's a male. It's just that Bob will fit into my organization better, stay longer, and do a better job." The employer can make the same argument about different wages paid for the same job. The employer's arguments may be legitimate—Bob *may* in fact be a better risk. To prove discrimination, we would have to show that the employer is treating people of equal ability, personality, motivation, and intelligence differently, solely because of sex, race, or age.

What the Numbers Tell Us about Exploitation and Discrimination

What is the evidence for exploitation and discrimination? We can divide it into three categories: Income differences, differences in unemployment rates, and differences in education.

Income Differences between Women and Men

Table 11-3 has a double purpose: (1) to compare women workers' incomes with men's, and (2) to show whether or not these income differences have narrowed over time. Although the dollar differences are important, the ratio shown on line 3 tells the story. Women's incomes are about 60 percent of men's. Between 1970 and 1980, the ratio stayed essentially the same. If we check the increases in income from 1970 to 1980, we find that female workers' incomes increased 2.13 ($11,591 ÷ $5,440) times, whereas men workers' incomes increased 2.09 ($19,173 ÷ $9,184) times. Not much change, either way you look at it.

The difference in income between male and female workers is undoubtedly the result of both wage and job discrimination. One study provides support for

Table 11-3. Median* Money Income of Full-Time Male and Female Workers, 1970 and 1979

	1970	1980
1. Women (full-time workers)	$5,440	$11,591
2. Men (full-time workers)	$9,184	$19,173
3. Ratio of women's incomes to men's (line 1 ÷ line 2)	.59	.60

*The median is the middle figure of a series of figures when they are arranged in order of size. In the series 2, 3, 5, 7, 8 and the series 2, 3, 5, 7, 28, the median is 5 even though the mean (the sum of the figures divided by the number of figures) changes from 5 to 9 in the first to the second series. Thus, the median is less influenced by extremes than is the mean. If the median dollar income of the male wage earners in 1980 was $19,173, one-half of the male wage-earners received more than $19,173 and one-half received less.
Source: Statistical Abstract of the United States, 1982–1983.

both conclusions. Two sociologists, James N. Baron of Stanford and William T. Bielby of the University of California at Santa Barbara, studied 400 business firms between 1968 and 1979. They found that 60 percent of the women employed would have to change jobs in order to equalize the distribution of sexes in each job.[6] Their other conclusions:

- In more than half the firms studied, no women were found to share identical job assignments with men, an indication that women may have been prevented from getting better jobs. None of the companies had both men and women working in every job task.
- Economic discrimination against women was not just unequal pay for equal work (wage discrimination) but also unequal access to better jobs (job discrimination).

Income Differences: White Families versus Black Families

Table 11-4 also uses median money income as the measure—this time comparing white *families* with black *families* (instead of comparing *individual* workers as in Table 10-3). Table 11-4 differs from Table 11-3 in one other respect: The income figures have been corrected for price changes so that the dollar figures for 1981 have the same purchasing power as those for 1970; that is the meaning of "constant 1981 dollars" in the title of the table.

Table 11-4. Median Family Money Income in Constant 1981 Dollars—By Race

	1970	1981
(1) All black families	$14,707	$13,266
(2) All white families	23,975	23,517
(3) Ratio of blacks' incomes to whites' (Line 1 ÷ Line 2)	.61	.56

Source: Statistical Abstract of the United States, 1982–1983.

This time the table shows a definite change between 1970 and 1981. The income gap between black families and white families has grown larger, as line 3 indicates. Note that family incomes in both categories showed a *decrease* in purchasing power (because the income figures have been corrected for price changes). This decrease in family income gives us one view of the economy's poor performance in the 1970s. The decrease also hurt black families more than white families. Black families' incomes dropped 9.8 percent; white families', 1.9 percent.

Table 11-5. Unemployment Rates in Percentage of Civilian Labor Force by Age, Sex, and Race, December 1981

	White	Blacks and other minorities
Males		
16–19 years	20.2%	37.4%
20 years and over	6.9	14.6
All males	7.7	16.3
Females		
16–19 years	17.7	40.8
20 years and over	6.4	13.1
All females	7.4	15.0
Both sexes	7.7	15.7
Both sexes, both races	8.8	

Source: Economic Report of the President, 1982

Unemployment Differences

The recent history of unemployment rates follows the income pattern, less income for women and blacks, higher unemployment rates for women and blacks. Table 11-5 shows this picture, including a category for teenagers.

Table 11-5 contains a surprise. The unemployment rates for white women are less than those for white men in every category. Does that mean that women are finally finding their rightful place in the labor market? Hardly. A glance back at Table 11-3 reminds us that female workers are still making only 60 percent of the earnings of male workers. If, by some chance, employment opportunities are improving for women (very doubtful), the opportunities must be in low-paying jobs. Table 11-5 further confirms the plight of black and other minority workers. In December 1981, the overall unemployment rate for everyone was 8.8 percent. Among white workers, only teenagers exceeded this average rate. All of the black unemployment rates were well beyond it. The unemployment rates of blacks of both sexes were more than double those for whites. And finally, we can easily see that all teenagers, but mainly black teenagers, were in need of help.

Differences in Education

One of the most important reasons for differences in hiring and paying people lies in the amount of formal training they have had in school or college. What is the relationship of education to income and to possible exploitation or discrimination? Table 11-6 compares male and female incomes with education for the year 1980.

Table 11-6 certainly verifies the idea that income and education rise together. In both sexes, those with five or more years of college receive about four times the amount received by those with less than eight years of elementary school.

The income ratios again show that women lag far behind, regardless of their education. Women with one to three years of college receive less than men with an eighth-grade education. Women with five or more years of college receive only $525 more than male high school graduates. However, the income

Table 11-6. Educational Attainment and Median Money Income by Sex, 1980 (all persons 18 years old and over)

	Women	Men	Income ratios women/men*
Elementary school			
Less than 8 years	$3,634	$7,035	.52
8 years	4,177	8,960	.47
High school			
1–3 years	4,242	9,924	.43
4 years	6,080	14,583	.42
College			
1–3 years	6,985	15,674	.45
4 years	10,119	22,173	.46
5 or more	15,108	26,927	.56

Source: Statistical Abstract of the United States, 1982-1983.

* Readers will wonder why the incomes in this table are so much lower than those shown in Table 11-3. The reason for the difference lies in the fact that Table 11-3 considers full-time workers only; Table 11-6 looks at "all persons over 18," many of whom may be working part time or not working at all.

Table 11-7. Highest Educational Attainment for Persons over Age 25 (1981)

Percent of each group completing . . .	White		Black		Spanish-surname	
	Men	Women	Men	Women	Men	Women
Less than 4 years of high school	28.0	28.9	46.8	47.3	54.5	56.4
4 years of high school	34.1	42.4	31.2	32.1	24.5	27.9
Less than 4 years of college	15.7	14.9	13.9	12.4	11.3	9.8
4 or more years of college	22.2	13.8	8.2	8.2	9.7	5.9
Totals	100.0	100.0	100.0	100.0	100.0	100.0

Source: Statistical Abstract of the United States, 1982–1983.

ratio column reveals that women's incomes improve relative to men's—somewhat—if they obtain five or more years of college.*

This brings us to Table 11-7, which considers only educational attainment (not income) by sex and race. The table answers the question: What percentage of women have only a high school education and what percentage have at least graduated from college? (This time three groups are reported: white, black, and Spanish surname.)

---

* From a survey of the years 1979, 1980, and 1981, the Census Bureau concluded that an 18-year-old man who gets a college degree will earn $1,190,000 in his lifetime compared with $861,000 for a man with a high school diploma, a difference of $329,000. Comparable figures for women were $523,000 and $381,000, with a difference of $142,000. Because women in the study worked 10 years less than men, 28 years versus 38 years, we cannot conclude that the large income differences are entirely the result of discrimination. But, if years of work were the only determinant of lifetime income, we would expect women's earnings to be 74 percent (28 ÷ 38 years) of men's, not 44 percent ($523,000 ÷ $1,190,000), as actually observed for female and male college graduates. For more details see "College Degree Worth More to Men than Women," *Los Angeles Times,* 14 March 1983, Pt. I, p. 5.

The table clearly shows that, in 1981, white people obtained the most education, and that black people obtained more education than Spanish-surnamed people. And in every category except one, the percentage of males who had finished four years of college was larger than the percentage of women. The one exception was that the percentage of black women who had finished college was the same as that for black males (8.2 percent).

Interestingly, the percentage of women who graduated from high school but who had no further education was greater than that for men, in every category. But, particularly among white people, there was a large difference among men and women who had completed four or more years of college. The percentage of white men who received four or more years of college was 1.6 times (22.2 ÷ 13.8) that for white women.

What is the significance of these data? Education undoubtedly affects the demand for labor. However, if for any reason our society excludes some people from getting an education, some of the observed income differences come from *discrimination in education*. Although most educational institutions try hard not to discriminate, it takes money to go to school, and so we run into a circular problem. Low incomes deprive people of education, and people with less education have lower incomes.

Moreover, education becomes more costly as people continue their education, because (1) fees and tuition costs increase with each year of education, and (2) the opportunity cost of staying in school increases. When one goes through college, the income sacrificed (usually called *foregone income*) while one is in school is estimated to be 50 percent of the cost of a college education. Consequently, education, particularly higher education, tends to exclude (exclusion principle) those with lower incomes. Attitudes of uneducated parents may also contribute to lower incomes by discouraging their offspring from getting an education.

THE ECONOMIC THEORY OF DISCRIMINATION

The tables in the preceding section do not prove that exploitation or discrimination exists. The evidence is circumstantial, but it is so overwhelming that we can imagine no other explanation for the income differences that occur. In this section we will assume that discrimination does in fact exist and show what economic theory has to say about it.

Let's assume to start with that you, the Dazzle toothpaste entrepreneur, are a humane person, quite willing to hire the best, most qualified workers, regardless of race or sex. Figure 11-1(**a**) shows an employer's downward-sloping demand curve for labor, an indication that he will hire more workers as the wage falls. The supply curve for labor is upward sloping, an indication that more workers will offer themselves for work as the wage rises. W_{ND} represents the wage rate paid by a nondiscriminating employer; Q_1 is the number of workers hired.

Now, we'll assume that you are male and that you have a jealous wife (named Emily) who can't stand having you spending your days with pretty young things. She insists you fire them all and hire men only. Figure 11-1(**b**) shows what happens.

There is no reason for your demand to change, but the supply is reduced because now only male workers are available. With the decrease in supply, you, the employer will have to pay a higher wage, W_D (for discriminating wage).

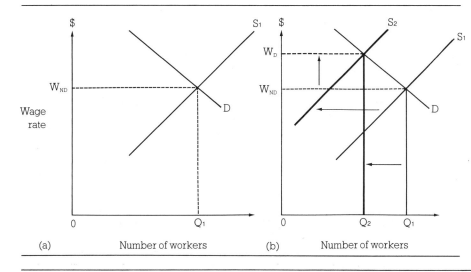

Figure 11-1.
(a) The demand for and supply of workers facing a nondiscriminating employer. (b) The employer discriminates against women.

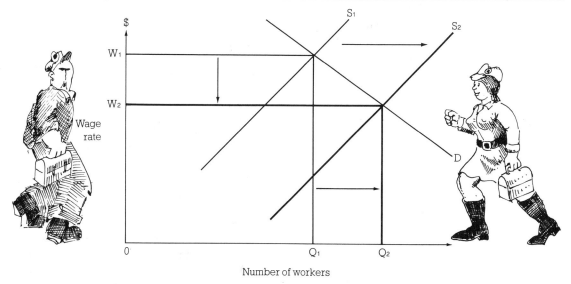

What do the women you have fired do? They will have to seek jobs elsewhere, in, for them, less attractive places to work, undoubtedly at lower wages. Figure 11-2 illustrates this change in whatever industry agrees to hire the women.

Figure 11-2 shows that, for this industry, the availability of additional female workers—at every wage rate—increases. The supply of workers shifts to the right. The wage falls—in the absence of unions—from W_1 to W_2 and the number of workers demanded increases from Q_1 to Q_2. This figure suggests the final outcome: The women hired will make less than they did before and they will probably work in secondary labor markets where there is little job training, high turnover, and poor pay.

What about Dazzle toothpaste and jealous Emily? You are now paying higher

Figure 11-2.
The women find work in another factory.

wages than before discrimination. If you are in a highly competitive industry, you will find yourself hard put to compete with nondiscriminating firms that pay lower wages. As time goes by, you may find that your very economic surviv- al depends on your ability to show Emily that your fidelity is everlasting so that you can hire the women back. Thus, in highly competitive situations, employ- ers may be forced to give up discriminatory practices.

One way to appreciate the effects of discrimination in labor markets is to imagine what would happen if farmers decided not to use some very good land just because it was black and grew their crops on "whiter" (and less produc- tive) land. Yields would be lower, and, as a result, production costs per unit would rise. Prices would be higher, and customers of such farmers would eat less well. Ultimately, we would hope, the discriminating farmers would see the error of their ways and use the black land.

On the other hand, many areas in our business community are dominated by large firms (as we saw in Chapter 8). In some cases, these large firms can influence markets sufficiently—either by themselves or with the cooperation of like firms—to maintain high prices and wages to a degree that would permit continued discrimination. Consequently, it is appropriate for a market-price system's government to engage in programs that soften the effects of discrimi- nation, because discrimination can lead to lower incomes and even poverty for some people and unnecessarily high prices for everyone.

GOVERNMENT PROGRAMS TO SOFTEN THE BLOW

The government's efforts to soften the blows of discrimination come in two forms:

1. Laws like the Equal Pay Act and the Civil Rights Act have pressured business firms and public agencies (including schools and colleges) to be- come "equal opportunity employers." In many instances, administrators are designated as "affirmative action" officers. Their job is to make sure that women and members of minorities are given preference over white males. Yet, no results of these efforts are yet apparent in national statistics covering income differences among people of different sex or race.

2. Federal, state, and local governments are also engaged in massive efforts to redistribute cash income, and income in the form of food, medical care, and low-cost housing in favor of poor people. These efforts are not necessarily aimed at discrimination because poverty can be the result of other than discriminatory causes. But, in the course of helping poor people, those who are the victims of discrimination may be helped also. The money for these programs has to come from somewhere. That means, of course, that it has to come from taxpayers; money and aid "in kind" are taken from one group and given to another, a redistribution, by government, of everyone's income.

The more familiar of these programs are OASDI (Old Age, Survivors, and Disability Insurance—Social Security), Supplemental Security Income (SSI), Medicaid, Medicare, Aid to Families with Dependent Children (AFDC), unem- ployment compensation, and food stamps. Federal outlays for these programs and others, including public housing, were $271 billion in 1980, about 10 percent of the nation's total income. A massive effort indeed!

The Inefficiency of Antipoverty (Welfare) Programs

Yet, economists criticize many of these antipoverty programs for three reasons:

1. One of the criticisms of many welfare systems is that, if anyone in a family receiving welfare gets a job and earns $1,000, the subsidy (the welfare payment) is sometimes cut by as much as $1,000. Economists call this a 100 percent **marginal tax on work**. Such a tax is apt to destroy any incentive to work. Welfare recipients may be tempted to conceal earned income or simply may refuse to look for a job in the first place.

To get a clearer idea of what happens, imagine a woman with a family of three young children receiving Aid for Families with Dependent Children (AFDC). The father has disappeared (see item 2.) The mother receives assistance in the form of cash, food stamps, and medical care. If the woman finds a job, for every $100 she earns, she will have to pay $7 in Social Security taxes. Typically, she will lose about $35 in AFDC benefits and $25 worth of food stamps. Taxes (assuming no income tax) and lost benefits total $67; for every $100 she earns, she increases her net income by only $33. The "marginal tax rate on work" is thus 67 percent, a much higher rate than the maximum tax rate paid on earned income. (The maximum federal income tax rate on individuals, excluding Social Security taxes, is 50 percent.) So, why work?

2. Working fathers may leave the family so that the other members can continue to receive the full subsidy. For this reason, high marginal tax rates on earned income are accused of breaking up families.

3. Because welfare subsidies differ from state to state— even from city to city—poor families have an incentive to migrate from cities where welfare subsidies are meager to those where the payments are more generous. Many cities are already overburdened and overcrowded with welfare immigrants for this reason.

The fundamental problem with the present system of welfare payments is that they focus the recipient's attention on beating the system, not on becoming self-supporting. When some individuals are encouraged not to work, total national output and income are reduced: There will be less to distribute to anyone. In this sense, present systems are inefficient; the manner of redistributing income reduces the total available.

In 1962, Milton Friedman published *Capitalism and Freedom,** in which he proposed a plan to overcome the present "welfare mess." Many economists agree with Friedman's plan, called the negative income tax. It is designed to give welfare recipients more incentive to work, and thereby to increase the size of the total national output available to help those unable to care for themselves.

The Negative Income Tax

The **negative income tax** is one of many similar proposals. Since space does not allow discussing them all, we will confine ourselves to only the broad outlines of the negative income tax.

---

* Friedman is a well-known economist at the Hoover Institution (Stanford University). The book was published by the University of Chicago Press.

Table 11-8. 50 Percent Marginal Tax Rates with a Negative Income Tax

Earned income	Government subsidy	Total income
$ 0	$5,000	$5,000
1,000	4,500	5,500
2,000	4,000	6,000
3,000	3,500	6,500
4,000	3,000	7,000
5,000	2,500	7,500
6,000	2,000	8,000
7,000	1,500	8,500
8,000	1,000	9,000
9,000	500	9,500
10,000	0	10,000

The idea is extremely simple. Every adult or head of family fills out a federal income-tax form. If the family's income is above some level defined as the poverty dividing line, say, $5,000,* the family pays a tax. If the family's income is less than $5,000, the family receives a "negative tax" in the form of a subsidy from the federal government. If the family's earned income is zero, it receives $5,000.

One controversy involves how much to subtract from the subsidy when someone in the family goes to work and earns money. The negative income tax (NIT) concept is based on allowing those who do go to work to keep more of their earned income than under the present system; that is, abolishing the excessively high marginal tax rate on income from work.

Most suggested negative income tax plans propose marginal rates on earned income of from 30 to 50 percent. To illustrate, let us use 50 percent. The 50 percent marginal tax rate on earned income means that for every $1,000 earned by the family, the subsidy is reduced by 50 percent of that amount, or $500.

Table 11-8 illustrates how such a plan would work. In this example, the subsidy drops to zero when our family earns $10,000 per year. If the marginal rates were lower than 50 percent, there would still be some subsidy at even higher income levels. A 40 percent rate would push the zero subsidy figure to $12,500.** A one-third marginal tax rate would push it to $15,000. The *lower* the marginal tax rate, then, the *less* the subsidy is reduced with each increase in income.

What about all the state and local welfare plans now in existence? Milton Friedman's original idea was clean and pure in its simplicity. He would sweep away *all* present welfare plans, including the Social Security program, and substitute a single, federally administered, NIT formula. Presumably, this would alleviate the problem of poor people's migrating across the country in search of higher welfare payments. One of the great attractions of Friedman's idea was

---

* The $5,000 subsidy drops to zero when earned income rises to $12,500 because $5,000 is 40 percent of $12,500.

** The figure depends on the number of people in the family, and it changes each year with changes in the cost of living. In 1982, the poverty line was about $9,300 for a nonfarm family of four. See also Table 11-2.

Studies of government subsidy plans have had mixed results.

that it proposed a single, nationally administered approach to a national problem, and the bureaucracy for administering the NIT—the Internal Revenue Service—is already in place. Poor people in the South would be treated the same as those in the northern cities.

The NIT idea has led to much opposition. Poor people and social workers worry about what will happen when present programs are eliminated. Politicians worry about losing votes until the NIT takes over. Voters worry about the cost of the NIT, variously estimated at $10 billion to $30 billion. And thousands of local and state welfare workers worry about losing their jobs if existing bureaucratic empires were to be wiped out.

There are legitimate differences of opinion about the size of the marginal tax rate, the income level at which subsidies would go to zero, and the design of a progressive income tax that might be inserted into the formula. And, unfortunately, in one extensive study of the NIT in action, the results contradicted the expected benefits of the plan.

The Seattle-Denver Experiment[7]

The Department of Health, Education, and Welfare studied the NIT in Seattle and Denver for eight years. Beginning in 1970, 2,700 black, white, and Hispanic families were exposed to the plan. They were divided into three groups based on a subsidy at zero earned income. The subsidies were 50 percent, 75 percent, and 100 percent of poverty-line income ($6,200 for a family of four). Then each of those groups was divided in half: one half to be at a 50 percent marginal tax rate on earned income and the other half to be at 70 percent.

All other forms of welfare were taken away from the families, and the families were reimbursed for any Social Security taxes or taxes they paid on earned income. In this way, the experimenters hoped that their subjects would respond only to the incentives (or lack of them) of the NIT.

Another group of 2,000 families functioned as a control group—remaining on whatever welfare program they had had or continuing to struggle along on their own without any assistance.

The results were disappointing for supporters of the NIT. In all families but 435, the number of hours worked declined as compared with hours worked previously. The decrease in hours worked varied from 8 to 34 percent. The exceptional 435 families increased their hours of work by one percent, perhaps because they had powerful incentives to work: They were single-parent families headed by women; their subsidy at zero-earned income was only 50 percent of poverty-line income; they could keep 50 percent of any earned income.

You will recall that one criticism of many welfare plans is that they lead to a breakup of families. Typically, the father leaves home so that his earned income will not make his wife and children ineligible for welfare payments. Quite unexpectedly in the Seattle-Denver experiment, the families in the NIT group had a 60 percent *higher* rate of separation than the families in the control group. And in many cases it was the woman who left the family. Researchers speculated that for many women the extra cash had the effect of helping them escape from unpleasant marriages.

There were a few bright spots. As expected, the decline in hours worked was more pronounced at the higher (70 percent) marginal tax rate on earned income than at the 50 percent rate. Men, for example, worked 10.6 percent fewer hours when they lost 70 cents in benefits for every dollar they earned, as compared with 6.2 percent fewer hours for those "taxed" at the 50 percent rate.

Many of the participants used the financial support as an opportunity to seek extra training or find better jobs and, eventually, about 25 percent of the NIT families earned so much that they were no longer eligible for benefits. Examples cited included a Seattle mother of three who had never finished high school and who got a degree in psychology and a job with an opinion-research firm. Another Seattle woman attended acting school, and her husband composed music. "We are now self-sufficient income-earning artists," she wrote.

Supporters of the plan like Senator Daniel P. Moynihan have concluded that the NIT will still work if job opportunities are present, and if work requirements are *mandatory*. This conclusion reminds us that the NIT plan is designed for those who are employable—perhaps only 30 percent of all poor people, as you learned on page 219. Public assistance without a work requirement will still be necessary for the other 70 percent. And unfortunately, creating job opportunities for those on an NIT program is easier to talk about than to do.

SUMMARY

Labor exploitation exists when employees are paid less than they would be paid in perfectly competitive labor markets. Exploitation can be reduced or prevented if employers have to compete for an employee's services. Discrimination exists when workers with the same skills are treated differently in terms of hiring, promotion, or pay.

Although exploitation and discrimination are difficult to prove, existing data provide strong circumstantial evidence that women, teenagers, and minorities suffer from both practices.

There is a possibility that the market will force discriminating employers to cease discriminating. If such employers hire only white males, the supply of labor available to them will be restricted. They will have to pay higher wages, possibly, than their competitors pay. If so, competition will eventually force them to hire the best person for the job regardless of race or sex in order to bring their wage costs down. If competition does not work, there are government regulations like the Equal Pay Act and the Civil Rights Act of 1964 to pressure employers to treat everyone equally. However, data indicate that income distribution has not been affected by such legislation.

The negative income tax plan attempts to overcome many of the deficiencies of present welfare plans. Many economists believe it is the best way to redistribute income, but there are political difficulties in passing the necessary legislation. Moreover, one study, the Seattle-Denver study, has indicated the NIT will not cause the working poor to work more hours unless appropriate job opportunities are available. And finally, we have to remember that 70 percent of poor people may not be able to participate in the benefits of the NIT program because they are unable to work.

Discussion Questions

1. What are the entry barriers to the career you want to follow after college?

2. How can exploitation be reduced?

3. How many male secretaries are there on your college campus? Male tellers and clerks at your local bank?

4. If, as we suspect, there aren't many males in either job, is the absence of males evidence of discrimination? Of which kind of discrimination— job discrimination or wage discrimination? (This is a tough one. It's possible there is *no* discrimination. Can you explain why?)

5. If you were a dictator, what problems would you face in installing the NIT?

DID YOU EVER WONDER WHY . . .

. . . discrimination can lower living standards?

References

1. One well-known economist is especially concerned about our lack of understanding of this problem. See: Lester C. Thurow, *The Zero-Sum Society* (New York: Penguin Books, 1981).

2. Gurney Breckenfeld, "Has Reagan Hurt the Poor?" *Fortune,* 24 January 1983.

3. See Michael Harrington's review of: Ken Auletta, *The Underclass* (New York: Random House, 1982) in *New Republic,* 9 June 1982.

4. Al Gonzales, a spokesman for the National Association of Social Workers. Quoted in *Facts on File,* 23 April 1982.

5. Breckenfeld.

6. Reported by Bruce Keppel, "Sexual Segregation Prevails in Business, Study Shows," *Los Angeles Times,* 22 August 1982. The two professors called the 60 percent figure the "segregation index."

7. Described in U.S. Department of Health, Education, and Welfare, *Summary Report: Seattle-Denver Income Maintenance Experiment,* (Washington, D.C.: Government Printing Office, February 1978). Also summarized in "Welfare: A Surprising Test," *Newsweek,* 27 November 1978.

We turn now from our study of individuals and their problems like Fred's thirst for beer in the desert and Amelia's production and sale of coffee mugs, from individual companies like Velvetex, from industries like the egg industry, and from problems affecting particular groups of workers to a discussion of how the national economy operates as a whole. We leave the world of microeconomics and enter that of macroeconomics.

Two of the nation's main macroeconomic concerns are inflation and unemployment. The goal of Parts IV and V is to help you understand the

PART IV

THE MACRO VIEW AND THE ROLE OF GOVERNMENT

federal government's role in trying to solve these two difficult problems. Part IV consists of three chapters. To discuss the cures for inflation and unemployment, we must first explain how the nation's economic activity is measured. That is the job of Chapter 12. Chapter 13 uses these measures to describe the up and down swings of the nation's output and employment. Chapter 14 analyzes the government's role in our economic system—its relative size and its effect on our incomes. Part V describes the measures the federal government can take to reduce inflation and unemployment.

12

The National Economy: Measuring Its Performance

KEY WORDS

National income
  accounting
Gross National
  Product (GNP)
Transfer payments
Aggregate supply
Aggregate demand
Consumption
Investment
Government
  purchases of
  goods and services
Net exports
Disposable Personal
  Income (DPI)
Saving versus savings

Double counting
Intermediate products
Final product
Price indexes
  Consumer Price
    Index (CPI)
  Producer Price
    Index (PPI)
  Implicit price
    deflator
Base year
Real GNP
Real change
Nominal GNP
Real per capita GNP
Real per capita DPI

This chapter has one main purpose: To show how the total production of the United States is measured. This total will influence the number of jobs available. The total quantities of everything produced will also have some influence on the level of prices. Thus, measuring the total output of the United States is the first step in understanding unemployment and inflation. The chapter is divided into three sections: (1) The link between microeconomics and macroeconomics, (2) measures of income and output, and (3) the limitations of the Gross National Product (GNP) as a measure of change (or of progress).

THE LINK BETWEEN MICROECONOMICS AND MACROECONOMICS

In Parts II and III, you saw how many individual microeconomic markets operated. Some of these markets were for goods (coffee mugs or Dazzle toothpaste), and some were for resources (labor markets). In each of these cases we were examining a "micro" bit of the economy to find out how much of each product or resource might be supplied or demanded at different prices. We made no attempt to determine the total dollar value of *all* products produced; that is, we were examining individual pieces of a pie without trying to measure the size of the whole pie. Parts IV and V are involved with this latter point of view—the "macro" view.

Only by viewing the economy as a whole can we find out if all the individual markets for coffee mugs, for toothpaste, for whatever, add up to enough economic activity to give a job to everyone who wants one. And, only by viewing the economy as a whole can we examine the ups and downs of the average price level. Analyzing how individual micro markets helps us explain the behavior of prices for, say, coffee mugs. But that doesn't tell us much about the behavior of *all* prices. To examine the behavior of all prices we have to look at the total demands for and total supplies of everything—as well as the total amount of money available for spending. (This last issue is examined in Part V.)

Despite these apparent differences in micro and macro points of view, the two are inevitably interdependent. For example, the morale of an individual baseball player (the micro view) will certainly have *some* effect on the performance of the whole team (the macro view). And the performance of the whole team (the macro view) will certainly have an effect on the morale of an individual player (the micro view). Unemployment in a particular industry like the automobile industry (the micro view) will certainly affect national employment (the macro view), and the (micro) success or failure of any single industry affects the size of the macro "pie." The whole affects the parts, and the parts affect the whole.

Similarly, decisions by the federal government to influence the whole economy (the macro view)—perhaps by changing taxes or government spending—invariably have micro effects in particular markets. A decision by the federal government to spend more or less money is never neutral: Some groups of people, some industries, will be affected more than others. President Kennedy's decision to put a man on the moon spurred growth in particular industries. President Reagan's tax cuts and tax increases affected different groups of people differently. So did his widely debated increases in military spending at the expense of social programs like food stamps. Macro decisions inevitably translate into micro effects.

Most nations have a system of measuring their macroeconomic affairs.

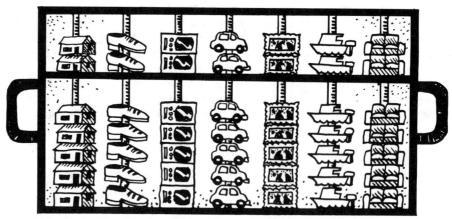

Moreover, micro decisions often have macro effects. Micro decisions that lead to technological breakthroughs might very well make the nation capable of producing a larger macro pie. Consider the huge industry that has been built upon the tiny silicon microchip.

Thus macro and micro changes in the economy are closely interwoven, and the difference depends on our point of view. The two aspects may be discussed separately, but in fact they are always interrelated.

A whole course in economics could be designed around just the micro effects of macro decisions. In this and the following chapters we will confine ourselves primarily to the *macro* effects of macro decisions. Moreover, we will assume that when the federal government acts, its decisions affect the whole macro pie. With a few exceptions, we will ignore the effects of the decisions made in Washington, D.C., on micro markets.

MEASURES OF INCOME AND OUTPUT

Most nations of the world keep track of their macroeconomic affairs—total output and income, levels of employment and unemployment, changes in the price level, rates of economic growth, and so forth. They need to know how things are going in order to determine whether government policies are helping the economy. The measuring system that is used in most parts of the world is called **national income accounting**.

Some of the major objectives of the system in the United States are:*

- To chart the progress (or lack of it) in the nation's output and income from one year to the next.
- To keep track of prices and unemployment.
- To report changes in the supply of money and credit.
- To report government spending, taxes, and changes in the national debt.
- To inform us where we stand internationally in relation to exports, imports, and the balance of payments.

*One of the best sources of this information is the annual *Economic Report of the President*, which is usually made available to the public each year in February. It covers the previous year and is divided into three parts: A report by the President, a report by his Council of Economic Advisers, and statistical tables covering the kinds of measures mentioned in our very brief list of the objectives of national income accounting.

There are five measures of the nation's output and income. The first three—*Gross National Product (GNP), Net National Product (NNP),* and *National Income (NI)*—deal with total output and total income. The last two—*Personal Income (PI)* and *Disposable Personal Income (DPI)*—deal with the money consumers have to spend or save.* We will consider only the first measure (GNP) and the last (DPI).

Gross National Product (GNP)

The **Gross National Product** is the largest and most inclusive of the five measures. It is an estimate of the dollar value of the goods and services produced in one year. Changes in income resulting from activities unconnected with production—for example, gains or losses in the stock market, income from crime, and income received in the form of transfer payments—are excluded.

Although not included in the Gross National Product (abbreviated GNP from now on), **transfer payments** have become an important part of many people's income. Transfer payments are not included in GNP because they are considered exchanges of money between taxpayers and recipients that have no effect on the "national product" or level of employment until the recipient decides to spend (or save) the money. Transfer payments are payments that governments (national, state, and local) make to people without receiving any *productive* service in exchange. These payments include welfare or unemployment insurance payments, the unpaid portion of food stamps, veterans' benefits, Social Security payments, subsidized medical care, and interest income paid to owners of government securities. At the end of 1982, transfer payments were running about $459 billion annually, of which $85 billion were interest payments to owners of government securities.

Now back to the GNP. The money total of everything supplied in the year we are measuring is called **aggregate supply**, and the grand total of *everything* supplied (produced) is our GNP. The money total that people spend during a year for newly produced goods and services (that is, produced during the year we are measuring) is called **aggregate demand**.

Economists usually take the view that aggregate demand determines aggregate supply because business firms base their supply decisions on what they expect demand to be. Following this line of argument, then, aggregate demand determines GNP. (There is also a school of thought that holds that supply can determine demand; we'll discuss this idea in Chapter 19.)

The total of everything produced, our GNP, can be measured, either (1) by assigning a dollar value to all the products or (2) by totaling the income everyone receives. The first approach is called the *expenditures approach* because it looks at patterns of spending. The second approach is called the *income approach.* The totals of spending and income have to match because all the money has to wind up somewhere.

The Expenditures Approach to Measuring GNP

Economists put everything everyone buys into four categories: *consumption, investment, government purchases of goods and services,* and *net exports.* Ag-

---

*NNP is GNP less all depreciation allowances. NI is NNP less indirect business taxes (sales and property taxes paid by businesses). PI is NI plus transfer payments, then minus corporate retained earnings, Social Security taxes, and corporate profits taxes.

gregate demand is the sum of these four kinds of spending, and because aggregate demand determines GNP, GNP is also the sum of these four kinds of spending. Let us consider these categories:

1. **Consumption**. This category represents the purchases consumers make in a given year for newly produced products (except for brand-new houses), plus purchases for services from people like doctors and plumbers.

2. **Investment**. This category consists of (1) the purchases of new houses by consumers, (2) purchases of capital goods by business firms—buildings, machinery, vehicles, filing cabinets, and other equipment, and (3) inventories. Production in process and finished goods that have not been sold are included in inventories, which are considered investments. Because each year usually begins with inventories representing production in the previous year, and because the measurement of GNP includes only the production of goods and services in the current year, we determine investment in inventory by subtracting the inventory at the end of last year from the inventory at the end of the present year. Only the net change in inventories is actually reported in the investment figure. Note that inventory changes can be either positive or negative.

When a soup company manufactures canned soup, the soup first becomes part of the company's inventory and then part of a grocery store's inventory. During this time in inventory, the soup is counted as an *investment*. When someone finally buys the soup, it is subtracted from investment and added to consumption. Such inventory changes help experts to program future production or to forecast changes in business activity and the level of employment.

The investment category also includes a fourth estimate: depreciation allowances (also called capital consumption allowances). Depreciation allowances are the means by which businesses compute the cost of capital goods, which wear out over time. (To subtract the whole cost at once from income would make production costs seem too high; to not subtract the cost at all would ignore capital costs entirely.) Suppose a machine costs $10,000. An accountant might estimate the machine's "life" at ten years. Having done so, she will label as depreciation one tenth of the cost of the machine per year ($1,000). This is a legitimate business expense that is deducted from income before computing the business' income tax. The investment category of the GNP includes the creation of new capital goods and an allowance for the replacement of those that have worn out.

To sum up: The term *investment* means the creation of capital goods and inventories. It does not mean the purchase of a stock or bond. Such purchases are acts of saving, and we'll use the term *financial investment* for them.

3. **Government purchases of goods and services**. Although this term includes all spending at every level of government, ranging from local spending for fire engines to federal spending for space shuttles, it does *not* include transfer payments.

4. **Net exports**. These are purchases by other countries of our products (like Coca-Cola) and services (like air travel) *minus* our purchases of theirs.

The Income Approach to Measuring GNP

All the money spent on consumption, investment, government purchases, and net exports winds up in someone's pocket. Who gets it?

Table 12-1. Simplified GNP, 1982 (in billions)

Income approach		Expenditures approach	
Wages (including payroll taxes and fringe benefits)	$1,855.9	Consumption	$1,972.0
Interest	265.3	Investment	421.9
Rent	34.1	Government purchases	647.1
Profit	281.2	Net exports	16.5
Depreciation allowances	356.8		
Indirect business taxes	264.2		
	$3,057.5		$3,057.5

Source: Economic Report of the President, 1983.

The answer is fairly simple. Economists put all income into four categories—wages, interest, rent, and profit. However, two kinds of expenditures are not counted as income: (1) Businesses set aside part of their profits for depreciation allowances, which are not considered part of profit in national income accounting. So depreciation allowances become a fifth category. (2) When we pay sales taxes at retail stores, the stores receiving that money have to forward it to the government. These "indirect business taxes" form a sixth category. Thus all money generated on the "expenditures" side of the GNP ledger ends up in *six* "pockets"—the four income pockets of wages, interest, rent, and profit, plus depreciation allowances and indirect business taxes.

A simplified GNP account for the year 1982 is shown in Table 12-1. The table indicates that we produced $3,057.5 billion dollars' worth of goods and services in 1982, an enormous quantity, probably double that of the Soviet Union, which has the world's next-largest GNP. Keep in mind that the $647 billion spent by all levels of government does not include $459 billion worth of transfer payments also spent in 1982. Notice also that net exports were positive, meaning that we exported more than we imported. More about the issue of net exports in Chapter 20.

Disposable Personal Income (DPI)

We have skipped over three measures of income (NNP, NI, and PI) to get to the one that matters most to consumers: **Disposable Personal Income (DPI)**. To get to DPI from GNP we first subtract from GNP all taxes, as well as monies corporations keep in the form of retained earnings and depreciation allowances. We then add transfer payments—payments such as veterans' benefits, welfare or unemployment insurance payments, Social Security payments, or interest income on government securities. The idea is to calculate the amount of money consumers have left to spend or save by subtracting from GNP monies people never see and the money they pay in taxes, but then adding the transfer payments that are so important to many Americans. Because transfer payments are included in DPI, economists usually say that DPI is a measure of *income received*, rather than a measure of *income earned*.

DPI is what is left after *all* taxes have been removed. This includes *personal taxes;* that is, income taxes, personal property taxes, inheritance taxes, and user taxes on vehicles (license plates and registration fees).

Table 12-2. Disposable Personal Income (DPI), 1982 (in billions)

Calculation of DPI	
GNP	$3,057.5
Minus all taxes and minus monies corporations kept	− 1,344.0
Plus transfer payments	+ 459.0*
Total DPI	= $2,172.5
How DPI was disposed of	
Consumption spending	$2,030.6
Personal saving	+ 141.9
	= $2,172.5

*See page 237.

Now that we have DPI, what does the consumer do with it? The consumer either spends it on consumption goods or saves it. (Remember that saving might be in the form of financial investments, but these do not constitute investment as economists use the term.)

What was DPI in 1982 and how did consumers divide it between consumption and saving? Table 12-2 summarizes what happened.

The table contains an important fact. In 1982 consumers spent 93.5 percent ($2,030.6 billion) of their DPIs and saved 6.5 percent ($141.9 billion). Since the end of World War II, this relationship has remained fairly stable, varying from about 95 to 92 percent for consumption and from 5 to 8 percent for personal saving. (Note that DPI = consumption + saving. Therefore, saving = DPI − consumption. This is a way of saying that **saving** is the unconsumed portion of income. Thus any income not spent—that is, put in the bank, stock market, or bonds—is saving. The term **savings** refers to one's accumulation of saving from all past years to the present.)

Economists pay considerable attention to these apparently small changes in consumption spending and saving for two reasons: (1) A change from 5 to 8 percent is a 60 percent increase in saving. Such a change nationwide means an important change in consumer attitudes about spending, an indication that jobs will become easier or harder to find. (2) Although these small changes are significant, knowing that consumption spending fluctuates in the area of 94 percent (plus or minus 1 to 2 percent) allows economists to make fairly accurate forecasts about how people will spend and save when DPI changes. If DPI increases by $10 billion because of some new government project, we can forecast that people will increase their spending by about $9.4 billion (94 percent of $10 billion) and their saving by about $600 million.

DIFFICULTIES . . . WITH MEASURING GNP

Collecting the data for measuring the nation's output is extraordinarily difficult. The Bureau of Economic Analysis of the Department of Commerce does most of this work. It must obtain its information from about 12 million business enterprises and many agencies of government. The results are statistical *estimates* and should not be interpreted as being exact. A famous mathematician, Oskar Morgenstern, once argued that the GNP estimate might be off by as

Estimates of consumption spending often include the problem of double counting.

much as 10 percent in either direction. Let us see why the GNP is subject to inaccuracies.

The Problem of Double Counting

Suppose that you, our honest, trustworthy, national income accountant, are busy one day trying to estimate consumption spending. You note the sales of cars priced at $12,000, but as you prepare to include such sales in the consumption category, you wonder if you should add to the $12,000 figure the cost of all the materials in the car, perhaps another $4,000, making the consumption-spending figure $16,000 per car instead of $12,000. Obviously, if you do, you'll be demoted to janitor the next day. The mistake involves what is called **double counting** because the $12,000 price necessarily includes the $4,000 worth of materials.

Materials used up in the production of any good are called **intermediate products**. The product that is produced is called the **final product**. Clearly, we want to avoid counting intermediate products and count only *final* products. Consequently, we try hard to estimate the value of all final products (and services) produced—excluding intermediate products—to arrive at GNP. A refined definition of the GNP is therefore: *The Gross National Product is an estimate of the value of the final goods and services produced during the year being measured.* The year may be a calendar year or a "fiscal year" (abbreviated FY). The fiscal year for the federal government is October 1 through the following September 30. (The FYs for the states may differ.)

. . . AND WITH USING GNP

GNP is the best measure we've got of the nation's total output and income. It is used to chart our progress or lack of it, as well as to compare ourselves with other countries. But the GNP measure is subject to at least six difficulties: (1) price inflation, (2) changes in population, (3) income distribution, (4) the comparison of how GNP is spent, (5) external costs, and (6) the "underground economy."

The Problem of Price Inflation

The term *inflation* as used here means a period of generally rising prices. With the exception of 1949, average prices have risen every year since 1940. Consequently, when GNP goes up, some or all of the increase reflects higher prices for the *same* quantities. Somehow, we have to take the effect of higher prices out of GNP to determine actual changes in the quantities of goods and services produced.

The process by which we take the effect of higher prices out of GNP is called *deflating the GNP*. Average prices are computed each year by a number of procedures and are published in the form of **price indexes**. There are three price indexes: (1) The **Consumer Price Index (CPI)** represents the average prices of some 400 retail products and services. (2) The **Producer Price Index (PPI)** represents product prices at the wholesale level. (3) The so-called **implicit price deflator**, a combination of both indexes, represents average price changes for the entire economy.

Because price indexes measure average price changes, there must be a starting point so that price changes can be measured relative to some particular year—called the **base year**. In the case of the implicit price deflator, the base year against which all others are presently compared is 1972.* A figure (price index) of 100 is arbitrarily assigned to the average price level for that year because that makes calculations simple. If (as it did) the implicit price deflator rose to 207 during 1982, you can conclude that prices rose 107 percent in 11 years. You can also say that what cost $1 in 1972, cost $2.07 in 1982.

Now let us use the index to tell us what happened after 1972. In 1972, GNP was $1,186 billion. In 1982, it was, as we have seen in Table 12-1, $3,057.5 billion. This makes an apparent difference of $1,871.5 billion, considerably more than double the GNP in 1972. We think, "Wow, that's progress!" Alas, not so.

The problem is that the apparent gain is false because in 1982 we paid more than twice as much as we did in 1972 for the same kinds of goods and service. To put it another way, each of those $3,057.5 billion bought considerably less in 1982 than in 1972. If the price of one pound of hamburger was $1 in 1972 and $2.07 in 1982, $1 in 1982 could buy only .483 pounds (1 ÷ 2.07) instead of a whole pound. The loss of about half a pound is indicated by the 51.7 percent (1.00 − .483) drop in the purchasing power of the dollar.

If each dollar in 1982 bought only 48.3 percent as much as it did in 1972, then the 1982 GNP was 51.7 percent too high. If we can find out how much the 1982 GNP could have bought at 1972 prices, then we can determine how much the country's total output increased (or decreased) in *physical quantities* of goods and services—not just in higher prices for the *same* quantities.

The procedure for taking the effect of higher prices out of the GNP figure is called "deflating the GNP"—just as if we were letting hot air out of a balloon. The formula for "deflating" the 1982 GNP to find its 1972 purchasing power is as follows:

$$\frac{\text{1982 GNP in}}{\text{1972 prices}} = \frac{\text{Base year implicit price deflator}}{\text{1982 implicit price deflator}} \times \text{1982 GNP in 1972 prices}$$

Because we have already noted that 100 ÷ 207 = .483, the formula becomes:

$$\$1,477 \text{ billion} = .483 \times \$3,057.5 \text{ billion}$$

---

*The base year for the Consumer Price and the Producer Price Index is 1967.

Table 12-3. Nominal and Real GNPs, 1978–1982 (in billions of dollars)

Year	Nominal GNP	Real GNP	Implicit price deflator
1978	$2,156.0	$1,437	150
1979	2,414.0	1,483	163
1980	2,626.0	1,481	177
1981	2,938.0	1,514	194
1982	3,057.5	1,477	207

Source: Economic Report of the President, 1983.

What does the $1,477 billion mean? It is the 1982 GNP expressed in dollars having the same purchasing power they had in 1972. Economists call the $1,477 billion figure **real GNP**. Or they may say that the 1982 GNP is now expressed in *constant dollars*, or in *real terms*. Further, the change from the $1,186 billion GNP in 1972 to the $1,477 billion figure in 1982 is a ***real change.*** The word "real" means that the income figures being used have been corrected for price changes.

Using constant 1972 dollars as the measuring stick, the real change from $1,186 billion in 1972 to $1,477 billion in 1982 is only $291 billion, instead of the "undeflated" change of $1,871.5 billion ($3,057.5 billion − $1,186 billion).

When we use GNP dollars that are *uncorrected* for price changes, like the $3,057.5 billion figure, economists refer to *money GNP, current dollar GNP*, or, most frequently, **nominal GNP**. Now we can see why the real change was so much smaller than the nominal change. *Nominal* GNP rose 2.58 times from $1,186 to $3,057.5 (3,057.5 ÷ 1,186), but prices more than doubled, cutting the apparent gain in nominal GNP to almost nothing. Table 12-3 compares other nominal and real GNPs in recent years.

The table reveals clearly that the "real" economy grew little during the 1978–1982 period; 1982 was worse than every year except 1978. Here we can see the numbers that lay behind the 10.1 unemployment rate in October 1982, the worst unemployment rate in 40 years. The macro pie simply wasn't growing fast enough to provide jobs for an expanding labor force.

What about Population Change?

Whether or not nominal or real GNP rises or falls, the number of people who must share the pie usually rises. If GNP doesn't rise fast enough to supply an expanding population, the pieces will have to get smaller. To uncover the effects of population changes on incomes, economists first change GNP into real terms, as we have done in the table, and then divide real GNP by population. The result is called **real per capita GNP.**

Let us compare 1972 with 1982. In Table 12-4 the figures in Column 3 result from dividing Column 1 by Column 2. Column 3 indicates that each person's share of GNP, corrected for inflation ("deflated"), increased by $718 over the eleven-year period, or about $65 per person per year.

A somewhat better measure of changes in well-being involves the **real per capita DPI.** Remember, although DPI includes transfer payments, it represents the consumer's net income after all taxes have been paid. It is our best measure

Table 12-4. Real per Capita GNP, 1972 and 1982 (GNP in billions of 1972 dollars, population in millions)

	Real GNP (1)	Population (2)	Real per capita GNP (3) = (1) ÷ (2)
1972	$1,186	210	$5,648
1982	1,477	232	6,366

of the money consumers have available for spending or saving. In 1972, real per capita DPI was $3,860, whereas in 1982 it was $4,544, an increase in real income of $684 over the eleven-year period. Real per capita DPI is a better measure of our economic status than real per capita GNP, because DPI includes the effects of taxes and transfer payments on our incomes. GNP does not.

The Problem of Income Distribution

Our difficulties are not over. Note that real per capita DPI or GNP figures are *averages*, obtained by dividing real income by population. Averages have a major failing; they conceal the way numbers are distributed.

Imagine two countries, A and B, which each have a GNP of $1,000 and a population of 10 people. Average per capita income is then $100 per person per year ($1,000 ÷ 10 people) in both countries. Now suppose that the $1,000 is fairly evenly divided in country A but that there is a king in country B whose annual income is $900. The other nine people in country B divide up the remaining $100, an average of about $11 per person. In country B, one person is rich while the others may be starving; nevertheless, country B's per capita income is still the same $100. The issue of income distribution is important whether we are comparing change in a given country from one year to the next or are making comparisons between countries.

Comparing How GNP Is Spent

Two examples will illustrate this additional problem: In 1944 and again in 1957, real per capita GNP was coincidentally about $2,600. But in 1944, we were engaged in all-out war, while 1957 was relatively peaceful. In 1944, spending for military services was about $75 billion, or 36 percent of GNP for that year ($75 billion ÷ $210 billion). In 1957, however, military spending was $39 billion, only 9 percent of GNP for that year ($39 ÷ $441 billion). Even though the real per capita GNP for the two years appears to be the same, the people in 1944 were giving up a much larger share of their incomes for military expenses and receiving necessarily much less for the civilian pleasures. When comparing per capita incomes in different years or making comparisons of different countries, we must consider the composition of GNP.

The same problem applies to differences in climate. Suppose a cold country like Greenland has the same real per capita GNP as Samoa. Which country is better off? In Greenland, much of the GNP is spent fighting for survival, whereas in Samoa more of it can be spent on pleasure.

This last point raises an interesting question. Does the fact that we have the largest GNP in the world really make us the richest country? Perhaps not. What does GNP really measure? It measures our desire for and effort to obtain goods and services. It may also measure our preoccupation with acquiring income

The production of automobiles leads to more than one kind of consumption.

and wealth or the pervasiveness of the "Protestant ethic" in our society. In any case, the GNP is a relatively poor measure of the quality of individual citizens' lives.

The Failure to Take External Costs into Account

Our comments so far about GNP are not intended to be criticisms of the concept. Rather, they are intended to show the limitations of the GNP estimate as a measure of change, and particularly as a measure of change in the standard of living of individuals. Recently, however, there has been a growing chorus of criticism of the way GNP is figured—directed mainly at the failure of GNP to take external costs into account.

For example, we count the sale of automobiles as a plus and add it to consumption. We also count the treatment of lung disease, which may have been caused by the exhaust from automobiles, as a plus and also add it to consumption (the purchase of medical services). Some economists now argue that, if the automobile causes damage, or if approach and landing patterns around airfields depress property values, or if a factory pollutes a stream, we should deduct the costs of correcting these problems from GNP rather than add them.

Besides deducting minuses we might also add pluses for external benefits not reflected in product or service prices. We could also add a plus for leisure time, a point to remember because the time spent working is getting shorter. It has also been suggested that we should deduct an allowance for the depletion of the earth's resources. Efforts are now under way to give us a revised GNP that will take these difficult but important considerations into account.*

---

*In one attempt to deal with this problem is the MEW—"Measure of Economic Welfare." The MEW concept subtracts from GNP not only pollution-related activities but also some government expenditures considered "regrettable," such as national defense, police forces, and fire departments. The MEW measure also subtracts a "disamenity premium" for the dissatisfaction one feels from living in crowded cities, while including large "pluses" for leisure time and work done in the home. Normative judgments are obviously involved here: One critic of the MEW notion has suggested that deciding what expenditures and activities are "good" and "bad" would require a "philosopher king." (Arthur M. Okun, "Should GNP Measure Social Welfare?" *Brookings Bulletin*, Summer 1971).

The Underground Economy

It stands to reason that the people in Washington can count as part of GNP only the transactions that are officially reported. But as we all know, countless unreported transactions take place every day involving services like housecleaning, home nursing care, gardening, and babysitting, as well as the earnings of undocumented immigrant workers in small nonunion factories and shops.

The reasons for failing to report payments in the underground economy are logical. One California woman who paid her babysitters $100 a week found that, over a year, Social Security taxes for *each* of them* amounted to $348.40, while $176.80 went for unemployment insurance, $130 for workers' compensation, and $41.60 for disability insurance—totaling $1,045.40 on wages of $5,200. On top of this, the employee became subject to income taxes. The employer, in addition to the cost, was required to prepare and mail four different forms for each of the four taxes, both quarterly and annually, to comply with government regulations. Basically, one lawyer commented, "You [an individual] and General Motors have to fill out the same forms."[1]

In addition to the unreported incomes earned by workers in these categories are the gigantic sums involved in transactions like illegal drug production and distribution, estimated at $79 billion in 1980.**[2] One example: Marijuana is believed by many to be the number-one cash crop in California. Attempts to verify this gossip proved interesting. Telephone conversations with experts in the Department of Justice, State of California, and the U.S. Forest Service brought admissions that any estimate of drug sales is guesswork. On the other hand, conversation with an expert at the U.S. Forest Service did produce some hard evidence of the amount of marijuana grown in California on *U.S. Forest Service land* in 1982: 387,001 plants, of which 55,561 were confiscated. A mature marijuana plant 10 feet tall can produce a crop with retail sales value of $3,500. Using $2,000 as an average per plant, the total value of the marijuana plants grown on U.S. Forest Service land was therefore 387,001 × $2,000 = $774 million. Assuming, as our expert did, that the production on U.S. Forest land was half of total production at most, the estimate for total sales in 1982 is about $1.5 billion. Keep in mind that this estimate is for California only. The value of *all legal crops* in California in 1981 was about $8 billion. The U.S. total for all crops in 1981 was about $83 billion.

In addition to *legal* but unreported transactions and *illegal*, unreported transactions, the underground economy includes transactions between people like a doctor who exchanges medical services for gardening and a patient who is a gardener. No money changes hands. The Internal Revenue Service never hears about it; no income or Social Security taxes are paid.[3]

Underground economies have existed for decades in many other countries, often in larger magnitudes than in the United States. The Soviet Union and its satellites are only one example. Hungary's underground economy is estimated at one third of its total production. Other examples include Italy, France, Belgium, West Germany, Denmark, Norway, Sweden, and Japan. We are again reminded of man's infinite ingenuity in bypassing rules that conflict with his self-interest.

---

*The employee and employer each pay an equal amount of Social Security taxes, so that, in this case, the total tax was actually $696.80, a good reason for not reporting from both points of view.

**The $79 billion figure is for illegal drug traffic only; it excludes income from other illegal activities like prostitution, gambling, and loan-sharking.

It is debated that unbridled capitalism works best—with no unions, regulations, or taxation.

The most authoritative estimate of the magnitude of this unreported underground economy in the United States was $420 billion for 1981, 14.3 percent of nominal GNP for that year. These estimates, according to one report, are "now being used to promote a highly debatable point—that capitalism works best without labor unions, job restraints, health and safety controls, and government taxation."[4]

The solutions to this problem will probably be long in coming. It's a ticklish issue for politicians. The cost of enforcement is high, and enforcement, if possible, might increase the numbers of those unemployed by increasing the cost of labor.

The failure of present accounting methods to include the underground economy in the GNP suggests that the GNP is understated, that we are better off than we think we are, and that the unemployment rate is less than that reported. On the other hand, when unemployment is over 10 percent, as it was in October 1982, many people become so discouraged they do not try to find work and are then not counted in the unemployment rate. In other words, there are good reasons why the real unemployment rate may be a good deal higher than the reported rate—and good reasons why it may be much lower. The measurement of unemployment and its consequences is considered in more detail in Chapter 13.

SUMMARY

This chapter has shown how the economy's total output and income are measured. The most inclusive measure is the Gross National Product (GNP). It is determined by everyone's total demand for goods and services—called aggregate demand. The idea is that, after correcting for mistakes in judgment, producers will gear their production to meet this demand. Total production is called aggregate supply.

Disposable personal income (DPI) is the best measure of a person's take-home pay, particularly after it is adjusted for inflation. Changes in "real" DPI are the best measure of economic growth.

There are many pitfalls in using these measures to assess change in human welfare. Among the pitfalls are the problems of double counting, price and population changes, GNP composition and income distribution, as well as external costs—the problem of treating the costs of economic activity (such as pollution) as if they were pluses. Finally, the GNP is incomplete because only those cash transactions officially reported are included. A large unreported underground economy exists.

Discussion Questions

1. If per capita GNP were $100 in Ethiopia and $5,000 in the United States, would you say that Americans were 50 times better off than Ethiopians?

2. Assume that your DPI in Year X is $7,000 and that Year X is the base year. In Year Y, your DPI is $10,000, but in Year Y the implicit price deflator is 130. How much has your real DPI changed?

3. If a rate of increase changes from 4 percent to 5 percent, how much has the rate changed?

4. If the rate of inflation is 10 percent, how long will it take to reduce the value of a dollar to 50 cents? (Hint: Use the "rule of of 72" in Chapter 1.)

5. What are the four kinds of spending that make up aggregate demand?

6. Why are aggregate supply and aggregate demand apt to be equal?

7. Why does aggregate demand determine GNP?

DID YOU EVER WONDER WHY . . .

. . . the government includes commercially grown vegetables in the GNP but not home grown?

References

1. Examples and quote from S. J. Diamond, "Red Tape Pushes Household Workers into the Underground Economy," *Los Angeles Times*, 24 January 1982.

2. *Facts on File*, 22 October 1982.

3. An extensive study of the underground economy and cheating on income tax was done by *Time* magazine in its cover story, 28 March 1983.

4. Thomas Brown, "The Shadow Economy," *Los Angeles Times*, 20 November 1980.

13

Changes in GNP, Employment, and Prices: Problems in the Macroeconomy

The previous chapter showed how the total output and income of the economy are measured. In this chapter we will use some of these measures to describe our two major macroeconomic problems—unemployment and inflation—and to begin the discussion of what can be done to cure them.

This chapter is divided into three sections: (1) A brief history of the performance of the U.S. economy; (2) a description of unemployment, how it is measured, and theories about why it occurs; and (3) a description of inflation, how it hurts or helps people in different ways, and why it occurs.

A BRIEF HISTORY OF U.S. ECONOMIC PERFORMANCE

We are going to look at our economic record with three measures in mind: Changes in business activity, changes in prices, and changes in unemployment.

The Record to 1930

The history of the United States, especially from the beginning of rapid industrial growth in the mid-nineteenth century, has been characterized by a number of ups and downs. In the years between 1854 and 1930 there were nineteen so-called business cycles, during which industrial production expanded and then declined. The periods of expansion averaged about two and one-half years; the periods of contraction averaged about one and two-thirds years.

During most of these years prices were either stable or actually fell. Amazingly, the consumer price index in 1929 was about what it had been in 1800. There were, however, short periods of inflation associated with wartime shortages. During the Civil War prices doubled in the North; during World War I prices almost tripled. *Sustained* inflation is a relatively recent problem.

The unemployment record has been uneven. During the years between 1890 and 1929, the average worker went through several periods of hardship. If we divide the 39-year span into periods of minimal unemployment (0 to 4.0 percent), moderate unemployment (4.1 to 7.0 percent), and severe unemployment (7.1 percent and over), we find that this worker would have spent

- 14 years with minimal unemployment
- 15 years with moderate unemployment
- 10 years with severe unemployment

Then came the crash.

The Great Depression*

The crash of the stock market in the fall of 1929 signaled the worst economic disaster the world had ever known. Most industrial countries suffered as much as the United States did. A few statistics will help dramatize what happened in the United States:

- By July 1932, some $74 billion, five sixths of the September 1929 total of common stock values, had vanished into thin air.
- The nation's money supply contracted by one third in the first three years of the Depression as 5,000 banks failed.

---

*Depression is hereafter spelled with a capital "D," because we reserve the term for the period of the 1930s. Let's hope that that period is the only period deserving of such a label!

- Total investment spending by businesses dropped from $16.2 billion in 1929 to *$1.4 billion* in 1933.
- GNP fell from $103.4 billion in 1929 to $55.8 billion in 1933.*
- Unemployment rose from 1.6 million workers in 1929 to 12.8 million workers in 1933 (25 percent of the labor force). The unemployment rate remained at more than 14 percent until 1941.

Space does not permit us to examine the causes of the Depression in any detail. However, they can be briefly described under four headings:

1. A decline in industrial production and housing construction following a post-World War I boom in the early 1920s.
2. An increase in consumer debt (occasioned by postwar buying on credit) that inhibited consumers from continuing to buy new houses and appliances.
3. Pricing of common stocks far beyond their real worth after a decade of speculation.
4. The inability or unwillingness of the Federal Reserve System to prevent the collapse of the banking system after the collapse of the stock market.

After the Depression

Recall that changes in GNP can occur simply because prices change. "Nominal" ("current dollar") GNP may rise even though the real quantities of goods and services produced have remained static or have even declined. Thus, *nominal* GNP is a poor measure of the quantities of goods and services produced and also of the level of employment. It is *real* (deflated) GNP that matters.

The Uneven Growth of GNP

There is no question that real GNP has grown since 1929. In 1972 ("constant") dollars, real GNP almost quintupled during the period 1929–1982 from $315 billion to $1,477 billion. However, this growth has been uneven. Table 13-1 shows the changes in *real GNP* from one year to the next since 1968.

Remember that real GNP means that the effect of price changes has been taken out of the numbers; all the GNP dollars have the same purchasing power that they did in 1972. And so we see that, measured in these terms, the real GNP actually fell four times in the 15 years shown.

These drops in real GNP also represent **recessions**, usually defined as a fall in real GNP over two or more *quarters*. The fall in real GNP for two *years* in a row, 1974 and 1975, and for two out of three years, 1980–1982, indicates that the recessions were particularly severe.

Business Cycle Theory: Trying to Forecast the Ups and Downs

The zig-zag picture of real GNP shown in Table 13-1 raises a fascinating question: Is there a pattern? Witch doctors, soothsayers, advisors to kings, and, yes, economists have tried for generations to discover such patterns in physical events (such as weather) and human behavior. If only one could know the pattern of, let us say, the stock market, one could buy low and sell high—and so presumably live happily ever after.

---

*Figures are in current dollars. Real GNP in 1972 dollars fell from $315.7 billion to $222.1 billion. Can you explain why are the latter figures so much higher than the current-dollar figures?

Table 13-1. Real GNP Changes, 1968–1982 (in billions of 1972 dollars)

Year	Real GNP	
1968	$1,052	
1969	1,079	
1970	1,075	◄————————— GNP drops
1971	1,108 ◄	
1972	1,171 ◄	————► then increases
1973	1,235 ◄	
1974	1,219 ◄	————► then drops twice
1975	1,202 ◄	
1976	1,298 ◄	
1977	1,370 ◄	————► then increases
1978	1,439 ◄	
1979	1,479 ◄	
1980	1,474 ◄	————— then drops
1981	1,514 ◄	————— then increases
1982	1,477 ◄	————— then drops

For roughly a hundred years, economists have been trying to predict changes in GNP by applying *business cycle theory.* The idea is that real GNP and levels of employment and prices go up and down in a wavelike or cyclical motion and that there is a regular and uniform time period between peaks and troughs. But no one is sure that such a cycle exists. We continue to live economic lives of uncertainty, lives during which predictions about the stock market, or any form of economic activity, continue to be full of risk. There are no sure things.

The problem is that what appear to be patterns are suddenly disrupted by unforeseen events like hurricanes, droughts, or wars. Such events are called **exogenous causes**. On the other hand, events that occur logically within the framework of a model are called **endogenous**. For example, when we spend more money because our incomes go up, the increase in spending is endogenously related to the change in income. But, *why* did our income change in the first place? If it changes because of an unforeseen, exogenous event like the discovery of oil in our backyard, an *exo*genous event has caused an *endo*genous event.

Despite these difficulties, it is of crucial importance to estimate as intelligently as we can what the future will bring and to plan for it.

The methods of economic forecasting are many. Records are kept of the number and age of automobiles and appliances that we own so that industry and government economists can estimate when we might want a new model. Pollsters measure "consumer sentiment" to detect feelings of pessimism or optimism and the readiness of consumers to buy. Recently, economists have developed computer models of the macroeconomy to help them visualize what may happen. Some of these models involve what are called economic indicators.

Economic indicators are series of data that economists believe are particularly helpful in estimating what is going to happen. There are three types: (1)

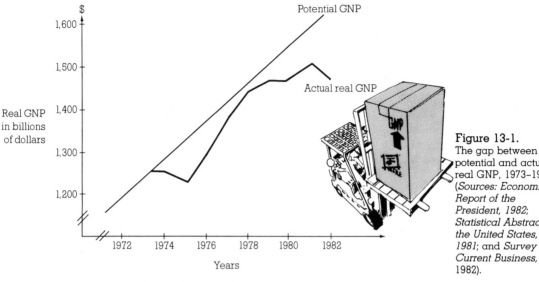

Figure 13-1.
The gap between potential and actual real GNP, 1973–1982. (*Sources: Economic Report of the President, 1982; Statistical Abstract of the United States, 1981; and Survey of Current Business,* July 1982).

Leading indicators show what is apt to happen several months in advance. Examples are average weekly overtime hours, capital spending for machines, and changes in inventories.* (2) *Lagging indicators* represent what has happened in the recent past and help to confirm or deny an upward or downward trend. Examples are the unemployment rate, labor costs per unit of output, and consumer installment debt. (3) *Coincident indicators* show current changes. Some examples are current dollar GNP, retail sales, and help-wanted advertisements.

But, sad to say, even these indicators may send out conflicting signals. Then the experts have to make judgments about which indicators have the greatest value.

Actual versus Potential GNP

Another way to visualize the performance of GNP is to compare what actually happened in real terms (**actual GNP**) with what the economy would have been capable of producing (**potential GNP**). Potential GNP, which has been calculated in recent years by the Council of Economic Advisors (CEA), is the amount that could have been produced each year with an annual increase in real GNP of roughly 3.5 percent per year.

Why 3.5 percent? The answer is somewhat complicated. Three-and-one-half percent is the growth rate that could be achieved: (1) If new entrants to the labor force found jobs, (2) if the unemployment rate were reduced to 5.5 percent, and (3) if an allowance is made for gains in the productivity of each worker (new and better machines, better methods, and so forth).

In Figure 13-1, the upper line represents potential GNP—the amounts that could have been produced given a steady 3.5 percent growth rate. The lower

---

*In April 1983, after the leading indicators had increased steadily for seven months, several expert economists announced that the 1980–1983 recession had "bottomed out."

line shows the amounts that were actually produced in real terms. One can see that actual and potential GNP are about the same until 1973. After that the doldrums set in, with actual GNP consistently lagging behind potential GNP, as shown by the shaded area. Many economists call the shaded area a gap; that is, a gap between what is produced and what could have been produced. Here we get a real inkling of what macroeconomic theory is all about. How can the gap be closed? This is the billion-dollar question that we will discuss in Part V.

In the 10-year period 1973–1982, the differences between potential and actual (real) GNP add up to about $590 *billion* worth of lost production and income. It is hard to appreciate how gigantic these numbers are. With that money, we could have built 5.9 million $100,000 houses! The point is that this production did not take place. It is permanently lost.

These large differences between potential and actual GNP mean that millions of people were unemployed. The next section is devoted to this problem.

UNEMPLOYMENT

In this section, we (1) show how unemployment is measured, (2) review what has been happening, and (3) explain the types of unemployment.

How Unemployment Is Measured

Every month, the Bureau of the Census determines who is employed and who is not by interviewing about 100,000 people in a statistical sample that includes people over 16 years of age in every state plus the District of Columbia.

To be counted as unemployed, you must meet these conditions: (1) You must not have worked during the interview week (called the *survey week*); (2) you must have been seeking a job during the previous four weeks; (3) you must have been available for work during the survey week (except for temporary illness). You would also be considered unemployed if you had been laid off (even though you had been told to report for work within 30 days). You would also be considered unemployed if you were waiting to report to a *new* job (one you'd found) within 30 days.

You are employed if (1) you are a civilian over 16 years of age who did a minimum of one hour's work for pay or profit during the survey week, (2) you worked 15 hours or more as an unpaid worker in a family enterprise, or (3) you were temporarily absent from a job for noneconomic reasons—illness, bad weather, vacation, or a labor-management dispute.

The **unemployment rate** is a percentage derived by dividing the number of people unemployed by the number of people in the civilian labor force. The civilian labor force is the sum of those employed (excluding members of the armed forces) plus those counted as unemployed. The unemployment rate for a whole year is based on yearly averages of the monthly surveys. In October 1982 there were about 110 million people in the civilian labor force. Of that number, 11 million were unemployed. The unemployment rate was therefore 10 percent (11 million ÷ 110 million).

Of course, the unemployment rate may not give us a true picture of who is *really* unemployed. A college student casually looking for work will be counted as unemployed if he or she has looked during the previous four weeks. On the other hand, a person who has looked desperately for work but who has quit looking out of discouragement will not be counted.

One noted economist, Lester C. Thurow, argued in October 1982 that, in addition to the 11 million officially unemployed, 1.5 million workers became too discouraged to look for work and dropped out of the labor force; another 2.1 million part-timers wanted full-time work. Still another 3.6 million part-timers did not want full-time work but did want more hours of work than they had. On the basis of such estimates, Professor Thurow argued that the true unemployment rate was actually 17 percent.[1]

On the other hand, some experts believe that the reported unemployment rate *overstates* the true rate. They point out that unemployment compensation is making unemployment an attractive alternative to work. One writer calls the unemployment that is induced or prolonged by unemployment compensation the "new unemployment."[2] The problem is that unemployment compensation payments have been tax free. If one works, income taxes and Social Security taxes commonly reduce one's earned income by at least 25 percent. Given that reduction, $600 per month in tax-free income is equivalent to $800 in earned income. If one earns $900 per month, one is only $75 better off by working than not working at all. (Taxes take 25 percent of $900, leaving $675.) Economists would say in this situation that the tax on work is really 75 percent, because one keeps only $75 (25 percent) of the extra $300 ($900 − $600) gained by working. These figures do not take into account the costs of working: carfare, better clothes, and so on. (One solution: Reduce the tax on earned income for those in low-income brackets and use some version of the negative income tax described in Chapter 11.)

The Cost of Unemployment

But even with unemployment compensation, the unemployed still suffer hardship. The average weekly unemployment check during 1981 was slightly over $100 per week, less than what could be earned even at the minimum wage. Moreover, in October 1982 only 4.3 million workers of the 11 million unemployed were still eligible for unemployment benefits. The rest were in trouble.

We should think for a moment about the cost of unemployment borne by these people. An unemployed person's skills deteriorate. Fear, frustration, and despair take over. Unemployed people lose their self-esteem. Often, unemployment leads to the break-up of families, alcoholism, and crime.

The Meaning of "Full Employment"

Before we look at the record, we should ask: What level of unemployment is considered acceptable? What level of *employment* should macroeconomic policy try to achieve?

The experts all agree that **full employment** does not mean zero unemployment. During the most intense year of World War II when the United States was supplying not only its own military forces but those of its allies, the unemployment rate was 1.2 percent of the civilian labor force—about 700,000 people.

Until the 1970s, the experts defined full employment as 4 percent unemployed. But during that decade, as more women and teenagers with less work experience entered the labor force, the 4 percent figure became harder to attain. (And it became more difficult for administrations in Washington to speak of "attaining full employment.") Gradually, presidents and their advisors had to adopt higher figures that did not make existing unemployment rates seem so harsh. And so now, a 5.5 percent rate of unemployment, or sometimes even 6 percent, is commonly accepted as the equivalent of full employment. In

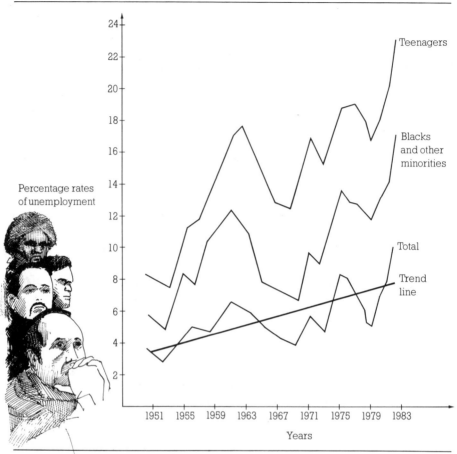

Figure 13-2.
Unemployment rates,
1951–1982.

fact, the term "full employment" may be disappearing. In its place, you will find references to "high employment," perhaps a politically less threatening term.

What Has Been the Record?

Figure 13-2 shows unemployment rates during the years 1951 through 1982. At first glance, the figure looks like three zig-zag lines. However, one can discern a pattern of four recessions—in 1961, 1971, 1975, and 1982. The figure also shows the drop in unemployment from 1951 to 1953 and from 1961 through 1969. In both cases we were involved with war, first the Korean War and then the Vietnam War. War seems to reduce unemployment.

We can also see that the lines zig together. Unemployment changes among blacks and teenagers coincide with changes in total employment. This pattern suggests that if we can bring down total unemployment, unemployment of blacks and teenagers will fall in absolute terms, though it will still be high relative to the overall figure.

At the bottom of Figure 13-2 we have drawn a trend line through the zigs and zags for all workers. Unemployment rates seem to be climbing. With each recession, business firms find more efficient ways of producing their products. When the recession ends, some of the workers laid off are not rehired. One case in point: Alone among the auto-makers, Chrysler made money in 1982. During the years 1978 through 1982, Chrysler cut its work force in half and reduced by 50 percent the sales it needed to make a profit. In the second quarter of 1982, Chrysler shipped 10 percent fewer cars than in the second quarter of 1981, but made five times as much money ($100 million versus $20 million).[3]

This example is but a sample of a general trend throughout the business community.[4] One possible reason: With the recovery of all industrial countries after World War II, the United States, once comfortably superior in many industries, is now exposed to tough international competition. In only one area are we still clearly in the lead: agricultural production. But, agriculture cannot be expected to absorb the unemployed. Because of mechanization, the number of people needed on farms drops every year. We have to find ways to compete harder in many areas, not just in agriculture.

Types of Unemployment

To explain why unemployment exists, economists have identified three very broad categories of unemployment: frictional, cyclical, and structural. As we examine each one, ask yourself, "What cure would I recommend? Would my cure be inflationary?"

Frictional Unemployment

Frictional unemployment occurs when workers are temporarily unemployed because (1) they are looking for a better job, (2) they are looking for a first job, or (3) they are temporarily laid off because of bad weather (in the construction industry), or model changeovers (in the automobile industry), or because the demand for their services is seasonal (migrant farmers, retail clerks).

This type of unemployment is often considered an indication that workers may be trying to accommodate to changing conditions by seeking education or different trades voluntarily, or employers may be seeking ways to satisfy changes in consumer demand. Thus, it is in a sense a desirable kind of unemployment.

Frictional unemployment can often be lessened by matching job-seekers with appropriate jobs. Research has shown that workers may remain voluntarily unemployed during at least part of their job-changing time. It is generally not in a worker's interest to take the first offer. The continuing job search can be thought of as an *investment* by workers in obtaining more information about the job market. In theory we can reduce this kind of unemployment by providing more information about alternatives, by lowering information costs borne by job-hunters, and by subsidizing relocation. Frictional unemployment is estimated to affect about 3 percent of the civilian labor force.

Cyclical Unemployment

Unemployment caused by generally poor business conditions is sometimes called **cyclical unemployment** because it is associated with the "trough" of a business cycle. Government policies designed to increase total output and spending can help cyclical unemployment. We will discuss these policies in the six chapters that make up Part V.

Structural Unemployment

The term **structural unemployment** means here that a particular industry is having difficulty or that a particular group of people cannot find jobs. Structural unemployment can occur because products are replaced by new ones (for example, adding machines and slide rules have been replaced by hand calculators). Or environmentalists may cause the closing of a pollution-creating factory. Or machines may replace labor (causing *technological unemployment*). Or industries like the automobile industry may guess wrong about the kinds of cars Americans prefer to buy. *Hard-core unemployment* is another form of structural unemployment. It refers to those who are unemployed because employers can't afford to hire uneducated people, people without skills, or people with special handicaps.

INFLATION

Our other major macroeconomic problem is inflation. It is *not* a separate problem from unemployment. The two problems are tangled like fishing worms in a can. As you will see, inflation can sometimes cause unemployment, with the two problems increasing in magnitude together. Sometimes they drift in opposite directions, as we saw in 1982 when the inflation rate came down but the unemployment rate went up.

In this chapter, we will confine ourselves primarily to describing of inflation and its causes. Some of the connections with unemployment will be mentioned, to be developed in more detail in Chapter 19.

As we noted on page 250, prices remained fairly level throughout the nineteenth century. Inflation did not become a chronic problem until after World War II. In this section we will show the recent record of inflation and discuss its effects on various groups of people.

Figure 13-3 shows how consumer prices have risen since 1933, the bottom of the Depression. Beginning in about 1965 (when the Vietnam War began to heat up), the rise in prices became much steeper.

Note that the base year of the Consumer Price Index (CPI) is 1967, when the CPI equals 100, and that the CPI at the end of 1982 was 289; in those 16 years consumer prices increased 189 percent, an average increase of about 7 percent per year.

Now, recall the Rule of 72 from Chapter 1. The rule tells us that in 10.29 years (72 ÷ 7) consumer prices will double if the inflation rate continues at that pace. This means that in 10.29 years the purchasing power of your dollar will be cut in half. And, it also means that, unless your savings account is earning at least 7 percent per year *after income taxes*, you're losing.*

Politicians like to say that inflation is a "tax" on everyone because rising prices cut everyone's purchasing power. But this is obviously not the case. When you buy something from a store at a higher price, your purchasing power may have been cut, but the store's income has gone up. Rising prices mean higher incomes for somebody. Consequently, the main effect of inflation is to *redistribute* real income and wealth rather than making everyone worse off. We will look briefly at six groups of people to see who wins or loses from inflation: (1) Savers, (2) taxpayers, (3) union versus nonunion employees, (4) creditors

---

*During 1982 it appeared that the annual inflation rate was dropping to around 5 or 6 percent. Perhaps, when you read this, the problem won't be so severe—we hope.

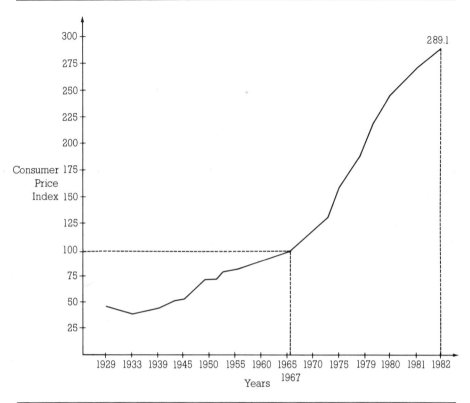

Figure 13-3.
The Consumer Price
Index, 1929–1982
(1967 = 100).

versus debtors, (5) those on fixed versus those on flexible incomes, and (6) anticipators versus nonanticipators.

Inflation: Who Wins and Who Loses?

Savers

We have already suggested that savers lose unless their interest income, after taxes, keeps up with inflation. If the interest income on your savings account is 6 percent, and your marginal tax bracket is 30 percent, you will have to pay 30 percent of that 6 percent (1.8 percent) to the government in taxes. Your net income on the savings account is now 6.0 − 1.8 = 4.2 percent. If the rate of inflation is, say, 10 percent, your savings account is losing 5.8 percent (10.0 − 4.2) per year. In about 12.4 years (72 ÷ 5.8), your savings account will be worth half of what it is today. The bank and the government win, you lose.

Taxpayers

If you receive a cost-of-living increase in your paycheck, you automatically pay a larger proportion of your income to the federal government and possibly to your state (this is called bracket creep). Winners are the government and people who whose earnings are not all in wages—they can take advantage of more tax loopholes. Losers are taxpayers whose incomes are mostly from wages and salaries. Various plans exist to prevent income tax from rising as a percentage of one's income. These plans are called tax indexing.

Union versus Nonunion Employees

Many union contracts have so-called *escalator clauses*—also called COLA (Cost of Living Adjustment) clauses—that provide the workers with automatic pay increases when the Consumer Price Index rises by an agreed-upon amount. The pay adjustments can occur every few months. Workers under such a contract win. The company may or may not lose, depending on its ability (its market power) to pass along the cost of such wage increases to the public in the form of higher prices. In general, workers belonging to strong unions win; those belonging to weak unions or to no union lose.

Creditors versus Debtors

Inflation may cause creditors (lenders) to lose and debtors (borrowers) to win. The debtor wins because each loan payment is worth less in *real* terms. The payments the creditor receives have successively less purchasing power. If, however, the creditor can anticipate the future course of inflation and charge an interest rate that covers it, then the creditor-debtor positions are reversed. We will take up this point again when we look at the last group.

Those Receiving Fixed Incomes versus Those Whose Incomes Vary

Here we are thinking about people living on relatively fixed incomes, such as pensions or life-insurance payments, versus the wage earner whose income will change. The fixed-income person loses as, each month, the pension check buys fewer groceries, less heating, and so on. To overcome this problem, one should, if possible, have a pension plan with automatic cost-of-living adjustments, like the escalator clauses in some union contracts.

Those Who Anticipate versus Those Who Do Not (or Cannot)

If you can anticipate inflation, you will win. If you don't or can't, you will lose. This holds for all groups. Corporations with the market power to do so can beat the gun by raising prices before costs go up. Unions can beat the gun, too, and so can creditors. But, according to the record, creditors have not done so well. One estimate is that the redistributional effects of inflation in favor of debtors have probably totaled at least $500 billion since World War II.[5]

Of course, knowing that inflation is coming and doing something about it are two different matters. The small-business entrepreneur may know what is coming but cannot raise prices because competition is too tough. The nonunion or weak union worker may realize that living costs are going up but may not have the market power to get a pay raise. Old people may know living costs are going up, but their incomes are too inflexible and too taken up with spending on "inflatable" goods and services (or increased rents or property taxes) to permit them to take any effective action.

It is odd but true that if people are successful in anticipating inflation and doing something about it, we will certainly have inflation. If we could get everyone to agree that there will not be any inflation, there would not be. This is another example of a self-fulfilling prophecy. If we all believe prices are going up, we will all try to buy before they go up. Then demand curves will shift to the right—forcing prices up. Business managers and unions will raise prices and wages, and inflation will result.

And so we are beginning to realize that long periods of inflation usually penalize those people least able to afford high prices and, further, that inflation

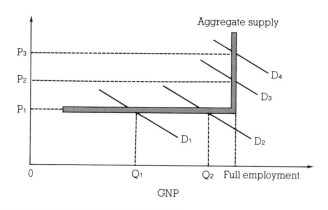

Figure 13-4.
Demand-pull inflation.

feeds on itself. Once we begin to accept inflation, the probability of continued, accelerating inflation increases.

The Causes of Inflation

Remember that inflation is a rise in average prices and that the Consumer Price Index has tripled since its base year in 1967. Five major types of inflation are recognized: (1) demand-pull, (2) cost-push, (3) profit-push, (4) bottleneck, and (5) inflation caused by increases in the money supply.

Demand-Pull Inflation

As the name suggests, prices can be pulled up if demand increases faster than supply increases. Figure 13-4 is a picture of **demand-pull inflation**. Increases in spending—which could come from any of the components of aggregate demand (consumption, investment, government purchases, or net exports)—help to shift demand from D_1 to D_2.

Prices may not change if GNP is far below full employment. When the economy is slack, as it was in the fall of 1982 (with 10 percent unemployment and 30 percent unused industrial capacity), increases in spending can lead to increases in output with no increases in costs or prices. (Because, according to demand-pull theory, business firms will be unable to raise prices when the economy is experiencing such hard times.) The quantities Q_1 and Q_2 represent this idea. Basically, one can hire more people and more resources of all kinds without causing prices to rise.

But when the economy reaches full employment, aggregate supply heads upward to indicate that producers will be unable to increase the quantities supplied, because at this point all the factories are working at full capacity. Consequently, when full employment is reached, any further increases in demand, as shown by D_3 and D_4, "pull" prices up from P_1 to P_2 and then to P_3.

Cost-Push Inflation

The demand-pull explanation for inflation would mean that inflation occurs only in times of prosperity. Inflation in *bad* times would be an impossibility.*

---

*Except in very special situations called "hyperinflation" to be mentioned briefly in Chapter 18-A.

No one doubted this "conventional wisdom" until a recession that occurred during 1957–1958. During this period, the unemployment rate rose from 4.1 percent in 1956 to 4.3 percent in 1957 and 6.8 percent in 1958. At the same time, industrial production fell 6.5 percent. On the other hand, prices, which had been almost stable during the preceding five years, rose 3.6 percent from 1956 to 1957 and 2.7 percent from 1957 to 1958.

Economists began to suspect that something was wrong with the demand-pull theory. Inflation was occurring during periods of rising unemployment and poor business. Their suspicion was confirmed by another business slow-down in 1969–1970, when industrial production fell 3.5 percent and unemployment rose from 3.5 percent to 4.9 percent, but prices increased almost 6 percent despite the business decline. Again in 1974 and 1975, prices rose an average of 10 percent, while unemployment averaged 7 percent during the two-year period. And in 1979, prices rose 13 percent, while the unemployment rate was stuck at 6 percent.

Something other than demand-pull was clearly responsible for rising prices during periods of high unemployment. The new theory was called **cost-push inflation**. The term "cost-push" implies that strong unions can force large corporations to grant higher wages, and these higher wages force employers to raise prices even during periods of business slowdown and rising unemployment. So inflation, the theory goes, is caused by the power of the unions.

The data tend to verify this conclusion. By looking at the dollar value of total output and comparing that figure with total wages, we can tell whether total labor costs went up or down. A simple example may help. Suppose in Year X you earn $50 a week producing $100 worth of Dazzle toothpaste. In Year Y, you get a raise to $60 and your production increases to $110 worth of Dazzle. What has happened to labor cost?

In Year X, labor cost is $50 ÷ $100 = 50 cents per $1 of output. In Year Y, labor cost is $60 ÷ $110 = 54.5 cents* per $1 of output. Given such an increase in labor cost, Dazzle's management will try to raise prices, contributing to cost-push inflation.

This simple example illustrates what actually did happen. Between 1970 and 1981, output per hour in manufacturing in the United States increased 74 percent. But compensation per hour increased 300 percent (!)—a net increase in labor cost of 19 percent *per year* during the twelve-year period.[6]

But cost-push inflation can also occur without any help from labor unions or management. The reason is our old friend the Law of Diminishing Returns (see pp. 154–155).

The law applies to the macroeconomy just as it does to individual firms. As we approach full employment, and as each factory begins to produce near capacity, several facts of life make further increases difficult, particularly in the short run. In any given factory, as more workers are hired, all workers will have less capital to work with (since it is spread out over a greater number) and will be less productive. They will be newer, less experienced, and therefore less skilled workers. And larger quantities of materials may be harder to find, as all factories together try to increase production.

---

*Can you see why labor cost went from 50 to 54.5 cents? Labor cost had to rise because your wages increased 20 percent (from $50 to $60), but output increased only 10 percent from $100 to $110. Note that the formula for labor cost here is: Labor cost = the wage divided by the firm's output (measured in sales dollars).

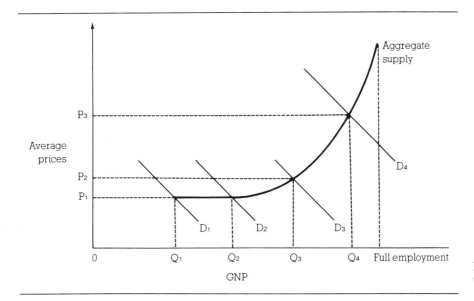

Figure 13-5.
Cost-push inflation.

As the costs of production rise, the supply curve begins to *curve* upward, meaning simply that higher prices are necessary to motivate producers to increase output. Figure 13-5 is a picture of cost-push inflation.

As in the demand-pull case, when GNP is very low and unemployment high, increases in demand from D_1 to D_2 cause no increases in prices. But when the Q_2 level of GNP is reached, union-management contracts and the Law of Diminishing Returns combine to curve aggregate supply upward—long before full employment is reached.

The upward curve tells us that producers will not produce quantities larger than Q_2 unless they (the producers) receive higher prices. Thus, if demand increases to D_3 or D_4, prices will be both "pushed" *and* "pulled" up to P_2 and P_3. Now demand-pull and cost-push forces are both at work. And note again that prices rise before full employment is reached.

But Figure 13-5 doesn't tell quite the whole story. Occasionally, events occur that are powerful enough to increase many producers' costs very suddenly. We have in mind the sudden increases in oil prices that occurred during the 1970s. (See "Bottleneck Inflation" that follows.)

When oil prices rise suddenly, almost everyone's production costs increase, because oil is such a widely used source of energy. When one source dominates to the extent that oil has, alternatives take time to develop. As a result, the increases in oil prices became a major cause of inflation during the 1970s. When such price increases occur, the whole aggregate supply curve shifts upward. At every level of output (GNP), producers require higher prices. Figure 13-6 shows what happens.

Figure 13-6 is the first macroeconomic figure that illustrates another dimension of the cost-push problem: *unemployment caused by inflation.** The figure shows aggregate supply *de*creasing from S_1 to S_2 as a result of the increase in oil

---

*This topic is discussed in more detail in Chapter 19.

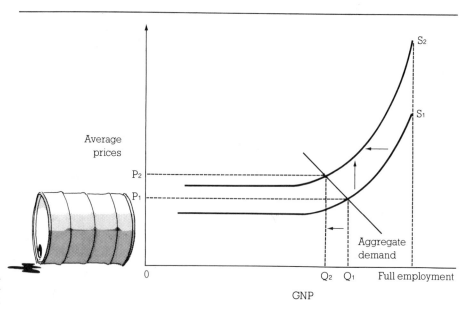

Figure 13-6.
Cost-push inflation—
another view.

prices. A higher price level is now associated with every GNP. Given any aggregate demand curve like the one shown, the quantities demanded will *decrease* with the increase in prices. GNP will fall from Q_1 to Q_2, and unemployment will increase as a result of the oil-price increases.

Profit-Push Inflation

The cost-push idea seems, at least partially, to blame the unions. The unions' retort is that large corporations have so much oligopoly or monopoly power that they can raise prices regardless of increases or decreases in cost, resulting in **profit-push inflation**.

Many observers believe a combination of cost-push and profit-push forces dictated the behavior of the U.S. automobile industry in the 1970s. General Motors, Ford, and Chrysler confidently granted the United Automobile Workers (UAW) generous raises, believing they (the manufacturers) could always cover increased costs with increased prices. Ultimately, the American companies lost out to foreign manufacturers who produced better cars at lower prices—and also produced the fuel-efficient cars Americans now wanted.

Figure 13-6 also helps to explain profit-push inflation. Assume the economy is operating at Q_1 GNP, a level far below full employment—perhaps during a recession with high unemployment rates of 7 to 8 percent. Nevertheless, large corporations, for profit-push reasons, raise prices from P_1 to P_2. How can they get away with this during a recession? You know the answer. A producer can raise prices so long as consumers can't find competitors who offer lower prices; that is, so long as demand for his product is inelastic. Even though the higher P_2 prices cause the quantity demanded to decrease, powerful corporations will enjoy an increase in total revenue. And these same corporations may be laying off workers while they are raising prices. This scenario gives us another view of the disease of the 1970s—rising prices *and* rising unemployment.

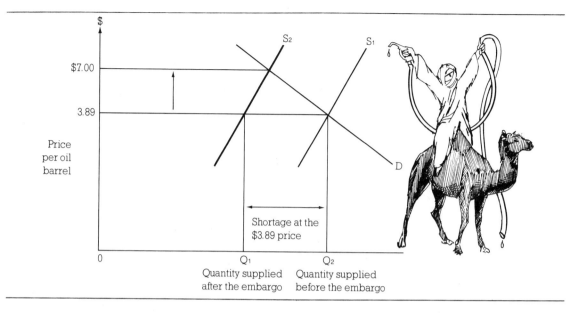

Bottleneck Inflation: A Special Case of Cost-Push Inflation

Bottleneck inflation occurs when there are severe shortages of important products. And as Figure 13-6 indicated, shortages of especially crucial products can cause inflation and unemployment. The Arab oil embargo in the winter of 1973–1974 is a classic example of bottleneck inflation. Notice that in Figure 13–7 the equilibrium price is at $3.89 per 42-gallon barrel of crude oil during 1973. Suddenly the embargo occurs; the supply curve for oil shifts rapidly to the left, leaving a shortage at the existing equilibrium price. Now at that price, there are large differences between the quantities available and the quantities demanded. The price rises rapidly so that by the end of 1974, one year later, the price had reached $7 per barrel. And, of course, this was only the beginning. The revolution in Iran caused another shortage in 1979. By 1982, as the OPEC cartel tightened its grip on world prices, the prices per 42-gallon barrel of crude oil was over $30. Because oil is not only an energy source but an important component of many products (especially plastics) and services, the rapid increase in the price of oil kicked off rapidly accelerating inflation during the 1970s. The oil crises were not the only reasons for accelerating inflation, but they were important ones (to be continued in Chapter 19).

Important events like two oil crises are called *external shocks* by economists. Resulting shortages send shock waves of higher costs and prices through the economy.

The foregoing four causes of inflation are rarely independent of one another. As crude oil prices began to rise in the 1970s, there was a corresponding rise in the prices of gasoline and diesel fuel. At the same time, the demand for diesel cars began to rise faster than for gasoline-using cars, as people discovered that diesel fuel was cheaper than gasoline and that diesel engines often provided more miles per gallon.

The prices of diesel fuel and diesel cars were pulled up by demand. And as

Figure 13-7.
Bottleneck inflation: The decrease in supply causes a shortage at $3.89; the price has to rise.

the number of diesel cars increased, gas stations offering diesel fuel engaged in profit-push increases. By late 1982, diesel prices were overtaking gasoline prices (even though diesel fuel costs less than gasoline to refine).

Inflation Caused by Increases in the Supply of Money

Many economists believe that the four types of inflation just discussed cannot exist unless, somehow, people are given more money to spend. The belief seems very logical. After all, our ability to buy anything like diesel fuel depends on the amount of money we have, not on whether diesel fuel is in short supply or on the desire of profit-minded oil companies to raise diesel prices. If we don't have the money, so the argument goes, our purchases will slow down regardless of cost-push or profit-push problems. And if our purchases slow down because of our inability to obtain enough money, business firms will be unable to raise prices. Thus, no inflation.

A real-world fact of life makes the money supply argument very persuasive, because the quantity of money available to the public is strongly influenced by the *Board of Governors of the Federal Reserve System.* The board has the power to make bank loans easier or harder to obtain. This control over bank loans has a powerful influence on the amounts of money we all have to spend. And so, yes, changes in the availability of bank loans can have an important effect on prices.

At this point we must limit ourselves to mere mention of the money supply argument. To understand it fully, you will need to read the latter part of Chapter 18 and Chapter 18A. There you will find a thorough explanation of the views of the *monetarists*—those who believe changes in the money supply are the primary cause of inflation.

THE IMPORTANCE OF UNDERSTANDING THE ORIGINS OF INFLATION AND UNEMPLOYMENT

The last two sections about unemployment and inflation have drawn a distinction between demand-side origins and other origins. To explain: Cyclical unemployment is caused by insufficient aggregate demand. Demand-pull inflation is caused by too much demand. If unemployment is cyclical or inflation is demand-pull, the federal government can help by increasing or decreasing aggregate demand through changes in taxes, government spending, or by changing the amounts of money available for loans at the banks. (The details of all of these maneuvers are in Part V.)

But if the origins of unemployment are frictional or structural, or the origins of inflation are cost-push or profit-push or are caused by external shocks, then the federal government's ability to help is more questionable. Solutions to these problems require knowledge of specific industries and types of labor.

Moreover, any attempts to solve unemployment or inflation involve a difficult trade-off. Attempts to reduce unemployment may increase inflation. Attempts to reduce inflation may increase unemployment. And finally, there is usually a time lag between the initiation of a government policy and its effect on the economy, so that when the policy begins to take effect, the problem for which it was designed may be long gone.

These are only a few of the difficulties facing any attempt by the federal government to solve national economic problems. Perhaps even more serious is the charge by many economists that federal government interference hurts more than it helps. The next two chapters about the economic role of government will help you to think about this argument.

SUMMARY

When we look at historical changes in real GNP, unemployment rates, and prices, we find that (1) changes in the rates of growth of real GNP show a zig-zag pattern, (2) unemployment rates appear to show an upward trend, and (3) prices have risen continuously since the Depression.

Unemployment may be frictional, cyclical, or structural, involving workers who are unemployed voluntarily between jobs, out of work because of a recession, or out of work because they are disadvantaged or because of problems in particular industries. Full employment is estimated as equivalent to a 5.5 percent rate of unemployment.

Inflation is a period of generally rising prices. From 1967 through 1982, average prices tripled. Those hurt by inflation are savers, creditors, nonunion workers, old people, and in general those without economic and political power sufficient to protect the purchasing power of their incomes during periods of rising prices.

Inflation is caused by increases in demand as the economy nears full employment (demand-pull), by increases in wages and prices initiated by labor-management contracts (cost-push), by the desire of business firms to increase profits (profit-push), by external shocks (bottleneck), and/or by increases in the money supply.

Discussion Questions

1. On the basis of this chapter, why do you think inflation is a recent phenomenon?

2. Which would you rather be: frictionally, cyclically, or structurally unemployed? List the types in order of preference with reasons for each one.

3. In which of the above cases could you expect the most help from the government? (A trip to a state or federal employment office would be worthwhile.)

4. If prices are rising at, say, 10 percent per year, which would you rather be? (Give reasons for each.)
   a. A stenographer
   b. A nurse
   c. A mechanic at a service station
   d. A clerk in a department store
   e. The owner of a hardware store
   f. A farmer
   g. A data processor

DID YOU EVER WONDER WHY . . .

. . . a discouraged person who quits seeking work is not counted as unemployed?

References

1. Lester C. Thurow, "The Cost of Unemployment," *Newsweek*, 4 October 1982.

2. Martin Feldstein, "The Economics of the New Unemployment," *Public Interest*, Fall 1973.

3. "Chrysler Makes a Comeback," *Newsweek*, 2 August 1982.

4. Robert Lubar, "Why Unemployment Will Hang High," *Fortune*, 14 June 1982.

5. G. L. Bach, "Inflation: Who Gains and Who Loses?" *Challenge*, July/August, 1974.

6. *Statistical Abstract of the United States, 1982–1983,* Table 663.

CHAPTER

14

The Economic Role of Government: Its Size and Impact

KEY WORDS
Fiscal policy
No-tax threshold
Federal revenue sharing
Marginal tax rate
Benefits principle
Average tax rate
Ability-to-pay principle
Tax loopholes
Progressive taxes
Flat tax idea
Proportional taxes
Tax shifting
Regressive taxes
Tax incidence

Chapter 13 presented the record of the U.S. economy's performance over the last fifty years or so. Our purpose was to emphasize the swings in GNP and to show how these changes affected unemployment and inflation. This chapter continues this examination of the record—but with a somewhat closer look. As you will remember from Chapter 12, GNP is composed of four kinds of spending: consumption, investment, government purchase of goods and services, and net exports. This chapter examines the government's role in total spending.

Why do we pick the role of the government for a whole chapter? The answer is that the government has the power to change the size of the GNP pie by changing the size or content of its spending or taxing. These changes then influence total spending by consumers or by business firms. And, of course, by far the largest unit of government is the federal government. Its spending and taxing decisions are like stones falling in a pool of water, sending rippling effects throughout the economy.

A PREVIEW OF WHAT IS TO COME

Although this chapter is going to be about the importance of government spending and of taxes in the macroeconomy, the discussion is leading toward an examination of **fiscal policy**. Fiscal policy is defined as changes in taxes and government spending, which may occur intentionally or automatically (as a result of previous decisions). Our ultimate goal is to help you understand the fiscal-policy measures the federal government can take to reduce unemployment and inflation. We will begin to analyze these measures in Chapter 15. Because the analysis of fiscal policy belongs in later chapters, we will to minimize our references to the Reagan administration's policies in this one. We want to postpone *that* discussion until you have all the tools of analysis ready to use.

This chapter is divided into three sections: (1) The growth of government spending, (2) patterns of spending and taxes, and (3) how taxes affect people with different incomes.

THE GROWTH OF GOVERNMENT SPENDING

Nine times out of ten when someone mentions "the government," we think, perhaps vaguely, of the complex of government agencies in Washington, D.C. But of course the government exists at all levels, represented by the President of the United States on down to the sanitation department of your city or town. In 1977, there were 79,913 units of government in the United States—one federal government, 50 states, and 79,862 local governments (counties, cities, school districts, and special districts for sewage, water, flood, and fire control). Therefore, unless we say otherwise, "government" in these discussions means all agencies of government at all levels.

Let's see how the spending and tax receipts of all of these levels of government have grown through the years. Then we'll examine the reasons for that growth. Table 14-1 summarizes the growth of total government spending and taxing from 1929 to 1982.

As you can see, the dollar growth of government has been staggering. But there's another way of looking at it. The country has grown too. A common method of analysis is to show government spending or taxing as a percentage of

Table 14-1. Total Government Tax Receipts and Expenditures (All Levels of Government), 1929-1982 (in billions)[a]

Year	Tax receipts	Spending[c]
1929	$ 11.3	$ 10.3
1940[b]	17.7	18.4
1950	69.0	61.0
1960	139.5	136.4
1970[b]	302.6	311.9
1980[b]	836.8	869.0
1981[b]	954.6	979.7
1982[b]	968.4	1,084.5

Source: Economic Report of the President, 1983.
[a]Unadjusted for inflation.
[b]Notice that in these years all levels of government spent more than they received. This excess of spending over receipts is called "deficit spending," a topic we'll discuss in later chapters.
[c]Includes transfer payments.

Table 14-2. Total Government Spending (All Levels of Government), 1940-1982 (in billions)[a]

Year	GNP	Government spending[b]	Government spending as a percentage of GNP
1940	$ 100.0	$ 18.4	18.4%
1950	286.2	61.0	21.3
1960	506.0	136.4	26.9
1970	872.4	311.9	31.7
1980	2,626.1	869.0	33.1
1981	2,922.2	979.7	33.5
1982	3,057.5	1,084.5	35.5

Source: Economic Report of the President, 1983.
[a]Unadjusted for inflation
[b]From Table 14-1

the nation's Gross National Product (GNP). In this way we can see the *relative* change in government spending. Table 14-2 does this.

We can see that spending has increased both absolutely and in relation to the nation's GNP. While the nation's GNP grew roughly 31 times ($100 billion up to $3,057.5 billion), government spending increased 59 times ($18.4 billion up to $1,084.5 billion).

What Has Caused the Growth in Government Spending?

1. *Increases in urbanization and population.* As countries become more industrialized and as people move from farms to cities, they can no longer handle many services individually; essentials like water supply, waste disposal, and such must be organized on a large, public scale. This tendency is reinforced as population increases and becomes more densely concentrated.

Between 1940 and 1982, the U.S. population grew from 132 million people to 232 million, an increase of about 1.5 million people per year. An increas-

BOX ESSAY
The Meaning of One Billion

The rate of government spending every hour is about $126 million. Now that we're involved with the macro, big picture, let's try to visualize the meaning of large numbers. One million is, of course, one thousand thousand. And one billion is one thousand million. (Our GNP of almost $3,100 billion in 1982 was equal to more than $3 trillion.)

Here are some ways to think about the size of one billion. A trip of one billion miles is equal to 4,000 trips to the moon. One billion hours equals 144,155 years. When all agencies of government annually spend almost $1,100 billion per year, the rate of spending every hour is about $126 million. At that rate of spending, $1 billion is spent in not quite 8 hours.

ing population that moves to cities leads to increasing demand for public services like trash collection, sewage systems, public schools, better means of transportation, public health delivery systems, and police and fire departments.

2. *Inflation.* When prices rise, so do costs for public services, necessitating ever larger government budgets.

3. *Demand for regulation.* We have already seen in Chapter 8 that businesses often demand protection from competition, while the public demands regulation to protect environmental quality and to keep products and working conditions safer. The extent and cost of government regulation is increasing rapidly.

4. *Transfer payments.* One reason for the growth in government spending has been the growth of transfer payments. Remember that these payments are government subsidies to industries (like the milk industry), interest payments to those who own government securities, and payments to people who are on welfare or who are unemployed. All these categories have grown, both absolutely and relatively. In 1960, transfer payments were $34 billion or 6.7 percent of GNP. By 1982 the numbers had grown to $445.5 billion, or 14.6 percent of GNP. Transfer payments grew more than twice as fast as GNP during the 1960–1982 years.

Before we conclude that this growth indicates an increase in compassion for the poor, remember that part of transfer payments are interest payments on government securities. These have grown tremendously with greater acceptance in Washington, D.C., with its recent policy of deficit spending. And interest payments on government securities go to people with incomes above the median who can afford the securities as part of their savings portfolios.* Even with these interest rates subtracted, though, we find that an increasing share of GNP was being spent on the poor, at least through 1982. Transfer payments other than government interest payments grew from 5.3 percent of GNP in 1960 to 11.8 percent in 1982.**

---

*When the U.S. Treasury pays interest to the owners of government securities, the Treasury has to raise the money by (1) taxing people or (2) by selling additional government securities to cover the interest payments. Some redistribution of income takes place whenever some people are taxed and some people receive that money. The effect of this taking and giving is mentioned again on page 345.

**The increase in aid to the poor may slow down under the Reagan administration. Another look at the numbers would be in order in 1984–1985.

Table 14-3. Tax Revenues as a Percentage of GDP* (1978) and GNP per Capita (1978) —Selected Countries

Country	Tax revenues as a percentage of GDP (1978)	Per capita GNP in 1977 dollars (1978)
Sweden	51.4%	$ 9,575
Netherlands	47.0	7,550
Belgium	44.1	8,371
France	39.6	7,385
West Germany	37.6	9,056
United Kingdom	34.0	4,519
Switzerland	31.6	10,121
Italy	31.3	3,515
United States	30.2	9,002
Japan	24.3	6,360
Spain	22.7	3,185

Source: *Statistical Abstract of the United States, 1981.* Tables 1556 and 1552.

*GDP stands for "gross domestic product." GDP is GNP minus the value of production owned by a country outside its borders; i.e., GDP for the United States is GNP minus the value of production of American firms in other countries.

The U.S. Tax Burden
Compared with That of Other Countries

By now you must be wondering how the size of the U.S. government compares with the size of government in other countries. It's difficult to compare spending because of statistical problems in determining what is, and what isn't, included. However, comparing tax burdens, rather than spending, gives us the picture of Table 14-3. We have included a column showing GNP per capita so that you can get an impression of the connection between taxes and income.

In general, Table 14-3 indicates that high incomes and high taxes can—but do not always—go together, an indication that the demand for public services may be proportional to high income. This conclusion tends to be borne out by the figures for less developed countries. Tax revenues as a percentage of total output are much lower than in the industrial countries shown in Table 14-3, and per capita incomes are much lower also. Typically, in these poor countries, government spending will be about 10 percent of total output, and their per capita GNPs will average around $500 to $1,000.

PATTERNS OF SPENDING AND TAXES

The budgets of the federal government and the other 79,912 units of government set the pattern of the taxes we pay and determine how our money is spent. We will look first at federal budgets and then at a combined budget for all state and local governments.

Federal Budgets

Each January, the President sends to the Congress his budget recommendations for the fiscal year beginning the following October 1. The Congress is legally empowered to change or eliminate programs in the President's budget or to add programs not requested by the President.

The freedom of either Congress or the President to change the budget in any given year is severely limited. When all past commitments are added up, about three-fourths of each federal budget has to be considered uncontrollable, or fixed.* The passage of each budget commits the federal government to continue payments for such important items as veterans' benefits, unemployment insurance and Social Security payments, and so forth. The federal government is also committed to pay interest on the public debt and to provide funds for construction projects for which contracts have been previously issued.

If you look at Table 14-4, you'll notice that the federal government spent a lot more—$188 billion ($848 billion − $660 billion)—than it took in in receipts. How does the government cover this deficit? By selling government securities—Treasury Bills, Treasury Notes, and Treasury Bonds. As you are probably aware, the federal government frequently runs a deficit in its annual budget, and there are constant outcries that it should "balance the budget." Every deficit adds to the national debt, adding to the anxiety of those who fear we are spending our way to bankruptcy. We will discuss the history of deficits and the consequences of the national debt in Chapter 17.

Where the Money Comes From, Where It Goes

Under tax receipts, we see the kinds of taxes the federal government collects. Taxes can be classified in a variety of ways, many of which are discussed later in this chapter. For the moment, note that taxes are compulsory payments we make either (1) on our incomes or (2) on the things we buy or have bought in the past.

In the federal budget most of the government's revenues come from taxes on income: the personal income tax, Social Security taxes, and taxes on income earned by corporations. Together, these three taxes accounted for 89.5 percent of the federal government's income. Excise taxes,** customs duties, estate taxes, and miscellaneous are taxes on the things we buy—like tires, alcoholic beverages, or cars from Japan.

The two most important categories of spending are "income security" and national defense. The category of income security includes Social Security, unemployment and retirement benefits, food stamps, grants for social services, and vocational rehabilitation. Actually, the 33.3 percent figure *understates* the emphasis the federal budget now places on helping people. When we add the 10.7 percent for health and the 2.9 percent for education and training, we reach a total of 46.9 percent of the budget. Back in 1974, this total was 29 percent.

The 28.9 percent earmarked for national defense is also an understatement. If we want to know the portion of the federal budget earmarked in 1984 for all wars—past, present, and future—we should add the 3.1 percent for veterans' benefits and services, some of the interest on the debt, and some of the items buried in "other" (such as space research). Altogether, war-connected expenditures for the 1984 budget were probably in the range of 35 to 40 percent, down from an estimated 50 to 60 percent during the Vietnam War years.

To the right of the 1984 percentages in Table 14-4, we have posted the percentage shares for the same items in the 1980 budget, just to see if anything

---

*See *Statistical Abstract of the United States, 1982–1983,* table 419. This table divides the federal budget into "relatively uncontrollable outlays" and "relatively controllable outlays." The estimated "uncontrollable" portion for 1982 was 75 percent.

**The term *excise taxes* refers to sales taxes on particular commodities like tires, alcoholic beverages, tobacco, and gasoline. Frequently, on such items, we pay a federal excise tax *plus* a state sales tax.

Table 14-4. The 1984 Federal Budget: Where the Money Comes From, Where It Goes*

	Billions of dollars (1984)	Percent of total (1984)	Percent of total (1980)
Tax Receipts:			
Personal income	$296	44.8%	45.1%
Social Security	243	36.8	32.0
Corporate profits	52	7.9	14.1
Excise	40	6.1	3.6
Customs duties, estate taxes, miscellaneous	29	4.4	5.2
	$660	100.0%	100.0%
Spending:			
Income security	$282	33.3%	33.6%
National defense	245	28.9	23.7
Interest on the national debt	103	12.1	10.7
Health	91	10.7	10.0
Education and training	25	2.9	5.6
Veterans' benefits	26	3.1	3.8
All other	76	9.0	12.6
	$848	100.0%	100.0%

*1984 figures are estimates made in 1982 by the Council of Economic Advisors. *Source: Economic Report of the President, 1983.* This table should not be confused with Table 14-2, which covered *all* levels of government through *1982*. Table 14-4 covers the *federal government only* in fiscal *1984*.

interesting is developing. One can see in 1984, the sharp drop in the percentage going to corporate profits taxes, reflecting tax cuts, and a sharp increase in excise taxes, reflecting higher federal taxes on commodities like tobacco.

Income security in 1984, takes a slightly smaller share, while national defense takes a larger share, even though older people are a constantly increasing part of our population. The increase in defense spending is an early indication of the Reagan administration's commitment to stronger military forces.

But there is always an opportunity cost for such increases. Education is down from 5.6 percent in 1980 to 2.9 percent in 1984. This decrease is also reflected in a drop in absolute dollars from a high of $31.4 billion in 1981 to $25.3 billion in 1984.

State and Local Budgets

Table 14-5 shows the combined budgets for all 50 states and the local governments within them. Estimated tax receipts and spending are for the period July 1, 1980, through June 30, 1981.

Table 14-5 presents quite a different picture from that of the federal government. Income taxes play a relatively small role in state and local budgets, whereas they provide the largest share of the federal government's income.

Table 14-5. Combined State and Local Budgets, 1979–1980

	Billions of dollars	Percent of total
General revenues:*		
Property taxes	$ 75.0	17.7%
Sales taxes	86.0	20.3
Income taxes	46.4	11.0
Corporate taxes	14.1	3.3
Licenses and miscellaneous fees	111.6	26.4
From the federal government	90.3	21.3
	$423.4	100.0%
Spending:		
Education	$145.8	35.8%
Highways	34.6	8.5
Public welfare	54.1	13.3
Police, fire, parks and miscellaneous	172.9	42.4
	$407.4	100.0%

Source: Economic Report of the President, 1983.

*Excludes income from publicly owned utilities and liquor stores and grants between states and local units.

Other kinds of taxes and fees give the states and local governments the money they need. But one of the important sources of income for the states and local governments is the federal government itself. As you can see, the federal government provided over one fifth of the income (21.3 percent) for states and local governments in the 1980–1981 year. That is a typical percentage; the range is from 18 to 22 percent. It is important to remember that trimming the budget in Washington, D.C., will certainly affect your state, probably your town, your college, and perhaps your own personal budget.

Federal Revenue Sharing

Federal contributions to state and local governments are called **federal revenue sharing**. The rationale for this flow of money from Washington, D.C., to state and local governments is this: As you saw in Table 14-4, most (44.8 percent) of the federal government's receipts comes from the personal income tax. Moreover, the federal government's tax receipts may rise faster than the increase in everyone's income, because income tax rates have been increasing faster than income.

On the other hand, state and local governments obtain most of their income from sales and property taxes and license fees. The problem is that as incomes rise, revenues from these three sources rise—*but not as fast as income.* When our paychecks go up, less of our income becomes subject to these kinds of taxes and fees. There are two reasons for this: (1) As our incomes rise, we tend to save a larger fraction of our incomes. Local government taxes generally don't affect money that isn't spent, although interest (or dividends or capital gains) may be taxed as part of income. (2) As our incomes rise, we tend to spend a larger fraction of our incomes on services like plumbers, tax accountants, law-yers, or dry cleaners. Our expenditures on these items often are not subject to sales taxes. And property taxes don't rise as fast as income increases. If we get a 20 percent salary raise, do we spend 20 percent more on housing? Probably not.

And so the federal government's receipts tend to rise faster than increases in income, while receipts for the states and local governments tend to increase sluggishly by comparison. Thus the rationale for federal revenue sharing.

But this apparently logical rationale for federal revenue sharing has been the subject of much disagreement. In the fiscal year 1980–1981, shown in Table 14-5, the states and local governments spent less money than they received: $407.4 billion spent, $423.4 billion received, leaving a surplus of $16.0 billion, a typical pattern because the states and local governments have had combined surpluses in every year since 1968. But in every year since 1969, the federal government has had deficits. The opponents of revenue sharing argue, under-standably, that the federal government is continuing to give the states and local governments money it doesn't have.

HOW TAXES AFFECT PEOPLE WITH DIFFERENT INCOMES

There are several issues that engage economists when they think about taxes: (1) Who should pay, (2) the relative burden of taxes on people with different incomes, and (3) taxpayers' efforts to shift the cost of taxes to others. This section is divided accordingly.

Two Principles of Taxation: Deciding Who Should Pay

There are two broad principles of taxation: the benefits principle and ability-to-pay principle. According to the **benefits principle**, the one who receives the benefit of a particular government service is the one who should pay (be taxed) for it. The gasoline tax is probably the best example of this. If you drive a car, the 10 to 15 cents per gallon you pay in gasoline taxes is intended for highway construction. This principle seems very fair. It is like buying a product in the free market for personal benefit.

Unfortunately, the benefits principle will not provide all the things we need, for two reasons: (1) Benefits are hard to measure and are often geographically distant from individual taxpayers; and (2) if all taxes were designed along benefits-principle lines, low-income people would be unable to obtain public goods such as education. (Costs per year per student in our public schools average around $2,000.)

Consequently, other taxes are designed to obtain more money from the rich than the poor—the **ability-to-pay principle**. The federal income tax as cur-rently structured is the best example of this kind of tax. As income rises, the average tax rate also rises, so that the rich not only pay more dollars but also a greater percentage of their income (assuming no tax loopholes—an important assumption).

The Relative Burden of Taxes

Taxes do not affect everyone equally. Some people are hit harder than others. Economists are interested in the *relative* burden of taxes on people of different income groups, and so they look at the taxes we pay as a percentage of the incomes we receive.

Some folks think there's a fourth type of taxes: oppressive.

Three Types of Taxes: Progressive, Proportional, and Regressive

When taxes are compared with our incomes, they are classified as progressive, proportional, or regressive. A **progressive tax** is one in which the tax as a percentage of income rises as income rises. The most common types of progressive taxes are inheritance taxes and income taxes.

Take two people, Mary Lovelace and Tom Strongheart. Tom's income is $10,000, while Mary's is $20,000. Tom's income tax will be approximately $1,200, while Mary's tax will be approximately $4,000. The tax is progressive, not because Mary's tax is higher in dollars, but because her tax is a higher *percentage* of her income. Mary's tax is 20 percent ($4,000 ÷ $20,000), while Tom's tax is only 12 percent ($1,200 ÷ $10,000) of his income. To be progressive, a tax must not only take a bigger bite in dollars as income rises, but also a bigger share (percentage). Now suppose that Tom's tax had been $2,000 with Mary's at the same $4,000. What kind of tax would that be? Not progressive, because the tax as a percentage of income hasn't changed. In both cases the tax is 20 percent. When the tax as a percentage of income stays the same, as income changes, the tax is called **proportional**. We will deal with proportional taxes a bit later in this chapter.

The corporate income tax is a hybrid—to some extent proportional, to some extent progressive. All corporations pay a 20 percent tax on the first $25,000 of taxable profit. The next $25,000 of taxable profit is taxed at a 22 percent rate. Thereafter, the rate is 46 percent. When we consider loopholes available to corporations (tax credits for new machinery or depletion allowances) plus tax-shifting to consumers through higher prices, it is difficult indeed to determine whether a corporation's income tax is progressive or proportional.

A **regressive** tax is one in which the tax as a percentage of income rises as income falls. The best example is a sales tax or an excise tax, but property taxes and payroll taxes can also be regressive.

The discussion that follows will take up progressive taxes, proportional ("flat") taxes, and regressive taxes in that order.

Table 14-6. Federal Tax Rate Schedule for Single Taxpayers, 1982 (selected tax brackets)

If line 5 is	the tax is	of the excess over
Not over $2,300	No tax	
over $6,500 but not over $8,500	$608 + 17%	$6,500
over $18,200 but not over $23,500	$3,194 + 31%	$18,200
over $41,500	$12,068 + 50%	$41,500

The Personal Income Tax Schedule

As Table 14-4 showed us, the personal income tax is by far the most important source of revenue for the federal government, accounting for about 45 percent of its receipts. The income tax is based on one's total income, from which many deductions can be made, the principal ones being IRA* savings accounts, state and local taxes, charitable gifts, and interest payments on mortgages and loans. The federal government also allows an exemption ($1,000 in 1982) for yourself and for each dependent. After all exemptions and deductions have been deducted from your total income from all sources, the remainder is called *taxable income*. When taxable income has been determined, a table is used to determine the amount you owe the government.

How the Schedule Works

Table 14-6 is a copy of a portion of the federal personal income tax schedule that single taxpayers filled out in the spring of 1983 for income received in 1982. The reference to "line 5" is to the taxable income that is left after all exemptions and allowable deductions are subtracted from the income single taxpayers received *before* the taxes that were withheld from their paychecks.

Note first that the table starts with a taxable income of $2,300, sometimes called the **no-tax threshold**. Individuals below that pay nothing.

Now let us see how the table works. Take three people: Joe Allen, whose taxable income is $7,500; Peg Jones, whose taxable income is $19,200; and Jackie Vanderbilt, whose taxable income is $51,500. We'll use Peg's income to show how the tax is calculated. Table 14-6 says that Peg must pay $3,194 plus 31 percent of the amount over $18,200. Therefore, she must pay $3,194 plus 31 percent of $1,000 ($19,200 − $18,200). Peg's tax is shown below:

	$3,194
31% of $1,000	+ 310
Peg's total tax	$3,504

Note that *two* tax rates are involved here. The 31 percent of Peg's last $1,000 of income is called the **marginal tax rate**. People often refer to the 31 percent as Peg's "tax bracket," but observe that this tax rate refers only to the dollars over $18,200, not to Peg's entire income.

But there is also an **average tax rate**; that is, Peg's total tax expressed as a percentage of her taxable income. In this case her average tax rate is $3,504 ÷ $19,200 = 18.3 percent. Table 14-7 shows marginal tax rates, average tax rates, and net income after taxes for Joe, Peg, and Jackie.

---

*IRA stands for "individual retirement accounts." Beginning in 1982, monies put into such accounts reduced one's taxable income. Be sure to discuss the details with your bank or a tax accountant.

Table 14-7. Tax Payments on Three Incomes

	Taxable income	Total tax	Marginal tax rate	Average tax rate	Net income after tax
Joe	$ 7,500	$ 778	17%	10.4%	$ 6,722
Peg	19,200	3,504	31	18.3	15,696
Jackie	51,500	12,068	50	34.1	34,432

Marriage and Taxes

What happens if Peg and Joe decide to marry? Their combined taxable income would be $19,200 plus $7,500 equals $26,700. On the 1982 schedule for married couples filing joint returns (not shown), we find that their tax will be $4,646. Their present combined tax is $3,504 plus $778 = $4,282. They will lose $364 ($4,646 − $4,282) by marrying. If they had had the *same* taxable incomes, they would have found that the penalty for marriage was even more severe.

Assume that Peg and Joe each have taxable incomes of $19,200. Their combined income tax would be double Peg's, or $7,008 if they remain single. If they marry, their joint return will show a tax of $8,571—a $1,563 annual penalty for giving up singlehood!

Income Tax Loopholes

The federal income tax schedule in Table 14-6 suggests that the income tax is extremely progressive, with marginal tax rates rising from 17 to 50 percent of taxable income. The entire schedule actually ranges from a low of 12 percent to a high of 50 percent. Most experts agree that the high rates rarely apply in the real world, owing to a number of **tax loopholes**. A loophole may be defined as a provision in the law that permits the taxpayer to reduce his or her taxable income or to receive income that is not taxed at all or that is taxed at a lower rate.

Back in the 1960s and 1970s when marginal tax rates went up to 70 percent, Nelson Rockefeller's federal income taxes averaged only 24 percent of his average annual taxable income of $4.7 million during the years 1964–1973.[1] Billionaire Bunker Hunt paid $9.65 between 1975 and 1977. Edwin S. Cohen, former Assistant Secretary of the Treasury, admitted that 112 Americans with incomes of more than $200,000 in 1970 paid no taxes for that year.[2] The Brookings Institution, a well-known economic research organization in Washington, D.C., once estimated that the highest *real* marginal tax rate was 32 percent, not the 70 percent marginal tax rate shown in the tax tables prior to 1981.

How do the more affluent manage to reduce their taxes? They use any of several loopholes: tax-exempt bonds, capital gains, and business-expense deductions.

Many municipalities and school districts issue *tax-exempt bonds* to finance new buildings, sewage-disposal plants, and so forth. These bonds earn an annual interest income for the bondholder that is often not subject to taxation. Tax-exempt bonds provide local governments with an important method of raising money. A person owning, say, $1 million worth of municipal or other tax-exempt bonds at 8 percent would receive $80,000 a year in income, and that income would be exempt from taxation by the federal government and often by

Tax loopholes cost the government billions of lost tax dollars.

state governments. The interest on U.S. government bonds is, however, subject to the federal income tax.

Capital gains are realized when a person sells stocks, buildings, land, or other assets for more than he or she paid for them. Sixty percent of the capital gain (the profit) from selling such an asset is tax exempt. The other 40 percent is taxed as ordinary income. Because only 40 percent of the capital gain is taxable, the maximum marginal tax rate on capital gains is really 20 percent (40 percent of the highest marginal tax rate of 50 percent).

Tax laws also provide important loopholes or subsidies in the form of *business-expense deductions.* Although the deductions are legitimate, the use of them may not be. People who own or manage a business are able to charge off to the business many of their everyday living expenses such as lunches, entertainment, the use of an automobile, and in some cases even the expenses of maintaining all or a portion of their homes.

All loopholes or deductions taken together cost the federal government over $200 billion in lost tax receipts in 1981.* The problem is that almost all taxpayers enjoy some of the loopholes, such as deducting interest on home mortgages and on installment contracts. But the problem is getting worse. By 1987, the federal government will lose through loopholes 86 cents for every dollar it collects in income taxes, up from 53 cents per dollar in 1977. Corporate loopholes will cost the Treasury $1.88 for every dollar collected, up from 50 cents in 1977.[3]

Proportional Taxes: The Flat Tax Idea

One idea to remedy the drain on tax revenues caused by tax loopholes is the **flat tax idea**, which received much notice and favorable comment in 1982. The idea is elegantly simple: Get rid of the loopholes and substitute an across-

---

* *Statistical Abstract of the United States, 1981.* Another $95 billion may have been lost from untaxed income generated in the "underground economy." *Fortune,* 26 July 1982.

Table 14-8. Impact of a $500 Sales Tax on Peg's and Jackie's Incomes.

	Peg	Jackie
Taxable income	$19,200	$51,500
Price of car	10,000	10,000
5% sales tax on car	500	500
Tax as a percentage of taxable income	2.6%	1.0%

the-board proportional tax of about 15 percent for the present income tax code. The money raised would be enough to run the federal government. The voluminous income tax code could be scrapped. Thousands of tax accountants and tax lawyers would have to find more productive work. (Many economists believe the resources used up in tax preparation are wasted.)

But, despite the attractiveness of the idea, most economists realize that it doesn't have "a snowball's chance." Opposition is bound to come from two sources: (1) Special-interest groups like corporations and homeowners will fight to keep deductions like interest on mortgages, special depreciation allowances, and tax credits. (2) Too many people will have higher tax rates than before. Joe, in Table 14-7, is an example. If the flat tax is 15 percent, Joe suffers an increase in his average tax rate. The problem is that there will be 21.5 million taxpayers in Joe's category in 1984.[4] Although many proposals exist to solve both sets of problems, and although the flat-tax idea has many supporters from both political parties, the experts see little chance for agreement and adoption in 1982. Nevertheless, some states like Massachusetts and Nebraska do have proportional ("flat") income taxes.

Regressive Taxes

Just to review: Progressive taxes take an increasing percentage of income as income increases. Proportional taxes take the same percentage, though a larger number of dollars, as income increases. Regressive taxes take a *smaller* percentage of income as income increases. We'll illustrate regressive taxes with three well-known types: sales taxes, property taxes, and payroll taxes.

Sales Taxes

Let us assume that Peg Jones and Jackie Vanderbilt each buy a $10,000 automobile. The 5 percent sales tax appears to be proportional because the percentage does not change, but note that the percentage applies to the *automobile*, not to the *purchaser's income*. The three terms "progressive," "proportional," and "regressive" involve the *relationship between the tax and the buyer's income*, not between the tax and the price of the item purchased.

What is the sales tax as a percentage of the buyer's income? The sales tax is 2.6 percent of Peg's income but only 1.0 percent of Jackie's. Because the percentage falls as income rises, the sales tax is a regressive tax. Table 14-8 shows the effect of this sales tax.

But, you may say, Jackie wouldn't buy a $10,000 car; she'd buy a $15,000 car. Oddly enough, it doesn't matter. Why? Because higher-income people will tend to save more, play the stock market more, and buy fewer things subject to sales (or property) taxes—*as a proportion of their incomes*—than will poorer people. Consequently, a smaller proportion of their income is subject to the

Table 14-9. Impact of $500 and $750 Car Sales Tax on Peg's and Jackie's Incomes.

	Peg	Jackie
Taxable income	$19,200	$51,500
Price of car	$10,000	$15,000
Car as percentage of income	52%	29%
5% sales tax on car	$500	$750*
Tax as a percentage of income	2.6%	1.5%*

*Note that in this case a regressive tax can produce a larger number of dollars—a reminder that it's not the dollars, but the *tax as a percentage of income*—that matters.

sales tax. As long as Peg spends a larger percentage of her income on a car than Jackie does, the tax is still regressive.

Table 14-9 shows that Peg's tax is still 2.6 percent of her income, while Jackie's tax as a percentage of her income is 1.5.

The secret of the regressivity of the sales tax is in line 3. Jackie, representing people with higher incomes, will spend a smaller percentage of her income (29 percent) on cars than will Peg, our representative of lower-income people.

One caution about any general conclusion that sales and excise taxes are necessarily regressive: Regressive effects can be lessened considerably if (1) food and other necessities are exempted and/or (2) the sales tax is made progressive by using higher rates for more expensive items—say, 15 percent on cars over $15,000, 10% on cars between $10,000 and $15,000, 7 percent on cars between $5,000 and $10,000, and so forth. Some economists believe that such progressive sales taxes, plus appropriate exemptions, may be preferable to income taxes as an efficient and fair way of collecting money because sales taxes are inescapable—there are no loopholes. The tax money is collected when the money is spent.

Property Taxes

Property taxes are usually levied by cities or counties to finance the affairs of all governmental units within their boundaries. Funds collected are used to pay each town's bills like administration, police and fire protection, and education. Counties also pay for their own administration and such countywide costs as community colleges, streets, flood control, welfare, and county libraries. The states generally determine the formulas used by the counties in levying property taxes, but property taxes are determined locally. Control by local voters creates differences among the states in their property-tax methods; there are even some differences among the counties of the same state.

Property taxes are regressive because, as with food, clothing, or transportation, a high-income person like Jackie will spend a smaller amount on housing—relative to her income—than will a lower-income person like Peg. A $50,000-income person like Jackie may spend three times her income ($150,000) for a house, while a $20,000-income person like Peg may have to spend five times her income ($100,000) for a house. So long as the property tax is expressed as a flat percentage of the value of the property, the property tax will be a larger share of Peg's income than of Jackie's.

Table 14-10. Payroll Taxes as a Percentage of Peg's and Jackie's Incomes.

	Peg	Jackie
Taxable income	$19,200	$51,500
Maximum taxable income under Social Security*	$29,700	$29,700
Tax rate	6.65%	6.65%
Social Security tax	1,276.80	1,975.05
Tax as a percentage of income	6.65%	3.8%

*An increase in the Social Security tax to 7 percent of the first $35,700 was under consideration in early 1983.

Payroll Taxes

Payroll taxes (Social Security and unemployment insurance taxes) are also regressive. For example, the 1981 tax rate for Social Security was 6.65 percent* of the first $29,700 earned. Consider the effect this has on Peg's and Jackie's incomes (Table 14-10).

In any comparison of people in different income groups, the Social Security tax will be regressive if some of the taxpayers earn less than the maximum taxed and some earn more. Among all those making less than the maximum, the tax is proportional. In this case, all of Peg's income is subject to the tax, while $21,800 ($51,500 − $29,700) of Jackie's income is exempt. The tax is bound to be regressive, as the last line of the table indicates.

Shifting the Tax Burden to Others

One of the most interesting questions about taxes is, Who pays them? The transfer of the burden from one enterprise to another or to the retail customer is called **tax shifting**. The final resting place of the tax burden is called **tax incidence**.

Suppose you buy a tube of Dazzle toothpaste for $1. The salesperson adds 5 percent to the price because of a sales tax. You pay $1.05. Apparently, you are the taxpayer. You are, but only indirectly. The store is the taxpayer because it must now send the money to some government agency. Economists call the sales tax an *indirect business tax* because the business is being taxed but passes the burden of the tax on to the consumer.

Now put yourself in the place of the retail store. The entrepreneur, having had a course in economics, realizes that the demand curve slopes down from left to right and that she will sell fewer tubes of toothpaste at $1.05 than at $1. She may say to herself: "If the demand for toothpaste is elastic, I'll not only sell less toothpaste, but my total revenue will fall if the price goes up." To the extent that the entrepreneur believes this to be true, she may decide to absorb some of the tax herself. She might decide to charge 98 cents instead of $1.00. Then the consumer would pay $1.03. The entrepreneur absorbs 2 cents, the consumer 3 cents.

*Effective January 1, 1984, the Social Security tax will become much less regressive, because one half of Social Security benefits received by those earning $25,000 or more will be subject to federal income taxes.

As a general rule, sales taxes are the most easily shifted. The ability of an enterprise to pass the cost of any tax along to buyers depends primarily on the elasticity of demand for the product. If demand is inelastic, the tax can be shifted; if it is elastic, the seller may have to absorb the tax. The final shares of the tax absorbed by sellers and buyers may involve an infinite variety of compromises.

Property taxes can be shifted if rental property or business property is involved, passing from landlords to tenants, or from business enterprises to consumers.

Personal income taxes are the most difficult to shift except in cases where the taxpayer is a member of a strong union. In this situation, the union may succeed in shifting some of the burden of income-tax increases to the employer by demanding and getting wage increases when income taxes go up. Then, depending on the employer's market power, he may be able to shift some or all of those income-tax increases to consumers (some of whom will be members of the union) in the form of higher prices. When consumer prices rise, the union may again demand higher wages—and so it goes. Nonunion employees may be left behind because they lack the power to increase their wages when losses in their take-home pay occur.

Redistributing Income: Does It Work?

Another way to ask this question is, What is the *combined* effect of taxes on people with different incomes? The best answer is, No one knows for sure.

Two economists, Joseph A. Pechman and Benjamin A. Okner, have estimated that only the wealthiest 3 to 5 percent of American families and the poorest 10 percent pay *more* than 25 percent of their income in taxes (all taxes, all levels). The families in between all pay about the same percentage (25 percent) of their income in taxes.[5]

But taxes themselves are only part of the picture. Taxes can be shifted; the poor may receive transfer payments, and the poor may also receive government services like subsidized public transportation that are not in the transfer payment category. Furthermore, we have to remember that *any* form of government spending probably favors people of different incomes differently. Who receives more benefit from freeways, schools, public hospitals, parks, police forces, fire departments—the rich or the poor? In some cases (public hospitals) the poor receive a larger share. But in others (police and fire protection of a large hilltop estate, for example), the rich receive a larger share. When all these factors are taken into account, the combined effect of all government spending and taxes becomes much less clear.[6]

SUMMARY

Government spending has increased from 18.4 percent of the nation's total output in 1940 to 35.5 percent in 1982. About one half of this is federal spending, which goes primarily for income security and national defense. State and local spending is mainly for education, highways, and public welfare. The principal source of government income at all levels is taxes—individual income, payroll, and corporate taxes for the federal government; sales taxes, federal grants, and property taxes for state and local governments.

Of all types of taxes, income taxes are the most progressive. Sales taxes, property taxes, and payroll taxes all tend to be regressive—that is, they take up a smaller proportion of the rich person's income than of the poor person's. State and local government taxes are mostly regressive, and the income from them has become increasingly inadequate. Federal revenue sharing has been adopted to help these governments meet rising needs.

Determining who bears the burden of a tax is difficult because the cost of taxes can be shifted to people other than the legal taxpayer. The final resting place of the burden of a tax is called tax incidence; to ask what is the incidence of a tax is to ask who really pays the tax. Sales taxes can be shifted most easily. Property taxes can be shifted where rental or business property is involved. Personal income taxes are the most difficult to shift.

Discussion Questions

1. Has defense spending been declining? Discuss.

2. Examine the following income-tax schedule. Is it progressive, proportional, or regressive? Why?

Income	Tax
$ 5,000	$ 500
10,000	800
15,000	1,050
20,000	1,200

3. How might sales taxes be made less regressive?

4. Is the property tax an example of the ability-to-pay principle or of the benefits principle? Discuss.

5. Can income taxes be shifted? (*Hint*: Would membership in a strong union affect your answer?)

DID YOU EVER WONDER WHY ...

... corporations do not *really* pay income taxes?

References

1. *New York Times*, September 24, 1974, p. 34.

2. Robert J. Samuelson, "Wealthy Tax-Nonpayers Widely Diverse Group," *Los Angeles Times*, 6 March 1972.

3. Robert S. McIntyre, "Flat-Rate Talk," *The New Republic*, July 19 and 26, 1982.

4. *Fortune*, 26 July 1982.

5. *Los Angeles Times*, 14 April 1974, p. 2.

6. Richard A. Musgrave and Peggy B. Musgrave, *Public Finance in Theory and Practice*, 2nd ed. (New York: McGraw-Hill, 1976), Ch. 16.

The purpose of the three chapters in Part IV was to set the scene for the action. In Part IV, the economy was measured, its performance was recorded, and the financial activities of the government were described. Part V is the part where the action to fight inflation and unemployment takes place. Part V is divided into five chapters as follows: Chapter 15 is about who should do the fighting. In particular, should the federal government be a participant? Chapter 16 describes fiscal-policy measures—changes in

PART V

MACROECONOMIC THEORY: FIGHTING INFLATION AND UNEMPLOYMENT

government spending and taxes—to fight inflation and unemployment. Chapter 17 reviews the arguments about the public (national) debt, because a growing debt is one of the side effects of government attempts to cure unemployment. Chapter 18 shows how the banking system fights inflation and unemployment. Efforts to control inflation and unemployment via the banking system are called "monetary policy." Finally, Chapter 19 takes up the trillion-dollar question: Can we have full employment without inflation?

15

The Economic Role of Government: The Great Debate

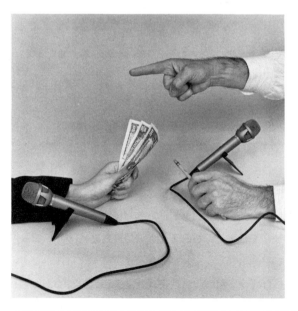

KEY WORDS
Classical economists
Classical school
Say's Law
Wage-price flexibility
Thomas Robert Malthus
Theory of Gluts
Keynesian revolution
Deficit spending
Budget surplus
The Employment Act of 1946
Supply-side economics
Public good

Whereas the last chapter described what the government does in fact do, this chapter examines the argument about the federal government's role in combating unemployment and inflation. No topic in economics is more subject to heated debate. One powerful school of thought argues that the federal government should do as little as possible, that when it does act, it usually does the wrong thing at the wrong time. This group emphasizes what can happen in free markets when the government interferes—as in the cases of rent control, dairy price supports, egg cartels, and oil price ceilings, already cited in Chapter 6. Still another equally powerful group believes the economy cannot take care of itself, that free markets do not necessarily provide full employment or an absence of inflation. The former school is usually represented politically by conservatives. This school captured the support of the country with the election of President Reagan in 1980. The other school, believing in a larger scope of government responsibility and action, is represented usually by liberal Democrats, those who supported the elections of Kennedy, Johnson, and Carter. These are the "line-ups" of the two teams making up the "great debate."

Pinning labels on people is dangerous; some Republicans are liberals, some Democrats are conservatives. We mention the labels to help you realize that, although this great debate began about 200 years ago, it continues today, more alive and heated than ever.

Before the two schools of thought originated, little thought was given to macroeconomic problems despite the considerable attention given to prices, wages, and interest rates by the Schoolmen in the Middle Ages. But around 1800, a group of economists called the classical economists began taking an interest in macroeconomic problems; they were the forerunners of modern conservatives. Later, in the 1930s, a British economist named John Maynard Keynes presented a different approach to macroeconomics. His views became so influential that he is regarded as the "messiah" of today's liberal Democrats.

This chapter is divided into three sections. The first two sections explain the views of the classical economists and of John Maynard Keynes, respectively. The third section summarizes current views about the functions of government.

CLASSICAL THEORY: LEAVE THE ECONOMY ALONE

Before the Great Depression of the 1930s, most economists accepted the view that a market-price system like ours could solve its own problems without government interference. Those who hold this view are called the **classical economists** or the **classical school**. The founder of classical theory was Adam Smith. Its other early supporters were British economist David Ricardo (1772–1823) and French economist Jean Baptiste Say (1767–1832). The classical economists believed not only that the economic system could take care of itself if left alone, but that there were automatic control devices in it, acting like thermostats, which would continuously move the economic system toward full employment without inflation.

The classical school's belief that a market-price system would always tend toward a condition of full employment is best explained by looking at the ideas of Jean Baptiste Say.

Say's Law: "Supply Creates Its Own Demand"

Say's major work, the *Treatise on Political Economy* (1803), contains a series of propositions that economists have called Say's Law of Markets or, more simply, **Say's Law**.

Say's Law is often reduced to a slogan: "Supply creates its own demand." The slogan means that the act of producing something immediately creates income (wages, rent, interest, and profit that are paid in the course of production), and that this income creates demand for something equal to the value of what was produced *because income is earned to be spent*.

To put it another way, in the course of producing a tube of Dazzle toothpaste to sell for $1, we will immediately create wages, rent, interest, and profit equal to $1, because $1 is the sum of the payments that went into its production.

The most important assumption in Say's line of reasoning was *that income is earned only to be spent*. The only reason any of us work for pay, according to Say, is to buy something with the income we earn. Thus, in Say's thinking, if the $1 of income created in the course of producing the tube of toothpaste is earned only to be spent, it constitutes *demand* for something worth $1. If we now consider the total production of *all* things, we can see that the total production of everything creates the income and demand necessary to buy everything. Thus the act of production (supply) creates equivalent income to be spent (demand).

Now the crucial point. Producers (suppliers) do not have to worry about demand, because everything they decide to produce will always be sold. If they are good Adam Smithians, motivated by self-interest to make as much money as possible, they will want to produce as much as possible. Consequently, they will offer jobs to all who want to work. There will be *no* unemployment. Note, furthermore, that aggregate supply will be at maximum output (at *potential GNP*), but no one need be concerned: Sufficient aggregate demand will be there to buy it.

The classical theorists led by Say answered every possible objection. If people did not want to spend their money on Dazzle toothpaste, for example, they would spend it on something else. Though Dazzle might lose sales and people would be laid off, these workers, it was argued, would soon find jobs elsewhere.

The Wage-Price Flexibility Argument

A loss enterprise like Dazzle would tend to recover even if resources did not shift from one industry to another. The reason is central to classical theory. Classical theory is based on the assumption of **wage-price flexibility**. Prices and wages are flexible enough, the classical economists believed, that in bad times they would fall. At lower prices and wages, buying and hiring would both pick up. Recovery from a recession would be automatic.

The classical economists believed the macroeconomy functioned exactly like the demand-supply diagrams of Chapters 5 and 6. If unemployment existed, the surplus of unemployed labor had to mean that wages were above equilibrium. The classical solution: Lower wages to the point where the quantities demanded by employers and offered by workers are equal.

Similarly, if unsold goods appeared on the shelves, prices had to be too high. Solution: Again, lower prices until equilibrium is reached.

Thus if the Dazzle toothpaste company is in trouble, classical theory says cut wages—say, 10 percent. The wage cut will allow management to cut prices 10

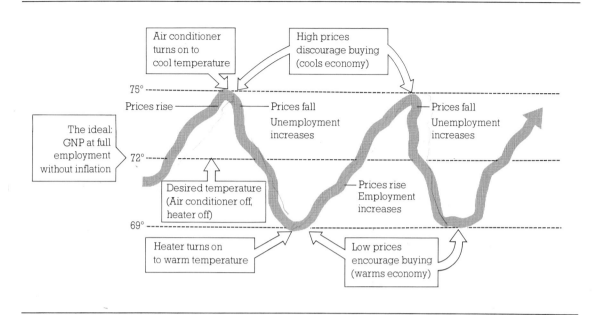

percent, and people will buy more Dazzle. The company will recover. Any unemployment will be temporary.

Figure 15-1.
Operation of the economy in classical theory.

The classical theorists believed that flexible wages and prices acted like a thermostat that would automatically keep GNP at a full-employment level without inflation. Think of a thermostat that automatically turns on the air conditioner during times of inflation to cool off the economy. (Rising prices discourage buying.) And when sales are sluggish (when the economy is too cold), the thermostat will turn on the furnace. (Falling prices encourage buying.) There may be fluctuations, but GNP always returns to full employment without inflation, as shown in Figure 15-1.

The Saving-Investment Argument

Even if people decided to save some of their income instead of spending all of it, flexible prices would take care of the problem. If people saved more, the banks would have more money to lend, the interest rate (the price paid for borrowing money) would fall, and when it did, borrowing by business managers for investment would increase. In fact, the interest rate at any given moment would arrive at an *equilibrium price* that would make the quantity of money saved equal to the quantity of money borrowed for investment. Thus, *all* income earned, or saved, would be spent, either by the people for consumption or by business managers for investment.

The essence of the classical argument, then, is that whereas industries may decline or blossom, the overall size of the industrial pie will always be sufficient to provide everyone with a job who wants one. There may be shifting around from one industry to another, but except for these temporary periods of adjustment, there will always be full employment. Anyone unemployed for any long period of time would be *voluntarily* unemployed.

Malthus's Objection to Classical Theory

Classical theory did not go unopposed, even in its own time. A famous British clergyman-economist named **Thomas Robert Malthus*** (1766–1834) is perhaps the first to have detected a difficulty in classical theory. Malthus's objection to classical theory is called the **Theory of Gluts**.

According to Malthus, if a $1 tube of toothpaste were produced and sold, workers would receive something *less* than $1 per tube because the entrepreneur would not hire them unless they produced a product worth *more* than the wage he or she paid them. Total wages paid all workers are therefore something less than the amount necessary to buy all the tubes of toothpaste and *all other* products produced. Consequently, even though income may be earned only to be spent, *total* earned income might not be enough to buy everything produced.

To illustrate: Assume GNP is $100 and that total wages are $80. How will the extra $20 worth of goods and services be sold? Malthus suggested an answer: All would be well *if* the consumption spending by those whom Malthus called "unproductive laborers" (service workers like school teachers) plus capital spending by entrepreneurs made up the difference between workers' income and the value of their production. But Malthus further believed that the capitalist-entrepreneurs' desire to make ever more money by enlarging their enterprises would periodically cause an overproduction of goods—a glut on the market. Because the demand by workers was never sufficient to buy everything produced, there would be periods of slowdown, unemployment, and general depression. Here we have the first objection to Say's law. Malthus recognized that $1 of supply does not necessarily mean $1 of demand.

Malthus's objection was buried by those who believed in the sanctity of classical theory. The idea that government interference might be necessary—or that uncontrolled capitalism might not work—found little support. Then came the stock market crash of 1929, heralding the Depression that engulfed this country and most other industrial countries.

The severity and length of the Depression in the 1930s helped to convince scholars and politicians that something was wrong with classical economic theory. The time was ripe for a new approach to macroeconomic problems.

THE KEYNESIAN REVOLUTION: THE ECONOMY NEEDS TO BE MANAGED

The new approach appeared in 1936. In that year, an English economist named John Maynard Keynes (pronounced "canes") published a book called *The General Theory of Employment, Interest, and Money*. Among economists, Keynes's book had such an explosive effect that its influence has been called the **Keynesian revolution**.

Keynes was strongly influenced by Malthus's idea that total demand might not be enough to provide full employment. He argued that the economy could get stuck at any level of unemployment and that there were no automatic forces that would help the economy recover from depressions or excessive inflation. Keynes's views inevitably led to the conclusion that the economy *could not*

---

*Malthus is much better known for his *Essay on Population*, in which he argued that population increases would eventually exceed food production. This argument is still taken seriously, particularly in less developed countries.

Economic debate includes the notion that it is up to the government to pull the economy out of a depression.

take care of itself. He believed it was the government's job to pull the economy out of a depression.

The frequent failure of aggregate demand to provide for full employment is at the center of Keynesian theory. If aggregate demand is high enough, the country will have full employment; if it is too low, we will have recessions and unemployment. Keynes's disagreement with classical theory can be summarized as follows.

Objections to the Wage-Price Flexibility Argument

Keynes had three main objections to the classical theory of wage-price flexibility:

1. Demand may be inelastic, and a decrease in price may not be offset by a proportionate increase in sales. Further, the classical argument assumes that demand does not change. In reality, if people get tired of a product, demand for it may decrease—may shift to the left—and if this happens, sales may not increase *at all* even when the price falls.

2. Keynes pointed out that if companies like Dazzle cut prices and wages by 10 percent (as on page 290), nothing really happens to help the economy. If all companies do this, the 10 percent price cuts won't help because everyone makes less money. The people's purchasing power remains the same. Dazzle and all the other companies would be stuck with whatever sales declines were occurring before the adjustments began. If there was unemployment before, it would continue. Aggregate demand could, therefore, get stuck at any level of unemployment.

3. Even if falling wages and prices could help, they would be unlikely to change in exactly the right proportions in the real world. For people to have *increased* purchasing power, prices would have to fall farther than wages.

BOX ESSAY
John Maynard Keynes

Englishman John Maynard Keynes (1883–1946)—he liked to be called Maynard—was the son of two Cambridge University professors. At the age of four, he was figuring out the economic theory of interest; at fourteen, he had a scholarship to Eton; at seventeen, he was a success at Kings College at Cambridge. After graduation, he came in second on the nationwide Civil Service Examination. (He would have placed first had his testers given him a better grade in economics, about which he knew more than they did.)

Following World War I, Keynes was one of the advisors who went to the Treaty of Versailles conference. Although he went to Paris as a representative of the Treasury, he was still only a member of the second echelon and could not engage in the peace negotiations himself. He could only stand by and watch helplessly as President Wilson was outmaneu-

vered by Clemençeau, who moved to break up Germany and exact a harsh penalty. Realizing that the signing of the Treaty of Versailles was inevitable, he resigned from the Treasury.

Three days before the treaty was signed, he started work on his book *The Economic Consequences of the Peace*. It was an attack on the treaty and the ineffectiveness, inadequacies, and inequities of the meeting. The book was an instant success, and his reputation as an economic prophet was secured.

By 1935, Keynes was known as one of the most brilliant economists and writers of modern times. He was so prolific that a list of his books, tracts, and essays fills 22 pages. Of main interest are his books on mathematical probability (1921), the gold standard and monetary reform (1923), the causes of business cycles (1930), and his book *The General Theory of Employment, Interest, and*

Money (1936), which consolidated all the theories of his previous books. *Time* magazine, devoting the cover story of its December 31, 1965, issue to Keynes, stated of *The General Theory*: "It is an uneven and ill-organized book, as difficult as *Deuteronomy* and open to as many interpretations. Yet for all its faults, it had more influence in a shorter time than any other book ever written in economics, including Smith's *The Wealth of Nations* and Marx's *Das Kapital*."

Keynes's ideas, which encompassed all aspects of economics, were the forerunners of macroeconomics as it is known today. His theories were not adopted overnight, however. Franklin D. Roosevelt, in 1934, was not the least bit impressed by lectures Keynes gave at the White House. Nevertheless, by 1946, Congress had adopted the Keynesian course of action with the passage of the Employment Act of 1946.

But, Keynes suggested, business firms will be more likely to try the reverse—to cut wages (or to lay off employees) more than prices—in an effort to maintain profits. And, if wages are cut more than prices, aggregate demand will certainly decline as everyone's purchasing power is reduced. Today, despite the niceties of all these arguments, economists recognize that *administered pricing* in large corporations and labor-management contracts tends to make both prices and wages inflexible—"sticky," as economists say, in the downward direction.

Objections to the Saving-Investment Argument

There are also three objections to the classical school's saving-investment argument with its interest-rate "thermostat."

1. Do entrepreneurs really invest more by borrowing savings because the interest rate falls? Keynes's answer was partly "yes" but mostly "no." The

interest rate is certainly an important cost of investment in a capital good or in any new venture, but the entrepreneur must believe that the new capital good will be profitable before borrowing the money at any interest rate. The *expectation of profit* is therefore the major determinant of investment, not the interest rate.

2. When people decide to save more, does the interest rate fall and are business firms apt to invest more? To this idea, Keynesian theory says, "Nonsense!" If people decide to save more out of the same income, it must mean that they are spending less. If, out of your $100 a week take-home pay, you decide to save $10 instead of $5, your consumption spending must necessarily drop from $95 to $90. If everyone saves more, total spending must fall. Business firms will see sales slackening, and, if anything, they will *reduce* investment spending, regardless of changes in the interest rate.

3. Even if most prices and wages were flexible in the downward direction, Keynes believed there was one price that would not fall far enough to help— the price of borrowed money; that is, interest rates. The interest rates we pay involve a combination of many considerations by the lender: (1) The fact that the lender deserves some reward for giving up the use of his or her money for a period of time; (2) the risk of nonrepayment; (3) the administrative costs of processing the loan plus a normal profit; (4) the lender's expectations about the change in the value of the money (inflation or deflation) when it is repaid. Keynes's reasoning was that some of these elements in interest rates tend to be rigid and that interest rates will not fall far enough to encourage business borrowing for investment even if the banks have more money to lend.

Keynesian Theory: "Demand Creates Supply"

Keynes's contribution to economic theory was the idea that aggregate demand—the grand total of all intentions to buy something—might *not* be sufficient to provide a job for everyone who wanted one. He argued that *demand creates supply*, not the reverse, in the sense that entrepreneurs produce only because they expect that demand for their goods and services exists. If these total intentions to buy were not enough to buy all of the goods and services produced, then enterprises would lay people off, aggregate demand would decline because of the decline in total income, and a recession or depression would result.

When aggregate demand lags, Keynes argued, it should be given artificial stimulation through tax cuts or increases in government spending. Keynes also recognized that aggregate demand could be changed by monetary policy—by controlling interest rates charged on loans and the total volume of loans. Low interest rates and a large volume of loans would increase aggregate demand. High interest rates and a small volume of loans would lower aggregate demand.

According to Keynesian theory, government spending should be increased enough to make up for any failure of consumption spending or investment spending to provide full employment. Keynes argued that, in times of unemployment, government spending should increase even if the government had to spend more than it was taking in through taxes.

Deficit Spending: When Government Spends More Than It Receives

When the government spends more money than it receives, it is engaged in

deficit spending. Where does the government get the money to spend? It borrows the money by selling government securities for the total of the deficit. The sale of government securities to cover deficit spending is called *deficit financing*. The securities are sold to individuals, businesses, and even government agencies, and the proceeds are spent on dams and highways; or on missiles, bombers, and submarines; or may even be given away in the form of transfer payments (welfare, Social Security, and the like). As the money is spent on goods and services produced by the private sector, employment rises and, according to Keynesian theory, the economy gradually recovers.

In most of the years since 1933, the federal government has spent more than it has received from taxes. For example, in 1982, the federal government's tax receipts were $618 billion, but it spent about $110 billion more than that. The $110 billion difference was deficit spending. This deficit was then financed by the sale of government securities. Each year that a deficit occurs, the *national debt* goes up by the amount of the deficit. (The national, officially called the "public" debt, is simply the grand total of all government securities in existence at any point in time. The public debt is discussed in detail in Chapter 17.)

The idea that the cure for unemployment is deficit spending was extremely controversial in the 1930s. Its logic is that when people buy government securities, they are transforming private savings in bank accounts or in the form of stocks and bonds into government securities. When the government spends the money it receives from the sale of securities, it spends money that would have been saved. In essence, the government converts inactive (savings) money to active spending. In theory, such spending adds to aggregate demand, causing GNP and therefore employment to rise.*

The Employment Act of 1946

Beginning in 1931, the federal government *did* run relatively small deficits, averaging $2 to $3 billion per year, not explicitly to bolster aggregate demand but to provide jobs in such programs as the Works Progress Administration (WPA) and the Civilian Conservation Corps (CCC). During World War II, federal deficit spending increased more than tenfold to pay for the war. With their savings, people bought *$210 billion* worth of government securities, permitting an equal amount of deficit spending. This enormous addition to aggregate demand caused *real* GNP to jump 10 to 15 percent *per year* during the war years. There was a corresponding drop in the unemployment rate to less than 2 percent in 1943, 1944, and 1945. For this reason, many economists believe that the deficit spending during World War II brought the country out of the Depression and showed that Keynesian theory actually worked.

But when World War II was over, people began to wonder if the drop in government spending would plunge the country back into a depression. Unemployment more than doubled in the years 1945–1946 (from 1,070,000 to 2,270,000). Furthermore, federal government spending dropped by more than half (from $84.6 billion to $35.6 billion). In 1945, the last year of the war, the deficit was $42.1 billion. In 1946, fifteen years of deficit spending stopped. Federal tax receipts in 1946 were $39.1 billion, while expenditures were only $35.6 billion. The government actually ran a surplus of $3.5 billion.

---

*Deficit spending adds to aggregate demand as long as it doesn't compete with private spending. We'll look at this point in later chapters.

Budget surplus may sound like a positive term, but it can be interpreted to have a negative effect on the economy.

A **budget surplus** occurs whenever the government's tax receipts exceed government expenditures. If, for example, the government collects $800 billion in taxes but spends "only" $795 billion of it, there is a $5 billion surplus. A surplus *may* be a withdrawal of money from the economy.* Such a withdrawal can have the same effect on the economy that increased saving by consumers or businesses has because the money ($5 billion in our example) may not be spent and may not find its way back to business firms in the form of purchases of consumer goods or capital goods.

A government surplus *may*, therefore, be interpreted as having a depressing effect on business activity and employment. It is just the opposite of a deficit, which adds to aggregate demand and helps the economy expand. The surplus in 1946, added to the tremendous reduction in government spending and the increase in unemployment, gave many people real cause for concern.

In 1946, many people were also worried about whether or not the peacetime economy would grow fast enough to absorb the millions of returning veterans. We should remember that aggregate demand is the sum of the four categories of spending—by consumers, by businesses for capital goods, by the government, and by net exports. When one of them drops—in this case the severe drop in government purchases—aggregate demand is more likely to fall than to rise, causing unemployment to increase still further.

Accordingly, Congress was motivated to pass the **Employment Act of 1946**, which states in part:

> The Congress hereby declares that it is the continuing policy and *responsibility* [emphasis added] of the Federal Government . . . to foster and promote . . . conditions under which there will be afforded useful employment opportunities, including self-employment, for those able, willing,

---

*Whether the surplus is a withdrawal of money from the economy depends on whether or not the Treasury keeps the surplus or uses it to pay back purchasers of government securities.

and seeking work and to promote maximum employment, production, and purchasing power.

The Act established a three-person Council of Economic Advisors (CEA), with an additional staff of professional economists to advise the President—mainly about the changes in taxes and government spending that might be necessary to carry out the intent of the act. The Act also established the Joint Economic Committee (JEC) of both houses of Congress to investigate a wide range of economic problems.

The Act is of paramount importance in our discussion of classical versus Keynesian theory. The Act says, in effect, that the market-price system cannot take care of itself and that the federal government will henceforth be responsible for managing the economy in such a way as to provide full employment.

The Employment Act of 1946 paved the way for almost total acceptance of Keynesian theory. *Time* magazine commented in December 1965 that economic policies in Washington were determined by followers of Keynesian theory. President Nixon said later, during his administration, "We are all Keynesians now." By the mid-1970s, however, Keynesian theory came under increasingly severe attack.

The Attack on Keynesian Theory

Keynesian theory had a problem. It was too easy. No politician wants to raise taxes, and so Congressional legislation—to build bridges, dams, freeways, to provide for antipoverty programs, to fight the Vietnam War—could all be deficit-financed, without pain, by selling government securities to people quite willing to buy them. Deficit spending was the next best thing to a free lunch.

The difficulty is that deficit spending can start the inflationary engine rolling by increasing the total demand for goods and services. And inflation became the major problem during the 1970s as a result of deficit spending for antipoverty programs, for the Vietnam War, and as a result of the two oil-price "shocks" of 1973 and 1979.

When inflation becomes a problem, Keynesian *theory* has an answer: Reduce total spending by raising taxes and cutting government spending. But in practice, such a course of action is politically very unpopular. Consequently, Keynesian theory is accepted when the major problem is unemployment but not when it is inflation.

Keynes's Own Views about the Causes of Inflation

As we have already noted, Keynes believed that if workers and factories were unemployed, deficit spending would add to aggregate demand. Increases in the government's demand for goods and services would encourage business firms to increase production. Consequently, increases in aggregate demand would lead to increases in aggregate supply. The macroeconomic pulse would speed up as business firms increased orders from *their* suppliers, and so forth. The quickening pace would ripple throughout the economy.

The increases in aggregate supply meant increases in GNP. Curiously, Keynes saw no danger from inflation until full employment was reached. Up to that point, changes in GNP would be *real* changes with no increases in prices. Inflation would occur only if aggregate demand continued to increase after the economy was fully employed.

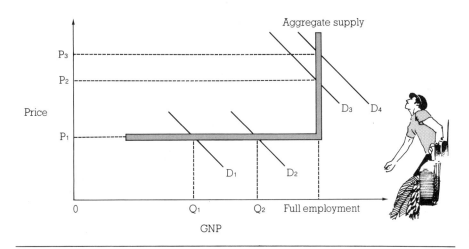

Figure 15-2.
Prices rise only at full employment.

· If inflation occurs only because of increases in demand at full employment, it must be of the demand-pull variety. On this point, Keynes and the classical economists were agreed. There could be only one kind of inflation—demand-pull—at full employment. Their big disagreement was about whether or not there could be sustained unemployment.

Because inflation presented no problems until full employment was reached, the Keynesian case for deficit spending posed no difficulties, provided deficits were not incurred during periods of full employment. Up to full employment, prices would not rise, and at full employment, there was no longer any need for deficit spending and thus, no problem with deficit spending.

This Keynesian-classical view of inflation is shown in Figure 15-2. Aggregate supply is flat all the way to full employment; then it rises vertically. Thus increases in demand (D_1 and D_2) in the flat section below full employment cause no changes in the price level. (Note the similarity of this view with the picture of demand-pull inflation shown in Figure 13-4, page 261). The increases in GNP from Q_1 to Q_2 are *real* changes. In the flat section, consequently, deficit spending does some *real* good. Only when the economy reaches full employment do further increases in aggregate demand (D_3 and D_4) pull prices up from P_1 to P_2 and P_3. But, in this vertical section, deficit spending is no longer necessary.

Neither Keynes nor the classical economists could foresee the pressures on prices from *cost-push* forces that began in the late 1950s or the upward pressures on prices from the oil-price shocks that occurred in 1973 and 1979. Against that background, deficit spending simply added to pressures on prices *long before full employment was reached.* Deficit spending became one of many causes of inflation, even when there was unemployment.

Even supporters of Keynes realized the difficulty. Professor John Kenneth Galbraith, one of Keynes's greatest admirers, had to admit that "the Keynesian remedy was asymmetrical; it would work against unemployment and depression but not in reverse against inflation."[1] Another Keynesian admirer, Professor Robert Lekachman, commented, "To start with, this variety of inflation [cost-push] rendered simple Keynesianism simpleminded."[2]

And so, because Keynesian theory works only some of the time, the conservatives took up the attack, and the great debate continued into the late seventies and early eighties. Today, in economics, the pro-Keynesians are called "post-Keynesians" or "neo-Keynesians." The conservatives are called "neoclassical" economists or, often, "market" economists, to indicate that they want free markets, not the government, to solve problems.

What about Say's Law?

With Keynes under attack, what has happened to Say's Law? Interestingly, Say's Law has enjoyed a revival. The law bolsters modern conservative thinking. The conservative argument is that the business community needs a freer rein to increase supply. Reducing government regulations that hassle business operations, lowering corporate taxes, and offering larger tax credits to spur investment should help business firms produce more goods and services. These increases in supply would lead, according to the argument, to increases in employment, to lower prices, and therefore to increases in everyone's purchases. GNP would rise. Prices would stay down, and employment would increase.

The argument is called **supply-side economics**. It holds that that fiscal measures (lower taxes) will increase supply. In essence, the argument is a restatement of Say's Law—increases in supply will result in increases in demand.

And so another aspect of the debate becomes apparent. Keynesian liberals emphasize increases in demand, "demand management," as it is often called. Conservative neoclassicists emphasize increases in supply or "supply management," a strategy that neatly dovetails with their desire for less government interference with the economy. We will see these two points of view again in Chapter 19.

THE FUNCTIONS OF GOVERNMENT

When we think about the proper functions of government, some additional refinement is clearly necessary. Do the conservatives-classicists mean they don't want *any* government interference? Certainly not. Even Adam Smith (see page 32), despite his faith in the "invisible hand," believed that the government should do many things for the people that a free, private market system would not provide. These "things" are now called **public goods**. Public goods are goods we consume together like highways, dams, or harbors, and services like national defense or police and fire departments. And Adam Smith recognized that it was to everyone's interest if everyone obtained some publicly supported education and if some public health measures were enforced. All these activities, Smith believed, were appropriate concerns of the government.

People of most political persuasions have little difficulty with Smith's general principles about the functions of government. But the impact of the Depression gave rise to a responsibility of government beyond those endorsed by the classical economists—responsibility for the economic health of the economy. And the despair of the Depression did "usher in" a new era of government legislation and regulation far beyond the scope of Smith's principles. The discipline of economics is not very helpful in analyzing the goodness or badness of these recent invasions into the conduct of business firms. The need for government intervention has become largely a value judgment dependent on the expressed needs of voters and of politicians. We know our market-price system has many faults, and that some government intervention is necessary, but only the voters through their representatives can tell us how much intervention is appropriate.

Given past legislation like the Social Security Act of 1935, many state and federal welfare measures, the Employment Act of 1946, unemployment compensation laws, various antitrust laws, laws to protect the environment, Medicare and Medicaid, and laws to ensure occupational and product safety, voters have recognized that our market system has failed in those areas. As a consequence, voters have decided that the appropriate economic functions of government are:

1. To protect the public against monopolistic or unhealthy business practices.
2. To protect the environment.
3. To provide goods and services the private economy is unlikely to provide.
4. To redistribute incomes to secure an adequate level of goods and services for all people in our society.
5. To provide stable prices, enough jobs, and sufficient economic growth to satisfy an increasing number of people who want continued improvements in their standards of living.

Of course the conservatives and the liberals will continue to debate the meaning of these functions. The difficulties of finding a consensus about how they should be translated into specific courses of action will continue long after this author has departed. Translating economic "principles into action," as the title of this book proclaims, inevitably runs into the hurdle of political reality.

In the next chapter we will take up the specifics of Keynesian theory in dealing with inflation and unemployment. In Chapter 19 we will present the case of the supply-siders.

SUMMARY

Despite the ups and downs of GNP, the classical economists like Adam Smith and Jean Baptiste Say believed that the free-enterprise economy had its own stabilizing mechanisms that made government macroeconomic policies unnecessary. Say's Law of Markets held that supply creates its own demand; that if consumers save more and buy less, interest rates would decline, causing entrepreneurs to borrow more for investment (expansion), eventually restoring full employment. These automatic adjustments are based on the assumption that the income from production in the form of workers' wages, profits, and interest rates would be spent. But workers try to save more when they expect hard times to come, while entrepreneurs also are often more influenced by their expectations for the future than by interest rates. As a result, attempted increases in saving may not be matched by increases in investment.

Modern economists led by John Maynard Keynes believe that the economy will not automatically take care of itself. When consumer spending decreases, or saving increases, interest rates may not fall and investment spending may well decrease if increased saving results in reduced consumer spending. Aggregate spending (total spending by consumers, investors, government, and net exports) will then decline, causing unemployment. The Keynesian fiscal cure for inadequate aggregate demand is deficit spending—government spending in excess of revenues from taxes.

Fears after World War II that the country would plunge back into the Depression of the 1930s led to the passage of the Employment Act of 1946, which charges the federal government with the responsibility for promoting full employment. The Act is a rejection of the classical belief that the economy can take care of itself.

Accelerating inflation in the 1970s brought Keynesian theory under attack when it became apparent that Keynesian tactics to control inflation were politically unpopular. Moreover, Keynes himself had not foreseen the problems caused by cost-push inflation. The attack on Keynes gained support from a new school of thought called supply-side economics.

Discussion Questions

1 What is Say's Law?

2. Why does Say's Law suggest automatic tendencies toward full employment in a market-price system?

3. "If product prices and wages fall far enough, unemployment can be avoided." Critically evaluate this statement.

4. Why does deficit spending increase aggregate demand?

5. On what point did the classical economists and Keynes agree?

6. Is Keynes being attacked because his theory was politically unpopular, or because it was wrong?

DID YOU EVER WONDER WHY...

... the Roosevelt Administration of the 1930s followed Keynes' policy even though Roosevelt opposed it?

References

1. John Kenneth Galbraith, *The Age of Uncertainty* (Boston: Houghton Mifflin, 1977), p. 225.

2. Robert Lekachman, *The Age of Keynes* (New York: Random House, 1966), p. 252.

16

An Introduction to Income Determination and Fiscal Policy

KEY WORDS

Income determination
Equilibrium income
(equilibrium GNP)
Unintended disinvestment
Actual investment
Intended investment
Unintended investment
Paradox of thrift
Spending multiplier
Marginal propensity to consume (MPC)
Marginal propensity to save (MPS)
Automatic stabilizers
Discretionary fiscal policy
Recessionary gap
Inflationary gap
Crowding out

At the end of Chapter 15, we saw an *apparently* fatal flaw in Keynesian theory: its overemphasis on unemployment and its failure to deal with inflation. Unfortunately, this flaw and the "great debate" between the neo-Keynesians and neoclassicists tend to conceal the great contributions Keynes made to economic theory: He helped us to understand what makes GNP and the level of employment go up and down. His analysis of the reasons for these changes is called **income determination**. A primary purpose of this chapter is to introduce you to the Keynesian model* of income determination. Once you understand the model, you can join the many debates about what to do about the economy. After we discuss national income determination, we will introduce the elements of fiscal policy: changes made in government spending or taxes to influence GNP.

We are obliged to omit from this chapter many interesting and controversial fiscal measures taken by the Reagan Administration, because the Reagan program involves both fiscal and monetary policy. Monetary policy, the control of aggregate demand through changes in the money supply and interest rates, is the subject of Chapter 18. Therefore, the discussion of "Reaganomics" will have to wait until Chapter 19. Given that limitation, this chapter emphasizes the *theory* of fiscal policy, whereas Chapter 19 endeavors to show how the theory works in practice.

This chapter is divided into four sections: (1) The theory of income determination: an overview, (2) income determination in the private economy, (3) the spending multiplier, and (4) income determination in the real world.

THE THEORY OF
INCOME DETERMINATION: AN OVERVIEW

The most important concept underlying the size of the nation's total income and its level of employment is the concept of **equilibrium income** or **equilibrium GNP** (the terms are interchangeable).

In Chapter 5, you were introduced to the idea of an equilibrium price at which the quantities demanded and supplied are equal, and also to the theory that an automatic mechanism causes market prices for products or services to move toward such an equilibrium price. (If the market price is above equilibrium, there is a surplus, and the price will tend to fall. If the market price is below equilibrium, there is a shortage, and the market price will tend to rise.)

This same concept applies to GNP. When *aggregate demand equals aggregate supply* (the sum total of all products and services produced), GNP is at an *equilibrium*, because everything that is produced will be sold. If business firms produce more than the value of GNP at equilibrium, inventories of unsold goods will simply pile up, because aggregate demand isn't sufficient to buy the excess production. If business firms produce less than the value of GNP at equilibrium, they will sacrifice the extra sales and profits they could have made.

Now, an important point. Although there will always be some price level or level of employment associated with any given equilibrium, the mere fact of equilibrium *does not* guarantee full employment or noninflationary prices. Aggregate demand and supply may be equal in the bottom of a depression or at the height of inflation.

---

*Keynesian theory is presented in graphical form in Chapter 16A.

However, the idea of an equilibrium income suggests that there is always some level of GNP toward which the economy tends to move, *because aggregate demand determines aggregate supply*. If aggregate demand exceeds aggregate supply, GNP and aggregate supply will increase. If aggregate demand is less than aggregate supply, GNP and aggregate supply will decrease, because people will be laid off as entrepreneurs cut production. Equilibrium exists only when aggregate demand and supply are equal. If we can estimate what this equilibrium level will be, we can estimate resulting levels of employment and prices—and then decide whether corrective measures are necessary.

Now the question arises: If changes in aggregate demand cause changes in aggregate supply, what determines the level of aggregate demand in the first place? Let's examine this question and then pursue the idea of equilibrium.

What Determines Aggregate Demand?

In Chapter 11, you saw that GNP is determined by the four kinds of spending that make up aggregate demand: (1) consumption spending by consumers, (2) investment spending by business firms (purchases of capital goods or inventories), (3) government purchases of goods and services, and (4) net exports (the difference between exports and imports).

So what determines demand in a market-price system on a national, aggregate scale? To put it another way, what determines the four kinds of spending that make up the GNP?

Consumption Spending by Consumers

Consumption spending usually accounts for about 65 percent of aggregate demand. Economists are agreed that consumption spending depends on a lot of things: the cost of borrowing, the price level, expectations of future price changes, the condition and quantity of durable goods (such as cars and washing machines) owned by the public. Most important, it depends on the size of present and expected paychecks—that is, present and expected DPI. After all, what, more than anything else, determines your decision to buy? *Your present income and your expectations about its regular arrival in the future.*

Investment Spending by Business Firms

Investment spending is usually around 15 percent of aggregate demand. It is determined partly by the cost of borrowing (the interest rate) but more than anything *by the business managers' expectations of future profit.* Business managers must believe in rising sales and profits before they will buy a new machine, erect a building, or increase the size of their inventories.

Economists believe that *investment* in capital goods or inventories is related to GNP just as your pressure on the gas pedal is related to how fast your car is moving. Of all kinds of spending, changes in investment spending have the greatest effect on changes in GNP—greater than changes in consumption, government purchases, or net exports. Consequently, federal policies to stimulate the economy are often aimed at encouraging business managers to spend for new factories, machines, or larger inventories. Such spending adds to the number of jobs available in the economy and increases the demand for labor.

Government Purchases of Goods and Services

Remember that government purchases *exclude* transfer payments but *include*

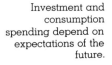

Investment and consumption spending depend on expectations of the future.

purchases by all levels of government—federal, state, and local. All levels are important "demanders" of goods and services. Government purchases (*excluding transfer payments*) average around 20 percent of aggregate demand.*

Net Exports

Net exports are important because export industries employ about 5 million people, but *net* exports are often close to *zero* percent of aggregate demand. (In 1982, exports were 11.4 percent; imports were 10.9 percent; thus, *net* exports were 0.5 percent.)

The Importance of Expectations

Note in our description of the four kinds of spending that consumption and investment make up 80 percent of total spending. These two kinds of spending determine the size and composition of private (rather than governmental) spending in a market-price system.

But now we are up against a puzzle. Consumption spending depends on present and expected income. Investment spending depends on present and future profit—another way of saying income.

If both depend on income, what determines income? Economists admit that the problem is circular. Income determines demand (consumption plus investment), and demand determines income. The answer to the puzzle is that

---

*The 20 percent figure here differs considerably from the 35.5 percent figure in Table 14-2, because transfer payments were included in that figure.

consumption and investment spending depend on expectations about the future that may or may not be favorable. If they are unfavorable, consumers will try to save more and spend less, and business managers will reduce all forms of investment. If the future looks bright, everyone will spend more, and as people spend more, incomes will rise and lead to further increases in spending.

The essence of Keynesian theory is that expectations determine spending, and expectations may or may not be optimistic enough to generate sufficient demand to give everyone a job who wants one. And if private expectations don't motivate people to spend enough, the theory holds, then the government must step in to bolster demand.

INCOME DETERMINATION IN THE PRIVATE ECONOMY

In this section we will concern ourselves only with how consumption spending and investment determine total income and employment. Consequently, we consider private spending only; government spending is temporarily excluded. Our excuse for this omission is that private decisions to consume or to invest represent 80 percent of total spending; we need to know the effects of those decisions. Net exports will be omitted from further mention in this chapter, purely to simplify the discussion.

Now let us imagine an economy with a GNP of $1,000 billion in which business firms spend their entire income on production for consumption or production for investment. Business spending for investment includes both capital goods and inventories. Now assume that the people want to buy $950 billion worth of consumer goods, and business firms want to spend $50 billion for investment. In this model with no government spending and no foreign trade, aggregate demand is therefore consumption spending (consumer demand) plus investment (business demand for capital goods and inventories): $950 billion + $50 billion = $1,000 billion. This demand will cause business firms to produce $1,000 billion worth of goods and services, $950 billion for consumers and $50 billion for one another. The $1,000 billion total is the total of all production; that is, it is aggregate supply. Consequently, the total value of what is produced—our aggregate supply—is our GNP. Further, as we saw in Chapter 12, GNP can be measured either as the sum of all spending (the "expenditures" method) or as the sum of all income (the "income" method).

Now, notice that with GNP and total income at $1,000 billion and consumer demand at $950 billion, the people must want to save $50 billion. And also notice that when the people buy $950 billion worth of the goods produced by business firms, $50 billion worth of business production will be left over for inventory or for the production of capital goods, both in the investment category. Consequently, the amount the people want to save is matched by the amount of business investment. If business firms *want* $50 billion in inventory in expectation of future sales and profits, we can say that desired saving equals desired investment.

The intention to save—to withhold some money from consumption—is matched by producers' intentions to withhold some production from consumption in the form of investment. As long as these sets of intentions match, the economy is in a state of equilibrium. What does this mean? It means that the people will continue to produce $1,000 billion worth of products and that their GNP will remain at $1,000 billion. When the economy is in an equilibrium

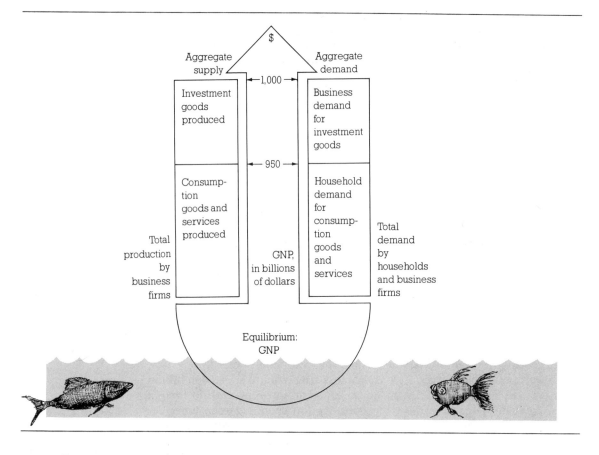

Figure 16-1.
Aggregate demand equals aggregate supply: a picture of equilibrium.

condition, aggregate demand equals aggregate supply. Figure 16-1 shows this equality of aggregate demand and supply.

Two Important Questions about Equilibrium

First, does everyone who wants a job have a job in the economy we have proposed? Not necessarily. Remember that equilibrium income can exist at *any* level of employment. The equilibrium condition merely means that GNP will tend to remain at $1,000 billion as long as the intentions of producers and consumers to divide up production and income remain the same. The $1,000 billion GNP could involve either depression or prosperity levels of employment.

Second, how is investment spending financed? Business sales for consumption are only $950 billion. Where do business firms who want to invest in larger factories or inventories get the other $50 billion? Answer: They get it by using money they have saved themselves (like undistributed profits) or by borrowing money saved by the public. (The availability of the public's savings at an attractive interest rate constitutes an extremely important complication that we'll have to postpone for later discussion.)

The point we want to stress here is that saving is the *unconsumed* portion of income. The fact that the people do not consume all of their income enables business firms to produce for investment as well as for consumption. Thus, *investment* also represents the *unconsumed* portion of income. Finally, the business savings and people's savings provide the funds that finance investment spending.

How Equilibrium Income Changes

Equilibrium income changes whenever the amounts of money that people (or business firms) *want* to save differ from the amounts of money that business firms *want* to invest. To see how these changes occur, let's assume that (1) the people want to save only $30 billion instead of $50 billion out of their total income of $1,000 billion; (2) all production for investment is for inventory; and (3) business firms continue to want to invest $50 billion in those inventories.

Now let us see what happens. If the people want to save only $30 billion, they must be planning to spend the remaining $970 billion for consumer goods. Business firms will now find that some of their investments in inventories have to be used to satisfy the increase in demand. Because production for consumption is set at $950 billion worth, an additional $20 billion worth must be taken from inventory. Stores will notice that some kinds of products have disappeared. To keep inventories at the intended value of $50 billion worth, the business firms will have to work longer hours and hire more people. The GNP is now in *disequilibrium*, in a state of change, because GNP will start to rise as production and incomes rise.

Intended and Unintended Investment

Let's pause for a moment to examine some details of this situation. Aggregate demand is always the sum of everyone's intentions to buy; that is, the goods and services that households intend to consume *plus* the amounts that business firms intend to invest in capital goods and in inventories. *These intentions may not always be realized.*

If households want to buy more than is being produced for them, business firms will see their inventories dropping below the levels they intend. In the preceding example, business firms intend to have $50 billion in inventories, but consumer buying causes inventories to drop $20 billion below that figure to $30 billion—exactly as if a shoe store had begun to run out of several sizes and styles. The unforeseen (or unintended) $20 billion drop in inventories has a name. It is called **unintended disinvestment**. (The prefix *dis* means "to reverse direction" as in *dis*own.)

After the $20 billion worth of unintended disinvestment comes out of the $50 billion in inventory, $30 billion worth of goods are left. Economists speak of this remainder as **actual investment** in contrast to the $50 billion of **intended investment** business firms wanted to have. Figure 16-2 summarizes this situation.

Figure 16-2 shows how aggregate demand exceeds aggregate supply by $20 billion. That $20 billion difference occurs because households want to consume $20 billion more than business firms intend to produce for them.

Figure 16-2 is extremely important because it helps to clear up some confusion about the causes of recession or prosperity. We often hear that people aren't buying enough or are buying too much or that businesses have overinvested or underinvested in plant and equipment. Not true. Figure 16-2 shows that the amount households want to buy ($970 billion) is matched by production for consumption ($950 billion) plus the amounts taken from inventories

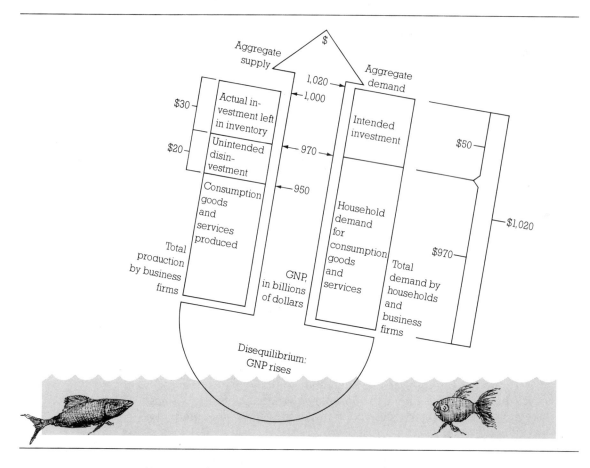

Figure 16-2.
Intended, unintended,
and actual
investment.

($20 billion). Therefore, the desire of people to consume $970 billion worth of goods and services was matched by actual production. Furthermore, the $30 billion households want to save is matched by the $30 billion actually invested (left) in inventories.

We can also visualize these differences in saving and investing by constructing a table. Table 16-1 divides the economy into two sectors—the business sector and the household* sector.

The table shows the differences between the amounts the people want to save (line 8) and the amounts business firms *intend* to invest (line 1). This difference leads directly to a difference between the amounts the people want to consume (line 9) and the amounts businesses *intend* to produce for them (line 4). Because line 9 exceeds line 4, businesses will increase production and GNP will rise.

Table 16-1 also reveals the same totals for aggregate demand and supply that are shown in Figure 16-2. Aggregate demand is the sum of the amounts the people intend to consume (line 9) plus the amounts business firms intend to invest (line 1). Demand always requires the *intention* to buy something, *not* to

---
*"Household" happens to be an official term meaning a group of people living and buying things together. In the household, people need not be blood related. We use the terms "households," "consumers," and "the public" interchangeably.

Table 16-1. Equilibrium Income Rises (all figures in billions of dollars)

Business firms			Households	
(1) Production intended for investment	$50			
(2) Minus unintended disinvestment	− 20			
(3) Actual investment in inventory left over	equals	+ $30	(8) Desired saving	$ 30
(4) Intended production for consumption	$950		(9) Desired consumption	$ 970
(5) Plus unintended disinvestment taken from inventory	+ 20			
(6) Total actually produced for consumption	equals	$ 970		
(7) Total production (GNP)		$1,000	(10) Total income (GNP)	$1,000

save. These intentions to buy consumption goods plus investment goods equal $1,020 billion. By contrast, the amount *actually* supplied (line 3 plus line 6), which is aggregate supply, totals only $1,000 billion. GNP will have to increase.

Equilibrium GNP Rises

And so now we have GNP rising because aggregate demand exceeds aggregate supply by $20 billion. Business firms will hasten to increase their orders from suppliers to build inventories back up to intended levels. More people will be hired, and total income will increase.

How large will the increase be? GNP will continue to rise until the intentions by households to spend and save coincide with the intentions of business firms to produce for consumption or for investment.

Two points have to be noted now: (1) Price increases may wipe out the gain, and (2) saving will change.

Price Increases May Wipe Out the Gain

As GNP rises, the level of employment will also rise, provided the economy is not at full employment. But what about prices? The question is reminiscent of the discussion back in Chapter 13 in connection with Figure 13-5 (see page 263). Whether or not prices increase depends on where equilibrium GNP is at the time of the increase in demand. Figure 16-3 illustrates:

If the increase in demand occurs when GNP is in the fairly flat section of the aggregate supply curve, between Q_1 and Q_2, prices will hardly increase at all, perhaps only from P_1 to P_2. The country is too depressed; too many people are out of work, and there is too much unused capacity in the factories. In this range, the increase in GNP will be almost entirely "real." But if the increase in demand occurs in the Q_2 to Q_3 range, then prices will increase for cost-push and profit-push reasons from P_2 to P_3.

Finally, suppose that, as in the previous example, aggregate demand exceeds aggregate supply by $20 billion and that this increase is shown in Figure

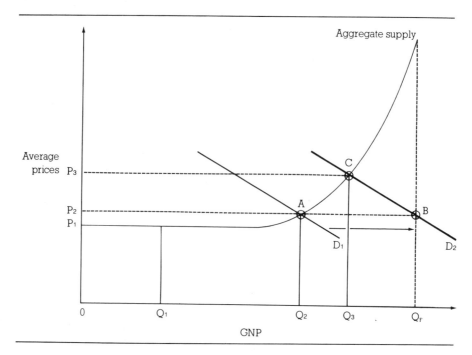

Figure 16-3.
GNP rises.

16-3 by the shift in demand from point A to point B. If that were the case, everyone would be happy because point B is at the full employment level of GNP, Q_F.

But, note that a new equilibrium at point B can occur only if prices remain at P_2. If prices rise to P_3, then at that price level, equilibrium GNP will be at point C, at output Q_3, which is still short of full employment. Thus, price increases for the same quantities of goods and services can wipe out some of the effects of an increase in demand.

Changes in Saving
In our assumed scenario where aggregate demand exceeds aggregate supply by $20 billion, GNP started to rise because the people decided to save less and buy more consumer goods than were being produced for them. The people's saving will now go through an interesting change. As production and incomes rise, the people will have more income from which *to spend more and to save more*. If GNP reached $1,010 billion, they might very well decide to spend $955 billion instead of the original $950 billion and save $55 billion instead of the original $50. The decision to save less leads eventually to the ability to save more.

If, at this new level of $1,010 billion, producers decide to produce $955 billion for consumption and $55 billion for inventory, a new equilibrium will be reached. The decisions of producers and consumers to divide total income coincide. When these two sets of intentions coincide, GNP will stop changing.

Equilibrium GNP Falls
As you might guess, equilibrium GNP falls if the people should decide to increase their saving and spend less. Let us go back to the $1,000 billion GNP.

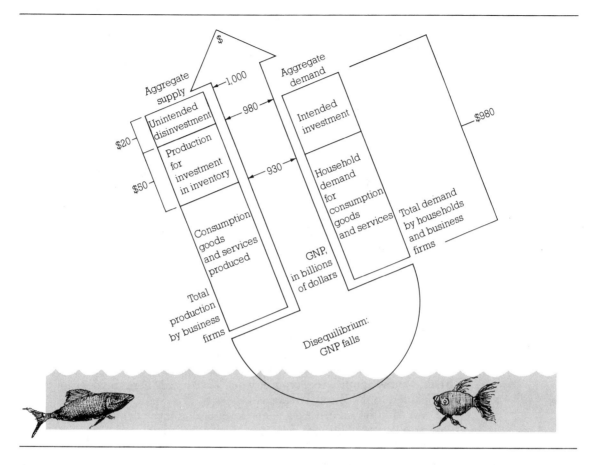

Suppose they decide to save $70 billion and spend only $930 billion out of their $1,000 billion income.

Production for consumption had been set at $950 billion, with $50 billion going into inventory. Now business firms are producing $20 billion too much. This extra $20 billion worth will be unsold and left on the shelves in the form of extra inventory. Inventories will rise from $50 billion worth to $70 billion. The extra $20 billion in inventory is called **unintended investment**. (No "dis" this time because inventories are going up, not down.)

Production will be cut back. People will be laid off and total income will start to fall below $1,000 billion. Again, this is disequilibrium.

GNP starts to move down as a result of the decision to save more and spend less. Aggregate demand is now less than aggregate supply. Aggregate demand is $930 billion (the people's desire to consume) plus $50 billion (production for intended inventories). Thus, $930 billion + $50 billion = $980 billion. Aggregate supply is still $1,000 billion; that is, $950 billion produced for consumption plus $50 billion produced for inventory. Figure 16-4 summarizes these changes. Compare this figure with Figure 16-2.

As GNP falls, workers will be laid off. Producers will produce less, and households will try to consume less and save more to prepare for possible unemployment. Aggregate demand and supply will both fall, and each new

Figure 16-4.
Aggregate demand fails to buy aggregate supply.

Table 16-2. A New, Lower Equilibrium (all figures in billions of dollars)

Business firms		Households	
Production for consumption	$900	Desired consumption by people	$900
Intended investment in inventory	+ 20	Desired saving by the people	+ 20
Total production (GNP)	$920	Total income (GNP)	$920

decrease in spending and employment will trigger more decreases. Again, we have to ask, "Where will the new equilibrium be? When will GNP stop falling?" The answer is that the new equilibrium level of income will occur only when the people's desire to spend or to save coincides with producers' desire to produce for consumption and investment. Table 16-2 shows a *possible* new equilibrium at $920 billion. (The figure is selected at random just to illustrate how all of the figures might fall.)

Again, two points should be noted:

1. The decision to save *more* led actually to a *lower* level of saving. As incomes fall, we may *want* to save more to prepare for a period of unemployment, but we are *unable* to. We have to spend a larger proportion of our reduced incomes in order to sustain ourselves. Thus the decision to save money may lead to less saving. This phenomenon is called the **paradox of thrift**. We saw another version of it when GNP rose. There the decision to save less led to the ability to save more.

2. An equilibrium can exist at any level of employment or unemployment. With a GNP at $920 billion, many people may be unemployed. They may want a job but be unable to find one. They may face poverty and even hunger. The real point is that GNP may remain at $920 billion as long as the intentions of consumers and producers to divide income remain the same.

Before continuing we should stop and ask, "What *does* determine total income and output?" A simple answer is that any total income and output are determined by the equality of aggregate demand and aggregate supply. But that answer is *too* simple, because it doesn't tell us why demand and supply change. Keynes's insight and great contribution was to show us that aggregate demand and supply change whenever intentions to invest are not matched by intentions to save.

But we are not quite done with the essentials of Keynesian theory. In his famous 1936 book, *The General Theory of Employment, Interest, and Money*, Keynes elaborated on an idea of a brilliant pupil and friend named Richard F. Kahn. The idea is called the multiplier. Kahn and Keynes showed that increases in aggregate demand would cause GNP to change by *more* than the change in demand. The next section explains this phenomenon.

THE SPENDING MULTIPLIER

In the example of a decline in GNP described in Figure 16-4, aggregate demand was $20 billion less than aggregate supply. As a result, GNP fell from $1,000 billion to the $920 billion suggested in Table 16-2. The $80 billion drop was caused by the $20 billion decrease in demand (and is four times the amount of the decrease). This phenomenon whereby GNP rises or falls by some multiple of a change in spending is called the "spending multiplier" to distinguish it from another multiplier that appears in monetary policy. The **spending multiplier** is defined as the multiple by which total income (GNP) increases or decreases as a result of an initial change in spending. You can see that, in the example above, the multiplier is 4, and also that the idea could hardly be more important. If we know the value of the multiplier we can estimate where the next equilibrium will be and also estimate the spending changes necessary to increase or decrease equilibrium GNP if need be.

The reason for the multiple change in GNP lies in the fact that any change in spending—by the government, households, or business firms—creates a *chain reaction* of further spending.* For example, Jackie Vanderbilt buys a new Cadillac from the local Cadillac dealer who buys his wife a new ring from the local jeweler who decides to take that trip to Hawaii he has been thinking about for years. The jeweler's trip to Hawaii adds to the profit of the airline, which then decides to give Sue Trueheart, one of its passenger agents, a raise. Sue then decides to add a room on her house . . . and so on.

The Arithmetic of the Multiplier

Keynes's analysis involved a good deal more precision than the example above. He wanted to know how much GNP would actually increase following a change in spending. He realized that the final increase in GNP (total income) would depend on what share of an increase in income each recipient would pass on to the next person. That is, how much of the increase in revenue from the sale of the Cadillac would the Cadillac dealer spend on the new ring? How much of the increase in revenue from selling the ring would the jeweler spend on the trip to Hawaii? The greater the amount each person passes on to the next person in the chain, the greater the value of the multiplier.

To arrive at the multiplier, we must introduce a Keynesian concept that at first will sound awesome—the **marginal propensity to consume (MPC)**. MPC is defined as the change in consumption that follows a given change in income. MPC is calculated by dividing the change in consumption by the change in income. Thus:

$$\frac{\text{change in consumption spending}}{\text{change in income}} = \text{MPC}$$

If, for example, you receive a raise of $100 per month, and out of that raise, you increase your consumption spending by $75, your MPC is:

$$\frac{\$75}{\$100} = .75 \text{ or } 75 \text{ percent}$$

What about the other $25?** Any money that is unspent automatically goes

---

*In these examples we are assuming that we are dealing with disposable personal income (DPI); that is, income after all taxes. Consequently, all income not spent has nowhere to go but into saving.

**We have to assume throughout this discussion that any change in spending is a *net* change in *total* spending throughout the whole economy. Thus, Jackie's decision to buy a Cadillac is a net increase in total car sales. Her purchase is not offset by someone else's decision to cancel a purchase of equivalent value.

Table 16-3 Jackie Starts a Chain Reaction

Rounds of spending (1)	New spending (2)	New saving (3)
1. Jackie gives the Cadillac dealer:	$20,000	
2. Out of this $20,000, the Cadillac dealer spends 75 percent on his wife's ring: and saves the other:	$15,000	$5,000
3. Out of this $15,000, the jeweler spends 75 percent on the trip to Hawaii: and saves the other:	$11,250	$3,750
4. The airline will use 75 percent of the $11,250 to give Sue Trueheart a raise: The airline will save the remaining:	$8,438*	$2,812*
5. Sue will use 75 percent of the $8,438 to add a room to her house: Sue puts the rest of the money in the bank:	$6,329*	$2,109*
6. At this point, total new spending is: And total new saving is:	$61,017*	$13,671*
7. The chain reaction will continue until the grand totals are:	$80,000	$20,000

*These figures are rounded to the nearest dollar.

into saving. The change in saving, relative to a change in income, is called the **marginal propensity to save (MPS)**. Thus MPS in this example is:

$$\frac{\text{change in saving}}{\text{change in income}} = \text{MPS} = \frac{\$25}{\$100} = .25 \text{ or } 25 \text{ percent}$$

Now let's return to the chain of spending that Jackie begins when she buys the new Cadillac. We'll assume that each person in the chain has an MPC of .75 and an MPS of .25. Finally, we'll assume that Jackie buys the new Cadillac for $20,000. Table 16-3 shows what happens.

Column 1 is called "rounds of spending" by economists. It shows the money changing hands five times, but of course in the real world, there will be a multitude of rounds. The grand totals on the last line indicate that each first-round figure will eventually be multiplied by 4. Total new spending is $80,000, or 4 times $20,000; total new saving will eventually be $20,000, or 4 times $5,000. The *spending multiplier* in this example is consequently 4.

The Multiplier Formula

Clearly, the grand total increase in spending and saving depends on MPC. The larger the MPC, the greater the fraction of each increase in income that is passed on to the next person, and the greater the increase in everyone's spending and income. We can also see that if the Cadillac dealer in round 2 had had an MPC of *zero*, he would not have bought the ring, and the process would have ended. Consequently, as MPC decreases toward zero, so will the total change in income. If, on the other hand, MPC increases, so will the change in total income. Therefore, the formula for determining the multiplier must include MPC.

If there are a large number of people in the economy, the formula for the multiplier is:

$$\frac{1}{1 - MPC^*}$$

If MPC is zero, then the multiplier equals:

$$\frac{1}{1 - 0} = 1$$

If, on the other hand, everyone's MPC is 75 percent, as in our model, then the multiplier is:

$$\frac{1}{1 - .75^*} = \frac{1}{.25^*} = \frac{100}{25} = 4$$

If MPC is .6, the multiplier is:

$$\frac{1}{1 - .6^*} = \frac{1}{.4^*} = 2.5$$

As MPC falls, the multiplier decreases because the amount of money passed on by each person in the economy is a smaller fraction of the money that person receives. If MPC falls, the increase in total income will be less, following any change in total spending.

The chain of spending beginning with Jackie's purchase of a Cadillac was, of course, a microscopic example of what occurs when the federal government increases spending for MX missiles, or space satellites. If the government increases its spending by $20 billion, the first recipients will spend some of that money and save some. The recipients of *that* money will in turn spend some of what they receive and save some. The eventual total change in GNP will be some multiple of the beginning change in spending, all depending on everyone's MPC.

Remember that the spending multiplier can operate either way: An increase in spending will produce an increase in total income (GNP) that is a multiple of the increase in spending. A decrease in spending will produce a decrease in total income (GNP) that is a multiple of the decrease in spending. It is this latter circumstance that we had in mind when we spoke on page 314 of the $80 billion decrease in GNP, from $1,000 billion to $920 billion, after the $20 billion decrease in demand.

INCOME DETERMINATION IN THE REAL WORLD

At this point we have to recognize that GNP is determined by more than private consumption and investment spending. The government has to be added to the model, keeping in mind that total government spending *including* transfer payments is about one third of GNP and about one fifth of GNP without them.

---

*You may have noticed that MPC plus MPS always add up to *one*. Therefore, the denominator in the formula $(1 - MPC)$ must equal MPS. Consequently, the formula for the multiplier $1 \div (1 - MPC)$ can be rewritten as $1 \div MPS$.

Of crucial importance is what happens to the multiplier in the real world. We need to know what the "real" multiplier is so that we can estimate the changes in GNP that will *really* occur following a change in spending. As you will now see, the normal activities of government in combination with some private tendencies greatly affect the multiplier.

The Multiplier in the Real World

When we look at our own behavior it would seem that the multiplier is very high—certainly a two-digit number, because a $100 raise means to most Americans an increase in spending of 95 percent of that amount. With an MPC of .95, the multiplier is 20 because $1 \div (1 - .95) = 1 \div .05 = 20$. In the real world, however, any change in total spending is multiplied only by about 2 within a period of one year. The reason for this large reduction from an apparent 20 to about 2 is that any change in total income (GNP) starts the operation of an automatic braking system. The "brakes" slow down changes in GNP in both directions. As GNP starts up, the brakes slow the increase; when GNP starts down, the brakes slow the decrease.

Several different kinds of brakes exist. The brakes are called **automatic** (sometimes *built-in*) **stabilizers**. What are they?

The Automatic Stabilizers

TAX RECEIPTS. As GNP falls, the federal government's tax receipts decline even faster, as individuals pay lower income taxes. Not only is there less income to tax, but the tax rates are lower as people's incomes fall. This phenomenon means that, in times of falling GNP, disposable personal income (DPI) will not fall so far, and therefore consumption spending (usually about 95 percent of DPI) will help to sustain aggregate demand in times of recession. The reverse is true in times of inflation. The higher income tax rates that accompany rising incomes will tend to slow the increase in DPI and also help to slow down the rise in prices.

From the point of view of low-income people apt to be hurt by a recession, the automatic stabilizers are a blessing, but from the point of view of a president, the automatic stabilizers may be an embarrassment. Why? Because government spending tends to grow in recessions while the government's income may remain unchanged or even decline. A simplified example explains:

Federal spending typically increases an average of 9 percent per year.* The federal government's tax receipts are usually about 20 percent of GNP. Assume that in 1982, tax receipts were $600 billion and spending was $700 billion, resulting in a deficit of $100 billion. (The figures approximate what actually occurred.) Now assume that, in 1983, GNP does not grow at all, so that tax receipts remain at $600 but spending grows by the usual 9 percent from $700 billion to $763 billion. The deficit is now $163 billion instead of $100 billion. The extra $63 billion adds to aggregate demand and, to some extent, protects the economy from slumping further. But, the extra deficit is an embarrassment to any administration trying to balance the federal budget.

UNEMPLOYMENT COMPENSATION PAYMENTS. In times of recession, unemployment compensation payments rise, again helping to prop up GNP. In 1982, a typical

---

*The average increase during the 33-year period 1950 to 1982.

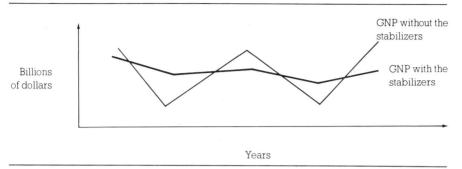

Figure 16-5.
The automatic stabilizers at work.

unemployed worker with a small family could receive $400 to $500 per month for as many as nine months. Think of where the unemployed would be without such help. Moreover, think of how such spending sustains the GNP in bad times. In prosperous times, of course, these payments fall, cooling the economy and slowing the tendency of prices to rise.

FARM PRICE-SUPPORT PAYMENTS. These also counteract the rises and falls of GNP by increasing in bad times, decreasing in good times.

SAVING. In the private sector, corporations sometimes use their retained earnings to pay out dividends in bad times in order to maintain an image of stability and integrity. These dividend payments help bolster DPI. By the same token, in bad times, families may try to maintain a given standard of living by using up their savings to maintain morale or keep up appearances. Both tendencies soften the effects of recession on consumption spending and aggregate demand.

NET EXPORTS. Even net exports *may* change in a way that slows the rate of growth of GNP when the economy is moving up and the rate of decline of GNP when the economy is moving down. When we are prosperous, we tend to buy more foreign products—cars, TV sets, tape recorders, French perfume, and so on. Rising imports reduce net exports and slow down the rise in aggregate demand. When aggregate demand falls, we buy fewer imports and net exports may rise, provided that other nations are not also suffering and do not block our exports with tariff barriers or nontariff barriers (something we will discuss in Chapter 20).

These are the important automatic stabilizers. We can visualize their effect on the economy by looking at Figure 16-5.

The preceding section indicates that, to an important extent, much of our fiscal policy—changes in government spending or taxes—is automatic. Economists believe that the automatic stabilizers dampen the movements of GNP by at least one third. Economists are also agreed, however, that the automatic stabilizers cannot do the whole job of maintaining full employment at stable prices and that other forms of deliberate, rather than automatic, policy measures are necessary. Moreover, the automatic stabilizers act in response to changes in GNP when such changes might not be desirable. For example, the stabilizers would slow down a period of recovery by increasing everyone's taxes.

When Congress or the President undertakes a deliberate fiscal policy change through new legislation, the subsequent change in fiscal policy is called **discretionary fiscal policy** because the action occurs at the discretion of the Congress or the President. The action is no longer automatic. From now on, we will confine ourselves to discretionary fiscal policy rather than to the automatic fiscal changes that occur as a result of the automatic stabilizers.

Discretionary Fiscal Policy

When private spending fails to maintain aggregate demand at full employment, the government can increase its own spending or reduce taxes. If the President's Council of Economic Advisors is worried about inflation, its members will suggest to the President that government spending be reduced and/or that taxes be increased in order to reduce private spending.

In the following discussion, we shall make two assumptions: (1) That if discretionary changes in government spending occur—*ceteris paribus*—everything else in the economy (such as taxes) remains the same, and (2) that if we decide to change taxes, government spending and all other components of aggregate demand remain the same. The primary reason for these assumptions is that the ability of deliberate changes in government spending to speed up or slow down the economy will be diminished if taxes are deliberately changed in the same direction. For example, if Congress insists on keeping the budget balanced and matches any increase in government spending with increases in taxes, aggregate demand is increased by the increase in government spending but decreased by the increase in taxes. The effect on aggregate demand will be stronger if we hold taxes constant and change only government spending.

Another word of explanation. If government spending and taxes start off equal, let us say at $700 billion each, and government spending increases to $710 billion with no change in taxes, there is deficit spending of $10 billion (and an increase in the public debt of that much). If government spending and taxes are both at $700 billion and government spending drops to $690 billion, then the Treasury runs a surplus of $10 billion. A deficit adds to aggregate demand. A surplus reduces it, just as if businesses or households decided to increase saving and reduce spending. Consequently, the relationship of government spending and taxes has an important bearing on equilibrium GNP.

Let us consider changes in government spending first and then changes in taxes.

Changes in Government Spending

Suppose that there is considerable unemployment. The Council of Economic Advisors estimates that equilibrium GNP must grow by $100 billion to provide full employment. How much deficit spending should there be? It all depends on the multiplier. If the multiplier is 2, deficit spending will have to be $50 billion.

To put this situation another way, aggregate demand is failing by $50 billion to provide the country with full employment. This insufficiency of demand to provide full employment has a name. It is called a **recessionary gap**. The gap can be filled by deficit spending.

If, on the other hand, GNP is already at full employment—say, $3,400 billion—and total spending by households, business firms and government agencies totals $3500 billion, aggregate demand exceeds aggregate supply at full employment. This unusual circumstance can occur if the additional spending is financed by borrowing (including the borrowing by the Treasury). Now the extra $200 billion worth of purchases will cause shortages in thousands of markets—for cars, typewriters, raw materials, and so forth. Prices will surely rise, and inflation will begin to accelerate.

The Council of Economic Advisors will now have to recommend that spending be reduced to bring prices down and to keep equilibrium at the full employment level of $3,400 billion. How much must spending be reduced to bring about a full-employment equilibrium at $3,400 billion? Again, it depends on the multiplier. Assume that the multiplier is 2.

To reduce aggregate demand by $200 billion, we must reduce government spending by $100 billion (200 ÷ 2). In this case, the amount by which spending must be reduced to provide equilibrium GNP at full employment without inflation also has a name. It is called the **inflationary gap**. In this case, the gap is $100 billion, and in this case we want to close the gap, not to fill it.

DIFFERENT MULTIPLIERS. There is always a question about what kinds of government spending should be increased in slow times or decreased in times of inflation. After all, the government can find many ways to spend our money— on defense, welfare, bigger salaries, or public projects like a Hoover Dam. Economists recognize that each type of expenditure will have a different effect on the economy. Each type will affect different industries, classes of workers, and geographical areas. And each type will have a different multiplier, meaning that the potency of the medicine varies with its type. In general, the principle is: To whatever extent the expenditure has a direct and lasting effect on jobs, the multiplier will be larger and the change in equilibrium GNP will be greater. Hoover Dam is an excellent example of very effective government spending.

The Dam was built during the Depression when millions were unemployed. Workers were less apt to be hired away from other firms, and more apt to become net additions to the labor force. The construction of the Dam directly involved thousands of workers and led to the employment of thousands afterward as industries blossomed in the areas where power from the Dam became available.

On the other hand, increases in transfer payments do not have as large an effect, because jobs are not directly created. Increases in federal employees' salaries are in the same category. And spending on national defense is also suspect. A recent study showed that every $1 billion the Pentagon spends causes the loss of 18,000 jobs that would have existed if consumers had been allowed to spend the money instead of the Pentagon.* Moreover, defense spending may drain away funds that could have been used for investment in projects that would enhance future employment like the Hoover Dam. On the other hand, defense spending can stimulate technological change along with the development of sophisticated weaponry.

---

* "Spending by Military Tied to Loss of Jobs," *Los Angeles Times*, 25 October 1982. The main reason given was that "the industries and businesses from which the military makes its purchases have a higher rate of inflation than . . . civilian industries. This means a dollar spent by the military stimulates less industrial activity than if the dollar was [*sic*] spent by the consumer."

Changes in Taxes

We can also fill or close the gaps by reducing taxes to give households more money to spend or by increasing taxes to reduce household spending.

Tax changes do not affect GNP as strongly as do changes in government spending. A look at income taxes will explain the point.

Remember that disposable personal income (DPI) is divided into consumption spending plus personal saving. When personal income taxes go up, our take-home pay (DPI) goes down by that amount. But our spending may not drop by the amount of the tax because we can pay part of the tax by taking the money out of savings. On the other hand, when taxes are cut, our spending will not increase by the amount of the tax cut, because we put some of the extra DPI into savings.

For example, suppose personal income taxes are cut by $10 billion as part of the government's discretionary fiscal policy to increase spending and employment. Also assume that taxpayers will change their consumption spending by 80 percent of any change in DPI, and change their saving by 20 percent of any change in DPI.* The $10 billion tax cut will then increase DPI by $10 billion and cause an $8 billion increase in consumption spending and a $2 billion increase in saving.

As far as aggregate demand is concerned, spending has changed by $8 billion, although the tax change was $10 billion. The multiplier effect will start with an $8 billion change in spending—not a $10 billion change. Consequently, the change in GNP will be 2 × $8 billion = $16 billion (not 2 × $10 billion = $20 billion).

The process looks like this:

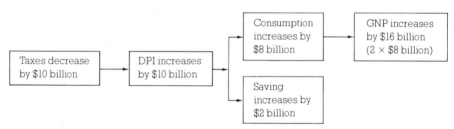

A tax increase works the same way. When personal income taxes are increased, DPI will decrease by the amount of the tax. Taxpayers will reduce their spending by some fraction (MPC) of the tax and get the rest of the money for the tax out of savings—just as many taxpayers have to do each spring prior to April 15. And so spending drops, but not by the amount of the tax. Tax changes do not affect GNP as powerfully as do changes in government spending, because part of the tax causes changes in saving—*not* in spending.

Just as there are different multipliers for different spending projects, different tax changes have different effects on GNP. The federal government can change excise (sales) taxes, Social Security taxes, corporate taxes, or personal income taxes. As we saw in Chapter 14, each of these taxes hurts or helps people in different income groups differently. In very broad generalities, tax cuts are usually biased in favor of either consumption spending or investment spending. Cuts in excise taxes and across-the-board cuts in personal taxes are

---

*Consequently, MPC is .8 and MPS is .2.

designed to help consumption; cuts in taxes of those in high income groups or cuts in business taxes are designed to help investment.

Which Method Is Better?

We can see that a desired change in aggregate demand can be achieved by changing either government spending or taxes. But which method should we choose? We know that government spending changes are more potent than tax changes, because tax changes usually involve changes in saving. But tax changes have an important feature: Once a tax change is enacted, the effect is quick. Everybody's DPI instantly changes (assuming that personal taxes are changed), because paychecks will go up when taxes withheld go down, or vice versa.

If the tax change is a tax reduction, who decides how the money will be spent? You do. On the other hand, when there is a change in government spending rather than a change in taxes, our political representatives decide where and how the money will be spent. This is not to suggest that your spending will be any wiser or more foolish than the government's, but it is a fact to consider. Some economists also believe that when the government spends the money the spending is always greater than it needs to be because of political logrolling. The senator who initiates a bill for federal programs in his state may have to agree to include projects in other states to obtain the votes of his colleagues.

Fiscal Policy Problems

TIME LAGS. One complication in the use of discretionary fiscal policy is the lag of a year or two between the time a new fiscal policy is launched and the time its effects take hold in the private economy. When the effects take hold, the problem may be over or the policy may be wrong for the period in which the effects materialize. For example, if gasoline taxes are increased to finance employment on highway renovation, the tax will be felt immediately by consumers when they buy gasoline for their cars, but the highway projects will take time to implement. The hiring may not occur for six months to a year. This example is a real one that began with a tax increase on gasoline in 1983 to finance future highway improvement.

CONFLICTING STATE AND LOCAL POLICIES. State and local fiscal policy may or may not coincide with federal policy. State and local governments may find it irresistible to offset expansionary fiscal policy. If state governors know that the federal government is going to increase everyone's income by reducing federal taxes or by deficit spending, they may think, "Ah, the people have more money. Now is the time to increase state taxes." Thus, state and local fiscal policy may offset or diminish the efforts of the federal government to accomplish its goal.

TAX CUTS TO REDUCE UNEMPLOYMENT. Corporations may be given tax cuts to give the economy a boost. These tax cuts in the form of extra depreciation allowances are usually designed to give corporations incentives to buy new machinery. The theory is that (1) the increase in investment spending will spur an increase in GNP and employment and (2) the new machines will produce greater quantities of goods, and these larger quantities will tend to reduce or at least slow down inflation. There are two problems:

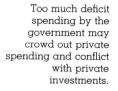

Too much deficit spending by the government may crowd out private spending and conflict with private investments.

First, such a tax cut will stimulate investment spending only if businesses expect sufficiently large increases in demand to buy the extra production the new machines will produce. The tax cut will not help if such an optimistic expectation is not present.

Second, the creation of new machines, if it *does* take place, will create jobs for the highly specialized technicians who build the machines. But when the machines begin to produce, they may replace workers. Over the life of the machines, the net, long-term effect may be to increase unemployment.

CROWDING OUT. Government spending may **crowd out**, or substitute for, private spending. If the federal government wants to give the economy a boost, it must be careful to find ways to deficit-spend that will not conflict with private industry. If government spending conflicts with private investment spending, then aggregate demand may not change as much as the President's Council of Economic Advisors would like. One example: government construction of a hydroelectric dam that private industry could have built.

Crowding out can also occur if deficit spending causes interest rates to rise. When the Treasury offers securities for sale, it will have to offer interest rates that are attractive enough to persuade buyers to put their savings into government securities instead of into financial institutions (savings and loan banks or commercial banks). These institutions will then have to compete for your savings by offering higher interest rates. We can visualize another demand/supply diagram in which the government's demand for funds shifts the demand for loans to the right and raises the price of loans (the interest rate) by causing a shortage of credit at the *old* interest rate.

As the interest rate rises, business firms will find that borrowing is more expensive. Individuals will find mortgage rates for home purchases and finance charges on installment contracts rising. Private spending will then drop. Government spending has, to some extent, crowded out private spending.

The rise in interest rates resulting from deficit spending may be a symptom of a larger problem. Total savings by private individuals and business firms typically runs around $500 billion. Normally, this money is available for private investment. But if the federal government deficit-spends at the level of, say, $200 billion, two fifths of all savings are taken from private sources and put into government securities for public projects. Crowding out can, therefore, occur simply by creating a shortage of funds for private investment.

The measure and extent of crowding out is still another subject of professional argument among economists.[1] The difficulty is that during a recession, a low level of investment spending occurs, not because of high interest rates, but because of lack of optimism about future profits. But if the economy starts to recover and business managers want to borrow, crowding out may occur and slow down progress toward recovery.

INFLATION AND THE AGGREGATE SUPPLY CURVE. Figure 16-3 on page 312 reminds us that the discretionary fiscal policy may produce changes that are not all "real." If the economy is operating in the upward bend of the curve, deficit spending may result in price increases rather than in real changes that help unemployment.

INFLATION AND POLITICS—A REMINDER. It is easy to get people to vote on expansionary fiscal policy—increases in spending or tax cuts—but tough to get them to do the reverse, to cut spending and raise taxes. Consequently, the reality of politics suggests that fiscal policy may be easy to apply in time of recession when the economy needs a boost, but very difficult to apply when the economy needs to slow down in times of inflation.

SUMMARY

Keynes's great contribution to economic theory was his analysis of what determines a country's total income. These determinants are intended saving and intended investment. If intended investment exceeds intended saving, GNP will rise, and vice versa. This interplay of intentions also determines the levels of aggregate demand and aggregate supply. When they are equal, equilibrium income or equilibrium GNP exists. But the fact of equilibrium does not mean that the economy has reached a desirable level. Equilibrium can exist in a recession. If equilibrium GNP is unsatisfactory, the government may have to seek fiscal policy measures to change the equilibrium.

Because of the fact that any change in spending starts a chain reaction of further spending, a spending multiplier exists. Changes in GNP that follow changes in spending are multiples of those changes in spending.

Fiscal policy refers to changes in government spending or taxes that change GNP. These changes may occur as a result of changes in taxes or transfer payments that occur automatically when GNP and total income change. Such changes are also called the built-in or automatic stabilizers because they help to level out the swings in GNP.

Deliberate actions by the President or Congress to change government spending or taxes for the purpose of changing GNP are called discretionary fiscal policy.

To change an unsatisfactory equilibrium, the government can change aggregate demand by changing taxes or spending. To increase aggregate demand in order to fill a recessionary gap, the government can reduce taxes and/or increase deficit spending. To reduce GNP (that is, to close an inflationary gap) the government can do the reverse.

Changes in government spending have a more potent effect on GNP than changes in taxes, but tax changes affect the economy more quickly than do changes in government spending.

Discussion Questions

1. Explain the statement "We have a fiscal policy whether we like it or not and whether Congress does anything or not."

2. Why are aggregate supply and GNP the same?

3. Why are expectations so important in Keynesian theory?

4. How do the automatic stabilizers affect the multiplier?

5. Why does Congress tend to increase aggregate demand more often than it decreases it?

6. Why might one prefer a tax reduction to an increase in government spending as a cure for unemployment?

DID YOU EVER WONDER WHY . . .

. . . a budget deficit, by itself, cannot cause inflation?

References

1. Keith M. Carlson and Roger W. Spencer, "Crowding Out and Its Critics," *Review*, Federal Reserve Bank of St. Louis, December 1975.

---

16 A
The Keynesian Cross

KEY WORDS
Keynesian Cross
Negative saving (dis-saving)
Consumption function
Income = spending line

There are many ways to illustrate the concepts of equilibrium GNP, aggregate demand, and aggregate supply. A graphical way, popular with many economists, is called the Keynesian Cross. A brief explanation of it is presented here to help you when you take other courses in economics.

The **Keynesian Cross** is simply another demand-supply diagram, but with a difference. All the demand-supply diagrams shown so far have price on the vertical axis and quantity (in physical units) on the horizontal axis. We could do this with GNP too, but the price level distorts GNP by concealing *real* GNP. Keynes bypassed the problem of price movements and concentrated on the relationship between demand and income.

Table 16A-1. DPI, Consumption, and Saving

DPI per week	C	S	
$100	120	−20	Dis-saving
150	150	0	Breakeven
200	180	+20 ⎫	
250	210	+40 ⎬ Positive saving	
300	240	+60 ⎭	

PATTERNS OF SPENDING AND SAVING

Keynes realized that, as income increases, so does spending, but *not as fast* as income. Imagine a worker who starts with a disposable personal income (DPI) of $100 per week and then, because of extraordinarily good luck, gets a series of $50 raises. Table 16A-1 shows how he or she divides each DPI into consumption spending (C) and personal saving (S).

The table shows that when our worker received $100, he or she spent $120. How can this be? By borrowing, using credit cards, automatic overdraft checking accounts, charge accounts, and so on. Most of us know it is easy to spend more than we make. When we do, we engage in what economists call **negative saving**, or **dis-saving**. Now we are in a position to display this information in a graph similar to a demand-supply diagram (Figure 16A-1).

THE KEYNESIAN DEMAND CURVE

Figure 16A-1 is a demand-supply diagram because the consumption-spending line is really a demand curve. The line shows the total dollar value of goods and services our worker wants to buy (demand) each week out of his or her income. The dollar total of the amounts the worker wants to spend at each level of income is measured on the vertical axis. Weekly income—DPI in this case— is measured on the horizontal axis. The official name for the consumption-spending-demand line is the **consumption function**.

Incidentally, note from the table and the graph that MPC (marginal propensity to consume) is .6 because consumption spending increases $30 with each $50 raise. Therefore, MPC is 30 ÷ 50 = .6, and the multiplier must be: 1 ÷ (1 − .6) = 1 ÷ .4 = 2.5. Because consumption spending increases by $30 with each $50 increase in income, that relationship dictates the slope of the consumption function. With each $50 move to the right, the consumption moves upward by $30:

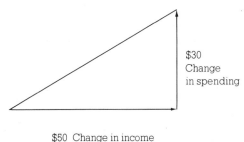

$30
Change
in spending

$50 Change in income

If we were describing a highway with a slope like this, we would say the highway has a 60 percent slope—again meaning that for every 50 feet of hori-

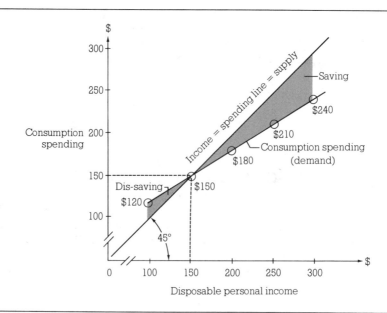

Figure 16A-1.
Spending (C) does not
increase as fast as
income (DPI).

zontal distance, the highway goes up 30 feet. Consequently, MPC (.6) describes the slope of the line.

Now let us draw a diagonal line halfway between the income axis and the
spending axis, so that at all points on this line income and spending are equal.
If an individual (or country) is not on the line, income and spending must not
be equal. We will call the diagonal line the **income = spending line**. But, as
you will see shortly, the income = spending line is also a measure of supply, so
that the two lines (the consumption function and the income = spending line)
criss-cross just like a demand-supply diagram.

Notice that the diagonal line bisects the right angle formed by the two axes.
Consequently, the diagonal line makes a 45-degree angle with either axis. If we
draw a perpendicular from any point on the income = spending line over to
each axis, a square will be formed. In other words, every point on the income
= spending line is equidistant from each axis. This is just another way of
showing that income and spending must be equal at every point on the income
= spending line.

Dis-saving is shown in Figure 16A-1 in the shaded area between the income
= spending line and the consumption-spending line at incomes below $150 a
week. At $150, our worker breaks even: consumption-spending = DPI and S =
0. Above $150, our worker saves. Now the income = spending line is above the
consumption-spending line.

THE KEYNESIAN SUPPLY CURVE

The consumption function is the demand curve. Where is the supply curve? To
make a long story short, the income = spending line is the Keynesian supply
curve. Here is why:

The horizontal axis represents DPI (disposable personal income), but it
could represent any measure of income like GNP. Now we remember that GNP

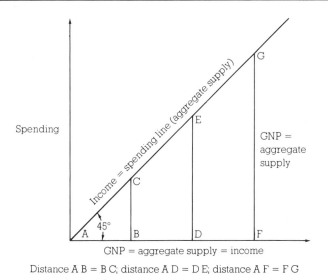

Distance A B = B C; distance A D = D E; distance A F = F G

Figure 16A-2.
The income =
spending line and the
horizontal axis are
both measures of
GNP, aggregate
supply, and total
income.

(measured by the "income approach") is the sum total of everyone's income, and that *that* total is also the value of all the final products produced (supplied) in one year. Consequently, the horizontal axis is a measure of both income and aggregate supply.

At any point on the income = spending line, if we drop a perpendicular to the horizontal axis, we will find that the distance from the income = spending to the horizontal axis is the same as the distance *out* the horizontal axis. Consequently, the perpendicular distance also represents aggregate supply. But, you say, the same thing is true of any perpendicular drawn to the vertical axis. Why doesn't the income = spending line also represent demand? The answer is that the line *does* represent demand—but *only at one point*, where the consumption function (demand) crosses the income = spending line. On the other hand, *any* point on the income = spending represents total income or aggregate supply. Figure 16A-2 illustrates:

When we put the two ideas together—that the consumption function is really a demand curve, and that the 45°-angle line is really a supply curve—the Keynesian Cross takes shape.

THE KEYNESIAN CROSS

Everything about Figure 16A-3 is essentially the same as Figure 16A-1. On the vertical axis we measure all four forms of spending added together: consumption, investment, government purchases, and net exports. The total of all this spending at each level of GNP is shown by the aggregate-demand line. The aggregate-demand line does not increase as fast as income because most of it (65 percent) is consumption spending, and we know that consumption spending in the real world does not increase as fast as income. The aggregate-demand line has the same relationship to the income = spending line that the consumption-spending line had in Figure 16A-1.

Figure 16A-3 is called a picture of the Keynesian Cross because of the cross formed by the aggregate demand and aggregate supply curves.

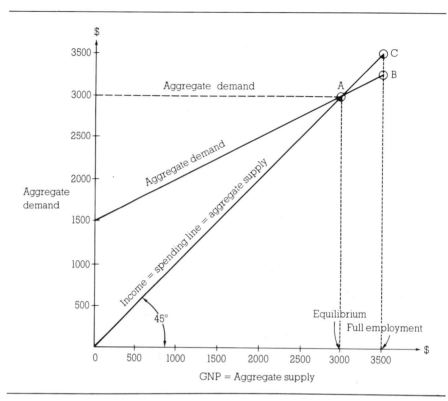

Figure 16A-3.
The Keynesian Cross
(all figures in billions
of dollars).

Notice that, up to the $3,000 billion GNP, aggregate demand is above aggregate supply. In *that* area, demand must exceed supply, and GNP will certainly increase. At $3,000 billion, demand equals supply: GNP has reached equilibrium. Beyond $3,000 billion, supply is greater than demand; at any level of GNP above $3,000 billion, there will be a surplus of unsold goods, employers will lay workers off, and GNP will slip back to the $3,000 billion equilbrium.

The difficulty with the $3,000 billion equilibrium is that it is $500 billion short of full employment. Unemployment rates will be unacceptably high. To get some or all of these unemployed workers hired, we must increase aggregate demand and create a new equilibrium GNP.

The Keynesian Cross and the Spending Multiplier

The Keynesian Cross is a useful device to illustrate the changes in spending needed to correct the situation shown in Figure 16A-3. In order to move the equilibrium GNP from Point A to Point C at full employment, we have to increase spending, but by how much? The spending multiplier provides the key. To put the question in terms of Figure 16A-3, we have to move equilibrium from Point A to Point C by increasing spending from Point B to Point C. So what is the distance from Point B to Point C?

In Figure 16A-3, MPC is .5, because aggregate demand begins at $1,500 billion and climbs another $1,500 billion as GNP increases to $3,000 billion. Thus, the change in spending is $1,500 billion given a change in income of $3,000 billion: MPC must be .5, and the spending multiplier must be $1 \div (1 - .5) = 1 \div .5 = 2$.

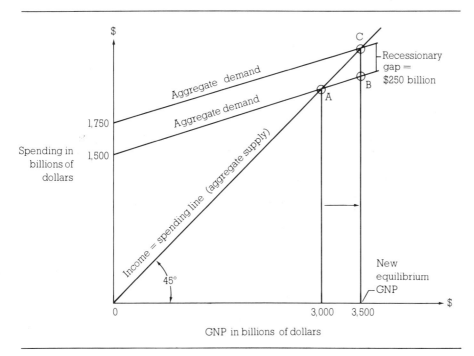

Figure 16A-4.
An increase in aggregate demand (based on Figure 16A-3).

If the multiplier is 2 and the desired change in GNP is $500 billion, the change in spending must be $250 billion. The distance from Point B to Point C is $250 billion. This distance illustrates a *recessionary gap*. The gap is defined as the amount by which aggregate demand must be increased to achieve equilibrium at full employment. Figure 16A-4 illustrates reaching full employment with deficit spending of $250 billion.

The Keynesian Cross diagram can also be used to explain demand-pull inflation. Suppose the diagram looks like Figure 16A-5.

Assume that the economy is at Point F, and that F represents full employment. The economy will want to reach an equilibrium at Point C, a GNP of 0E billions of dollars, because between F and E, aggregate demand exceeds aggregate supply. But the increase from F to E is impossible because the economy is already fully employed at F. Something has to give, because aggregate demand exceeds supply (as it might in a major war like World War II).

You have probably guessed what will happen: Nominal GNP will increase from F to E in the form of higher prices for the same quantities of goods and services that were produced at F. Real GNP won't change.

But now many groups of people will suffer from inflation, and something must be done. Aggregate demand will have to be brought down so that equilibrium will occur at F, not at E. Equilibrium will have to move from C to A. The amount by which aggregate demand needs to be brought down is indicated by the distance AB. That distance illustrates an *inflationary gap*. This gap is defined as the amount by which aggregate demand exceeds aggregate supply at full employment.

Some numbers may help. Suppose Point F is $3,500 billion, as it was in Figures 16A-3 and 16A-4, and that Point E is $3,800 billion. Thus the distance

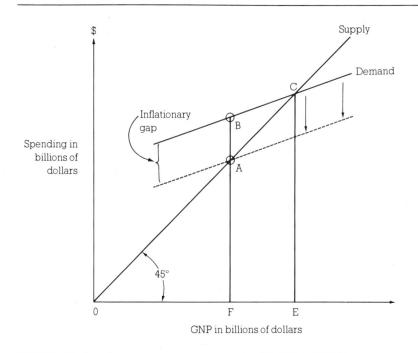

FE is $300 billlion (in higher prices). To calculate the amount of spending reductions needed—through outright reductions in government spending or increases in taxes—simply divide the $300 by the spending multiplier. If the multiplier is 2, we'll have to reduce demand by $150 billion, the distance AB. The new demand curve is shown by the dotted line.

At this point it would be nice to say, "Well, that's the Keynesian Cross, folks," and go to something else. Unfortunately, we can't. The Keynesian Cross has a major defect: It shows only one kind of inflation—demand-pull inflation at full employment. All changes in GNP up to full employment are assumed to be *real* changes with no changes in prices.

But we know now that long before full employment is reached, prices will rise for cost-push reasons. This fact of life seriously alters the simplicity of the Keynesian Cross analysis. To illustrate this point, let's go back to the recessionary gap shown in Figures 16A-3 and 16A-4. When we needed an increase in GNP of $500 billion, we deficit-spent $250 billion to fill the gap. We didn't say so, but the $500 billion increase in GNP was assumed to be a *real* increase with no change in prices. But what if prices do increase long before full employment is reached? We can show prices increases by curving the aggregate supply line upward as Figure 16A-6 indicates.

The upward curving supply curve means that beyond Point G, where the line begins to curve upward, changes in demand (from D_3 to D_4) don't produce much of a change in *real GNP*—only from C to D. Much of the increase in demand is weakened by price increases for almost the same quantities of goods and services.

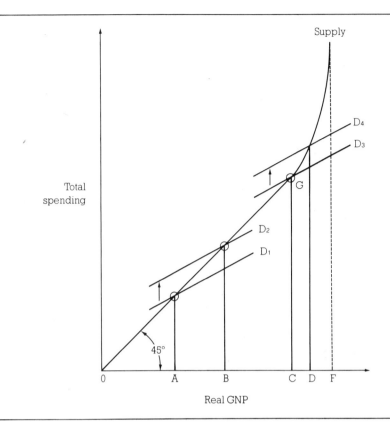

Figure 16A-6.
Aggregate supply
with rising prices.

Up to point G, the aggregate supply curve is straight, and we assume no price increases when demand increases. When demand increases from D_1 to D_2, the same increase as from D_3 to D_4, the increase in real GNP is from A to B, much larger than from C to D. Figure 16-3 in the main body of the chapter helps to explain the same point in a different way.

What is the significance of this defect in the Keynesian Cross? The significance is that to fill a recessionary gap and achieve a full-employment equilibrium, some inflation is inevitable, and some people will be hurt by it—typically, you'll remember, the people who can afford it the least. Furthermore, whenever the possibility of cost-push inflation is present (where the aggregate supply line curves upward) the increase in spending necessary to obtain any given increase in GNP is larger than the spending multiplier indicates. Recessionary gaps aren't as easy to fill as Figures 16A-3 and 16A-4 indicate. More about how to solve this problem in Chapter 19.

17

The Public Debt: Are We Spending Ourselves into Bankruptcy?

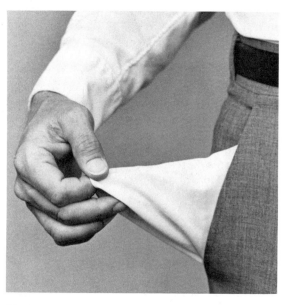

KEY WORDS

Public debt
Debt ceiling
Government securities
Net public debt
Internal debt
External debt
Annually balanced budget
Countercyclical budget
Functional finance
High-employment budget
  approach

Y ou will remember that the excess of government spending over tax revenues is called deficit spending. The United States Treasury raises this money by printing government securities and selling them to whoever will buy. (This is a simplified explanation of a very complex process.) The securities are promises by the Treasury to pay the owner of those securities some amount of money on some date in the future. The grand sum total of all of these promises to pay is the **public** (sometimes called national) **debt**.

Two preliminary points need to be made about the debt: (1) The public debt described in this chapter refers to the issuance of government securities *only by the federal government, not* by the states or local governments for such things as water or sewage systems. Consequently, think of the public debt as a *federal* debt. (2) Remember that the federal government sends a great deal of money each year (federal revenue sharing) back to the states and local governments—in fact, about 20 percent of their total income. Therefore, to some extent, the spending habits of the states and local governments are partly responsible for the federal government's need to raise money by selling government securities.

In this chapter, we will explain the arguments for and against the public debt. Often these arguments are filled with emotion. You hear some people say, "We are spending ourselves into bankruptcy," or "Sooner or later there will be a day of judgment," and so on. It is very important for all of us to understand what this is all about, since the public debt is debated more, by more uninformed people, than is any other topic in economics.

The chapter is divided into four sections: (1) Emotional arguments, (2) the size and ownership of the debt, (3) the four budget philosophies, and (4) some hard questions about the debt.

EMOTIONAL ARGUMENTS: "HEADING FOR BANKRUPTCY"

Critics of the public debt have plenty of fuel for their anxiety. Annual deficits incurred by the federal government are the rule rather than the exception. In the 55 years from 1929 to 1983, the federal government had deficits in all but eight. Since 1961, there has been only one year without a deficit (1969). The deficits in recent years have been particularly large—averaging around $100 billion per year. The fact that in the twenty-five years between 1946 and 1971 there were only two years when the deficits were more than $10 billion helps to give these numbers some perspective.

Many intelligent Americans are horrified at this spendthrift behavior. The people in charge in Washington are accused of fiscal irresponsibility and of driving us into bankruptcy. There are undoubtedly millions of Americans who share this concern. Senator John L. McClellan (D-Arkansas) once complained that those who control the economy are "callously and mercilessly burdening the livelihood and earnings of the generations that will follow us with a tremendous oppressive national debt." President Eisenhower worried that "we are stealing from our children in order to satisfy our desires of today."

SIZE AND OWNERSHIP OF THE DEBT

Now let's see how bad the problem really is. We'll look at the size of the debt and to whom the debt is owed and use this information to answer the emotional arguments about the "merciless burden" and bankruptcy.

Table 17-1. GNP and the Federal Public Debt in Selected Years, 1930–1982
(figures are in billions of current dollars)

Year	(1) GNP	(2) Federal debt	(3) Debt ÷ GNP (in percent)
1930	$ 90	$ 16	17.8%
1940	100	43	43.0
1945	210	259	123.0
1950	285	257	90.0
1955	398	281	71.0
1960	504	290	57.5
1965	685	321	46.8
1970	974	389	39.9
1975	1,516	544	35.9
1976	1,693	632	37.3
1977	1,900	699	36.8
1978	2,128	772	36.3
1979	2,369	834	35.2
1980	2,626	914	34.8
1981	2,922	998	34.2
1982*	3,058*	1,142*	37.3*

Source: Economic Report of the President, 1983.

How Large Is the Debt?

Table 17-1 shows how the debt has grown without interruption from a modest $16 billion in 1930 to over $1 trillion by the end of 1982, a more than 60-fold increase!

The Debt as a Percentage of GNP

Scary as the debt figures may seem, economists are more interested in the debt as a percentage of GNP than in its absolute size. For example, in 1930, when the debt was $16 billion, the GNP was $90 billion, and the debt as a percentage of GNP was therefore $16 billion ÷ $90 billion = 17.8 percent. During World War II, the percentage rose to 123, but by 1981 it had dropped to 34.2. In 1982, the percentage was apparently inching up to 37.3, where it was in 1976. The increase from 1981 to 1982 was probably the result of declining tax revenues as a result of the recession in 1981–1982 and a negligible growth in GNP. The automatic stabilizers were undoubtedly at work, causing a larger deficit during the recession and, consequently, a large addition to the debt while the change in nominal GNP was negligible (and *real* GNP actually fell).

The rationale for calculating the debt as a percentage of GNP is that this measure helps us to evaluate the advantages or disadvantages of going into debt and our ability to pay it off. Often, business firms go into debt to build new factories or stores; the success of the new venture measures the wisdom of going into debt. If the extra sales and profits generated by the expansion more than make up for the debt and help to pay it off, then going into debt was worth it.

If our GNP grows faster than the debt, the debt as a percentage of GNP must fall. The falling percentage shows that the debt has helped our GNP to grow, just as rising sales and profits validate a business firm's debt.

The Debt Ceiling

The last line of Table 17-1 shows the debt exceeding $1 trillion, a kind of sound barrier referred to disparagingly by most politicians. Can the Treasury continue to increase this number indefinitely? Apparently, yes. The Treasury operates under limitations imposed by the Second Liberty Bond Act, passed in 1917 to help finance World War I. The Act provides for a **debt ceiling**, beyond which the Treasury is not supposed to go. The ceiling was set at slightly over $7.5 billion.

Each year, the Treasury is faced with a crisis. Because government programs are politically so much easier to finance with deficits (sales of government securities) than with tax increases, every government budget since 1969 has failed to take in enough money to finance government spending. And so every spring the Treasury finds itself going broke.

What to do? Increase taxes? No, no, not that! Borrow more money from the people? Certainly. The people's government securities purchases are voluntary. The people want the interest income. The process is painless.

And so every spring, the Treasury asks Congress to raise the statutory ceiling on the debt. Congress is always glad to oblige. After all, the alternatives are either to cut spending or to raise taxes. Either way, *that* hurts. And so, through the years, the debt ceiling has been raised from the $7.5 billion limit to $1,143 billion as of September 30, 1982. By the time this book appears in print the ceiling will have had to be increased by another $200 billion or so.

Under these circumstances, can the government go broke? Probably not. As long as Congress has the power to tax and to raise the debt ceiling, and as long as the Treasury can sell new securities to replace the old ones, and, finally, as long as, in the last resort, the Treasury can print money to pay its bills—and its creditors accept the money—the country will not go broke. What matters most is the size of the debt compared with GNP. That relationship shows whether or not the debt helps or hinders the macroeconomy's performance.

The "Merciless Burden"

Economists dispose of the merciless-burden argument by pointing out that, although the next generation inherits the debt along with its obligation to pay interest to the owners of government securities, it also inherits the assets the securities represent. The debt and its interest cost are minuses, but the securities holders' assets in the form of the securities and interest income from the securities are offsetting pluses.

The merciless-burden argument was probably the result of the tremendous increase in the public debt during World War II. At the beginning of the war, the debt was $43 billion. In 1945, when the war ended, the debt was $259 billion.

Are we now bearing the burden of that war because it was financed by deficit spending rather than by wartime taxes? The answer is partly yes and partly no.

We have to consider this question from two points of view: (1) That of people living during the war and (2) that of people living in future generations. From the point of view of the people living as consumers in the 1941–

1945 period, they bore the real burden of the war. During 1942–1944, the most intense period of our involvement, consumption spending as a percentage of disposable personal income fell from the usual 92 to 95 percent to an average of 75 percent. Personal saving rose to a corresponding 25 percent of DPI. These percentages indicate that the people went without innumerable consumption goods—automobiles, appliances, nylon stockings, gasoline—so that resources could be released for war materials. A revealing statistic is that in the year 1940, before involvement in the war, we produced and sold 1 million passenger cars. During the three-year period 1942–1944, we produced only 25,000 passenger cars per year.

But people in future generations may also bear the burden of a war. In 1944, *half* of our GNP went to the war effort. Members of future generations will *forever* bear the opportunity cost of the war in the form of the rapid-transit systems, solar energy projects, hydroelectric dams, or capital improvements in public health and education that could have been created with the resources and talent that were burned up in the war.

The difficulty with this point of view is that if the debt had not been used to fight the war, could we have won it? The war and the debt transferred a burden (lost production and resources) to future generations but also a benefit (freedom from totalitarian rule).

Nevertheless, this discussion indicates that future generations *may* bear a burden from the debt. If the debt finances a use of resources (such as the Vietnam war) that, it can be argued, holds no benefit for future generations, then the future generations do bear a burden with no offsetting benefit. If the debt finances the development of projects such as solar energy, future generations will bear the opportunity cost of using resources in that particular way, but they will also have the benefit of the solar energy. The question of burden or benefit depends on one's value judgments about how the funds obtained from the sale of government securities are spent.

Interest on the Debt

The Treasury must pay the owners of the debt interest on the securities. This interest, estimated at $85 billion in 1982, must be obtained from taxpayers or from the sale of more securities (which will further increase the interest cost of the debt). Consequently, the interest cost of the debt must be included in every federal budget. On the other hand, when the securities become due, the Treasury can simply print up new securities and sell them to people to obtain the money to pay off the old ones. This is one reason the debt rarely, if ever, goes down.

The enormous interest cost of the debt that must be paid to the holders of government securities creates more fuel for worry about the debt. Consequently, economists also compare the interest cost of the debt with GNP. In 1982, the interest cost of the debt ($85 billion) was 2.8 percent of the $3,058 GNP of that year. Whereas the debt itself as a percentage of GNP seems to be growing slowly, the interest cost as a percentage of GNP has grown substantially. Back in 1973, for example, the interest cost (then $26.6 billion) was 2 percent of GNP, 29 percent less than the 1982 percentage. The increase in the interest cost percentage is the result of rising interest rates. In 1973 the average interest *rate* on the government securities making up the debt was 5.9 percent. In 1982, the average rate was about 11 percent—almost double.

Table 17-2. Ownership of the Federal Debt, August 31, 1981

	Securities holdings in billions of $	Percent of total
(1) Individuals	$140.2	14.3%
(2) Commercial banks	115.0	11.7
(3) Corporations	38.0	3.9
(4) Savings banks and insurance companies	26.1	2.7
(5) State and local governments	86.2	8.8
(6) Federal Reserve Banks	124.5	12.7
(7) U.S. Government Accounts	199.0	20.3
(8) Foreign governments and individuals	73.9	7.5
(9) Miscellaneous*	177.3	18.1
Total	$980.2	100.0

Sources: Economic Report of the President, 1982 and *Treasury Bulletin*, October 1981.

*Miscellaneous includes nonprofit institutions, corporate pension funds, and securities brokers.

As we have already seen, the period 1973–1982 was one of considerable inflation. And because inflation erodes the purchasing power of our savings, the Treasury had to offer high interest rates to offset the inflationary "penalty" borne by people who decided to save in the form of government securities.

The rising interest cost of the debt is apt to have unfortunate side effects. When we pay taxes to give the debt-owners their interest, a very large redistribution of income takes place. This shift of income from taxpayers to debt-owners raises a difficult question about whether or not the debt makes the rich richer and the poor poorer. We will reserve this question for the last section of this chapter.

To Whom Is the Debt Owed?

The public debt is owed to the owners of all outstanding **government securities**. Consequently, those who own the securities that make up the debt are the creditors. The U.S. Treasury is the debtor.

(Most people are used to talking about government bonds rather than government securities. "Securities" is the broader term used to describe *all* the government's IOUs, regardless of the amount of time that passes before the Treasury—the debtor—must repay the buyer—the creditor. Securities that mature in one year or less are called *Treasury bills*; securities that mature within a one- to five-year time span are called *Treasury notes*. Finally, *Treasury bonds* are long-term IOUs that take more than five years to mature.)

Private and Public Ownership of the Debt

But now let's see who the creditors of the $980.2 billion* public debt were on August 31, 1981 (Table 17-2). Several items in the table deserve mention. Note that much of the public debt is not owned by private individuals and partner

*This figure is less than the over-trillion dollar figure in Table 17-1, because it's an estimate of the debt made one year earlier than the estimate in Table 17-1.

ships. Amazingly, the federal government buys some of its own government securities (line 7). The federal government accumulates money in the Social Security fund and the highway trust fund prior to spending the money for Social Security benefits and new highways. The administrators of these funds may legally purchase government securities to help the Treasury and earn interest, but they cannot use the funds for investment in the private sector.

Because government agencies own so much of the federal debt, some experts argue that we should separate the amount of the debt owed to the public from the portions of the debt owed to government agencies. In the government agency category we could lump the U.S. securities owned by state and local governments (line 5) and those owed by the Federal Reserve District Banks (line 6) with those that U.S. government agencies own (line 7) and call this total a portion of the debt that is not owed to the public. The three lines total $409.7 billion. Subtract that figure from the $980.2 billion total and we have left $570.5 billion owed to the public. This last figure is sometimes called the **net public debt**.

Are We Spending Ourselves into Bankruptcy?

Now that you know to whom we owe the debt, you will find it easier to understand why ultimate bankruptcy is extremely improbable. The bankruptcy argument involves a misunderstanding. The existence of the debt does not make the country any richer or poorer. The wealth (or poverty) of the country is measured in terms of such resources as factories, houses, appliances, and vehicles, plus our human capital. Our trillion-dollar debt does not change the quantity or quality of resources in the country one bit.

We have seen that the lenders (creditors) are the people who own the securities and that the borrower (debtor) is the Treasury. But because the Treasury, like any government agency, is supported by taxpayers, taxpayers are the real borrowers (debtors). Consequently, one portion of the nation (taxpayers) owes the debt to another (the owners of government securities), who are *also* taxpayers. No matter how large the debt becomes, the indebtedness it represents for all taxpayers is offset by the assets (the securities) held by some taxpayers.

Thus, the public debt is a debt *owed to ourselves.* It is as if one member of a family were indebted to another member of the same family. The family's total wealth is unaffected by the intrafamily debt. Economists refer to this largest part of the public debt as **internal debt**.

Because most of the public debt is internally held, its existence will not lead to bankruptcy. Why, then is this argument so popular? Undoubtedly, because we worry, with good reason, about debts *outside* the family.

Buried in Table 17-2 (line 8) is an important exception to the idea that the public debt is *internal.* About 7.5 percent of the public debt is held by non-U.S. owners.* This indebtedness is **external**. When the foreign-held securities become due, we will be taxed the amount necessary by the federal government to send resources to the creditor countries. An external debt, therefore, reduces the real wealth of the debtor in favor of the creditor. Also external are most of the debts we worry about as consumers—private debts in the form of charge accounts, appliance or car loans, and mortgages.

---

*An interesting tidbit: Of the $73.9 billion worth of U.S. securities owned by foreigners, $5.7 billion worth were denominated in West German marks or Swiss francs. These securities were issued in 1978 and 1979 when the U.S. dollar was weak and seemed a poor risk. *Treasury Bulletin,* July 1982, p. 73.

Table 17-3. Private Debt in the United States, 1960 and 1981 (in billions)

	1960	1981
Corporate debt	$154	$1,177
Individual debt	264	1,918
Totals	$418	$3,095

Source: Statistical Abstract of the United States, 1982–83, Table 816.

To judge any debt as "bad" or "good" presents a problem. To the extent we can persuade oil-rich countries to send us their oil in exchange for government securities, we can enjoy the benefits of having warm homes, plentiful electrical power, ration-free supplies of gasoline, and so forth. Our present standard of living rises when our suppliers give us credit. If it were not for mortgages, car loans, and other installment types of loans, most of us would be unable to afford many important and necessary purchases until late in life. As always, there is a benefit side and a cost side in any decision to go into debt.

Because the internal public debt is so much maligned, a look at total private (external) debt makes an interesting comparison. Table 17-3 reveals that our 1981 private debt totaled $3,095 billion. That is about *three times as large as* the public debt of $998 billion of the same year.

Private debt has also grown faster than public debt during the 1960–1981 period—7.4 times for private debt versus 3.4 times for the public debt. During this same period, GNP grew 5.8 times.*

We must keep in mind that public indebtedness is accomplished by borrowing individual or corporate savings. When the borrowed money is spent, it becomes available for consumption or investment spending. Borrowing helps aggregate demand grow, which helps incomes grow, which helps people save, which provides funds for loans, which in turn helps aggregate demand, and so on.

Consumer indebtedness, particularly from installment buying, is one of the *indicators* (see page 253) that economists use to forecast what is happening or is going to happen to GNP. If consumer indebtedness rises, then consumers must be increasing their consumption spending. But if consumer debt rises less rapidly in any month than it did the month before, economists worry that spending may be slackening. Even "worse," if Americans start to pay off old debts faster than they take on new ones, retail stores find their unsold inventories piling up. A business slowdown and rising unemployment rates are sure to follow, and that is what happened during the 1974–1975 and 1981–1983 recessions.

At this point you must be wondering, "How can the politicians in Washington almost always spend more than tax receipts and get away with it?" Good question. Let's see how the philosophy of government spending has changed over the years.

FOUR FEDERAL BUDGET PHILOSOPHIES

There are four different philosophies of government finance pertaining to the public debt: (1) The annually balanced budget, (2) the countercyclical budget,

---

*All these comparisons come from the data shown in Table 17-1 or Table 17-3.

(3) functional finance, and (4) the federal high-employment budget approach. Let us discuss each in turn.

The Annually Balanced Budget

The philosophy of the **annually balanced budget** says simply that taxes should always equal government spending; a debt should never arise. Prior to the general acceptance of Keynesian theory in the 1960s, any presidential candidate who did not promise to keep the budget in balance was beaten before he started. Americans often equate indebtedness with sin.

Many economists now believe, however, that a budget that always balances spending with taxes is the worst possible course of action for the health of the economy. It will contribute to inflation in times of prosperity and will deepen and prolong recessions. The key to this argument lies with the automatic stabilizers. In times of growing prosperity, the federal government's tax revenues automatically rise because of increases in income tax collections. If the federal government then pursues the annually balanced budget philosophy, it will use this opportunity to increase government spending. The increase in government spending will add to an already increasing aggregate demand and contribute to inflation.

When the economy starts slipping downhill into a period of poor sales for business and increasing unemployment, tax collections automatically fall. If the federal government is then forced to reduce spending to keep the budget in balance, the reduction in spending will subtract from aggregate demand and make matters worse.

Despite these objections, Senate Joint Resolution 58 was passed by the Senate in early August 1982. The resolution called for an amendment to the U.S. Constitution requiring Congress to balance federal spending with federal tax revenues (no deficits) in every federal budget. Spending could exceed tax revenues only if the nation was at war or if three fifths of *all* members of Congress (not just those present) voted to do so. (One senator—Daniel P. Moynihan—remarked that we would have to declare war on Iceland every year to continue our deficit spending.)

At the time the resolution was passed, much was happening to bolster the case for the amendment. Future deficits were forecast in the $100–200 billion range. Tight money and high interest rates, the result of crowding out (see page 325) and anticipated inflation, had severely cut borrowing and spending and industrial production. Large deficits seemed to be the culprit. Milton Friedman, probably the most famous conservative economist in the country, called the amendment "excellent."[1] But other economists were strongly in opposition. George L. Perry called the budget amendment a "travesty,"[2] because it would destroy the automatic stabilizers and make recessions worse: "If Congress is surprised by an unexpected recession . . . it cannot, except through a three-fifths vote, allow for the increase in unemployment compensation payments that will automatically occur."

With considerable division of opinion in Washington* and with 38 (three fourths) of the states needed to support the amendment, it seems doubtful at

---

*On October 1, 1982, the House passed the resolution, 236 in favor, 187 against, not enough in favor to provide the two-thirds majority necessary to send the amendment to the states. For a thorough analysis, see Gardner Ackley, "You Can't Balance the Budget by Amendment," *Challenge*, November-December 1982.

The annually balanced budget philosophy says that taxation and government spending should be equal.

this writing that the resolution will go much further. The *real* "bottom line" is that to balance the budget and bring a halt to deficit spending would require massive tax increases and massive spending cuts, a package few members of Congress want to support.

The Countercyclical Budget

You are probably already saying to yourself that the federal government should reduce spending in times of inflation and should run a deficit by increasing spending without increasing taxes in times of recession. If so, you are advocating a countercyclical policy. A **countercyclical budget** means that the federal budget should counteract the swings in aggregate demand by reducing spending in times of inflation and increasing it in times of recession or depression.

Unfortunately, there are two reasons why this beautiful idea will not work. First, the swings in aggregate demand are apt to be uneven; the ups do not necessarily match the downs, either in height or in duration. There is no way of knowing whether the surpluses accumulated during periods of prosperity will match the increases in the debt incurred during periods of depression or recession. Second, the countercyclical philosophy has no provision for helping our GNP grow enough to provide jobs for a growing labor force.

Functional Finance

The **functional finance** philosophy stresses the federal government's obligation to achieve the goals stated in the Employment Act of 1946. It views deficit spending and a growing debt as matters that are of secondary importance to the primary functions of government—providing for full employment, maintaining stable prices, and helping to solve many domestic social and economic problems. Thus, this philosophy emphasizes particular problems that need solving whether deficits are incurred or not—problems such as poverty, substandard housing, pollution, and inadequacy of rapid transit.

The High-Employment Budget Approach

The problem with any federal budget is that it may operate to prevent the economy from reaching full employment. A simple example will help. Assume a small country named Belgravia has an unemployment rate of 10 percent. As measured in crowns, its domestic currency, Belgravia's GNP is 300, its government's tax receipts are 60, and its government spending is 70. Clearly, the government is running a deficit of 10 crowns per year.

A good Keynesian would take one look at these numbers and say, "Not to worry. The deficit will add to aggregate demand and bring Belgravia out of its slump. The unemployment rate will certainly come down."

Unfortunately, economists now realize that the solution to Belgravia's unemployment rate isn't that easy. The deficit will probably help the GNP grow, and yes, the unemployment rate will start to come down. But as these trends appear, the automatic stabilizers will go to work. Government spending will tend to decrease as welfare payments, unemployment compensation payments, and farm price-support payments become less necessary. And as the economy's pace quickens, more people will go to work, they will pay more taxes, and the government's tax receipts will automatically increase. In fact, the deficit may automatically disappear, and at high levels of employment, the government's tax receipts may exceed its spending. A surplus at high employment could develop. Belgravia's tax receipts could exceed its government spending by, say, 10 crowns, when the economy becomes prosperous.

But, when tax receipts are 10 crowns more than government spending, the net effect on total income must be *negative*, because the people are collectively giving more to the government than the government gives back to them. The *surplus* of tax receipts over government spending will eventually reduce aggregate demand and prevent the economy from reaching full employment.

To avoid such a surplus before the economy reaches a high-employment level, economists try to estimate what the deficit or surplus *would be after* a high-employment level of GNP is achieved. If this calculation indicates that a surplus would occur, then present tax rates should be cut. Notice that this policy holds that a current deficit should be made *even larger* in order to prevent a *surplus* from accumulating at some time in the future. Conversely, an estimate of high-employment tax receipts and government spending that shows a *deficit* would indicate that present tax revenues should be raised in order to avoid future demand-pull inflation.

This approach to federal budget making is called the **high-employment budget approach** because it urges politicians to design tax and spending policies that will produce a balanced budget at high employment. The approach is noteworthy because (1) it accepts the view that *future* budget surpluses may be a reason for larger deficits today (and consequent increases in the public debt), and (2) it emphasizes budget planning over a period of years, rather than hasty policy decisions based on present circumstances.

The last two philosophies provide some logic for an ever-growing debt, but as you well know by now, every decision has its cost; there is no such thing as a "free lunch." Let's see what some of the real costs of the debt are.

SOME HARD QUESTIONS ABOUT THE DEBT

So far, the arguments about the debt make a growing debt seem painless, even necessary, with the possible exception of the 7.5 percent held externally. The remainder of this chapter is devoted to four problems with which the professionals have difficulty.

Redistribution of Income

The debt may cause a redistribution of income away from low-income people to high-income people, because the owners of government securities probably have higher-than-average incomes. (One clue: The richest *one* percent of the people owned *sixty* percent of all bonds, including corporate bonds, in 1972.) Consequently, when all taxpayers have to pay the $85 billion or so in interest income to the owners of government securities, a large redistribution of income undoubtedly takes place.

We should be reminded, however, that this argument pertains only to the tax side of the question. When the money is spent, people in lower income groups may benefit, for example, from such projects as rapid transit or federally subsidized housing.

The Debt and Inflation

The second argument about the debt concerns its effect on inflation. The existence of an *un*changing public debt has *little* or *no* effect on inflation. That is, if our trillion-dollar public debt did not increase or decrease in size during the year, the federal budget would have to be balanced, and whatever level of aggregate demand existed at the time would be unaffected. The price level is affected when the debt *grows* as the result of deficit spending during the year. The reason is that deficit spending adds more to people's incomes (in the form of income from sales to the government or income from transfer payments) than the government takes away from the people by taxing them. Thus, the government-spending component of aggregate demand *may* grow without any offsetting decreases in consumption, investment, or net exports. The resulting increases in aggregate demand can lead to higher prices.

Inflation caused by increases in aggregate demand resulting from deficit spending is particularly aggravating if the economy is at or near full employment. Remember that *any* spending by the government means that the government is buying goods and services in private markets. If suppliers are already producing as much as they can, the demand for goods and services by government agencies will cause suppliers to raise prices on the same quantities of goods and services. No one except the suppliers wins in this game.

If, on the other hand, there is high *un*employment, increased government spending will cause suppliers to increase production and hire more people. *For a time*, while the economy gathers steam, prices may remain at their previous levels. This scenario was the one Keynes foresaw as the way out of the Depression.

Deficit Spending Can Be Self-Perpetuating

The third argument about the debt again has to do, not with the size of the debt itself, but with deficit spending. Deficit spending can act on the economy like a drug that is increasingly addictive. The problem is that politicians don't want to have to balance a budget (*any* budget, federal, state, or local) if to do so means a cut in spending or an increase in taxes. Any such change will cause pain for some interest group, and that pain may be translated into less financial support and fewer votes for the politicians in the next election.

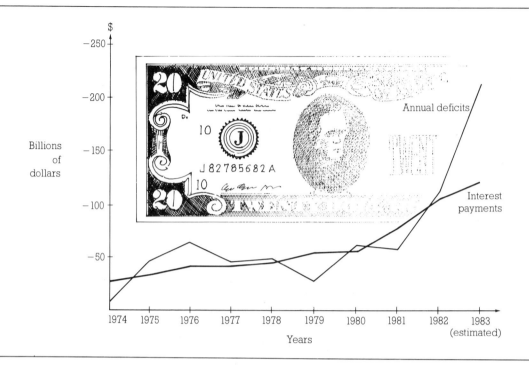

$

Billions
of
dollars

−250

−200

−150

−100

−50

Annual deficits

Interest
payments

1974 1975 1976 1977 1978 1979 1980 1981 1982 1983
(estimated)

Years

Figure 17-1.
Recent increases in
deficit spending and
interest payments on
the public debt.
(*Source: Economic
Report of the
President, 1983.*)

Consequently, Congress usually prefers to finance deficits with more borrowing from the people (more sales of government securities). And when the old securities become due for repayment by the Treasury, new securities are issued to raise the necessary money. And as the debt grows as a consequence, the interest payments on the debt also grow. And again, Congress would much rather finance the interest payments by selling still more government securities, leading to still larger interest payments. And on and on. The only way the process can be interrupted is to cut government spending and/or to raise taxes, but the pain of withdrawal is too awful to consider.

Figure 17-1 shows annual deficit spending and interest payments during the ten-year period, 1974–1983. The deficit-spending figures are for each year. The interest-payment figures are the payments made each year by the Treasury to owners of the total accumulated debt for *all* years. As you can see, the interest payments increase continuously, because, in recent years, the debt has increased continuously, because of our taste for deficit spending. The trend of annual deficit spending is also up, although some years show less deficit spending than others.

Crowding Out, or When Deficit Spending Doesn't Reduce Unemployment

So far we have noted the debt and deficit spending can (1) redistribute incomes, (2) cause inflation, and (3) be addictive. The fourth "hard" question about the debt is called crowding out, a topic already mentioned in Chapter 16. As you will remember, crowding out means that deficit spending may "crowd out" private spending.

When the Treasury sells new government securities (to replace old ones, to finance interest payments, or simply to finance a new deficit), the Treasury often has to sweeten the new offering with higher interest rates. And when the Treasury offers higher interest rates, corporations have a more difficult time selling securities to the public to finance *private* investment. Then business managers may decide to postpone investment spending until borrowing becomes cheaper. The government spending component increases, but at the expense of a drop in investment spending. Aggregate demand and the level of employment may not change at all.

Evidence of this possibility is at hand. If deficit spending, *by itself,* can reduce unemployment, then why didn't it help during the 1980–1983 recession? During those four years, the unemployment rate averaged around 9 percent, while the four-year total for deficit spending was a gigantic $436 billion. Certainly, the unemployment rate should have come down.

The most widely accepted reason for the failure of the unemployment rate to come down was the crowding-out effect. Throughout the four-year period, private spending by consumers and business firms was sluggish. For example, purchases by consumers of durable goods like automobiles in 1982 were (in real terms) less than they were in three of the four previous years. Investment spending by business firms in 1982 was less (again in real terms) than in all previous years back to 1976. A drop in investment spending is particularly significant to economists, because the drop indicates a lack of willingness by business firms to expand their operations. Clearly, business firms were unwilling during this period to provide new jobs. And so we have an instance where deficit spending—even massive deficit spending—did not help to reduce the unemployment rate.

The crowding-out argument is intimately connected to monetary policy, the subject of the next chapter. If the monetary authorities make loans easy to obtain and interest rates for borrowers low (and the authorities can do this), then private spending by consumers and by business firms can continue unabated *even* while the Treasury is borrowing for deficit spending. But if the monetary authorities make loans hard to get and if interest rates are kept high (and the authorities can do this too), then borrowing by the Treasury for deficit spending will compound a felony already under way. The supply of money available to the public for loans is made triply scarce by Treasury borrowing, by the monetary authorities' restrictions on the growth of the money supply, and by the high interest rates that result from such a monetary policy.

Thus, from our recent experience with crowding out, we have learned two important lessons: (1) Crowding out can hurt, and (2) deficit financing à la Keynes can reduce unemployment only if the monetary authorities are making it easy for borrowers to obtain money for loans. Monetary and fiscal policy have to work together.

SUMMARY

The federal government has spent more than it has taken in in most years since 1929, with a resultant increase in the public debt to over $1 trillion in 1982. Some people believe the debt is leading the country into bankruptcy or causing a "merciless burden" to fall on future generations. However, unlike most private debts, the public debt is largely internal; that is, it is owed by all taxpayers to some of their number (securities holders who are also taxpayers). Only about 7.5 percent of the total debt is owed to foreign investors.

Some people argue that the government should always operate on an annually balanced budget, but such a policy would exaggerate the ups and downs of the business cycle. Some economists say that federal budgets should be planned to counteract the business cycle by increasing spending above tax revenues in times of recession and increasing taxes above spending in times of inflation. Other economists argue that governmental financial policies should be used to attack social problems such as unemployment, poverty, urban decay, and pollution; the resulting changes in the public debt should be of secondary concern. This policy is called functional finance.

Finally, some economists believe that deficit spending is valid, because it helps GNP move toward high employment. If GNP is at or near high employment, the automatic increases in tax collections that come from an expanding economy will erase the deficit and may even produce a surplus.

There are serious arguments against the debt: (1) It contributes to the unequal distribution of income; (2) it contributes to inflation; (3) it may become addictive and cause ever larger increases in the debt; and (4) it may crowd out private spending.

Discussion Questions

1. Evaluate the following statement: An individual who is steadily accumulating debt is probably in trouble, but a country that is in debt is probably in good economic health.

2. Why is an annually balanced budget apt to aggravate the ups and downs of inflation and unemployment?

3. What would happen to the economy if we instituted a tax program to pay off the entire debt?

4. Is the sale of $500 million worth of bonds by the American Telephone and Telegraph Company to build new exchanges an internal or external debt? How would you judge whether or not this indebtedness is economically worthwhile?

5. How big can the public debt become? If the debt continues to get bigger, are we in danger of going bankrupt? Discuss.

DID YOU EVER WONDER WHY . . .

. . . the United States has a positive net worth even though it has such a large debt?

References

1. *Newsweek*, 13 September 1982.

2. *Los Angeles Times*, 3 August 1982, Part IV, p. 3. (Perry is a senior fellow at the Brookings Institution, a Washington, D.C. economics think tank.)

18

Monetary Policy: Changing the Money Supply to Change Aggregate Demand

KEY WORDS

Monetary policy
Federal Reserve
    System (the Fed)
Gold Reserve Act
    of 1934
M_1
Currency in circulation
Demand deposits
    (checking accounts)
Credit
Fractional reserve
    system
Required reserves
Excess reserves
Deposit multiplier
Federal Reserve
    District Bank
Board of Governors

Federal Open Market
    Committee
Federal Reserve Notes
Interdistrict Settlement
    Fund
Federal Deposit
    Insurance
    Corporation (FDIC)
Depository Institutions
    Deregulation and
    Monetary Control
    Act of 1980
Easy-money policy
Tight-money policy
Open-market
    operations
Discount rate
Prime rate

So far we have concentrated on fiscal policy—the theory, mechanics, and consequences of changing aggregate demand through changes in government spending or taxes. In this chapter we explore the other major method of raising or lowering aggregate demand to combat recession or inflation—monetary policy. **Monetary policy** is the manipulation of the money supply for the purpose of changing aggregate demand. In the United States, monetary policy is formulated and carried out by the Board of Governors of the **Federal Reserve System (the Fed)**.

It will help to keep in mind two central, easy-to-understand theories upon which monetary policy is based: (1) If borrowing is made easy, total spending (aggregate demand) should increase. (2) If borrowing is made difficult, then spending should stop rising and may even fall.

Of the two sets of policies for changing aggregate demand—fiscal and monetary—the public is generally more aware of changes in discretionary fiscal policy. That is because changes in government spending and taxes are often "front page news" and may directly affect us as taxpayers or as members of the business community. On the other hand, the public is rarely aware of changes in monetary policy, because the Board of Governors (hereafter we'll simply say the Board) conducts its meetings in secret. When the results of these meetings are made public, thirty days later, they are usually reported on the back pages of our newspapers.

Nevertheless, the decisions of the Board probably affect us as much as discretionary fiscal policy does—if not more—because the Board has the power to make borrowing easy or difficult. In fact, so powerful is the Board that there is much debate about whether it ought to be so independent. As of the end of 1983, the Board could change the volume of loans by billions of dollars—in secret and as often as once a week—without having to obtain the consent of Congress or the President.

This chapter is divided into six sections: (1) What makes money, money? (2) how money is defined in monetary policy; (3) how the banks can create money; (4) how the Federal Reserve System is organized; (5) what the Board does to influence aggregate demand; and (6) does monetary policy work? An appendix, Chapter 18A, presents another great debate (like that in Chapter 15) about monetary policy.

WHAT MAKES MONEY, MONEY?
OR, WHAT GIVES MONEY ITS VALUE?

Explaining what makes money, money is not as easy as it might seem. We are so used to thinking of the bills in our wallets as money that we seldom stop to think about what makes them acceptable to merchants or creditors when we want to buy something or pay off a debt. Yet paper money is a relatively recent development.

All kinds of commodities have been used as money in different countries at different times: salt and grain in ancient times; gold and silver—first "raw" and then as coins; tea and cheese (China); fishhooks (Alaska); bristles from the tails of elephants (Portuguese West Africa); cocoa beans (Mexico); and cigarettes (in wartime prison camps and in Europe after World War II).

From these examples we get a hint of the *fundamental* answer to the question, What is money? Money is whatever people will take in exchange for goods and services and as payment for debts. In more formal terms, money functions

Fishhooks were once used as money in Alaska.

as a *medium of exchange*—among members of a tribe or nation or among nations. It also functions as a *store of value.*

Not every commodity serves one or both of these functions equally well. Indeed, that is why the need for a medium of exchange arose so early in human history—about as soon as people began bartering (trading) with one another and with neighboring groups.

Remember how Jane Pennyworth had to sell her eggs for what she could get on market day? Her eggs were perishable. They were also fragile. And although eggs are much alike, they are not *uniform*—nor are they readily *divisible.*

If Jane had to barter her eggs—that is, exchange them directly for another commodity—she would have to find a "barter partner" who (1) needed eggs right away, and (2) had something of equal value to give in exchange.

Consider a herdsman in ancient times who had a cow or goat to trade and who wanted, say, a fine flint knife for scraping hides. If the toolmaker (or flint knapper) wanted a whole goat, well and good. If not, there was a problem. Goats are somewhat portable, somewhat storable (they must be fed), and not very evenly divisible. The toolmaker, as you can see, was in a much better position—his product was *durable, portable,* relatively *divisible* (that is, as small objects like spear tips), relatively *uniform,* and widely *acceptable.* Many people needed knives, axes, or spear tips. And so, perhaps, some enterprising herdsman traded off a goat for a batch of spear tips that *he* then traded off one at a time for berries, or a woven basket, or rabbitskin boots from the tanner.

The toolmaker's products became money. They fulfilled some principal requirements for a medium of exchange: durability, divisibility, acceptability, reproducibility, and convenience. They could serve as a *unit of account,* as a *measure of relative value* (one goat equals ten spear tips; one basket of berries equals one spear tip); and as a *standard of deferred payment* (let me have some berries for this party and I'll pay you a spear tip when I've sold my goat).

From this we can see how people came to use precious metals for money. They fulfilled the criteria for both a medium of exchange and a store of value very well—especially gold, which is extremely durable, quite scarce (meaning that a small unit has a high exchange value), readily divisible, uniform and—in the form of coins—reproducible. (Think how difficult it would be to use lead for money or, say, copper—just imagine carrying your spending money in the form of pennies.)

Eventually people began storing their gold in some centralized, guarded place—often with a goldsmith—from which they got receipts. Trading the receipts (paper) was much more convenient than trading the metal—and from there it was a relatively short step to paper money such as we use today. Those who stored the money found they could meet their customers' withdrawals without keeping all the stock of gold on hand; they lent it out at interest (also in the form of receipts). And thus originated the very complex system of fractional reserve banking, which you will learn about in this chapter.

In the early days of paper money, the paper currency was *backed by* deposits of gold or silver, and gold and silver coins remained in circulation. A paper bill could be exchanged for its face value in precious metal coins at any bank. In the United States (and in many other countries), however, paper money and base-metal coins are no longer backed by gold or silver.

Our paper money *was* exchangeable for gold *or* silver until 1934.* During the early years of the Depression, Americans exchanged large quantities of paper money for gold. When the stock of gold held by the Treasury sank to disturbingly low levels, Congress passed (in 1934) the **Gold Reserve Act**. The Act stopped the redemption of paper money (five-dollar bills and up) for gold. Later, in 1963, Congress halted the redemption of one-dollar bills for silver. And in the late 1960s, copper and nickel replaced silver in our coins.

So, if our money is backed neither by gold nor silver, what *does* back it? The answer is that our money is backed by our faith that it will buy us goods and services. Money is valuable because we all *believe* it has purchasing power and accept it as a medium of exchange. The value of money is determined entirely by the quantity and quality of the goods and services we can obtain with money, not by its backing.

The purchasing power of money is determined by its scarcity relative to the supply of goods and services it can buy. As money becomes more plentiful relative to supplies of goods and services, prices are apt to rise and money tends to lose its value (inflation). As money becomes less plentiful relative to available supplies of goods and services, it becomes more valuable.

Because the relative scarcity of money is important to its value, and because the quantity of money in circulation is no longer limited by supplies of gold or silver, what or who controls the quantity of money in circulation? Answer: The Board of Governors of the Federal Reserve System. Now perhaps you can appreciate what enormous power the Board has. Although we have been discussing the role of paper money in our society, monetary policy, which concerns the manipulation of the money supply to influence aggregate demand, is concerned with many forms of money in addition to the paper bills in your wallet.

---

*Until then, the government could not print money beyond a legally specified ratio of the gold and silver in the Treasury to the amount of currency in circulation. Thus, expansion of the money supply was limited.

Money is valuable because we have faith in its purchasing power.

To understand monetary policy, we must therefore consider the different forms of money—like cash, checks, and savings accounts—that make up the money supply.

HOW MONEY IS DEFINED IN MONETARY POLICY

Monetary policy is based on an assumption: Changes in GNP can be engineered by changing the money supply. This assumption involves one of the great puzzles of monetary policy—what measure of the money supply should be used? Which ingredients in the money supply have the greatest effect on aggregate demand?

Determining "essential ingredients" is a problem typical of the social sciences. When we find that more-educated people have higher incomes than less-educated people, is it because of their education, intelligence, or hard work, or is it because their parents were rich, their father was president of the company, or the family was especially attuned to the "Protestant ethic" of work? Which variable is the most important determinant of income?

In the same way, research economists try to sift out the particular ingredients in the money supply that are most closely linked to changes in aggregate demand. And there are lots of ingredients to choose from: money in banks, money in circulation, checking accounts, money in credit unions, travelers' checks, money in money market funds, American money in foreign bank accounts, charge accounts, savings accounts, equities in life insurance policies, government securities that can be easily cashed in, and so forth.

You will note that credit cards are not included in this list. Why? After all, they perform the primary function of money. They enable the credit-card user to exchange a promise to pay (like a check) for some good or service. The problem is that the Fed doesn't know how to measure or classify credit-card purchases. No one knows when the credit-card user actually pays for a purchase. The user of "bank" cards, like Visa or MasterCard, and many "store" cards like Sears, may pay a bill promptly at the end of the month or may postpone complete payment indefinitely by making installment payments. Because of these unknowns, credit cards are not classified as money. However, from the point of view of the seller, a credit-card purchase *is* money. The seller receives money promptly from the credit-card company, and as far as the seller is concerned, a sale has taken place. The seller's inventory drops by one monkey wrench, electric guitar, or whatever. And the national income accountant agrees with the seller. A sale was completed, money changed hands, and the transaction was recorded as part of the "consumption" total under the "expenditures approach" (see Table 12-1). And the money the seller receives from the credit-card company will appear in various categories on the "income" side of the account. Credit cards are "neither fish nor fowl nor good, red herring." People use them like money, but the Fed does not treat them as money when it calculates the money supply.

There are now four ways to describe the money supply, and there is much debate about which one has the greatest effect on aggregate demand. However, the first and most common definition of the money supply is called M_1.

The M_1 Formula

M_1 is defined as currency in circulation plus checking accounts.* **Currency in circulation** includes all of the coins and paper money not sitting in some bank but in the possession of the public, whether in a wallet, cash register, cookie jar, or mattress.

Even though the currency in banks seems easy to obtain by withdrawing it from some account, it is not counted as being in circulation. Furthermore, counting the currency in commercial banks and checking accounts would involve double counting. When you obtain $100 in cash by cashing a $100 check, the checking account portion of M_1 goes down by $100 and currency in circulation goes up by $100. M_1 does not change. If, prior to your writing the check, M_1 were to include both the $100 in the bank vault and the $100 in your checking account, M_1 would be $100 too high. We cannot have it both ways.

Checking accounts require no explanation except that they are called **demand deposits** by the banks, an indication that the banks must deliver a depositor's checking account to the depositor instantly upon the depositor's demand. (Savings accounts, which are not included in M_1, are usually called savings deposits when held by individuals and, sometimes, "time deposits" when held by businesses, because the bank can take time, if it wishes, to fulfill the depositor's request for the business firm's money.)

Other Measures of Money

The intent of the definition of M_1 is to describe the purchasing power that is instantly available to the public without borrowing (without using credit cards, charge accounts, overdrawn checking accounts, and the like) and without having to convert time deposits or other financial assets (stocks, securities, insur-

---

*In recent years, in addition to commercial banks, many financial institutions like credit unions and savings banks have been given the right by law to have checking accounts. M_2 includes all of these accounts—in fact, every account from which the account holder can make withdrawals by an "instrument" (check) payable to someone else. (At this writing, there is still one exception: Money market funds, on which checks can be written, are not included in M_1. They are included in M_2. See Table 18-1.)

Table 18-1. M_1, M_2, M_3, and L as of June 1982 (in billions of dollars)

M_1	
Coins in circulation (approx.)	$ 13.0
Paper money (Federal Reserve Notes) in circulation	120.0
Total currency in circulation	$ 133.0
Demand deposits (checking accounts)	319.0
Total M_1	$ 452.0
M_2	
M_1 plus "small" savings accounts less than $100,000 and money market funds	$1,908.0
M_3	
M_2 plus "large" savings accounts over $100,000	$2,295.0
L (estimate)	
M_3 plus commercial paper, U.S. accounts in foreign banks, and government securities	$2,800.0

Source: Federal Reserve Bulletin, August 1982, Table 1.21.

ance policies, and so forth) into cash. Other official measures of the money supply are designated as M_2, M_3, and L. Table 18-1 breaks down M_1 into three components and then shows the totals for M_2, M_3, and L. (Don't add them all together because M_2 includes M_1; M_3 includes M_2, and L includes M_3.)

Table 18-1 illustrates a point to keep in mind: The importance of demand deposits in our society and in M_1. As of June 1982, demand deposits were 71 percent of M_1, with currency in circulation making up the other 29 percent. The fact that demand deposits compose 71 percent of M_1 is especially important. The Federal Reserve System has little direct control over the amount of currency in circulation, but it can change at will the 71 percent of the money supply that constitutes demand deposits. Consequently, our discussion of monetary policy will emphasize changes in the demand-deposit component of M_1.

Credit

Before we continue, we must point out a distinction between money, as we have defined the term, and credit. The term **credit** (which means "I trust" in Latin) refers to a creditor's belief that a borrower will repay a loan. Consequently, credit appears on the scene anytime anyone is given an obligation to repay a loan, credit-card balance, or charge account, by someone else, the creditor.

In Chapter 17 you saw the gigantic extent of public and private debt in the United States. This indebtedness is a mountain of credit, involving someone's belief that someone else will pay. Owners of government securities believe the government (taxpayers) will pay. Private lenders to corporations and individuals believe their loans will be paid.

And loans can cause M_1 to grow. When you borrow money from a bank, to pay for a car, for example, the bank will usually add the amount of the loan to your checking account. By doing so, the bank has created credit in the form of increased funds in your checking account (your demand deposit), which will add to M_1. This is one way M_1 can grow.

HOW THE BANKS CAN CREATE MONEY

The key to creation of money by the banks is their ability to lend out some of the money that is deposited in them.

Let us assume that you deposit $1,000 in a commercial bank and ask for a demand deposit in that amount. The bank gives you a checkbook showing that you have $1,000 in a demand-deposit account and puts the money in what is called its *reserve account.*

As long as the money sits in the reserve account, it earns no interest for the bank. But banks are privately owned corporations that are in business to make money. The bank is eager to put as much money as it can immediately into some form of financial investment that earns interest. In modern economies, banks operate under what is called a **fractional reserve system**. They are legally required to keep only a fraction of their reserves. The Board has the power (within limits set by Congress) to select the specific percentage of demand deposits the banks must keep at all times. That portion of their reserves that the banks must keep is called **required reserves**.

How the Fractional Reserve System Works

In the following example of how banks create money, we will assume that the required reserve percentage for all banks is 10 percent of demand deposits. This means that, whether demand deposits go up or down, the bank must keep a minimum of 10 percent* of demand deposits in reserves. But it can lend money out (create credit) or buy stocks or bonds with the other 90 percent and thereby earn interest income.

Let us assume that Jane Pennyworth wants to borrow some money from the bank where you deposited the $1,000. We will call your bank Bank A.

How much can your bank lend? With a deposit of $1,000, it must keep $100 (10 percent) in reserves, but it can lend out the other $900. The amount that the bank can lend over and above its required reserve is called **excess reserves**.

The Banks Lend Money

Now let us assume that Bank A wants to lend its excess reserves of $900 and that Jane qualifies for a loan of this amount for the purchase of chicken feed. (In the real world, the bank would rarely lend out all of its excess reserves.)

We shall now assume that Jane wishes to have the loan in the form of a demand deposit (checking account). Bank A is happy to oblige.

Now the point. When Jane receives her $900 loan in the form of a demand deposit, demand deposits increase by $900 and thus the money supply also increases by $900. M_1 has increased by $900 because your $1,000 demand deposit is still there. Amazingly enough, a commercial bank *creates money out of thin air* when it makes a loan.

What happens when Jane buys the feed with the $900? We shall assume that she pays Jake's Grain and Feed with a check for $900. Jake deposits the check, we shall assume, in a bank other than Bank A, called Bank B.

Now what happens? Bank B sends the check to the nearest Federal Reserve District Bank. The District Bank keeps an accounting of all reserves held by member banks in its district. Accordingly, the District Bank will add $900 to Bank B's reserves and subtract $900 from Bank A's reserves.

---

*Required reserves of 10 percent are fairly close to real-world requirements, as you will see on page 364.

After the District Bank completes its calculation of each member bank's reserves, the canceled check is returned to Bank A and eventually finds its way back to Jane in her bank statement. The processing of the check by the Federal Reserve System is called check clearing. Whenever a check is cleared, the bank against which it is drawn loses reserves; the bank in which it is deposited gains reserves.

What has happened to the money supply? It has still increased by $900. The $900 is no longer in Bank A but is now in Bank B.

Now let us repeat the process. How much can Bank B lend out of the $900? It must keep 10 percent of the $900 in reserves, or $90. It therefore has excess reserves of $810 ($900 minus $90) that it can lend out. We shall pretend that it lends $810 to a Mrs. Stevens.

When Bank B lends the $810 to Mrs. Stevens, the money supply (M_1) increases by another $810. Note that Jake still has Jane's $900 to spend. And in addition to the $900 available to Jake, $810 is available for Mrs. Stevens.

Keep in mind that M_1 equals the currency in circulation *plus* demand deposits. The demand-deposit portion of M_1 has increased by $900 plus $810, or $1,710. It all happened because Banks A and B could create credit.

Now let us assume that Mrs. Stevens uses her $810 loan to buy a rowboat and an outboard and the boat dealer has an account with still another bank, Bank C. When the boat dealer deposits Mrs. Stevens' check for $810 in Bank C, the process can be repeated again. Bank C has to keep 10 percent of the $810, or $81, but the remaining $729 ($810 minus $81) are excess reserves. Bank C can lend out the $729. If it does, M_1 goes up by $729.

The Deposit Multiplier

You can see that your original $1,000 can result in at least three loans—$900 to Jane, $810 to Mrs. Stevens, and $729, assuming Bank C decides to lend it. We have a chain reaction going, just like the spending chain back in Chapter 16. The only difference is that this time it is a lending chain. In short, we have *another* multiplier.

We called the multiplier in Chapter 16 the spending multiplier. It showed how GNP could increase or decrease by a multiple of a change in spending. This time we are involved with a change in M_1. M_1 can change by a multiple of an initial change in deposits.

We call this multiplier the **deposit multiplier**. Here's a definition: *The deposit multiplier is the multiple by which demand deposits (in all banks) increase or decrease following an initial change in demand deposits.* The formula for the deposit multiplier is:

Deposit multiplier = 1 ÷ the required reserve expressed as a decimal

Thus, in our example where the required reserve is 10 percent, the deposit multiplier is:

Deposit multiplier = 1 ÷ 0.10 = 10.

When the deposit multiplier is 10, demand deposits will rise by ten times the first deposit. Table 18-2 shows the final totals, assuming that all banks act the way Banks A, B, and C did.

What about the effect on M_1? When you deposited your $1,000 in Bank A, the net effect on M_1 was zero, because the increase in Bank A's deposits was can-

Table 18-2. The Deposit Multiplier in Operation

Bank	Demand deposit portion of M_1	Loans	Reserves
A	$1,000	$ 900	$ 200
B	900	810	90
C	810	729	81
Subtotal	$2,710	$2,439	$ 271
All other banks	7,290	6,561	729
Final totals	$10,000	$9,000	$1,000

celled out by the withdrawal of $1,000 from currency in circulation. Thus, we cannot count the deposit of $1,000 in Bank A as part of the $10,000 increase. The net increase is actually $9,000, all of it the result of bank loans.

If, however, the $1,000 had been deposited in Bank A in some manner that *did not subtract from the existing money supply*, then we could call the entire $10,000 a net increase in M_1.

As we shall see, the Board of Governors of the Federal Reserve System has a way of doing just that. The new deposit does not involve a check drawn on any bank, nor does it involve the deposit of currency.

Contracting the Money Supply

The money supply can also contract by a multiple of a withdrawal. Suppose Bank A has made its $900 loan to Jane. Having done so, Bank A has no more money to lend. Its excess reserves are gone. Its reserves are down to the minimum the Board of Governors allows. Bankers would say Bank A is "loaned up." Now suppose someone comes along and insists on withdrawing any amount of money.

The only currency (cash) Bank A has in its reserve account is $100. All other monies are out on loan. If Bank A hands over any money, its reserves will be below the required minimum.

Consequently, Bank A will have to sell some of its assets (for example, some stocks and bonds), or it will have to allow some loans to mature without re-lending the money.

Suppose now that the people who buy these assets or repay loans write checks on other banks to pay Bank A. Then these other banks will lose demand deposits, and when the checks are cleared the other banks will lose reserves in those amounts, too.

The first withdrawal can start a chain of withdrawals from demand-deposit accounts resulting in a chain of losses from bank reserves. If the first withdrawal happens to be $1,000, all the numbers in Table 18-2 become negative. The final changes are −$10,000 in demand deposits, −$9,000 in loans, and −$1,000 in reserves.

As you might guess, the Board of Governors of the Federal Reserve System has a way of starting the withdrawal process. The Board has a way of taking money out of the banks in such a way that the money is *not deposited in any bank*. Consequently, such withdrawals have the effect of letting some of the M_1 evaporate into "thin air." M_1 will shrink by a multiple of the Board's withdrawal. In conclusion, any action the Board takes to expand or contract M_1 will be multiplied by the deposit multiplier.

The Deposit Multiplier in the Real World

We picked a required reserve of 10 percent because that figure approximates the required reserve for large banks in the real world. Therefore, according to the deposit-multiplier formula, the deposit multiplier should be 10 (1 ÷ .10 = 10). But in the real world, the deposit multiplier is only about 3. Consequently, if the Board initiates a change of $1 billion in M_1, the final change in demand deposits will not be $10 billion; the change will be "only" about $3 billion. (The reduction from 10 to 3 reminds us of the reduction in the spending multiplier caused by the automatic stabilizers.) In this case, two major factors reduce the deposit multiplier:

1. The borrowing and spending in Table 18-2 assumed that each bank wants to lend out *all* the money it can. When the country is in a recession, and the risk of nonrepayment of loans rises, the banks may decide to "sit" on any extra money they receive and let excess reserves rise. Such actions reduce the amount received by each succeeding bank in the chain. The totals and the multiplier will be less to that extent.

2. The borrowing and spending in Table 18-2 assumed that all transactions were by check and that the checks were always deposited in another bank. After the check is deposited, the bank receiving the check also receives new reserves and can lend out most of the new reserves, thereby creating more new money. But, if anyone in the chain converts a check to cash, the chain may be interrupted, because the cash may remain in circulation. If the cash remains outside the banks, the banks can't use the money for additional loans.

Real-world data indicate that such "leakages" (in economic jargon) to cash have become increasingly common in recent years. Between 1974 and 1981, currency in circulation grew by 82 percent while demand deposits grew only 14 percent. One possible reason for the increasing need for cash: The need for an unrecorded means of payment in the underground economy (see page 246).

HOW THE FED IS ORGANIZED

Now we need to see how the Fed is organized; then we can see what the Board does to change M_1. Most industrial countries have a so-called *central bank*: the Bank of England, the Bank of France, the Deutsche Bundesbank of Germany, the Gosbank in the Soviet Union, the Nippon Ginko in Japan. These banks perform a variety of functions, such as issuing paper money, clearing checks, handling their government's checking account, assisting with international balance-of-payments problems, and supervising the operations of banks in their respective countries. In the United States, the Federal Reserve System District Banks are our central bank.

District Banks

The Federal Reserve Act of 1913 was adopted primarily with the support of the Progressive Party, which did not want control of our central bank to be subject to the influence of the financial giants of New York City or any eastern industrial city. Thus, they decided to divide the country into twelve Federal Reserve Districts, with a central bank in each one.

As the country grew in commercial complexity, the twelve District Banks found they needed help in other major cities within their districts, and gradual-

Figure 18-1.
The Federal Reserve System: boundaries of Federal Reserve Districts and their branch territories (Alaska and Hawaii are in District 12). (*Source: Federal Reserve Bulletin.*)

ly they acquired a total of twenty-four branches. Consequently, our central bank is now divided up into thirty-six parts sprinkled across the country. The map in Figure 18-1 shows the twelve districts, the twelve cities in which the main District Banks are located, and the cities where the branch banks are located.

The **Federal Reserve District Banks** in the Federal Reserve System are known as "bankers' banks." Individuals cannot borrow money there or open a checking account, but the District Banks perform many services (see the next section) for the commercial banks in their districts.

The System operates like a set of twelve clubs, in the sense that they are district associations to which member banks belong, but the District Banks also supervise the conduct of their members through bank examiners.

Membership in the System

The Federal Reserve System is organized in such a way that it has been called a quasi-public agency. Like any corporation, a commercial bank is owned by stockholders. Upon joining the System, the member commercial banks are required to buy stock in their respective district banks equal to 3 percent of the money stockholders have invested in the member bank. Another 3 percent is subject to "call" from the Fed (a possible disadvantage of joining). However, member banks receive dividends from the profits of the System, up to a maximum of 6 percent of their invested capital. Profits earned by the System in excess of 6 percent are turned over to the U.S. Treasury.

The Federal Reserve System therefore rests on a foundation of private ownership, with private stockholders owning stock in member banks and member banks owning stock in the District Banks. To supervise the system, however, there is a seven-member Board of Governors appointed by the U.S. President. Thus, the System is both public and private in character.

Because the Federal Reserve Act is federal legislation, it could and did require that all commercial banks chartered by the federal government join the System. Any commercial bank with the word "national" in its name belongs to the Federal Reserve System. However, the banks chartered by the states have the option of joining or not joining, as they please.*

The Board of Governors

The **Board of Governors** of the Fed is composed of seven people whose backgrounds may be in finance, industry, commerce, or agriculture. In practice, they are usually in some area of finance. They are usually appointed by the President of the United States for a fourteen-year term. Consequently, several Board members may represent the political views of a previous President and a political party different from that of the current President. The fourteen-year terms are staggered so that every two years a Board member retires and a new one is appointed.

Coordinate Bodies of the Board

In carrying out its policies, the Board is assisted by the Federal Advisory Council and the **Federal Open Market Committee**. The Council, which consists of twelve members, one from each district, helps to provide the Board of Governors with data to guide its decision making.

The Open Market Committee is composed of the seven members of the Board of Governors and five presidents of District Banks. The president of the New York City District Bank is a permanent member. The other four presidents serve annually and are elected by presidents of the other eleven District Banks in such a way that different areas of the country are represented. The committee's power is thus divided between the Board of Governors and the presidents of the District Banks, but the seven-member Board constitutes a majority of the twelve-member Committee. As we shall see later in the chapter, the activities of the Open Market Committee are the Board's most important instrument for changing M_1.

The Board has a close relationship with each of the twelve District Banks. The president and vice-president of each District Bank are appointed subject to approval by the Board of Governors. Having approval of these appointments enhances the overall power of the Board and helps to improve the channels of communication with each of the Districts. Figure 18-2 illustrates the organization of the system.

Functions of the Fed

Aside from the methods the Board uses to control M_1, the Fed issues our paper money, called **Federal Reserve Notes**. It handles the check-clearing mechanism** not only within each district but across the country through the **Interdistrict Settlement Fund**. In so doing, the Fed not only handles the bookkeeping involved in adding to and subtracting from reserves as checks are cleared, but it keeps most member banks' reserves in its possession. We do so much of our business by check that the commercial banks need keep only about 2 percent of their demand deposits on their premises in the form of cash (called "vault cash" or "till money"). The rest is kept by the Fed. This proce-

---

*Prior to 1980, a commercial bank was defined as a bank holding checking accounts. But as you will see, many types of financial institutions now hold checking accounts, and so the term commercial bank no longer has much meaning.

**All banks now, whether members of nonmembers of the System, have equal access to the Fed's check-clearing services.

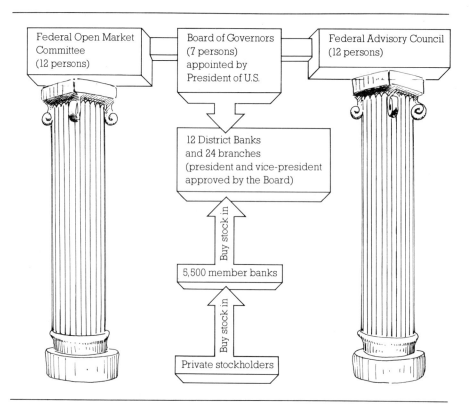

Figure 18-2.
Organization of the
Federal Reserve
System.

dure helps the Fed keep track of reserves, provides much more physical safety for the money, and enables the Fed to sort the money continuously for counterfeit or worn-out bills.

Whether a bank's reserves are on their own premises in the form of till money or on deposit with the Fed, they belong to the member bank and jointly serve to determine the bank's reserve position relative to the required minimum.

The Fed acts as an agent for the federal government by (1) handling the sales of *new* government securities issued by the Treasury (for the purpose of deficit financing), (2) issuing currency, and (3) holding some of the Treasury's deposits.

Deposit Insurance

All members of the System are required to buy insurance from the **Federal Deposit Insurance Corporation (FDIC)**, which insures each demand deposit and time deposit in commercial banks up to $100,000.* The banks pay an insurance premium equal to one-twelfth of 1 percent of their deposits for this insurance. Nonmember banks also buy this insurance. Almost 99 percent of all deposits in commercial banks are covered by FDIC insurance. Because of public confidence in FDIC, a bank panic or a run on a bank of the kind that was so common during the Depression is now considered improbable. Savings and

---

*If your demand deposit or savings accounts total more than $100,000, you can set up other accounts in your spouse's name or jointly with your spouse or a relative and so cover all of your deposits with insurance.

loan institutions also insure deposits up to $100,000 per depositor with the Federal Savings and Loan Insurance Corporation (FSLIC).

Recent Strains on the System

The Board's primary monetary-policy function is to control the purchasing power of the public. Prior to the 1970s, that purchasing power *was* largely under the control of the Board. The Board held the reins because the Board controlled the banks that held checking accounts.

But during the 1970s, the Board lost some of this control for three major reasons:

1. Before the 1970s, only banks designated as commercial banks could have demand deposits (checking accounts). Savings banks were barred from this action. But during the 1970s, savings banks, mainly in New England, began offering so-called NOW accounts. (NOW stands for *n*egotiable *o*rder of *w*ithdrawal.) This device enabled savers to write an "order" to pay a third party from their savings accounts. Any piece of paper that performs that function is in fact a check. And so, increasingly, the savings banks were offering *interest-earning* checking accounts. The commercial banks, however, were prohibited by law from offering interest on *their* checking accounts. The commercial banks lost some depositors to the savings banks, and when the money left the commercial banks, it disappeared from M_1 and went to an institution that was not under the Board's control.

2. Increasingly, demand deposits in commercial banks became a poor measure of the public's purchasing power. Installment buying with credit cards increased. And the banks attracted new customers by offering overdraft accounts (often called "check-loan" accounts) as well as procedures whereby depositors could quickly switch funds from saving to checking accounts and back to saving—all so the depositor could earn some interest on money normally held in checking accounts. In addition, the rise of money market funds enabled the public to switch funds back and forth, in and out of demand deposits, to or from interest-earning accounts. (Money market funds enabled small depositors to earn high rates of interest previously available only to savers with accounts of $100,000 or more held for stipulated times. The money funds combined deposits from many small savers—$500 or more—into large blocks to purchase these large CDs, or certificates of deposit, and deducted a small management fee. To combat the outflow, banks eventually received legal permission to offer a similar service.) With all the switching going on, how could the Board tell *what* M_1 was, or *where* it was?

3. The final blow was that the Federal Reserve System was losing members. At a time when the required reserve was 16.5 percent for large member banks, nonmember banks in some states were permitted to maintain required reserves against demand deposits of as little as 6 percent. Such banks had much greater opportunities for profit because they could invest as much as 94 percent of their depositors' money. Although these banks are extreme examples, the required reserves of nonmember banks were, on the average, 2 or 3 percent less than for member banks—an important advantage in finding extra profit.*

---

*When Chicago's Oak Park Trust and Savings Bank withdrew its $9 million reserves from the System in May 1979, its earnings rose in 1979 by $300,000. See *Time*, 9 January 1980, p. 90.

At the end of 1982 there were about 15,000 commercial banks in the United States, of which 5,500 belonged to the Fed. One might think that the Federal Reserve Club was of no great consequence because its membership accounted for only 37 percent of all U.S. banks. However, the banks that did belong were evidently relatively large banks: about 70 percent of all demand deposits in the United States were deposited with them.

But the Fed was worried. Back in 1950, there had been 6,873 members; each year, more banks left the system. Chairman of the Board Paul A. Volcker told the Senate Banking Committee on February 4, 1980, that during 1979, 69 banks had left the System with total deposits of $7 billion. He expressed concern that the System's membership might decline to the point where monetary management would be "seriously disrupted." Finally, on March 31, 1980, Congress solved the Fed's problem by passing the **Depository Institutions Deregulation and Monetary Control Act of 1980**.

The Depository Institutions Deregulation and Monetary Control Act of 1980

The Monetary Control Act is a landmark in the field of banking. The purpose of the Act was not only to solve the Fed's problems but to "deregulate" the banking industry.[1] Henceforth, the sharp distinctions between commercial banks, savings banks, and even credit unions would blur and perhaps disappear. Each of these banking sectors was allowed by the Act to compete harder for the other sector's business. The major provisions of the Act are:

1. The Act brings under the Board's control all banking institutions holding what the Act called "transactions accounts" except those institutions that manage money-market funds. A transactions account is a deposit from which the depositor can make a withdrawal by a "transferable instrument" (check) payable to third persons. In addition to the commercial banks already in the system, this provision gave the Board control of savings and loan institutions and credit unions with checking accounts, and of nonmember commercial banks.

2. The Act specifies required reserves for all institutions holding transactions accounts. For small banks with deposits under $25 million (a figure to be gradually increased), required reserves of 3 percent are specified; for larger banks, 12 percent. The 12 percent figure is reasonably close to the 10 percent figure used in our explanation of the deposit multiplier. The Board is allowed to vary this figure between 8 and 14 percent, and "in extraordinary circumstances" it can increase the reserve requirement for both large and small banks by as much as 4 percent. By making reserve requirements uniform, the Act immediately wiped out any advantage in being a nonmember of the Federal Reserve System. And, in 1982, six state banks joined the System.

3. The Act establishes a committee* that is instructed to phase out interest rate ceilings in a six-year period for all types of deposits carried by the financial institutions covered by the Act. This provision is especially significant because it allows the banks and credit unions to compete for the public's savings on a more equal basis among themselves, and, in particular,

---

*Called the Depository Institutions Deregulation Committee; composed of the Secretary of the Treasury and the chiefs of the Federal Reserve Board, Federal Deposit Insurance Corporation, Federal Home Loan Bank Board, and the National Credit Union Administration.

to compete for the public's money that has been going to money market mutual funds. In December 1982, the Committee invaded the money funds' province by allowing the banks to pay unrestricted interest rates on checking accounts with minimum balances over $2,500 and on savings accounts over that same figure.* Thereafter, the battle for the public's money would become intense.

When competition is intense, prices (in this case interest rates) offered by competitors tend to become uniform. The more uniform they become, the less reason depositors have to shift funds from one institution to another. And with all of these institutions offering interest on checking accounts, the public would have less reason to switch funds back and forth between checking and saving accounts or to or from money market fund accounts.

Thus we can see the broad intentions of the Act. The Act increased the power and scope of authority of the Board and made the rules of the game the same for all the players. And the Act tried to make M_1 easier to measure by reducing the public's incentives to switch money from one type of account to another.

MONETARY POLICY: WHAT THE FEDERAL RESERVE BOARD DOES TO INFLUENCE AGGREGATE DEMAND

As you will see very shortly, the Federal Reserve Board does *not* change M_1 directly; the Board does so indirectly by changing bank reserves. When the banks lend and relend the money that the Board adds** to their reserves, the deposit multiplier goes into action, and M_1 changes by a multiple of the change in bank reserves. Thus, if the Board wants to give the economy a boost, it will increase bank reserves on the theory that such an increase will give the banks more money to lend, which will then tend to lower interest rates, which in turn will tend to stimulate more borrowing and spending by business firms. Such a policy is called an **easy-money policy**. If, on the other hand, the Board wants to cool the economy in times of inflation, the Board will reduce bank reserves, depriving the banks of money to lend, causing interest rates to rise and borrowing and spending to decline. Such a policy is called **tight money**.

The Board has three methods, called *quantitative controls*, at its disposal for lowering or raising bank reserves: (1) Through its participation in the decisions of the Open Market Committee, called *open-market operations*, and through direct control of (2) the discount rate, and (3) the required reserve. These measures are called quantitative controls because they all act on total bank reserves.

The Board can also exercise a variety of so-called selective or qualitative controls. For example, it can determine down payments (called *margin requirements*) that we must make when we buy stock in the stock market. And, it can exert informal pressure on bankers through what is called *moral suasion*. Moral suasion can also refer to the powerful effects speeches by Board mem-

---

*Up to this point the money market funds had had a clear advantage: They required relatively low minimum balances and paid higher interest than the banks were allowed to pay. After the Committee's action, the money funds were at some disadvantage, because their deposits (unlike those in the banks) were uninsured. But, the money market funds retained one advantage: They were not required to hold money in reserve. During 1982, the banks complained about this advantage, and future legislation could still wipe it out.

**We're assuming the Board adds to reserves here. The Board can reduce reserves just as easily.

bers (usually the Chairman of the Board) have on public attitudes. When a Board chairman says, "Tight money is coming," business executives listen and react accordingly.

Open-Market Operations

By far the most important and frequent method of changing bank reserves is **open-market operations**—the buying and selling of government securities in the open market by the Board's Open Market Committee. Government securities in the *open market* are securities that have already been sold by the U.S. Treasury to individuals, corporations, banks, or insurance companies and are owned by someone in the private economy. They are to be distinguished from new government securities purchased from the Treasury. Thus, open-market operations are the buying and selling of government securities held by people or institutions in the private economy. Once in the private economy, many of these so-called marketable government securities change hands. They are bought and sold at prices that fluctuate around the face value of the security, depending on the forces of demand and supply. We can trace the effects of open-market operations on the economy via a series of steps.

The Open Market Committee Decides the Economy Needs a Boost to Reduce Unemployment

- Step 1. The Committee will buy government securities in the "open market." We'll assume the committee's decision is to buy $1 billion worth of $10,000 Treasury bills.
- Step 2. The Committee looks at the fluctuating price of these securities in the open market, which might be $9,500 each,* and offers to buy $1 billion worth at a price of $9,600 each.
- Step 3. The Committee makes the offer** to a select group of stock and bond brokers who specialize in very large transactions. If the brokers were not successful in getting owners of securities to sell to the Fed, the Committee would offer a price higher than $9,600, but we'll assume that the brokers do find sellers.
- Step 4. The Committee buys the $1 billion worth of Treasury bills and pays the brokers for them. The brokers give the securities to the Committee and pay the sellers with the Fed's money. Where does the Fed get the money for this purchase? The fascinating answer is that the Fed does not get it from *anywhere*. It simply writes checks amounting to $1 billion on itself. These checks are not written on any checking account. (It is just as if you wrote a check with no money in the bank.)
- Step 5. When the checks are received by the brokers, the brokers deposit the checks in their banks.
- Step 6. The banks send the checks to the Federal Reserve Banks for "clearance."
- Step 7. The District Banks honor the checks by adding the amount of the checks to each bank's reserves. (Why would the Fed honor the checks?

---

*We are using short-term Treasury bills here as an example. The Treasury promises to pay the owner the full $10,000 at time of maturity, but the bill is sold at a discount. The difference between the discounted price and the bill's face value determines the bill's interest rate (which can fluctuate).

**We are overlooking an organizational detail. The actual buying and selling is done by the "Trading Desk" of the New York District Bank. The Open Market Committee sets the policy.

Table 18-3. Multiplier Effect of the Open Market Committee's Purchase of $1 Billion Worth of Treasury Bills (in millions)

Banks	Demand deposits	Loans	Reserves
A's (first round)	+ $ 1,000	+ $ 900	+ $ 100
B's (second round)	900	810	90
C's (third round)	810	729	81
Subtotals	$2,710	$2,439	$ 271
All other banks	7,290	6,561	729
Totals	$10,000	$9,000	$1,000

The Fed wrote them in the first place!) Consequently, the initial effect of a $1 billion open market purchase is an increase in bank reserves of $1 billion.

■ Step 8. Now that the banks have $1 billion in new reserves, they will lend some of the money out. Assume again as in Table 18-2 that the reserve requirement is 10 percent. Table 18-3 shows what happens.

In Table 18-3 we see the final effect of the Open Market Committee's action. The purchase of $1 billion is deposited in the Bank A's. As they lend 90 percent of the money, it is deposited in Bank B's, which relend 90 percent of the amount they receive, and so forth. The final change in demand deposits (and in M_1) is $10 billion, ten times the original transaction by the Open Market Committee. But remember that the real-world deposit multiplier is 3. Table 18-3 somewhat overstates reality. In the real world, M_1 will increase by $3 billion.

In Table 18-2, the cash deposited in the Bank A's caused no immediate change in M_1 because the cash was traded for a demand deposit. But in Table 18-3, in the case of open-market purchases, the $1 billion deposited in the Bank A's is a net addition to M_1 of $1 billion ($1,000 million). After the banks lend and relend these new deposits, M_1 will increase by $10 billion, assuming that the banks lend out all they can and that there are no leakages to cash.

Note in Table 18-3 that bank reserves go up by $1 billion. Consequently, economists often say that the Treasury bills were paid for by increasing bank reserves. In whatever way you think about it, remember that the securities were paid for *without drawing a check* on any bank account. When the Open Market Committee's checks arrived, they were new additions to M_1.

What happens to interest rates? Assuming that the demand for loans does not change, interest rates should fall, because the banks now have excess reserves to lend. In Figure 18-3 the supply curves represent the supply of M_1 before and after the securities purchase; D represents the demand for loans and/or money. The supply curves of money slope up from left to right under the theory that people will deposit more money in the banks as the interest rate rises—thus increasing the quantity of money available for loans. The increase in M_1 shifts supply to the right by $3 billion (using the real-world deposit multiplier of 3) from a hypothetical supply of $450 billion to $453 billion. Given no change in demand, interest rates will fall from, we will assume, 14 percent to 12 percent. The fall in interest rates will presumably stimulate borrowing and spending. If spending *does* increase, GNP will rise by a multiple of the change in spending,

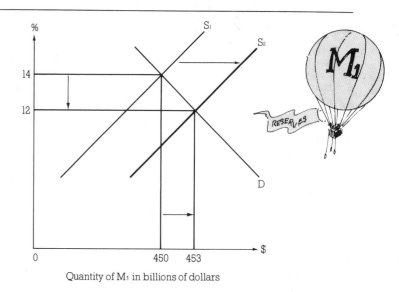

Figure 18-3.
Interest rates fall as
reserves and M_1
increase.

owing to the *spending multiplier.* (The deposit multiplier has caused M_1 to change by a multiple of the Open Market Committee's transaction.) The original goal—the reduction of unemployment—should come to pass as a result of the Committee's purchase of Treasury bills in the open market.

The Open Market Committee Decides to Slow the Economy Down to Reduce Inflation

If the Open Market Committee is worried about inflation, it can reverse the whole process by selling government securities in the open market. How will it get people to buy? It will sell a $10,000 security at an attractive price; say, $9,300. When the Open Market Committee sells, some of M_1 and bank reserves will vanish into thin air because demand deposits go down when the buyers of the securities write checks to pay the Fed and the Fed reduces bank reserves as the checks are cleared.*

As bank reserves decline, the banks have to sell assets and reduce loans to maintain required reserves, and M_1 declines by a multiple of the securities sale by the Open Market Committee. If the Open Market Committee sells $1 billion in securities, member bank reserves and the Fed's holding of government securities will both drop by $1 billion, but M_1 will drop $3 billion, assuming a real-world deposit multiplier of 3.

Thereafter, interest rates will tend to rise because the banks have less money to lend. The check writing by securities buyers causes reserves to drop, and particularly excess reserves to drop. The money supply curve shifts to the left. Assuming no change in demand, interest rates will rise. The banks will become more selective about whom they lend money to. The rise in interest rates will slow down spending (consumption and investment spending) by making loans

---

*This description is somewhat oversimplified. The Committee can dampen inflationary tendencies by *reducing* the *purchases* of government securities in the open market. The Committee does not actually have to *sell* them.

more expensive, and the economy will become less subject to inflation. If the Open Market Committee overreacts, aggregate demand may decline too much, and unemployment may rise.

Because the Open Market Committee is free to buy and sell as it chooses, and because its transactions are so frequent, its decisions must be delicate ones. Overreactions in either direction may have serious consequences.

Changing the Discount Rate

The second, and much less important, way of influencing bank reserves is by changing the **discount rate**—the rate of interest paid by banks* to the Fed when they borrow money from the Fed.

When a member bank that has loaned all of its excess reserves wishes to increase its interest income, it can present evidence of its ownership of loans, stocks or bonds, or other assets as security for a loan from the Fed. Provided that the Fed agrees to the loan, the member bank can lend out still more money with the money obtained from the loan.

Let us assume that the Fed decides to lend $1,000 to the member bank. The Fed may now engage in a common practice in lending—one that could happen to you. If you borrow $1,000 from your bank for one year at 15 percent interest, the bank may subtract (or discount) the 15 percent ($150) from your loan so that you receive only $850, but you must pay back $1,000. You actually pay 17.6 percent interest because you are paying $150 for the use of $850. This practice is called discounting, and the rate of interest actually charged (the 17.6 percent) is called the discount rate.**

The Board of Governors has the authority to determine the discount rate on the Fed's loans to member banks. By raising or lowering the discount rate, the Board can encourage or discourage borrowing by the member banks.

The discount rate is widely publicized, yet member-bank loans are small compared with the money supply. At any time, the Fed's loans to member banks amount to about $1 billion. In a money supply of about $500 billion, such loans amount to only one-fifth of one percent of the money supply. So the effect of the discount rate is largely political and psychological. To whatever extent changes in the discount rate affect excess reserves and the volume of loans, the deposit multiplier will again cause a change in M_1 that is a multiple of the initial change in borrowing by the banks.

You will also see many references to the **prime rate** in the newspapers. The prime rate is the interest rate that commercial banks charge their biggest and best borrowers—large corporations. If the prime rate is 12 percent, the chances are that you or any individual will have to pay at least 18 percent for a loan. The prime rate is determined by the demand for and the supply of money in the banks for large loans.

Changing the Required Reserve

Within the legal range, the Board of Governors is also free to choose the required minimum that member banks must keep in reserves. Changes in the required reserve within the legal range of 8 to 14 percent are considered very

---

*The Monetary Control Act extended this borrowing privilege to all nonmember banks, a possible reason why nonmember banks might now wish to join the System.

**The real-world discount rate in May 1983 was 8.5 percent. The 17.6 percent approximates the interest rate borrowers would pay for a *personal* loan.

strong medicine and occur very infrequently. It was once estimated that increasing required reserves by one-half of one percent would force banks to withdraw $500 million from circulation, resulting in a $1.5 billion (3 times $500 million) reduction in M_1. Between November 1972 and enactment of the Monetary Control Act, the required reserves were increased only five times, each time by less than 1 percent.

To sum up: If the Board of Governors wants to increase GNP, it will buy securities, and/or lower the discount rate, and/or lower the required reserve. If the Board wants to slow the economy down—to reduce inflation—it will sell securities, and/or raise the discount rate, and/or raise the required reserve.

Does Monetary Policy Work?

Just as fiscal policy has its problems (noted at the end of Chapter 16), monetary policy also has its problems. To focus on them, let's remember that monetary policy is based on the theory that (1) changes in bank reserves cause changes in bank lending and interest rates and (2) these changes in lending and interest rates change aggregate demand. The experts have noticed seven major problems with the theory:

1. The Board's performance in the past indicates that it has great difficulty in meeting its own objectives. For example, the Board announced in December 1982 that its open-market activities would permit M_1 to grow from about $475 billion to about $490 billion, and M_2 from about $1,950 billion to about $2,050 billion, during the following seven months. Instead, M_1 grew to about $515 billion, and M_2 to about $2,100 by July 1983. The *actual* increase in the two measures of the money supply was much higher than the Board's own goals permitted.

2. The Board has only partial control of interest rates. Interest rates, like any price, are determined by demand and supply. The Board can change supply but not demand.

3. Because of this problem, the Board's open market operations sometimes produce results that are the opposite of those intended. A decision to give the economy a boost by expanding bank reserves, for example, may at first lower interest rates. But if the change makes the business community more optimistic about the future, or more concerned about future inflation, demand for credit will increase, and interest rates will certainly rise. Everyone will want to borrow, to "beat the gun," before interest rates *do* rise. Thus the expectation that interest rates *may* rise will *cause* them to rise (a good example of a self-fulfilling prophecy). We have a paradox: A policy intended to lower interest rates may result in higher ones. Conversely, higher interest rates can eventually lead to reduced interest rates if the economy slows down as a result of tight money and if the demand for credit drops.

4. Interest rates *do* influence spending, but they are not *the* most important determinant of spending. Spending by business firms is influenced most of all by the prospect of future profit, not the interest rate. Spending by consumers is influenced most of all by feelings of optimism about their jobs, their future income and wealth, not the interest rate.

5. As the recession in 1980–1982 has shown us, monetary policy is a more powerful weapon for reducing aggregate demand than for increasing it. For example, in its desire to curb inflation, the Board severely cut the rate of

BOX ESSAY

Interest Rates Aren't Always What They Seem

As we saw in Chapter 15, any interest rate tries to do four things: (1) Reward the lender for giving up the use of money; (2) compensate the lender for any rise in prices that will reduce the purchasing power of his money when the loan is repaid; (3) cover the paperwork costs of making the loan, including checking the borrower's credit; and (4) give the lender something extra to cover the risk of non-repayment.

With (2) in mind, economists often speak of interest rates in two ways: (1) the "nominal" rate, and (2) the "real" rate. The nominal rate is the rate the bank quotes when you borrow, and it is the rate usually given in newspapers or official reports from the government. The "real" rate is the nominal rate *minus* the rate of infla-

tion as measured by the Consumer Price Index. The figure included here shows the behavior of the nominal rates on personal loans from 1978 to the first quarter of 1983.

The figure is interesting because it shows that the *nominal* prime has come down to roughly what it was in late 1978. But the *real* rate is still higher than all the years prior to 1981, and the nominal rate on personal loans is still very high.

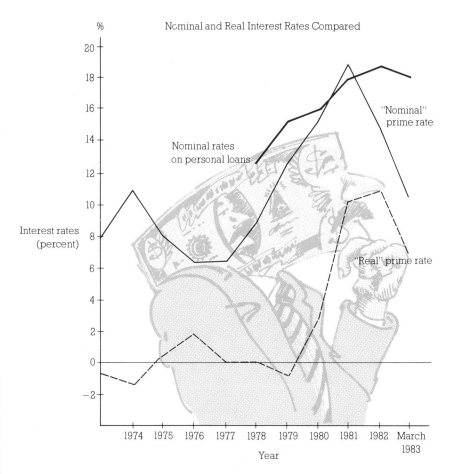

Nominal and Real Interest Rates Compared

Nominal rates on personal loans

"Nominal" prime rate

"Real" prime rate

Interest rates (percent)

Year

March 1983

Nominal and real interest rates compared. (*Source: Economic Report of the President, 1983;* "Big Rates for the Little Guys," *Time,* 4 April 1983.)

growth of M_1. From October 1981 to January 1982, the Board had been expansionary, allowing M_1 to grow at an annual rate of 15 percent per year. But in the first half of 1982, the M_1 growth rate dropped to less than 1 percent.[2] When their excess reserves were suddenly reduced, the banks made loans very hard to get, and interest rates reached record levels. Thousands of business firms failed and, as we have noted, unemployment reached the highest rates (10.8 percent) since the Depression of the 1930s.

Economists sometimes use the old saying "You can lead a horse to water, but you can't make him drink" to describe the one-sidedness of monetary policy. By that, they mean that a strong tight-money policy designed to raise interest rates (open-market sales of government securities, increased reserve requirements, and increased discount rates) will reduce member-bank reserves and M_1 and will slow down the economy. But, if the Board wants to give the economy a boost with an *easy* money policy (open market purchases, lower reserve requirements, and lower discount rates), it can increase bank reserves, but it cannot *force* the banks to lend the money. Particularly in a time of depression, the banks may want to be very conservative about lending money. Thus, monetary policy may be more effective as a contractionary than as an expansionary weapon.

6. Economists recognize that a tight-money policy may affect the economy unevenly, that it discriminates against particular industries such as the construction industry and especially against home building and buying. A tract developer typically operates on borrowed money, and the home buyer typically finances his or her purchase with a mortgage. Both the selling and buying ends of the business depend on borrowed money, and the interest rate becomes an important cost in the transaction.

Here's a quick example of what high interest rates mean to a home buyer. Assume an average single-family residence is priced at $100,000. Assume the buyer pays $20,000 down and obtains an $80,000 mortgage. At an interest rate of 18 percent, typical in mid-1982, the monthly payments will be $1,200 for 30 years. (Total payments are then $432,000.) Assuming the general rule that mortgage payments should be one third or less of the family's income, a family would have to earn over $40,000 per year to be eligible to buy an *average* house. In 1982, only 10 percent of all families qualified for such a house: a grim outlook.

7. Any change in U.S. monetary policy is bound to have international effects. Tight money and high interest rates will attract foreign deposits, thereby increasing the foreign exchange value of dollars relative to foreign currencies. This effect will make travel overseas attractive for Americans but will make all American products more expensive for foreigners to buy. The latter effect hurts our exports, now accounting for 13 percent of GNP, and causes layoffs in all the industries involved with selling goods and services overseas. We alluded to this problem back in Chapter 1 (see Figure 1-1).

SUMMARY

Monetary policy is the manipulation of the nation's money supply to influence aggregate demand. Money can be any generally accepted medium of exchange. There are several definitions for the money supply, but the most commonly used one is M_1, the total of all coins and paper money (Federal Reserve Notes) in circulation plus checking accounts. Checking accounts, called demand de-

posits, constitute about three quarters of M_1. Monetary policy is carried out through the activities of banks that hold checking accounts.

Banks are permitted to have fractional reserves, which means they can lend out a large fraction of the money deposited with them. In the process of lending, new checking accounts are created. The creation of deposits through loans adds to M_1. All banks together can increase M_1 by a multiple of any deposit that is not withdrawn from some other bank. This multiple, or deposit multiplier, is estimated to be about 3. If money is withdrawn, M_1 will collapse by a multiple of the withdrawal.

Only 37 percent of all commercial banks are members of the Federal Reserve System, but these banks hold about 70 percent of all demand deposits. The Federal Reserve System issues paper money, carries the federal government's checking accounts, handles the sale of government securities for the Treasury, supervises member banks, and clears their checks. The Federal Reserve System's Board of Governors, a seven-member board appointed by the President, runs the system.

The Depository Institutions Deregulation and Monetary Control Act was passed in 1980 to give the Board greater control of the money supply and to prevent banks from leaving the Federal Reserve System. The Act enables the Board to specify the same reserve requirements for all banks and removes ceilings from the interest rates banks pay to depositors. All banks are thereby made more competitive.

The Board uses three quantitative methods to change bank reserves—open-market operations, changes in the discount rate, and changes in the required reserve. If the Board wants to control inflation, it may sell government securities in the open market and/or raise the discount rate and the required reserve.

These measures are called tight-money policies. If the Board wants to give the economy a boost, it pursues easy-money policies by buying government bonds in the open market and/or lowering the discount rate and required reserve.

The Board's power is primarily controlled by its own integrity and by the Congressional prerogative to review Board policies every six months. Nevertheless, there have been many attempts to put the Board under the control of the executive branch.

Monetary policies may be more effective in reducing aggregate demand than in expanding it, and certain industries like housing may suffer more than others during periods of tight money.

Discussion Questions

1. How do commercial banks create money? If the reserve requirement were 100 percent, could the commercial banks create money? Can they create more money if the reserve requirement is 15 percent than if it is 20 percent? Why or why not?

2. Assume that a commercial bank has $1 million in demand deposits, that the reserve requirement is 20 percent, and that the bank actually has $350,000 in reserves. How much can the bank lend?

3. What happens to XYZ Bank's reserves if a depositor writes a $100 check and the check is deposited in QRS Bank? What happens to QRS's reserves?

4. How can banks pay off depositors in a fractional reserve banking system? (Answer in terms of the safety of deposits.)

5. Where does the Fed get the money to make open market purchases?

6. What effect does the U.S. Treasury have on monetary policy?

7. List all of the measures you would propose as a member of the Board of Governors in times of inflation. Explain why your proposals might or might not work.

8. Why might the policies of the Board of Governors be more effective when they are contractionary than when they are expansionary? Explain.

DID YOU EVER WONDER WHY ...

. . . it is possible for a bank robbery to increase the money supply?

References

1. Details are from *Congressional Quarterly*, 12 April 1980.

2. Milton Friedman, "An Aborted Recovery," *Newsweek*, 23 August 1982. See also *Economic Report of the President, 1983*, Table B-61.

18A

The Great Debate about Monetary Policy

KEY WORDS
Monetarists
Hyperinflation
Monetarist rule
Equation of exchange

This appendix is really a continuation of the great debate, first outlined in Chapter 15, between the classical economists and the followers of Keynes. Today, in connection with monetary policy, the classical view is maintained by a group of economists called the **monetarists**, while the Keynesian view is maintained by the neo-Keynesians. The monetarists tend to be politically conservative. They believe that monetary weapons to change aggregate demand are very powerful and that, consequently, the role of fiscal policy can be justifiably reduced. This conclusion naturally fits their desire to reduce the size of the federal government. The neo-Keynesians, on the other hand, usually argue that monetary policy is considerably less important in managing the economy than is fiscal policy. The debate between the two schools of thought centers on (1) the independence of the Board of Governors, and (2) the effectiveness of monetary policy.

THE INDEPENDENCE OF THE FEDERAL RESERVE BOARD

The ability of the Open Market Committee to create new money through open-market purchases raises a fascinating and important question. Now that the committee no longer has to pay any attention to the gold supply backing for the dollar, what prevents it from expanding M_1 by *any* amount? Instead of $1 or $2 billion, why not add $10 billion or a $100 billion? If the Open Market Committee wanted to, it could do just that, and we would soon be so flooded with new money that our money would become almost worthless, like German money after World War I and Hungarian money after World War II. A condition called **hyperinflation** (skyrocketing prices) would occur. This kind of inflation is so rapid it is hard for us to imagine. In the German inflation of the 1920s, prices went up so fast that factory workers were paid daily and given time off each morning to buy groceries before the prices went up (i.e., the Mark went down) at noon. The government was printing *trillion*-Mark notes.

There is no *legal* limitation on the Board's freedom to expand the money supply. When asked what did limit the Board's open-market purchases, the manager of a District Bank once told the author, "Only the integrity of the people on the Board." In other words, the Board can, if it wants to, increase the money supply by any amount. It can also *reduce* the money supply by any amount, and if it wanted to, it could create a severe recession.

There is no doubt that the Board has enormous power. Once in office, Board members are as immune from the influence of the President and his cabinet as are the Supreme Court justices. Only an Act of Congress can change the independence of the Board. And such independence was undoubtedly the intent of members of the Progressive Party who supported the Federal Reserve Act. They wanted to put the Board into a kind of political vacuum apart from the interests of bankers in the twelve districts and independent of political storms in Washington, D.C. Nevertheless, there is an occasional attempt by members of Congress to change the law and put control of the Board in the executive branch of government.

Former Chairman of the Board Arthur Burns, whose term of office was 1970 to 1978, gave this strong answer (perhaps with Watergate in mind) to those who wish to make such a change:

> I doubt that the American people would want to see the power to create money lodged in the Presidency—which may mean that it would in fact be exercised by political aides in the White House. Such a step would create a potential for political mischief or abuse on a larger scale than we have yet seen.[1]

Under the present system, making the Fed more subservient to the wishes of the President or the Congress is not easy, because the Fed doesn't depend on Congress for appropriations. Income from its own operations more than supports the system. In fact, the Fed annually turns over to the Treasury $5 to $7 billion in surplus funds. On the other hand, the Board is required, since 1978, to report semiannually to the Congress its targets for changes in the money supply. And the Open Market Committee makes public at each monthly meeting its operations for the previous thirty days.

Nevertheless, these gestures fail to satisfy some of the Fed's most influential critics. The recession of 1980–1982 raised the temperature of the argument because the Board's tight money policies during most of 1982 were blamed for creating the worst recession and the highest unemployment rates since the Great Depression.

Liberal economists like Lester C. Thurow and Robert Lekachman have argued* that the Fed should be part of the executive branch under the Secretary of the Treasury. In that organizational location, the Board chairman would have to obey the President's orders, and the President would be fully responsible for the Board's activities.

The monetarist-conservatives, led by Milton Friedman, believe that changes in the money supply are so powerful in determining changes in GNP and the level of employment that no one should have the power to tinker with the

---

*Thurow in *Newsweek*, 5 July 1982; Lekachman in the *Los Angeles Times*, 5 October 1982. Thurow once remarked that because we give the President the ultimate power to push the nuclear button, we ought to give him the power to supervise monetary policy.

Table 18A-1. Real GNP, M_1, and Consumer Prices (real GNP and M_1 in billions)

Year	Real GNP (1972 dollars)	M_1	Consumer Price Index
1970	$1,085.6	$216.5	116.3
1982	1,475.5	478.5	289.1
Percent change 1970-1982	+35.9%	+121 %	+148.6%

Source: Economic Report of the President (1983).

money supply. And moreover, they say, the Board of Governors has usually done the wrong thing at the wrong time.

THE MONETARIST'S CASE

The monetarists argue that the basic source of inflation is that the quantity of money grows faster than in output. Let's now present the monetarist case. What is the evidence? Table 18A-1 tends to show they are right.

The table clearly shows that, while real GNP (real output) grew about 36 percent from 1970 through 1982, M_1 grew more than three times as fast and prices increased more than four times as fast as real output. The monetarists seem to be right, and they blame the Board for inept management.

The Monetarist Rule

Here is what the monetarists prescribe: Let the Board take whatever quantitative measures are necessary to increase the money supply at a steady rate of 4 percent per year, in good times and bad—no deviations. (This monetarist prescription is called the **monetarist rule**. The 4 percent increase is based on the assumption that this is the increase in *real* GNP necessary to provide enough jobs for the new people entering the labor force plus those displaced by machines.) Thus, the monetarist position says, "Let the Board continue in its present role, but limit it to a goal that never changes."

Supporters of the monetarist view hold that the steady 4 percent growth in the money supply would act like a countercyclical governor on an engine— acting constantly to prevent it from slowing down too much (recession) or speeding up too much (inflation). Opponents of the monetarist view argue that depriving the Board of its power in this manner would prevent the Board from acting quickly during times of urgent need. The winter of 1976–1977 is a good example. Snowstorms in the Midwest and Northeast forced plants to close and increased unemployment. The same winter brought drought and threatened economic disaster to the West. During such times, the opponents would argue, the Board must be free to expand the money supply quickly via open-market purchases or reductions in required reserve.

THE KEYNESIANS VERSUS THE MONETARISTS

At this point, the outlines of this debate come sharply into focus: The monetarists tend to emphasize the role of money in managing the economy. The Keynesians tend to emphasize fiscal policy in managing the economy. If the monetarists are right, we don't need a big government playing discretionary fiscal games; the Board has all the weapons needed to tinker with the economy.

When confronted with what seems irrefutable monetarist evidence in Table

18A-1, we can imagine the Keynesians saying something like this: "The table doesn't prove a thing; if we look more closely at the numbers we find that money growth and inflation are not that closely linked. During the years 1978, 1979, and 1980, the money supply increased all right, but the rate of money-supply growth declined each year: 8.2 percent, 7.4 percent, and 6.5 percent, respectively. But during that period of declining money growth, the annual inflation rate *accelerated* from 7.6 percent to 11.3 percent to 13.5 percent. Not much of a connection."

"Not so fast!" say the monetarists. "The link between the money supply and inflation can be seen better by looking even more closely. The high rate of inflation in 1980 comes not from the 12-month money growth of 6.5 percent but from the fact that from May 1980 through October 1980, the money supply grew 16 percent!"

The preceding paragraph indicates what bothers the monetarists the most: an unstable money supply. Unstable monetary growth makes planning for the future difficult. No one wants to be caught short by inflation, and so business firms and banks hedge by keeping prices and interest rates high. One indication of the instability was the behavior of the prime rate. During the late 1950s and 1960s the prime rate changed about once a year. In the late 1970s it changed an average of once a month. In 1980 it changed almost forty times in one year. Professor Friedman's comment: "Unstable and rising monetary growth has been the major reason for the correspondingly unstable and even more rapidly rising inflation."[2]

The Equation of Exchange

The **equation of exchange** is another view of the argument between the monetarists and the Keynesians. The equation expresses a relationship between the money supply, the price level, and GNP. The equation looks like this:

$$MV = PQ$$

In macroecononomic terms, if M_1 is $500 billion and GNP is $3,000 billion, M_1 has to be re-spent six times to buy the $3,000 billion worth of goods and services that GNP represents. The number of times M_1 turns over to equal GNP is called the *income velocity* of money. It is abbreviated *V*.

Thus, $M_1 \times V$ = GNP. Notice that M_1V represents the willingness of people to spend money; therefore, M_1V is another way to measure *aggregate demand*.

GNP is also the sum of all prices times quantities. If we abbreviate the prices of everything as P and the quantities of everying produced as Q, then GNP = PQ. And because PQ represents the *value* of everything produced, PQ is another way to measure *aggregate supply*. And finally, therefore, the equation of exchange is a way to show that aggregate demand (M_1V) equals aggregate supply (PQ).

Let's translate the equation with a simple example: Pretend the whole economy produces only one product, $3,000 home computers. That's our price level, P. And now pretend that 1 billion of them are produced. That's Q. Thus, PQ = GNP. And if M_1 is $500 billion and V is 6, then M_1V also equals the GNP of $3,000 billion.

The equation is sometimes helpful in explaining inflation. Over the last 25 years, V has shown a tendency to increase from about 2 to 6. This means that people are willing to spend their money faster. An income velocity of 2 means that people will turn M_1 over twice a year, or every six months. If V is 6, M_1 turns over every two months.

On the average, the quantity of goods and services produced (Q) changes slowly—about 3 percent per year in real terms. Therefore, a double cause of inflation could exist: Prices will certainly increase if the money supply (M_1) *and* income velocity (V) increase faster than increases in the quantity of goods and services (Q) produced. When this combination of events occurs, economists say, "There is too much money chasing too few goods." Inflation is bound to occur.

But, again, the Keynesians and the monetarists argue about the equation. The monetarists tend to believe that V is relatively constant. If V is constant, then any change in M_1 will cause a proportionate change in PQ (GNP). Therefore, say the monetarists, changes in the money supply are *the* crucial factor in GNP changes.

The Keynesians argue that because V is a variable, changes in the money supply are not that important. If, for example, the Board tries to give the economy a boost by increasing the money supply, V could drop and nothing would happen. Abbreviated, the situation would be this: $M_1\uparrow V\downarrow$ = GNP (no change). To bolster their case, the Keynesians cite the rise in V from 2 to 6 over the years as well as declines in V during recessions.

But again, in rebuttal, the monetarists argue that the change from 2 to 6 was part of a long-run predictable trend. Thus, knowing the trend in V, the Board could still change GNP by changing the money supply.

But . . . but . . . but . . . the Keynesians counter with two more arguments:

1. Even small changes in *V, not in* M_1, can cause very large changes in GNP. If V changes by 10 percent, say, to 6.6 from 6.0, the change in GNP is $300 billion, from $3,000 billion ($500 billion [M_1] × 6) to $3,300 billion ($500 billion × 6.6).

2. While the monetarists argue that changes in the money supply change GNP, the Keynesians argue that the cause-and-effect relationship could run the other way. Changes in GNP caused by other than monetary changes (fiscal changes in taxes or government spending or changes in expectations) could cause changes in the money supply. When GNP declines, less borrowing and spending reduces the money supply by reducing money-creation by the banks. And vice versa; greater optimism increases borrowing, spending, and GNP. Money-creation by the banks increases. And so, the Keynesians argue, the cause-effect chain runs from GNP change to money supply change, not the reverse.

References

1. Arthur F. Burns, "The Independence of the Federal Reserve System," *Challenge*, July-August 1976, p. 23.

2. *Newsweek*, 20 August 1979.

19

Fighting the Problem of Stagflation

KEY WORDS
Stagflation
Phillips Curve
Accelerationist view
Natural rate of unemployment
Discomfort Index
Tax-based incomes policy
    (TIP)
Laffer Curve
Rational expectations
The "rules" approach

T his chapter—the last of the chapters about macroeconomic theories and problems—concerns our most perplexing difficulty: how to have full employment without inflation. The difficulty is that fiscal and monetary efforts to reduce unemployment tend to be inflationary; fiscal and monetary efforts to reduce inflation tend to increase unemployment. And in the last ten years or so, inflation and unemployment rates have *both* increased.

The appearance of high prices plus high rates of unemployment that has characterized our economy in recent years is called **stagflation** to indicate a combination of stagnation and inflation. The discussion of stagflation is divided into two sections: (1) A description of the disease and (2) some possible cures.

A DESCRIPTION OF THE DISEASE

One of the most provocative ideas in economics is that there is a trade-off between inflation and unemployment. The idea is that we can reduce unemployment by increasing aggregate demand, but that will increase the rate of inflation. Or we can reduce the rate of inflation by reducing aggregate demand, but that will increase unemployment.

The Phillips Curve: Trading Inflation for Unemployment— or the Reverse

Our recognition of the trade-off comes from a study of British wages and unemployment rates between 1861 and 1957 published in 1958 by British economist A. W. Phillips. Phillips showed that wages rose when unemployment rates were low and fell when unemployment rates rose. Because wage rates often determine production costs and prices, economists in this country soon adopted the practice of using Phillips' idea to show an inverse relationship between average annual inflation rates and unemployment rates.

The trade-off between inflation rates and unemployment rates is illustrated by a curve called the **Phillips Curve**. An imaginary Phillips Curve is shown in Figure 19-1 on the next page.

Point A on the curve shows that we could have zero unemployment, but the rate of inflation would be a horrendous 16 percent. At the other extreme, point D shows that we could have a zero inflation rate, but the rate of unemployment would be a horrendous 20 percent. Points B and C are intermediate points. At point C, things are better than at point D—in fact about what they were in 1976. The inflation rate is 6.4 percent, but the unemployment rate is 8 percent— considerably above the full-employment rate of 5.5 percent shown at point B. We can get to point B by increased spending, but only at the cost of having the inflation rate rise to 10 percent.

Figure 19-2 shows what has happened to the Phillips Curve in the real world. Note that during the years 1960–1965, events do seem to follow a Phillips Curve. Thereafter, however, chaos sets in and the pattern disappears.

What Happened after 1965?

Look at the dots for 1966, 1967, 1968, and 1969. If you look only at those years, the Phillips Curve is not a curve at all: It is a straight vertical line. What does that mean?

Remember that Phillips' idea was that an increase in the rate of inflation would reduce the rate of unemployment, and vice versa. During the late 1960s, the rate of inflation clearly went up, but the drop in unemployment was negli-

Figure 19-1

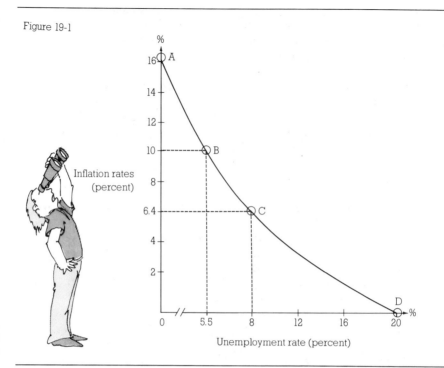

Figure 19-1.
An imaginary Phillips
Curve.

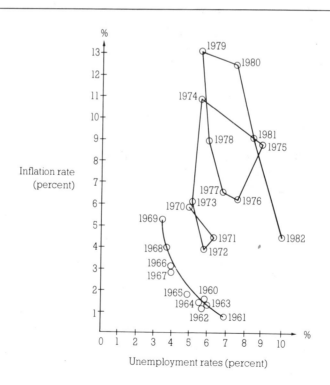

Figure 19-2.
The Phillips Curve in
chaos.

gible. What had seemed a clear pattern became clouded when an increase in the inflation rate did *not* reduce the rate of unemployment. At the time, no one worried, because the unemployment rates in those particular years were below the 5.5 percent full-employment rate. Demand-pull inflation was undoubtedly the cause.

After 1969, the pattern disappears. The rates of inflation have been higher (except for 1971 and 1972) than in the 1960s, and the unemployment rates have usually been higher than 5.5 percent. If we can glean anything from Figure 19-2 it is that the curve (if there is one) seems to be shifting to the right. If this is the case, either every inflation rate will be associated with a higher rate of unemployment, or every unemployment rate will be associated with a higher rate of inflation. A black picture!

But, even though Figure 19-2 seems to shoot down Phillips' concept, his basic idea is by no means dead. Most economists believe that inflation and unemployment rates *are* inversely related when the time span involved is fairly short, say a year or two. For example, the inflation rate was a very high 13.3 percent in 1979, when the unemployment rate was a reasonable 5.8 percent. When the Fed's tight-money policies brought the inflation rate down to 3.9 percent in 1982, the unemployment rate climbed to a record high (in December) of 10.8 percent. Thus, in the short run, at least, the Phillips trade-off exists. We cannot seem to have the best of both worlds—full employment *and* a low inflation rate.

Long-Run Theories

Although most economists agree that the Phillips trade-off is valid for a time-frame of a few years, there is much debate about the Phillips Curve in the long run—over periods of 20 to 30 years. One school of thought argues that the Phillips Curve is really a line starting at some point on the horizontal (unemployment rate) axis and headed straight up from that point. The starting point most often mentioned is 6 percent. Thus, according to this argument, over a long time, and regardless of the inflation rate, the unemployment rate will tend toward an average of 6 percent.

The reasoning goes like this: If the unemployment rate is above 6 percent, a politically sensitive administration will engage in expansionary fiscal policy (tax cuts and increases in spending) and easy monetary policy (decreases in bank reserves and lower interest rates). These measures will encourage borrowing and spending. As aggregate demand increases, business firms will enjoy sales and profit increases, more workers will be hired, and the unemployment rate will drop.

But soon the increases in demand will cause prices to rise, and many workers will find that their nominal* wages lag behind the inflation rate. They will see that their *real* wages are falling. Thereupon, many workers, particularly those in strong unions, will bargain for higher wages. If they succeed, labor costs will increase, business profits will decline, and business firms will be forced to lay off newly hired workers. The unemployment rate will rise again toward the original 6 percent. At this point, the workers have received wage increases that match the rise in prices; thus, the end result is that their real

---

*Nominal wages are the dollar amount of one's wages. Real wages are nominal wages adjusted downward to account for price increases. The concept is the same as that of deflating nominal GNP to find real GNP.

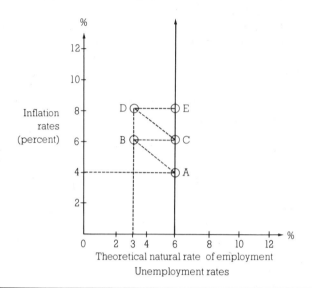

Figure 19-3.
The natural
unemployment rate
(the long-run Phillips
Curve).

wages haven't changed and the level of employment is just what it was before
the friendly government tried to help. The one change that *has* occurred is that
now prices are higher than they were before the process began. If the government should make another attempt to reduce the unemployment rate, the process will be repeated. The end result will be no improvement in unemployment but a *still higher* rate of inflation.

Figure 19-3 illustrates the process. Point A represents the starting point. The
inflation rate is an acceptable 4 percent; the unemployment rate is at 6 percent.
Now assume that the government tries to reduce unemployment by increasing
deficit spending. The resulting increase in aggregate demand *does* reduce un-
emloyment, but as unemployment drops, prices begin to rise. The economy
moves from point A to point B, where the unemployment rate is now 3 percent,
but the inflation rate has risen to 6 percent. But now, because prices are higher,
workers demand higher wages. When they succeed in getting them, business
profits decline, workers are laid off, and the unemployment returns to 6 percent at point C. But point C represents a higher inflation rate, 6 percent, than
does point A. Nevertheless, the government may try to reduce unemployment
again. If it does, the economy will move from point C to D and then to E. But
again, inflation is still higher. Now the inflation rate is 8 percent.

Does this view of the Phillips Curve mean that it doesn't exist? Not quite.
The short-term movements from A to B and from C to D are Phillips-Curve
movements because they show a trade-off of higher inflation rates for lower
unemployment rates. But according to Phillips' opponents, these short-term
movements are temporary and unstable.

The long-term view that the Phillips Curve really isn't a curve at all but a
straight, vertical line is called the **accelerationist view** because it explains
how inflation gets started and then accelerates. Notice that the accelerationist
view holds that fiscal and monetary policies do no good in the long run because the unemployment rate, despite some zig-zags, stays at 6 percent. Conse-

quently, the accelerationist view is usually endorsed by conservatives, who prefer to believe that *discretionary* (as opposed to automatic) fiscal and monetary policies are really powerless to change the unemployment rate and that in the long run, such policies only contribute to inflation. The Keynesians, on the other hand, stress the short-term validity of the Phillips Curve and usually reject the notion that we are stuck in the long run at some particular rate of unemployment. Thus, the Phillips Curve is another aspect of the many-faceted monetarist-Keynesian debate.

Why Six Percent?

Another argument within the accelerationist view concerns the location of the vertical line. The location of the line is obviously of tremendous importance because the line tells us that there is an *equilibrium rate of unemployment toward which the economy will tend to move*, regardless of discretionary fiscal and monetary policies. The apparent reason that the line is located at 6 percent is that 6 percent *is* about the *average* rate of unemployment over the 22-year period 1961–1982. Whether or not we should accept the 6 percent figure is a matter of individual judgment. Some economists believe that 6 percent is the sum of a reasonable amount of *frictional* plus *structural* unemployment. Others recognize that averages can be misleading. What is the equilibrium number of legs on a human being? We answer: two legs. Most people tend to have two legs. But what is the *average* number of legs? Something less than that.* The 6 percent figure is misleading because it is only an average; the figure conceals the distribution of the numbers. In 14 years of the 22-year 1961–1982 period, the unemployment rate was less than 6 percent, reaching a low point of 3.5 percent in 1969.

Despite these arguments, the 6 percent figure is called the **natural rate of unemployment**. The term refers to the rate of unemployment that will exist after business and labor have adjusted fully to the inflation rate. It is the unemployment rate that will exist after workers have had the chance to keep their nominal wages even with the inflation rate, and after business firms have had the chance to establish levels of hiring based on those wages.

The concept of a natural rate of unemployment, particularly one as high as 6 percent,** is distasteful. Acceptance of the idea is like an admission that we have an incurable disease. We need to know more about whether the natural rate is valid, why it is located where it is, and—if it is valid—how it can be lowered. The logic of the natural rate does suggest one unattractive way to reduce it: Make sure that wage increases never equal the rate of inflation. If so, real wages will decline, business profits will increase,*** and more workers will be hired—as long as their wage demands are less than the inflation rate. Unfortunately, as the next section suggests, the natural rate of unemployment is increasing, if anything.

---

*This example about averages is taken from a remark by a well-known American philosopher, Joseph Wood Krutch.

**Back in the 1950s and 1960s, most economists believed that 4 percent was the "natural" rate, and that 4 percent was the equivalent of full employment.

***Business profits might increase temporarily if real wages fall, but either of two things will surely happen. Labor will realize it is losing its share of the national pie and demand more; and/or, labor will view its loss of real income as a good reason to reduce purchases, in which case aggregate demand and GNP will fall, and unemployment will rise. These consequences will probably, in the short run at least, shift the natural rate of unemployment to the right.

Table 19-1. Arthur Okun's Discomfort Index (average annual rates)

Years	Inflation rates	+	Unemployment rates	=	Discomfort Index
1961–65	1.3		5.5		6.8
1966–70	4.5		3.9		8.4
1971–75	5.6		6.1		11.7
1976–80	9.3		6.8		16.1
1981–82	6.4		8.7		15.1

Source: Economic Report of the President, 1983.

The Discomfort Index

Under the theory that inflation and unemployment rates are both measures of macroeconomic failure, Arthur M. Okun, Chairman of the Council of Economic Advisors under President Lyndon B. Johnson, suggested that we add the inflation and unemployment rates together and call the sum the **Discomfort Index**. When we do that, an interesting picture of increasing discomfort emerges.

Table 19-1 shows the Discomfort Index over five-year periods from 1961 to 1980 and for 1981–1982. The table shows what it was like to live in the good old days of the 1960s—"good" *provided* one was not involved with the war in Vietnam. In both five-year periods in that decade, the unemployment rates were the equivalent of full employment, and the inflation rates seem very reasonable when compared with later ones. We can understand why economists—particularly Keynesian ones—lived in a rosy glow of self-satisfaction. They believed they had found the keys to prosperity.

But since that decade, the Discomfort Index has almost doubled, giving us another view of the apparent rightward shift of the Phillips Curve and, perhaps, a rightward shift of the natural unemployment rate. What went wrong? A number of explanations have been offered:

1. During the period from 1965 to 1969, while we were fighting the Vietnam War, the Johnson Administration engaged in $42.5 billion worth of deficit spending, not only to fight the war but also to finance a variety of new "Great Society" measures to help the poor. None of this additional spending was offset by tax increases. And the additional spending (adding to aggregate demand) came during a time when the unemployment rates were *less* than the full-employment rate of 5.5 percent. Prices began to rise. Prior to the 1965–1969 period, the inflation rate was less than 2 percent per year. By 1970 the inflation rate was 5.5 percent.

2. The Nixon Administration's system of price controls, in effect from 1971 to 1973, collapsed from political pressure, a collapse that resulted in higher-than-before-controls rates of inflation when the lid came off. (The inflation rate was 3.4 percent in 1972, 8.8 percent in 1973, and 12.2 percent in 1974!)

3. Shipments to the Soviet Union of almost our entire grain reserve in 1972 led to skyrocketing food prices.

4. The doubling and quadrupling of oil prices following the OPEC oil embargo in the winter of 1973–1974 contributed to higher prices for everything.

Inflation and
unemployment rates
added together is
called the Discomfort
Index.

5. The excessive stimulation of demand during the 1970s by government deficit spending and "easy" money put still more upward pressure on prices.

6. The productivity of labor declined, leading to higher labor costs and prices.

7. Ineffective fiscal and monetary policies increased inflation without helping unemployment—the accelerationist view.

These seven reasons help to explain the recent surge of prices, but what do they have to do with unemployment? In particular, why does the unemployment rate seem to be increasing over the 22-year period?

Reasons for Long-Term Increases in Unemployment

We cannot know for sure if the following developments have caused the natural rate of unemployment to increase, along with the actual rate, but they probably have:

1. We have had at least four post-World War II recessions. During each one, business firms have found cheaper methods of production that have made it unnecessary to rehire 100 percent of laid-off workers when the recession was over.

2. Advances in electronics have made such labor-saving changes possible.

(We're thinking of the mechanization and computerization of many manufacturing and information-processing functions.)

3. More women and teenagers have entered the labor force. In 1960, 59.4 percent of the population over age 16 wanted to work. In 1980, the percentage had increased to 63.8 percent. This increase was the result of increased job participation by women and teenagers, both groups more prone to unemployment than male adults. (See the discussion of full employment on page 255.)

4. Unemployment compensation payments have made unemployment an attractive alternative to work.

5. Minimum wage laws have tended to throw young people and unskilled workers out of work.

6. High initiation fees have restricted union membership, and have sometimes prevented employment when union membership was a prerequisite for the desired job.

7. Occupational licenses, like a license to be a barber, have made it difficult to enter into an occupation.

8. And finally, the continuing presence of inflation can, by itself, cause unemployment. This last development is illustrated by the following anecdote:

Once upon a time the Chaffey College newspaper ran an article about the college athletic budget. Some of the reported dialogue with the basketball coach was as follows:

Press: How much is Chaffey College's athletic budget?
Coach: Our budget fluctuates between $50,000 and $60,000. They increase it by a certain percentage as the cost of living goes up. In other words, they give us an 8 percent increase in budget, but we find out that we're getting pinched, because the cost of the product has gone up 18 percent in a single year. A basketball that I could buy five years ago for $10 would now cost about $16. The price has gone up, but the increase in our allotment hasn't gone up. So, instead of buying six basketballs, we're only buying four now.[1]

That is by no means the end of the story. Inflation caused the purchase of basketballs to drop from six to four. The business firm that supplied the basketballs will lose sales. Workers will be laid off. The spending multiplier will cause GNP to fall by a multiple of the initial drop in spending. An increase in prices had led to an increase in unemployment. And, obviously, we cannot blame the coach. He did what he had to do. But stagflation was on its way.

SOME POSSIBLE CURES

We're going to comment on five possible cures for stagflation: (1) Wage and price controls, (2) tax-based incomes policies, (3) job creation by the government, (4) supply-side economics, and (5) fiscal and monetary policy according to rules. The first three ideas tend to be supported by Keynesians, the last two by conservatives. But this division of opinion into two camps oversimplifies the complexities of the stagflation problem. Here and there we find the Keynesians and the conservatives in agreement.

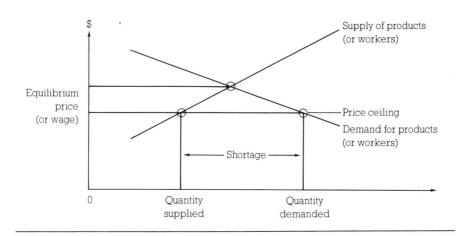

Figure 19-4.
A picture of a price or wage ceiling.

Wage and Price Controls

Simply stated, this cure requires the government to set ceilings on prices and wages because nothing else will work. The argument is based on the fact that the American industrial scene is dominated by giant corporations and unions who have so much market power that their prices and wages cannot be controlled in any other way. For example, in 1977, one-tenth of one percent of all corporations owned 66.5 percent of all U.S. corporate assets. In 1978, 42 percent of all union workers belonged to the eight largest unions (out of a total of 174 unions).[2] Wage bargaining and pricing policies involving these giant combinations are immune, so the argument goes, to the forces of competition and to general economic conditions affecting the rest of the economy. They can engage in cost- or profit-push inflation almost as easily as OPEC can raise its prices. Economist Robert Lekachman sums up the argument this way:

> The diagnosis implies the therapy. We desperately need permanent statutory authority to establish criteria for wages and prices, and a permanent federal agency to apply and administer these standards. . . .
>
> The sooner we all face the inescapable fact that our more-or-less "free" economy is a mélange of forces, some of them exceedingly powerful, the sooner we shall arrive at two necessary conclusions: In a time of dangerous inflation, we urgently require mandatory restraints on prices and incomes; and, at all times, government must have in reserve the authority to react quickly to inflationary threats. We shall all be better off for the realization.[3]

The Case against Controls

The argument against controls reminds us of the effect of any price ceiling (Figure 19-4). Remember that a price ceiling is the *maximum* allowable price. The government initiates the price ceiling because it believes the equilibrium price will be inflationary. The inevitable results: Suppliers will curtail the quantities supplied. (During the Nixon Administration's experiment with price controls, cattle ranchers tried to keep their beef cattle on the hoof rather than sell them. The stores rapidly ran out of beef.) On the other hand, buyers will want to buy more than is being supplied and will end up (1) having to buy something else, (2) standing in line for what is available, or (3) finding a way around the law (black market activities). Economists refer to such consequences as distortions in the allocation of resources.

The opponents of controls cite a long history of their failure, going all the way back to the Roman emperor, Diocletian. In A.D. 301 Diocletian, angry at high prices and the profiteering tactics of merchants, issued an edict setting maximum prices and wages for all important articles and services in the Empire.

> The Edict was until our time the most famous example of an attempt to replace economic laws by governmental decrees. Its failure was rapid and complete. Tradesmen concealed their commodities, scarcities became more acute than before . . . riots occurred, and the Edict had to be relaxed to restore production and distribution. It was finally revoked by Constantine.[4]

Despite this calamity, the urge to control prices and wages by statutory and other means has continued. A giant bureaucracy of 60,000 officials, the Office of Price Administration (OPA), supervised controls during World War II. When controls were lifted in 1946, the country suffered the highest annual inflation rate in 60 years (18.2 percent). President John F. Kennedy tried "jawboning" to keep the annual inflation rate under 3.2 percent. This kind of effort, continued by President Johnson, dwindled away after a strike in 1966 by aircraft mechanics gave them raises of 5 percent.

President Nixon tried controls again between 1971 and 1974. But these gradually were weakened as one business firm or union after another complained that they were being left behind by the firms or unions that had gotten large increases before the controls were instituted. Princeton economists Alan S. Blinder and Willian J. Newton concluded that by "early 1975 the 1971–1974 controls had actually increased inflation by almost one percent over what it would otherwise have been during those years."[5]

In more recent times, President Jimmy Carter attempted to hold prices and wage increases below 7 percent, but his guideline was ignored by the Teamsters, who won a 9 percent increase in 1979. Thereupon (perhaps to save face), the Carter administration boosted the guideline to 9.5 percent, only to find that overall price increases in 1979 averaged 13 percent.

The supporters of wage and price controls respond to all this by saying, "Of course, the controls are going to be tough to enforce, but (1) we need to place controls only on large corporations and unions, and (2) the controls must be left on *indefinitely*, to wipe out any expectation by the participants that they can recover lost wages or profits after the controls are removed."

In the past there was a general understanding that controls were temporary. This understanding encouraged interest groups to exert political pressure on the president to remove controls, and it led to an explosion of prices and wages when they were lifted.

Tax-Based Incomes Policy

In the early 1970s, economists Henry C. Wallich and Sidney Weintraub proposed a variant of wage and price controls called a **tax-based incomes policy**, abbreviated **TIP**. The idea was this: The President and his advisors would select a guideline rate of permissible inflation, perhaps 5 percent. Thereupon, a corporation would be penalized if its average annual wage increase exceeded the guideline. If the corporation granted annual wage increases of, say, 7 percent, the excess of 2 percent over the guideline would be added to its corporate income taxes by some multiple of the excess. If the multiple were 2, then the corporation's profits would be taxed an additional 4 percent (2 $\times$ 2 percent).*

The authors of the plan argued that wages and prices usually maintain a constant relationship; that the control of wages under their TIP plan would also control prices.

The main advantage to the plan was that it gave corporations a "bottom-line" incentive to control wages while leaving the details to individual companies. The plan was analogous in this sense to the "effluent charge" idea (see Chapter 6) for controlling pollution, in that penalties were specifically linked to the offense. In both cases, the corporations that knew best how to adapt to a problem were given an incentive to solve it. The TIP plan was another market solution to a public problem.

The arguments against the plan were (1) that the plan seemed to be a way to increase corporate profit at labor's expense, and (2) that the cost of any tax penalties might ultimately be shifted to consumers in the form of higher prices. In the latter case, the corporation could be a "bad guy" at no expense to itself, and the tax penalty would contribute to additional inflation.

Job Creation by the Government

We mention this idea because in the spring of 1983 federal gasoline taxes were increased 5 cents a gallon with the intention of raising $5 billion per year for six years. This money was to finance the repair of highways, bridges, and the like—all to provide jobs for 320,000 unemployed workers. Congress and the Administration were desperate to make some gesture to the 12 million people out of work.

Unfortunately, past and present histories of such plans provide little basis for support:[6]

1. The Works Progress Administration (WPA) employed 8 million people during the Depression in the 1930s, but there is no evidence that this employment helped to end the Depression. The Depression ended with the military build-up and government spending that went into World War II.

2. President Kennedy's public-service jobs bills, designed to ease the 1960–1961 recession, did not benefit a substantial number of recipients until three years later.

3. The $6 billion Local Public Works Program designed to ease the 1974–1975 recession did not peak until three years later. An analysis of the program in 1979 by the Office of Management and Budget found that only 12 percent of the jobs and 2 percent of the money went to persons previously unemployed.

4. Although many liberals and conservatives supported the December 1982 effort, President Reagan's own Council of Economic Advisors didn't like it. Martin Feldstein, CEA chairman, pointed out that the program might result

---

*A later variation suggested by Arthur Okun called for rewarding "good" corporations that stayed under the guideline with tax credits. Thus, some economists favored the "carrot" rather than the "stick" approach.

in a net *loss* of 30,000 to 100,000 jobs. The problem was that the public would lose $30 billion over six years in taxes, and that the resulting drop in private spending would cost more jobs than the government could create. The reason is that prevailing union wages are usually 10 to 30 percent higher than what the average American earns, and the federal jobs program involved paying union wages. Thus $1 given to the program would provide less employment than if spent by the average private citizen.

These histories remind us of two problems:

1. Spending projects take time to design and implement. If the financing of the program begins at once, and the benefits of the program are slow to arrive, the public is first penalized and then later given a benefit—one that may not be appropriately timed.

2. "There is no such thing as a free lunch"—as economists love to tell us. There is always an opportunity cost: If the job program is financed by taxes, the opportunity cost is measured, probably, by the lost consumption spending that might have been directed elsewhere. If the program is financed by the sale of government securities, the opportunity cost will probably be the decrease in private investment that might have been financed by the private saving that went, instead, to the government. Here again we are thinking of "crowding out."

Supply-Side Economics

The 1970s produced a new line of inquiry into the stagflation problem. Keynesian theory had taken a beating. Demand management via fiscal or monetary policy got a black eye because it was easy for politicians to support expansion (more spending and jobs for everyone) but very difficult to go into reverse to fight inflation.

The new line of inquiry was beautiful in its simplicity. If demand management doesn't work, perhaps we ought to look at *supply*. If we can get supply to increase, given no change in demand, prices will fall. And at lower prices, people will buy more and we will have less unemployment. And even if demand increases, as long as supply increases faster than the increases in demand, prices will still fall.

How do we go about increasing aggregate supply? Before we start, let's take one more look at a demand-supply model of the economy. Figure 19-5 is similar to the cost/profit-push diagram on page 264.

In Figure 19-5, the two solid arrows pointing upward indicate cost- or profit-push inflation. Higher prices are charged at every level of output so that when aggregate supply shifts upward, real GNP drops back from Q_1 to Q_2. The trick is to reverse the arrows—to help suppliers produce every quantity at lower prices (P_1 instead of P_2). At lower prices, the quantities demanded will increase from Q_2 back to Q_1. Business firms will produce more and hire more people. The result will be an ideal combination of lower prices and less unemployment. The dotted arrows in Figure 19-5 show these changes.

How Do We Produce This Desirable Situation?

The supply-sider's answer is simple and direct: Cut taxes. The supply-siders present two arguments for their answer:

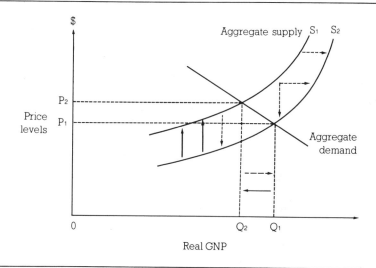

Figure 19-5.
Cost- or profit-push inflation.

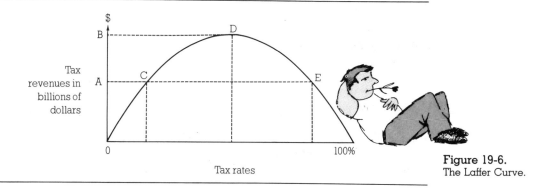

Figure 19-6.
The Laffer Curve.

1. Taxes contribute to inflation because business firms incorporate taxes in their prices. Taxes create a "wedge" that forces a gap between the actual costs of production and the prices firms finally charge.

2. Taxes create disincentives for work. Heavy tax burdens make people wonder, "Why work harder if I have to give a large share to the government?"

The Laffer Curve

The so-called Laffer argument is crucial. It is based on an idea called the Laffer Curve, named for its originator, Arthur Laffer, professor of economics at the University of Southern California. The **Laffer Curve** illustrates the idea that high tax rates will so reduce incentives to work that the government's tax revenues will decline, whereas low tax rates may actually increase incentives to work and thereby increase tax revenues. The Laffer Curve is shown in Figure 19-6.

At the two ends of the curve, tax revenues would be zero. Tax revenues would, of course, be zero when tax rates are zero, but revenues would also be zero if the tax rates were 100 percent, because no one would have any incentive to work. Therefore, argues Professor Laffer, there must be some optimum tax rate in between the two extremes where tax revenues are maximum and where people are motivated to work hardest.* That rate is shown at point D, with maximum revenues opposite D at point B. Professor Laffer's belief is that we are presently at some point on the curve like E, and that therefore a lowering of tax rates to D would increase tax revenues from A to B. Moreover, we could lower the tax rates all the way to C and do just as well as at E.

If Professor Laffer is right, the results would indeed be beneficial:

1. Tax revenues would increase, and the deficit would be reduced, thereby reducing the crowding out effect.

2. With more spendable income after taxes are reduced, people would spend and save more, and business firms would find more money to invest in new projects. More people would get jobs, transfer payments would fall, and the budget would be brought into better balance than at higher tax rates.

3. Everyone would have less reason to avoid taxes, and there would be less unreported "underground" income.

The Laffer-inspired tax cut also would provide an avenue toward the supply-siders' (and conservatives') ultimate objective: to reduce the size of government. Specifically, the supply-siders hoped to reduce the share of the GNP spent by the federal government by one or two percentage points.** To that extent, the supply-siders hoped to return a portion of the nation's economic activity to free markets.

A tax cut would make such a cut in government spending possible. (Without a tax cut to help the people, a cut in government spending would be politically unwise.) The particular cuts the supply-siders had in mind were (1) transfer payments like unemployment insurance that might dull workers' incentives to work, and (2) environmental and safety regulations that kept production costs up and profitable opportunities down. This last argument was an important pillar in the supply-siders' program to increase supply.

Objections to the Laffer Curve

Because the idea of the tax cut is the keystone of the supply-siders' case, we need to review contrary opinions about it. Unfortunately, no evidence exists to prove Professor Laffer right. We can all agree that the two extremes of the curve are logical, and some economists will agree that a curve might well exist, but no one knows where on the curve the nation is, if the curve does, in fact, exist.

Opponents of the Laffer Curve give three reasons for their opposition:

1. No data exist to show the shape of the Curve or our location on it. The Curve might look like Figure 19-7.

If the curve looks like the one in Figure 19-7, tax revenues will not be at the maximum (point D) until the tax rate is at some very high rate like at point R, very close to 100 percent. Consequently, any tax cut, either above or

---

*Note that we could put GNP on the horizontal axis instead of tax revenues and the curve would look the same, at least according to Laffer's theory. High tax rates above some point would reduce GNP. Low rates would increase it up to some point.

**Federal budget outlays as a percent of GNP in 1982 were 23.8 percent.

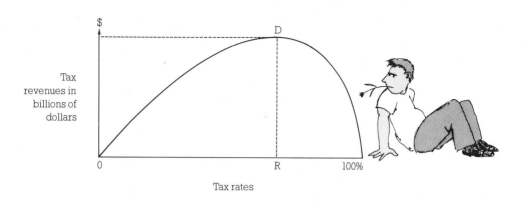

below point R, would *de*crease tax revenues, not increase them. We have to know the shape of the curve and where we are on it to know whether or not a tax cut will do any good.

Figure 19-7.
Another Laffer Curve.

2. No data exist to show that the curve is stable—that what is true for last year will also be true for this year or next year.

3. The experts have very mixed opinions about tax rates and incentives. Some believe that higher tax rates make at least some of us work harder to maintain a given level of disposable personal income. Even the relationship of tax rates and the incentive to invest is difficult to analyze. High tax rates may actually encourage investment in new ventures because subsequent losses can be used to reduce personal or corporate income taxes. The higher the marginal tax rate one is in, the bigger the tax saving from such a loss. Furthermore, there is no evidence that the overall tax burden on the people of a nation depresses their standard of living. Some countries like the Scandinavian countries have higher per capita incomes than we do as well as higher tax rates.

To sum up: The bottom-line difficulty with all of these pro and con arguments is that even though there is no proof the supply-siders are right, there is no proof that they are wrong, either. The supply-siders have given the economics profession much to consider and to debate, particularly because they were joined in 1981 by a President who shared their views. At this writing, President Reagan's first term in office is about half over. During those two years the supply-siders took quite a beating. From the point of view of economic analysis, no period in our history is more interesting or instructive and so we want, briefly, to tell the economic story of that time.

The Reagan Experience, 1981–1983

The program initiated by President Reagan in 1981 was designed to please the conservatives of the country. Accordingly, his administration and his program embraced supply-side *and* monetarist policies, with emphasis on (1) the tax rate, (2) cuts in federal spending, and (3) efforts to control inflation. As it turned out, all three parts of the program developed problems.

Table 19-2. Federal Income Taxes in 1980 and 1984 Before and After the Kemp-Roth Tax Cut (for married individuals filing joint returns)

Taxable income	Total income tax		Tax saving	Tax saving as a percentage of taxable income
	1980	1984		
$ 8,000	$ 786	$ 693	$ 93	1.2%
15,000	1,823	1,581	242	1.6
30,000	5,607	4,762	845	2.8
60,000	17,705	15,168	2,537	4.2
80,000	29,989	26,104	3,885	4.9

Source: *1981 Prentice-Hall Federal Tax Guide,* August 1981.

The Tax Cut

The tax cut, usually called the Kemp-Roth* Bill, was enacted in 1981. The bill was designed to cut personal income taxes by 25 percent over a period of three years. Additional tax breaks for depreciation and new investment were given corporations. The tax cut was adopted, in the spirit of the Laffer Curve, with the hope that lower tax rates would increase spending, saving, and investing, and at higher GNP levels, tax revenues would increase.

Almost immediately, the tax cut produced a furor. Analyses of the tax-cut bill indicated that it favored people with high incomes. Table 19-2 provides a sample.

Table 19-2 clearly shows that the critics were right. The tax cut gave larger dollar savings to higher-income people; that was to be expected. But the tax saving as a percentage of income also rose—an indication that the tax cut was regressive. Another way to see the same point is to note that as income increases 10 times from $8,000 to $80,000, the tax saving increases 41.8 times from $93 to $3,885. One columnist commented: "It seems that when Reagan talks about lower taxes, he is not addressing the 96 percent of families making $50,000 or less."[7] The same columnist suggested that supply side theory might be a smoke screen for cutting taxes at the very top. However, since 44 percent of U.S. families had incomes of $25,000 or more in 1981, many people did benefit from the cut. And personal savings—one goal of the cut—did increase to $140 billion in 1982 from $130.2 billion in 1981.

Cuts in Federal Spending

The hoped-for reduction in the size of the federal government did not materialize. The Reagan administration *did* cut federal nondefense spending, but Reagan was also determined to increase defense spending under the theory that U.S. military strength was falling below that of the Russians. Given this rationale, the Reagan administration determined to increase military spending in *real terms* by more than 40 percent between 1980 and 1985. As a proportion of all federal spending, defense spending would rise from 23 percent in 1980 to 36 percent in 1985.[8] And because of the increases in defense spending, the Congressional Budget Office estimated that defense spending as a percentage of GNP would increase from 22.6 percent in 1980 to 23.2 percent in 1985.

The changes in the mix of federal spending from nondefense to defense

---

*The official name was the Economic Recovery Tax Act of 1981.

generated more criticism: First, military spending is notoriously costly because there is little competition among suppliers. Second, increases in military spending tend to draw resources away from the private economy where they may be more productive. (A technician may benefit the average person more by making toasters than by making missiles.) Third, the opportunity cost of increases in military spending was measured by a decline in spending for the poor. Food stamps were cut by more than $2 billion in 1982; Medicaid was cut almost $2 billion; the school lunch program was cut by 30 percent; $1 billion (above 20 percent) was cut from aid to families with dependent children (AFDC), a program involving 4 million households.

Efforts to Control Inflation

During 1981 and the first seven months of 1982, the Federal Reserve Board kept money tight in an effort to combat inflation. As we have noted elsewhere, the battle against inflation was successful. The inflation rate was cut in half. But the tight-money policy kept interest rates at record highs: The prime rate stayed above 15 percent during much of the period.

The result was a severe recession. Business failures in 1982 reached record levels (over 20,000), at least partly because of the high cost of borrowing money. Auto sales and residential sales hit the lowest levels in 20 years. Wall Street reacted by sending the Dow Jones average down 20 percent between July 1981 and July 1982. The unemployment rate hit the highest level since 1939. And we have already seen on page 347 in Chapter 17 how devastating the effect of tight money was on investment spending by business firms and on purchases of consumer durables like automobiles. Tight money made the U.S. dollar strong in international markets, which was disastrous for other countries as *their* depositors moved money to U.S. deposits, thereby depriving their own business firms of money for investment. Foreign banks had to compete with U.S. banks by offering high interest rates, thus depressing their own economies. The recession became worldwide.

Tight money and high interest rates in the U.S. meant that any deficit spending would crowd out private spending. If money is "easy," the Fed Board can reduce crowding out by making money more easily available. Even if the Treasury borrows a lot, money is still left for business firms and consumers to borrow and spend. But when money is tight, private spending is crowded out by Treasury borrowing.

As 1982 drew to a close, attention in Washington shifted to unemployment, the recession, and future deficits. As long as the recession continued, the automatic stabilizers would enlarge the deficits. The tax cut would combine with lower taxable incomes to reduce tax revenues. The Administration's insistence on heavy defense spending would keep federal outlays up.

At this point, the Fed Board changed its policies and made money easier to obtain. Interest rates on all kinds of loans came down. The prime rate fell to 11.5 percent in late 1982. The drop in interest rates, however, produced no optimism that the recession would suddenly end.

On August 19, 1982, the Reagan administration persuaded Congress to pass a measure designed to reduce deficits. Major provisions of the act were further ($15 billion) cuts in federal health and welfare programs and a $98.3 billion tax *increase.* The $98.3 billion was to come from a doubling of the Federal excise tax on cigarettes to 16 cents a pack, an increase in the federal tax on telephone service, an increase in taxes on unemployment benefits, and an increase in federal taxes on airline passenger tickets. The tax increase meant an about-face in terms of the Laffer Curve and supply-side policies.

During his first two years in office, Reagan produced a contradictory set of goals: to cut taxes, to increase military spending, and yet to balance the budget. The latter goal became an impossibility as tight money and the recession reduced economic activity. Supply-side economics never had a chance. Yes, there was a tax cut, but tax revenues did not increase as the Laffer Curve had predicted. And ultimately, when taxes were raised, Laffer and supply-siding were abandoned.

One thought about the Reagan experience keeps coming to mind: Tight money reduced inflation but crippled the economy. The unemployment-inflation relationship was a trade-off, just as Professor Phillips had told us. Inflation could be brought down but only at the cost of increased unemployment. We are still searching for a painless cure for inflation, but the possibility that there is one seems remote.

Fiscal and Monetary Policy According to Rules

This is the fifth and last category of cures for stagflation. As the heading of this section suggests, this "cure" holds that fiscal and monetary policy should be conducted according to *rules*. The rules argument is based on the accelerationist theory presented in Figure 19-3. *That* theory holds that in the long run, discretionary monetary and fiscal policies will be ineffective; that no matter what the federal government does, the unemployment rate will tend toward the natural rate of unemployment.

A recent variant of the accelerationist view is called **rational expectations**. The rational expectations view is that the effectiveness of fiscal and monetary policies depends on what people expect to happen. If fiscal and monetary policies are initiated to reduce unemployment, everyone (workers, management, school teachers, and bankers) will expect prices to rise as a result of the government's expansionary efforts. Workers will ask for raises, managers will raise prices, bankers will raise interest rates. The end result is that the same GNP gets produced at a higher price level; no increase in *real* GNP occurs. The *expectation* of inflation frustrates the effort of the government to increase real output and the level of employment.

This scenario is the same as that of the accelerationists, but the rational expectationists, as they are called, go two steps further:

1. One more look at Figure 19-3 will help to explain this point. The rational expectationists believe that the short-run swings from A to B and from C to D will be minimal; that everyone's expectations of coming inflation will develop so rapidly that the economy really will move only straight up through points A, C, and E. In other words, the Phillips Curve doesn't exist *at all*, even for short periods of time. Thus, discretionary monetary and fiscal policies are *totally* ineffective, for *any* period of time.

2. But as if that conclusion weren't enough to seal the fate of the manipulations in Washington, the rational expectationists also believe that discretionary fiscal and monetary policies can make matters worse. For example, suppose that business sales and profits are down and that unemployment is

If business managers wait for signals from Washington, the expectationists believe it worsens a recession.

increasing. Business managers aren't stupid; they know that, sooner or later, discretionary monetary and fiscal policies will have to help. In response to that thought, business managers *wait* for expansionary signals from Washington and postpone their investments until the expected tax cuts and/or easier money at lower interest rates arrive. But this kind of behavior, the rational expectationists argue, will make any recession worse while the business community waits for the signals.

The "Rules" Approach

What to do? The rational expectationists prefer **the rules approach**. They want to take the "discretionary" out of monetary and fiscal policy. Both sets of policies, they argue, should be conducted according to rules.

1. We have already encountered the monetarist rule in the previous chapter: The money supply growth should be set at a constant rate, the rate to coincide with the desired rate of growth for *real* GNP. The rate most often cited is 4 percent per year. Under this rule, the Board would be deprived of its discretionary power to change the money supply unless its actions coincided with the desired growth rate.

2. Fiscal policy should also be conducted according to rules. Automatic changes in tax rates could be used to augment the automatic stabilizers. Thus, with each X percent increase in unemployment rates, cuts in income tax rates of some percentage would automatically go into effect. With each Y percent increase in, say, the consumer price index, income tax rates would

automatically increase by some percentage. This latter event would help to slow any price-level increases caused by rational expectations.

Conclusions

Where does all this leave us? As with the arguments of the supply-siders and their Laffer Curve, there is no proof that Americans react as rationally or as quickly as the rational expectationists suggest. If the latter are right, the federal government has no business manipulating the economy. Few economists, other than the rational expectationists, are ready to go that far.

Nevertheless, recent history has taught us two lessons and suggested a third:

1. Tight money *can* bring down the rate of inflation.
2. There *is* a Phillips Curve, in the short run at the very least. When the tight money of 1981–1982 brought the inflation rate down from over 13 percent to 4 percent, the unemployment rate climbed from an average of 7.1 percent in 1980 to 10.8 percent in December 1982. No one has yet found a painless cure for inflation. We will have to wait and see if unemployment can in turn be reduced without an increase in the inflation rate from 1983 on.
3. The "suggested" lesson is that, although the "rules" school has many opponents, unstable and politically motivated fiscal and monetary policies *can* accentuate the business cycle. Many economists would agree that both fiscal and monetary policy have been subject to unnecessary zigs and zags, usually leading to overcorrection at the wrong time. Even though the "rules" approach may be too rigid, we need to make less frequent and smaller course changes than have been occurring.

SUMMARY

Stagflation, the simultaneous appearance of unemployment and inflation, is a relatively recent phenomenon that first appeared in the late 1950s. The elimination of stagflation poses special problems because efforts to reduce inflation may increase unemployment and vice versa.

The Phillips Curve is used to describe the trade-off between inflation and unemployment. In recent years, this trade-off has apparently disappeared because increases in the rate of inflation are not associated with reductions in unemployment. Both inflation and unemployment seem to be rising—an indication of stagflation. Nevertheless, the 1982 experience indicates that in the short run, the inflation-unemployment trade-off exists.

The accelerationist view holds that the Phillips Curve is really a series of variations around a vertical line set at the natural rate of unemployment. This view is an attempt to explain accelerating inflation.

Several explanations have been offered as to why unemployment rates seem to be increasing. Among these explanations is increased job participation by women and teenagers.

Some possible cures for stagflation are (1) wage and price controls, (2) tax-based incomes policies, (3) job creation by the government, (4) supply-side economics, and (5) discretionary fiscal and monetary policy conducted according to rules. The first three of these cures have serious shortcomings, while the last two depend on assumptions yet to be proved true by data.

Most economists still agree that there is a cost for reducing the inflation rate in terms of increased unemployment.

Discussion Questions

1. Why does the Phillips Curve seem to be a perfect curve up to 1965 and then disappear?

2. What are the arguments pro and con about the natural rate of unemployment?

3. Can you find any evidence in your city or town to show that:
   (a) inflation causes unemployment?
   (b) high interest rates hurt business?
   (c) recession overseas hurts a local business?

4. What is the main argument *in favor* of the Laffer Curve?

5. Why is the Laffer Curve subject to so much criticism?

6. Does this criticism mean that the Laffer Curve is useless? In what way is the idea useful?

7. Why did the Reagan program fail during 1980–1982?

8. How are rational expectations and the "rules" approach related?

DID YOU EVER WONDER WHY . . .

. . . there were price controls during World War II?

References

1. Mike Balchunas and Russell Ingold, "We Can Always Use More Money," *Panther Press*, Chaffey College, Alta Loma, CA, 17 October 1975.

2. *Statistical Abstract of the United States, 1978*.

3. Robert Lekachman, "The Desperate Need for Wage-Price Curbs," *Los Angeles Times*, 1 February 1980, Pt. ii, p. 5. With permission from *Los Angeles Times*. See also his book *Inflation* (New York: Vintage Books, 1973).

4. Will Durant, *Caesar and Christ* (New York: Simon and Schuster, 1944), pp. 642–643.

5. "Infatuation with Controls," *Time*, 25 February 1980, p. 77.

6. Details from *Newsweek*, "Twelve Million Out of Work," 13 December 1982.

7. Jane Bryant Quinn, "The Tax-cut Lottery," *Newsweek*, 11 May 1981.

8. James Fallows, "Endless Deficits," *Atlantic Monthly*, April 1982.

We have come full circle. In Chapter 1 we discussed the problem of an increasing population demanding increasing quantities of food and other resources. In Chapter 5 we were reminded again that the world's increasing demands for energy must be kept in line with global supplies. Now, we are going to look at the same problems from an international perspective.

Somehow, the world's nations will have to find a way

PART VI

INTERNATIONAL ECONOMICS: OUR LINKS WITH OTHER COUNTRIES

to develop their economies cooperatively and peacefully. No longer can the United States or any country sit back and pretend that the economic problems that threaten to destroy, say, Bangladesh, have no bearing on the welfare of its own citizens.

This last part looks at these problems in two ways: (1) international trade between nations—mainly from the point of view of the United States, and (2) the economic challenges of the eighties.

20

The Economics of International Trade

KEY WORDS
Production possibilities table
Principle of comparative advantage
Tariff
Nontariff barriers (NTBs)
Most-favored nation (MFN)
  principle
General Agreement on Tariffs
  and Trade (GATT)
Trade Expansion Act of 1962
Organization for Economic
  Cooperation and Development
  (OECD)
Trade deficit
Trade surplus
Floating exchange rates
Currency depreciation

The reasons for trade between nations are the same as those for trade between individuals. Someone once said that we live by "taking in one another's washing." Plumbers hire income-tax acountants, and income-tax accountants hire plumbers. We depend on what others produce in countless ways. This morning when you got up, you perhaps drank coffee from Brazil with sugar from the Philippines. Your shoes may have come from Korea, your clothes from Taiwan. Your car is probably made with steel from Japan, runs on tires made from Malaysian rubber, and is powered by oil from the Middle East.

If specialization and exchange were unavailable and if each of us had to be self-sufficient, we would be reduced to scratching a living from the earth with the most primitive tools. Imagine trying to be self-sufficient without electrical power, automobiles, housing, and medical care—all provided by the specialized skills of others.

This same reasoning applies to trade between nations. The more nations use the specialized skills of others, the wealthier all nations become. The less we depend on the specialized skills of other countries, the more we try to be self-sufficient, the more money we will spend producing goods for which we lack the resources or skills. We could spend $15 a pound growing coffee in climate-controlled hothouses if we wanted to. But this lavish use of our own resources is unnecessary and foolish if we can buy coffee for $4 a pound from Brazil.

Unfortunately, nations are less apt to accept this harmonious view of living together than are individuals or regions within nations. Differences in wealth (resources), in language, currencies, customs, and religion, as well as differences arising out of past international conflicts over territory, serve to make nations wary of one another and less able to give up the notion of self-sufficiency. Purely from the standpoint of economics, however (overlooking considerations of national defense), we can say that the freer the trade, the better the result is for everyone.

This chapter is divided into five sections: (1) The economic theory of specialization and exchange, (2) obstacles to free international trade, (3) the mechanics of trade, (4) the international value of the dollar, and (5) floating exchange rates, tight money, and jobs. An appendix called "The Money Side of International Trade" follows this chapter.

THE ECONOMIC THEORY
OF SPECIALIZATION AND EXCHANGE

Adam Smith was one of the first to understand the benefits of specialization and exchange. He realized that it takes time to start a task, stop it, switch to another task, and so on. He realized that people would lose much less start-and-stop time if they had only one job to do, and that they would gradually become much more proficient if they could concentrate on that task, rather than trying to perform many others as well.

Smith explained this idea in a famous passage about making straight pins for sewing:

> To take an example, therefore from a trifling manufacture . . . the trade of
> a pin-maker; a workman not educated to this business . . . could scarce,
> perhaps, with his utmost industry, make one pin in a day, and certainly
> could not make twenty. But in the way in which this business is now
> carried on . . . one man draws out the wire, another straights it, a third

cuts it, a fourth points it, a fifth grinds it at the top for receiving the head; to make the head requires two or three distinct operations; to put it on is a peculiar business, to whiten the pins is another; it is even a trade by itself to put them into the paper; and the important business of making a pin is, in this manner, divided into about eighteen distinct operations . . . all performed by distinct hands. . . . I have seen a small manufactory of this kind where ten men only were employed, and where . . . they could make among them . . . upwards of forty-eight thousand pins, each might be considered as making four thousand eight hundred pins in a day.[1]

But what does this division of labor in a pin factory have to do with international trade? Smith's famous answer to this question is that "the division of labor is limited [only] to the extent of the market."[2] He meant that if the market is very small, as in a small village, the opportunities for division of labor will be small. There will not be enough demand for shoes to permit someone to do nothing but make shoes or to permit many other specialties to be self-supporting. It is only because the market is big enough to absorb 48,000 pins a day that we can have ten men doing nothing but making pins, or one man doing nothing but sharpening the wire to a point.

If the market encompasses the whole world, then consumers can enjoy the enormous gains from production divided into the minutest of tasks. Thus, a world market with an international division of labor is at the core of Smith's belief in international free trade.

Just as the pin factory helped Adam Smith to see the benefits of specialization and trade, a model called the **production possibilities table** helps today's economists analyze the benefits of specialization and exchange.

The Production Possibilities Table

Remembering that the reasons for specialization and exchange apply to individuals, cities, states, and regions, as well as to nations, let's assume a model involving Sue and Tom Makepeace. The young couple own and operate a restaurant that specializes in pita-bread hamburgers made with shredded onions and tomatoes, and omelettes made with herbs and grated Swiss cheese. Sue and Tom are, each of them, good at making the hamburgers and omelettes. But a question arises: Which one of them should make the hamburgers and which one should make the omelettes?

We must now make some assumptions about what economists call production possibilities. The production possibilities of an individual, state, or nation are the various combinations of products that can be produced, assuming (1) a certain level of technology, (2) a certain quantity of resources, (3) a certain quality of resources, and (4) the full-time occupation (full employment) of the individual, state, or nation in producing its products.

Assuming that these four variables do not change, the problem of opportunity cost arises. Because Sue is fully employed (assumption 4), she is totally busy making hamburgers and/or omelettes. Any decision Sue might make to prepare and cook another omelette will mean that she will be unable to prepare and cook some hamburgers. The opportunity cost of doing the omelettes is measured by the loss of some hamburgers, and vice versa.

How many hamburgers are lost when Sue does the omelettes? We'll assume that she can cook two omelettes in the time that it takes her to make four

Table 20-1. Sue's Omelettes-Hamburgers Production Possibilities (per hour)

Possibility	Omelettes	Hamburgers
A	0	12
B	2	8
C	4	4
D	6	0

Table 20-2. Tom's Omelettes-Hamburgers Production Possibilities (per hour)

Possibility	Omelettes	Hamburgers
A	0	9
B	1	6
C	2	3
D	3	0

hamburgers; the production of each omelette therefore involves the sacrifice (opportunity cost) of two hamburgers. This constant relationship of one omelette for two hamburgers is maintained throughout all Sue's working hours. The assumption that Sue can always cook another omelette at the sacrifice of two hamburgers is called the *assumption of constant cost.*

Table 20-1 is a production possibilities table. It shows four different combinations (possibilities) Sue is capable of producing per hour, using all of her time, resources, and skills. The table has two extremes. Possibility A tells us that if Sue were to spend no time at all cooking omelettes, she could make twelve hamburgers. The other extreme, possibility D, shows that, if Sue were to spend all her time cooking omelettes, she could cook six omelettes but make no hamburgers. Notice that the relationship of two omelettes for four hamburgers is maintained with each possibility. Every time Sue decides to cook two more omelettes, she must sacrifice four hamburgers. Thus, Sue's opportunity cost for cooking each additional omelette is always two hamburgers. Table 20-2 shows the same information for Tom.

The Principle of Comparative Advantage

Now the question is, should Sue and Tom specialize, with one person doing the omelettes and the other the hamburgers? The answer isn't easy, because Sue is actually better than Tom at both chores. But we can decide by looking at opportunity cost. We know that every time Sue cooks another omelette she must give up two hamburgers. What about Tom?

Whenever Tom decides to cook another omelette, he must give up (opportunity cost) three hamburgers. Thus, the opportunity cost of cooking omelettes is *less* for Sue.

Does it work the other way? Yes. Whenever Sue decides to make four more hamburgers, we can see that she must sacrifice two omelettes. Her opportunity cost in making each additional hamburger is the loss of half an omelette. Whenever Tom decides to make three more hamburgers, he must sacrifice one omelette; if Tom makes *one* more hamburger, he loses one third of an omelette. Because one third is less than one half, the opportunity cost for making hamburgers is less for Tom. Clearly, it is cheaper in terms of opportunity cost for Sue to cook the omelettes and for Tom to make the hamburgers. They have an economic reason for specializing.

When an individual or nation is superior at producing one product, that individual or nation is said to have an *absolute advantage* in the production of that product. In the Sue-Tom example, Sue has the absolute advantage in both tasks. She can make more hamburgers and can cook more omelettes than Tom can. But identifying who has an absolute advantage does not necessarily tell us who should specialize in which product. For example, a lawyer may be an expert typist, far better than anyone she can hire to do her typing. The lawyer has an absolute advantage in typing. But does that mean the lawyer should do her own typing? Obviously not. The opportunity cost of the lawyer's typing will be much higher than the opportunity cost of typing done by a hired typist. (The lawyer might lose thousands of dollars in fees while typing her own briefs. The hired typist's opportunity cost while typing for the lawyer would be measured by the highest hourly wage—perhaps $10 an hour—he might earn while typing for someone else.)

Thus, the answer to the question, "Who should do what?" lies in the opportunity costs of specialization. If one country, or individual, has lower opportunity costs than another in the cooking of omelettes, for example, then it should cook omelettes. This conclusion leads us to the **principle of comparative advantage**.

A country, or individual, having lower opportunity costs than others in the production of some product is said to have a comparative advantage in the production of that product. Moreover, if the participants in a *specialization-exchange relationship* permit each party to specialize in making the product in which that country or individual has the comparative advantage, both parties will benefit.

The Benefits of Specialization and Exchange

Suppose that before specialization and exchange, Sue and Tom are both operating at possibility C. Sue cooks four omelettes and makes four hamburgers; Tom cooks two omelettes and makes three hamburgers. Therefore, before specializing, their combined production is six omelettes and seven hamburgers. If they specialize, with Sue doing all the omelettes (six omelettes and no hamburgers)

Table 20-3. The Benefits of Specialization and Exchange

	Omelettes	Hamburgers
Before specialization at Possibility C		
Sue	4	4
Tom	2	3
Total	6	7
After specialization		
Sue	6	0
Tom	0	9
Total	6	9
Gain	No gain	+ 2 hamburgers

while Tom does all the hamburgers (nine hamburgers and no omelettes), there is a clear gain of two hamburgers.

The secret of the principle of comparative advantage is that benefits may be obtained by specializing when there is a difference in opportunity costs. In this case, Tom has the comparative advantage in making hamburgers, even though Sue can do more hamburgers than he can in the same time (twelve hamburgers versus nine hamburgers). Table 20-3 summarizes the benefit they obtain through specialization and exchange.

The principle of comparative advantage works just as well for nations as it does for individuals. If the Japanese have a comparative advantage in the production of, say, television sets, relative to the United States, the production of television sets in this country will involve a greater sacrifice of the other products we *could* have made (opportunity cost) than for the Japanese. American consumers will benefit by being able to buy lower-priced Japanese TV sets. (Of course, American television manufacturers will be unhappy, but a decline in their sales will release resources for the production of goods where *we* have a comparative advantage, like farm machinery.)

When, however, the complications of transportation costs, differences in quality, and consumer demand are introduced, the basic principle remains the same—but specialization may not be complete. The two countries will probably continue to produce some of both products and exchange some of both.

Although specialization and the principle of comparative advantage provide sound reasons for international trade, many nations still seek to benefit their economies by erecting various obstacles to trade. In the last two decades particularly, many efforts have been made to overcome some of these obstacles.

OBSTACLES TO FREE INTERNATIONAL TRADE

There are two kinds of obstacles to trade: tariff barriers and nontariff barriers. Both are important because they interfere with the operation of the principle of comparative advantage.

Tariff Barriers

A **tariff** is simply a tax on imported products. The tariff may be a percentage of the product price or it may be a flat fee for a given quantity of the product

($1.25 per twelve-bottle case of French wine). Tariffs fall into two general categories—revenue tariffs and protective tariffs. *Revenue tariffs*, like most taxes, are designed to provide the government with revenue. Typically, they are levied against products a country does not have, such as tin, coffee, and bananas in the case of the United States. *Protective tariffs*, on the other hand, are designed to protect a particular industry from foreign competition by taxing the foreign product so that its price will no longer be so competitive.

Tariffs are not only a barrier to trade; they may also support a less-efficient industry at the expense of more efficient ones and may cause higher prices for consumers. If, for example, the Italians can produce shoes at a lower opportunity cost than Americans can, and the United States taxes each imported pair of Italian shoes, the tax will cause the American retail price of Italian shoes to rise, making them less competitive with American shoes (the intent of the tariff). Because the taxed Italian shoes now cost more, American shoe buyers will buy more American shoes, causing the shoe factories to hire more people and use larger quantities of all resources. Resources will flow to the protected industry.

But, to the extent that resources flow to that industry, another industry in which Americans are more efficient—perhaps golf-ball production—is deprived of these resources. Moreover, consumers will have to pay more for imported shoes because of the tariff *and* more for domestic shoes because the tariff protects U.S. shoe manufacturers against foreign competition. And American consumers will also lose because golf-ball producers will have to pay more for resources and charge higher prices for golf balls. The primary beneficiaries of the tariff will be the owners of shoe-manufacturing firms and their employees.

Nontariff Barriers

We talked about barriers to entry in a local or national economy in Chapters 8 and 9. What if highly skilled entrepreneurs are prevented from producing something that they are particularly good at making because the patent rights to some crucial part are owned by someone else? What if an excellent typist cannot get a job because he or she is black? What if a skilled typesetter cannot get a job because the local typographer's union will not accept new members? These situations illustrate barriers to entry. Barriers to entry prevent the principle of comparative advantage from working among individuals, and industries—and also among nations.

Nations have created a vast array of rules and regulations that are not tariffs but that accomplish the same purpose. These **nontariff barriers (NTBs)** undoubtedly cause more serious distortions of world trade and the free operation of the principle of comparative advantage than tariffs do. Furthermore, while tariff rates have come down, NTBs seem more meddlesome than ever.

It was once reported that Kentucky Fried Chicken could be sold in Japan, but not if the chickens came from Kentucky—or from anywhere except Japan, for that matter. Japanese customs inspectors politely explained that all non-Japanese chickens have skin diseases. There are Kentucky Fried Chicken establishments in Japan now, but the chickens have to be Japanese.

In France, an imported tractor can't be sold if it runs faster than 17 miles per hour. In Germany it is 13 mph. In the Netherlands it is 10 mph. The point, of course, is that these countries want to develop their own tractor-manufacturing industries.

The *Los Angeles Times* once reported that "you can ship fresh fruit from America to the Common Market, but don't be surprised if it never gets unloaded. The customs inspector may be ill or off duty when the cargo arrives. The fruit spoils on the ship."[3]

There are six common kinds of nontariff barriers:

1. *Import quotas* set an absolute limit on the quantity of a product one country allows itself to buy from another. Quotas are often regarded as even more harmful to American consumers than tariffs, although both import quotas and tariffs can raise prices.

2. *Export subsidies*, either through direct governmental grants to an industry or tax breaks, may enable a domestic producer to export goods at a price no foreign competitor can match.

3. *Dumping*—selling a product abroad for less than its price at home—may result from export subsidies.

4. *Buy-at-home policies* may require that products be clearly labeled with the country of origin, and considerable pressure may be put on consumers to buy domestic products.

5. *Rigid health and safety standards* may be designed less to protect health than to prove that products from other countries are unhealthy or unsafe.

6. *Preferential trading arrangements* may favor some countries and discriminate against others. The Reciprocal Trade Agreements Law of 1934 includes a **most-favored nation (MFN) principle** under which a trade concession granted to one nation may be granted to all other trading partners. The granting or withholding of the MFN benefit has, occasionally, been used as a weapon.

Arguments in Favor of Tariffs and Import Quotas

There are five common arguments in favor of tariffs and import quotas (the most important nontariff barrier): (1) That these barriers protect domestic employment, (2) that they help diversify industry, (3) that they protect infant industries, (4) that they protect American workers against "cheap foreign labor," and (5) that they protect defense industries. For each argument in favor, there is a counterargument.

Tariffs and Quotas Protect Domestic Employment

This argument recognizes the importance of net exports in aggregate demand. If imports rise, net exports drop and Americans lose jobs because they no longer produce the products brought in by importers. Therefore, the argument goes, we must use tariffs or quotas to reduce imports.

The position seems logical enough, but it overlooks several facts of life. All nations cannot maintain an export surplus. International trade is a two-way street. One nation's exports are another's imports. If one nation is to have a favorable trade balance, some other nation must have an unfavorable balance, and that nation will experience rising unemployment. A nation in this situation must increase its exports, but if it cannot, because of tariff walls or quotas in other countries, it will very likely try to reduce its own imports with similar restrictions. As countries with unfavorable trade balances retaliate, the exports of all countries will decline and the world will be worse off.

We must also remember that if a certain country is to buy American farm machinery, it must have acquired a supply of U.S. dollars to pay the machinery manufacturers. How does that country get the dollars? Only by Americans buying something from it. When Americans buy Japanese cars, the Japanese accumulate dollars because Americans have to buy yen with dollars and the yen are then given to the Japanese manufacturer. The Japanese can then use the dollars to buy American products.

Tariffs Help Diversify Industry

Another argument for tariffs is that we must protect some industries in order to preserve the diversification of industry. This argument holds that we should not allow the principle of comparative advantage to persuade us to put all of our eggs in a few baskets.

There may be some truth to this argument, but it seems hardly relevant in diversified economies like those of the United States or other industrial countries. For countries that are heavily committed to one crop—coffee in Brazil, cotton in Egypt—the argument assumes greater importance. But the cost of diversifying and protecting new industries with tariffs may be very large. And the consumer always pays that cost.

Tariffs and Quotas Protect Infant Industries

This argument calls for the protection of new industries until they become established. Again, the argument makes little sense in the United States. Moreover, a protected infant industry may never grow up. Once it is protected, such an industry frequently puts great political pressure on Congress to continue the protection and may provide heavy financial support for sympathetic congressmen during their election campaigns. The infant-industry argument may, however, have some relevance for less-developed countries, which need to produce a greater variety of their own products.

Tariffs and Quotas Protect American Workers against "Cheap Foreign Labor"

According to this argument, the more cheap goods we let in, the more American wages will fall in competition with the "cheap foreign labor" of the exporting country. Our standard of living will go down as the wages of others go up, it is said.

Economists reject this argument as completely fallacious. First, the influx of cheap goods helps American consumers, a great many of whom are workers. Low-priced products extend the purchasing power of the dollar; real wages rise as a result.

Second, the cheap-labor argument ignores the fact that labor cost is only one of many costs of production. American labor is highly paid, but American workers use enormously productive machines (capital goods). If a $10-an-hour American laborer produces 1,000 units per hour, the average labor cost per unit is 1 cent. If a laborer earning 50 cents per hour in a poor country produces only 10 units per hour because of the absence of capital goods, the labor cost per unit is 5 cents.

Finally, the American worker earns more than the worker in the poor country because, in addition to having the machine, he or she knows how to use it.

The watch industry keeps watch to defend its role in the national defense.

Tariffs and Quotas Protect Defense Industries

This argument is a tough one. If America is on the brink of war, it may make sense to protect industries that are closely connected with national defense.

But there are many pitfalls. The benefits of being self-sufficient in defense-connected industries are extremely hard to measure. The trade-off of any such benefit is the immediate loss of good will in the countries from which the United States might have bought large quantities of defense-connected supplies. Further, how does one always know whether or not the industry really is a necessary part of national defense? Any industry can claim this role—as has the American watch industry, on the theory that the skills of Amerian watchmakers need to be maintained for possible work on military gadgets in time of war.

One possible solution to this argument and several of the others is to give outright subsidies to those industries that voters decide need protection instead of protecting them with tariffs or quotas.

Trade Agreements in the Last 50 Years

Tariff rates have dropped since the 1930s. In the early years of the Depression, Congress passed the *Smoot-Hawley Tariff Act*, which raised American tariff rates on imports to 52.8 percent of their value. Countries around the world retaliated, and the result was a breakdown in international trade.

In 1947, in a move to liberalize trade, the United States signed a treaty with 23 other countries called the **General Agreement on Tariffs and Trade (GATT)**. GATT, now an organization of 81 nations, has been successful so far in the realm of tariff rates but has been less successful with nontariff barriers such as import quotas.

The United States supported its commitment to GATT with the **Trade Ex-**

pansion Act of 1962, under which the United States and the European Common Market agreed to lower substantially or eliminate entirely tariffs on those products on which they together had 80 percent or more of the world's trade. The Trade Expansion Act has led to many rounds of talks about reducing tariff rates, which in 1982 averaged around 8 percent of the value of imported products. Averages can be misleading, however, because they conceal the effects of high rates relative to low rates. Average tariff rates are calculated only on the basis of the values of goods that actually enter a country. If a product is blocked partially or completely from entering a country because of a high tariff rate, its resulting decline as an import will so reduce the revenues collected on it that the high rate will not noticeably affect the average of all rates.

Although progress has been made in lowering tariff rates, the NTBs have proved much more difficult to eliminate. The United States has been inclined to favor not GATT, but the **Organization for Economic Cooperation and Development (OECD)**, formed in 1960, as a more appropriate institution for liberalizing trade.*

Prospects for the Future

In the United States, the battle lines are drawn between the advocates of freer trade and advocates for increased protection. On the one hand, firms producing military hardware for export to other countries, firms producing agricultural equipment, and grain farmers are for free trade because all of them are interested in exporting: They know that in order to export, the United States must import and maintain friendly trade relations around the world.

The leaders of the protectionists are the industrial unions—steelworkers, glass-bottle blowers, textile workers, machinists, theatrical employees, and merchant seamen. They worry about competition from imports of goods and services (the use of foreign ships in the case of the seamen). The United Automobile Workers (UAW) is in a difficult position because the union represents some workers who are for and others who are against free trade. (Workers producing weapons and agricultural equipment on the free-trade side face opposition from automobile workers who would like to keep out foreign cars.)

Concern about persistently high unemployment rates is leading to a new wave of protectionism all over the world. In the United States, protectionism has taken several forms:

1. So-called trigger-price mechanisms that automatically trigger increased tariffs on imports like steel when these imports reach a certain percentage of domestic sales.

2. "Domestic content laws"** that would require foreign auto-makers with sales in the 100,000 to 150,000 car range to show that at least 25 percent of the average wholesale price of their cars was produced in the United States. The percentage minimum would rise to 90 percent for foreign companies selling more than 150,000 cars in the United States.

3. Voluntary acceptance by the Japanese of quotas on shipments of their

---

*OECD members are all of the noncommunist European countries plus Australia, Canada, Finland, Iceland, Japan, Turkey, New Zealand, Yugoslavia, and the United States, a total of 24 countries.

**The measure, called The Fair Practices in Automotive Products Act, was widely endorsed by members of Congress, but it had not passed by year's end, 1982.

cars to the United States. To avoid an all-out trade war with the United States, the Japanese agreed (under pressure) on April 1, 1981, to limit their shipments of cars to the United States to 93.3 percent of their 1980 shipments.

The Consequences of Protectionism

Whenever any country erects barriers to incoming trade, there is always a danger of retaliation by other countries. If a trade war results, international trade will decline, GNPs will drop, unemployment will rise, and consumers will suffer from higher prices. The United States and its trading partners went through a trade war in the 1930s, the result of which was to make the Depression even worse.

Today, the United States is dependent on the smooth functioning of international trade as never before for two major reasons:

1. Our exports have increased to 13 percent of GNP, up from 6.6 percent in 1970.* Job losses from imports—as in the automobile industry—are highly visible, but much less visible is the fact that employment related to industrial exports increased by 47 percent or 1.5 million jobs, in just three years from 1977 to 1980. If exports had not soared during that period, the total number of manufacturing jobs in the United States would have declined by about 1 million instead of increasing by about 500,000. All told, about 5 million jobs are involved with American exports.

2. We depend on other countries for materials that are essential to manufacturing: 100 percent of columbium, strontium, and industrial diamonds come from other countries. More than 90 percent of our manganese, tantalum, bauxite, cobalt, and chromium is imported. In fact, we depend on other countries for 23 of the 36 materials labeled strategic. Shortages of any of these materials would seriously cripple industrial production.

Trade Barriers Benefit a Few at the Expense of Many

Trade barriers help the industries they protect—for a while, assuming that other competing countries don't retaliate. The problem is that trade barriers may help one group of workers that can be easily identified but hurt many other masses of workers working in assorted industries where they cannot be easily identified.

A case in point is the domestic-content proposal to help the U.S. auto industry. Douglas Fraser, the UAW president, commented that the measure would save 941,000 jobs—a large, highly visible group of people.

Much less visible are the 5 million people working in export-related industries who would be hurt by countries seeking to block our exports if the domestic content measure is passed. American consumers would suffer because the domestic content measure is expected to add 10 percent to the cost of cars by 1984.[4]

Finally, the domestic content measure skirts the real problem: Production of cars is cheaper in other countries. American auto manufacturers are already trying to solve that basic problem by making cars elsewhere. Arrangements are already in place whereby Chrysler and General Motors import Japanese cars. General Motors has begun importing 400,000 engines a year from Mexico. Ford

---

*By comparison, Japan's exports as a percentage of its GNP were not much larger—14.5 percent in 1980.

will begin in 1983 to import 740,000 engines annually from Mexico, Japan, West Germany, and Austria. Our point is that laws designed to restrain a market-price system—such as the domestic content measure—will provoke intelligent entrepreneurs to circumvent them.

As you will see in the next section, international trade requires reciprocity. If we are to *sell* our products to other countries, we have to buy from those countries. *Our* purchases provide them with the dollars they need to buy from us. If we are to *buy* from other countries, we have to sell to them. *Their* purchases provide us with the foreign currencies we need to buy from them.*

THE MECHANICS OF TRADE

This section helps to show how other countries acquire dollars when they sell to us, and how we acquire their currencies when we buy from other countries. As you will see, the Japanese acquire dollars by persuading us to buy their products; for example, Datsuns. By the same token, we can buy Datsuns if we have a supply of yen, and we obtain those yen by selling the Japanese something they need; say, soybeans.

Importing Datsuns, Exporting Soybeans

The mechanics of buying Datsuns from a Japanese manufacturer are many and varied, but it all comes down to this: The Datsun manufacturer wants to be paid in yen, not dollars. He wants a demand deposit in a Japanese bank in yen so that he can write checks to pay his expenses. Similarly, the American producer exporting soybeans wants dollars to be paid into his demand-deposit account in his local bank.

We can illustrate the process of international buying and selling by showing only the final steps in the transaction. To do this, we will imagine two banks: a U.S. commercial bank, called Mainstreet Bank, and a commercial bank in Japan, called Nippon Bank. The American importers of Datsuns and the American exporters of soybeans have their demand-deposit accounts in Mainstreet Bank. The Japanese exporters of Datsuns and the Japanese importers of soybeans have their demand-deposit accounts in Nippon Bank.

We now want to show one common way of financing the import of a Datsun by an American firm and the export of soybeans by an American company to a Japanese importer.

We will begin with the purchase of one Datsun automobile by the American importer. Keep in mind that the American has dollars to spend, but the Datsun Company wants to be paid in yen. We will assume that the Datsun Company wants 1.2 million yen for one Datsun (excluding all shipping costs and tariffs). How much is that? The exchange rate will tell us. In late 1982, the exchange rate was 240 yen per dollar. The dollar price of the Datsun in Japan is therefore $5,000 (1.2 million ÷ 240).

- Step 1. Our American importer writes a check for $5,000 on his demand-deposit account in Mainstreet Bank.
- Step 2. The check in dollars is now sent to the Datsun Company in Japan.
- Step 3. Of course the Datsun Company wants yen, not dollars. The Datsun

---

*These statements are true in principle but not always true in fact when applied to the United States. The reason is that many countries use the U.S. dollar for international exchange; consequently, it's usually more important for other countries to sell to us (which gives them dollars) than to buy from us.

Company therefore asks Nippon Bank to credit its demand-deposit account with $5,000 worth of yen (1.2 million yen).

■ Step 4. Nippon Bank now sends the American importer's $5,000 check to Mainstreet Bank in the U.S. There, Mainstreet Bank gives Nippon Bank a demand-deposit account for $5,000. Nippon Bank now has $5,000 in a U.S. bank that it can offer its Japanese customers, those who may want dollars for purchases in the U.S. If it were not for such an eventual Japanese demand for dollars, a Japanese bank would have no reason to pay out yen (to the Datsun company) upon receipt of an American check drawn in dollars.

Let us look at the American export of $1,000 worth of soybeans to a Japanese importer (for resale to a Japanese manufacturer of soy sauce). The process goes into reverse. The American firm wants $1,000.

■ Step 1. Now, because Nippon Bank has a demand deposit in dollars in Mainstreet Bank, the Japanese importer can buy a $1,000 check from Nippon Bank drawn on Nippon Bank's American account. The check will cost the Japanese importer 240,000 yen ($1,000 × 240), which Nippon Bank will deduct from the importer's account.

■ Step 2. The $1,000 check is now sent to the Soybean Company in the United States.

■ Step 3. The Soybean Company deposits the check in Mainstreet Bank. The Soybean Company's account goes up by $1,000.

■ Step 4. Mainstreet Bank clears the check by deducting $1,000 from Nippon Bank's demand-deposit account.

You may have noticed a peculiarity in this example: Nippon Bank has an account in Mainstreet Bank but not vice versa. In the real world this happens because other countries are accustomed to using dollars as an international medium of exchange. However, this condition is not necessary. Mainstreet Bank could have a deposit in yen in Nippon Bank. We have selected an approach that emphasizes the customary use of dollars.

This example has been deliberately rigged to illustrate the typical pattern of our trade with Japan. We bought more from the Japanese (the $5,000 Datsun) than they bought from us (the $1,000 worth of soybeans). For the past twenty years our total imports from Japan have been greater than our total sales (exports) to Japan.

Why, if the Japanese continue to pile up dollars from their exports to the United States, are they willing to continue to accumulate dollars in their accounts? A probable answer: The Japanese need these dollar accounts for their Japanese customers who may wish to buy in the United States or who may wish to use these dollars for purchases in any country. As the Japanese supply of dollars increases, however, we can visualize that banks such as Nippon Bank will become more and more reluctant to pay out yen to Japanese exporters such as the Datsun Company in exchange for deposits in dollars in the United States.

The excess of purchases from foreign countries over sales to foreign countries is called a **trade deficit**. An excess of sales over purchases is called a **trade surplus**. There is a *trade imbalance* whenever purchases and sales are not equal.

At this point, the question arises, why are trade deficits or surpluses important? The answer is that they are important because they affect the international value of our dollars. If trade deficits persist, the international value of the dollar will fall. We will find that foreign products like Japanese cars and television sets, and also travel in other countries, have all become more expensive. A trade surplus means the reverse, but even a trade surplus will cause some concern, because the surplus will mean that the international value of the dollar is rising. Then, we will find that all our products and services (such as air travel) have become more expensive for foreigners. Our exports are apt to suffer, and the jobs of 5 million American workers in export industries may be threatened. All of these concerns mean that changes in the international value of the dollar can have a direct bearing on our welfare.

THE INTERNATIONAL VALUE OF THE DOLLAR

The international value of a dollar is *measured* by the number of Japanese yen, German marks, French francs, and so on, it will buy. The amount of foreign currencies the dollar will buy measures the quantities of foreign goods and services it will buy. These quantities are the "real" measure of the international value of a dollar. But what *determines* the amounts of another country's currency a dollar will buy?

The answer to that crucial question lies in the Datsun-soybean example. The more we want Datsuns, the more dollars we will offer for a given number of yen. To put it another way, the more we want Datsuns, the *fewer* yen the Japanese will offer for each dollar. These statements may sound complicated, but they illustrate a simple fact of life: The more we want apples, the more the price of apples will increase, and at higher prices, each of our dollars will buy fewer apples. And of course, the same goes for increases in the Japanese demand for our soybeans. When the Japanese demand for soybeans increases, the Japanese will offer more yen for each dollar.

Therefore, the international value of the dollar depends entirely on our demand for foreign goods and services, and on foreign demand for our goods and services. As one would expect, our demand for foreign goods and services, and foreign demand for our goods and services, change daily. Consequently, exchange rates change daily. The official term is **floating exchange rates**, meaning that exchange rates are free to float (to change) as determined by international changes in demand.

When Exchange Rates Float

Prior to the arrival of floating exchange rates in the early 1970s, exchange rates were determined by international agreement tying the currencies of almost all noncommunist countries to an agreed-upon price of gold. The role of gold in international exchange rates is discussed in an appendix that follows this chapter. Suffice it to say here that the role of gold in international trade has almost disappeared and that exchange rates in most noncommunist countries are as free to change as any price is free to change (assuming no government-set price floors or ceilings). For example, if a U.S. trade deficit persists, the Japanese will not exchange as many yen for each dollar as they did before. If the exchange rate is free to float, it will change. When the American importer of Datsuns decides to buy another Datsun, he may find that Nippon Bank will pay out only 200 yen for each dollar deposited in the United States instead of 240. In international jargon, the yen has floated upward, the dollar downward.

Currency Depreciation

When the number of yen given by the Japanese for each dollar drops, as in the previous example, from 240 to 200, the U.S. experiences a **currency depreciation**. Do not be deceived by the drop in the number of yen per dollar. Before the depreciation of the dollar, the yen was worth 1/240 of a dollar. After the drop, one yen was worth 1/200 of a dollar, a *larger* amount. In this example, the dollar has depreciated 40 yen or about 17 percent (240 − 200 = 40 and 40 ÷ 240 = 16.67 percent).

If there is a 17 percent depreciation of the dollar relative to the yen, what happens to the price of Datsuns? Remember from page 416 that the Datsun Company still wants to be paid 1.2 million yen for one Datsun. Before depreciation, $5,000 would buy 1.2 million yen. If the dollar is worth only 200 yen, the new Datsun price to Americans will be $6,000 (1.2 million ÷ 200). Not everyone will be happy. American consumers lose, and the Datsun Company may not sell as many Datsuns. But what about the Soybean Company? Before depreciation, the Japanese importers of soybeans had to pay 240,000 yen to obtain the $1,000 for the purchases of soybeans. Now Japanese importers need pay only 200,000 yen to obtain $1,000. The price of soybeans has dropped—not in the United States, but in Japan. The Soybean Company should enjoy an increase in exports to Japan, and Japanese purchasers of soybeans and soy sauce should see a drop in the Japanese retail price of these products.

Notice that when the dollar depreciates relative to the yen, Datsuns, Toyotas, and Hondas all become more expensive for American buyers and, consequently, a lesser threat to U.S. auto-makers. The prices of American cars begin to look relatively more attractive. When the dollar depreciates, American producers, like the Soybean Company, have the chance to increase their exports to other countries as the dollar drops in value relative to other currencies. But as exports continue to increase, the international price of dollars will increase and the whole process will go into reverse.

Thus, depreciation of a country's currency tends to inhibit imports by raising the prices of imported goods and to spur exports by making its goods less expensive abroad. Exporters favor depreciation of their currencies and deplore appreciation, whereas importers favor appreciation and oppose depreciation.

FLOATING EXCHANGE RATES, TIGHT MONEY, AND JOBS

If you do read the appendix following this chapter, you will find that the trade deficit for 1981 was $29.4 billion. More recent data indicate that the trade deficit in 1982 was $36.1 billion,* and preliminary estimates for 1983 indicate that the deficit will be much larger. All these deficits are supposed to trigger an automatic fall in the international value of the dollar. The deficits mean that we are buying much more from other countries than they are from us. As these other countries accumulate dollars, the dollar is supposed to fall, and as the dollar falls, American prices begin to look good to foreigners, and the trade deficit is supposed to disappear. American exports pick up. American exporting companies hire more people. That's the theory. Figure 20-1 is an overview of the way floating exchange rates are supposed to work:

Over the past few years the theory hasn't worked. The dollar *gained* in strength with its major trading partners during the years 1980–1982 from 5 (Canada) to 73 percent (Sweden).** In the case of West Germany, for example, $1 exchanged for 1.72 marks in early 1980; in late 1982, $1 was worth 2.5 marks. This was fine for American travelers, but seen from the German point of view, American products became 45 percent more expensive. American exports to Germany would be hurt, not helped, and the trade deficit would worsen.

Why didn't floating rates help? To put it another way, why didn't trade deficits cause the dollar to float downward? Something was going on that prevented steps 3, 4, and 5 in Figure 20-1 from operating according to the theory.

The answer lies in the enormous flows of currency in and out of international banks. These flows are apparently much larger and more complicated than the requirements of trade indicate. Instead, the international flows of currency follow the dictates of interest rates and the needs of brokers dealing internationally in stocks and bonds. With the imposition of tight money by the Fed and the resulting high interest rates in the United States, American banks attracted some of these flows, estimated at $53 billion in 1982.[5] Because every deposit in dollars tends to strengthen the dollar, our trade deficits refused to disappear and floating rates failed to reverse the process as shown by step 7 in Figure 20-1. American firms lost export business and Americans lost jobs with those export firms.

As 1982 ended, a mixture of forces was at work. The Fed's tight money

---

*This figure has no apparent connection with the *positive* figure for "net exports" shown in Table 12-1. The reason is that the Table 12-1 figure includes a very large plus: income from overseas investments. This plus wipes out the trade deficit and leaves a positive figure for net exports. That "plus" is not included here.

**The Federal Reserve Board of Governors commented in their 1982 *Annual Report* that "beginning with the upsurge in the second half of 1980, through the end of 1982, the weighted average value of the dollar rose more than 40 percent. . . ."

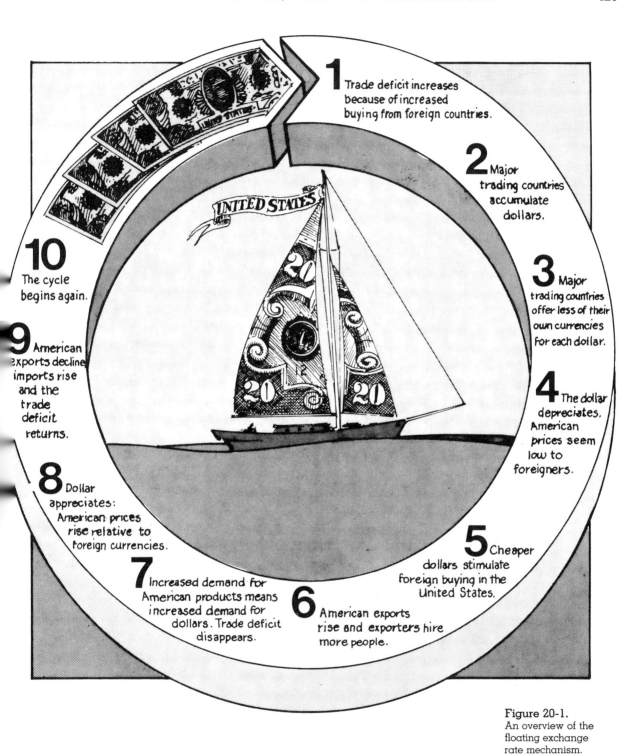

1 Trade deficit increases because of increased buying from foreign countries.

2 Major trading countries accumulate dollars.

3 Major trading countries offer less of their own currencies for each dollar.

4 The dollar depreciates. American prices seem low to foreigners.

5 Cheaper dollars stimulate foreign buying in the United States.

6 American exports rise and exporters hire more people.

7 Increased demand for American products means increased demand for dollars. Trade deficit disappears.

8 Dollar appreciates: American prices rise relative to foreign currencies.

9 American exports decline, imports rise and the trade deficit returns.

10 The cycle begins again.

UNITED STATES

Figure 20-1.
An overview of the floating exchange rate mechanism.

policies had brought inflation rates down to an annual rate of 4 percent. American prices, relative to prices in other countries, should begin to look more attractive, even given a strong dollar. But other forces were at work, too. The Fed dropped its tight money policy; interest rates fell. (The prime rate fell almost 50 percent in the second half of 1982.) The effects of falling interest rates on the dollar were uncertain at year's end. And always, lurking behind the scenes, was the chance that Congress would be pressured into enacting protectionist policies—bringing with them retaliation and diminished trade for everyone.

SUMMARY

Adam Smith argued that free trade permits an international division of labor whereby consumers can enjoy the benefits of products made more cheaply abroad than at home. According to the principle of comparative advantage, even when a country is superior at producing everything, there are still many products it should buy from other countries. Despite the country's superiority, there may be differences in the opportunity cost of specialization relative to other countries, thus providing a logical basis for specialization and exchange.

Trade restrictions fall into two broad categories—tariffs and nontariff barriers. Since 1934, the United States has passed legislation and participated in treaties that have helped lower tariff rates. The most important pieces of legislation are the Reciprocal Trade Agreements Act of 1934 and the Trade Expansion Act of 1962. Treaties with other countries have led to U.S. participation in the 81-nation General Agreement for Tariffs and Trade (GATT) and the 24-nation Organization for Economic Cooperation and Development (OECD). Although these efforts have helped lower tariff rates, nontariff barriers in the form of import quotas, licenses, "buy-American" campaigns, and so forth are apparently more difficult to deal with. Concern in the United States about high unemployment rates is leading to a new wave of protectionism.

To the extent that trade restrictions interfere with the operation of the principle of comparative advantage, a nation's real wealth and income may suffer. Trade restrictions in the long run lead to retaliatory measures in other countries and thus to a general breakdown in the international division of labor.

When two countries want to trade, they must first buy each other's currencies so that they can pay for the product they want in the currency of its producer. When they buy the currency of another country, they give their own currency in exchange.

If country A buys more goods and services from country B than B buys from A, A has a trade deficit with B, and as a result, A's supply of B's currency will dwindle and B's supply of A's currency will grow. Conversely, if A has a trade surplus with B, A's supply of B's currency will increase and B's supply of A's currency will decrease.

Exchange rates of most noncommunist nations float in response to the forces of demand and supply for each other's goods and services. Floating rates can serve as an automatic adjustment mechanism to eliminate deficits and surpluses.

Discussion Questions

1. What is the "wealth of a nation"?

2. If Tom can make two beds in the same time that it takes him to wash and dry twenty dishes, and Sue can make three beds in the same time that it takes her to wash and dry twenty-seven dishes, who has the absolute advantage in what? Who has the comparative advantage in what? How should they divide up the two tasks? Explain.

3. Why do average tariff rates fail to reflect high tariff rates?

4. Why would exporters favor depreciation of their own country's currency?

5. How do floating exchange rates serve as an automatic control mechanism? Is there any evidence that floating rates don't work?

6. What, if any, might be the relationship between a depreciation of the dollar and the level of employment in the United States?

DID YOU EVER WONDER WHY . . .

. . . wheat is grown in Kansas?

References

1. Adam Smith, *An Inquiry into the Nature and Causes of the Wealth of Nations* (Chicago: Great Books Series, Encyclopedia Britannica, 1952), p. 287.

2. Ibid., p. 3.

3. Sterling F. Green, "Maze of Tariffs, Taxes Traps Free World Trade," *Los Angeles Times*, 3 May 1972.

4. Department of Commerce estimate in "An Enormous New Problem," *Los Angeles Times* editorial, 29 July 1982.

5. "The Dynamite Issue," *Newsweek*, 30 May 1983.

KEY WORDS

Special drawing rights (SDRs)
International Monetary Fund (IMF)
Balance-of-international-
payments account
Merchandise trade balance
Current account balance

20A
The Money Side of International Trade

This appendix is devoted to four topics, closely related to international trade, but which you may not have time to absorb in a one-term course. They are: (1) Prices and the principle of comparative advantage, (2) the demise of gold in international trade, (3) the International Monetary Fund, and (4) the Balance of International Payments account.

Table 20A-1. United States and France: Production Possibilities in Golf Balls and Wine

Production possibilities	United States		France	
	Golf balls	Wine	Golf balls	Wine
A	0	6	0	9
B	3	4	2	6
C	6	2	4	3
D	9	0	6	0

Table 20A-2. United States and France: Opportunity Cost in Golf Balls and Wine

United States	France
9 golf balls = 6 bottles wine	6 golf balls = 9 bottles wine
1 ball = .67 bottles	1 bottle = .67 balls
1 bottle = 1.5 balls	1 ball = 1.5 bottles

PRICES AND THE
PRINCIPLE OF COMPARATIVE ADVANTAGE

How are decisions made about importing certain quantities of products from abroad and exporting others to foreign countries when prices and exchange rates are taken into account? In Chapter 20, we used the Sue-Tom example to illustrate the principle of comparative advantage, which encourages countries to specialize in producing certain products and then to exchange them for others.

However, the Sue-Tom illustration was limited to physical units (omelettes and hamburgers). No prices were used. Nor did we consider what would happen if Sue and Tom belonged to different countries and used different currencies. In this section, we will show the connections among production possibilities, the principle of comparative advantage, and prices expressed in different currencies.

In order to show how prices, production possibilities, and the principle of comparative advantage are related, let's design another production possibilities table (Table 20A-1). This time, we will replace Sue and Tom with the United States and France. The two products are golf balls and wine instead of omelettes and hamburgers.

Keep in mind that in any discussion of production possibilities we assume that these are combinations of products that can be produced at full employment. Thus, if either country wants to produce more golf balls, it must take resources away from wine and vice versa.

As Table 20A-1 shows, the United States can make nine golf balls if it pours all of its resources into golf-ball production, but France can make only six. On the other hand, France can make nine bottles of wine with complete specialization; the United States can make only six. Table 20A-2 shows the situation in terms of opportunity cost. Because specialization in golf balls has a lower opportunity cost (comparative advantage) in the United States than in France, the United States should specialize in golf balls. France on the other hand, has the comparative advantage in wine. (Americans give up only 6 bottles of wine to make 9 golf balls; the French have to give up 9 bottles of wine for only 6 golf balls. But the French give up only 6 golf balls to make 9 bottles of wine, whereas the Americans have to sacrifice 9 golf balls for only 6 bottles of wine.)

The United States will trade golf balls for wine as long as the French will exchange more than two thirds of a bottle of wine for each golf ball (the opportunity cost, measured in lost wine, of producing one more golf ball in the United States); France will trade wine for golf balls as long as the United States will exchange at least two thirds of a golf ball for each bottle of wine (the opportunity cost of a bottle measured in lost golf balls in France).

The stage is set. Let us now relate the prices of individual golf balls and bottles of wine, using the exchange rate of 5 francs per dollar. The price of one golf ball in the United States is $1.20; the price of a bottle of wine in France is 6 francs. When U.S. exporters sell one golf ball to the French, the French pay 6 francs to get the $1.20 golf ball (overlooking shipping costs). The Americans can now use those 6 francs to buy a bottle of wine in France.

Are both countries happy? Yes. The Americans are happy to get one bottle of wine for one golf ball because their opportunity cost of producing each additional bottle of wine is 1.5 golf balls. The French are happy to give up a bottle of wine for a golf ball because their opportunity cost of producing golf balls is 1.5 bottles of wine.

All is well so far. Now suppose that the United States buys more wine (measured in dollars) than the dollar value of French purchases of golf balls. The result is a U.S. trade deficit in which the French accumulate dollars and we lose our supply of francs. From our point of view, the decrease in our supply of francs will cause the price of francs as measured in dollars to rise. From the French point of view, the increase in their supply of dollars will cause the price of dollars as measured in francs to fall. As the French accumulate dollars, they begin to look less and less favorably upon the dollar.

Suppose that because of a persistent trade deficit with France the dollar will buy only 4 French francs instead of 5. Now $1.20 will buy only 4.8 francs. In order to buy the 6 francs that a bottle of wine costs, we will have to pay $1.50. If we decide to buy the wine at this price, the French have $1.50 with which to buy our $1.20 golf ball. They can now obtain 1.25 (one and one quarter) golf balls in exchange for one bottle of wine.

Now, the final question arises. Will the Americans be willing to give up 1.25 golf balls (instead of one) to obtain a bottle of French wine? Yes, they will. In the United States, the opportunity cost of producing one bottle of wine is still 1.5 golf balls. Therefore, even at 1.25 golf balls per bottle of wine, it is cheaper for the United States to specialize in golf balls and trade them for French wine.

But when we add the real-world costs of shipping to the increased price of French wine, we may find that the drop in the value of the dollar makes the importation of wine too expensive. The French will probably lose sales, and American consumers will switch to New York or California wines. American winery owners will be happy, but American consumers will undoubtedly have to pay more for American as well as French wine because the American wine producers will not have to compete as hard as before.

THE DEMISE OF GOLD IN INTERNATIONAL TRADE

Up until 1971, the U.S. trade position seemed secure. We had always managed to have a trade surplus. But in 1971 we had our first trade deficit in 93 years. It amounted to *minus* $2.3 billion. (In 1981 it was almost 13 times larger: *minus* $29.4 billion.).

Until August 15, 1971, gold served as an international medium of exchange,

Table 20A-3. Decline in the U.S. Stock of Gold in Selected Years, 1949–1982 (in billions)*

Year	U.S. gold stock
1949	$24.6 billion
1953	22.1
1957	22.9
1961	17.0
1965	13.8
1970	11.1
1982 (August)	11.1

Sources: Economic Report of the President, 1979, and Federal Reserve Bulletin, September 1982.

*In official prices ranging from $35 to $44 per ounce.

and all currencies were expressed in terms of a quantity of gold. For example, suppose that the U.S. Treasury announces that one dollar is worth 1/40 of an ounce of gold. The official price of gold in the United States is then $40 per ounce. And further suppose that the French announce that one franc is worth 1/200 of an ounce of gold. The official price of gold in France is then 200 francs per ounce.

When all currencies are expressed in terms of gold in this manner, we can determine how valuable they are in terms of one another. In the example above, $40 = 1 ounce of gold in the United States; 200 francs = 1 ounce of gold in France. Therefore, $40 = 200 francs, $1 = 5 francs, and 1 franc = 20 cents (one fifth of a dollar).

The domestic price of gold in each of the 124 nations belonging to the International Monetary Fund (IMF) (see next section) determined international exchange rates until 1973. Moreover, until August 15, 1971, the United States agreement with the IMF member nations was that we would give any country that was holding dollars one ounce of gold for every $35 it held. The generally accepted theory was that the agreement to redeem dollars for gold guaranteed the strength of the dollar.

On August 15, 1971, President Nixon made a speech during which he announced "Phase One," the government's attempt to halt inflation with direct price and wage controls. In that speech, the President also announced that the United States would no longer redeem dollars held by foreigners with *gold*.

Why did he do it?

President Nixon had a good reason for his action. We were running out of gold as a result of having had to redeem some of the dollars owned by other countries in order to finance our balance-of-payments deficits. Table 20A-3 shows what has happened to the U.S. supply of gold since 1949.

Our gold disappeared for one basic reason: Other countries accumulated far more dollars than our accumulations of their currencies. By 1972, 80 billion U.S. dollars were held in foreign accounts. Until President Nixon's action, these dollars could be redeemed for gold—and often were.

There were four main causes of this foreign accumulation of dollars:

1. As our industrial trading partners recovered from World War II, they began to outsell us in international markets. Often they sold more to us than

In 1971, Nixon refused the exchange of U.S. dollars held by foreigners for gold.

they bought from us. Other countries accumulated dollars, just as the Japanese did in the Datsun-soybean example in Chapter 20.

2. American travel overseas contributed to the outflow of dollars.

3. Private investment overseas by American multinational corporations added to the exit of dollars.

4. And, finally, U.S. government spending overseas, particularly for military purposes like the NATO armies and the rental of Air Force and Navy bases, added to foreign holdings of dollars.

Following President Nixon's refusal to exchange dollars for gold, gold gradually began to lose its importance in international trade. There were several significant events along the way:

1. You will remember from Chapter 18 that the United States abandoned the gold standard for its own citizens back in 1934 and also made it illegal for Americans to own gold.

2. The major trading countries decided in 1967 (the Rio de Janeiro agreement) to supplement gold with **special drawing rights (SDRs)** because world supplies of gold were insufficient to support growing world trade.

3. In 1975, the U.S. government reversed its 1934 decision to prohibit the private ownership of gold. Thereafter, the U.S. Treasury began to auction off its gold stocks—typically, 1.5 million ounces at a time—to anyone wanting to buy.

4. In the Jamaica agreement of 1976, the IMF members agreed to abandon gold as a measuring stick and to use SDRs only—the value of SDRs to be determined by a "basket" of sixteen major currencies. Further, the IMF was authorized to auction off one third of its gold holdings, the original value to

be returned to the contributors, but the profits to be given to less-developed countries (LDCs). Finally, the Jamaica agreement endorsed floating exchange rates: The world's major currencies were allowed to find their value relative to one another without reference to gold—or even to SDRs. Henceforth, the demand and supply for one another's currency determined exchange rates.

And so gold gradually "died," particularly during the 1970s, largely because the wealthiest trading nation of the world refused to exchange its currency for gold. But we should hasten to add that gold is very much alive in private markets. In December 1979 the free-market price of gold reached $800 per ounce. South African one-ounce gold coins called "Krugerrands" became a popular form of saving in anticipation of continuing gold-price increases. And there are many economists who still prefer the stabilizing effects of gold as a measuring stick rather than the floating rates that may change the value of one's currency daily.

THE INTERNATIONAL MONETARY FUND

As its name indicates, the **International Monetary Fund (IMF)** is a fund of monies deposited by member nations—the nations that are not members of the communist bloc. Each country deposits an amount of gold and an amount of its own currency in the Fund. These sums, called *quotas*, are determined by each country's income and wealth. The United States has by far the largest quota—about 25 percent of the total.

Since then, the IMF has served the function of a world central bank, as the Federal Reserve Bank does in the United States. Its primary function is to lend currencies to member nations who have deficit problems. If a country has used up its supply of German marks, for example, but still wants to buy more German products, it can apply to the IMF for a loan of German marks. Such a loan is usually in the form of a *repurchase agreement*, in which the borrowing country buys the marks with its own currency but agrees to repurchase its currency, with some other currency acceptable to the IMF, at some future date—usually three to five years. The borrowing country must also pay a small interest charge.

The IMF is rarely loved for its help. The developing countries' problems typically involve a combination of trade deficits and inflation. Before the developing country gets the IMF loan, the IMF insists that the developing country's government take stringent steps to correct the country's problems. Before lending Mexico $3.9 billion in early 1983, the IMF insisted that Mexico trim its budget deficit to one fifth of its 1982 size in three years. To do this, the Mexican government began a painful program of firing 1,000 government employees. In both Zaire and Jamaica the IMF stands for wage controls, government austerity, and unemployment. Opposition political parties make hay by promising to get the IMF out of the country. Nevertheless, the IMF's requirements usually help developing countries to obtain not only IMF loans but additional funds from other sources. In recent years, according to one source, the IMF has become the financial market's "Good Housekeeping Seal of Approval."[1]

THE BALANCE OF INTERNATIONAL PAYMENTS ACCOUNT

Governments try to keep track of all money and credit that flows into or out of their countries so that they can predict what is apt to happen (1) to exchange

Table 20A-4. U.S. Balance of International Payments, 1981 (in billions)

I. Current account transactions resulting in U.S. ownership of foreign currency		
(1) Exports	+ $236.3	
(2) Investment income (net)	+ 33.0	
(3) Other services (net)	+ 7.5	
(4) Total	+ $276.8	
II. Current account transactions resulting in foreign ownership of U.S. dollars		
(5) Imports	− $265.7	
(6) Private gifts and government grants	− 6.6	
(7) Total	− $272.3	
III. Current account balance		+ 4.5
IV. Private capital flows (net)		− 25.9
V. Changes in U.S. international reserves		− 5.2
VI. Statistical discrepancy		+ 26.6
VII. Balance of all the pluses and minuses		$ 0.0

Source: Federal Reserve Bulletin, September 1982.

rates, (2) to their "credit rating" (their ability to borrow) with the IMF, and (3) to their stocks of international reserves. For these purposes, nations keep a **balance-of-international-payments account**.

A nation maintains a balance-of-international-payments account to record all transactions with other countries in a given year. In the United States, the account is kept by the Department of Commerce for the three purposes just mentioned. Our balance-of-international-payments account is an attempt to measure not just U.S. exports and imports, but all transactions that lead to a loss of dollars to foreign ownership or to a gain in U.S. ownership of foreign currencies.

The transactions that lead to these outflows or inflows of money are numerous. When General Motors buys control of an Opel factory in Germany, GM must first buy German marks with dollars. This leads to an increase in dollar deposits owned by Germans, just as the U.S. purchase of a Datsun leads to an increase in dollar deposits owned by Japanese. On the other hand, if the GM investment in Opel is profitable, the profits return to the United States via the purchase of dollars with marks so that American owners of GM stock can receive dividend payments in dollars.

There are a host of other ways dollars flow into or out of our control. If we fly on a French airline, sail on a Greek cruise ship, catch a train in Spain, buy British insurance, put money into a Swiss bank, or send money to relatives in Israel, we are buying foreign currencies with dollars and causing the dollar holdings of foreigners to increase. And if foreigners use our services or travel in this country, we obtain increased deposits of their currencies.

All these transactions involve private individuals or enterprises. We must also take into account government spending—rent payments for Air Force or Navy bases overseas; grants or loans to other countries; payments to foreign countries for food, utilities, and foreign labor for the servicing and maintenance of our bases and diplomatic embassies or missions. Table 20A-4 is a simplified version of all these dollar flows in 1981.

When you read newspaper references to this summary of international transactions, often there will be a mention of the **merchandise trade balance**, in this case, line 1 minus line 5 (+$236.3 billion − $265.7 billion = −$29.4 billion). And you will also see references to the **current account balance** (line III). The +$4.5 billion shown here is the difference between lines 4 and 7. Note here that our income from foreign investments (line 2) wipes out the trade deficit of −$29.4 billion.

The private capital flows (line IV) were largely bank loans to foreigners in 1981 (made in order to give them a supply of dollars).

Finally, note that on line VII the account "balances." All the pluses and minuses add up to zero. This is because in international accounting, there is a plus for every minus. Our export of soybeans to Japan is a plus, but their payment to us is a minus. Thus, it is incorrect to think of any plus or minus as either "bad" or "good." However, look at line VI. Line VI shows that all *known* transactions in 1981 actually added up to a *minus* $26.6 billion. But we also know that *somehow* the minus figure was paid for by an inflow of foreign monies seeking dollar deposits; that is, by "a continuing demand for dollar assets that is operating through channels that are not well covered in the reporting system."[2] Here we have evidence of the large inflow resulting from our high interest rates mentioned on page 420.

DID YOU EVER WONDER WHY . . .

. . . Karl Marx might have been surprised to learn of Russia's Communist revolution?

References

1. David Rogers, "International Monetary Fund," *Los Angeles Times*, 18 December 1980.

2. Federal Reserve Board of Governors, *Annual Report, 1982*, p. 26.

21

Economic
Challenges of the Eighties

The 1980s will be a crucial decade that may well determine the ability of human beings to survive on this planet. A bewildering number of crises confront us: The ability of our own nation to cure stagflation, the challenges posed by continued rivalry between Marxist societies and mixed systems, the struggle of poor countries to become richer, the effects of dwindling supplies of resources like oil, trade deficits, the consequences of increases in pollution or population, the pressure on world food supplies, and the increases in world spending for arms. And more.

From this list of issues, we're going to extract two we think are extremely important because each involves elements common to all the listed problems. Accordingly, the chapter is divided into two sections: (1) The challenge of poverty in the developing countries and (2) the increases in world spending for arms.

COPING WITH WORLD POVERTY: THE DEVELOPING COUNTRIES

This section is about poverty among nations. Poverty is, of course, a relative matter. Whenever there is any inequality in the distribution of income, some people will always be poor *relative* to others. But much of the world is so abjectly poor that some observers speak of *absolute* poverty—"a condition of life so degraded by disease, illiteracy, malnutrition, and squalor as to deny its victims basic human necessities."[1]

Almost 1 billion people—one quarter of the world's population—are in this category. A quarter of a million people in Calcutta are homeless. They eat, live, and die in the streets. Three million people in Bolivia out of a total population of 5 million have a life expectancy of 30 years. The average Bolivian eats less than half an ounce of meat per year; in effect, the peasant population is too poor to eat any meat at all.

What Is a "Developing Country"?

Several terms are used to describe countries that are poorer than others: "underdeveloped countries," "third world countries," sometimes even "fourth" or "fifth world countries." Economists have no specific dividing lines or explicit definitions of such terms. A nation's position is usually determined by dividing its GNP by population (per capita GNP) so that there is a "ladder" of countries from rich to poor—from $20,250 per person per year in Kuwait to $110 per person per year in Bangladesh in 1979.

Usually, all countries are classified as either "developed" or "developing," with about two dozen countries in the first category and all the rest in the second. The dividing line is *approximately* $1,000 per person per year, but such a division is arbitrary and often unrevealing. We know that GNP says little about the quality of life. Moreover, a per capita GNP figure conceals the distribution of income within a nation. For example, per capita GNP in Brazil was about $2,000 in 1980, but 30 million of Brazil's 110 million people had average annual incomes of only $77. And so we are left with an imperfect measure of a nation's standard of living, as the next section emphasizes.

The Trouble with Comparing per Capita GNPs

When we use per capita GNPs to compare countries, we find ourselves trapped by numbers that are of little help in describing real differences in standards of

GNP comparisons between countries are misleading.

living. Not only is GNP an imperfect measure of welfare or progress *within* a country, as we saw in Chapter 12, it has even less meaning when used for comparisons between countries. Two examples will clarify this point:

1. In a poor, less-developed country like Tanzania with a per capita GNP of $260 per year, the $260 figure is imperfect because it is based primarily on cash transactions. But much of such a country's production and consumption will typically involve little or no cash. The people in Tanzania's villages feed themselves out of their own production, just as the people in the Chinese communes do. Therefore, in most cases, per capita GNP figures in poor countries understate their true incomes. Of course, that doesn't mean such people are rich. We could double the numbers, and these people would still be abjectly poor by any standard.

2. In the fall of 1978, the author had the good fortune to spend three months in New Zealand with an opportunity to observe and compare New Zealand life-styles with ours. At that time, New Zealand's per capita GNP was about half the United States' per capita GNP. But, it would have been very foolish to conclude that New Zealanders' standard of living was half that of the average American. Fresh food prices were generally half of U.S. prices, so that with much lower wages, the New Zealanders ate just as well as or better than we do. Housing costs (rents and home purchase prices) were also about half of ours. Education, medical care, and retirement pensions were all provided from a highly progressive schedule of income taxes. One real-life example, that of a highly skilled construction worker who retired at age 60. At the time of retirement, he earned $3.80 per hour, by our standards abysmally low after a lifetime of work. Nevertheless, he owned a home and automobile free and clear, had $50,000 in the bank, and began receiving a

Table 21-1. World GNP at Market Prices and Average GNP per Capita (1979), and Population (mid-1979), by Income Group

Per capita income group	Population (millions)	GNP (billions of $)	Average GNP per capita ($)
Less than $330	2,037	$ 464	$ 230
$330–$759	388	185	477
$760–$3,249	642	1,047	1,590
$3,250–$7,589	547	2,568	4,690
$7,590 and over	567	5,892	10,390
Totals	4,181*	$10,156	

Source: 1981 World Bank Atlas.

*This figure is about 150 million too low because population data are unavailable in some countries.

pension of 80 percent of his highest earnings. He and his wife were comfortable and content, traveled overseas occasionally, and had no financial worries.

Offsetting these amenities, the prices of manufactured, imported products like automobiles were very high by U.S. standards. But the problem is, how does one evaluate these differences in life-styles? Can one say that Americans are better off than New Zealanders or vice versa? The question is impossible to answer. Nevertheless, the GNP per capita method of comparison among different countries is the method most commonly used.

In one attempt to improve on the GNP per capita measure, economists have devised an index called the **Physical Quality of Life Index (PQLI)**. The PQLI is a composite of a nation's life expectancy, infant mortality, and literacy. The index is 97 for Sweden, 94 for the United States, 35 for Bangladesh. The index reveals the weaknesses of looking only at GNP per capita: GNP per capita in Saudi Arabia is a healthy $11,000 (1980), but its PQLI is only 28. For that reason Saudi Arabia is usually classified as a "developing" country.

This section reviews the plight of the developing countries. It describes the distribution of the world's income; discusses the reasons why the developed countries, particularly the United States, should be concerned with world poverty; analyzes the two major problems of population increase and lack of capital; and presents some conclusions.

Distribution of the World's Income

Just as income is unevenly distributed in the United States, so is it unequally distributed throughout the world. Table 21-1 shows the distribution of the world's income in 1979.

Table 21-1 shows that in 1979 total world population was 4,181 million (4.2 billion) people and that total world income was $10,156 billion ($10.2 trillion). Average income throughout the world was therefore about $2,400 per person. But the table shows that about half the people are in the lowest category where average income was $230, while 13.6 percent of the people (567 ÷ 4,181) received 58 percent ($5,892 ÷ $10,156) of total income. While we in the United States account for about 5 percent of total world population, we receive about 30 percent of total income.

A further difficulty is that the gap between rich and poor countries is getting wider. During the 20-year period between 1960 and 1979, per capita GNP grew at an annual rate of 1.8 percent in the 36 poorest countries. The comparable annual per capita growth rate among the 18 richest countries was close to 4 percent. Using the rule of 72, a 1.8 percent growth rate will yield a doubling in 40 (72 ÷ 1.8) years. A 4 percent growth rate means a doubling every 18 years.

Even if the growth rates were the same in the two groups, the gap would widen. Assume that the annual per capita growth is 4 percent for both groups and that the poor group starts with a per capita income of $300 and the rich group with $10,000, a beginning difference of $9,700. After doubling in 18 years, the poor group's annual per capita income will be $600, the rich group's will be $20,000, a difference of $19,400. We have to draw the uncomfortable conclusion that the income gap is almost certain to widen and that the relative unhappiness of people in the developing countries is almost certain to increase—unless the rich countries take strong measures to help.

Why Should We Be Concerned?

Aside from the moral issues involved, self-interest provides several basic arguments for our concern with the problems of developing countries. In one way or another, they are our problems too.

Our Need for Strategic and Other Materials

An industrial society like the United States cannot function without certain raw materials. Some examples are oil, asbestos, bauxite (aluminum ore), chrome, cobalt, copper, lead, manganese, nickel, petroleum, platinum, silver, tin, and titanium. Many of these essentials come from the developing countries, and our dependence on other countries keeps growing. In 1950 we relied on other countries to provide us with more than half of our needed supply of four of thirteen strategic materials. By 1985 we will want more than half of our supply of *nine* of the thirteen from other countries.

Many of the developing countries are following the lead of OPEC and forming cartels to control supplies (and prices) of bauxite, tin, coffee, bananas, tea, rubber, and pepper, to name a few. The United States will have to form new relationships with cartel countries to whom it formerly dictated prices.

The Need for Political Stability

It is sometimes said that "only the rich can afford democracy." Consider a nation of starving, uneducated people. It is easy for them to turn to an authoritarian political party or a dictator, whether of the left or the right, who persuades them that he or she can solve their problems. If the dictator becomes the source of international tension, or even war, as in some of the African or Latin American states, the peace of the world may be threatened. No one (rich) nation like the United States can afford to permit a people's suffering to threaten the development of a stable political order throughout the world. Economic assistance to poor nations reduces the risk of internal revolution and military adventurism.

Time Is Running Out

In a world of growing populations and declining food reserves, the time left to solve the world's poverty problems is getting short. The world's population is increasing at the rate of 64 million per year now, rising perhaps to 100 million per year by the year 2000.[2] Roughly 87 percent of these new mouths to feed will be in the developing countries. Some experts believe that if we don't act *now* to solve the problems of population and environmental pollution, the human race will begin to starve and suffocate by the middle of the twenty-first century.

The Revolution of Rising Expectations

Some of our responsibility to help less-developed countries stems from the imperialism of the nineteenth century—the empire period of mother countries and colonies. The United States turned Cuba into its supplier of sugar; Brazil, Colombia, and Central America into its suppliers of coffee and bananas; Chile and Venezuela into its suppliers of copper, nitrates, and oil. And of course the United States was not alone in molding other countries and colonies into one-crop, one-resource economies that were dependent on their mother countries for capital goods. In most cases, the capital goods that were supplied by the United States and other mother countries were for the purpose of assisting the production of one crop or resource. Dependency on "mother" was encouraged, diversified development discouraged.

But as time went on, the colonies became aware that there was a double standard of existence. The imperialists who were visible on the scene lived in mansions and treated the people in the colonies like servants. The imperialists brought with them all the props of development—varied diets, refrigeration, automobiles, country-club enclaves. It was natural for the colonial peoples to demand a new life-style.

What has taken centuries of development in the rich countries, from the Renaissance through the Industrial Revolution, the poor countries want *now*. The result has been called a **revolution of rising expectations**. The poor recognize the need for *power* to control their own destinies and we must recognize this need as legitimate.

Problems That Must Be Solved—And Some Solutions

The developing countries share a number of common problems, any or all of which may be present in any given country. We will take up two of them,* and in each case give some idea about what might be done. The two problems are (1) increases in population that can wipe out any gains in food production, and (2) the difficulty of obtaining all forms of capital—financial, tangible (machines), and human (skilled workers) and of putting this capital to work.

Population and Poverty

The world's population was 4.6 billion in 1981, and that figure was about *1 billion* more than it was in 1960. This last billion was added in *just 17 years*.

Many of the developing countries face ruinous rates of population increase, high rates of infant mortality, and relatively poor life expectancy. For example, the average annual population growth rate in the United States, 1970–1981, was about 1 percent per year. The Rule of 72 tells us that at the rate, the United States population will double in 72 years. By contrast, the comparable rate in India was 2.2 percent per year during the same period. Consequently, India's population will double in 32.7 years (72 ÷ 2.2) unless the Indians manage to

---

*Military spending by developing countries is discussed in a later section of this chapter.

In China, women and men are discouraged from marrying at an early age to help control population growth.

slow the rate down. The average rate for all developing nations was 2.1 percent during the six year period 1975–1980.[3]

To persuade people of the developing countries to slow their rates of population increase is essential—and enormously difficult. In most such countries, adults want and often need large families. The children can help perform manual labor in the fields and support their parents as their parents grow old. Children are the "social security system" in poor countries.

But if the result of economic aid is to keep people alive longer (better food, health care, sanitation) so that more people reach reproductive age and produce more offspring, then the benefits of aid will be swept away in the rising tide of population. Consequently, massive programs to educate the people to have smaller families are a prerequisite for development and for aid.

The People's Republic of China has shown that such a massive educational program can work. In China, premarital sex is frowned upon; women are discouraged from marrying until age 25 and the men until age 28. Families are encouraged to have only one child. Free birth-control devices, abortions, and vasectomies are easy to obtain. In overcrowded Szechwan province with a population of 90 million, parents are offered extra rice rations and cash bonuses for stopping at one baby. China's new goal is to halve its rate of population increase from 2 to 1 percent per year.[4]

Singapore has also instituted a successful plan of imposing penalties on couples who have more than three children. The working mother forfeits maternity leave; the delivery fee is higher. The couple that has more than four children gets a lower priority for choice of primary school and the lowest priority in obtaining subsidized public housing.

It may also be much cheaper for a rich country to help a poor country develop by subsidizing a population-control program than by paying for a program to increase production. Remember that welfare is usually measured by comparing per capita GNPs, and that a nation's per capita GNP is determined by dividing GNP by population. We can make per capita GNP go up by increasing the country's GNP, by reducing its population, or by trying to do some of both. Most economists believe that it is far cheaper to raise a country's per capita GNP by reducing its population—*because the cost of preventing a birth is as little as one dollar per adult per year.*

Dr. Stephen Enke comments, "The moral is clear: If the objective is higher income per head, money spent to reduce births will be as much as 100 times more effective than money invested to raise output."[5] Here is a simple example. Assume GNP is $100,000 and population is 1,000. Per capita GNP is therefore $100,000 ÷ 1,000 = $100. The developing country now receives a grant from rich countries of, say, $500 to build a factory. Because of increased production, GNP increases by $100 to $100,100. Per capita GNP is now $100,100 ÷ 1,000 people = $100.10. The people are 10 cents per capita better off than before. Now suppose instead that the $500 is used to reduce population and that population is reduced by 100 people. Per capita GNP is now $100,000 ÷ 900 = $111.11. The people are now $11.11 per capita better off, roughly 100 times better off than they were with their 10 cent increase following the $100 increase in GNP.

Obtaining and Using Capital

Assuming the developing country tries to increase production (as well as slow its rate of population increase), it can choose any or all of three paths: (1) It can make sure that everyone is working as hard as possible—that there is no "disguised unemployment" involved in make-work jobs or working so inefficiently that fewer people could do the same amount of work. (2) It can follow the lessons of Adam Smith's pin factory by reorganizing the work in order to obtain a greater division of labor. (3) It can acquire tangible capital (machines) or human capital (educated know-how) to increase the productivity of its labor force. Let's look at the third option, as economists do.

THE NEED TO SAVE IN ORDER TO OBTAIN CAPITAL. Let us assume that a developing country does not want or need massive amounts of capital, but *some* capital in small amounts is necessary. How does a developing country go about getting it? A simple model will help.

Assume that a poor country has a GNP of $100 million, that production of food is $100 million, and that the people eat all the food they produce. Under these conditions, total income is $100 million and the people consume the entire $100 million. Saving is zero and so is investment, because all production is devoted to consumption, a not unusual situation in a very poor country.

So long as all the people are busy producing food, none of them can be released to produce capital. There are two exceptions to this line of reasoning: (1) If there is disguised unemployment in the fields, people *can* be released without lowering food production. (2) People might learn how to produce more food by reorganizing the work (through a better division of labor, for example) without having to obtain more capital.

At this point an expert from the United Nations arrives and shows the agricultural workers how they can reorganize their work so that some of their people can be released for creation of capital goods. But how are these workers released from food production to be paid? Somehow, the poor country's government will have to find additional funds by taxing the people (*forced* saving) or by borrowing someone's savings (even the savings of people or of governments in other countries) to finance the investment in capital goods. The crucial point is that the creation or acquisition of capital (machines, factories, etc.) is made possible by funds that are saved; that is, by income *that is not spent on consumption.*

Now the question is, what good will the investment in capital goods do?

The **capital-output ratio** helps to explain. The capital-output ratio is the ratio (measured in dollars) between the cost of capital and the annual income it produces. In the United States, the capital-output ratio is about 3:1. That is, $3 worth of capital will produce about $1 worth of income per year. In other words, $3 worth of saving will permit investment of $3, which will, in turn, produce $1 worth of income per year. If this ratio held in our simple model of a developing country, $15 worth of investment would produce $5 worth of income annually.

The problem is that, in a developing country, the capital-output ratio is more likely to be 5:1. This means that it takes *$5* worth of capital to produce $1 worth of annual income. Each dollar's worth of capital operates less efficiently in a poor country than in a rich one. If the developing country invests $15, it will get $3 worth of income, not $5. To obtain $5 of extra income, it would have to invest *$25*, not $15. And to invest $25, it would have to *save $25.*

The developing country is therefore in a tough spot. It has to save more than a rich country does to obtain the same extra dollar's worth of income. And saving—refraining from consumption—is far more difficult when one is hungry than when one spends only a modest portion of one's income for food (17 percent in the United States).

A word about why the capital-output ratio is so much higher in a developing country. If the capital-output ratio is 3:1, a capital investment produces enough income to pay for itself in three years, a return of 33 1/3 percent. When the ratio is 5:1, the return is considerably less—20 percent. Why so much less? In a developing country, if a capital good, say, an electric generator, breaks down, it may take days to find someone (or find spare parts) to fix it. The efficiency of capital depends on the condition of a country's **social overhead capital** or **infrastructure** (its transportation and communication systems), as well as on the know-how of its workers. All these forms of human and nonhuman capital are of better quality in rich countries than in poor ones and improve the return on capital investments in the rich countries.

THE NEED TO SAVE IN ORDER TO EXPORT. A developing country also has to save if it wants to buy capital goods from other countries. Let us return to our simple model again. If GNP is $100, and consumption is $100, the country has nothing to export. It is consuming all of its income. As we saw in Chapter 20, this means that a developing country is unable to obtain the Swiss francs, German marks, Japanese yen, or U.S. dollars it will need to buy capital goods from these industrial countries.

Thus, a developing country must export to obtain the international reserves with which it can pay for capital goods from other countries. And to export, it must save. It must refrain from consuming some of its production.

If a developing country is unable to export, it will have to obtain foreign exchange through loans or grants from richer countries. But this approach has its own difficulties. The money has to come from somewhere, and lenders usually want to be paid back. The developing countries who do not have the means to pay back such loans are in trouble, as the next section indicates.

THE FINANCIAL CAPITAL PROBLEM. The financial plight of the non-OPEC developing countries became highly visible following the OPEC oil embargo of 1973. The developing countries' ability to import capital and other necessities worsened badly as (1) they had to pay higher and higher prices for oil and (2) the international markets for their exports became sluggish as a result of the worldwide recessions of 1974–1976 and 1980–1982.

By 1982, developing countries had borrowed almost $500 billion from other countries. The bankers are particularly worried about middle-income cases— like Brazil, Mexico, Argentina, Venezuela, Nigeria, Peru, Poland, and China— who owe $310 billion of the total. These debts are worrisome for American banks because the debts represent substantial portions of their total loans. Any delay in prompt repayment makes the banks fear for their own economic health and for their ability to finance loans for American industry. The problem is also very severe for non-oil producing developing countries who owed a total of $100 billion in 1982, up from $39 billion in 1978. For them, one official noted that their "choice will be either lowering their living standard or cutting their development programs. Neither choice is any good."[6]

These indebted countries had a particularly difficult time during the 1980–1982 years. They had a hard time improving their balance of payments for two reasons: (1) The worldwide recession reduced the demand for their products, and (2) high interest rates in the United States attracted foreign capital to the United States that might have otherwise been invested in the poor countries.

Here, in the latter instance, we find one of the many interconnections between countries. Deficit spending in the United States on top of the Fed's tight-money policies led to high interest rates in the United States, which in turn not only caused crowding out in the United States but hurt the developing countries. To help the poorer countries recover, Martin Feldstein[*] believes that we must be prepared to run trade deficits with the poorer countries; that is, we must buy more from them than we sell to them. The resulting trade deficits with these countries would then give them the dollars they need to pay their debts, and also the dollars they could use to buy the capital goods they so desperately need.

In an attempt to solve their financial plight, many of the developing countries have formed alliances such as the **Group of 77**.[7] The Group of 77 has made three kinds of proposals: (1) a general debt moratorium, which would permit them to make *no* debt payments over some period of time; (2) agreements for "indexing" their commodity prices to the prices of the industrial goods they buy,[**] and (3) the creation of a "common fund" to finance the stockpiling of the commodities they sell.

All three plans have problems. A debt moratorium might bankrupt the banks that loaned the money. An indexing arrangement designed to help all less-

[*]Martin Feldstein is a Harvard professor of economics and is currently (1983) President Reagan's chairman of the Council of Economic Advisors. His comment is taken from *Newsweek*, 30 May 1983.

[**]An indexing plan would enable a developing country selling, say, coffee, to raise coffee prices 10 percent if the United States (or any supplier) selling capital goods to it raised its prices 10 percent.

developed countries could only by the "sheerest coincidence," as one scholar pointed out, be appropriate for any one country taken singly.[8]

The third plan would establish a common fund that would finance the stockpiling of commodities produced by the developing countries in times of excess supply and replenish the fund by selling the stockpile when the quantities demanded exceeded the quantities being currently produced. Again, there are formidable obstacles—principally, getting all the participants to agree on their initial contributions to the fund and on the quantities they would produce. The "common fund" idea would involve all of the difficulties our egg producers faced back in Chapter 6 (stemming from the urge to undersell or outproduce one another)—with the further difficulty that we are talking now about many different countries with different national aspirations. Still, the "common fund" idea is probably the best chance for the less-developed countries to provide themselves with a steady income.

MORE AID FROM THE RICH? The United States could probably extend more **official** (government) **development aid (ODA)**. Many governments give larger percentages of their GNPs (though not more money in absolute terms) to the developing countries than does the United States.* Private investment by rich countries in the developing countries can also provide the latter with capital goods and higher wages. But the pattern of private U.S. investment overseas has shifted from development of natural resources in the developing countries to manufacturing in other rich countries. In the 1890s, the bulk of our private overseas investment was in the developing countries. Now only about 25 percent of our overseas investment is, and the percentage appears to be falling. Conscious effort by government agencies to encourage U.S. corporations to invest in the poorer countries would help. Needless to say, this is not easy. The developing country may very well treat outside investment as a return to colonialism, and the corporation might easily consider the possibility for native takeover too risky.

A COMMENT ON HUMAN CAPITAL. The developing countries are desperately in need of a literate population for informed decision making and for the know-how to operate and maintain complicated forms of tangible capital. Before people can be trained in, say, soil chemistry, they have to be able to read. If a country's labor force is illiterate, its labor force can perform only the simplest tasks—usually manual labor in the fields.

Let's compare our illiteracy rate with India's. In the United States only 1 percent of the people over age 15 can neither read nor write in any language. In India, the comparable figure is 66 percent. In 1977, the average illiteracy rate in 100 developing countries was 50 percent.

The apparent solution is for the developed countries to send technicians, teachers, and medical doctors to the developing countries—much like the United States' Peace Corps program. The idea seems attractive on its surface, but there may be an unintended effect. Educational training divides people into classes: some get left behind and income differences grow. Perhaps the

*In 1980 we gave about $5 billion, 0.19 percent of our 1980 GNP. As a percentage of GNP, our giving ranked thirteenth out of seventeen developed countries.

first efforts to help developing countries should be those that disturb the status quo the least.

INTERMEDIATE TECHNOLOGY. The most innovative solution to all of these capital problems comes from a British economist, E. F. Schumacher.[9] Schumacher's solution is to send very modest forms of capital called intermediate technology to the developing nations.

The term **intermediate technology** means a simple tool, the operation of which can be easily understood by an illiterate peasant in a developing country. Dr. Schumacher's prescription: A tool that enhances a worker's energy by, say, 1 horsepower, rather than 300. Dr. Schumacher and his group of scientists have developed a $16 hand-operated metal-bending machine that Nigerian villagers use to make agricultural tools; the cheapest non-hand-operated machine available to do the same job requires electricity and costs $1,750. Other forms of intermediate technology the group has developed are machines that make egg cartons from recycled paper, old tires adapted for use on oxcarts, and a 20,000-gallon water tank that costs Botswanans $40 to build. Use of such tools will not transform a developing nation into a U.S.A. tomorrow, but it will start it on a path of gradual growth.

The use of simple tools has several advantages: (1) They do not require large amounts of human capital (skill or training); (2) they will not displace workers; (3) they will not require large amounts of saving; (4) they will not be hard to manufacture or fix; (5) they will not require large amounts of energy; (6) the purchase of such tools—if the tools have to be purchased—will be less of a financial burden than will the purchase of large machines.

What Conclusions Can We Draw?

The first conclusion is that there is *no* general conclusion that will fit all of the developing countries except one: They must all learn how to reduce their rates of population increase. The second conclusion is that economic analysis can only go so far. Many of the poor countries' problems are political, social, and religious. We cannot, for example, tell the Hindus in India to eat their Brahman bulls when the bulls are sacred.

We have ignored the whole area of politics in this discussion. If a country has a dictator or has, at least, an authoritarian bureaucracy (as does the Soviet Union), it can order its people to eat less, have fewer babies, and save more for investment. And at present, authoritarianism *is* attractive to many less-developed countries, which want to get a job done *now* and believe democracy is too slow. They could be right.* But the cost of such a direction would have to be measured over the long pull in terms of loss of personal freedom and the political instability that can occur when dissenters disagree with the authorities.

There is one particular argument we want to discuss. Some people say, "We can't possibly help them all. Let's try to select the ones who are most likely to make it."

Such a policy is called **triage**, a French noun meaning "choice." The term was used by the French during World War I to describe the method of choosing

---

*The remarkable record of the Chinese in feeding, housing, educating, and providing health care for their people is an example of what can be done with modified central planning. Moreover, the Chinese experience shows that survival is possible with very little outside help.

those individuals among the wounded who might profit from the scarce medical resources that were available. The implication is that the rest must be abandoned.

Other variants of this suggestion exist. One writer likens the world to a lifeboat containing a few rich people while masses of poor people swim outside the lifeboat in the ocean.[10] Any attempts to help the poor will increase their number and increase the likelihood that they will climb into the lifeboat and sink it.

Other writers don't go to the extent of saying that the poor countries will sink us, but they insist that at least the quantity of aid that will materially help them has got to make us poorer. As Professor Gunnar Myrdal says, "The blunt truth is without rather radical changes in the consumption patterns in the rich countries, any pious talk about a new world economic order is humbug."[11]

Another theory is that Americans just will not give that much anyhow. If, for example, Americans are asked to help, it would require that they go on "producing like Americans" but be content to consume much smaller amounts. But this is impossible, because the act of producing is inextricably involved with the act of consuming. To produce, we consume food, transportation, health services, appliances, houses; we take vacations—all activities that replenish us and give us the incentive for further production.[12]

These are tough arguments, but if we agree with them, we consign millions of people to hunger, misery, and death. Moreover, it is possible that these statements are guilty of a fallacy. The fallacy is the assumption that the supply of resources, the space in the lifeboat, is *fixed*; that any gift of resources, or of space in the "lifeboat," will subtract from what is left for the occupants. Consequently, we must hope that knowledge will *expand* the quantities of resources and the size of the lifeboat. By so doing, there can be more for everyone.

WORLD MILITARY SPENDING

Part of the problem in helping the developing countries results from the fact that rich and poor nations alike are caught up in an arms race. The superpowers fear one another; many poor countries fear everyone. Both groups feel that they must have their arsenals of weapons. The result is a catastrophic waste of resources that could otherwise be used to raise everyone's standard of living.

The topic is appropriate for the last chapter of an economics text because military spending has micro, macro, and international implications. Micro effects occur because government purchases of military products distort the prices in all markets where such purchases occur. Furthermore, the prices paid by the government are often higher than those paid in the private economy because of cost overruns or the failure of government agencies to obtain competitive bids. Then, insofar as military spending contributes to aggregate demand, it has macro effects because it contributes to employment. The connection between military spending and employment has caused some critics to wonder if we are beginning to accept military spending as necessary for economic health. Finally, as you will see, military spending creates international rivalry, which tends to be self-perpetuating.

The discussion will be divided into two sections: (1) The size and consequences of military spending and (2) the arms race.

The Size and Consequences of Military Spending*

Total world military spending in 1982 amounted to more than $650 billion, about 6.5 percent of total world GNP. This amount is more than the total income of the poorest 50 nations of the world of that year.

World military spending in real terms is more than twelve times as great as it was 50 years ago, and the character of the spending is shifting in favor of sophisticated weaponry and away from personnel. This shift is not helping employment in the countries that produce the hardware (mainly the United States, the U.S.S.R., France, the United Kingdom, and West Germany), because the hardware is produced by skilled personnel working in high-technology firms. The main effect of the spending is therefore to draw skilled people who do not lack employment away from nondefense industries.

One study in the United States estimated that a billion dollars spent on defense in 1975 would have created 76,000 jobs in defense industries, compared with 80,000 jobs for local expenditures on health and 104,000 jobs for local expenditures on education. The study concluded that defense spending "creates less employment than other forms of spending."

The Military-Industrial Complex

In 1961, in his farewell address, President Dwight D. Eisenhower warned the country of the danger of a "military-industrial complex." By that term, the President meant that military spending could become so economically and politically important in terms of employment, money, and votes, to so many Americans and their political representatives, that Congress would be obliged to

---

*This section relies heavily on Olof Palme, et al., "Military Spending: The Economic and Social Consequences," *Challenge*, September-October 1982. The article is Chapter 4 of the report of the Independent Commission on Disarmament and Security Issues that began meeting in Vienna from early 1980. Palme is a former prime minister of Sweden. Commission members were from communist and noncommunist countries.

vote for ever-increasing military budgets whether the nation needed them or not.

Despite Eisenhower's warning, defense spending accounts for more than half the general federal revenues.* The military-industrial complex employs 30 percent of the nation's mathematicians and one of every four scientists and engineers, a development that helps explain America's failure to compete with other industrial nations in civilian markets.

With 10 percent of all jobs in the country dependent on defense spending, politicans are pressured, "out of fear for their political lives,"[13] to vote for weapon systems whether or not they are considered effective. One example is the B-1 bomber program which, despite misgivings in the Pentagon itself about the need for the plane or its effectiveness, now involves contractors in seventeen states producing parts for a fleet of one hundred B-1s at a minimum price of $280 million each.

Military Spending in the Developing Countries

In rich and poor countries alike, the opportunity costs of military spending can be imagined in the public projects aimed at health, education, and welfare that are sacrificed. But in many developing countries, these costs directly mean the difference between life or starvation.

From 1971 through 1980, the developing countries increased their share of world military spending from 19 percent to 25 percent of the total. One is apt to conclude that most of the spending was done by oil-rich countries, but the oil-exporting countries accounted for only one third of all military spending by the developing countries. During the 1970s both the oil and non-oil developing countries doubled their military spending in real terms. Two countries with per capita incomes below $200 in 1979 (Ethiopia and Somalia) imported more than $1 billion worth of arms. Arms imports by these two developing countries accounted for 14 percent of their combined national income. The dollar amount of the imports was equivalent to the income of 36,000 people in developed countries but to 5 *million* people in the two African countries.

The developing countries are less able to pay for arms than they used to be. During the 1970s the developing countries were able to finance their purchases with a combination of aid from the developed countries and shipments to them of strategic materials. These adjustments "seem less likely in 1982," the Palme study (see footnote, p. 444) concludes, because:

1. Worldwide recession dropped the prices of the primary commodities the developing countries exported.

2. Developing countries that did not produce oil lost most of their supplies of developed countries' currencies (international reserves) as the price of oil increased about fifteen times during the 1970s.

3. The developed countries and oil-exporting developing countries, which were previously counted on for foreign aid, were less likely to give it as their own revenues declined during the recession.

4. High interest rates increased the burden of the developing countries' foreign debt. More and more of their precious international reserves had to

---

*By "general" revenues, we mean tax revenues not already earmarked for a specific purpose like revenues from Social Security taxes. By 1986, military spending is expected to be *60* percent of general tax revenues.

be used to make debt payments instead of to improve the welfare of their people.

The Palme report concludes by stating that "all countries are hurt if military spending reduces the economic well-being of major participants in the world economy. All are hurt if military demand on government finances limits aid or commercial bank lending to developing countries."

The Arms Race and the "Prisoners' Dilemma"

The outlook for the future is not especially heartening. There is evidence that world military spending will continue to rise and that distrust among the great powers will result in continued increases in the development and production of nuclear weapons.

The "**prisoners' dilemma**" helps to explain why nations fear one another and why the arms race may well continue—despite continuing efforts to slow the arms race like the SALT talks of 1979 and the start of talks in 1982.

Here's the dilemma: Once upon a time, in the mythical country of Belgravia, two men were captured and accused of attempting to kidnap the King's beautiful daughter. The evidence against them was incomplete. The King was furious and put great pressure on the prison warden to determine the guilt of at least one of the prisoners.

The two prisoners were well-known partners in crime named Sleazy Sam and Dirty Dan. Guessing that both men were actually guilty, the warden devised a scheme to get at least one of them to incriminate the other. He had Sam brought to his office. The warden told Sam that if he would incriminate Dan at least one day before Dan incriminated Sam, then he, Sam, would be given freedom and a $1,000 reward. Thereupon, Sam was told, Dan would be hanged. The warden also informed Sam that Dan would be given the same offer. "And what if we should each incriminate the other on the same day?" Sam asked. "Then you will each keep your life, but you will get 10 years in prison." "And if we should both remain silent, your Excellency?" Sam asked. "Then both of you will be set free—without any reward, of course. But will you bet your neck that Dan—that crook—will not hurry to accuse you and pocket the reward? Now go back to your solitary cell and think about your answer until tomorrow." Dan, in his interview, was told the same, and each man spent the night alone considering his dilemma.[14]

The alternatives available in the prisoners' dilemma are usually displayed in a matrix diagram that looks like Figure 21-1. The diagram indicates that if both prisoners remain silent, they both go free (square 1). But the one who accuses the other first goes free and receives a reward, while the other is hanged (squares 2 and 3). Finally, if they accuse one another simultaneously, both will spend 10 years in prison (square 4).

What is the logical decision for them to make? Call for the warden and accuse the other as quickly as possible. First, note the arrows. Sam can improve his lot by moving from square 1 to square 2, where, by accusing Dan, he will receive his freedom and a reward. Similarly, Dan can improve his lot by accusing Sam (moving from square 1 to square 3). The second point is, of course, that only by accusing the other can each prisoner be sure of keeping his life.

The tragic point is that both could go free if they remained silent. But can they afford to? They cannot, unless they have absolute faith that neither one

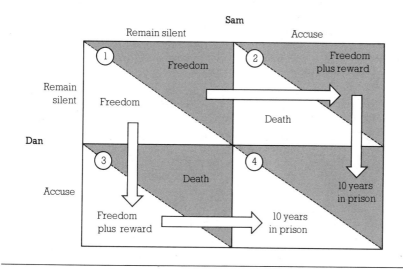

Figure 21-1.

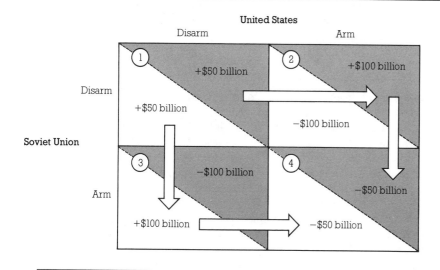

Figure 21-2.

will doublecross the other and tattle on the other first. In short, mutual distrust is the nub of the problem.

The prisoners' dilemma has many other applications, but our purpose is to show how it applies to the arms race. Let's pretend that the two countries (instead of two prisoners) involved are the United States and the Soviet Union and that they have a choice between disarming or building rockets at a cost of $50 billion to each country. If one country builds the rockets and the other does not, the country that arms will be in a position to command trade agreements that will give it a $100 billion advantage (and the country that disarms a $100 billion disadvantage). Finally, if both disarm, each will be $50 billion better off (by not having to spend the money on rockets). Figure 21-2 summarizes the situation.

What will they do? If they could trust each other, they would disarm. But again notice the arrows. Each country can improve its situation by moving from disarmament (square 1) to arming (squares 2 and 3). In an atmosphere of distrust, however, neither can afford to be the disarmed country if the other has armed. The unfortunate result: both arm (square 4), and each is $100 billion worse off than in square 1 (−$50 billion versus + $50 billion).

Only by changing the climate of distrust can the major powers break through the dilemma of the two prisoners and agree to live in square 1. But enemies cannot trust each other when each one behaves in such a way as to justify the other's distrust. When the United States and the Soviet Union display visible mutual distrust, as in containment policies, expansionist moves, and increasingly sophisticated weaponry (the Trident submarine and the Cruise missile), the distrust can only reinforce their dilemma and oblige them to move to square 4. Because each nation believes the other is an enemy, the other nation becomes, in reality, an enemy, and each must arm in self-defense.

The arms race is what social scientists call a **negative sum game**. Most of the games we play for competition and enjoyment, like poker, chess, or tennis, are called **zero sum games** because there is a winner (a "plus") and a loser (a "minus"). The pluses and minuses balance out to zero. But in an arms race everyone loses; the combined result is two (or more) minuses. But, one wonders, won't there be a winner and a loser in case of war? The answer isn't clear—even for past wars. The answer is particularly in doubt if the world becomes involved in nuclear war.

SUMMARY

The world is divided into two groups of countries—developed and developing. There is no exact definition of a developing country because countries exist at every level of income. In general, by "developing" we mean countries with incomes lower than $1,000 per person per year and particularly those countries with high levels of illiteracy and low life expectancies.

There are several reasons for helping these countries: (1) Our dependence on the strategic materials they supply; (2) the need to promote world political stability; and (3) the urgent nature of the developing countries' needs.

Most developing countries have common problems: Dependence on one or two crops, lack of machinery, difficulty in obtaining capital, the need to save in order to export (to obtain the foreign exchange needed to buy necessities), population increases that keep per capita incomes low, illiteracy, and excessive financial indebtedness to other countries. Of all of these, the needs to reduce the rate of population increase and to obtain capital are the most important.

Some argue that helping the developing countries will destroy us, that too many people will try to climb into the lifeboat. Others argue that the amount of aid necessary to do them any good would require a radically lower level of consumption in the rich countries, and that Americans would not be willing to sacrifice that much anyway. These arguments are fallacious in that they assume the quantities of food and other resources to be fixed. If we can expand total supply, there should be more for everyone.

World spending for defense exceeds spending for education or public health. The production of military products and services is apparently the world's largest industry, and it is growing. Defense spending is increasing at a more rapid rate among the low-income (developing) countries than among the richer (developed) countries. Rivalry and distrust among the major powers seem to be rising, as evidenced by inability to reduce spending on nuclear delivery systems.

Discussion Questions

1. Imagine that you are with a group of people on an island, cut off from contact with the rest of the world. How would you increase per capita consumption? Could you manage this democratically or would a dictator be necessary?

2. There may be some forms of sophisticated capital a developing country cannot produce by itself (a computer, perhaps). How should it go about obtaining the computer from another country? What options does it have?

3. Why do families in rich countries have fewer children than families in poor countries?

4. Explain Enke's argument.

5. How are the "lifeboat" and "triage" arguments similar?

6. Explain the prisoners' dilemma. How might it apply to the advertising strategies of large companies?

DID YOU EVER WONDER WHY . . .

. . . India benefits from having Americans buy into its firms?

References

1. Robert S. McNamara, "The Moral Case for Helping the World's Poor," *Los Angeles Times*, 28 September 1973, Pt. ii, p. 7.

2. See Nathan Keyfitz, "World Resources and the Middle Class," *Scientific American*, July 1976; "Running Out of Food," *Newsweek*, 11 November 1974; Lester R. Brown, "The World Food Prospect," *Science*, 12 December 1975; Thomas Y. Canby, "Can the World Feed Its People?" *National Geographic*, July 1975; and Douglas N. Ross, *Food and Population: The Next Crisis* (New York: The Conference Board, 1974).

3. *Statistical Abstract of the United States, 1981.*

4. *Los Angeles Times*, 2 April 1979, Pt. i, p. 16.

5. Stephen Enke, "Economic Development through Birth Control," *Challenge*, May/June 1967.

6. Robert V. Roosa, "The Debts of the Poor: Preventing the Crash," *The New Republic*, 22 January 1977.

7. Jon McLin, *The Group of 77*, American Universities Field Staff Report, 1976.

8. Roosa, "The Debts of the Poor."

9. E. F. Schumacher, *Small Is Beautiful* (New York: Harper & Row, 1973).

10. Garret Hardin, "Lifeboat Ethics: The Case Against Helping the Poor," *Psychology Today*, September 1974.

11. Gunnar Myrdal, "The Equality Issue in World Development," *World Issues*, October/November 1976.

12. Keyfitz, "World Resources and the Middle Class."

13. "The Complex Complex," *Los Angeles Times*, 10 July 1983.

14. Karl Deutsch, *The Analysis of International Relations* (Englewood Cliffs, N.J.: Prentice-Hall, 1968), p. 120.

Glossary

A

Ability-to-pay principle A principle of taxation holding that taxes should be collected from people in accordance with their ability to pay. Best example: the personal income tax. (14; 276)

Absolute change See *Relative and absolute changes*. (7; 126)

Accelerationist view The belief that the federal government's attempts to reduce unemployment will fail and serve only to increase the rate of inflation. (19; 384)

Actual GNP An estimate of what the economy actually produces in one year. The estimate may be expressed in "nominal" or "real" terms. Usually compared with "potential" GNP. See potential GNP, nominal GNP, and real GNP. (13; 253)

Aggregate demand The total demand to buy all goods and services. In modern theory, aggregate demand is the sum of consumption spending for goods and services, business spending for capital goods (investment) and inventory, government purchases, and net exports (export minus imports). (12; 237)

Aggregate supply Everything actually produced. (12; 237)

Alienation A feeling by workers that their jobs (and lives) are meaningless and that they are powerless to change their condition. Attributed to Karl Marx's criticism of capitalism. (3; 43)

Allocative efficiency An allocation of resources such that the prices charged cause all industries to buy and use resources up to the point where the social benefit conferred by the last unit produced is equal to or exceeds the social cost of producing it. (6; 121)

Annually balanced budget One of four philosophies of government budgets. A government's budget should always be balanced; government spending should always equal tax revenues. Under this philosophy, a public debt would never exist. (17; 342)

Automatic (built-in) stabilizers Changes in taxes and government spending that occur automatically to stabilize the ups and downs of economic activity. (16; 318)

Average tax rate The income tax rate on one's entire taxable income rather than on the last increment of income. (14; 278) See *Marginal tax rate*.

Average variable cost (AVC) Variable costs are those costs that vary with the number of units produced. *Average* variable costs are total variable costs divided by the number of units produced; that is, average variable costs are variable costs per unit. (8; 154)

B

Balance-of-international-payments account Measures all international inflows and outflows of money. Includes spending for imports and exports (the trade balance), overseas investments, and government spending abroad. (20A; 429)

Barriers to entry Anything that prevents the free movement of a resource. Typical barriers are franchise agreements, discriminatory hiring policies, occupational licenses, patent rights, and capital requirements (necessary to start a business). (5; 71)

Base year The year against which all other years are compared for changes in the average price level. Base-year-average prices are given an index number of 100. The base year for the implicit price deflator for the GNP is 1972; for the consumer price index, 1967. (12; 242)

Benefits principle A principle of taxation holding that an individual who pays a tax should receive the benefit when the government spends that money. Best example: the gasoline tax used for road building benefits drivers who paid the tax. (14; 276)

Board of Governors Seven-person board that supervises the Federal Reserve System and its member banks. Board members are appointed by the U.S. President for fourteen-year terms. (18; 361)

Bottleneck inflation Price increases that occur when there are severe shortages of important products. (13; 265)

Brigade See *Commune*.

Budget surplus The reverse of a deficit. A surplus occurs when tax revenues exceed government spending. (15; 297)

C

Canon Law The writings of the Schoolmen, which included rulings on the just price, the just wage, and the doctrine of usury. (2; 24)

Capital One of the three factors of production; the buildings, machines, and other equipment used in production. (2; 29)

451

Capital formation See *Investment.*

Capital-output ratio The ratio between an amount of capital and the amount of income it produces. If $9 worth of capital produces $3 worth of income, the ratio is 3:1. (21; 439)

Capitalism A system in which most things are privately owned, where people are free to choose their occupation, where the kind and amount of production is determined by prices and people searching for a profit, and where there is a substantial amount of competition. (3; 37)

Cartel A group of business firms producing the same product or service who, with or without permission of law, agree on output and price to avoid price competition. Example: U.S. airlines operating under regulation by the Civil Aeronautics Board. (8; 165)

Ceteris paribus A Latin expression meaning "all other things equal." Social scientists use this expression to indicate that all conditions not specifically mentioned in a model remain the same. (4; 60) See *Model.*

Classical economists Economists, beginning with Adam Smith, who believe that a market-price system would have full employment provided its government did not interfere. (15; 289)

Clayton Act of 1914 Made several business practices illegal, including price discrimination, rebates, exclusive sales contracts, and interlocking directorates. (9; 188)

Closed shop A workplace where an employer may hire only those who are already union members. (10; 205)

Coefficient of elasticity The number obtained when the percentage change in quantity is divided by the percentage

change in prices. If the coefficient is two, the percentage change in quantity is double that of the percentage in price. When the coefficient is greater than one, demand is elastic; less than one, inelastic; equal to one, unitary elastic. (7; 129)

Command/planning systems See Traditional systems.

Commune Rural administrative unit in China. May encompass 50,000 acres of land on which 70,000 people live. Further subdivided into brigades and teams. (3; 49)

Communism Often used to refer to the Soviet Union's political system and other totalitarian systems. However, in Marxist theory, the term refers to a system of no command planning, where the working class owns and operates the means of production. (3; 40)

Communist Manifesto An appeal written in 1848 by Karl Marx and Friedrich Engels to persuade workers to overthrow capitalists. (3; 42)

Complementary goods Goods that go together, such as automobiles and tires, phonographs and records, typewriters and typewriter ribbons. (7; 79)

Concentration ratio Usually the fraction of an industry's total sales made by the four (sometimes eight) largest firms. (8; 158)

Consumer Price Index (CPI) An index of measuring the average price level of the goods and services typical urban workers buy. The prices of some 400 items are measured in different parts of the country. The average is expressed by an index number; 100 is the index number for the base year, 1967. A new index number is computed monthly. (12; 242) See *Price index.*

Consumer surplus The surplus of satisfaction consumers receive over and above the amount they pay for a good, when they would have been willing to pay a price higher than the equilibrium price. (9; 183)

Consumption One of the four components of aggregate demand, including everything consumers buy *except* housing. (12; 238)

Consumption function Official name for the consumption-spending-demand line (16A; 327)

Cost The time and effort expended to obtain a good or service desired. (1; 8)

Cost-benefit analysis Comparison of expected costs with expected benefits of a decision. (1; 11)

Cost-push inflation Rising prices that occur when firms and unions have sufficient market power to increase prices and wages independent of the forces of demand and supply, even in times of recession or rising unemployment. (13; 262)

Countercyclical budget A philosophy of government budgets stating that government spending and taxing should counteract the ups and downs of the economy by engaging in deficit spending in times of unemployment and running a surplus in times of inflation. (17; 343)

Credit Refers to the trust extended by lenders to borrowers that a loan will be repaid. (18; 355)

Crowding-out The possibility that government borrowing for deficit spending may "crowd out" private spending by driving interest rates up, thereby making private borrowing and spending more expensive. (16; 324)

Currency in circulation Coins and paper money in the

possession of the public, *not* in a bank account. (18; 354)

Currency depreciation A fall in the international value of a country's currency as a result of a decline in demand for the country's exports. The equivalent of a currency floating downward. (20; 419)

Current account balance Exports of goods and services plus income from overseas investments minus imports of goods and services, minus income from foreign investments in the United States, minus private gifts to foreign individuals, and minus government grants to other countries. (20A; 430) See *Balance-of-International-Payments Account.*

Cyclical unemployment General unemployment because of poor business throughout the country. Associated with the trough of a business cycle. (13; 257)

D

Debt ceiling The limit to the size of the public (national) debt legislated by Congress. (17; 337)

Deficit spending Government spending that exceeds tax revenues, is financed by selling government bonds, and leads to increases in the public debt. (15; 295–296)

Demand The number of units of a good or service a buyer is willing to purchase during some period of time and at various prices. (5; 72) See *Demand schedule* and *Demand curve.*

Demand curve A graph of a demand schedule. The vertical axis always shows the price per unit, and the horizontal axis shows the quantity demanded at each price. (5; 75) See *Demand schedule.*

Demand deposits Checking accounts. (18; 354)

Demand-pull inflation Price increases that occur as a result of increases in aggregate demand when the country is at full employment. (13; 261)

Demand schedule A schedule showing the quantities of a good or service a buyer will buy during some period of time and at various prices. (5; 73)

Deposit multiplier The multiple by which demand deposits (in all banks) increase or decrease following an initial change in demand deposits. (18; 357)

Depository Institutions Deregulation and Monetary Control Act of 1980 An Act designed to give the Board of Governors of the Federal Reserve System greater control of banks outside the System and also to make all banking institutions more competitive with one another. (18; 364)

Derived demand The demand for any factor of production. The demand for the factor is "derived" because it orginates from and depends on the demand for the good or service the employer is producing. (10; 196)

Direct relationship A relationship in which two variables increase together. (4; 62)

Discomfort Index The sum of the inflation and unemployment rates. (19; 386)

Discount rate The interest Federal Reserve district banks charge on loans to member banks. (18; 369)

Discretionary fiscal policy Changes in taxes or government spending undertaken deliberately by the President and Congress to boost or slow down the economy. (16; 320)

Discrimination Job discrimination exists when an employer's hiring or promoting decision is based on sex or race.

Wage discrimination exists when an employer pays workers differently for doing the same job. (11; 220)

Diseconomies of scale Diseconomies of scale occur when companies lose efficiency by becoming too large, by failing to keep close track of operations or by purchasing large quantities of supplies that increase costs. (8; 157)

Disposable Personal Income (DPI) Personal income minus personal taxes (income taxes, personal property taxes, gift and inheritance taxes). (12; 239)

Double counting One of the problems involved in estimating GNP. If we counted, for example, the value of steel in a car and the price of the car in GNP, we would be counting the steel twice. (12; 241)

E

Easy-money policy Action by the Federal Reserve Board to increase bank reserves on the theory that such an increase will give the banks more money to lend, which will then tend to lower interest rates, which in turn will stimulate more borrowing and spending by business firms. (18; 365)

Economic indicators Data that helps predict events in the macroeconomy. Leading indicators, such as overtime hours and changes in inventories, show what is likely to happen several months in advance. Lagging indicators, such as the unemployment rate and consumer installment debt, show what has happened in the recent past. Coincident indicators, such as current dollar GNP and retail sales, show current changes. (13; 252–253)

Economic profit The amount of profit left over after all explicit and implicit costs have been deducted from total revenue. (8; 149)

Economic system   A body of laws, habits, ethics, and customs that a group of people observe to satisfy their material wants. (1; 18)

Economics   A social science that analyzes the expected effects of private and public decisions on human material welfare. (1; 15)

Economies of scale   See *Internal and external economies of scale.*

Effluent charges   Charges imposed on a producer or user for every pound or gallon of waster he allows to pollute the air or water. (6; 120)

Employment Act of 1946   An act that gave the federal government responsibility for promoting full employment. The Act rejects the classical idea that the economy can take care of itself. (15; 297)

Enclosure movement   From the Middle Ages to about 1850, large landowners fenced their estates, and brought in thousands of sheep, forcing the serfs to leave the land. (2; 28)

Endogenous causes   Factors within an economic system that cause changes in economic activity. Examples are: changes in investment spending following the depreciation of capital goods or changes in consumption spending following changes in income. (13; 252)

Entrepreneur   The person who takes the risk to start a new enterprise. (2; 30)

Equation of exchange **($M_1V=PQ$)**   The money supply times income velocity equals the average price level times the quantities of things produced. Both sides of the equation also equal GNP. (18A; 378)

Equilibrium income (equilibrium GNP)   A level of GNP at which aggregate demand is sufficient to buy everything produced (aggregate supply).

Because GNP moves toward equilibrium, experts can forecast if GNP is about to rise or fall. (16; 304)

Equilibrium price   The price at which the quantity supplied equals the quantity demanded. If the price is above or below equilibrium, automatic forces will usually cause the price to return to equilibrium. (5; 93)

Excess reserves   Reserves in excess of the legal minimum banks are required to keep that a bank is free to lend or use for financial investments. (18; 356)

Exclusion principle Recognition of the fact that any price will exclude those people, who cannot afford to buy or do not want to buy from buying. Also used in connection with situations where people cannot be excluded, like pollution. (5; 72)

Exogenous causes   Factors external to an economic system, as in hurricanes or droughts, that cause changes in economic activity. (13; 252)

Explicit costs   Costs involving an actual payment of money to someone. (8; 147) See *Implicit costs.*

Exploitation   Exists when workers are paid less than they would be paid in a market where employers bid competitively for their services. (11; 220)

External costs (or benefits) See *External effects.*

External debt   An external debt is owed by one economic unit to another as in an individual's debt to a store or one nation's debt to another. When paid, the debtor become poorer, the creditor richer. Most private debts (charge accounts, bank loans) are external debts. (17; 340)

External effects   Effects on people outside the seller-buyer transaction. External benefits are those that are beneficial to

society, such as education; external costs are harmful effects, such as pollution. (6; 118)

F

Factors of production   All resources are divided into three factors of production: land, labor, and capital. (2; 27)

Federal Deposit Insurance Corporation (FDIC)   Insures deposits up to $100,000 so that if a bank fails, depositors will not lose their money. Commercial banks belonging to the Federal Reserve System must buy this insurance. (18; 362)

Federal Open Market Committee   Twelve people, including the seven board members of the Federal Reserve System and five presidents of district banks, who buy and sell government securities for the purpose of increasing or decreasing the money supply. (18; 361)

Federal Reserve District Banks   The Federal Reserve System is the U.S. central bank and includes twelve district banks, which have a combined total of twenty-four branches. The district banks and their branches are nicknamed "the Fed." (18; 360)

Federal Reserve Notes   U.S. paper money, called notes because they are issued by Federal Reserve district banks even though they are printed by the Treasury. (18; 361)

Federal Reserve System (the Fed)   A nationwide network of twelve regional Federal Reserve (district) banks with twenty-four branches, each serving a particular U.S. geographical area. Its policies seek to provide monetary conditions favorable to business and employment, maintain the purchasing power of the dollar, and help the economy grow. (18; 350)

Federal revenue sharing
Monies given to the states each year by the federal government. (14; 275)

Final product The price paid by the final user of a product excluding intermediate products. GNP is an estimate of final products and services produced in one year. (12; 241)

Fiscal policy Changes in taxes and/or government spending that cause changes in total output and spending and that may be automatic or deliberately undertaken by the President and/or Congress. (14; 269) See *Automatic stabilizers* and *discretionary fiscal policy*.

Fixed costs Costs, such as rent, taxes, insurance, or interest on loans, that do not fluctuate with changes in a factory's output. (9; 171)

Fixed supply Occurs when the quantity supplied does not change with changes in price. Examples of fixed supply are famous paintings or the quantities of anything in existence at a moment in time such as freeway space, parking spaces, hospital beds, houses. (9; 176)

Flat tax idea A proposal to eliminate tax loopholes by substituting an across-the-board proportional tax of about 15 percent for the present personal income tax code. (14; 281)

Floating exchange rates International currency exchange rates that are free to change as a result of changes in demand or supply for goods, services, or currencies in international trade. (20; 419)

Foregone income The income one could have earned while going to school. Estimated to be 50 percent of the cost of a college education. (1; 11)

Fractional reserve system A system in which banks are required to keep only a fraction of their reserves. (18; 356)

Free good A good that exists in such abundance that greater use of it by one person does not subtract from its availability to everyone else. (1; 8)

Frictional unemployment Unemployment that occurs because workers have difficulty shifting from a declining industry to a rising one. Classical theory admits the problem but argues that unemployment will be temporary. (13; 257)

Full employment Usually said to exist when 94.5 percent of the people who want jobs have them. Thus, a 5.5 percent unemployment rate is the equivalent of full employment. (13; 255)

Functional finance A philosophy of government budgets: The need to guarantee jobs for a growing labor force and to finance public works, like rapid transit, in good times or bad, may require deficit financing on a permanent basis. Acceptance of the functional finance philosophy indicates acceptance of a growing public debt. (17; 343)

Functional graph A picture of the relationship between two variables. (4; 60)

G

General Agreement on Tariffs and Trade (GATT) An organization of eighty-one countries formed in 1947 to reduce barriers to trade. (20; 413)

Gold Reserve Act of 1934 Set the price of gold at $35 per ounce to prevent hoarding of gold. (18; 352)

Gosplan The central economic planning agency in the Soviet Union. (3; 44)

Government purchases of goods and services One of the four components of aggregate demand that refers to spending by all levels of government—local, state, and federal—but excludes transfer payments. (12; 238)

Government securities Government securities (often called bonds) are (1) Treasury bills that mature in less than one year, (2) Treasury notes that mature in one to five years, and (3) Treasury bonds that take longer than five years to mature. (17; 339)

Gross National Product (GNP) The sum of consumption, investment, government purchases of goods and services, and net exports. GNP is determined by aggregate demand. (12; 241)

Group of 77 An organization of 77 countries (most of them, but not all, are less-developed countries) to help poorer countries obtain financial aid. (21; 440)

H

High-employment budget approach The surplus of tax revenues over government spending the federal government might have if the economy were operating at high employment. High employment usually means a 5.5 percent (or less) rate of unemployment. This is one of the four budget philosophies relative to the public debt. (17; 344)

Hyperinflation A rate of inflation that accelerates—as in Germany after World War I and Hungary after World War II—when a government must print ever-increasing amounts of money to finance operations because the people are too poor to tax. Result: money becomes worthless. (18A; 375)

I

Implicit costs The opportunity costs borne by a business for employing its resources in a particular way. These costs are measured by what the firm could have earned with the entrepreneur's labor (implicit wages), the entrepreneur's land (implicit rent), the entrepreneur's capital (implicit capital), and depreciation. (8; 147) See *Normal profit.*

Implicit interest   Interest one could have earned on money tied up in a business (or home). (8; 148)

Implicit price deflator   A large price index combining both wholesale and retail prices that is used to correct (deflate) GNP for the effects of inflation. (12; 242) See *Price index.*

Implicit rent   The rent one could have earned by renting out one's property instead of using it. (8; 148)

Implicit wages   Wages one could have earned on a job other than the job one has. (8; 148)

Income   See *Wealth.*

Income determination Keynes' analysis of the reasons for changes in GNP and the level of employment. (16; 304)

Income effect   The effect a falling or rising price has on our ability to buy more or less with a given income. (5; 74)

Income=spending line   A 45-degree angle line that bisects a right angle formed by a spending axis and an income axis. At all points on the line, spending and income are equal. (16A; 328)

Inflation   A general rise in prices. (1; 4) See *Cost-push inflation* and *Demand-pull inflation.*

Inflation psychology   A state of mind tending to intensify any existing inflationary conditions. If people believe prices are rising, they will try to buy more before the prices do rise; they will also increase their wage demands to keep up with increases in the cost of living. The increases in demand cause

prices to rise even faster, resulting in further increase in demand. Thus, the belief that prices are rising contributes to their increase and constitutes a self-fulfilling prophecy. (5; 81)

Inflationary gap   The amount by which spending must be reduced to provide equilibrium GNP at full employment without inflation. (16; 321)

Information costs   A barrier to entry in the sense that if information about a product, service, or entrepreneurial opportunity is difficult or costly to obtain, resources will be prevented from moving to those activities most desired by society. (8; 151)

Intended vs. actual investment   Intended investment means the amounts of money business firms want (intend) to spend for capital goods and inventories. Actual investment may differ from these intentions if slack sales cause inventories to rise above intended levels (unintended investment), or if brisk sales cause inventories to fall below intended levels (unintended disinvestment). (16; 309)

Interdistrict Settlement Fund   A check-clearing mechanism operated by the Federal Reserve System for the processing of checks that are written in one district and cashed in another. (18; 361)

Intermediate products Products used in the production of others; for example, steel in a car. In computing GNP, the value-added method is used to eliminate intermediate products that might otherwise be double-counted. (12; 241)

Intermediate technology The invention and creation of simple tools and machines that an LDC can make itself and that will not cause technological unemployment. The idea comes from E.F. Schumacher's

influential book, *Small is Beautiful.* (21; 442)

Internal debt   A debt owed by one member of a family to another member; by one branch of a corporation to another; by some people in a nation to others in the same nation. The existence of such a debt does not change the wealth of the family, corporation, or nation because payment involves a transfer of income within an economic unit. The public debt is mostly internal. (17; 340)

Internal and external economies of scale.   An internal economy of scale occurs when an x percent increase in all inputs results in an increase of more than x percent in output. External economies of scale occur when factories receive benefits external to their operation like better streets or the movement of a supplier closer to them. (8; 156)

International economics   The study of the problems of international trade and the unequal distribution of income around the world. (1; 15)

International Monetary Fund (IMF)   An international financial institution that provides funds as they are needed to its member nations and attempts to stabilize exchange rates in order to encourage international trade. The IMF was created by the Bretton Woods (New Hampshire) agreement of 1944. (20A; 428)

Inverse relationship   A relationship in which one variable decreases as the other increases. (4; 62)

Investment   The creation of tangible capital and/or the production of goods for inventory, including business spending for all capital goods, inventories, and business and personal spending for buildings. (12; 238)

J

Just price   As defined by the Schoolmen, whatever the community thought a product was worth (the "common estimate"). (2; 24)

Just wage   As defined by the Schoolmen, no more than is necessary to maintain a worker's present station in life (or that of his parents). (2; 24)

K

Keynesian Cross   Formed by the crossing of the income-spending line by a line that represents aggregate demand, to show that aggregate demand may be greater than, or less than, total income. (16A; 329–330)

Keynesian revolution   The revolution in economic theory following the publication of John Maynard Keynes' book, *The General Theory of Employment, Interest, and Money.* The book was revolutionary because it argued that an economic system could get stuck at any level of unemployment; and that market price economic systems do not automatically provide everyone who wants to work with a job, as had previously been argued by the Classical economists. (15; 292) See *Classical economists* and *Say's Law.*

L

Labor-Management Relations Act of 1947   See *Taft-Hartley Act.*

Labor-Management Reporting and Disclosure Act   See *Landrum-Griffin Act.*

Labor productivity   A measure of output per worker per hour. (10; 196)

Labor union   An association of workers who join together to negotiate a labor-management contract with an employer. (10; 200)

Laffer Curve   Based on the idea that high tax rates will so reduce incentives to work that the government's tax revenues will decline, whereas low tax rates may actually increase incentives to work and thus increase tax revenues. (19; 393)

Landrum-Griffin Act (1958)   Officially known as the Labor-Management Reporting and Disclosure Act. Aimed at making the internal operation of unions more democratic and preventing union bosses from using funds to their own advantage. (10; 206)

Law of demand   As the price falls, the quantities demanded by buyers will increase. Price and quantity are inversely related (5; 73)

Law of Diminishing Returns   When increasing amounts of one resource are added to other resources, with one or more of the latter held constant in both quantity and quality, a point will be reached where successive increases in output will become more difficult to achieve. (8; 154)

Long run   A period of time long enough for entrepreneurs to vary all of the costs of production including the costs of acquiring additional stores or factories or cost-reductions from the sale of stores or factories. (9; 171–172)

M

M₁ M_1 One definition of the money supply. The sum of currency (coins and paper money) in circulation plus demand deposits (checking accounts). (18; 354)

Macroeconomics   The study of the functions of the whole economy, particularly the whole economy's ability to provide enough jobs, a fair distribution of goods and services, and an average price level that does not rise too fast (inflation). (1; 15)

Malthus, Thomas Robert (1776–1834)   English economist, best known for his beliefs that population would increase faster than the food supply subjecting the world to periods of disease and famine, and that a market-price system would have periods of unemployment caused by overproduction and underconsumption. (15; 292) See *Theory of Glut.*

Mao Tse-tung (1884–1976)   Leader of the People's Republic of China. Tried to enforce economic equality for the people. (3; 48)

Marginal cost   Defined as the change in total cost when one more unit is produced. (9; 174)

Marginal product   The extra production achieved when one unit of a resource is added to another that is held constant in quantity and quality. (8; 154)

Marginal propensity to consume (MPC)   The change in consumption that follows a given change in income, calculated by dividing the change in consumption by the change in income. (16; 315)

Marginal propensity to save (MPS)   The change in saving relative to a change in income, calculated by dividing the change in saving by the change in income. (16; 316)

Marginal revenue   The addition of total revenue when one more unit is old. (9; 174)

Marginal tax on work   The income lost as a percent of income earned when a person on welfare earns income for work performed. (11; 227)

Marginal tax rate   The percentage income tax paid on the last dollar of one's income rather than on one's total income. The last dollar defines one's tax bracket. The marginal tax rate applies only to one's tax bracket. (14; 278)

Market Any method by which, or place at which, buyers can communicate with sellers to negotiate a price. (2; 21)

Market period A period in which all costs are in the past and the product is ready for sale. (9; 171)

Market power The power buyers or sellers can exert over other buyers or sellers to control the market price. (5; 94 and 8; 147)

Market-price system See *Traditional system.*

Market socialism A system that combines some form of market-price system with public ownership of major enterprises. (3; 39)

Marx, Karl (1818–1883) German political philosopher and socialist who predicted the collapse of capitalism. He believed that greedy capitalists would try to extract more and more profit from workers who were paid as little as possible. Overproduction and subsistence wages would create chronic deficiencies in aggregate demand leading to worse and worse depressions and finally revolution by the working class (the proletariat). Author of *Das Kapital (Capital).* (3; 40)

Merchandise Trade Balance The difference between exports and imports of merchandise, excluding exports and imports of services. (20A; 430) See *Balance-of-international-payments account.*

Microeconomics The study of the functioning of the individual parts of the economy, like individual consumers, business firms, and unions, in contrast to the study of national problems like unemployment and inflation. Micro-economic theory is concerned with how prices are determined and their effect on the production, distribution, and use of goods and services. (1; 15)

Model A simplified version of the real world requiring a set of assumptions. (4; 59)

Monetarist rule A belief of the monetarists that the Federal Reserve Board should take whatever measures necessary to increase the money supply at a steady rate of 4 percent a year, with no deviations. (18A; 377)

Monetarists Economists who believe that monetary policy is more important than fiscal policy in changing the price level or level of employment. (18A; 375)

Monetary policy Control of interest rates and borrowing through control of the money supply. Like fiscal policy, monetary policy is employed to increase or decrease aggregate demand. It is based on the theory that aggregate demand can be made to rise or fall with changes in the money supply; that changes in the money supply cause changes in interest rates, which make borrowing for spending more or less expensive. (18; 350)

Monopolistic competition An economic system in which entry barriers to an industry are still low, as in pure competition, but in which brand names are used to convince buyers that a brand-name product is better than one without a brand name. When brand names are used, firms often compete by advertising special ingredients rather than prices. (8; 153)

Monopoly Exclusive control of an industry by one firm (seller). Examples: the only movie theater in a small town; a utility with no competitor. (8; 160)

Monopsony Exclusive control of a market of sellers by one buyer. Monopsony exists when a firm or industry sells its entire output to one buyer, the monopsonist. (9; 186)

Most-favored-nation principle Holds that trade concessions granted to one nation will be granted to all other trading partners. The principle was inaugurated by the Reciprocal Trade Agreements Law of 1934 and has been included in all noncommunist trade agreements since then. (20; 411)

N

National income accounting The accounting system used to measure a nation's total output and income. (Also called social accounting.) (12; 236)

National Labor Relations Act See *Wagner Act.*

Natural monopoly When one firm can produce the total quantity sold cheaper than two or more firms and usually refers to a utility. (8; 160)

Natural rate of unemployment The rate of unemployment that will exist after business and labor have adjusted fully to the inflation rate; thought to be 6 percent based upon average unemployment rates from 1961 to 1982. (19; 385)

Negative income tax A proposal to give each family that earns an income below the poverty line a negative tax in the form of a subsidy from the federal government. (11; 228)

Negative saving (dis-saving) Results from private spending that exceeds income. If we spend more than we make we have to borrow or take money out of savings. (16A; 327)

Negative sum game A game in which everyone loses; the combined result is two minuses. Used to describe the arms race. (21; 448)

Net exports One of the four components of aggregate demand. The difference between exports and imports. If exports exceed imports, the difference adds to aggregate demand, but if imports exceed exports, as they did in 1971 and 1972, the difference subtracts from aggregate demand. (12; 328)

Net public debt The total federal debt minus the amount borrowed by government agencies. (17; 340)

Nomenklatura A secret roster of the privileged people in the Soviet Union who can obtain groceries, housing, cars, and vacations not available to the ordinary Soviet citizen. (3; 48)

Nominal GNP GNP uncorrected for price changes; also called money GNP or current dollar GNP. (12; 243)

Nonprice competition Competition among competing brands, not in terms of price, but in terms of special ingredients or services. Usually indicates competition in the form of advertising. (8; 154)

Nonrenewable resource A resource that exists in some finite amount and cannot be renewed or replenished. Best example: oil. (6; 115)

Nontariff barriers (NTBs) Barriers to trade where no tariff is imposed. Examples: Import quotas, import licenses, export subsidies, dumping, buy-at-home policies, health and safety standards, red tape, preferential trading arrangements. (20; 410)

Normal profit The profit that an entrepreneur must earn to equal the income that he could have earned if he had used his own resources (his labor, land, and capital) in some other occupation. Regarded as a cost of production—the opportunity cost of using the entrepreneur's own resources. (8; 148)

Normative reasoning A decision or judgment about whether or not something is desirable; e.g. prices are too high. (4; 59)

No-tax threshold The minimum level of taxable

income at which one must pay an income tax. (14; 278)

O

Official (government) development aid (ODA) Financial aid extended by governments rather than from private sources. (21; 441)

Oligopoly The domination of an industry by three or four very large firms (sellers). Any one of them is large enough to influence the price of the others. (8; 157)

Open market operations The purchase or sale of government bonds on the open market by the Federal Open Market Committee. Bonds purchased or sold on the open market are owned by commercial banks, corporations, or the public. (18; 366)

Open shop A workplace where an employer could assert the right to hire anyone, whether union member or not. (10; 205)

Opportunity cost, trade-off The value of an opportunity or alternative that is sacrificed when a decision to do something is made. Sometimes called alternative cost or trade-off. What do we trade off (lose) in exchange for obtaining something we want? (1; 9)

Organization for Economic Cooperation and Development (OECD) An organization of twenty countries formed to liberalize trade. (20; 414)

Origin On a graph, the intersection of the horizontal and vertical axes. (4; 62)

P

Paradox of thrift The paradox in which a desire by the people to increase their saving and spend less results in reduced saving; their desire to spend more and save less leads to increased saving. (16; 314)

Perfect competition Perfect competition exists in an industry in which each firm is so small that it cannot influence the market price, all firms make the same product, resources are instantly mobile, and knowledge of more profitable opportunities is immediately and freely available. (8; 150)

Perfect elasticity When the smallest increase in price affects the quantities demanded, the demand curve is perfectly elastic. (7; 137)

Perfect inelasticity When the price does not affect the quantities demanded, the demand curve is perfectly inelastic. (7; 137)

Phillips Curve A curve that describes the inverse relationship (trade-off) between inflation and unemployment: The more we try to reduce prices by reducing aggregate demand, the more unemployment will rise—the price of full employment is a high rate of inflation. (19; 381)

Physical Quality of Life Index A composite of three measures of a nation's life expectancy, infant mortality, and literacy. (21; 434)

Positive reasoning A conclusion drawn from observations; e.g. people buy less at higher prices than at lower prices. (4; 59)

Potential GNP The amount that could have been produced each year with an annual increase in real GNP of about 3.5 percent per year. (13; 253)

Poverty Poverty exists when a nonfarm family's income is less than the cost of a nutritionally balanced diet multiplied by three. The income that just equals that amount is often called the "poverty line." Estimated poverty-line income for a nonfarm family of four in 1982 was $9,287. (11; 217)

Price ceiling A maximum price set by government legislation. (The price can fall, but it cannot rise above the ceiling.) Examples are wage or price ceilings. Shortages often result from price ceilings. (6; 110)

Price discrimination The practice whereby a seller sells the same (or almost the same) product or service to different buyers or even the same buyer, at different prices. (9; 181)

Price-elastic The responsiveness of buyers (demanders) or suppliers to changes in price. If the response is large relative to the price change, the good is said to be price-elastic. If not, it is price-inelastic. (7; 125)

Price floor A minimum price legislated by the government. (The price can rise above the price floor, but it cannot fall below it.) Examples are minimum wage laws and farm-price supports. Surpluses often result from price floors. (6; 107)

Price index Measure of average prices relative to a base year. Base-year-average prices are given an index number of 100. If ten years later average prices have risen 50 percent; the new price level is given an index number of 150. There are three indexes: The consumer price index (retail items), the producer (wholesale) price index, and the implicit price deflator for the GNP. The latter is an all-inclusive composite of retail and wholesale prices used to correct GNP for price changes (deflate the GNP). (12; 242)

Price-inelastic See *Price-elastic*.

Price taker A purely competitive firm that must accept (take) the market price because the firm is too small to influence the price. (8; 147)

Primary job market Jobs

requiring skill, investment by employers in training, avenues for promotion, career possibilities for employees, and low turnover. (1; 10)

Prime rate The rate of interest commercial banks charge their biggest and best customers (large corporations). The prime rate is usually the lowest interest rate obtainable on loans. (18; 369)

Principle of comparative advantage According to this principle, an individual or nation should specialize in producing products where the opportunity cost of specialization is lower than that of other countries. (20; 408)

Prisoner's dilemma The idea that when two people or two companies or two nations do not trust each other, they follow much more costly courses of action than if they cooperate. (21; 446)

Private (internal) costs Costs borne by the producer or user in producing, using, or disposing of a product. Term does not include external costs borne by society in connection with pollution. (6; 117)

Private labeling The practice whereby a manufacturer permits a retail store to sell the manufacturer's product under the store's brand name, rather than the manufacturer's. (9; 186)

Producer Price Index (PPI) Measures average prices at the producer's or wholesale level. (12; 242) See *Price index*.

Production possibilities table Shows the different combinations of products individuals or countries can produce at full employment. (20; 406)

Profit-push inflation Price increases initiated by powerful corporations in search of higher profits. (13; 264) See *Cost-push inflation*.

Progressive taxes Taxes in which assessment as a percentage of income rises as income rises. Best example: personal income taxes. (14; 277)

Proletariat Karl Marx's term for the working class. (3; 42)

Proportional taxes Taxes in which the assessment as a percentage of income remains constant. If everyone paid 10 percent of income, the amount collected would rise as income rose, but the tax rate would remain the same; that is, in proportion to income. (14; 277)

Public debt Total of all government securities (bonds) in existence. The bond-holders are the creditors, having lent money to the Treasury when they purchased the bonds. The Treasury (representing the people) is the debtor. (17; 335)

Public goods Goods that the people consume together— highways, dams, or harbors, and services like national defense or police and fire departments. (15; 300)

Q

Quality circle A small group of workers who meet regularly to identify and solve worksite problems. A Japanese concept of labor management. (10; 211)

R

Rational expectations A theory that holds that workers quickly realize the effects of present and expected inflation on their real wages; that when this (rational) realization occurs, workers will react by either (1) demanding higher pay for their present jobs or (2) seeking jobs with higher pay. (19; 398)

Real change Change that occurs in income or GNP after the income or GNP has been deflated (expressed in constant dollars). Thus, a real change denotes that the data have been correlated for inflation. (12; 243)

Real GNP The current GNP deflated; that is, expressed in dollars having the same purchase power they had in 1972. (12; 243)

Real per capita DPI A deflated DPI divided by population. (12; 243)

Real per capita GNP A deflated GNP divided by population. (12; 243)

"Real" terms Measurement of the cost of a purchasing decision not by money, but by the value of the actual goods or services sacrificed. (1; 9)

Recession A fall in real GNP over two or more quarters. (13; 251)

Recessionary gap The insufficiency of demand to provide full employment. (16; 320)

Regressive taxes Taxes in which the assessment as a percentage of income rises as income falls. Best examples are sales taxes, personal property taxes, and social security taxes. (14; 277)

Relative and absolute changes An increase of from 4 to 6 quarts is an absolute change of 2 but a relative change of 50 percent: the change of 2 relative to the starting number 4. Absolute changes do not reflect relative importance; a change from 8 to 10 is also an absolute change of 2, but this time the change is only 2 relative to 8, or 25 percent. (7; 126)

Required reserves The percentage of demand deposits (or savings accounts) the Board of Governors of the Federal Reserve System requires member banks to keep at all times. (18; 356)

Revolution of rising expectations After slumbering for centuries in poverty, the LDC's now see how people in the richer countries live. The people in the LDCs have begun to want and to expect rapid increases in their standards of living. (21; 436)

Robinson-Patman Act of 1936 Instituted to prevent wholesalers from giving extra discounts to chain stores, but left three legal loopholes for price discrimination. (9; 188)

Rule of 72 A rough guide as to how many years it will take a number to double at some rate of increase or interest rate compounded annually. If the interest rate is 6 percent, divide 72 by 6. The answer is 12, indicating that it will take about 12 years for whatever number you started with to double. (1; 7)

Rules approach Argument by the rational expectationists that monetary and fiscal policy should be conducted according to rules. (19; 399)

S

Saving The unconsumed portion of one's income or the portion of a business firm's income it elects to keep. (12; 240) See *Savings.*

Savings The accumulation of past saving. (12; 240) See *Saving.*

Say's Law Expressed as a slogan: "Supply creates its own demand." The act of producing something creates the income and the demand to buy it; thus, all goods produced are sold and there is no unemployment. (15; 290)

Scarcity "Scarcity" arises because people generally want more than is available at any given time. Because our wants exceed the supply of everything available, we are always faced with having to choose some things at the expense of giving up others. Scarcity gives rise to opportunity cost. (1; 8)

Schoolmen In the Middle Ages, an elite group of priests who formulated Church doctrine. (2; 24)

Secondary job market Jobs requiring little skill or training, characterized by low wages, poor working conditions, layoffs, little chance for advancement, and high turnover. (1; 10) See *Primary Job Market.*

Self-fulfilling prophecy Occurs when the belief that something will happen causes it to happen. (5; 81)

Short run A period of time in which entrepreneurs can vary some costs such as labor or materials but not others such as taxes or interest payments on bank loans. (9; 171)

Shortage A condition in which the quantities demanded exceed the quantities supplied. (5; 91)

Shut-down point The point at which a firm's total revenue is equal to total variable costs in the short run. If total revenue does not exceed total variable costs in the short run, the firm should cease to operate. (9; 173)

Social costs The total burden to society of production, use, and disposal of some good. Social costs are made up of the private costs to sellers and buyers plus the costs of external effects. (6; 118)

Social good An indivisible good that cannot be sold unit-by-unit, and nonbuyers cannot be excluded from the market, as in the light of a lighthouse. When the light is turned on, everyone will see it whether they have paid for the lighthouse or nor. (2; 34)

Social overhead capital The transportation, power, and communications systems a society needs to facilitate production and distribution of goods and services. Also called infrastructure. (21; 439)

Socialism An economic system in which the major industries, like steel, coal, oil, transportation, electricity, telephone, and telegraph are owned and operated by the government. Socialism may involve a democratic or totalitarian political system. (3; 38)

Special Drawing Rights (SDRs)   Sometimes called "paper gold." SDRs are additional funds created by the IMF that can be used to purchase member nations' currencies. (20A; 427)

Spending multiplier   Any change in spending will cause a chain reaction in spending so that the final increase in total income (GNP) is greater than (a multiple of) the original change in spending. The number of times the change in spending is multiplied to equal the change in total income is the spending multiplier. Thus, if the multiplier is 2.5 and the change in spending is $10 billion, the change in total income (GNP) is $25 billion (2.5 times $10 billion). (16; 317)

Stagflation   The simultaneous presence of recession (stagnation) and inflation. (19; 381)

Structural unemployment Unemployment caused by poor business in a particular industry. (13; 258)

Substitute goods   Goods that compete with one another (are good substitutes for each other), like two brands of coffee. (5; 79)

Substitution effect   As the price of a product falls, consumers substitute the product for others and find more uses for it. (5; 74)

Supply   The number of units a supplier (producer or seller) of a product will offer for sale at various market prices during some period of time. (5; 83) See *Supply schedule* and *Supply curve*.

Supply curve   A graph of a supply schedule. The price per unit is on the vertical axis. The quantities supplied are on the horizontal axis. (5; 85)

Supply schedule   A schedule of prices and quantities showing the quantities supplied at each price during some period of time. (5; 84)

Supply-side economics   A theory that holds that supply should be increased via business tax cuts and reduced government regulation as a cure for stagflation. (15; 300)

Surplus   A condition in which the quantity supplied exceeds the quantity demanded. (5; 91)

T

Taft-Hartley Act   Declared the closed shop illegal but permitted the union shop; gave the states the right to pass "right-to-work" laws banning the union shop; and provided a no-strike 80-day "cooling-off" period for industrial disputes in some industries. (10; 206)

Tariff   A tax imposed on imported products by the government of the importing country. (20; 409)

Tax-based incomes policy (TIP)   Federal government policies designed to give incentives to corporations for holding down price and wage increases (tax breaks) or punishment (tax increases) for letting prices and wages exceed certain limits. (19; 390–391)

Tax incidence   The final resting place of the burden of a tax. Often a taxpayer does not bear the burden of a tax if he can shift the burden (cost) of the tax to someone else. (14; 283) See *Tax shifting*.

Tax loopholes   Provisions in tax laws that permit taxpayers to avoid income taxes. Best examples: tax exempt securities,

taxes on capital gains, and business-expense deductions. (14; 279)

Tax shifting   The transfer of the burden of a tax to someone other than the taxpayer. Taxes may be shifted backward by retailers to wholesalers (or manufacturers) or forward by retailers to customers. (14; 283)

Team   See *Commune*.

Theory of gluts   Malthus's idea that we would have periodic recessions because of gluts (oversupplies of unsold goods) on the market. The gluts would be caused by insufficient aggregate demand, a result of the fact that total wages paid are less than the total value of everything produced. (15; 292)

Theory Z   An American version of a Japanese form of labor-management organization based upon worker goals and motivation, prompt feedback, clearly formulated personnel policies, and regular revision of employee goals. (10; 210)

Tight-money policy   Action by the Federal Reserve Board to reduce bank reserves, depriving banks of money to lend and causing interest rates to rise and borrowing and spending to decline. (18; 365)

Time-series graphs   Two-variable graphs in which one variable is always some measure of time such as weeks, months, years. Useful for displaying historical data. (4; 64)

Total revenue   The total amount of money received by a company from the sale of a good or service. Equals price times quantity. (7; 125)

Trade deficit   An excess of imports over exports. (20; 418)

Trade Expansion Act of 1962   An agreement with the Common Market countries to lower tariffs on products where the Common Market and the United States together had more than 80 percent of the world's trade. (20; 414)

Trade-off See *Opportunity cost.*

Trade surplus An excess of exports over imports. (20; 418)

Traditional, command/planning, and market-price systems Traditional systems answer the what, how, and for whom questions by copying the decisions of previous generations. Command/planning systems answer the questions with a national, centrally made plan. Market-price systems answer the questions via the forces of demand and supply which determine prices. (2; 19, 20)

Transfer payments Unemployment insurance payments, farm price support payments, social security payments, welfare payments, and interest paid on government bonds. Sometimes thought of as payments by government to recipients who have not rendered any productive service during the year being measured. (12; 237)

Triage French term meaning "choice." Refers to the suggestion that we should help the LDCs that can be helped and forget the rest. (21; 442)

Turnover tax A sales tax used by Soviet planners to encourage or discourage consumption of particular items. Has averaged as much as 44 percent of the retail price. (3; 45)

U

Unemployment rate A percentage derived by dividing the number of people unemployed by the number of people in the civilian labor force. (13; 254)

Unintended disinvestment A drop in inventories below desired (intended) levels because of an unanticipated increase in sales. (16; 309)

Unintended investment An increase in inventories above desired (intended) levels because of an unanticipated drop in sales. (16; 313)

Union shop An agreement under which newly hired workers do not have to be union members before hiring but must join the union in some specified time after being hired. (10; 206)

Usury The practice of lending money to earn interest. (2; 24)

V

Variable A quantity whose numerical value is allowed to change. (4; 60)

Variable costs Costs that change with a firm's output. (9; 171)

Variable pricing Occurs when different prices are charged for the same product or service. (9; 176)

Variable supply Supply is variable when entrepreneurs can change the quantities they supply in response to changes in demand. (9; 176)

W

Wage-price flexibility The classical argument that, if workers are laid off during an economic slowdown, wages and prices will fall. When they do, employers will hire more people. People will buy more products, and full employment will be restored. (15; 290)

Wagner Act Gave the workers the right to form unions. (10; 205)

Wealth versus income Wealth consists of assets one owns, such as real estate, bank accounts, stocks, bonds, equities in life insurance policies, and personal property. Income is the flow of dollars that one receives, most often in the form of paychecks for work. (11; 214)

Z

Zero sum game A game in which there is a winner and a loser; the pluses from winning and the minuses from losing balance out to zero. (21; 448)

Index